Tolley's
SSAS, SIPPS and FURBS
(Directors' Retirement Benefits)

by

Alec Ure
Senior Pensions Consultant

Barry Bolland
Technical Manager, SSAS/SIPP Division,
HSBC Actuaries and Consultants Ltd

GW00775898

Members of the LexisNexis Group worldwide

United Kingdom	Butterworths Tolley, a Division of Reed Elsevier (UK) Ltd, 2 Addiscombe Road, CROYDON CR9 5AF
Argentina	Abeledo Perrot, Jurisprudencia Argentina and Depalma, BUENOS AIRES
Australia	Butterworths, a Division of Reed International Books Australia Pty Ltd, CHATSWOOD, New South Wales
Austria	ARD Betriebsdienst and Verlag Orac, VIENNA
Canada	Butterworths Canada Ltd, MARKHAM, Ontario
Chile	Publitecsa and Conosur Ltda, SANTIAGO DE CHILE
Czech Republic	Orac sro, PRAGUE
France	Editions du Juris-Classeur SA, PARIS
Hong Kong	Butterworths Asia (Hong Kong), HONG KONG
Hungary	Hvg Orac, BUDAPEST
India	Butterworths India, NEW DELHI
Ireland	Butterworths (Ireland) Ltd, DUBLIN
Italy	Giuffré, MILAN
Malaysia	Malayan Law Journal Sdn Bhd, KUALA LUMPUR
New Zealand	Butterworths Asia, WELLINGTON
Poland	Wydawnictwa Prawnicze PWN, WARSAW
Singapore	Butterworths Asia, SINGAPORE
South Africa	Butterworths Publishers (Pty) Ltd, DURBAN
Switzerland	Stämpfli Verlag AG, BERNE
USA	LexisNexis, DAYTON, Ohio

© Reed Elsevier (UK) Ltd 2001

Any Crown copyright material is reproduced with the permission of the Controller of Her Majesty's Stationery Office. Any European material in this work which has been reproduced from EUR-lex, the official European Communities legislation website, is European Communities copyright.

A CIP Catalogue record for this book is available from the British Library.

ISBN 0 7545 1225 8

Typeset by Kerrypress Ltd, Luton, Bedfordshire
Printed by Clays Ltd, St Ives plc

Visit Butterworths LexisNexis *direct* at www.butterworths.com

Foreword

There is no doubt that this rather awkwardly-named book has become the resource to turn to when exploring the mysteries of those crucial acronyms, which are at the core of advanced pension planning for the better paid.

For many years in the distinguished hands of John Hayward, it is now in the equally distinguished care of two very experienced and able practitioners in the SSAS and SIPP fields, with decades of practice between them.

SSASs have now been going for over a quarter of a century; SIPPs are newer but fast-growing and have been used as the prototype for the introduction of stakeholder pensions. These and the innumerable varieties of FURBS (including SUBURBS and UURBS) are all part of a growing trend against the use of intermediaries in pension arrangements, with costs being disclosed and transparent, and specialists in administration, investment, law and actuarial science all separately managing and charging for their services. This drive to avoid commission arrangements, coupled with the urge by an increasing number of clients to defer the obligation to buy an annuity at the present seemingly low rates, has lead to the increase in the use of these very sensible pensions vehicles.

With increased use has sadly come some minor abuse (see e.g. *Allan v Nolan [2001] 60 PBLR*, or *Roux [1997] STC 781*). Such abuse in the context of this sphere of activity is very low; but it has lead to unparalleled supervisory requirements both by the IR SPSS and, more recently, by other regulators. This complexity is driven largely by the understandable paranoia of the Revenue, which now thankfully shows signs of abating. Nonetheless, sometimes draconian requirements on these creative schemes have been imposed.

These requirements, together with the recent increase in the complexity of the rules relating to the division of pension spoils on divorce, the problems resulting from self-assessment and of course the onerous requirements of the *Pensions Act 1995*, mean that the need for professional guidance is greater than ever before. Indeed, recent experience with the increasingly stringent Occupational Pensions Regulatory Authority has indicated that they seem to be targeting SASSs for special treatment, and are not prepared to take on board the not unreasonable argument that the regulator should not be the medium for settling business disputes. The fines, disqualifications and other penalties relating to SSASs are now one of the main activities of the regulator.

Nonetheless, despite this excess of regulation, and despite the various caps on the amounts than can be put into the schemes (and in the case of FURBs arrangements, because of the existence of arbitrary and unnecessary limits) there is no doubt that the popularity of these high-value self-managed arrangements is growing.

This book, written in the usual straightforward, simple yet authoritative style of the authors is now firmly in the canon of classic pensions literature; the fact that it is in its fifth edition speaks of its immense value to the pensions community. For this edition Alec Ure, who has made good use of his background with the IR SPSS, is joined by Barry Bolland, who runs a substantial portfolio of SASSs and SIPPs for one of the largest firms of actuaries and consultants.

This book will, as with previous editions, find a prominent place on my desk and be used almost daily. It is a technical tour-de-force, and both a testament to the determined efforts of its dedicated authors and a reproach to the way in which our regulators express their requirements. It deserves to sell in its thousands.

Robin Ellison
National Head of Pensions
Eversheds

Preface

Who would have thought that a mere two years after the publication of the fourth edition of this book a wholesale updating would be necessary? During those two years there have been major changes. The Pension Schemes Office (PSO) has been subsumed into a somewhat awkwardly titled new "business stream" known as Inland Revenue Savings, Pensions, Share Schemes (IR SPSS). It has managed to issue fifty-five Pensions Updates in that period (three more than were issued in the four years from the issue of Update No. 1 in 1995 to Update No. 52 in 1999).

The changes affecting SSASs include: finalizing the proposals (mentioned in the fourth edition) for changes in the role of the pensioneer trustee, which came into force in August 2000; developments concerning the early retirement problem for directors (viz. the *Venables* case); proposals for additional requirements in relation to loanbacks; and the more recent proposals to impose a statutory "whistle-blowing" requirement on trustees, including the pensioneer trustee.

The major legislative changes over the last two years have been those affecting SIPPs, in particular the new tax regime for personal pensions/defined contribution schemes/stakeholder schemes under *Chapter IV Part XIV of ICTA 1988*, and a whole raft of regulations including those relating to investments, reporting requirements and transfers. These have been incorporated into this edition. There have also been changes affecting both SSASs and SIPPs, e.g. the requirements for pension sharing on divorce.

Without doubt, there will be further changes in the future that will affect SSAS, SIPPs and FURBS. The single biggest effect could well be simplification, to which the Inland Revenue appear to be more committed than they have been in previous attempts to reduce the complexities of the rules relating to tax approved schemes. However, as things stand at the present time, I do expect SIPPs to continue to increase in popularity generally, and in particular with directors and high-net worth individuals who want a pension scheme that is both flexible and under their personal control. This may well be at the expense of SSASs, including existing schemes, as more and more individuals start out with a SIPP, transfer to SIPPs from SSASs, or their SSASs are converted to SIPPs under the new regulations.

The book remains the one place to find the complete picture for SSAS, SIPPS and FURBS, having been given such a firm foundation by John Hayward, to whom I offer my best wishes as he 'eases up' towards a well-earned retirement.

There are a number of people I wish to thank. The first is my co-writer Alec Ure, whom I have known since 1984, when he was my first manager at the then Superannuation Funds Office. My thanks for his kind invitation to join him on updating the book and for his calming influence when deadlines were fast approaching! Next, my wife Rachel, for all her help and patience, and my children Dan, Joe and Eve for putting up with a 'non-participating' and at times, 'grumpy' dad for quite a few weekends. For their help in clarifying certain difficult areas of the chapters I rewrote, I would like to thank my present colleague John Wilson, and friends and former colleagues involved in the SSAS, SIPPS, and FURBS fields: Kate Ragnauth, Ian Stewart, Nick White and especially John Richardson. I would also like to thank my 'boss' John Andrews for all his support and encouragement.

Barry Bolland
Technical Manager, SSAS/SIPP Division
HSBC Actuaries and Consultants Limited   October 2001

I am delighted to be joined in the fifth edition of this book by Barry Bolland. It was a daunting task to find someone to replace John Hayward's experience and considerable expertise. However, Barry is without doubt a worthy successor, and his involvement in, and knowledge of, SIPPs and the APT have been of particular value. As Barry states, the book has required significant updating in order to reflect the surprising number of changes since the last edition was published in May 1999. Amongst other things, the changed role of the pensioneer trustee, developments in UK law and practice and the encroachment of European law into pensions and employment rights have been described in this edition. All this should be of help to the reader.

Our thanks to Teresa Sienkiewicz of KPMG for updating chapter 12 and to our publishers. Also, to the Inland Revenue, Opra and other regulatory bodies for the added value that has been given to this book by the reproduction of their guidelines and of relevant legislation.

Alec Ure
Senior Adviser, Employee Benefits Department, Gissings
(formerly Senior Consultant, Bacon & Woodrow)   October 2001

Contents

Contents

Contents

Contents

Contents

Table of Cases

Table of Statutes

Table of Statutory Instruments

Abbreviations

ABI	—	Association of British Insurers
ACT	—	Advance Corporation Tax
AIM	—	Alternative Investment Market
APT	—	Association of Pensioneer Trustees
AVC(s)	—	Additional Voluntary Contribution(s)
CA	—	Companies Act 1985
CBBR	—	Clearing Banks Base Rate
CGT	—	Capital Gains Tax
COMP	—	Contracted-out Money Purchase
CTO	—	Capital Taxes Office
DSS	—	Department of Social Security
EPP(s)	—	Executive Pension Plan(s)
EU	—	European Union (formerly European Community)
FA	—	Finance Act (followed by the year)
F(No 2)A	—	Finance (No 2) Act 1987
FICO	—	Financial Intermediaries Claims Office
FSA	—	Financial Services Authority
FSA 1986	—	Financial Services Act 1986
FSAVC(s)	—	Free-standing Additional Voluntary Contributions
FURBS(s)	—	Funded Unapproved Retirement Benefit Scheme(s)
GAD	—	Government Actuary's Department
GN(s)	—	Guidance Note(s) (issued by the Institute of Actuaries, Faculty of Actuaries or the Inland Revenue)
IBA(s)	—	Industrial Buildings Allowance(s)
ICTA	—	Income and Corporation Taxes Act 1970 or 1988
IHT	—	Inheritance Tax
IMRO	—	Investment Management Regulatory Organisation Limited
IPT	—	Insurance Premium Tax
ISD	—	Investment Services Directive
JOM(s)	—	Joint Office Memorandum (Memoranda) (followed by the number and paragraph) — succeeded by Memorandum and PSO Updates
LIFFE	—	London International Financial Futures and Options Exchange
LO(s)	—	Life Office(s)
MFR	—	Minimum Funding Requirement
NAPF	—	National Association of Pension Funds
NESI	—	New Enterprise Support Initiative

NICO	—	National Insurance Contributions Office (formerly Contributions Agency)
OAC	—	Ordinary Annual Contribution(s)
OEICS	—	Open ended Investment Company
OFEX	—	Off exchange
OFT	—	Office of Fair Trading
OPAS	—	Occupational Pensions Advisory Service
OPB	—	Occupational Pensions Board
OPRA	—	Occupational Pensions Regulatory Authority
PIA	—	Personal Investment Authority
PMI	—	Pension Management Institute
PN(s)	—	Practice Note(s) (issued by PSO, e.g. PSO Booklet IR12)
PQ	—	Parliamentary Question
PRP	—	Profit Related Pay
PSA	—	Pension Schemes Act 1993
PSI	—	Pension Scheme Instructions (followed by the paragraph number)
PSO	—	Pension Schemes Office
RPI	—	Retail Price Index
SC(s)	—	Special Contribution(s)
SCO	—	Special Compliance Office
SERP	—	State Earnings-Related Pension
SERPS	—	State Earnings-Related Pension Scheme
SFO	—	Superannuation Funds Office (now the Pension Schemes Office)
SI	—	Statutory Instrument
SIB	—	Securities and Investments Board (now Financial Services Authority)
SIPPS(s)	—	Self-Invested Personal Pension Scheme(s)
SORP	—	Statement of Recommended Practice (issued by the ASC)
SP	—	Statement of Practice (issued by the Inland Revenue)
SPG	—	SIPP Provider Group
SSA	—	Social Security Act (followed by the year)
SSAP	—	Statement of Standard Accounting Practice (issued by the ASC)
SSAS(s)	—	Small Self-Administered Pension Scheme(s)
SSAS GN	—	Small Self Administered Schemes Guidance Notes (followed by the paragraph number)
TCGA	—	Taxation of Chargeable Gains Act 1992

TMA	—	Taxes Management Act 1970
UK	—	United Kingdom
USM	—	Unlisted Stock Market
UURBS	—	Unfunded Unapproved Retirement Benefit Scheme
VAT	—	Value Added Tax

Table of Publications

Inland Revenue Statements of Practice

Other Publications

Department of Social Security Leaflet PP1
  'Thinking about Personal Pensions?'

Department of Social Security Leaflet PP3
  'A Guide to the Financial Services Act for Employers'

Department of Social Security Booklet
  'The 1995 Pensions Act'

The Pensions Ombudsman: How he can help you

Retirement Provision Freedom of Management and Investment of Funds Held by Institutions for Retirement Provision—COM91(301)

Communication on the Internal Market for Pension Funds

Chapter 1

Introduction

About this book

1.1   The first edition of this book was written by John Hayward ten years ago. It was about pension provision for controlling directors through small self-administered schemes. Such schemes are widely known throughout the pensions industry and the authorities that regulate pensions as SSASs. John Hayward's book rapidly became the most widely read work on the subject. Since those early days, and under John's vigilant guidance, the scope of the book has been extended significantly. Although it remains the most authoritative source of reference for SSASs, it now also covers the following areas:

* self-assessment for self-administered occupational pension schemes;

* Opra;

* the Ombudsman;

* relevant case law;

* VAT;

* self-invested personal pension schemes, known as SIPPS;

* stakeholder schemes;

* funded unapproved retirement benefit schemes, known as FURBS;

* unfunded unapproved retirement benefit schemes, known as UURBS;

* the *Welfare Reform and Pensions Act 1999*;

* the rules that apply to data protection.

1.2   Because of the nature of SSAS membership, the Inland Revenue places special restrictions on administration, documentation, investments, funding, reporting and winding-up of those schemes. Some of the restrictions have been imposed on SIPPS in similar form. The relevant areas are covered in detail in later chapters.

In any book about pension schemes, that are approved under *ICTA 1988, Pt XIV*, it is necessary to understand the basis of taxation of occupational pension schemes in the UK. Generally SSASs are subject to the same legislation and guidelines as all other occupational pension schemes. Thus, having explained the legislation, which applies to SSASs in CHAPTER 2, the documentation and benefit structure which applies generally to all approved occupational pension schemes is examined in CHAPTERS 3 and 4 and any particular relevance for SSASs is highlighted. The application of the legislation to SIPPS is somewhat different to that which applies to occupational pension schemes, and the differences are described in CHAPTER 14. Additionally, CHAPTER 15 deals exclusively with the general tax legislation that applies to unapproved schemes, both funded and unfunded.

Background

1.3   Until 1973 the directors of private companies could not be members of an occupational pension scheme because of the specialist tax legislation that applied to controlling directors (broadly, someone controlling more than 5% of the ordinary share capital of a company). Such directors were treated as self-employed for pension purposes and could only provide tax approved pension, lump sum and death benefits for themselves *via* retirement annuity contracts through *ICTA 1970, ss 226, 226A* (known as '*section 226* policies') which are now embodied in *ss 619–621*. Retirement annuity contracts were not sold after 30 June 1988, although contracts that were set up before 1 July 1988 could, and still do, remain in existence. The retirement annuity contract market was effectively filled by the personal pensions product which emerged on 1 July 1988, and which has now extended to the stakeholder pension scheme (see CHAPTER 14).

1.4   Self-administered pension schemes existed prior to 1973, but their members were all at arm's-length or, if the members held director status, they were likely to be directors of public companies where it is not usual or possible to hold 5% of the equity due to the financial implications of cost.

1.5   *FA 1973, s 15(a)* and *Sch 22* changed the position of controlling directors radically. This repealed the legislation forbidding controlling directors from being members of tax approved pension schemes and introduced the concept of the 20% director (now controlling director). The definition of a controlling director is contained in APPENDIX 10. The way was now open for controlling directors to become members of:

(a)   those self-administered schemes that were already in existence;

(b)   insured schemes; and

(c)   new self-administered schemes that were suitable for their entry.

1.6   The Inland Revenue rapidly became aware that controlling directors could manipulate their pension benefits in certain areas, e.g. their levels of remuneration and dates of retirement. Accordingly restrictions were introduced into the Inland Revenue's Code of Practice (PN) to limit the scope for abuse. It is important to note however that no restrictions were placed on scheme investments by the new legislation or PN at that time.

1.7 The Life Offices (LOs) were quick to offer insured schemes to controlling directors, but there were distinct disadvantages to this type of scheme. They lacked flexibility. Although contributions would be high because of high salaries, the expense loading was commensurately high. There was no ability to control the investments and large sums of money could be lost to a company with no facility to re-invest in itself. With no Inland Revenue restrictions placed on investments, the advantages of a self-administered scheme for controlling directors with themselves as the trustees soon became apparent. SSASs were born in the mid-1970s and their numbers multiplied very quickly.

1.8 The potential for tax avoidance was exploited, particularly in the area of investments and loan backs to the company and connected parties, often on advantageous terms, and these became prominent features of the early SSASs. The Inland Revenue (through the Superannuation Funds Office, later named the PSO) became concerned at the growing number of SSASs and the abuse that was taking place on an ever-increasing basis. The Revenue's remedial reaction was to publish the Joint Office Memorandum No 58 (JOM 58) in February 1979, the PSO's original Statement of Practice for SSASs (see CHAPTER 2).

1.9 The first SSASs were marketed by various insurance agents, pension consultants, actuaries etc. The LOs were noticeable by their absence. When the latter realised in the late 1970s the potential for SSASs they began to enter the market. At first the LOs offered hybrid self-administered schemes i.e. partly self-invested and partly invested in life policies. However, to compete with the growing numbers of SSASs, they soon began to offer wholly self-administered schemes while retaining some input into the administration of such themselves.

1.10 There are various forms of LO SSASs, including what became known as a deferred SSAS, where a scheme is set up as an insured one with the facility to convert later to a partly or wholly self-administered scheme. LO SSASs still have a good share of the total SSAS market, but the majority of SSASs are operated by advisers who, in the main, are made up of consultants, brokers, actuaries and banks.

The advantages of SSASs

1.11 It is necessary to examine the main financial and commercial advantages of a SSAS in providing retirement benefits for controlling directors and not just the tax advantages. Some of the advantages have been mentioned in 1.7 and 1.8 and these, together with other advantages, deserve to be looked at in greater depth.

1.12 A SSAS offers a facility for the directors of a private company to be the trustees of a pension scheme to which they belong as members. They have almost complete control (apart from certain restrictions imposed by the Inland Revenue, including the appointment and responsibilities of a pensioneer trustee (see 2.35 to 2.58) and by the Department for Work and Pensions (DWP) formerly the Department of Social Security (DSS)). This is a very compelling reason for establishing a SSAS. There are clearly areas where the Inland Revenue and the DWP impose investment restrictions, but these are not unduly onerous. The trustees themselves can decide within limits the various investments they want to make, unlike an insured scheme where the contributions are paid to a LO and the LO decides on the investments to be made.

1.13 It is quite possible for the director-trustees to be the managing trustees responsible for the day-to-day running of the scheme, including the investment decisions. However, this is subject to the requirements that are laid down in 2.49 to 2.55. The pensioneer trustee does not have to be a managing trustee. The sole function of the pensioneer trustee used to be described as that required by the Inland Revenue (see 2.36), that is the prevention of the scheme's winding-up except in accordance with the rules. It is now clear that the pensioneer trustee does, in practice, have wider role to play. However, a SSAS may also provide protection to directors in a takeover situation, particularly if the SSAS is set up for the directors of a public company.

1.14 One drawback to self-invested small self-administered schemes naturally is the additional work involved compared with an insured scheme (where the LO is paid to manage everything). The trustees will still need advisers and many SSAS consultants provide a full service from being pensioneer trustee to providing professional and investment advice within the parameters of approval. Companies need to weigh up the costs involved. The total costs of running a SSAS need to be compared with those of an insured scheme. The contributions to an insured scheme will usually include 'hidden' administration expenses, as very often a breakdown of the expenses and the real pension contribution is not known, whereas with a SSAS all the expenses and the contributions will be known. The administration costs of a SSAS plus contributions should be less than premiums paid to a LO thereby making a SSAS more cost effective. The administration expenses are also allowable as deductions for corporation tax purposes.

1.15 A very strong point in favour of SSASs as opposed to insured schemes or SIPPs is a higher level of opportunity to assist the sponsoring company with its business. The facility to re-invest the contributions paid to the SSAS in loans to the company is widely used and of great benefit to a company's business. Not only will the contributions have obtained relief from corporation tax, but the interest on the loan will also attract relief when the company pays it. The trustees can reclaim any tax deducted from interest payments where the interest is paid net of tax. The trustees may also invest in shares of the company, subject to certain limits. This can be very useful where shares are being passed on in a family company and there is no immediate purchaser to hand. It is therefore an effective way for the family to retain control. Another common method of using a SSAS as a vehicle for investing in the company is for the trustees to purchase commercial property and lease it back to the company. This assists in several ways. If the company cannot afford to purchase property, the trustees may well be able to do so. The separate ownership of property by the trustees affords protection to the company should it be taken over or wound up. Furthermore:

(a)   a leaseback arrangement with the company ensures it has premises from which to operate;

(b)   the rent it pays the trustees is allowable as a deduction for corporation tax;

(c)   whilst it is in the hands of the trustees the rent is tax free.

Also, the trustees will not incur capital gains tax (CGT) on the property when they dispose of it.

1.16   If a small family company wants to take advantage of the above investment opportunities it would be difficult to do better than a SSAS. Additionally, provision of retirement benefits later can be combined with a SIPP by transferring the assets, where acceptable, to a SIPP to enjoy the income drawdown facility, subject to any overfunding restrictions.

Tax advantages

1.17   All approved pension schemes enjoy tax advantages of various kinds. However, SSASs can be more tax efficient than other pension schemes, as explained in 1.15. Nonetheless, it is important to bear in mind that the use of a SSAS as a vehicle to achieve tax avoidance will not satisfy the test of '*bona fide*' established for the sole provision of relevant benefits (that is, there must be no duality of purpose to any approved pension scheme). For instance, the tax reliefs which are incidental to the establishment and administration of a scheme are not perceived as constituting tax avoidance. PSI 2.2.1 mentions that if contributions are not excessive in relation to the emerging benefits, and the scheme is not otherwise used to obtain an unacceptable tax advantage, this will be accepted as legitimate tax avoidance. However, the deliberate use of a scheme primarily to achieve tax avoidance, particularly a SSAS where the opportunity exists to a greater extent to maximise the tax opportunities, will inevitably lead to conflict with IR SPSS and perhaps loss of the scheme's approval.

1.18   PSI warns that pension schemes may be used to obtain tax advantages that Parliament did not intend to give, and describes some of the problems that may confront IR SPSS together with some of the remedies (PSI 2.2.2 and 2.2.6). Of particular relevance to SSASs is IR SPSS's concern with pension scheme investments. Self-administered schemes, particularly SSASs, are looked at more closely regarding their investments because the trustees (and, indirectly, the company) control the investments. PSI 2.2.6 claims that most avoidance problems arise with SSASs and refers IR SPSS examiners to the SSAS Guidance Notes (see 2.15).

1.19   A tax advantage which is available to a SSAS is in the area of inheritance tax (IHT). By building up assets in their own SSAS the director members can usually transfer substantial sums to the next generation free of IHT under discretionary provisions in the scheme rules (see 3.29).

1.20   The tax reliefs available to SSASs are explained in 1.21 to 1.28, but it must be remembered that these are generally available to all types of pension schemes, e.g. the treatment of income received by LOs and gains on assets which are all exempt from tax in their exempt pensions business, and therefore there is no perceived advantage to a SSAS here compared with an insured scheme.

1.21   Company contributions are allowable as deductions for corporation tax purposes under *ICTA 1988, s 592(4)*. Ordinary annual contributions (OACs) are deductible in the company's accounting period in which they are paid. Any other contributions (special contributions) may, at the discretion of the Inland Revenue, be spread over a period (see 9.33 and 9.34).

1.22   The contributions paid to the scheme by the company on behalf of the members are not liable to tax under Schedule E in the hands of the members by virtue of *ICTA 1988, s 596(1)(a)*.

1.23   Any personal contributions paid by members to a scheme are allowable as an expense for Schedule E purposes in the year in which they are paid under *ICTA 1988, s 592(7)*. The maximum permitted personal contribution is 15% of gross earnings for a year (*ICTA 1988, s 592(8)*). It is interesting to note that in only a small number of SSASs do the members actually make personal contributions, a feature acknowledged in PSI 4.1.2.

1.24   The income of the scheme is exempt from income tax at the basic and additional rate under *ICTA 1988, ss 592(2)* and *686(2)* respectively. This means that rent and interest received gross by the trustees are not subject to tax and that tax deducted from dividends, interest etc. before payment to the trustees can be reclaimed. However, the amount of tax credit that can be reclaimed on dividends received after 5 April 1993 was changed by the *Finance Act 1993*. By way of background information, for 1992/93 the tax credit that can be reclaimed from 1993/94 to 1 July 1997 is 25% of the dividend plus the tax credit. From 1993/94 to 1 July 1997, with the changes to assist companies with surplus advance corporation tax, the value of the tax credit that can be reclaimed is 20% of the dividend plus the tax credit. With effect from 2 July 1997 the payment of tax credits in respect of UK dividend distributions was abolished by *F (No 2) A 1997, s19*.

1.25   There is no CGT chargeable on any gains realised on the disposal of an asset by the trustees under *TCGA 1992, s 271(1)(g)*.

1.26   Underwriting commissions received by the trustees are generally exempt from income tax by virtue of *ICTA 1988, s 592(3)* but only to the extent that they are applied for the purposes of the scheme (see PSO Updates Nos 33 and 64).

1.27   Under *ICTA 1988, s 56(3)(b)* the trustees are exempt from income tax on profits on gains from transactions in certificates of deposit to the extent that the deposits are again held for the purposes of the scheme.

1.28   Any income or capital gains derived from dealing in financial futures or traded options are exempt from CGT and income tax under *TCGA 1992 ss 271(1)(g)* and *659A* respectively.

1.29   Any fees derived from stock lending are exempt from income tax from 2 January 1996 under *s 129B* introduced by *Finance Act 1996, s 157*.

1.30   The tax reliefs given in 1.21 to 1.29 will be affected in future if the Scottish Parliament exercises its tax varying powers. Careful consideration would then need to be given to the advantages and disadvantages of any differences in the tax rates in Scotland and the remainder of the UK.

1.31   There are various tax exemptions, which apply to payments made from a SSAS. These will be covered in CHAPTERS 3 and 4 together with the taxation of some payments made.

1.32   Having looked at the advantages of establishing a SSAS, the company with the benefit of its advisers can decide on how the vehicle is to provide the level of benefits within Inland Revenue limits in the most tax efficient way for itself and the directors/members.

SSASs and the future

1.33   The various advantages of SSASs, explained in 1.12 to 1.29, have been and remain major selling points for this type of pension scheme since their inception. This is despite the following:

(a)   the development of the PSO's (later, IR SPSSs) practice in this area since the publication of JOM 58 over 20 years ago;

(b)   the *1991 Regulations* from the Inland Revenue (see 2.2);

(c)   the *1992 Regulations* from the DWP, which are covered in 11.33 to 11.45 below and which restrict SSASs in some areas;

(d)   the 1996 restrictions on funding (see 9.14 to 9.27);

(e)   the requirements of the *Pensions Act 1995* (see 11.70 to 11.89);

(f)   the competition from SIPPS (CHAPTER 14);

(g)   the recent restrictions on pensioneer trustees in PSO Update No 69; and

(h)   the recent tightening on transfer payments.

1.34   The DWP regulations, and in particular the *1991 Regulations* from the Inland Revenue contained measures which restricted the activities of SSASs and the establishment of new ones. The increase in the number of SSASs thereafter was not be as great as it had been until the 1990s. However, as will be seen from later chapters in this book, important concessions were won from both the Inland Revenue and the DWP after their proposals for SSASs were initially published and exemptions were gained from many of the provisions of the *Pensions Act 1995* (see CHAPTER 11). The future for SSASs remains good, particularly with the concession given by the PSO in 1994 allowing the purchase of annuities to be deferred to age 75 (see 4.97 to 4.108), although this is matched by the income withdrawal facility available to SIPPS since 1995 (see 14.118 to 14.155).

SSASs still remain the most tax efficient vehicles for providing retirement benefits for the directors of private companies as well as for directors and senior executives of large companies. They may not remain as unassailable as they once were, but they continue to offer significant areas for unique planning opportunities.

1.35   It is to be hoped also that SSASs will benefit in future along with all other occupational pension schemes from the Inland Revenue's proposals to simplify its tax legislation. These are currently under active discussion with the pensions industry.

Chapter 2

Inland Revenue Legislation and Guidelines

Introduction

2.1   This chapter is primarily concerned with the legislation and practice drafted by the Inland Revenue that govern SSASs. DWP legislation, other UK pensions legislation, the role of Opra and the Ombudsman, the role of other UK regulatory authorities and the *Pensions Act 1995* are all covered by CHAPTER 11. A new CHAPTER 16 has been added to the book for the purpose of describing the applicability of EU law and directives to UK pension provision.

2.2   SSASs are subject to the following legislation and guidelines:

(*a*)   *ICTA 1988* and successive *Finance Acts*;

(*b*)   Practice Notes (PN) and Updates (formerly Memoranda or Joint Office Memoranda (JOM));

(*c*)   Changes in Practice such as those published following the Parliamentary Question (PQ) raised in July 1984 (APPENDIX 2);

(*d*)   Pension Schemes Instructions — Examiners' Manual and Small Self-Administered Schemes Guidance Notes;

(*e*)   Consultative Document of September 1987 (APPENDIX 3).

(*f*)   *The Retirement Benefit Schemes (Restriction on Discretion to Approve) (Small Self-Administered Schemes) Regulations (SI 1991 No 1614)* (APPENDIX 4) — referred to as the '*SSAS Regulations*' throughout this book for convenience — and other regulations;

(*g*)   The enhanced role of the pensioneer trustee, which was laid down in PSO Update No 69.

ICTA 1988, PN and Updates

2.3   *ICTA 1988, Part XIV* has been revised over the years by way of a consolidation of all the past, and the present, statutes that relate to UK pension provision generally. *Section 591* is of particular relevance as it gives the

Inland Revenue the wide ranging discretionary powers that it applies assiduously to SSASs. PN Pt 20 and the *SSAS Regulations* described in 2.2(f) are the main statements of practice for SSASs. However, IR SPSS's underlying objections to certain features of a SSAS stem from *ICTA 1988, s 591* and the application of the '*bona fide* established . . . sole purpose' test provided in *s 590(2)(a)*. This is because the controlling directors in a SSAS are also the members and trustees, which presents an infinite variety of opportunities and arrangements for the PSO to challenge on the grounds of duality of purpose. Indeed, the sole purpose test was re-emphasised in July 1997 with an amendment to PN 1.4 pointing out that continued approval would be dependent on the sole purpose test being maintained. PN 1.1 was also amended stating that the Practice Notes would not bind the PSO if a scheme was involved in, or used for the purpose of tax avoidance. Both amendments were clearly designed as warnings to SSASs.

2.4   The legislation in *ICTA 1988* applies generally to all pension schemes and not just to SSASs. There are not many exemptions for SSASs in this legislation. Notably SSASs are exempt from the prescribed valuation requirements under the surplus legislation, but approved SSASs are not exempt from the 35 (previously 40) % tax charge if a surplus is repaid to the employer. PN also applies generally to all schemes including SSASs, laying down the PSO's guidelines under its discretionary powers, and until the issue of JOM 58 (APPENDIX 1) in February 1979, the *FA 1970* and its successors together with PN were all there were to guide the practitioner in administering SSASs from their advent in the mid–1970s. Since *ICTA 1988* there have been various changes introduced by successive *Finance Acts*, and an exclusive part 20 has been inserted in PN for SSASs. The *Finance Act 1994* is of particular relevance because *s 105* thereof enables regulations to be made relating to the furnishing of information and documents and for penalties to be imposed for failure to provide them. These regulations were made on 4 December 1995 (see 3.71) and provide for penalties to be imposed from 1 January 1996.

2.5   The principal guidelines for the operation of SSASs were laid down in JOM 58 and these still apply through their incorporation into PN 20 together with *SI 1991 No 1614* and subsequent regulations and Updates. They set out how SSASs should be administered, what practitioners and trustees are expected to do and the boundaries, transgression beyond which may prejudice the approval of a SSAS. However, the PSO was very careful not to delineate specific 'no-go' areas so far as investments are concerned until more recent times, preferring to keep such guidelines in general terms, but specifically warning against using SSASs as vehicles for tax avoidance without spelling out the precise nature of that avoidance. This lack of a definition of unacceptable tax avoidance continued with the change to PN 20.10, now renumbered 20.12, in July 1997 (see 2.45). Thus, there is guidance on the membership, the appointment of a pensioneer trustee, scheme investments with loanbacks to employers provided certain criteria are met, investment in shares of the employer, non-income producing assets, trading, purchasing of annuities, insurance of death benefits, funding, specific prohibition on loans to members and transfer requirements etc. Each of these is a subject by itself and is covered in this and later chapters.

2.6   JOM 58 remained the PSO's principal statement of practice for SSASs for twelve years, until the *SI 1991 No 1614 Regulations* were made in July 1991, Memorandum 109 was published in August 1991 and the latter was incorporated into PN 20 in October 1991. Throughout that period the PSO continually made it clear that additional conditions may be imposed in a particular case if the facts warrant it. This continues to apply under IR SPSS.

2.7   Some later JOMs had particular relevance to SSASs – most notably JOM 59 because it covered death benefits payable in respect of controlling directors (see 4.77 to 4.98) and JOM 90 and the accompanying application form which required that all initial actuarial reports or advice must be submitted to the Inland Revenue at the time of the application for approval (see 3.70). These are now incorporated in PN 20.17 and PN 18 respectively. JOMs and Memoranda up to No 120 are also now incorporated in PN, with the exception of Memoranda 95, 101 and 118. Several later Updates have particular relevance to SSASs and are mentioned in the relevant sections of this book.

2.8   It is appropriate to mention two other aspects of the legislation before leaving *ICTA 1988*. The vast majority of SSASs seek the Inland Revenue's approval under its discretionary powers that are contained in *ICTA 1988 s 591*. Yet *s 590* is available for mandatory approval of SSASs just as it is for other types of schemes. It is hard to imagine such an application being made because of the severe restrictions in *section 590*, but it may be the only avenue available to the controlling directors of an investment or property company and members of their families to whom discretionary approval under *s 591* is not available.

2.9   The other aspect is a more sinister one and it is to be hoped practitioners do not get involved with it too often, namely *s 591B(1)*, formerly *s 590(5)* and the Inland Revenue's power to withdraw approval. This particular piece of legislation was clarified in the *F(No 2)A 1987*. Prior to this the PSO had the power to withdraw approval, but a grey area existed as to the actual effective date of withdrawal of approval. *S 591B(1)* makes it quite clear that if a scheme has indulged in an unacceptable practice, and the scope for SSASs to do this is much greater than for any other type of scheme, approval may be withdrawn from the date when the transgression occurred or 17 March 1987, whichever is the later. The legislation was further amended by *Finance Act 1995, s 61* which introduced *ss 591C* and *D* and the 40% tax charge on scheme funds as a measure to prevent trust-busting (see 10.13 to 10.24). *Sections 591C* and *D* were subsequently amended by *FA 1998, s 92* and *Sch 15* to strengthen these anti-trust busting measures (see 10.4 to 10.33). CHAPTER 10 deals with the withdrawal of approval generally.

Subsequent changes in practice

2.10   As the Inland Revenue's experience has grown over the years with the increasing number of SSASs, its discretionary practice has also developed and further guidelines have been promulgated, although not necessarily via Memoranda and Updates. It has been usual for the PSO, now IR SSPS, to inform the various representative bodies concerned, mainly the Association of Pensioneer Trustees (APT), from time to time of practices it finds unacceptable or to clarify certain areas, particularly investments. By 1984 several changes had been communicated which were not included in Memoranda.

2.11   Following a Parliamentary Question (PQ) asked in July 1984, the Inland Revenue published to various representative bodies a list of changes in practice that had taken place since February 1979 regarding SSASs (APPENDIX 2). The list was made freely available to practitioners at the time. The main changes notified were the restrictions on trustees' borrowings to three times the OAC paid, an employer was restricted to one SSAS only for its controlling directors and the value of shares in the employer should be aggregated with loans to the employer for the purposes of the 50% loanback test. It is important to note that these changes were not all effective from July 1984, they applied from the date when the PSO (now IR SSPS) first announced them publicly. For instance the trustees' borrowings limit commenced in January 1983 (see 7.70 to 7.72). The latest requirements that relate to borrowings and loanbacks are described later in this book, Additionally, PSO Update No 55 deals with insured loanbacks and the PS8 certificate that has to be signed by the employer and all of the trustees of the scheme. The regulations confirm that a further SSAS will not be approved by IR SPSS under its discretionary powers if another SSAS currently exists for the company. If a SSAS is being wound-up IR SPSS will not approve another SSAS for the same employer until the winding-up is complete. Furthermore, if an employer wishing to set up a SSAS is already participating in another employer's SSAS, it will have to withdraw from the latter before its own SSAS can be approved.

2.12   There were no further major changes in practice by the Inland Revenue in relation to SSASs since 1984 until the *Regulations* were promulgated in July 1991, although it may have been felt there had been changes in some areas simply because searching enquiries were fielded on certain fronts. This was more the result of a sharpening up of the (then) PSO's attitude to some aspects rather than any announced changes, something which has continued to the present. For example, that office pursued with some vigour outstanding triennial actuarial reports on SSASs, noticeably after the surplus legislation was enacted. However, it could not rely on the surplus legislation to wave the big stick, but only cite the administration of the scheme as not being in accordance with the approved rules in producing an actuarial report every three years. With effect from 1 January 1996 the production of triennial actuarial reports was been made statutory by the *Retirement Benefits Schemes (Information Powers) Regulations (SI 1995 No 3103)* (APPENDIX 5). The most significant recent developments have been:

(a)   the publication of an IR SPSS consultation paper on a proposed *Compliance Strategy for self-administered Schemes;*

(b)   the potential impact of the *Data Protection Act 1988*, which is described in CHAPTER 10;

(c)   the declaration of an intent to publish clear guidelines in a forthcoming Update on the extent of the Inland Revenue's discretion (that is, to clarify the matters on which the Inland Revenue may exercise discretion, and those on which the ground rules should already be clear); and

(d)   the establishment of a steering group, due to report in February 2003, with a remit to introduce an initiative entitled *Cutting the Red Tape for Pension Schemes.*

Additionally, a new form PS20 is being introduced for completion by trustees which will inform IR SPSS of the names and particulars of professionals and other advisers to a scheme.

Open Government

2.13   With the increase in Open Government, the Inland Revenue published two booklets. The first in the Personal Taxpayer Series IR120 is entitled 'You and the Pension Schemes Office'. This reproduced the Taxpayer's Charter and set out the standard of service customers could expect from the (then) PSO. The IR120 also provided advice also on how to complain if a practitioner was not satisfied about the way in which a case had been handled. If a feature remained unresolved after considerable correspondence or negotiations between a practitioner and the Inland Revenue , or there was undue delay, the IR120 advised the practitioner to ask for the matter to be reviewed by a senior officer. If the practitioner remained dissatisfied or the problem had not been resolved the matter should be raised in writing with the PSO Director (formerly the PSO Controller). If the practitioner was still not happy with the

Director's decision then he could put the matter in writing to the Inland Revenue Adjudicator's Officer. The PSO Director has been replaced by the IR SPSS Business Director, but the ongoing versions of this publication continue to be useful reference points.

2.14   The second booklet was a guide for members of tax approved schemes entitled 'Occupational Pension Schemes PSO1'. As mentioned, the booklet was intended for scheme members rather than practitioners. It was aimed at those who want to know more about the rules which apply to approved occupational schemes and their benefits, but who did not t have a working knowledge of the requirements. The booklet covered pension schemes generally and was therefore of general application to SSAS. Again, the ongoing versions of this publication continue to be useful reference points.

2.15   PSO Update No 13 mentioned that as part of the publication of all Inland Revenue Department internal manuals under the Code of Practice on Access to Government Information, the PSO's general examiner's manual and SSAS manual would be made available publicly. The PSO's general examiner's manual, the Pension Scheme Instructions (PSI), was as a result published by Tolley in May 1996, and whilst the instructions are particularly relevant to all occupational pension schemes they should not be overlooked in relation to SSAS. They reveal the way in which PSO (now IR SPSS) examiners operate and how they reach decisions on cases and problems relating to occupational pension schemes. The insight they provide into Inland Revenue pension practice is invaluable to any pension practitioner, and the good practitioner cannot afford to overlook them. It is most advisable to look at any salient point to understand how the Inland Revenue may react, and then to advise clients accordingly. The PSI are there to be used as essential weapons in the adviser's armoury. They are referred to throughout this book wherever it is appropriate to do so.

2.16   Tolley first published the Small Self-Administered Scheme Guidance Notes (SSAS GN) in December 1996. They are an essential tool for all SSASs practitioners. They explain how Inland Revenue examiners operate and reach decisions on SSASs. They interpret the practice in PN20 and compliment it throughout. They should be consulted whenever a SSAS problem is researched. SSAS GN are also quoted throughout this book where relevant. It is important to bear in mind though that the PSI and SSAS GN are for internal guidance within IR SPSS and their contents have not been agreed with any representative bodies. Consequently they cannot be relied upon 100% as statements of the PSO's practice in a contentious case.

Consultative document

2.17   It was inevitable with the passage of time since JOM 58 was issued and the increase in numbers of SSASs that the Inland Revenue would eventually look at the adequacy of its guidelines on SSASs and the streamlining of procedures. So with the enactment of *paragraph 3(5)* of *Schedule 3* to *F(No 2)A 1987*, (now *s 591(5)(6)*), enabling the Inland Revenue to make regulations to prescribe additional conditions for the approval of pension schemes, the opportunity was taken in September 1987 to publish a draft discussion document outlining the (then) PSO's intentions in the SSAS area (APPENDIX 3). The time passed for practitioners and representative bodies to make their representations and it was three years before the next development took place in July 1990 when draft regulations were published. Further representations were received on the draft regulations and some of these were incorporated in the *Regulations* laid before Parliament on 15 July 1991 as the *Retirement Benefits Schemes (Restriction on Discretion to Approve) (Small Self-administered Schemes) Regulations 1991 (SI 1991 No 1614)*. These *Regulations* came into effect on 5 August 1991.

The *1991 Regulations*

2.18   The important point to note about the *Regulations* is that they limit IR SPSS's discretionary powers in prescribed circumstances. For example, they restrict the power of the trustees to borrow money and sell certain investments. They also require the administrator to provide information and documents to IR SPSS at the time certain transactions and investments are made. There are many important points stemming from the regulations and the accompanying Memorandum 109 now subsumed in PN 20 that will be explained in the various chapters where the particular investment or feature of a SSAS is covered.

2.19   It is also important to note the position of JOM 58 following the publication of the *Regulations* and the subsequent revision of PN in October 1991. As Memorandum 109(5) explained where the *Regulations* and Memorandum 109 overlapped JOM 58, the new provisions prevailed. Thus some of the guidelines covering the PSO's discretionary practice in relation to SSASs in JOM 58 remained in existence after 5 August 1991 and all the guidelines in JOM 58 continued to apply to SSASs established before that date with some exceptions under the transitional arrangements (see 2.22 to 2.23). Memorandum 109(21) mentioned that JOM 58 would be cancelled when the revised PN was published later in 1991 containing a detailed explanation of the effect of the *Regulations* and of the PSO's practice regarding SSASs. When the revised edition of PN was published in October 1991 the accompanying Memorandum 110(25) stated that PN 20 described the PSO's practice in relation to SSASs together with an explanation of the effect of the *Regulations* and that JOM 58 should now be regarded as cancelled. In the event a few aspects of JOM 58 do not appear in PN 20 or the regulations, but nonetheless they do remain as part of IR SPSS's discretionary practice. These omitted aspects are highlighted in the relevant parts of this book, as they can be important.

2.20 The *Regulations*, and correspondence in September 1994 between the Inland Revenue and the APT, generally clarified the applications of discretion and statute to SSASs, but some grey continued to give rise to difficulties of interpretation. These matters are highlighted in the relevant parts of this book. A summary of the main changes brought about by the *Regulations* may be found at APPENDIX 36.

2.21 Because of the marked change in emphasis from discretionary practice to regulation regarding SSASs after 5 August 1991 in CHAPTERS 5 to 7 of this book covering investments, IR SPSS's practice from 5 August 1991 is described both in relation to the regulations and discretionary practice. IR SPSS's discretionary practice as it applied prior to 5 August 1991 to SSASs is also described.

Transitional arrangements under the *1991 Regulations*

2.22 Those SSASs approved by 5 August 1991 which hold assets at 15 July 1991 which are prohibited by the *Regulations*, but permitted under the previous discretionary practice, are provided with an exemption in the *Regulations*. Such assets may be retained after 5 August 1991, but if sold later may not be replaced. They may also be sold to scheme members, despite the ban on such transactions from 5 August 1991 (see 2.34 and 6.50), provided the disposal is at a full open market value.

2.23 SSASs established prior to 5 August 1991, but not approved by the Inland Revenue by that date, were permitted under the *Regulations* by virtue of *section 591(A)* introduced by *FA 1991, s 35,* to undertake transactions with members or their relatives prior to 5 August 1991. However, where the asset concerned was acquired on or after 15 July 1991, when the *Regulations* were actually made, but before 5 August 1991, the asset could not subsequently be sold to a member. The asset must have been held prior to 15 July 1991 to enable it to be sold subsequently to a member. In addition to this category of SSASs, an investment that was not consistent with the *Regulations* could only be retained, assuming it satisfied the Inland Revenue's guidelines at the time, if it was held before the regulations were made on 15 July 1991. This effectively means that a SSAS established on 16 July 1991 could not make a loan to an employer of more than 25% of the value of the scheme's assets (see 5.10). The Inland Revenue later granted an easement to the transitional arrangements for both approved SSASs and those yet to be approved where contracts were exchanged prior to 15 July 1991 but completion took place later. Such transactions are regarded as pre-regulations. This recognised that property transactions are a two-tier process involving both exchange of contract and later completion. A summary is provided in APPENDIX 36 regarding the main changes introduced by the *Regulations* with particular regard to approved and unapproved SSASs and those awaiting approval which fall within or outside the transitional arrangements.

Other Regulations

2.24   Several statutory instruments have been promulgated since 1991 that affect SSASs. Of particular relevance are:

(a)   the *Retirement Benefits Schemes (Restriction on Discretion to Approve) (Small Self-administered Schemes) (Amendment) Regulations (SI 1998 No 728)*;

(b)   the *Retirement Benefits Schemes (Restriction on Discretion to Approve) (Excepted Provisions) Regulations (SI 1998 No 729)*;

(c)   the *Retirement Benefits Schemes (Restriction on Discretion to Approve) (Small Self-administered Schemes (Amendment No 2) Regulations (SI 1998 No 1315)*;

(d)   the *Personal Pension Schemes (Conversion of Retirement Benefit Schemes) Regulations (SI 2001 No 1315)*;

(e)   the *Personal Pension Schemes (Transfer Payments) Regulations (SI 2001 No 114)*.

Additionally, there will be new investment regulation under the forthcoming *Financial Services and Markets Act* and a proposed *Regulated Activities Order.*

SI 1998 No 728 amended the definition of a small self-administered scheme (see 2.27) and the formulae for borrowing and lending by the trustees of a SSAS (see 7.58 and 5.8) allowed non-commercial ground rents and locked the pensioneer trustee into that appointment (see 2.37). *SI 1998 No 729* merely disapplies parts of the *1991 Regulations* amended by *SI 1998 No 728. SI 1998 No 1315* further amended the formulae for borrowing and lending by the trustees of a SSAS (see 7.57 and 5.8) and added a further category disqualifying a pensioneer trustee from acting (see 2.40).

2.25   There is one further statutory instrument, the *Retirement Benefits Schemes (Information Powers) Regulations (SI 1995 No 3103)* (APPENDIX 5) which is of relevance to SSAS, although it applies in the main to all occupational pension schemes. This introduced with effect from 1 January 1996 a requirement to furnish information and documents (see 2.4) by certain deadlines, failing which penalties may be imposed. Regarding SSASs, it required triennial actuarial reports to be produced (see 2.12) within one year of their effective date and imported the 90 day reporting requirements from the *1991 Regulations* (see 3.75), in consequence of which, the *1991 Regulations* were further amended by *SI 1998 No 728* (see 2.24).

Definition of 'small'

2.26   There obviously has to be some cut-off point in the number of members of a self-administered pension scheme below which the PSO's guidelines will apply, and this number is twelve. A SSAS is therefore generally a scheme with less than twelve members. The great majority of SSASs have between one to three members and when the former 20% director, rather than the current controlling director, definition applied it was not possible to have more than five such directors in the scheme. However, there are some SSASs which include arm's length employees in their membership apart from family directors and once the total membership goes above eleven the question arises of whether the guidelines in PN 20 and regulation restrictions should apply. PN 20.1 and SSAS GN 2.10 are quite clear on this. If the scheme is providing maximum benefits for the family directors and derisory benefits for the arm's length employees, then the PSO is likely to take the view that the latter members are included in the scheme solely as makeweights to get round the restrictions imposed by PN 20 and the regulations. The scheme is still therefore small and the restrictions apply.

2.27   On the other hand a self-administered scheme set up for less than twelve members, who are all at arm's length from each other, from the employer and from the trustees, may not necessarily be subject to the restrictions of PN 20 and the regulations (SSAS GN 2.11). This could apply for instance to a scheme set up by a large public company for its senior executives who have no sizeable shareholdings in the company and where the trustees are totally independent. In fact the definition of a SSAS in the *Regulations* as amended by *SI 1998 No 728* allows such a self-administered scheme to escape from its provisions. This is because a SSAS is defined as a self-administered scheme with less than twelve members, where at least one of the members is connected to another member or to the trustee, or to the employer in relation to the scheme and some or all the income and other assets are invested other than in insurance polices. On the other hand PN 20.1 mentions that schemes with twelve or more members, which the PSO has insisted are subject to PN 20, will not escape the provisions of the *Regulations*. It is always best in these circumstances to approach the PSO for its decision that PN 20 and the *Regulations* will not apply to such a scheme. The process can lead to argument though with individual examiners whose interpretation of the situation can vary. Therefore the PSO agreed with the APT in 1985 that where this issue became contentious it should be referred to a senior officer in the PSO for his consideration.

2.28   It is possible because of the Inland Revenue's wide discretionary powers for that office to require only certain aspects of the regulations or PN 20 to be met in relation to a self-administered scheme with less than twelve members. For instance, just the ban on loans to members or on residential property might apply, each case being looked at on its merits. However it should be noted that any SSAS restrictions applied in these circumstances are purely under the Inland Revenue's discretionary powers (SSAS GN 2.10) and cannot be enforced under the regulations. Regarding self-managed funds see 2.33 to 2.34.

2.29   Occasionally a self-administered pension scheme's membership falls below twelve, quite fortuitously, perhaps because there are now fewer active members and the rest have retired or withdrawn and taken their retirement benefits. No special action under PN 20 will normally be required if this happens unless one of the scheme's active members is connected with another member or a trustee of the scheme or any participating employer (SSAS GN 2.11).

2.30   Obviously, conditions for running a self-administered pension scheme outside the confines of PN 20 with more than eleven members will be less restrictive, yet when contemplating an increase in membership to more than eleven it is necessary to be aware of the additional requirements imposed by the surplus legislation in 1986 regarding actuarial valuations being prepared on the prescribed basis which does not apply to SSASs, the DSS (now the DWP) *1992 Regulations* on self-investment (and the relevance of European directives in that respect) and the provisions of the *Pensions Act 1995* from some of which SSAS are exempt.

2.31   The definition of a SSAS in the regulations includes a self-administered pension scheme whose assets are invested other than in insurance policies (see 2.26). This therefore includes an insured scheme whose only self-administered asset may be a bank account. However, in these circumstances scheme monies held in a current account, whether interest bearing or not, with a bank or building society will not be treated as an investment otherwise than in insurance policies if the monies are so held for incidental purposes (SSAS GN 2.4). Member's voluntary contributions may also be invested in a building society account earmarked for the member concerned (PSI 4.3.9). Thus by concession the IR SPSS will regard such a scheme as an insured scheme for approval purposes. It will not be a SSAS for the purposes of the regulations so the various restrictions and reporting requirements will not apply. Its documentation may nonetheless permit self-administration (SSAS GN 2.9), it may include a pensioneer trustee if so desired and it may have a rule allowing pensions to be paid from the scheme for five years following retirement only if it was established prior to 5 August 1991.

2.32   Reference is made in paragraphs 1.9 to 1.10 above of small schemes administered by LOs which permit self-administration, but where scheme monies are wholly invested in insurance policies from the outset. These are generally known as deferred SSASs. As soon as the trustees of such a scheme invest other than in insurance policies the scheme will immediately become subject to the regulations (SSAS GN 2.9). If this happens, IR SPSS must be notified at once and details of the non-insured investments supplied. A deferred SSAS established before 5 August 1991, but not granted formal approval by then is allowed to retain the five year deferral facility (see 4.95). A deferred SSAS established after 5 August 1991 that later becomes a SSAS must make a genuine and significant switch to self-administration. By this IR SPSS expects at least 25% of the assets to be invested outside of insurance policies for at least five years before retirement.

2.33   There are also insured earmarked schemes, known as self-managed funds, where the policies are linked to an individual fund for each scheme. The investments of each individual fund are normally selected by the employer or trustee, subject to the LO's agreement, but are made and held in the name of the LO. These are not SSASs within the definition of the regulations (SSAS GN 7.2), but under its discretionary powers IR SPSS applies some of the provisions of the regulations to them (PN 16.46), e.g. on borrowings, banned investments and transactions, and loans and they have to submit a schedule of their investment fund and a statement of their funding position every 3 years (SSAS GN 7.5).

2.34   For schemes established as self-managed funds before 31 December 1992, both approved and not approved by that date, they had to insert in their governing documents by 4 August 1994 the provisions in the regulations relating to borrowings, banned investments and transactions and loans. They were allowed to retain investments already made, provided they were acceptable under previous PSO practice. Such investments may subsequently be sold to whoever the trustees wish, including members and their relatives, on an arm's length basis at full market value as allowed for SSAS under the transitional arrangements (see 2.22). Self-managed funds set up on or after 1 January 1993 are not granted formal approval unless their governing documents contain the provisions in the regulations relating to borrowings, banned investments and transactions, and loans.

The pensioneer trustee

2.35   The Inland Revenue was concerned from the start of SSASs in the 1970s that there was considerable potential for the members to walk off with the assets, the members also being trustees of the scheme and directors of the participating company. The (then) PSO therefore insisted on the appointment of an independent trustee to every SSAS who would ensure the scheme was only wound up in strict accordance with its rules upon the unanimous agreement of all the trustees. The (then) PSO rested its argument on the very old case of *Saunders v Vautier [1835–42] All ER 58* (see 2.46).

2.36　Thus was created that unique name of 'pensioneer trustee'. It was important to note at the time that whilst the pensioneer trustee is a general trustee of a SSAS he did not have to be a managing trustee. His only function could have been solely in relation to agreeing to the winding-up whilst the other trustees deal with the day to day running of the scheme, making investments etc. However, in reality most pensioneer trustees found themselves handling the administration side particularly with the Inland Revenue and giving advice to the other trustees and companies involved. As will be seen later in this chapter, there has been a significant increase in the role and the regulation of pensioneer trustees in recent times.

2.37　There is provision in the *Regulations* that one of the trustees must be a pensioneer trustee. It is also provided that where the pensioneer trustee no longer qualifies to act as such or ceases to be a trustee of a SSAS, IR SPSS should be notified within 30 days and a successor appointed within 60 days. In addition IR SPSS must be notified of the successor's appointment within 30 days and a copy of the document removing and appointing the pensioneer trustee sent to IR SPSS within 30 days.

2.38　The position of pensioneer trustees was changed dramatically from 7 April 1998. PSO Update No 41 (6–10) announced measures to strengthen substantially the role of pensioneer trustees to limit the opportunities for abuse, particularly where they had been removed without replacement or transactions were undertaken without their knowledge. *SI 1998 No 728* deleted *Regulation 9* of *SI 1991 No 1614* with effect from 1 April 1998 and substituted the following requirements for a SSAS:

(a)　one of the trustees must be a pensioneer trustee;

(b)　the pensioneer trustee's appointment shall only be capable of termination:

　(i)　by the death of the trustee;

　(ii)　by an order of the court;

　(iii)　by withdrawal of pensioneer trustee status by the Inland Revenue;

　(iv)　where the pensioneer trustee has committed a fraudulent breach of trust, unless the pensioneer trustee is replaced by another pensioneer trustee at the same time as the termination.

If the circumstances at (b)(i) to (iii) occur, the appointment of a successor pensioneer trustee has to be made within 30 days of the date of termination.

In addition the Inland Revenue still has to be notified within 30 days of the successor's appointment in all these circumstances and provided with a copy of the document removing and appointing the pensioneer trustee. The latest changes in the Inland Revenue's requirements for pensioneer trustees were announced in PSO Update No 69, and incorporated into PN under an announcement in PSO Update 90. They are described in detail in 2.56.

2.39 For SSASs approved on or before 17 March 1998 the provisions of *Schedule 15* override scheme rules regarding the circumstances in which a pensioneer trustee's appointment may be terminated. For SSASs not approved by 17 March 1998 or established thereafter their rules have to contain the provisions regarding the termination of a pensioneer trustee's appointment (see 3.58).

2.40 *SI 1998 No 1315* added a further category to the circumstances in which the termination of a pensioneer trustee's appointment is permitted provided a replacement is effected within 30 days (see 2.24). This is where a pensioneer trustee is the subject of a prohibition or suspension order, or is disqualified under the *Pensions Act 1995* or the *Pensions (Northern Ireland) Order 1995* from being a trustee. This subsequent amendment must also appear in the rules of a SSAS (see 2.39 and 3.58).

2.41 The requirements in 2.39 and 2.41 effectively place a fetter on a pensioneer trustee wishing to resign of his own free will. He has to ensure someone replaces him immediately, but not if the SSAS has yet to receive tax approval. His relationship with the client may however have broken down or he may be dissatisfied with the operation of a SSAS by his co-trustees or his fees may be unpaid. There could be problems in finding a successor in these circumstances. The APT has made representations to the Inland Revenue at the apparent unfairness of this 'lock-in', but has been informed the position is not negotiable. However, it emerged from the discussions with the Inland Revenue that pensioneer trustees are free to include in the rules of a SSAS something to the effect that if a pensioneer trustee wishes to resign and a replacement cannot be found within a certain period, then the SSAS will commence winding-up. Additionally, it now seems clear that Opra does not feel that it is able to resolve matters in the area of the removal of trustees from SSASs in cases of dishonesty.

Qualifications

2.42 PN 20.4 states that it is necessary for the pensioneer trustee to be an individual or body widely involved with occupational pension schemes and having dealings with IR SPSS So apart from individuals, both corporate bodies and partnerships can qualify. At least 50% of the directors of a corporate trustee should be capable of being pensioneer trustees in their own right. The acid test is having wide involvement with pension schemes and dealings with IR SPSS. There are many people who are actively involved with all sorts of pension schemes who do not deal with the IR SPSS and despite their expertise would be turned down. They have also to demonstrate dealings with IR SPSS over a period of time though not necessarily on SSASs. The application to IR SPSS for pensioneer trustee status should provide details of the individual's experience with pension schemes generally and of particular schemes where correspondence, discussions or negotiations have taken place with IR SPSS over a period of several months. If an individual is seeking pensioneer trustee status in his own right, having left a LO or an actuarial firm where he was an employee engaged in dealings with IR SPSS, the PSO will not grant pensioneer trustee status until the individual has been involved on his own account with IR SPSS for several months. This is very much a chicken and egg situation, but it is possible for an individual branching out on his own to become an approved pensioneer trustee within a year provided he becomes involved with IR SPSS during that period. It does mean, however, that on his own SSAS portfolio, he must appoint an approved pensioneer trustee meanwhile.

2.43   IR SPSS qualifications do not as yet imply a test of anyone's professional competence and it stresses this point if for some reason it turns down an application where perhaps there is a lack of dealings with IR SPSS. If IR SPSS is satisfied that pensioneer trustee status can be granted it asks the individual to complete an undertaking that he will not consent to the termination of a SSAS of which he is a trustee except in accordance with the approved terms of the winding-up rule, so not only does the pensioneer trustee have to give this undertaking individually, but also each SSAS's rules must contain a provision in relation to the termination of the SSAS that the trustees must act unanimously i.e. *nem con*.

2.44   The pensioneer trustee's role had previously been seen to be solely to prevent the winding-up of a SSAS except on the terms of the trust. The pensioneer trustee had not been a 'watchdog' for the Inland Revenue in any area other than the improper termination of the scheme, but this is changing for the future (see 2.49 to 2.58). IR SPSS places great reliance on the pensioneer trustee undertaking, which has recently been extended (see 2.58). It has stressed that any pensioneer trustee involved in deliberately engineering the loss of tax approval of a SSAS can expect to lose its pensioneer trustee status. It is also clear that if a pensioneer trustee is involved in arrangements to circumvent the provisions of the regulations its pensioneer status can be revoked. For instance, Case 12 in the National Audit Survey APPENDIX 2 mentions loss of pensioneer trustee status where the (then) PSO's ban on loans to scheme members was circumvented.

2.45   PN 20.10 (now PN 20.12) originally recorded that the Inland Revenue reserved the right to withdraw pensioneer trustee status should the circumstances warrant it, without recording what those circumstances might be. Then, in July 1997, apparently as a result of the case of *R v IRC ex parte Roux Waterside Inn Ltd [1997] STC 781*, the *Roux* case (see 10.21 to 10.25), PN 20.10 (now 20.12) was amended by stating that an example of circumstances warranting withdrawal of pensioneer trustees status would be if the individual or corporate pensioneer trustee or any of its directors or staff were found to be involved in or promoting tax avoidance whether or not the avoidance related to pension schemes. No definition of unacceptable tax avoidance was provided, but the (then) PSO indicated to the APT that if the tax reliefs referred to in PN are obtained only for the purposes for which they are intended and no attempt is made to circumvent tax charges payable in the circumstances intended, withdrawal of pensioneer trustee status should not occur.

2.46   The circumstances envisaged in PN 20.12 clearly cover the use of pension schemes to obtain tax advantages Parliament did not intend to give (see 1.18), but promoting tax avoidance elsewhere clearly envisages a much wider field and the Inland Revenue has provided no firm advice in this connection. Fortunately, most pensioneer trustees are pension consultants, actuaries, solicitors or LOs and therefore not generally engaged in giving tax advice, but some are accountants who themselves or via other departments in their firms provide tax advice. They may be more vulnerable to the strictures in PN 20.10, and may find the general concept of tax avoidance enunciated in the House of Lords in *IRC v Willoughby [1997] STC 995* useful. This states:

> *'The hallmark of tax avoidance is that the taxpayer reduces his liability to tax without incurring the economic consequences that Parliament intended to be suffered by any taxpayer qualifying for such a reduction in his tax liability, whereas the hallmark of tax mitigation, on the other hand, is that the taxpayer takes advantage of a fiscally attractive option afforded to him by the tax legislation and generally suffers the economic consequences Parliament intended to be suffered by those taking advantage of the option'.*

Saunders v Vautier [1835–42] All ER 58

2.47   This particular case is important because it involved a trust where all the prospective and contingent beneficiaries combined to enforce the winding-up of the trust and the payment of the trust monies to themselves. Its implication for pension schemes is that such an action is directly opposed to the purpose for which they are established and to the spirit behind the legislation. If IR SPSS were not to interpose an independent trustee in a SSAS, any request from the members of the scheme, who are limited in numbers, to wind it up on the lines of *Saunders v Vautier* could result in the funds being distributed to them contrary to IR SPSS requirements. The appointment of a pensioneer trustee is therefore intended to block such a request from the members. It is generally felt nonetheless that the likelihood of a combination of all the beneficiaries to wind-up a scheme is most remote and that IR SPSSs insistence on the appointment of a pensioneer trustee is not absolutely necessary. However, the presence of an independent trustee does provide a deterrent to the beneficiaries combining to wind-up the scheme. Pensioneer trustees also have a vested interest in preserving the system because it provides them with a discrete area of the pensions scene in which to practise their expertise and they do have a direct avenue to IR SPSS via the APT on any subject related to SSASs.

2.48   So far as corporate pensioneer trustees are concerned, if such a company establishes a SSAS for its own directors, IR SPSS will insist that an entirely separate pensioneer trustee is appointed. The pensioneer trustee on this SSAS cannot be the practitioner's own pensioneer trustee company or any of the directors even if they are qualified to act as pensioneer trustees in their own right. The restriction is contained in the regulations and PN 20.8.

The future for pensioneer trustees

2.49   It must be recognised that the appointment of a pensioneer trustee may not prevent the illegal winding-up of a SSAS by the other trustee(s) and the subsequent mis-appropriation of the assets. In the unlikely event that the other trustees are minded to wind-up a SSAS other than in accordance with its rules, or actually do so, the pensioneer trustee until 7 April 1998 (see 2.38) was always able to resign to protect his status with the PSO. To prevent this it always was a sound precaution for the pensioneer trustee to be a co-signatory to the bank account of a SSAS. This is now a requirement (see 2.57(k)). Many pensioneer trustees have become something akin to a 'watchdog' by their very involvement in the administration of SSASs and are well aware that IR SPSS expects them to be well versed in Inland Revenue practice and to use their good offices to see that this practice is observed. The consultative document as long ago as 1987 acknowledged something of this, particularly the service pensioneer trustees provide the (then) PSO in discouraging the more unacceptable proposals of employers, and it re-affirmed that the pensioneer trustee's main function would continue to be prevention of a premature winding up.

2.50   The Inland Revenue however announced in PSO Update No 41, as part of its measures to strengthen the role of the pensioneer trustee and limit the opportunities for abuse, proposals regarding the future approval of pensioneer trustees and their role. The background for the proposals appeared to be countering tax avoidance and trust-busting (see 10.10 to 10.26), and the increasing member of injudicious loans granted by the trustees of SSASs which later became irrecoverable (see 5.34 to 5.39), with a degree of increased status for pensioneer trustees. The proposals were published together with a draft Update (APPENDIX 6) in March 1998. The main proposals have largely been overtaken by the terms of PSO Update No 69 (see 2.57, 2.58). For information, the original proposals were:

(a) pensioneer trustees should be registered as co-owners of SSAS assets, and mandatory signatories to all SSAS bank accounts;

(b) pensioneer trustees must not consent to any actions taken by SSASs that are inconsistent with approval, and must report them to the Inland Revenue;

(c) pensioneer trustees must demonstrate the monitoring procedures that they have in place;

(d) to tighten up the appointment of pensioneer trustees, and be more active in withdrawing pensioneer trustee status where appropriate;

(e) pensioneer trustees to inform IR SPSS regularly of the names of the SSASs for which they act as pensioneer trustee;

(f) to restrict the extent to which pensioneer trustees can delegate their powers as trustees; and

(g) pensioneer trustees must inform IR SPSS of any proposal of which they are aware either for them to resign or be removed.

2.51 The draft Update contained additional proposals. In future, to gain pensioneer trustee status, the practitioner would have to demonstrate a current wide personal involvement with SSASs and a knowledge of Inland Revenue requirements regarding the approval and continued approval of SSASs evidenced in at least 20 schemes. If corporate pensioneer trustee status is applied for, the directors of the corporate trustee must have the experience required of an individual pensioneer trustee.

2.52 The draft Update mentioned that the current undertaking of a pensioneer trustee not to agree to terminate a SSAS other than in accordance with its approved winding-up rule was no longer an adequate safeguard against abuses of the pensions tax reliefs. So the undertaking was to be amended, and a list of its terms is contained in 2.58 below.

2.53 IR SPSS has issued publicly a list of all approved pensioneer trustees, something it has always steadfastly refused to do, regarding such information as confidential until now. Details of the availability of the list are given in 2.56. A list is also available from the secretary of the APT for anyone seeking to appoint a pensioneer trustee. It should be borne in mind that whilst most pensioneer trustees are members of the APT, a few are not.

2.54   Some of the proposals at 2.50 to 2.53 are still subject to discussions between IR SPSS and APT and although the increased role of the pensioneer trustee will bring him into the area covered by the *Financial Services Act 1986* and may require him to be authorised if he was not before. This point awaits clarification. It is apparent that the discussions so far have produced some watering down of the proposals. For instance, the 'whistle-blowing' requirement for pensioneer trustees (see 2.50(b)) has been dropped, although the Inland Revenue has stated that it will not stand in the way of a pensioneer trustee who does wish to take such a course of action. The Inland Revenue has also stated that it is exploring the possibility of extending *SI 1995 No 3103* (the *Information Regulations*) to give statutory protection to pensioneer trustees from facing action for a breach of confidentiality. IR SPSS have recently been asking pensioneer trustees how many of their schemes have co-signatories to their scheme bank accounts. This is interesting because, although the consultative document in 1987 proposed that pensioneer trustees notify the Inland Revenue of any SSAS transactions which were likely to infringe the requirements for approval, It was omitted from the *Regulations* presumably because there would be a problem for solicitors over confidentiality.

Revisions to PN, Pt 20

2.55   Part 20 of PN has been extensively revised in order to reflect the changes to IR SPSS practice in recent months. The section contents are as follows:

(a)   Introduction, paras. 20.1–20.3, dealing with the definition of a SSAS and the reason why special conditions apply;

(b)   The trust and the pensioneer trustee, paras 20.4–20.16, dealing with the rights of beneficiaries and the appointment and removal of the pensioneer trustee;

(c)   Further requirements for the pensioneer trustee, paras 20.17–20.33, dealing with the involvement of the pensioneer trustee in scheme assets;

(d)   Funding, paras 20.34–20.44, dealing mainly with contributions and annuities;

(e)   Investments, paras 20.45–20.51, dealing mainly with the *SSAS Regulations*;

(f)   Loans to members and connected persons, para 20.52;

(g)   Self-investment, paras 20.53–20.66;

(h)   Purchase of assets from a members, connected persons or an employer, paras 20.67–20.75;

(i) Shared investments and trading, paras 20.76–20.79;

(j) Serious ill-health, and employer in liquidation, paras 20.80–20.83.

The list of pensioneer trustees

2.56 The list of approved pensioneer trustees can now be found on the IR SPSS website under *www.inlandrevenue.gov.uk/pensionschemes/apt-list.htm*. The APT are actively in contact with IR SPSS regarding any omissions or incorrect data contained in the current version.

The enhanced role of the pensioneer trustee

2.57 The enhanced role of the pensioneer trustee was announced in PSO Update No 69. The salient points are as follows:

(a) the requirements in 2.42 concerning the qualifications that are required in order to obtain pensioneer trustee status are restated;

(b) in accordance with PN 20.5, any applicant for pensioneer status must have involvement with at least 20 SSASs;

(c) it is necessary to demonstrate that proper management systems and procedures are in place;

(d) IR SPSS will monitor the management of schemes;

(e) an undertaking must be signed by the pensioneer trustee (in the case of a corporate trustee, all the directors must sign, and there must always be at least one individual who holds a position of authority in order to ensure that the conditions in (c) are met);

(f) the individual undertaking is attached to the Update as Appendix A, and the corporate undertaking is attached to the Update as Appendix B;

(g) the undertaking must be accompanied by a list of all schemes for which the pensioneer trustee acts, renewable on an annual basis;

(h) an outline specification for (g) to be sent in electronic format is attached to the Update as Appendix B;

(i) a pensioneer trustee can lose his status if the undertaking is not completed (there was a 90 day timescale for existing pensioneer trustees as at 29 August 2000);

(j) a pensioneer trustee must, together with the other trustees, be a registered owner of all of the scheme's assets;

(k) a pensioneer trustee must be a co-signatory to all scheme bank accounts unless they only give rise to a liability (a subsequent APT request that a bank account could be solely under the control of the pensioneer trustee has been rejected), and IR SPSS auditors will make appropriate checks;

(l) a pensioneer trustee must authorise the conversion of any scheme assets into cash, and ensure that the monies are paid into the scheme bank account;

(m) a pensioneer trustee must ensure that his name is on any document that evidences a scheme's interest in land or property, whether registered within or outside of the UK, or there must be a legally binding restriction on property to achieve the same;

(n) the restriction in (m) in respect of property in England and Wales should be registered at HM Land Registry on form 75;

(o) the restriction in (m) in respect of property in Northern Ireland should be registered at the Land Registers of Northern Ireland (a "caution" will not suffice);

(p) the restriction in respect of property in Scotland should be in accordance with (m) above;

(q) the requirement that a pensioneer trustee shall be a co-owner of land in Scotland or Northern Ireland shall only apply after the cessation of any existing charge to secure a loan against that land with a bank or financial institution;

(r) the monies from cash repayments of loan interest must be paid into the scheme bank account;

(s) loans made on or after 1 October 2000 should evidence that the pensioneer trustee is a party to the agreement;

(t) loans made prior to 1 October 2000 need not evidence that the pensioneer trustee was a party to the agreement, and this exemption shall apply to rolled-over monies as long as no further monies are lent;

(u) shares, unit trusts and investment management arrangements must be registered, or re-registered, to show that a pensioneer trustee shall be a co-owner of land in is a co-owner of the asset;

(v) the pensioneer trustee must be a signatory to any management agreement between the trustees and the fund manager or broker, and any proceeds must be paid into the scheme bank account;

(w) the pensioneer trustee need not be a signatory to any nominee account, unless the account can be accessed by the trustees;

(x) the requirements in (v) and (w) apply to other management arrangements where shares are held by a nominee on behalf of the trustees and any share transactions undertaken on non-UK stock exchanges that may require the share certificate to be registered in the name of a recognised nominee;

(y) where shares are registered in the name of CREST it will suffice if written arrangements ensure that they cannot be transferred out of the control of the appointed fund manager (other than in the normal course of managing investments) without written consent from the pensioneer trustee;

(z) insurance policies and annuity contracts entered into on or after 1 October 2000 should evidence that the pensioneer trustee is a party to the documentation, and any proceeds may only be paid out if the pensioneer trustee agrees in writing to the insurer;

(aa) insurance policies and annuity contracts in place prior to 1 October 2000 need not evidence that the pensioneer trustee was a party to the documentation;

(ab) any other assets must show that the pensioneer trustee is a co-owner;

(ac) borrowings entered into on or after 1 October 2000 should evidence that the pensioneer trustee is a party to the documentation;

(ad) borrowings entered into before 1 October 2000 need not evidence that the pensioneer trustee was a party to the documentation;

(ae) all member and employer contributions, and monies and money transfers, must be paid into a scheme account to which the pensioneer trustee is a co-signatory;

(af) payments of the following nature may be made by the trustees under standing orders or direct debits from the scheme bank account if previously authorised by the pensioneer trustee:

 (i) pensions (but not lump sums);

 (ii) premiums on insurance policies;

 (iii) rents and rates;

 (iv) standing charges for gas, electricity, telephone bills, mortgages, loan repayments, ground rents, bank charges, employer contributions direct to an insurance policy, etc;

 (v) pension increases;

(ag) the pensioneer trustee must be a co-signatory to the following:

 (i) transfer payments;

 (ii) pension scheme refunds;

 (iii) payment of benefits not in pension form;

 (iv) other non-regular payments;

(ah) scheme documents must be revised if they do not permit the pensioneer trustee to be a co-signatory in the designated areas;

(ai) schemes will not be approved if they fail to meet the above conditions.

Pensioneer trustee undertaking

2.58   The pensioneer trustee undertakings for individual and corporate trustees are appended to PSO Update 69. The main terms of the undertakings are:

(a)   pensioneer trustees must not consent to any actions taken by SSASs which are inconsistent with the approved terms of the scheme, the legislation or published Inland Revenue practice;

(b)   pensioneer trustees must inform IR SPSS of any proposal of which they are aware either for them to resign or be removed;

(c)   pensioneer trustees must not agree to the termination of a SSAS unless it is in accordance with the scheme provisions or, where the scheme is not yet approved, with published Inland Revenue practice;

(d)   pensioneer trustees must not delegate their powers to other trustees, or body or person acting on behalf of such trustees (other than banks, building societies and professional managers authorised under the *Financial Services Act* legislation), if the delegation is for the purpose of infringing the terms of approval, the scheme documentation or published Inland Revenue practice;

(e)   pensioneer trustees must not delegate their powers unless the delegate is informed of the terms of the undertaking and the pensioneer trustee has made all reasonable efforts to ensure that the delegate has given the trustees an undertaking that corresponds with the terms in (a);

(f)   pensioneer trustees must undertake to provide IR SPSS, at least annually, with details of PSO reference numbers, and the names of their schemes and the sponsoring employers.

Chapter 3

Documentation and approval

Introduction

3.1   This chapter covers the various documents required for a SSAS, including the latest requirements to provide divorce provisions, what should appear in SSAS documentation, the procedure for applying to IR SPSS for approval and the main reporting requirements.

Establishment of a SSAS

3.2   To obtain approval it is necessary to establish a SSAS under irrevocable trusts. The reason for this is to alienate the pension scheme completely from the company so that on any later change of mind the company cannot reclaim the scheme funds placed in the trust. The trust may be established either by deed or by company resolution. SSASs are invariably established by deed (see 3.4 to 3.9), but if a company resolution is used a suggested resolution may be found at APPENDIX 6. An important initial step in this process is to ensure that the company's memorandum of association contains the power required to establish a pension scheme. If the requisite power is absent, it is preferable to amend the memorandum by special resolution. A suggested clause for insertion in the memorandum to provide this power may be found at APPENDIX 7.

3.3   The (then) PSO had not permitted a SSAS to be established within six months of a member's normal retirement age if the company concerned already had an existing insured scheme for the member. IR SPSS was concerned that in these circumstances the aim would be to make a transfer from the insured scheme to the SSAS and take advantage of the annuity purchase deferral facility (3.42). As the prior consent of the PSO must now be obtained before a SSAS is permitted to make or receive transfer payments (see 4.62), and SSASs may defer purchase until age 75 (if so documented), this restriction has become rather academic.

Interim deed

The position prior to 6 April 2002

3.4   It was not always practicable to establish a SSAS *ab initio* by a definitive deed particularly if it needs to be tailored to suit the circumstances or if time is of the essence to pay the first contribution before the company's year end and so qualify for tax relief. So an interim trust deed has been used to establish a SSAS instead. This procedure will only be available in very limited circumstances after 6 April 2002, as shown later in this paragraph. The interim deed should declare that the trust is irrevocable, set out the main purposes of the scheme and provide the trustees with appropriate powers of investment and administration. As the trust established by the interim deed is a common trust fund, the deed should also make it clear that all income and capital of the trust is available to provide benefits for the members. The definitive deed (see 3.14) containing the detailed rules and provisions could follow later and it was usual for the interim deed to provide for this to be executed within two years. For schemes established after 5 April 1993 it was required that definitive documents be adopted within two years. Failure to provide definitive documentation within two years could have led to the withdrawal of the provisional tax reliefs. This was reinforced by PSO Update No 17(8) where, after 5 April 1997, schemes operating on interim authorisation from before 6 April 1995 would have their application for approval withdrawn (see 3.67). PSO Update No 73 referred back to PSO Update No 17 and shortened the reminding procedure following which an application for approval shall be regarded as having been withdrawn. A flowchart was appended to the Update, showing the timing of the reminders.

The position after 6 April 2002

IR SPSS announced, in Pensions Update No 103, that a definitive deed and rules must accompany all applications for approval from 6 April 2002. This means that it will be necessary for practitioners to have in place appropriate SSAS deeds and rules for their clients for execution *ab initio* after 6 April 2002. The only exception will be where a SSAS is set up as a result of the sale of an employer or part of an employer's trade, which can give rise to complexities in the take-over of business. IR SPSS have stated that schemes that are entitled to use the interim stage for documentation will be required to use more extensive interim documentation than in the past. Further details of the procedure will be issued by the end of the year 2002.

3.5   It is necessary for the interim deed to include an approved pensioneer trustee among the trustees.

3.6 *Documentation and approval*

3.6 It is also recommended that an interim deed contains sufficient provisions to satisfy the *Preservation Regulations* regarding the operation of SSASs (see 11.2 to 11.5).

3.7 It is also advisable, if the trustees wish to make any employer-related investments before the definitive deed is executed, to include a rule in the interim deed permitting the trustees to make such investments (see 3.46 and 11.33 to 11.37).

3.8 At present, the interim deed does not need to include lengthy rules as to how the scheme should be operated until the definitive deed is executed (but see 3.15) provided there is an outline prepared by the advisers. The trustees should bear in mind, however, that until the definitive deed, which contains the detailed rules, is executed they may have to approach IR SPSS beforehand on certain matters in the absence of rules.

3.9 It is very important to ensure that the date the interim deed is executed is either before or the same date that the first contribution is paid to a SSAS. This will ensure that when the scheme eventually obtains approval from IR SPSS, relief from corporation tax is given on the initial contribution, as the effective date of approval cannot be earlier than the date of execution of the interim deed. If a contribution was paid to the trustees prior to the date of the interim deed it would not qualify for relief under *s 592(4)*, but may possibly be allowed as a deduction for Schedule D purposes by the company's inspector of taxes. Because the tax concessions would not be available there could also be taxation implications for the scheme members in respect of the amount of the contribution paid on their behalf as a result of the application of *s 595(1)(a)* and for the trustees in relation to any income received from investments derived from the contribution in the period prior to the effective date of approval as they may not be able to claim exemption under *s 592(2)* (see 10.34, to 10.35 and 10.39).

A revised version of PN(1997) was issued with PSO Update No 28 on 29 August 1997. This Update contained an important statement. PN 18.10 was amended to state that any schemes, which are not documented within two years of inception, should be treated for tax purposes as FURBS from commencement date. The Inland Revenue's view was that ample warning of this had been given in PSO Update No 17. In the first steps towards expediting the production of definitive documentation, the Inland Revenue set deadlines for schemes to provide documentation for cases, which had run well over the two year interim period. It provided special certificates to assist those schemes that had wound up or were paid up without full documentation. Any schemes which failed to meet the deadline would have their application for approval treated as having been withdrawn from outset and would be treated as FURBS as stated above.

Just as surprising was the statement in PSO Update No 29 that late applications for approval would result in similar treatment (see 3.67). Both matters gave rise to concern, because it is the inspector of taxes who has the right to determine the tax status of a scheme that has not received approval, not IR SPSS. Indeed, IR SPSS was not the author of the unapproved schemes brochure contained in APPENDIX 59.

In the case of the establishment of a new scheme, the administrator has three months to apply to the Inspector of Taxes for FURBS status if that is what he desires. Clarification is still awaited on why IR SPSS (at the time of the Updates, the PSO) considers that it has these powers, and whether or not it considers that it is empowered to determine the status of schemes which have either lost approval or fail to obtain approval. There are cases where trustees may consider it to be more advantageous to have their scheme classified as a discretionary trust rather than a FURBS.

The NIC position must also be considered (see 15.20(*f*)). The Contributions Agency's Press Release dated 15 March 1999 stated that provisions are contained in the new regulations which concern approved schemes and those at interim stage. The regulations are the *Social Security (Contributions and Credits) (Miscellaneous Amendments) Regulations 1999 (SI 1999 No 568)*. If key criteria are met at interim stage, NICs will not be chargeable. If they are not met, but the scheme is subsequently approved, they may be refunded. The main criteria concern a valid application for approval, contributions not to exceed a maximum of 53 primary Class 1 contributions at the primary percentage payable on earnings at the upper earnings limit for that year, commutation not to exceed a three-eightieths accrual rate up to a maximum of forty years, aggregation with connected schemes and *Regulation 9* of the *SSAS Regulations* (see APPENDIX 4) to be satisfied. However, the criteria shall not apply to a SSAS to which *Regulation 3* (see APPENDIX 4) of the *SSAS Regulations* applies.

Members' announcement letters

3.10   These must be sent to IR SPSS when applying for approval. They stem from *s 590(2)(b)* which requires that every member must be given written particulars of all essential features of the scheme. The particulars can be given in the form of a short announcement, a letter, and a booklet or in a copy of the trust deed and rules. In a SSAS it is usual to provide the particulars in an announcement letter to each member. This is done at the commencement of the scheme and whenever a new member joins the scheme.

3.11   The main areas that should be covered in an announcement are set out as follows:

(a)   Main benefits:

- on normal retirement;
- on death in service;
- on death after retirement;
- on withdrawal from service;
- on early retirement;
- on late retirement;
- any options at retirement (e.g. commutation to provide a lump sum).

(b) Pension increases.

(c) Members' contributions:

- amount;
- arrangements for their collection;
- effect of temporary absence.

(d) Financing details:

- the basis of the company's contributions.

(e) Legal constitution:

- documentation;
- reference to the legislation under which the scheme is or will be approved.

(f) Operational details:

- the administrator;
- the trustees;
- the managing trustees.

(g) Amendment:

- the powers of amendment and how amendments may be effected.

3.12 Announcement letters quite often describe the basis of a member's interest in the scheme. As a SSAS is a common trust fund (see 3.4) it is most important that a member's interest is correctly described and that the description avoids the earmarking of specific assets to a member in order to preserve the common access integrity of the trust fund. A member's interest lies against all the assets of the scheme and not against any specific asset. The assets are therefore usually allocated notionally by the actuary to each member to avoid earmarking apart from any policies in respect of the member or assets specifically representing the investment of a member's personal contributions. The terms 'member's credit', 'member's interest' or 'contribution credit' are often met with and usually defined in the definitive deed and possibly the announcement letter. Wherever it appears, the definition must avoid any suggestion of earmarking.

Actuarial documentation

3.13   It is essential that on the establishment of a SSAS an actuarial report is prepared or actuarial advice is provided on the funding of the scheme as this must be sent with the initial application for approval to IR SPSS (see 3.59). The form of the report or advice is described in 9.3 to 9.50.

Definitive documentation

3.14   Whereas the use of the interim deed procedure previously allowed a scheme to be established quickly and for the lengthier definitive deed containing the detailed provisions and rules of the scheme to be drawn up later, this is no longer an option for most schemes. Sometimes a document is tailor-made to suit the particular scheme concerned, and it is possible to submit draft definitive documentation to IR SPSS prior to execution of an agreed definitive deed. However, this practice is generally not adopted with SSASs because of the widespread use of 'model deeds' (see 3.47 to 3.52).

3.15   IR SPSS issued Pensions Update No 100 on 18 June 2001. This Update sets out the position with regard to the abandonment of schemes that have not been approved, and of approved schemes. The main criteria that apply are:

(a)   a SSAS that has not yet received approval may be abandoned, subject to IR SPSS approval, if it is fully insured, the trust provisions allow for abandonment and no member has more than 2 years of qualifying service;

(b)   in the case of (a), the policies must be surrendered, employer premiums must be returned to the employer and employee contributions to the members and any provisional tax reliefs will be withdrawn;

(c)   the cancellation of a policy during a cooling off period is not in itself sufficient reason for a scheme to be treated as having been abandoned;

(d)   approved schemes can only be abandoned if IR SPSS cancels approval (for instance, if there has been a change from employed to self-employed status since approval was granted);

(e)   if there has been no change in circumstance, the trustees may wish to make the scheme paid up or to wind it up in accordance with its provisions;

(f)   the trustees are satisfied that the trusts allow it.

Contents of definitive deed

3.16 The definitive deed is usually in two parts. The first part (the trust powers) containing the clauses sets out the trustees' powers and discretions and provisions for winding-up the scheme. The second part, the rules, often a schedule, contains the rules that cover eligibility, contribution and benefit details, and sets out Inland Revenue limits on benefits. There is however no set format as to which provisions should appear in either part.

3.17 The deed should include all the usual clauses and rules which IR SPSS expects for a self-administered scheme set up under irrevocable trusts seeking discretionary approval. There are certain requirements that must appear in the deed so far as IRPSS is concerned.

3.18 In the preamble to the deed IR SPSS will expect to see that one of the trustees is an approved pensioneer trustee, otherwise this appointment should appear in the body of the deed for the scheme concerned.

3.19 There must also be a rule providing for actuarial valuations to take place at intervals of no more than three years (PN 20.15).

3.20 Somewhere in the deed, either in the provisions as to the powers of the trustees or for winding-up the scheme, there must be a provision that in the event of winding-up the scheme this can only be done in accordance with the rules on the unanimous decision of all the trustees. The agreement of the pensioneer trustee must be sought to the winding-up (see 2.35).

3.21 From 5 August 1991 when the *SSAS Regulations* came into effect, the governing documentation had to contain the provisions in the regulations that relate to borrowings, trustee/member transactions, certain investments, loans, the pensioneer trustee and reporting requirements. A period of three years until 5 August 1994 was allowed under *s 591A(2)* to execute the appropriate documentation for those SSASs already approved at 5 August 1991. Approval lapsed if executed definitive documentation was not in place by 5 August 1994. SSASs not approved at 5 August 1991 must have had these provisions in their documentation before approval was granted.

These *Regulations* have since been amended, as described in 3.50. Schemes not approved on or before 17 March 1998 are required to satisfy the new requirements before approval will be granted (see 3.58). However, if an application for approval was made prior to the issue of PSO Update No 45 on 24 July 1998, and the procedures described in 3.58(a) to (d) are met, the PSO will consider granting approval.

For schemes approved after 17 March 1998, and before the issue of PSO Update No 45 on 24 July 1998, which do not reflect the second set of SSAS regulations referred to in 3.50 (*SI 1998 No 1315*) these should be incorporated as soon as possible, and no later than when other changes are made.

Schemes approved after 24 July 1998 and future applications for approval are dealt with in 3.58(e) to 3.58(h), and schemes approved on or before 17 March 1998 are dealt with in 3.58(j) to (m).

Other requirements

3.22 There is a whole series of provisions and rules that may or may not be included in the definitive deed depending on the circumstances of the scheme. IR SPSS will not insist on them all, but where they do appear in the deed there are certain requirements to be met because controlling directors are members of the scheme and special limitations apply to their benefits. In addition, because the scheme is self-administered certain other provisions will be expected by IR SPSS to be written into the deed. Readers are referred to the 'Trust Deed, Rules and Checklist' published by the National Association of Pension Funds (Notes on Pensions No 21) which provides guidance in drafting a trust deed and Chapter 1 of Tolley's Taxation of Pension Benefits. The main points remaining for consideration include:

(a) scheme name, commencement date, interpretation and a recital listing earlier documentation (and whether timescales for documentation have been exceeded);

(b) powers of appointment and removal of trustees, their own powers (including investment powers), proceedings and scheme administration;

(c) powers of appointment and removal of the scheme actuary and accountant;

(d) a provision for actuarial reviews;

(e) powers to close, freeze or wind up the scheme;

(f) contributions, trustees' costs and indemnification;

(g) death benefits, including discretionary distributions and member nominations;

(h) an amendment power; and

(i) eligibility and temporary absence, benefits and limits, transfers and buy outs.

The points in 3.22 to 3.43 refer to matters which particularly concern SSASs.

3.23 Any deeds affecting the scheme, including interim and definitive deeds, should be engrossed by a solicitor.

3.24 The trustees should normally be given wide powers of investment in the definitive deed, unless it is intended to be a wholly insured scheme.

However, investment in policies should not be overlooked in drafting the investment clause. Even though the SSAS may be separately administered from a LO it is always advisable to have provision for making investments in insurance policies. As trustees may borrow (see 7.56 – 7.74) it is essential for them to have powers to raise loans and mortgages, quite apart from the restrictions which apply thereto from the regulations and which must also be in the rules. A specimen investment clause may be found at APPENDIX 8.

However, a word of warning must be given in connection with rebated and shared insurance commissions. IR SPSS are concerned that commissions, which are passed on to clients by IFAs or other intermediaries, may not be used to enhance the value of scheme funds. PSO Updates No 31, 33 and 64 express concerns about the use of some pension schemes for tax avoidance. PSO Update No 33 deals with insurance commissions in some detail. In particular, any benefit that is gained must be retained in the scheme if approval is not to be lost. PSO Update No 33 also warns about the unacceptability of an advantage gained by virtue of a misrepresentation of annual premium levels, and PSO Update No 64 explains that the concern is wide-ranging and includes such business as the purchase of annuities.

3.25   Because the trustees of a SSAS are permitted to sell certain investments held prior to 16 July 1991 to scheme members (see 2.22) and those members may be trustees of the SSAS, the definitive deed should contain a provision allowing the trustee beneficiary to benefit himself. This is necessary to prevent a trustee placing himself in a conflict of interests. In *Bray v Ford [1896] AC 51* it was held that a person in a fiduciary position is not, unless expressly provided, entitled to make a profit. This principle was upheld more recently in the case of a pension scheme in *Re Drexel Burnham Lambert UK Pension Plan [1995] 1 WLR 32*. The problem has been resolved by *Pensions Act 1995, s 39*. No conflict arises for member trustees who benefit by the exercise of discretionary powers vested in them, merely because they are members of the scheme.

3.26   It is important to stipulate who should appoint the trustees and who should remove them. This power is usually vested in the principal company. In the event of the company being sold or liquidated this power would reside with the new owners or the liquidator. Therefore before such events occur the trustees and company could consider amending the power to appoint the trustees by conferring that power on the trustees themselves subject to the provisions of the *Pensions Act 1995* where appropriate.

3.27   This conveniently leads to the power to amend the definitive deed (see 3.22(f)) which should be written into the deed. It is usual for this power to be subject to the agreement of the principal company. A specimen clause containing powers of amendment may be found at APPENDIX 9. Any deed of amendment should be sent to IR SPSS after execution for its acceptance.

3.28   It is usual for the rules to include various definitions to facilitate interpretation (see 3.22(a)). Such definitions must include controlling directors (see APPENDIX 10) and final remuneration (see 4.16), which is most relevant to controlling directors. The rules may also allow for each year's remuneration to be increased in line with the RPI (the Glossary, in Appendix 1 to PN). Pensions in payment may be increased in line with the RPI, or 3% per annum, tested on a year-on-year basis (PN 9.1) provided there is such a provision.

3.29   IR SPSS has always had fears of an irregular distribution of death benefits should the principle in *Saunders v Vautier* be applied. To reduce such risks IR SPSS requires scheme rules to provide that lump sum death in service benefits and lump sum guarantee payments should be distributable at the trustees' discretion among the usual range of individuals and bodies that may be designated for this purpose. The discretionary power afforded to the trustees in this area will of course free the lump sum payments from IHT (*Inheritance Tax Act 1984, s 151*). However, the general IR SPSS practice precluding a discretionary distribution of a benefit payable on death in service on or after age 75 of a controlling director would still apply. This latter point must be written into the rules of a SSAS as explained in PN 11.12.

3.30   There must be a scheme rule providing for full commutation of pension where the member is in exceptional circumstances of serious ill-health if such a benefit is to be provided at all (PN 8.15). This is subject to the agreement of the Inland Revenue for controlling directors (PN 8.20). This is because no arm's length relationship exists in a SSAS and there is no life office interest. In other cases for ordinary employees it can be left to the trustees to satisfy themselves regarding the circumstances of the case. The reference to IR SPSS for approval of full commutation must be made at least 14 days before the payment of the proposed benefits and accompanied by proper medical evidence (see 3.83). That evidence should show that the member's life expectancy is very short because of a terminal illness. Showing that the member is incapacitated or has a life expectancy reduced to a few years will not be sufficient to secure full commutation. The member's life expectancy must be unquestionably short, i.e. less than one year (APPENDIX 5). Full commutation in these circumstances should be dealt with expeditiously including the reference to IR SPSS and IR SPSS can be expected to respond promptly. It will do so initially by telephone and then confirm in writing or disagree. If nothing is heard within 14 days practitioners are entitled to assume the proposals are satisfactory.

3.31   It is most advisable to have a rule allowing the trustees to make and receive transfer payments. Its wording should not only allow transfers between occupational pension schemes, but should also allow payments to be made to and received from personal pension schemes. Transfers must not be made in either direction without prior IR SPSS approval (see 4.62). Such a rule is not only important during the continuance of a scheme, but it will also be of importance if the scheme is to be wound-up (see 3.38). Specimen clauses for making and receiving transfers may be found at APPENDIX 11.

PSO Updates No 21 and 26 explain the provisions which will apply in the event of reinstatement in an occupational pensions scheme where mis-selling of personal pension schemes is in point.

3.32   It is also advisable to have rules allowing other companies to adhere to, and withdraw from, the scheme. This will allow subsidiary and associated companies to participate. Such participation is usually effected by a deed of adherence, but it may also be effected in the interim deed or definitive deed. A specimen deed of adherence may be found at APPENDIX 12.

3.33   Originally, if the rules of a SSAS provided for pensions increases linked to increases with the RPI, money to finance the increases could be retained in the fund, provided such increases were not at a fixed rate of 3 per cent. IR SPSSs practice in this area, however, has developed to the extent that pensions increases awarded during the period between retirement and securing the pension should be secured at the time the pension is secured and increases awarded subsequently are secured at the time of the award. This development was published following the PQ of July 1984 (APPENDIX 2) and the rules should take this into account. See 3.28 concerning maximum increases.

3.34   On securing pensions in SSASs, PN 20.42 mentions that where a contingent spouse's or dependant's pension is to be provided the rules may allow either for the spouse's or dependant's pension to be purchased at the same time as the member's pension or its purchase may be deferred until the earlier of the date on which the deceased member would have attained age 75 or the attainment of age 75 years by the spouse or dependant. However, if the rules provide for the widow's pension to be payable to the woman who is the member's wife at his retirement, not as at the date of his death, the spouse's benefit must be secured by an annuity at the same time as the member's benefit is secured. The further conditions that apply are similar to those for member's annuity deferrals, and are described in 3.42 and 3.43.

3.35   For SSASs already approved at the time the *F(No 2)A 1987* and *FA 1989* were enacted, the various amendments they contained are covered by the legislative over-rides and later amendments. The main regulations are in the *Occupational Pension Schemes (Transitional Provisions) (Amendment) Regulations 1993 (SI 1993 No 3219)*, the *Retirement Benefits Schemes (Continuation of Rights of Members of Approved Schemes) (Amendment) Regulations 1993 (SI 1993 No 3220)* and the *Retirement Benefits Schemes*

(Tax Relief on Contributions) (Disapplication of Earnings Cap) (Amendment) Regulations 1993 (SI 1993 No 3221). Such amendments were required to be made to scheme rules by December 1996, but PSO Update No 5 confirmed it would no longer be necessary by then. However, it is desirable to include these provisions in the rules in order to promote compliance with the tax requirements and schemes are encouraged to amend their rules at the first opportunity. For any SSASs established prior to this legislation and not yet approved by IR SPSS, and for all SSASs established afterwards, the provisions of both *Finance Acts* must be included in the rules, and the changes described in 3.58.

3.36 The *Retirement Benefits Schemes (Restriction on Discretion to Approve) (Additional Voluntary Contributions) Regulations 1993 (SI 1993 No 3016)* which came into force on 27 December 1993 restrict the repayment to a member of surplus funds arising from the provision of benefits under a scheme to which a member pays AVCs. These regulations prevent IR SPSS from approving a scheme until its documents contain provisions requiring the administrator to comply with the requirements of the regulations. SSASs which received approval prior to 27 December 1993 initially had three years to incorporate the necessary provisions into their definitive deeds otherwise approval would have automatically been lost under *s 591A*. Following representations the PSO (now IR SPSS) indicated (PSO Update No 5) that it was prepared to disapply this deadline in relation to schemes other than Free Standing Additional Voluntary Contribution Schemes (FSAVCS), i.e. SSASs in this instance, if the APT or other representative bodies give an assurance that a voluntary code of practice will be widely adopted. SSASs are expected to make rule amendments at the first practicable opportunity and comply with *SI 1993 No 3016* in the meantime. Any non-compliant SSASs are recommended to make the required rule amendments as soon as possible to ensure that the risk of automatic loss of approval is avoided. Transfers must not be made in either direction without prior IR SPSS approval (see 4.62).

3.37 The provisions for winding-up a SSAS, always subject to the agreement of the pensioneer trustee, should cover all the circumstances where this can occur i.e. payments of benefits to the last member, withdrawal of a participating company, sale or liquidation of the principal company. In fact it was an IR SPSS requirement that on the liquidation of the principal company a SSAS should be wound-up (APPENDIX 2).

This was confirmed in the response to the Parliamentary Question in July 1984 (APPENDIX 2), following which the APT and the Association of British Insurers were issued with the following statement:

"The scheme documentation should provide that, in these circumstances, the scheme will be wound-up or partially wound-up if appropriate and the proceeds used in accordance with the documentation to purchase or

transfer accrued benefits of members, any surplus being returned to the employer. Any other course should be subject to the specific approval of the Board of Inland Revenue."

APT Newsletters Nos 101, 106, 113 and 114 had originally reported that IR SPSS had conceded that SSASs may continue without a principal employer, and that schemes approved before 29 April 1991 were exempt. As later stated, the latter was not the case at the time. The PSO (now IR SPSS) had objected to the continuation of a scheme in such circumstances since at least 1983. It may have been possible for the SSAS to remain paid up, but that would be subject to the agreement of the Inland Revenue and to any conditions that it may require.

The Inland Revenue finally relented on the point, and announced in PSO Update No 70 that a SSAS may continue in existence after the employer has gone into liquidation if the rules so permit. If the employer is also the administrator, a new administrator must be appointed.

3.38   The winding-up provisions should cover all the options available to the trustees for meeting the liabilities of the scheme. Members' benefits including those of contingent beneficiaries should be secured if they are already in payment and also if they have reached normal retirement age. They may be provided with early retirement benefits if they have reached age 50. Otherwise the options available are to purchase deferred annuities, or make transfer payments to other occupational schemes or personal pension schemes. There may be some circumstances in which winding-up may be delayed, for example by uncertainties about asset values and liabilities. The PSO is willing to permit two stage transfer payments in unusual situations, and its requirements are laid down in detail in PSO Update No 40. A rule amendment may be necessary for this to take place.

3.39   The priorities as to which members' benefits are to be dealt with first, e.g. pensioners, current members or leavers, may be specified and, in the event of insufficient funds, provision made as to how the funds are to be apportioned between the members. If there are more than sufficient funds, provision to increase benefits to Inland Revenue maxima should be included or use made of a general augmentation provision.

3.40   The expenses of realising assets and of winding-up the scheme may be met from scheme funds if the rules so provide. This can be useful where the company is in liquidation with no funds of its own. There must be a rule providing for any balance of funds to be returned to the company if there is a surplus in the scheme after payment of all benefits and expenses. Such a refund is subject to tax at 35% (40% prior to *FA 2001*–see 9.51). IR SPSS must be notified on form PS199 (see APPENDIX 13) in all cases where a SSAS is winding-up.

3.41 Sometimes the winding-up of a SSAS can occur before the definitive deed has been executed and the scheme has been approved by the IR SPSS. Obviously approval will still be required in these circumstances. Until February 1992 a short deed or trustees' resolution reciting what had occurred, confirming that since its establishment the SSAS had been administered in accordance with the requirements of the Inland Revenue and incorporating the provisions of the *Regulations*, was acceptable to IR SPSS. Since then IR SPSS has required a formal trustees' declaration adopting the PSO model rules for SSASs (see 3.47 to 3.51) and certifying that the administration has been consistent with Inland Revenue approval. A specimen declaration may be found at APPENDIX 14. The execution of the trustees' declaration, even if two years after the execution of the interim deed, should ensure that provisional tax reliefs are maintained until approval is granted (see 3.4) provided IR SPSS was approached before the two-year period expired.

Annuity purchase

3.42 Pensions Update No 97 announced that, pending the provision by IR SPSS of standard wording to take account of the flexible provisions for annuity purchase that were described in PSO Update No 54, a scheme or buy-out policy may adopt an overriding grandfather clause to reflect the flexible provisions that are now enshrined in PN, App XII. The standard wording should have issued by the time this book goes to press as, by virtue of PSO Update No 66, schemes provisions should be introduced within two years of the facility being made available to a member. IR SPSS will not need to see the amendment if the standard wording is used, and the form PS176, PS 5 or PS6 (as appropriate) is submitted to that office.

A maximum benefit check was specified in para 17 of PSO Update No 54. However, it is no longer necessary for the benefit style chosen to be adopted when the annuity is purchased at a future date.

The new provisions (which broadly follow the arrangements for personal pension schemes) are more flexible than the existing deferral provisions, and SSASs can chose whichever method they wish. The two methods are described below.

The old method of deferral

SSASs are allowed to pay pensions from their resources for up to five years from a member's retirement if the pension is guaranteed for five years and there is a lump sum guarantee payment prospectively distributable to the member's dependants or legal personal representatives in the event of death. As an alternative, from 4 February 1994 IR SPSS agreed to a further easement of the five-year concession to allow the purchase of pensions to be deferred to age 75 irrespective of the retirement age of members. For SSASs in existence prior to 5 August 1994 this alternative rule may be adopted instead of the five-year rule. For all SSASs established after 4 August 1994 the age 75 deferral rule must be adopted if they wish to take advantage of the purchase deferral. The deferment of purchasing pensions on retirement must be written into the rules in all cases, and any policies or buy-out policies if required, otherwise it cannot be deferred.

The new method of deferral

If any income is already being drawn down, there must be a recalculation on the new basis even if there has been a recent review or the pension is reduced as a result. Again, the facility must be written into the rules in all cases, and any policies or buy-out policies if required, otherwise it cannot be used. The main criteria are:

(a)   any over-funding must be dealt with when the benefits come into payment, and on final annuity purchase;

(b)   the test for buy-out policies will be the date on which the benefits first become payable;

(c)   for the purpose of calculating maximum benefits, allocation of benefits under PN 12.5 must not take place until annuity purchase;

(d)   the pension available for drawdown will be calculated by use of GADs tables for a single life basis only;

(e)   drawdown may apply to the total benefits or a part of the pension may be purchased as an annuity, with drawdown applying to the remainder;

(f)   Inland Revenue limits apply to the amount of pension and the pension equivalence of any lump sum taken;

(g)   subject to (f), a lower and upper range applies, being 35% to 100% of the annuity that could have been purchased at the relevant time;

(h)   PAYE must be applied;

(i)   pensions in payment must not cease, although they may vary each year within the specified range;

(j)   if there is a direct relationship between the pension and the lump sum, the latter must be based on the amount of pension drawn before any allocation or commutation;

(k)   there must be (at least) triennial reviews after the start of drawdown if the pension has not been secured, employing the GADs tables;

(l)   following the review in (k), the amount of pension must be within the 35% to 100% range;

(m)   restrictions on insured schemes are laid down in PN, App XII;

(n)   if the member is concurrently a member of more than one scheme or buy-out policy, where permitted, drawdown may be taken from one but not from the other subject to the normal timing requirements;

(o)   if there was a shortfall on Inland Revenue maxima when the drawdown first commenced, the sponsoring employer may pay additional contributions at any time and secure additional benefits and /or pension increases;

(p)   if (o) applies, and an annuity has already been secured, the additional benefits may be deferred and drawdown may commence on those benefits in accordance with the principles laid down above;

(q)   if the pension in payment has to be valued for retained benefits purposes, it should be valued on the maximum amount capable of being withdrawn.

The old method of deferral (spouses and dependants)

3.43   Subsequent to the arrangements at 3.42, IR SPSS has allowed a similar deferral regarding the purchase of contingent spouse's and dependants' pensions from 22 June 1995. Thus, instead of the five-year deferral rules, if a SSAS adopts the rule allowing the purchase of members' pensions to be deferred until age 75, the same rule can incorporate a provision that where the member dies whilst in receipt of a pension from the scheme, a surviving spouse's or dependant's pension may be paid from the scheme instead of being purchased immediately. Purchase of the surviving spouse's or dependant's pension may be deferred until the earlier of the attaining by either of age 75 or the date the deceased member would have attained 75. The background and IR SPSS's requirements in respect of the alternative rules at 3.42 and in this paragraph, are set out in 4.97 to 4.107.

The new method of deferral (spouses and dependants)

If any income is already being drawn down, there must be a recalculation on the new basis even if there has been a recent review or the pension is reduced as a result. Again, the facility must be written into the rules in all cases, and any policies or buy-out policies if required, otherwise it cannot be used. The conditions in 3.42 (a) to (q) also apply to spouses and dependants.

Additionally:

(a)   if a member dies during drawdown, he or she is treated as having died in retirement, subject to special conditions where AVCs have come into payment;

(b)   any five year guarantee must be elected at commencement of drawdown;

(c)   the amount in (b) may be calculated as if the member had opted for 100% withdrawal;

(d)   if an annuity is purchased in the guarantee period, any guarantee attached to it should be reduced proportionate to the time that has elapsed since drawdown commenced;

(e)   any survivors' pension benefits, together with any own right pensions, shall be subject to the limits that applied as at the member's death (PN 12.2, 12.3), and any surplus dealt with under the normal rules;

(f)   the beneficiary may commence drawdown in accordance with the principles laid down above, and those principles, where appropriate, shall apply in the event of the death of the beneficiary during a period of drawdown.

Model drawdown documentation was provided under Pensions Update No 105.

Preservation and equal treatment

3.44   The *Preservation Regulations* (see 11.2 to 11.4), particularly the entitlement to short service benefit, must be included in the definitive deed. With the demise of the OPB on 5 April 1997, the actuary became responsible for preparing detailed tables of the uniform accrual method and the scheme method of calculating short service benefit in accordance with the *Preservation Regulations*. Any permitted alternatives to short service benefit either on termination of the member's service or the winding-up of the SSAS must also be included. So the purchase of an approved 'Section 32' buy-out policy needs to be included together with provisions for transfers out and pension increases. The buy-out policy legislation was changed on 1 July 1994 (see 4.61) so those insurance policies are no longer subject to prior approval. However, the rules of a SSAS that restrict the trustees to the purchase of approved buy-out policies do not have to be amended unless they wish to purchase post–30 June 1994 policies. IR SPSS will not object if the trustees wish to purchase such policies pending the amendment of the rules. Neither will IR SPSS withhold the approval of a scheme whose rules contain the former prior approved formula.

3.45   The rules should comply with the equal treatment requirements (see 11.52 to 11.55). These require membership to be open to both men and women on the same terms as to age and length of service needed to become a member and whether membership is voluntary or compulsory. PSO Updates No 27 and 68 describe changes to Inland Revenue practice to enable schemes to comply with equal treatment requirements. The main decisions by the European Courts of Justice which are referred to are *Coloroll, Ten Oever, Moroni, Neath, Roberts* and *Vroege. The Pensions Act 1995, ss 62 and 66 and*

The Occupational Pension Schemes (Equal Treatment) Regulations 1995 (SI 1995 No 3183) brought the requirements within UK statute law with effect from 1 January 1996. In brief, the Updates consider equal benefits from 17 May 1990; the acceptance of sex-based actuarial factors on commutation, transfers, funding, etc. and the admission of part-timers retrospectively (see also 11.56). A claim for part-time membership could, following the ruling in the case of *Preston v Wolverhampton Health Care NHS Trust [2001] PLR 39*, in the House of Lords on 8 February 2001, go back to 8 April 1976, and the reaction of IR SPSS is awaited to the latest developments. SSASs usually provide that membership is at the invitation of the company that will satisfy the equal access requirements. The unfair maternity and family leave provisions of *Social Security Act 1989, Sch 5* were brought into effect on 23 June 1994 by the *Social Security Act 1989 (Commencement No 2) Order 1994 (SI 1994 No 1661)*. These provisions are over-riding. It is good practice to include a rule affording women members the protection of this legislation and the *Employment Rights Act 1996, s 71.* (see 11.33 to 11.39) and the later legislation described in 11.57.

3.46   Employer-related investments of more than 5% of the value of the fund cannot be made unless there is a scheme rule which provides for them and which states that all the members of the scheme must agree to such investments in writing.

Model deeds

3.47   The practice of agreeing model deeds for SSASs with the Inland Revenue has been established since the late 1970s. It is clearly economical, as mentioned in PN 18.15, for a practitioner with a portfolio of SSASs to have model documentation of some sort so that it may be used on all schemes in almost the same format apart from names, dates etc. This applies to all the different practitioners including LOs and can embrace definitive deeds, deeds of amendment and members' announcement letters. If model documentation is agreed beforehand with IR SPSS and submitted on particular schemes later it also greatly facilitates the examination procedures in IR SPSS and can lead to much quicker approval of schemes. To this end IR SPSS has agreed a model deed procedure whereby practitioners can approach and agree with the standards section of IR SPSS a model deed to be used on all of the practitioner's SSASs.

3.48   The time taken to agree a model deed with the standards section will very much depend on the contents of the deed and whether or not they can be agreed without further correspondence and negotiation. The definitive deed will require all the usual clauses and rules IR SPSS expects for a scheme set up under irrevocable trusts seeking discretionary approval. The essential and other main requirements have been covered in 3.17 to 3.46 and will not be dealt with again.

3.49   Having agreed a model deed with the standards section the procedure on individual schemes is very simple. The deed is executed with the names and dates inserted for that scheme, but it does not have to be sent to IR SPSS. Instead it is mandatory to send a documentation certificate in lieu (see 3.58). PN 18.14, 18.15 describe the procedure. Even where a document in its present form is not suitable for this procedure the standards section will advise how it can be revised to bring it within the procedure. The standards section will confirm that all model deeds come within the procedure at the time negotiations on the model are completed. If there are any variations in the model each variation will be treated as a separate agreed model and given a different reference number. Rule amendments intended for use on a large number of SSASs and agreed by the standards section are suitable for this procedure. If a non-model deed is used on a SSAS or a copiously amended deed is executed it has to be submitted to IR SPSS general section and will take longer to be examined and accepted.

3.50   Model deeds need updating from time to time and the standards section will agree amended versions of definitive deeds if approached, for example the substantial amendments necessitated by the *F(No 2)A 1987* and the *FA 1989* and the later amendments to the over-rides (see 3.35), the amendments required by the surplus *AVC Regulations* (see 3.36) and any change to the rules to adopt the deferral of pension purchase until age 75 (see 3.42 to 3.43). The divorce provision requirements are also described separately in 3.95. It is probably better to agree a totally new model deed where major changes are intended rather than a model deed of amendment as the former is more likely to be economical. The standards section may indicate that it will only agree a new model deed anyway. The standards section will not otherwise agree one-off amendments for use on individual SSASs. Thus the documentation procedure (see 3.49) is not available for this type of amendment. A package of model rules was issued by the PSO standards section in December 1991 incorporating the changes introduced by the regulations for use by practitioners. This has since been updated, as shown in the following paragraph. A model rule is also available to cover the deferral of the purchase of members' and dependants' pensions (see 3.42 and 3.43).

Two sets of regulations, *SI 1998 No 728* and *SI 1998 No 1315* (see 2.24) were announced in PSO Updates No 41 and 45. A revised version of part 5 of the Inland Revenue's model rules can be obtained from the standard documents section of IR SPSS and may be used by any SSAS irrespective of whether or not it has been documented using a model deed. Current versions of IR SPSS model rules for use by practitioners are contained in Appendices 15 and 16.

3.51   Many SSASs used the interim deed procedure but it is unlikely to be possible to agree with the standards section any new model interim deed, and the documentation procedure described in 3.58 is not available for interim deeds. Equally, a short definitive deed *ab initio* (see 3.15) with no interim period at all is unlikely to meet current standards. It is important to understand the distinction between 'model' deeds and 'standard' deeds agreed with the standards section of IR SPSS. They are not the same. Model deeds are not for instance agreed with LOs and large pensions practitioners for their other schemes. Moreover model deeds are not likely to receive the in depth examination apparently accorded to standard deeds.

3.52 It was found that because model deeds can be agreed in a relatively short period and are used on the vast majority of SSASs, IR SPSS was most unlikely to adopt the deed of indemnity procedure (PN 18.11 and 18.12) which was available to large self-administered schemes where approval could have been held up for a considerable period pending agreement of a standard deed or a one-off definitive deed. The removal of the interim period from 6 April 2002 will now make this matter academic.

Application for approval

3.53 IR SPSS's requirements for the approval are set out in *section 604*. PN, paras 18.1–18.14 contain IR SPSS guidelines for the procedure to be adopted.

3.54 Applications for approval of SSASs must be made to IR SPSS in writing using the prescribed form PS176 signed by all the trustees and accompanied by form PS176 (A/T) (see PSO Update No 47 and APPENDIX 17), and must be accompanied by certain documents. All applications for approval should be made to the IR SPSS. The timing of the application is also crucial to obtaining the appropriate tax reliefs.

3.55 The PSO (now IR SPSS) operates very strict procedures regarding applications for approval that can be seen from PN 18.6. This mentions that applications not made on the appropriate form fully and accurately completed and accompanied by the appropriate undertaking and documentation will not be accepted as valid applications for approval. Thus if the form PS176 is left blank in places or entries are made such as 'not known' or 'to follow' the application will be returned. Only a resubmitted complete application will constitute a valid application for approval and the date on which IR SPSS receives it will constitute the date of application for approval for statutory purposes. Any delay here may therefore affect the eventual effective date of approval and the tax reliefs that flow therefrom. See 3.9 concerning the possible automatic treatment of a scheme as a FURBS by IR SPSS.

3.56 The form PS176 requires considerable information that is mainly self-evident and only those parts most relevant to SSASs will be looked at more closely in this book. As one would expect full details of controlling directors are required and other schemes of the employer.

3.57   Section M of the form refers to the accompanying documentation. A copy of the executed interim deed is required to be sent and a copy of the definitive deed if it has been executed at this stage. Copies of the members' announcement letters should also be provided (see 3.10 to 3.12). If each member's letter is the same IR SPSS should be able to accept a copy of one letter with an explanation that they are identical for all members.

3.58   If the definitive deed is a model the standards section reference should be clearly quoted (see 3.49) to facilitate examination. If the model deed comes within the documentation certificate procedure outlined in PN 18.4 then a completed certificate PS5 (APPENDIX 18) must be sent with the application for approval if the deed has been executed at that stage or the completed certificate should be sent later when the deed is executed. A completed certificate PS6 (APPENDIX 19) must be sent at the application stage or later as the case may be for model rule amendments agreed with the standards section. Both certificates must be fully completed to show the IR SPSS reference number allocated to the document being used and confirmation is required from the signatory that the document has been used for the specific purpose designated. Where model rules include the amendments required by the surplus *AVC Regulations* and other legislation (see 3.50) certificates PS5 or PS6 (see APPENDICES 18 and 19) should be endorsed as explained below. Where deferral of the purchase of members' or dependants' pensions (see 3.50) applies, this should be indicated. Practitioners who send certificates PS5 or PS6 without a covering letter may enter their reference number for the scheme at the top right-hand corner of the certificate. There is no need under this procedure to send a copy of the definitive deed or deed of amendment itself.

By way of background information, IR SPSS requirements for different circumstances following the changes to *SSAS Regulations* described in 3.50 were as follows (the main principles still apply to future changes to accommodate new changes to practice and legislation):-

Schemes not approved on or before 17 March 1998

In general, schemes not approved on or before 17 March 1998 had to satisfy the new requirements for approval. However schemes for which application for approval was made before 24 July 1998 could seek to give confirmation in accordance with (a) to (e) below that the scheme had been amended to incorporate the current requirements in order that IR SPSS could consider granting approval:

(a) if a previously agreed model deed was being used, certificate PS6 could be used as described above for the purpose of providing such confirmation. For amendments made after 24 July 1998, where the current version of part 5 of the model rules described in 3.50 was being used, paragraph (*a*) of the certificate should have been amended to read:

'that the rules of the above scheme were amended on..................................
by an amendment which accords in all respects with the revised and amended part 5 of the Inland Revenue Model Rules'.

This approach was also permissible for use of a previously agreed standard rule amendment that was being amended by incorporation of the part 5 changes;

(b) certificates PS6, which were amended in line with PSO Update No 41 (15) and were sent to the PSO before 24 July 1998, would be accepted as confirmation of the incorporation of the first set of regulations (*SI 1998 No 728*) referred to in 3.50;

(c) once the standards section of IR SPSS had agreed an up-to-date revised model deed with a practitioner, certificate PS6 could be used without amendment, subject to the insertion of the appropriate reference number as described above;

(d) if a scheme was documented by a previously agreed model deed and subsequently amends that deed by a non-standard amendment, or a scheme had not adopted a previously agreed model deed, a copy of the amending document had to be be sent to IR SPSS stating whether the changes entirely reflect revised part 5 of the model rules. If they did not, but reflected only the requirement to include the statutory changes referred to in 3.50, the amending document had to be marked up to show where it deviated from the model rules.

Applications for approval after 24 July 1998

PSO Update No 45 requested that future applications for approval, where no interim stage is involved, be delayed until IR SPSS have confirmed that the rules to be adopted meet all current conditions (subject to 3.62). Additionally, for future applications:

(e) certificate PS5, as described above, may be used for providing confirmation that schemes which adopt model deeds that do not satisfy the new conditions have been amended. If the current version of part 5 of the model rules described in 3.50 is being used, paragraph (b) of the certificate should be amended by inserting after the SF or PS reference number the words 'amended in accordance with the revised and amended part 5 of the Inland Revenue Model Rules';

(f) certificates PS5, which were amended in line with PSO Update No 41 (15) and were sent to IR SPSS before 24 July 1998, will be accepted as confirmation of incorporation of the first set of regulations (*SI 1998 No 728*) referred to in 3.50;

(g)   once the standards documentation section of IR SPSS has agreed an up to date revised model deed with a practitioner, certificate PS5 may be used without amendment, subject to the insertion of the appropriate reference number as described above;

(h)   if a required amendment is made other than by adoption of the current version of part 5 of the model rules, a copy of the amending document must be sent to IR SPSS stating whether the changes entirely reflect revised part 5 of the model rules. If they do not, but reflect the SSAS regulatory changes, the amending document must be marked up to show where they deviate from the model rules.

Schemes approved on or before 17 March 1998

(i)   PSO Update No 41 required such schemes to incorporate the overriding tax legislation which applies the tax regimes described in 4.12, as appropriate, and the requirements of *SI 1998 No 728* (see 3.50), in their documentation. This requirement was extended by PSO Update No 45 to include *SI 1998 No 1315*. Amendments to scheme documentation must be made:

'at the earliest convenient opportunity, and.. if the scheme rules are being amended in any other way'.

Compliance with the regulations is required as a condition of continued approval;

(j)   schemes, whether or not they are documented by model deeds, may use the updated part 5 of the model rules described in 3.50. If a model deed has not been used in the past, this must be explained in the letter that accompanies the executed amending documentation;

(k)   if part 5 is not used (and the amending rules reflect only the requirement to include the statutory changes referred to in 3.50 or a bespoke version, and the overriding legislation referred to in 4.12 as appropriate), this must be stated in the covering letter to IR SPSS. The amending document must be marked up to show where it deviates from the model rules;

(l)   if a scheme was documented by a model deed, the certificate PS6 may be used amended as appropriate, as described in 3.58(*a*). In this connection, PSO Update No 45 draws specific attention to paragraph 6 of the letter which accompanied the first revised part of the model rules (APPENDIX 15).

3.59   The requirement to forward a copy of the actuarial report on which the funding of the scheme is based is most important for a SSAS. If the full initial report has not been prepared by the time the application is made for approval then a copy of the actuarial advice provided on the establishment of the scheme must be provided instead. A list of the current investments of a SSAS is also required.

3.60   The composite undertaking which had to accompany the application for approval of all SSAS established before 1 January 1996 (form SF176(U)) was completed by the administrator who thereby undertook to notify various circumstances to the PSO (now IR SPSS) before taking any action. With the advent of the information powers procedures from 1 January 1996 (see 3.71 to 3.91) the undertaking was abolished and the reference to it in the form PS176 should be ignored and has been removed from later printings.

Timing of application for approval

3.61   *Section 604(1)* requires an application for approval to be made before the end of the first year of assessment for which approval is required. However, for schemes established shortly before the end of the tax year there may not be sufficient time to obtain and prepare the full information for submission to IR SPSS by 5 April. A concession is allowed for schemes in these circumstances, which extends the period for making an application by up to six months after the end of the tax year.

3.62   The following table that appears in PN 18.5 sets out the 'period of grace' allowed for applications for approval to reach IR SPSS.

Date scheme established	*Date by which application must be received by IR SPSS*
In the 6 months ending 5 October	by the following 5 April
In the month ending 5 November	by the following 5 May
In the month ending 5 December	by the following 5 June
In the month ending 5 January	by the following 5 July
In the month ending 5 February	by the following 5 August
In the month ending 5 March	by the following 5 September
In the month ending 5 April	by the following 5 October

3.63   All schemes therefore have at least six months from inception in which to apply for approval to include the tax year in which the scheme was established. Those schemes set up in the first six months of the tax year in fact have from six to twelve months in which to make application for approval.

3.64   Sometimes a newly established SSAS may invest in property or make loans or borrow money in the fourth to sixth month before its application for approval has to be made. Such transactions are reportable to IR SPSS however within 90 days (see 3.75). It is not a requirement of IR SPSS to receive reports of such transactions prior to the application. It will accept that, where the 90 day limit has expired before the application has been made, the reporting regulations have not been breached provided the appropriate fully completed form is submitted with the application by the application deadline.

3.65   It is important to note that although formal application for approval may be deferred under these time concessions, a scheme's approval under *s 592(1)(a)* cannot pre-date its establishment under irrevocable trusts. Equally it is important to note that a late application will lose the appropriate tax reliefs as the scheme's effective date of approval will be no earlier than the 6 April or the sixth of the month as the case may be following the date the scheme was established. The loss of tax reliefs in these circumstances is explained in 3.9 although it may be possible to have the company's contribution paid before the effective date of approval allowed as a deduction for corporation tax purposes. See 3.9 concerning the possible automatic treatment of a scheme as a FURBS by IR SPSS.

Provisional reliefs

3.66   In the circumstances where an interim period is permissible prior to formal approval (see 3.4), the position is as described in this paragraph and 3.67 and 3.68. The time taken to obtain formal approval from the PSO for a SSAS can vary considerably. It will depend to some extent on the execution of a definitive deed and the satisfactory outcome of IR SPSS enquiries into investments and other features of the SSASs. The company cannot obtain relief meanwhile on contributions paid, but the company's inspector of taxes may hold over the tax in respect of the contributions until such time as the scheme is formally approved. The trustees cannot obtain repayment of tax deducted from income received. They are unlikely to be assessed, however, on income received without deduction of tax.

The net pay arrangement, as described in the Revenue booklet 'Employer's Guide to PAYE', can be applied to the members' contributions once the application for approval is accepted. It is essential that the main features of the scheme have been communicated to the members in writing. Any premiums under insured schemes may be referred to pensions business.

3.67   The position prior to the changes described in 3.4 is as follows. The National Audit Office Report in 1991 and subsequently the Public Accounts Committee were critical of the length of time during which many schemes have been obtaining provisional tax relief before approval was given. As a result the PSO (now IR SPSS) stated that all schemes established after 5 April 1993 should aim to adopt definitive documentation within two years otherwise the provisional tax reliefs would be lost.

In May 1996 the PSO (now the IR SPSS) wrote to all practitioners whose schemes were established more than two years previously and where no definitive deed had been produced. It urged execution of the definitive deed failing which the application for tax approval would be withdrawn. This was followed up by PSO Update No 17. As a result the PSO set deadlines for schemes to achieve the documentation deadlines for existing schemes, and provided special certificates to assist those schemes which had wound up or were paid up without full documentation. Any schemes which failed to meet the deadline would have their application for approval treated as having been withdrawn from the outset. By virtue of the revised wording of PN(1997) 18.10, which issued with PSO Update No 28, such schemes would be treated as FURBS from inception (see 3.9). Late or incomplete applications were also likely to cause tax loss in the early days of the scheme's life, as the date of approval would only have effect from the date when all the required data was provided. Prior to that date the scheme would be treated as a FURBS. This is still the case.

3.68 As trustees were not able to reclaim tax until approval was granted a SSAS was at a disadvantage compared with an insured scheme where a LO is allowed to invest premiums received in its tax-exempt pension funds and obtain relief on a provisional basis. The trustees may therefore not have felt it worthwhile investing in equities to start with, but to invest where interest was paid gross. Bank deposits and gilts can be arranged to pay interest gross as they are not 'relevant deposits' for the purposes of *s 479*. Similarly building society accounts can be held by the trustees and interest paid gross under the arrangements set out in *s 476(7)* and *regulation 4(1)(f)* of the *Income Tax (Building Societies) (Dividends and Interest) Regulations 1990 (SI 1990 No 2231)* as amended by the *Income Tax (Building Societies) (Dividends and Interest) (Amendment) Regulations 1994 (SI 1994 No 296)*.

3.69 Formal notification of approval is sent by IR SPSS to the applicant. At the same time IR SPSS sends instructions to the appropriate tax districts to put the tax reliefs into effect. This will normally result in reliefs being granted retrospectively to the effective date of approval where the interim period had been authorised (but see 3.67). An additional copy of the notification of approval is also provided so those claims may be made to the appropriate tax districts for tax relief. The trustees may also expect, if they qualify, to receive a repayment supplement representing interest on tax repaid to them.

The approval letter is a valuable document, and both the trustees and the practitioner should keep a permanent copy stored in a safe place. It should not be held on files that are likely to be archived or destroyed at a later date.

Reporting requirements

3.70   There are various reporting requirements imposed upon the administrator of a pension scheme. Some of the requirements are of general application and are contained in a chart appended to PN by way of Appendix VIII. Others are statutory, and these are covered in 3.71 to 3.93. The requirement to appoint an administrator is laid down in *section 590(2)(c)* and *section 611 AA*. The administrator must be resident in the UK.

3.71   Until 1 January 1996 the reporting requirements stemmed from the undertaking given on application for approval (see 3.60) and *s 605(1)*. From 1 January 1996 the undertaking was abolished, *s 605(1)* ceased to have effect and a new reporting regime brought into effect. This was done by the *Finance Act 1994, s 105 (Appointed Day) Order 1995 (SI 1995 No 3125)* under powers contained in *Finance Act 1994, s 105(5)*. At the same time *SI 1995 No 3103* (Appendix 5) was promulgated setting out the requirements for furnishing information and documents with effect from 1 January 1996. The amended legislation also provides for penalties to be imposed for failure to comply (see 10.54 to 10.59).

3.72   As a result of the changes at 3.71, two non-statutory requirements remain the responsibility of the administrator. These are making application for approval (see 3.53 to 3.65) and complying with the Inland Revenue undertaking (see 3.60) where appropriate.

3.73   *Section 605(1A)* to *(1E)* and *605(2)* to *605(4)*, and *SI 1195 No 3103* set out the current reporting requirements for all occupational pension schemes, i.e. for insured and self-administered schemes. These are covered insofar as SSAS are concerned in 3.74 to 3.93. Some of the more specific reporting requirements stemming from *SI 1995 No 3103* are covered in the paragraphs relating to the feature or the investment concerned.

The administrator should normally sign the report, but where there is more than one person, that person may sign on behalf of the others (PSO Update No 39). The other persons must have given written authorisation for such person to sign on their behalf, and this should be sent to IR SPSS on the first occasion on which such person becomes the sole signatory. IR SPSS should be told if the arrangement changes.

3.74   Actuarial valuation reports with an effective date of 1 January 1996 or later must be produced to IR SPSS within one year of the effective date (see 9.57 to 9.72). Under *SI 1995 No. 3103*, with effect from 1 January 1996, the requirement is that self-administered schemes should submit to deadlines without notice or reminder from the Inland Revenue. In fact, IR SPSS issues one stock reminder to the practitioner nine months after the effective date and one to the administrator one month before it becomes overdue. Further details of IR SPSSs practice in this area are described in 9.54 to 9.61.

3.75 Under the *1991 Regulations* previous reporting requirements are imposed on the administrator. These requirements have been deleted from the *1991 Regulations en bloc* and may now be found in *SI 1995 No 3103*. The requirement remains within 90 days of certain prescribed transactions by the trustees for the administrator to furnish IR SPSS with details of acquisitions of land, loans to the company and associated companies, unquoted shares, borrowings, and purchases of property from, and sales to, the company and associated companies and leases thereto. There is an exception to the 90 days reporting requirement for prescribed transactions that take place in the fourth to sixth months of the existence of a newly established SSAS (see 3.64).

These requirements are intended to provide IR SPSS with a more up-to-date picture of the assets of a SSAS and to prevent trustees from concealing dubious features for considerable periods of time.

PSO Update No 48 describes IR SPSSs requirements concerning loans (see CHAPTER 5), borrowing (see 7.56 to 7.73), non-cash transactions (see CHAPTER 7), property leases (see CHAPTER 6) and related IR SPSS forms. PSO Updates Nos 41 and 45 refer to the changes brought about by *SI 1998 No 728* and *SI 1998 No 1315* (see 2.24).

3.76 There can be problems, however, for advisers in obtaining the information to be reported to IR SPSS in 90 days. Some legal documentation, particularly involving the Land Registry, can take longer than three months to be produced. IR SPSS had granted a concession regarding the production of leases, because it recognised these can take some time to be agreed between parties. This was withdrawn on 26 November 1997 (see 6.14).

3.77 From 1 January 1996 the admission of a new employer to any scheme must be reported to IR SPSS within 180 days of the end of the scheme year in which the admission took place.

The report should be made on form PS274 (APPENDIX 20) and accompanied by a certified copy of the Deed of Adherence (APPENDIX 12).

3.78 Any subsequent changes that occur to the details previously supplied regarding a participating employer, must also be reported to IR SPSS within 180 days of the end of the scheme year in which the change occurs. Notification under this heading would include a change to the employer's name and address, withdrawal from participation, cessation of trade or of association with other participating employers.

3.79 *Documentation and approval*

The report of the change should be made on form PS256 (APPENDIX 21).

It should be noted that in respect of the reports due here and at paragraph 3.77 above, the administrator might be called upon to provide copies of any books, documents and other records in connection with the reported events.

3.79 Special contributions (SCs) paid to a SSAS after 31 December 1995 must be reported to IR SPSS within 180 days of the end of the scheme year in which they are paid. The report must be made on the form PS251 (APPENDIX 22). The amount of the special contribution to be reported is half of the earnings cap at the end of the scheme year in which the SC is paid or the employer's ordinary annual contribution (OAC) to the SSAS, whichever is the greater. SCs to finance pensions increases are excluded from being reported. Once reported SCs may be spread as deductions for corporation tax purposes (see 9.32 to 9.38). IR SPSS's rules for spreading were changed on 30 May 1996 by PSO Update No 16 (see 9.38). PN 5.8 to 5.10 was revised accordingly. Because the aggregation provisions of IR SPSS 's procedures for spreading SCs paid before 1 January 1996 relate to all the schemes of the employer, and its latest procedures are specific to the scheme in question, reports of SCs will need to be made on the old print of form PS251. SCs for all later chargeable periods should be reported on the latest print of form PS251 (APPENDIX 22). Reports of SCs on form PS251 are still required, even if the SC is less than the minimum figure to be spread, for compliance audit purposes. It should be noted that in connection with reports of SCs the administrator might be called upon to produce copies of any books, documents and other records in support.

The PSO (now IR SPSS) also provided clarification in PSO Update No 16 of possible difficulty of interpretation of *SI 1995 No 3103*. Where the chargeable period and scheme year do not coincide it may appear that a SC paid early in a chargeable period has a reporting deadline before that chargeable period has ended. However, the requirement to aggregate with other SCs to the scheme in the same chargeable period and test against the OACs paid to the scheme in that period means that it may not be known until after the reporting deadline has passed whether or not it was reportable. The following example illustrates the point:

- The employer's chargeable period ends 31 August 1998

- The pension scheme year ends 31 January 1999

- The SC reporting date is 180 days after the end of the scheme year = 30 July 1999

If a SC was paid in January 1998 it may not *prima facie* be reportable until 30 July 1998. If another SC were paid in August 1997 it would be reportable together with the SC paid in January 1998. A SC paid in August

1998 has a reporting deadline of 30 July 1999, but the SC paid in January 1998 could now be reported late, although its reporting deadline was 30 July 1996. IR SPSS accepts this position is unreasonable and will interpret the time prescribed for reporting under *Regulation 7(2)* of *SI 1995 No 3103* as being 180 days after the end of the scheme year in which the chargeable period, during which the SC was paid, ends. The limit of one-half of the earnings cap for reporting purposes in *Regulation 7(3)(b)* of *SI 1995 No 3103* refers to the earnings cap applicable at the end of the scheme year and not the earlier one.

3.80 Regarding SCs paid to a SSAS prior to 31 May 1996, PN5.10 applies. This requires all SCs greater than £25,000 and the employer's total OACs to all its schemes to be reported to IR SPSS after the end of the employer's accounting period in which the SC was paid on form PS251. There was no deadline for such a report unless IR SPSS gave 30 days notice for production of details under *s 605(1)(a)(b)*. The spreading arrangements for such SCs is explained in 9.32 to 9.38.

3.81 The admission of a controlling director (see APPENDIX 10) to membership of a SSAS from 1 January 1996 must be reported to IR SPSS within 180 days of the end of the scheme year in which the admission occurs. This requirement also includes anyone who was a controlling director for 10 years prior to membership or an existing member who becomes a controlling director. The request should be made on form PS255 (APPENDIX 23). The form PS255 does not have to be completed when application for approval is made as the application form (APPENDIX 17) includes member details of controlling directors.

In connection with reports relating to controlling directors, the administrator may be asked by IR SPSS to supply copies of relevant books, documents or other records. These could include records of issued share capital and details of directors' meetings.

There is still a requirement to report the admission of a controlling director to membership prior to 1 January 1996 or where a member became a controlling director before that date, but there is no deadline for doing so.

3.82 Where a controlling director retires on the grounds of incapacity (see 4.93), IR SPSS must be approached for approval to pay the incapacity benefits. This must be done at least 28 days before the payment of the proposed benefits and accompanied by copies of any documents relating to the administrator's decision to permit such benefits, including medical reports and other medical evidence (*SI 1995 No 3103, Regulation 9*).

The application should be made to IR SPSSs Compliance Audit Section who can be expected to respond promptly. It will do so initially by telephone and then confirm in writing or disagree. If nothing is heard in 28 days administrators are entitled to assume the proposals are satisfactory and the benefits can be paid.

3.83 Where a controlling director retires on the grounds of serious ill-health and payment of a wholly commuted lump sum is to be paid, approval must be sought from IR SPSS at least 14 days before the payment of the proposed benefits (*SI 1995 No 3103, regulation 9*). The circumstances and detailed procedure are explained in 3.30, including the timescale for IR SPSSs response. Once again, IR SPSSs Compliance Audit Section is responsible, to whom details of the tax deductible (see 4.93) should also be sent.

3.84 The administrator has always been liable to deduct tax in relation to various payments made from a SSAS. In respect of the following payments made after 31 December 1995, the administrator must within 30 days after the end of the tax year in which the payment was made, make a return to the Inland Revenue of:

- repayment of an employee's contributions;
- commutation of an employee's pension;
- payment to or for the benefit of an employee or his personal representatives out of surplus voluntary contributions; and
- refund of a surplus to an employer.

Failure to do so may result in the imposition of penalties under *TMA 1970, s 98*. The initial penalty is £300 and there is a daily penalty of £60 until the matter is put right. Persons who fraudulently or negligently give incorrect information in connection with the requirements of *Regulation 10* of *SI 1995 No 3103* (APPENDIX 5) shall incur a penalty of £3,000.

The return accounts for the tax deducted by the administrator in these circumstances, but it is the trustees who will be ultimately liable to pay the tax. The return will continue to be sent to the inspector of taxes using either the repayment claim form R63N (APPENDIX 24) if a claim for repayment of tax is being submitted, or the form 1(SF). For SSASs that do not submit income tax repayment claims annually to the inspector of taxes, IR SPSS must be informed on the form 1(SF) (APPENDIX 25).

It should be noted that this return is totally separate from the self-assessment tax return completed by the trustees (see 3.94 and 8.45).

The form 1(SF) is no longer issued automatically. The onus is on the administrator to obtain a copy from IR SPSS or the inspector of taxes if a chargeable event has occurred. On completion, the form should be sent to the inspector of taxes or, where this information is not held, to the PSO examiner. The appropriate form for insured schemes, under *Regulation 11*, is the 2(SF).

3.85 In respect of payments made from a SSAS prior to 1 January 1996 from which tax was deductible by the administrator, these were reportable to the Inland Revenue but there was no deadline for such a report unless 30 days' notice was given for production of details of the payments under *s 605(1A)(a)(b)*.

3.86 There is a requirement from 1 January 1996 for the administrator, trustee, participating companies and providers of administration services, to produce certain information, make it available for inspection and retain certain records (see 3.87 to 3.91). These requirements are clearly aimed at facilitating IR SPSS's increasing compliance audit function.

The exemptions of SSASs from some of the more arduous requirements of the *Occupational Pension Schemes (Scheme Administration) Regulations 1996 (SI 1996 No 1715)* are listed in 11.89.

3.87 If IR SPSS serves a notice, the following information, including any supporting documents, must be supplied within 28 days:

• all monies received or receivable; or

• all investments and other assets; or

• all monies paid or payable.

IR SPSS expects to issue such notices only where it has difficulty obtaining the information in the first place. The supporting documents requested could be bank statements, share certificates and other legal documents.

3.88 Where IR SPSS serves notice, books, documents and other records must be made available for inspection within 28 days. The records to be made available relate to:

• all monies received or receivable; or

• all investments and other assets; or

• all monies paid or payable; or

• any annuity contract securing benefits.

3.89 To underpin IR SPSSs powers to call for or inspect records, there is a requirement from 1 January 1996 for records to be retained for six years from the end of the scheme year in which the transaction or event took place. The records are books, documents and other records relating to:

3.90 *Documentation and approval*

- any monies received or receivable; or
- any investments and other assets; or
- any monies paid and payable; or
- any annuity contract securing benefits; or
- details of controlling directors.

These records are to be retained by the persons mentioned in 3.86.

3.90 The records at 3.89 are those relating to accounts, actuarial reports, 90 day reporting, admissions of new employers and controlling director members, chargeable events, SCs, incapacity and serious ill-health. It is interesting to note that whilst there is a requirement to retain scheme accounts, there is no requirement to provide them to IR SPSS unless requested. Such requests may be expected in connection with the examination of actuarial reports and scheme investments as mentioned in PSO Update No 9. The accounts are, however, a statutory requirement under the *Disclosure Regulations* (see 11.9) and their production is the responsibility of the administrator. The inspector of taxes may also request them in connection with a repayment claim.

3.91 In addition, the records at 3.89 are to be kept for six years where they relate to the:

- provision of any benefit to a member and/or dependant;
- refund of contributions to an early leaver;
- payment of contributions to a scheme by an employer and employee;
- payment by the trustees to any participating employer;
- payment of a transfer value or purchase of an annuity;
- acquisition and disposal of any asset;
- and undertaking of any transactions for the purpose of the scheme;
- receipt of income from the assets of the scheme and from trading.

3.92 It will be most advisable where a practitioner loses the administration of a SSAS, to hand over all documents relating to changes of the principal employer and trustees after 1 January 1996 to the new practitioner to avoid being liable for production of such records. There is an exclusion in *SI 1995 No 3103* for persons who no longer act for a scheme and have passed all the relevant information to their successor.

3.93 Prior to 1 January 1996 there was a requirement for the administrator to provide certain information under *s 605(1A)(c)* within 30 days' notice given by IR SPSS. This is not now likely to be invoked in respect of events and features that arose before this in view of the new regime brought about by *SI 1995 No 3103*. However, scheme accounts were required under *s 605(1A)(c)* as part of the approval process, so for schemes established before 1 January 1996 this provision could still apply.

Self-assessment requirements

3.94 Self-assessment was first applied to the trustees of some pension schemes in the tax year 1996/97 (see 8.46 and 8.47). A set off of tax due against the other liabilities of the trustees or administrator is not permitted.

Self-assessment applies to the trustees of tax approved self-administered in the same way that it does to other taxpayers, and the self-assessment legislation covers the power to require pension scheme accounts to be produced (TMA 1970, s 8A).

Scheme administrators do not fall within self-assessment. They are covered by the reporting requirements described above.

Divorce requirements

3.95 Pensions and divorce law has been going through major developments in the UK. Under the *Matrimonial Causes Act 1973,* as there is often a lot of equity tied up in the net value of joint matrimonial property, including pension schemes, it is permitted for a divorce settlement to be made by distributing other assets so that pensions rights are kept intact. Alternatively, financial provision orders may require a scheme to pay part or all of any lump sum or pension payments directly to a member's former spouse at the time they come into payment. The Petitioner's financial resources, earning capacity and age will need to be considered.

Under the recent *Welfare Reform and Pensions Act 1999*, and the *Finance Act 1999* there is a sharing (previously known as splitting) concept. The *Finance Act 1999* contains details of the changes made to Inland Revenue discretionary practice in order to accommodate the introduction of family law and social security law that is intended to enable such a clean break to be made between parties in a pension sharing divorce settlement.

PSO Update No. 60 first addressed the Inland Revenue's position on divorce and pension rights, and Nos. 62, 76 and 84 provided detailed explanations and specimen rule amendments for adoption by approved schemes, Pensions Update No. 84 particularly focussed on the calculation of pension debits for money purchase schemes. There is a new Part 6A to PN that sets out the requirements for those who acquire pension rights from their former spouse under the *Welfare Reform and Pensions Act 1999* provisions that came into

3.95   *Documentation and approval*

force on 1 December 2000, and a new Appendix XIII to PN which describes how to calculate maximum limits if pension rights are reduced by a pension sharing order. The Capital and Savings Division of the Inland Revenue are currently looking at the calculation of pension debits on divorce, in order to ensure that Inland Revenue limits cannot be exceeded.

Chapter 4

Benefit Structure

Introduction

4.1   As mentioned in 2.8 the vast majority of SSASs apply for discretionary approval under *ICTA 1988,* s *591* from IR SPSS. This is because under *s 591* IR SPSS can exercise its discretion to approve higher levels and types of benefits than those that are provided under *s 590*. Under *s 590* approval is mandatory and benefits are very restricted, with no potential for uplift from basic accrual level. The full benefit limitations for uplifted benefits under *s 591* approved schemes are set out in PN and various subsequent Updates. This chapter highlights the main benefits and their limitations and explains them further subject to what has already been stated in CHAPTER 3 on the rule requirements applicable to them. It also explains the position of ex-gratia payments made on retirement and IR SPSS's requirements where the securing of pensions is deferred.

4.2   The maximum benefits that may be paid will always depend upon the rules and it cannot be stressed enough how important it is when drafting the definitive deed and the rules thereunder to allow for the maximum level of benefits in all circumstances. Amendments can always be made later to extend the benefits to the PSO permissible limits, but these take time and may, in the meantime, delay the payment of a benefit unless the augmentation provisions are wide enough to allow it.

4.3   It is always possible before a member retires to seek IR SPSS's agreement to the payment of benefits unless tax avoidance is at issue. Full details of the calculations involved should be provided. However, IR SPSS will only give confirmation to the benefits being paid on the basis of the information supplied and this will not preclude a benefit audit check later. This is because responsibility for paying benefits within Inland Revenue limits rests with the administrator.

4.4   It should also be borne in mind that SSASs are usually money purchase schemes (sometimes referred to as defined contribution) schemes as opposed to final salary schemes. They may well provide benefits based on final salary, but the exemptions accorded to money purchase schemes under *PA 1995* could be lost. Money purchase schemes mean that the level of benefits to emerge will depend on the level of contributions paid by the company and the member and the amount of growth of those contributions once invested.

From April 1988 it was compulsory for all occupational pension schemes (including SSASs) to permit members to make additional voluntary contributions (AVCs) up to 15% of gross earnings in any year. From April 1987 the amount and timing of the AVCs can be varied in accordance with the employees' wishes. From 26 October 1987 AVCs can be made outside the pension scheme and such payments are called Free-standing Additional Voluntary Contributions (FSAVCs).

However, controlling directors cannot be members of a FSAVC scheme. If a member of such a scheme becomes a controlling director, he must stop his contributions and his options with regard to the acquired benefits are to:

(a)   take an additional pension;

(b)   take a *s 32* buyout policy; or

(c)   allow a transfer payment to the SSAS once he becomes a member.

Commuted lump sums are not available in respect of new AVC or FSAVC arrangements made after 7 April 1987 and it is only possible for these benefits to be taken as an income pension.

4.5   In a final salary scheme sometimes referred to as a defined benefit scheme the level of benefits to be provided are based on the length of service, the definition of final remuneration and the fraction of final remuneration to which a member is entitled. The fraction may be based solely on length of service with the principal employer or together with service from associated employers or may include previous service with another employer from whose scheme a transfer payment has been received. The benefit structure will need to take into account the different regimes which apply (see 4.10 to 4.15). Continued rights members, if they were 20% directors, had normal retirement ages set at a minimum age of 60 (both male and female members) whereas other female members could have a normal retirement ages date of 55 onwards. Also the uplifted scales for pension and lump sums in PN 7.40 and PN 8.25 respectively may be used for pre–17 March 1987 members with continued rights.

4.6   There are several reasons why a money purchase basis is preferred for SSASs. The main reasons though are those of cost. The financial commitment of the company to fund a final salary scheme can be financially burdensome. In addition salary increases entail increased contributions to meet the final salary commitment. Any underfunding at the time a member retires would have to be met by payment of a special contribution which in turn may require to be spread as a deduction for corporation tax purposes (*s 592(6)*). The advent of the minimum funding requirement as a result of the *Pensions Act 1995*, and its likely successor under the recent Myners report, (see 11.81 to 11.84 and 11.89) is also likely to be too burdensome for a final salary SSAS.

4.7   A money purchase scheme is however still subject to Inland Revenue limits on the level of benefits it may provide. Thus a SSAS is usually funded on a money purchase basis with a target of maximum Inland Revenue limits. The member's credit or contribution credit in these cases representing the member's interest in the scheme from which benefits will be paid is limited to no more than the Inland Revenue maximum.

4.8   The maximum benefits for which it is possible to fund depend upon the actuarial assumptions which are made in determining the level of contributions to be paid to the scheme (see 9.7 and 9.8) and the maximum benefits which the Inland Revenue will allow.

Normal retirement age

4.9   Controlling directors, like any arm's length member of a SSAS, may have their normal retirement age set at any time between the ages of 60 to 75 (PN 6.6). The concession for women with pre–1 June 1989 continued rights to have a normal retirement age of 55 (see 4.5) does not apply to female controlling directors. It should also be noted that the lower retiring ages available in some employments do not apply to controlling directors as they will still be able to carry out their 'directing' of the company after the activity for which an early retirement age is acceptable has ceased.

4.10   Four member regimes currently exist. They are described in 4.12. The categories of members are referred to as pre–1987 Members, 1987 Members, 1989 Members and Full 1989 Members. Most joiners of SSASs join schemes which were set up after 14 March 1989 or become members of schemes on or after 1 June 1989. They fall to be treated as Full 1989 Members, and it is that tax regime which is described first. There are few members who fall to be treated as 1989 Members, and that regime is described last.

4.11   Continued rights members may elect to be subject to the 1989 tax regime. This can be particularly beneficial on early leaving if a member's earnings are not above the earnings cap (see 4.28 to 4.32), but it is irrevocable so caution is needed. There is a statutory right under *ICTA 1988* for 1987 Members to elect, and an option can be written into the scheme rules as a right for pre–1987 Members. The election must be made to the administrator no later than:

4.12   *Benefit Structure*

(a)   the date on which the benefits become payable;

(b)   the date on which the benefits are bought out or transferred to another scheme;

(c)   age 75.

4.12   An uplifted rate of accrual of benefits is permissible for different categories of membership. The different tax regimes and the uplifted rates which apply to each category are described in (a) to (d). Final remuneration, and retained benefits, are explained for ease of interpretation in 4.16 to 4.27 and 4.40 respectively.

(*a*) Full 1989 Members (members of schemes established on or after 14 March 1989 and members of other schemes who joined on or after 1 July 1989 or who have elected to be subject to these limits)

Employee contributions

- Employees may contribute 15 per cent of remuneration per annum, subject to the earnings cap.

Pension at normal retirement age

- The maximum pension at normal retirement age (including pension equivalent of any lump sum) is 2/3 × final remuneration after 20 years service. Where service is less than 20 years, it is 1/30 × final remuneration for each year of service.

Lump sum at normal retirement age

- 2¼ × the initial annual rate of actual pension (including pension secured by AVCs and FSAVCs paid during the period of membership of the scheme) before commutation or any allocation to spouses' and/or dependants' benefits.

Early retirement on grounds of ill-health

- The benefits are:
    (i)   the maximum potential pension that could have been provided at normal retirement age based on actual final remuneration;
    (ii)   2¼ × initial annual rate of pension before commutation or allocation.

Normal early retirement benefits

- The benefits are:
  (i)   a pension of 1/30 × final remuneration × years of service, subject to a maximum pension of 2/3 × final remuneration;
  (ii) a lump sum of 2¼ × the initial annual rate of actual pension (before commutation or allocation).

Leaving service

- The benefits are:
  (i)   a deferred pension equal to the ordinary early retirement pension based on final remuneration at date of leaving service and revalued in deferment;
  (ii) a deferred lump sum of 2¼ × the initial annual rate of actual pension (before commutation or allocation).

Late retirement

- The benefits are:
  (i)   a pension of 1/30 × final remuneration × years of service up to a maximum of 20/30;
  (ii) a lump sum of 2¼ × the initial annual rate of pension (before commutation or allocation).

Death-in-service lump sum

- 4 × final remuneration, or remuneration (see the definition in 4.77, 4.78) plus a refund of employee's contributions (with interest).

Death-in-service pension

- 2/3 × the maximum potential pension which could have been provided for the member at normal retirement age. This benefit may be paid to the surviving spouse. In addition to this benefit, or a lesser amount of benefit, pensions may be paid to the dependants of the member. The maximum aggregate benefit payable to a surviving spouse and dependants, or all dependants, is the member's own maximum pension as described above. In the absence of a surviving spouse the maximum pension payable to one dependant is the same as may be paid to a surviving spouse.

Death after retirement pension

- 2/3 × the maximum pension which could have been provided for the member at retirement, increased in line with the Index (no commuted lump sum is available). This benefit may be paid to the surviving spouse. In addition to this benefit, or a lesser amount of benefit, pensions may be paid to the dependants of the member. The maximum aggregate benefit payable to a surviving spouse and dependants, or all dependants, is the member's own maximum pension as described above. In the absence of a surviving spouse the maximum pension payable to one dependant is the same as may be paid to a surviving spouse;

- A guarantee payment may be paid as described in 4.84.

AVCs

- The additional benefits purchased shall be paid in pension form, except that a commutation lump sum may be paid (subject to the overall limits) if the employee had entered into the AVC arrangement prior to 8 April 1987;

- Surplus AVCs may be repaid to the employee after tax at the rate shown in Appendix has been deducted. This equates to a tax credit at the basic rate only.

Retained benefits

- In most cases pensions must be aggregated with any retained benefits to assess whether the 2/3rds limit is exceeded;

- A retained benefits test is not required for the lump sum calculation or dependants' benefits, and no retained benefits need to be taken into account for new entrants on or after 31 August 1991 who earn less than ¼ of the Earnings Cap in their first year of membership.

(*b*) Pre–1987 Members (joiners before 17 March 1987)

Employee contributions

- Employees may contribute 15% of remuneration per annum.

Pension at normal retirement age (including the pension equivalent of any lump sum)

- 2/3 × final remuneration after ten years' service. Where the member's service is less than ten years, the fraction of final remuneration is determined from the following uplift table:

Years of service	*60ths*
1–5	1 per year
6	8
7	16
8	24
9	32
10	40

Lump sum at normal retirement age

- 1½ × final remuneration after 20 years' service. Where the member's service is less than 20 years, the fraction of final remuneration is determined from the following uplift table:

Years of service	*80ths*
1–8	3 per year
9	30
10	36
11	42
12	48
13	54
14	63
15	72
16	81
17	90
18	99
19	108
20	120

Early retirement on grounds of ill-health

- The benefits are:
  - (i) the maximum potential pension which could have been provided at normal retirement age;
  - (ii) the maximum potential lump sum which could have been provided at normal retirement age,

  both based on actual final remuneration.

Normal early retirement benefits

- A ratio of completed service to potential service, multiplied by the maxima shown in (i) and (ii) immediately above, is applied. Final remuneration is determined at actual retirement.

4.12 *Benefit Structure*

Leaving service

• A deferred pension equal to the ordinary early retirement pension based on final remuneration at date of leaving service and revalued in deferment. This is commutable within normal limits on retirement.

Late retirement

• Either a pension of:

(i) 1/60 × final remuneration × years of service (if 40 years have been served by normal retirement age, an additional 1/60 for each later year of service may be accrued up to an overall total of 45/60); or

(ii) uplifted benefits at normal retirement age, plus interest (see above table) to retirement,

and either a lump sum of:

(i) 3/80 × final remuneration × years of service (if 40 years have been served by normal retirement age, an additional 3/80 for each year of later service up to an overall total of 135/80); or

(ii) uplifted lump sum at normal retirement age plus interest (see above table) to retirement.

For controlling directors there is a restriction on the amount of additional benefits which can be accrued before age 70 (see 4.74).

Death-in-service lump sum

• 4 × final remuneration, or remuneration (see the definition in 4.77 and 4.78), plus a refund of employee's contributions (with interest).

Death-in-service pension

• 2/3 × the maximum potential pension which could have been provided for the member at normal retirement age. This benefit may be paid to the surviving spouse. In addition to this benefit, or a lesser amount of benefit, pensions may be paid to the dependants of the member. The maximum aggregate benefit payable to a surviving spouse and dependants, or all dependants, is the member's own maximum pension as described above. In the absence of a surviving spouse the maximum pension payable to one dependant is the same as may be paid to a surviving spouse.

Death after retirement pension

• 2/3 × the maximum pension which could have been provided for the member at actual retirement, increased in line with the Index (no commuted lump sum is available). This benefit may be paid to the surviving

74

spouse. In addition to this benefit, or a lesser amount of benefit, pensions may be paid to the dependants of the member. The maximum aggregate benefit payable to a surviving spouse and dependants, or all dependants, is the member's own maximum pension as described above. In the absence of a surviving spouse the maximum pension payable to one dependant is the same as may be paid to a surviving spouse.

- A guarantee payment may be paid as described in 4.84.

AVCs

- The additional benefits purchased and treatment of surplus AVCs shall be as described for Full 1989 Members.

Retained benefits

- In most cases pensions must be aggregated with any retained benefits to assess whether the 2/3 limit is exceeded.
- A retained benefits test is also required for the lump sum calculation.
- A retained benefits test is not required for dependants' benefits, and no retained benefits need to be taken into account for new entrants on or after 31 August 1991 who earn less than ¼ of the earnings cap in their first year of membership.

(c) 1987 Members (members of schemes established before 14 March 1989 who joined between 17 March 1987 and 31 May 1989 inclusive)

Employee contributions

- Employees may contribute 15% of remuneration per annum.

Pension at normal retirement age (including the pension equivalent of any lump sum)

$2/3 \times$ final remuneration after 20 years' service. Where the member's service is less than 20 years, $1/30 \times$ final remuneration $\times$ years of service.

Lump sum at normal retirement age

- The lump sum may be enhanced above the basic rate of 3/80 accrual (up to 'uplifted 3/80' level) in proportion to a pension enhancement which is above the 1/60 basic rate.

75

Early retirement on grounds of ill-health

- The benefits are:
    - (i) the maximum potential pension which could have been provided at normal retirement age;
    - (ii) the maximum potential lump sum which could have been provided at normal retirement age,

    both based on actual final remuneration.

Normal early retirement benefits

- A ratio of completed service to potential service, multiplied by the maxima shown in (i) and (ii) immediately above, and based on final remuneration at actual retirement.

Leaving service

- A deferred pension equal to the ordinary early retirement pension based on final remuneration at date of leaving service and revalued in deferment. This is commutable within normal limits on retirement.

Late retirement

- Either a pension of:
    - (i) $1/60 \times$ final remuneration $\times$ years of service (if 40 years has been served by normal retirement age, an additional 1/60 for each later year of service up to a total of 45/60); or
    - (ii) $1/30 \times$ final remuneration $\times$ years of service up to a maximum of 20/30 at normal retirement age, plus interest (see above) to retirement,

    and either a lump sum of:
    - (i) 3/80 up to a maximum of 135/80 as for pre–1987 Members; or
    - (ii) a higher cash formula enhancement in proportion to the pension.

For controlling directors there is a restriction on the amount of additional benefits which can be accrued before age 70 (see 4.74).

Death-in-service cash sum

- $4 \times$ final remuneration, or remuneration (see 4.77 and 4.78), plus a refund of employee's contributions (with interest).

Death-in-service pension

- $2/3 \times$ the maximum potential pension which could have been provided for the member at normal retirement age. This benefit may be paid to the surviving spouse. In addition to this benefit, or a lesser amount of benefit, pensions may be paid to the dependants of the member. The maximum aggregate benefit payable to a surviving spouse and dependants, or all dependants, is the member's own maximum pension as described above. In the absence of a surviving spouse the maximum pension payable to one dependant is the same as may be paid to a surviving spouse.

- A guarantee payment may be paid as described in 4.84.

Death after retirement pension

- 2/3 × the maximum pension which could have been provided for the member at retirement, increased in line with the Index (no commuted lump sum is available). This benefit may be paid to the surviving spouse. In addition to this benefit, or a lesser amount of benefit, pensions may be paid to the dependants of the member. The maximum aggregate benefit payable to a surviving spouse and dependants, or all dependants, is the member's own maximum pension as described above. In the absence of a surviving spouse the maximum pension payable to one dependant is the same as may be paid to a surviving spouse.

AVCs

- As for pre–1987 Members.

Retained benefits

- In most cases pensions must be aggregated with any retained benefits to assess whether the 2/3 limit is exceeded.
- A retained benefits test not required for the lump sum calculation, this is contained in the pension formula in PN 8.25.
- A retained benefits test is not required for dependants' benefits, and no retained benefits need to be taken into account for new entrants on or after 31 August 1991 who earn less than ¼ of the earnings cap in their first year of membership.

(*d*) 1989 Members – (members of schemes approved before 27 July 1989 who joined on or after 1 June 1989 or who have elected to be subject to the limits which apply to such individuals, or Members of schemes established before 14 March 1989 which were not approved before 27 July 1989 and who joined the scheme before 1 June 1989).

- The benefit regime is the same as for 1987 Members except that the earnings cap and the lump sum enhancement of 2¼ × initial rate of actual pension apply by overriding statute.

• The application of the earnings cap has effect not only on the calculation of the member's pension, lump sum and death benefits under the scheme, but also on the maximum remuneration on which the member may make contributions into the scheme in order to augment his or her benefits.

General – trivial commutation

Whenever a pension comes into payment, or on winding-up, trivial pensions may be wholly commuted. "Trivial" means the aggregate of all benefits (including the pension equivalent of lump sums) in respect of the employment not exceeding £260 per annum (PN 8.12). Under PN 8.14 a pension already in payment may be wholly commuted if the threshold increases sufficiently, or at state pension age if the total pension including any revalued GMP does not exceed the threshold. Scheme rules may be revised to provide for the above if the member agrees. Any tax that may be incurred is described in *ICTA 1988, s599* and PN 17.27. It is not necessary to notify IR SPSS of any actions under the above guidelines.

Commutation factors

4.13   In commuting a pension to provide a lump sum commutation rates are necessary to determine the cash value provided by each £1 of pension given up. For members joining pension schemes from 1 June 1989 or those who joined before then but who opt for the post *Finance Act 1989* regime a commutation factor of 12:1 must be used irrespective of age, sex or escalation rate. For members with continued rights the commutation rates differ according to age and escalation rates. The commutation factors acceptable to IR SPSS for schemes not using enhanced factors are set out in PN 7.54 and are as follows:

Age	Factor Range
60	10.2–11.0
65	9.0–9.8

The factors may be interpolated by a factor of 0.02 per month. PN 7.55 explains the position for schemes using enhanced factors. GADs has recently reviewed the tables, and a copy of the new table of enhanced factors is attached to PSI, Part 82, by way of Appendix A thereto.

4.14   The interaction of pensions and lump sums is an important aspect of the decision to be made on retirement. It may be that the member's credit is no more than can provide a lump sum. Or the member's credit may be less than the sum needed to provide maximum benefits. A balance may therefore have to be struck between taking the maximum cash and a smaller pension or no lump sum and the maximum pension. The member has to decide if the residual pension which will be taxed under PAYE will be sufficient. A decision will also have to be taken on whether to take a level pension or one increasing annually up to the Index. Whilst the cash lump sum is tax-free, once invested the income it generates will become taxable. However if it is invested to purchase a further annuity to supplement the residual pension there could still be a financial advantage as the capital element of the annuity would be tax-free and only the interest element taxable.

Continued rights

4.15 Some measure of protection was needed for members following the changes to the tax regimes brought about by the *F(No 2)A 1987* and the *FA 1989* so that they would not be disadvantaged in certain circumstances e.g. a move on promotion from the company's scheme of which they were members prior to 17 March 1987 or 1 June 1989 to another scheme of the company after those dates. A list of the instances where the restrictions will not apply may be found in Appendix III to PN.

Final remuneration

4.16 It can be seen from 4.12 how important the member's final remuneration is in the calculation of the benefits payable on retirement and in other circumstances. The definition of final remuneration of a controlling director or other employee and its application needs explanation at this stage.

Under the Glossary to PN, the main requirement is that final remuneration must be no greater than either:

(a)   the highest remuneration for 1 of 5 years prior to cessation of pensionable service, being basic pay for that year plus a three or more year average of fluctuating emoluments (unless received for a shorter period for averaging purposes) expiring at the end of that year. Fluctuating earnings may include profit-related pay (whether or not relieved from tax), benefits in kind, overtime, bonuses and commissions etc. which are assessable to tax under Schedule E. They may be increased by the rise in the Index to the end of the basic pay year; and

(b)   the yearly average of total emoluments for any three or more consecutive years ending not more than ten years before cessation of pensionable service.

and that (b) shall apply to controlling directors, not (a).

Having determined final remuneration, it is necessary for purposes of benefit calculation to take into account retained benefits. These are also defined in the

4.17   *Benefit Structure*

Glossary to PN. Retained benefits include approved relevant benefits, but exclude refunds of contributions, from earlier periods of employment or self-employment whether alone or in partnership which have been retained from schemes or under contractual entitlements which have received tax privileges.

Retained benefits are not taken into account for determining spouses and dependants benefits.

4.17   Once a controlling director enters the 13–year period prior to normal retirement age the level of remuneration should be closely watched. There will need to be a consecutive three-year period somewhere in these 13 years that will provide the final remuneration figures on which benefits will be based. The last three years in this period may not provide the best figures if the company is unable to sustain a director's remuneration at previous levels. Fortunately dynamisation helps in this situation as earlier years' remuneration may be increased in line with the Index. However, where a director's remuneration fluctuates from one year to another finding three consecutive years that produce the best results can create problems.

4.18   The following example illustrates how complicated it can be to arrive at the best period of three years. Here it is assumed the controlling director retired aged 60 on 31 December 2000. The indexation figures are not intended to be precise, they are used for demonstration only.

Example

Year ended	Basic remuneration	Fluctuating remuneration	Total	Increased by RPI	Three year average
31.12.88	£23,000	nil	£23,000	£38,466	
31.12.89	£25,000	£600	£25,600	£41,100	
31.12.90	£23,000	£600	£23,600	£35,792	£38,453
31.12.91	£32,500	nil	£32,500	£45,823	£40,905
31.12.92	£30,000	£500	£30,500	£38,780	£40,132
31.12.93	£35,000	£500	£35,500	£43,360	£42,654
31.12.94	£30,000	£1,000	£31,000	£36,560	£39,566
31.12.95	£40,000	£1,500	£41,500	£48,080	£42,666
31.12.96	£45,000	£2,000	£47,000	£53,288	£45,976
31.12.97	£25,000	nil	£25,000	£27,291	£42,886
31.12.98	£45,000	£1,500	£46,500	£49,705	£43,428
31.12.99	£50,000	nil	£50,000	£51,601	£42,865
31.12.2000	£50,000	£1,000	£51,000	£51,000	£50,769

It can be seen that the three years which ended in 31 December 2000 give the highest average final remuneration (£50,769) for any three consecutive years ending in the ten-year period prior to retirement. The next best average is for the three years ended 31 December 1996 (£45,976).

For Full 1989 Members and 1989 Members the earnings cap has effect (see 4.28 to 4.30).

4.19 It is always best to smooth out the troughs and peaks of remuneration if at all possible as one really good year on its own may not come into the reckoning if remuneration on either side of it is substantially less. Another point to watch is where no remuneration is paid. This should not be allowed to happen for too long because, although the director's service may still be pensionable, nil remuneration in any of the last three consecutive years will reduce the final benefits and it may be treated as part-time service (see 4.53 and 4.54).

4.20 The date the particular years end that is used for calculating final remuneration is flexible provided it falls in the ten years prior to the retirement date. It may be convenient to use company years, tax years, the three years ending on retirement or on any other convenient date.

4.21 The remuneration itself which makes up the final remuneration is generally any earnings paid by the company which are subject to tax under Schedule E. There are some restrictions and exceptions as will be explained later. It is therefore most important that in framing the definition of pensionable earnings in the rules everything that is permissible to be included should be brought within the definition. Thus not only basic salary should be pensionable, but so should bonuses, fees, commission, benefits-in-kind and contributions to a FURBS (whilst permissible) etc. Controlling directors are most likely to be in receipt of taxable benefits-in-kind and other remuneration which may fluctuate from year to year, and will be averaged over the best three consecutive years anyway. For non-controlling director members these so called 'fluctuating emoluments' cannot be taken for one year only unlike basic remuneration, but must be averaged over three consecutive years. If a fluctuating emolument was paid in a single year only and is to be included in final remuneration, the agreement of IR SPSS must be sought.

The PN Glossary definition of final remuneration permits on account pension and lump sum payments to be made if it is not possible to calculate precisely final remuneration at the date the benefits become payable. When a balancing payment or payments occur, interest may be paid and limits must not be exceeded. The interest will be taxable on the recipient under Schedule D Case III.

4.22 Because directors of private companies are able to control the remuneration paid to them, the three-year averaging was imposed in the 1970s to limit their ability to increase their remuneration just before they retired. Further restrictions are imposed by *Sch 23, para 5(3)*. These restrictions ensure that not only are controlling directors at the time of their retirement restricted to the three-year averaging, but they will also be subject to this if they held that position at any time in the last ten years.

This prevents a director relinquishing control just before he retires and using the best year in the last five for final remuneration purposes. The same restriction as to final remuneration also applies to any other employees whose remuneration since 6 April 1987 exceeds £100,000 p.a.

4.23 For members who joined a scheme after 17 March 1987 their final remuneration used to determine the cash lump sum must not exceed £100,000 under *Sch 23, para 6(2)*. This means that the maximum cash lump sum payable to such members on retirement after completing the minimum 20 years service is £150,000. The final remuneration figure of £100,000 is capable of being increased from time to time in an order made by the Treasury (*s 590(3)*) but no such order has yet been made.

Under the table for calculating early payment of lump sums for 1987 Members, this limit applies to D and E of the formula. Prior to the issue of PSO Update No 48 the PSO view was that it applied to items B, C, D and E.

4.24 *Section 612(1) ICTA 1988* debars the inclusion of certain forms of remuneration from the calculation of final remuneration for all employees for 1987/88 *et seq*. These forms of remuneration include any sums chargeable to tax under *s 148 ICTA 1988* (popularly known as 'golden handshakes') and share options. Remuneration paid in the form of unit trusts and taxed under Schedule E may still be included in final remuneration, but it will probably be a fluctuating emolument. An employer's contribution paid to an unapproved pension scheme and taxed on the member under Schedule E (at least for the present) may also be included in final remuneration in relation to that member's membership of the same employer's tax approved pension scheme (see 15.19(e)).

4.25 The Glossary to PN excludes from final remuneration any sums chargeable to tax under Schedule E that arise from the acquisition or disposal of shares or from a right to acquire shares except where the shares or rights giving rise on or after 17 March 1987 to liability under Schedule E were acquired before that date. It is unlikely that this will have any effect on SSASs established by private unquoted companies as they probably do not have share option or incentive schemes. However, some SSASs are established for the senior directors of large public companies and this restriction may have considerable impact.

4.26 Payments made under *s 148, ICTA 1988* are usually for termination of employment or office and compensatory by nature. The first £30,000 of such payments is normally tax-free and the excess subject to tax under Schedule E.

It is the excess element which cannot form part of the final remuneration even though it is subject to Schedule E tax.

4.27 The definition of final remuneration in the Glossary to PN includes Profit Related Pay (PRP). The total amount of any PRP is pensionable (PSI 6.4.1), but must be treated as a fluctuating emolument. Employers, however, usually wish to calculate contributions and benefits by reference to notional 'shadow pay', i.e. the pay an employee would have received had the PRP scheme not been introduced. Benefits can be promised and calculated by reference to 'shadow pay' provided they do not exceed the Inland Revenue maximum. However, any notional element cannot be included in final remuneration. Members' personal contributions may also be calculated by reference to 'shadow pay' provided they do not exceed 15% of actual pay for the year concerned. In the event it is unlikely that a member of a SSAS will be a member of the employer's PRP scheme as directors are not eligible to be members of PRP schemes.

Tax relief for profit-related pay has now been phased out. The timescales that applied in the run down period were:

(a) prior to 1 January 1998, no change to the £4,000 ceiling on relief;

(b) between 1 January 1998 and 31 December 1998, the ceiling was reduced to £2,000;

(c) on or after 1 January 2000, no relief is available.

The earnings cap

4.28 *FA 1989* also introduced other far-reaching effects on pension schemes. It brought in legislation which, like *F(No 2)A 1987*, over-rides the rules for schemes approved by Royal Assent to the bill (27 July 1989). It had the effect of limiting pensionable earnings to the earnings cap (see 4.29), limiting the maximum approvable accelerated accrual of lump sums (see 4.31) and simplifying the calculation of maximum benefits on early/late retirement or leaving service (see 4.57, 4.61 and 4.75).

4.29 *Section 590C* was introduced by *FA 1989, Sch 6 para 4*, and restricts pensionable earnings for the years 1989/90 *et seq* used in the calculation of maximum benefits based on final remuneration to the 'earnings cap'. The restriction applies to the aggregate of benefits from all approved schemes in respect of all service with the company or associated companies. Concurrent service is not counted twice, so it is not possible to obtain benefits based on the level of the earnings cap from each of a series of associated companies.

Allowance is made in the legislation to increase the level of the earnings cap annually in line with the Index. The limit may be found in APPENDIX 26.

4.30   The 'earnings cap' applies to all schemes established on or after 14 March 1989. It does not apply to members of schemes who joined before 1 June 1989 where the scheme was already in existence before 14 March 1989 except in the circumstances provided in the *Retirement Benefits Schemes (Continuation of Rights of Members of Approved Schemes) Regulations 1990 (SI 1990 No 2101)* for employees considered to have continuity of membership from before the relevant date. Remuneration above the 'earnings cap' may be pensioned through an unapproved pension scheme without prejudicing the approval of a scheme already approved or one seeking approval (see CHAPTER 15).

4.31   *FA 1989, Sch 6 para 23* limits the maximum approvable accelerated accrual of lump sums for all members of schemes established after 14 March 1989. It does not apply to members of schemes who joined before 1 June 1989 where the scheme was already in existence prior to 14 March 1989. The limit is 2.25 times the initial amount of pension payable before commutation or allocation in favour of dependants (see 4.12). A member who joined the scheme after 17 March 1987 and before 1 June 1989 and who is subject to the old limits may elect to be subject to the new maxima (see 4.11), but this would entail being subject to the earnings cap also.

4.32   *Sections 590, 590A, 590B* as amended by *FA 1989, Sch 6 para 3(3), 4* contain rather complicated legislation defining associated employments and connected schemes to prevent the capping restrictions being circumvented. Broadly where a holding company/subsidiary company relationship exists or another company acquires the whole of the previous participating company, the member's remuneration will not be subject to the cap on any future re-structuring of the company and its pension scheme. Service pre- and post–14 March 1989 will remain continuous and therefore aggregable. However, where these relationships do not exist, particularly where another company participates in a scheme after 14 March 1989 and is only an associate of the other company and they both remunerate the member, pensionable service cannot be counted as continuous and aggregated for benefit calculation purposes.

Finance Act 1989, s 37 **and final remuneration**

4.33   Until 5 April 1989 all emoluments assessable to income tax under Schedule E were either assessable on a receipts or earnings basis. Broadly this meant that emoluments were assessable in the year in which they were paid or made available unless the taxpayer elected to have them assessed for the year in which they were actually earned. Thus a bonus, fees or commission received on 1 December 1988 in respect of a company's year ended 30 March 1988 would have been assessable under Schedule E for the tax year 1987/88 if an election to be assessed on an earnings basis had been made. The earnings basis once adopted could not be changed from year to year.

4.34 In calculating final remuneration for pensions purposes it did not matter whether a receipts or earnings basis had been adopted for Schedule E purposes as the amounts used for basic earnings and fluctuating emoluments followed the amounts assessed or assessable to Schedule E.

4.35 From 6 April 1989 the Schedule E position was changed by *ss 202A* and *202B* inserted by *FA 1989, s 37*. With effect from 6 April 1989 the earnings basis of assessment was abolished. From that date all emoluments are assessable to Schedule E on a receipts basis regardless of the year in which they were earned. The effect of this change did, however, mean that a bonus etc. paid or voted on or after 6 April 1989 in respect of a company's year ended prior to that date was assessable to Schedule E both under the old earnings basis for the year in which it was earned and under the new receipts basis for the year in which it was paid or voted.

4.36 To avoid this double assessment there were relieving provisions in *FA 1989, s 38*. These provided for a taxpayer to elect to remove emoluments assessed on an earnings basis prior to 6 April 1989 from any Schedule E assessment and for them to be assessable solely on the receipts basis. The election had to be made to the Inland Revenue before 6 April 1991 and only applied to emoluments paid or voted on or after 6 April 1989 and before 6 April 1991 in respect of a company's year ended prior to 6 April 1989.

4.37 The Inland Revenue issued a Statement of Practice (SP 1/92) on 3 January 1992 extending the time limit for an election where a claim in writing was made within three months of the issue of a Schedule E assessment for the year 1988/89 or 1989/90 whichever is issued later and where a taxpayer was unable to meet the time limit for reasons beyond his or her control. The time limit for elections by the employees and directors of Lloyd's underwriting agents in respect of bonuses and commissions relating to profits for periods before 6 April 1989 was 6 April 1994.

4.38 If an election was made regarding any emoluments paid or made available between 6 April 1989 and 5 April 1991 which would have been assessable to Schedule E under the old earnings basis for 1988/89 or earlier years, and the final remuneration on which pension scheme benefits are based includes remuneration for 1988/89 or earlier years, then the retirement benefits will be reduced as the emoluments concerned cannot be included in remuneration for 1988/89 or earlier years.

4.39 The information in 4.33 to 4.38 is now only likely to have impact on those persons who have previously transferred out or bought out benefits.

Retained benefits

4.40   Retained benefits exclude refunds of contributions, but include benefits from earlier periods of employment or self-employment whether alone or in partnership which have been retained from schemes or under contractual entitlements which have received tax privileges. The Glossary to PN provides a full list. For ease of reference, the main sources are:

- retirement benefits schemes;
- relevant statutory schemes;
- *S 608* schemes;
- 'corresponding' overseas schemes, as described in *s 596(2)(b)*;
- retirement annuity contracts or trust schemes approved under *section 620*, or personal pension schemes (other than ones which receive minimum contributions only) which relate to or related to relevant earnings from the current employment or previous employments including periods of self-employment whether alone or in partnership;
- transfer payments from overseas schemes held in a retirement benefits scheme, a relevant statutory scheme, a personal pension scheme or a retirement annuity contract.

Benefits transferred to another scheme or bought out, whether or not in the UK, are treated as retained benefits, but benefits from a wholly concurrent employment or occupation are not generally considered to be so. The Glossary to PN explains the treatment of the latter benefits in some detail with regard to members with and members without entitlements to continued rights.

For controlling directors who are not entitled to continued rights, benefits from retirement annuity contracts or personal pension schemes arising from premiums or contributions paid out of relevant earnings from the current employer are aggregable with benefits provided by the current employer. In other circumstances they are retained benefits.

A benefit from a transfer from an occupational pension scheme of the current employer to a personal pension scheme, to the extent that it relates to service with the current employer, is treated as an aggregable benefit for the purpose of PN 7.25 to 7.28.

Retained benefits include the pension equivalent of any benefit from relevant sources not in pension form. If the total of all benefits is less than £260 they can be ignored. When considering lump sums as retained benefits, a total amount of less than £2500 can be ignored.

For lump sum death benefits, retained benefits means the lump sum death in service benefit. This benefit may be ignored if it does not exceed £2,500 in total with the exception of any element received from a transfer from an occupational pension scheme. Returns of fund from personal pension schemes and retirement annuity contracts may also be ignored, but lump sums in respect of transfers into personal pension schemes out of approved occupational pension schemes or relevant statutory schemes will continue to be treated as retained benefits.

Retained benefits are not taken into account for determining spouses and dependants benefits.

Ex-gratia payments on retirement

4.41 With effect from March 1991 IR SPSS (previously the PSO) have held that an arrangement by an employer to pay ex-gratia relevant benefits to an employee constitutes a retirement benefit scheme within *s 611* and that all such payments will be treated as unapproved pension schemes and taxed accordingly, subject to certain exceptions.

4.42 Such an arrangement may be approvable by IR SPSS under *s 590* or *591*, if it meets certain criteria. IR SPSS's guidelines on ex-gratia payments may be found in PN 23. Additionally SP 13/91 makes it clear that ex-gratia payments on retirement or death made after 31 October 1991 will normally come within the tax rules for pension schemes. So, provided an application for approval is made to IR SPSS (see 4.44) they can be made tax-free as lump sums subject to the maximum lump sum permitted. The term 'arrangement' may be a prior formal or informal agreement, a decision at a meeting, where a personnel or other manager makes an ex-gratia payment under delegated authority, or where it is common practice built up over a period of time.

4.43 The ex-gratia payments which come within the scope for approval are pensions, lump sums, gratuities and similar benefits given where someone retires or dies, in anticipation of retirement, after someone has retired or died in recognition of past service, or as compensation for a change in conditions of continuing employment (not as compensation for loss of employment). Severance payments on genuine redundancy or loss of office are not relevant benefits and fall within *s 148, ICTA 1988* for tax purposes (see 4.26). Other ex-gratia lump sum payments which the PSO will not approve are taxable in full and do not qualify for the £30,000 exemption.

4.44 IR SPSS will give approval to ex-gratia payments without the need for a formal contractual scheme created under trust. The conditions for approval are that the employee receiving the ex-gratia payment is not already a member of his or her employer's tax approved pension scheme unless the ex-gratia payment is made on retirement and the pension scheme provides benefits only on death in service. In addition the payment must satisfy the normal requirements for tax approval of a pension scheme. A separate application form PS 60 (APPENDIX 27) should be used for each ex-gratia payment for which approval is required. Where a payment is made before confirmation of approval is received the employer should deduct tax under PAYE and when approval is granted the employee will be able to claim repayment of the tax deducted.

4.45 Provided the conditions for approval at 4.44 are met and the total of all lump sum payments from all associated employers made in a tax year in connection with the retirement or death do not exceed one-twelfth of the earnings cap for that year (see 4.28 to 4.32) an arrangement to pay a single ex-gratia lump sum to an employee does not have to be submitted for approval. In these cases the payments will nonetheless be treated as from an approved pension scheme.

Continuous service

4.46 It is not only important to establish that service pre- and post–14 March 1989 for a controlling director is continuous to avoid the earnings cap (see 4.28 and 4.29) but it is also important from the point of view of funding and the continuation of the scheme. IR SPSS lays down much stricter criteria for controlling directors than for arm's length employees in this area. For the arm's length employee, who has no control over his employer's business, if that business is taken over and the employee's position before and after the change is essentially unchanged, service with both employers can be treated as continuous service in the present employer's pension scheme (but see 4.53). As controlling directors can clearly influence their company's affairs IR SPSS's criteria for them in PN 7.15 to 7.21 and in subsequent pronouncements are more restrictive, and a claim for continuous service to apply must be made to IR SPSS on form PS 155 (see APPENDIX 28 and Pensions Update No 101). The previous requirement that a controlling director must be a controlling director of both the old and the new company has now been removed, and it is sufficient if the individual simply holds the office of director of the other employer. The form PS 155 gives guidance as to whether or not a request is worthwhile making.

4.47 If a company with a SSAS is sold or goes into receivership or liquidation it is always advisable as far as possible to find a successor company to continue the SSAS. Alternatively a transfer of benefits can be made to an associated company's scheme. In both instances if IR SPSS's criteria can be met continuous service will increase the member's maximum benefits.

4.48 To satisfy IR SPSS there has to be a succession of trade. This is more easily met where the former and present employing companies are associated within the same trading group. They can be in a holding company and subsidiary company relationship or both subsidiary companies of the same holding company. If these circumstances are not met then it may be possible to establish continuous service through a community of interest. It should be noted however that whilst the controlling director is the common link between the companies, the fact that he or she may be a director and controlling shareholder of both companies is not the essential linking factor so far as IR SPSS is concerned.

4.49   The community of interest criterion is quite separate from the holding/subsidiary company relationship and continuous service for a controlling director does not depend on both sets of criteria being met. Where a community of interest applies IR SPSS requires that there has been a succession of trade from one employer to the other and at least 75% of the vendor's liabilities have been assumed by the purchaser. For the succession of trade to be acceptable the new employer should have acquired from the old employer the business assets, property, goodwill, contracts, staff, etc. This information together with the circumstances of the change should be presented to IR SPSS for confirmation that continuity exists and continuous service is applicable. It is recommended that a deed of adherence is not executed where another company is to be brought into a SSAS until IR SPSS signifies that it may participate and continuous service is applicable.

4.50   IR SPSS accepts that where a single business is broken up into a number of businesses it is not unreasonable to accept that the 75% of liabilities test is met if these liabilities are allocated to the new businesses. It is clearly concerned that loans made by SSASs to a participating company may be left unpaid on such company's winding-up and its controlling directors may get the benefit of continuous service with another company that does not assume the liability. Thus it is not prepared to accept continuous service for controlling directors where the liabilities of the previous company are not taken over by the successor company unless the purchase price for a buy-out of part of the business takes into account the fact that the liabilities will be retained by the vendor. In such cases the claim for continuous service to IR SPSS must be supported by a copy of the sale agreement setting out the details.

4.51   IR SPSS has confirmed that where the original business is split between one or more new businesses it will look for not less than 75% of the liabilities of the old business going forward. This means for example that where 65% is allocated to one new business and 10% to another, continuous service will apply for a controlling director of either new business provided he or she was employed by the original business and IR SPSSs other criteria are satisfied. If all the liabilities of the old business are met prior to the transfer then the 75% test does not come into the picture.

4.52   Although PN 7.15 to 7.21 and Pensions Update No 101 lay down IR SPSS's main requirements for continuous service to apply for a controlling director, the contents of 4.67 to 4.73 should also be considered in the light of the tough stance being taken by IR SPSS and the Revenue compliance units.

Concurrent and part-time employment

4.53   Concurrent service is mentioned in 4.29. This and part-time service often apply to controlling directors who may be directors also of associated companies within the same SSAS or totally unassociated companies in other schemes or which do not participate in other schemes at all. Problems can arise where, although the periods of service are concurrent, the time spent in each employment and remuneration received fluctuates considerably or one employment ceases and another commences outside the scheme. No remuneration may also be paid at certain times from any of the concurrent employments. This can cause difficulties in arriving at an accurate number of years full-time service on which benefits are to be based. Where all the concurrent employments run together in the same scheme there should be no difficulty. In other circumstances where there are concurrent employments special consideration will need to be given. Full-time service of more than 10 or 20 years to obtain maximum pension or lump sum benefits may need to be substantiated to IR SPSS where concurrent or part-time employments are involved.

The Inland Revenue announced in PSO Update No 42 that it is concerned that continuous service is being sought when the individuals involved have in fact been in concurrent service rather than consecutive service. If, for example, a director becomes a director of an associated company whilst remaining a director of the original company, continuous service does not apply and PN 16.52 to 55 are in point.

4.54   Benefits may be provided for part-time employees by reference to years of part-time service and remuneration therefrom as explained in PN 7.24. The administrator was obliged to notify the PSO (now IR SPSS) under the terms of the old undertaking (SF176(U)) where there had been a change before 1 January 1996 from part-time to full-time service or *vice versa* if the part-time service is to be converted to its full-time equivalent in calculating benefits. There is no such requirement in relation to such changes which occur on or after 1 January 1996. Appendix V to PN explains how, where following full-time service, part-time service and remuneration up to retirement may be converted to their full-time equivalents and aggregated. This cannot be used however for calculating benefits in respect of remuneration which includes emoluments as a director.

Early retirement

4.55 Until recently, early retirement benefits could be taken at any time within ten years of a member's normal retirement age. This effectively means that benefits may be taken at any time after age 50 if the member retires. A female controlling director cannot retire early after age 45 as her minimum normal retirement age is 60 (see 4.5 and 4.9), although an arm's length female member with pre–1 June 1989 continued rights and a normal retirement age of 55 could retire early after age 45. Retiring early can be an attractive proposition for a controlling director particularly if the company is being sold, especially as CGT retirement relief is now available from age 50 (*Finance Act 1996, s 176*). The benefits are, however, scaled down as would be expected in comparison with those payable at normal retirement age, and see 4.73 also in this connection. The scheme cannot be funded by the employer on the basis of the benefits payable at any age between 50 and 60 years even if it was always the intention of the director to retire early. It must be funded on the basis of benefits payable on retirement at normal retirement age. It is possible however for a member who intends to retire early to pay voluntary contributions to the scheme to fund the extra costs of early retirement (PSI 4.3.7) if the scheme rules so permit.

However, before any early retirement benefits are paid out, it will be necessary to be certain that the PSO regard the retirement as *bona fide* if the tax implications in 4.70 are to be avoided.

4.56 The maximum pension payable on early retirement for a member with continued rights is set out in PN 7.47 with the formula for its calculation and is reproduced below.

The maximum immediate pension (including the annuity equivalent of any lump sum) is either 1/60th of final remuneration for each year of actual service with a maximum of 40, or if this is more favourable, the amount calculated by the formula:

$\frac{N}{NS} \times P$ where:

N is the number of actual years of service with a maximum of 40

NS is the number of years of potential service to normal retirement age and may be limited to 40

P is the maximum pension approvable had the employee served until normal retirement age.

Any restriction for retained benefits must be made in arriving at P before multiplying by the fraction N/NS and the retained benefits should normally be taken into account at their current value rather than their prospective value at the scheme's normal retirement age.

4.57   The maximum benefit payable on early retirement in lump sum form is either 3/80ths of final remuneration for each year of actual service with a maximum of 40, or if this is more favourable, the amount calculated by the formula:

$\frac{N}{NS} \times LS$ where:

N is the number of years of actual service with a maximum of 40

NS is the number of years of potential service to normal retirement date and may be limited to 40

LS is the maximum lump sum receivable had the employee served until normal retirement date.

Any restriction for retained benefits must be made in arriving at LS before multiplying by the fraction N/NS and the retained benefits should be valued as at paragraph 4.56 above.

For members who joined on or after 17 March 1987 the formula N/NS × LS may only be used if the total benefits have been calculated on a similar basis. PN 8.28 includes a table showing the calculation method (see also 4.23).

4.58   The restrictions on remuneration used to calculate pension and lump sum benefits introduced by the *F(No 2)A 1987* and incorporated in *Sch 23, paras 2(2), 3, 5(3), 6(2)* (see 4.12, 4.22 and 4.23) and by *FA 1989, Sch 6 para 4* (see paragraphs 4.28 to 4.32) should be taken into account where appropriate.

4.59   An alternative basis for calculating benefits on early retirement allows an accrual rate of 1/30th of remuneration for each year of service to be used instead of 1/60th up to a maximum of 20/30ths and subject to it not exceeding 2/3rds of final remuneration when aggregated with any retained benefits. This basis does not apply to members who withdraw voluntarily from scheme membership but continue in service with the company. Members with continued rights have the option to be granted retirement benefits on the *FA 1989* tax regime basis (see 4.11).

4.60   In 4.17 the importance was stressed of ensuring a period of three consecutive years remuneration in the last thirteen years was maintained at the highest level possible to achieve maximum benefits. It may be that the best three years of a director's remuneration were before age 50 and helped by dynamisation these may influence the decision to retire early. The band of highest earnings could be lost at normal retirement age and any increase in benefits they generate on early retirement may compensate for the proportionate reduction then suffered due to the scaling down of early retirement benefits.

Leaving service

4.61 If a member of a SSAS leaves employment before normal retirement age several options are available regarding the member's accrued benefits. If the member is over 50 years old, early retirement benefits may be paid (see 4.55 to 4.61). Benefits may be left in the scheme and taken at normal retirement age. A deferred annuity may be purchased or a pension transfer made to the member's new occupational pension scheme or to a personal pension scheme. To comply with the EU's Third Life Insurance Directive, under *s 591(2)(g)* insurance policies such as those underlying a deferred annuity no longer need the prior approval of the Inland Revenue after 31 May 1995. The trustees must satisfy themselves though before purchase that a particular buy-out annuity contract provides only suitable benefits. In 1995, in line also with the moves to allow a free market in the EU, further legislative changes were made to allow annuities to be purchased from insurance companies established in every EU country (see 4.96).

Transfers, including leaving service

UK transfers

4.62 Prior approval must be obtained from IR SPSS before a transfer is made to a SSAS (PN 10.24(a)). The information required by that office was set out in Appendix 2 to PSO Update No 17. There is an exception for death in service term life policies (first announced in PSO Update No 25 (16)).

Prior IR SPSS consent must also be obtained for transfers out of a SSAS (PSO Update No 31, and No 36 with attached Appendix 1 listed the information required to be sent).

New transfer forms for SSASs were introduced by PSO Update No 93 with effect from 6 April 2001. They are coded PS 7050F and PS 7050T. However, these forms may become redundant as there may be a change to the *Information Powers* (see Appendix 5) that will remove the need for prior consent, but require large transfers to be reported after the event. This will accord with the desire of the Inland Revenue to continue to move towards self-regulation in matters of pension administration.

Transfers to and from Personal Pension Schemes are governed by *the Personal Pension Schemes (Transfer Payments) Regulations 2001 (SI 2001 No 114),* which contain transitional provisions for transfers in process as at 5 April 2001. These regulations have resulted in smaller maximum transfer values will result under GN11, and this matter is under discussion with various representative bodies in the pensions industry and the Inland Revenue.

4.62 *Benefit Structure*

It should be noted that there are limitations on transfer payments for controlling directors and individuals whose remuneration exceeds the earnings cap who are members of personal pension schemes (PN 16.17 to 16.24, PN, APP XI and paragraph 11.7(b) of IR 76 guidance notes). Transfer payments made from a SSAS to a personal pension scheme may therefore limit the amount of the transfer that may be used to pay a lump sum from a personal pension scheme. This is to prevent a transfer being used to maximise the advantage of the tax-free lump sum in a personal pension scheme. A transfer payment must not exceed the amount calculated by reference to *regulation 6(3)* of the *Personal Pension Schemes (Transfer Payments) Regulations 1988 (SI 1988 No 1014)*.

Transfers are not permitted once benefits have come into payment (PN 10.22), except where a member has left pensionable service prior to normal retirement age and has deferred the receipt of benefits until state pension becomes payable. This restriction does not apply where employers are restructuring their pension arrangements, although even in those circumstances a transfer to a personal pension scheme or from an insured scheme to a SSAS is not permitted.

Overseas transfers

For transfers to overseas schemes (for which forms PS119, 120, 121 or 122 must be completed, as appropriate), PSO Update No 49 clarifies the meaning of the expression 'a change of job', Appendix VI to PN contains details of IR SPSS's main requirements, and further detail is given in PSO Update No 82. The trustees or administrator of the UK scheme should keep records of transfers for six years. The provisions of the *Welfare Reform and Pensions Act 1999* which apply to overseas transfers are set out in the *Pension Sharing (Pension Credit Benefits) Regulations 2000 (SI 2000 No 1054)*. The person with credit rights must consent to the overseas transfer, must have emigrated permanently from the UK and must have received a benefit statement. In addition, the receiving scheme must be an occupational pension scheme or a personal pension scheme.

Where the conditions are met, IR SPSS will not require notification in ordinary occupational pension schemes. However, in the case of controlling directors and high earners (members earning more than £95,400 for the tax year 2001–2002), IR SPSS's consent will still be required. Special conditions apply to persons employed by European Union Institutions, Staff of International Bodies of the European Union, members of the European Investment Bank Staff Pension Scheme and members of the European Patent Office Pension Schemes. It may also be possible to make a transfer to an overseas equivalent of a personal pension scheme if the provider and the transferring member are located in the same jurisdiction (see IR76).

Transfers to United States Qualifying Plans are usually impractical for tax reasons even if the US Plan is willing to accept the transfer payment.

Transfers in late retirement — background

4.63 Until the issue of its announcement in a letter to the Chairman of the APT, and practitioners, on 15 May 1998 that 'it has been decided that the prohibition on making transfers once Normal Retirement Date has been reached . . . be removed forthwith . . . the ban on transfers *after* benefits have come into payment . . . will remain in force', the Inland Revenue did *not* permit transfers to be made out of an approved scheme after normal retirement age had been attained. The previous announcements were mainly conveyed to the pensions industry by means of earlier versions of PN.

This gave rise to some difficulties in the past, in particular as to how the restriction interplayed with the ability to represcribe normal retirement age under PN. In this connection it must be remembered that PN is not a binding statement of practice (the wording contained in the introduction to PN begins:

"These notes relate only to schemes for which approval is sought under the exercise of the Board's discretion. They give only general guidance on how that discretion is exercised and reflect the tax position at the time of writing. It should be borne in mind that they are not binding in law and the Board may find in a particular case that there may be special circumstances justifying different treatment, subject of course to any Regulations which restrict the Board's discretion. The Board will not be bound by these notes where a scheme is involved in or used for the purposes of tax avoidance."

Any attempt to circumvent the Inland Revenue's normal requirements by reference to PN is likely to be unacceptable to IR SPSS. There are circumstances under which represcription of normal retirement age is not permissible for continued rights members and circumstances where prior IR SPSS clearance must be sought. In the remaining circumstances, in which IR SPSS consent need not be obtained, it will still be necessary to approach that office for guidance if there is any apparent conflict with its other published or known practice.

Because of the ongoing problems facing practitioners in this area, in particular with regard to past cases which are currently under review, the following summary of past PSO (now IR SPSS) practice has been included (this information could also be of value in any appropriate cases of litigation):

Developments on transfers after normal retirement age/ retirement

- PN (9/91). 10.21: this permitted transfers to be made between approved and tax advantaged pension arrangements, with a minimum of restriction, subject to the following:

(a)   no transfers to be made after benefits have come into payment, except on the reconstruction of an employer's pension arrangements as described in (*b*) below;

(b)   if the exception in (*a*) above is in point, the benefits under the successor scheme should be in the same form as, and not less than in, the transferring scheme;

(c)   no transfers under (*c*) may be made into a personal pension scheme.

The restructuring issue was announced by Memorandum No 104 in March 1991. ˉ

- PN (12/93). 10.21: this extended the restriction on transfers in PN (9/91) to prohibit the making of transfers after normal retirement age, whether or not the employer's pension arrangements were being reconstructed. This reflected current PSO working practice at the time.

- PN (1/95). 10.21: this stated that the prohibition of the making of transfers after normal retirement age did not extend to re-structuring, to accord with PN (9/91) above. However, in this circumstance, once normal retirement age has been reached it cannot be altered under the receiving scheme. Additionally, on reconstruction, the prohibition on transfers to a personal pension scheme was extended to prevent transfers from an insured scheme to a SSAS at such time.

- PN (7/97). 10.21 and 10.22: this reflected PN (1/95), with the following change: transfers after normal retirement age were permitted for deferred pensioners, subject to the PN 10.8 requirements on permissible payment dates for such members. PSO Update 13 announced this in March 1996. Under PN 10.24(a) no transfer was permitted to a SSAS without consent (PSO Update No 10 in November 1995).

- PN (11/97). 10.21 and 10.22: as for PN (7/97). The removal of the restriction on transfers after normal retirement age on 15 May 1998 is described at the beginning of this paragraph 4.63. No transfers from SSASs, without consent, was introduced by PSO Update No 31 in September 1997.

- PN (2001). 10.22 to 10.24 as for PN (11/97). No transfers after benefits have come into payment is subject to an exception. This will be permitted if the benefit in payment is an AVC benefit paid in accordance with the arrangements described in PN, App XII, Pt II.

Developments on the re-prescription of normal retirement ages

A circular letter was issued to practitioners by the Inland Revenue on 31 October 1988, and Memorandum No 108 issued in August 1991. The PSO (now IR SPSS) did not need to be informed of a change of normal retirement age if it was within the agreed range for that scheme, and not within 5 years of the new normal retirement age if it was being lowered. Additionally, no prior reference was required for Full 1989 Members.

However, IR SPSS may at any time look carefully at a raising of normal retirement age in the circumstances of the case concerned (for example, if a member had already ceased to accrue scheme benefits).

- PN (9/91). 6.8, 6.10 and 6.14: confirmed Memorandum No 108, but replaced the expression 'lowered' normal retirement age with 'altered' normal retirement age.

- PN (12/93). 6.10 and 6.14: as for PN (9/91). PN 6.14 was not changed from the 9/91 version. Additionally, no change to normal retirement age could be made once a member had reached that age under Memorandum 117. This reflected PSO working practice at the time.

- PN (1/95). 6.10 and 6.14: as for PN (12/93). No change could be made once the member had attained normal retirement age was emphasised by PN 6.14.

- PN (7/97). 6.11 and 6.15: as for PN (1/95).

- PN (11/97). 6.11 and 6.15: as for PN (1/95).

It must be noted that, although IR SPSS has relented on the issue of making transfers after normal retirement age, it is necessary to confirm to that office that any such transfers are permitted by the rules of the scheme concerned.

Maximum benefits on leaving service

4.64 The maximum benefits payable on leaving service in respect of pensions and lump sums are set out in PN 10.9, 10.10 and 10.15–10.18. The calculations are similarly based to those used for early retirement benefits. However, if the member's actual service is less than 10 or 20 years for pension purposes and 20 years for lump sum purposes, the benefits payable should not exceed the maximum approvable at normal retirement age for the same service in accordance with the accrual tables in PN 7.40 and 8.25 respectively (see 4.12).

4.65 The alternative basis for calculating benefits on early retirement described in 4.59 is also available for deferred benefits on leaving service.

Early retirement on or after leaving service

4.66 The decision whether or not to take benefits on early retirement or leaving service is one for individual scheme members to make in the light of their own circumstances and the scheme rules. A leaver must wait until age 50 or later before early retirement benefits can be paid. An employee aged over 50 must leave the service of the employer operating the pension scheme concerned before receiving early retirement benefits.

4.67   Leaving service for ordinary employees used to be clear cut. For directors and senior executives, particularly controlling directors of private companies, it was not so clear whether they had left service. Their pensionable service does not cease, even if their remuneration ceases. They remain in pensionable service whilst they are full time directors and their service only ceases on relinquishing their director's appointment. In the past, if they are 50 or more, they had to give up their appointment as an executive director to obtain early retirement benefits. They did not necessarily, however, have to dispose of their shares in the company. They could continue in service with the same company as non-executive directors (usually part-time) or in a lesser role and still receive early retirement benefits (It is essential to document the change formally and notify Companies House within 30 days).

The PSO (now IR SPSS) began to take a much firmer line some years ago, matters coming to a head in 1997 when it maintained that the view that is described in 4.70 reflected its past practice. There were many protestations from the pensions industry, and some decisions were challenged. The *Venables* case, which is described below in 4.70, has relaxed IR SPSS's grip on directors' pension provision significantly for outstanding and future cases.

4.68   Other arrangements for leaving service may be considered and these may involve senior executives as well as directors. For instance, employment may commence within an associated company or the individual concerned may become a self-employed consultant. Such arrangements are prone to critical examination by either IR SPSS or the inspector of taxes or come to IR SPSS's attention via its compliance audit function. It should be remembered that the company's return is available publicly to IR SPSS and inspector.

4.69   To preserve a director's early retirement benefits in payment from taxation of the lump sum and suspension or repayment of the pension, it is essential to demonstrate that the director's new role is not the former role in disguise and not a device to circumvent IR SPSS's early retirement requirements. Working for an associated company which charges a fee to the director's former company for the services previously rendered to the former company could well prejudice the position of early retirement benefits in payment. Also providing the same services to a separate management services company is likely to put early retirement benefits in jeopardy. This latter approach is particularly vulnerable to challenge in the future. Inland Revenue Press Release No 35 dated 9 March 1999, has drawn specific attention to the Inland Revenue's concern about the potential for tax avoidance in running such companies. It is most important that they are set up for bona fide reasons and, whilst running them, the developments over the next couple of years should be observed closely.

4.70 The circumstances in which a member's service may be regarded by IR SPSS as continuous are described in 4.46 to 4.52. However, a few years ago, problems began to be encountered in endeavouring to demonstrate that a director or employee has effectively retired.

There was a hardening in the Inland Revenue's attitude towards cases of re-commencement of employment by persons who have already received retirement benefits. As a worst case scenario, approval was lost, and/or tax charged on lump sums at full *Schedule E* marginal rates on the individuals concerned. The situation first arose with regard to controlling directors of SSASs, but the Inland Revenue extended their hard line to all employees later on. This was most surprising at it occurred at a time when the Green Paper of 1998 had stated an intent to introduce the flexible payment of pensions from occupational pension schemes between ages 50 and 75. Additionally, in an answer to questions by two MPs during a Standing Committee debate on the Finance Bill in June 1998, the Economic Secretary stated that it was *'quite a simple matter as to whether a scheme had paid a benefit as authorised by its trust deed and rules'*, implying that if the rules do permit such an action then the benefit may be paid.

The main resistance from the PSO (now IR SPSS) seemed to be founded on the basis that a continuation in service of a director was tantamount to ongoing pensionable service. Re-employment with the same company could be deemed to include associated or successor companies. Some different scenarios which helped in countering IR SPSS objections are listed below:

(a) *Reconstruction of the company — no change of ownership*

   (i) a change in the structure of a company (e.g. a change in directors/shareholders) does not in itself constitute a change in the nature of service. If the company subsequently sets up a new scheme, members may join that scheme if invited to do so. They will automatically enjoy continued rights, as appropriate, whether or not they transfer their benefits into the new scheme.

   (ii) if members do transfer their benefits, and the transfer represents a second or subsequent transfer of continued rights, IR SPSS's consent must be obtained (prior consent applies to all SSAS transfers in any event, and to all schemes under Appendix III of PN).

   (iii) continuous service can apply (PN 7.15 to 7.21) if the members continue to do the same job as before (this also applies if the business has been taken over or merged — see (b) below).

(iv) if pensionable service under the scheme ceases and the member is entitled to deferred benefits, under new PN, benefits may only come into payment (subject to the 50 year age requirement) when the member leaves the employment to which the benefits relate. The PSO (now IR SPSS) considers that this also applies to pre- 29 November 1991 cases which are covered by the old PN. However, past working practice often relied only on a cessation of 'pensionable service', and many schemes were so documented and approved.

Any benefits deemed to have been wrongly paid out are likely to be treated as follows:

- pensions in payment must cease (as they will have been subjected to Schedule E tax, the Revenue should not be concerned with past payments);

- any lump sums paid out shall be chargeable to tax under Schedule E on the recipients as unauthorised payments under section 600 'if not expressly authorised by the Rules'.

(b) *Change of ownership of company or part of a business*

(i) if the company is sold to another company, the members can remain in the scheme with a successor company, or join another scheme as described above. Whether or not continuous service will apply is dealt with in 4.46 to 4.52. If employees are issued with new or revised contracts of employment, early retirement benefits may be acceptable to IR SPSS. IR SPSS will refuse to permit the payment of early retirement benefits where the 'job' and company are deemed to be unchanged or directorships remain.

(c) *Early retirement benefits, followed by re-employment*

Where persons re-enter a scheme or employment in a different or reduced capacity following early retirement, IR SPSS may seek to impose tax charges as described in (a) above. This can extend to schemes of associated employers.

IR SPSS does not consider that it has the resources to check whether or not every case involving early retirement is genuine. It is important, therefore, for the trustees to satisfy themselves as to whether or not early retirement is in point, and it may be necessary to seek guidance from the inspector of taxes in some cases. Under PN 10.8 payment is not possible unless the employees have, or are deemed to have, left service or actually retired.

The Venables case

Some legal guidance was at last obtained on the meaning of retirement in the outcome in case of *David John Venables and the Trustees of the Fussell*

Pension Scheme v Michael John Hornby (HMIT) [2001] All ER 126. This case was heard by the Special Commisssioners on 18 September 2000, and it helps to resolve some of the matters raised above. The main issue was whether or not a non-executive director can be considered to have retired, the relevance of the precise terms of the scheme to the issue and the relevance of *Article 14 of the European Human Rights Convention.* The Special Commissioner found for the Inland Revenue and the assessment and determination were upheld, subject to an increase due to an arithmetical error. The case was appealed to the High Court, supported by the APT, and the judgment went against the Inland Revenue. The judge defined the meaning of retirement as "withdrawing from active work". A further point of interest in the case was the judge's view on the applicability of the *Hillsdown Holdings Plc v IRC [1999] STC 561* case to an unauthorised payment from a pension trust. He felt that the recipient of such a payment could be held to be a constructive trustee. Thus, if the recipient pays the money back to the trustees there is no effective payment to him and therefore there is no taxable payment.

4.71   Directors and senior executives quite often become self-employed consultants to their former employers on retirement or retirement at normal retirement age. So far as early retirement benefits are concerned, they should not be affected if their self-employed consultancy status is genuine. If their consultancy is exclusively to their former employer, or they are still fulfilling the same role they performed when employees, then the inspector of taxes may challenge their *Schedule D* status and, if successful, Schedule E will apply to their consultant's earnings. Such a ruling would be brought to IR SPSS's attention because service with the employer would not have ceased and the early retirement benefits should not have been paid. In these circumstances, any cash lump sum paid would be liable to tax under Schedule E as an unauthorised payment (*s 600(2)*). It is understood that IR SPSS will not allow, due to a change in its policy in 1995, repayment of the lump sum to redress the position. The pension paid would also have to cease and be deducted from any later payment on normal retirement unless tax approval was withdrawn from the scheme if the circumstances warranted it.

4.72   It is recommended that sound professional accountancy advice is sought when changing to self-employed status, where an individual has hitherto worked as an employee and proposes to work for the same employer on a Schedule D basis. To ensure Schedule D status, it is advisable to provide consultancy services to a wider clientele and not exclusively to a single client, e.g. the former employer.

4.73   It is important to be aware of any potential claim to CGT Retirement Relief from age 50 onwards that scheme members and their advisers have in mind. Such a claim could be prejudiced if a director took early retirement benefits before the date from which CGT Retirement Relief was later claimed.

To preserve the position for CGT Retirement Relief purposes, the member must remain a director of the company, i.e. a non-executive director. If early retirement benefits are taken, the company must remain a family company and the director devote at least ten hours per week to service of the company (*TCGA 1992, s 163*).

With the introduction of tapering relief under *FA 1988* (see APPENDIX 61) from 6 April 1998, CGT Retirement Relief is to be phased out over 5 years from that date. This will be achieved by a progressive reduction of the thresholds for exemption and the 50 per cent exclusion.

Retirement after normal retirement age

4.74   As a result of the introduction in 1989 of the alternative basis for calculating benefits on early retirement (see 4.59) it was no longer appropriate to allow increases above the maxima on late retirement which had applied before then. In late retirement it had been possible to accrue extra years of service as if the actual retirement date were the member's normal retirement age; or to accrue additional years at 60ths up to 45 if service at normal retirement age was 40 or more years; or to grant an actuarial or RPI increase for the period of deferment. (Only if the first option was available prior to age 70 in respect of controlling directors, and if that member had already taken his or her lump sum, his or her pension was restricted to RPI). Increases to benefits in late retirement are now limited to 1/30th of final remuneration for each year of service to bring benefits up to 2/3rds of final remuneration or by reference to final remuneration at actual retirement where that is higher than at normal retirement age.

4.75   Controlling directors often continue in service with their company beyond normal retirement age. They may take benefits at normal retirement age nonetheless in both pension and lump sum form and these will eventually have to be taken into account in calculating their benefits on final retirement. If a lump sum is taken at normal retirement age, however, then on further retirement no further commutation is permitted because lump sums cannot be paid in instalments.

4.76   All members with normal retirement ages of 75 or above and these can only be members with continued rights, must take all benefits at normal retirement age rather than at actual retirement age if later.

Death benefits

4.77   On a member's death in service before reaching normal retirement age a lump sum may be paid of up to four times final remuneration. As it is assumed a member's death in these circumstances could not have been foreseen the definition of final remuneration is not so restricted as for benefits payable on retirement. This is particularly useful in the case of controlling directors.

4.78 Final remuneration can be defined here as:

(a) the annual basic salary immediately before death; or

(b) basic salary in (a) plus the average fluctuating emoluments during the three years up to the date of death; or

(c) total earnings fixed and fluctuating, paid during any period of twelve months falling within three years prior to death.

4.79 The lump sum is payable free from IHT provided the scheme rules are worded so that the exercise of discretion in paying the lump sum is vested in the trustees to pay the benefits among a wide class of beneficiaries (see 3.29). Provision should be made for members to complete an expression of wish regarding to whom the lump sum benefit should be paid in the event of their death. An example of an expression of wish may be found at APPENDIX 29.

4.80 In addition to a lump sum benefit spouse's and dependants' pensions may be provided subject to a total of 2/3rds of the member's final remuneration. The maximum pension for any one person however is limited to 4/9ths of final remuneration which would usually be payable to the surviving spouse. Dependants means any persons who were financially dependent on the deceased at the date of death. Children are considered to be financially dependent if under age 18 or in full time educational or vocational training. It is possible for a woman living with the deceased at the time of death who was not a lawful wife to receive a dependant's pension instead of a spouse's pension.

Insurance of death benefits

4.81 In a large self-administered scheme because of the wide spread of membership and size of the fund it is possible to pay out benefits from the fund should a death in service occur. However, in a SSAS with one or two members and especially in its early years, such cover does not fully exist in the fund to pay out benefits in the event of an unexpected death. So IR SPSS has allowed for insurance cover to be provided for this eventuality. Term assurance is usually used for this purpose and it will not be subject to the Insurance Premium Tax (see 13.55 to 13.57).

4.82 PN 20.37 states that all death-in-service benefits must be insured to the extent that they exceed the value from year to year of the member's interest in the scheme based on his accrued pension and other benefits. There are two points to note from this. The first point is that such insurance is not compulsory and if insurance cover is required it is not a rule requirement. It is important to understand that if insurance cover is not provided then the amount of any death-in-service benefits will be limited to the member's interest in the scheme provided that does not exceed the Inland Revenue maxima. The second point to bear in mind is that the insurance cover provided should not, when added to the member's interest in the scheme, exceed the Inland Revenue maxima. It follows from this that if maximum death-in-service benefits are to be provided, the level of insured cover should decrease over the years as further contributions are paid and the value of the member's interest increases, even after allowing for increases in remuneration.

4.83 There will be instances where it is not possible to obtain insurance cover of this nature i.e. the member has an impaired life and is uninsurable or the premiums quoted are prohibitive. If such a member died in service the death-in-service benefits would be limited to the member's interest in the fund, but it may be possible to approach IR SPSS after the death to ascertain if it would allow a special contribution to be paid to the scheme to fund for the balance of death-in-service benefits up to the maximum permitted.

Death benefits in retirement

4.84 If a member's pension has been secured following retirement a lump sum may be payable under a guarantee attaching to the pension. IR SPSS allows a guaranteed pension to be paid for up to ten years after retirement. If the guarantee is limited to five years from retirement a lump sum will become payable on the member's death within that five years equal to the balance of pension due at the end of the five-year period.

4.85 The lump sum is also payable free of IHT (see 4.79) provided the trustees have discretion as to its disposal.

4.86 Following the death of a member a dependant's pension may be provided to the spouse. It may already have been secured at the time the member's pension was purchased and will come into payment automatically or it can be secured following the member's death or if the member was receiving a pension from the scheme, its purchase may be deferred until the earlier of the attaining by the dependant of age 75 or the date on which the deceased member would have attained age 75, or increased to the maximum allowable. The limits as set out in PN 11.7 allow pensions to be provided up to 2/3rds of the maximum pension approvable for the deceased member before any lump sum commutation at retirement and as if the deceased had no retained benefits from earlier occupations. The maximum pension so calculated may also be increased in line with the RPI from the date on which the deceased's own pension became payable.

4.87 If a leaver dies before normal retirement age having deferred benefits in the scheme, a cash lump sum and spouse's and dependant's pensions may be paid. PN 10.19 explains any lump sum benefit payable will be governed by the practice relating to death-in-service benefits in PN Part 11 and based on final remuneration at the date of leaving. PN 10.19 also explains spouse's and dependant's pensions may be provided as explained in PN Part 11 except they are to be calculated by reference to the deceased member's maximum approvable deferred pension.

4.88 Where a member dies in service after normal retirement age, PN 11.10 allows maximum benefits to be provided on the basis of death in service generally (see 4.77, 4.78 and 4.80) or in the case of a member with continued rights on the basis that the member had died in retirement having retired the day before the date of death.

Ill-health

4.89 If a member's retirement is caused by incapacity benefits may be paid immediately whatever the age. Pension and lump sum benefits are higher than those allowable than on early retirement as the benefits may be based on the fraction of final remuneration the member could have received had service continued until normal retirement age. Incapacity is defined in the Glossary to PN and *SI 1995 No 3103* as physical or mental deterioration bad enough to prevent members from following their normal employment or seriously impairing their earnings capacity. It does not mean simply a decline in energy or ability.

4.90 It is a matter for the trustees, subject to 4.91, to decide on the evidence available to them if early retirement benefits due to incapacity can be paid. Such benefits are enhanced in these circumstances providing a greater tax free cash lump sum and pension. If someone who has taken incapacity early retirement benefits is re-employed in a lesser role than before, their incapacity benefits would not then be affected by their re-employment. Their pension may have to be suspended if the circumstances giving rise to incapacity no longer existed.

4.91 When controlling director members of a SSAS intend to retire after 1 January 1996 on incapacity grounds, IR SPSS must be notified in writing at least 28 days before any proposed incapacity benefits are paid. The procedure is set out in 3.82. IR SPSS can be expected to look critically later at the position of directors who have taken incapacity benefits, particularly the enhanced tax-free lump sum, if they have continued in some executive role or as a self-employed consultant with the company. The inspector of taxes may well closely consider the consultancy role (see 4.71) as to whether or not Schedule E status has effectively been relinquished.

4.92   If Schedule E status is deemed to have continued or a director's role remains undiminished after taking incapacity benefits, the tax-free lump sum or the enhanced element of it may be in jeopardy. IR SPSS may seek to tax it under Schedule E as an unauthorised payment (see 4.71). The pension will have been taxed anyway, but that may not prevent repayment to the trustees of any excessive element and the possible imposition of a penalty under *Finance Act 1994, s 106* up to £3,000 on the administrator or director personally for making a false representation to obtain the increased benefits.

4.93   Where a member is in exceptional circumstances of serious ill-health, full commutation of the member's pension is permissible. The rule wording and IR SPSS requirements are explained in 3.30 and 3.83 respectively. A lump sum paid in these circumstances is subject to a tax charge under *section 599(1)* on the excess of the lump sum payable less the maximum lump sum which would otherwise have been payable on grounds of incapacity. Thus, if the full commutation produces a lump sum of £300,000 and the maximum lump sum permitted on grounds of incapacity was £200,000, tax would be payable on the excess of £100,000 at 20% and accounted for by the administrator to the Inland Revenue.

If a member takes this option it is also possible to avoid inheritance tax (see 4.79).

Payment of pensions

4.94   Before JOM 58 was published the rules of a SSAS had to provide for a member's pension to be secured immediately it became payable by the purchase of a non-commutable, non-assignable annuity from a LO. There were certain exceptions for impaired lives (see 4.83) and pension increases (see 3.33 and 3.34). The main reason for this requirement was to prevent scheme members demanding the termination of the scheme in any way they chose, particularly as this situation was more likely to occur where all or most of the members had retired. However, the PSO (now IR SPSS) recognised that such a risk was no more significant during the first five years of retirement than it was during service if the emerging pension was guaranteed for five years and there was a lump sum guarantee payment prospectively distributable to the member's dependants or legal personal representatives in the event of death.

4.95   As a result this requirement was changed if the rules provided for an annuity to be purchased within five years of the member's retirement. The five-year period is very useful indeed. It allows members' pensions to be paid from the scheme during that period. They must be paid because they are mandatory following retirement apart from the exceptions in PN 10.8. The trustees need to ensure there is sufficient in the fund to pay the pension at the correct level and they will be required to deduct PAYE (see 4.110). Most importantly it allows the trustees to choose the most propitious time to purchase the annuity, when rates are more favourable, and also time to realise an investment which may take a while to sell as its value may be currently depressed. On the negative side is IR SPSS's imposition of the restrictions on loans, borrowings and share purchases during deferral up to age 75, as described below, to apply to 5 year deferral cases by virtue of PSO Update No. 63.

4.96   Until 1 May 1995 the trustees had to purchase annuities on retirement or deferred annuities from an authorised company. Since 1 September 1995 this includes any insurance company established in the EU. This change was introduced by *Finance Act 1995, s 59*. *Section 659B* was introduced providing a new definition of an authorised insurance company and the Inland Revenue's requirements if it is used for purchasing annuities. This defines an insurance company as including a European Community (note not 'EU') company that lawfully carries on long-term business or provides long-term insurance in the UK through a branch here if appropriate. It is not clear if a scheme's rules will require amending before an annuity is purchased from another EU country insurance company. European legislation may over-ride this requirement.

4.97   There is a new method of deferral for members, spouses and dependants, which is described in 3.42 and 3.43. As the existing method may still apply, the details are given below.

In February 1994 the PSO (now IR SPSS) agreed to a further easement of the five-year concession to allow the purchase of annuities for retiring members to be deferred to age 75 irrespective of their retirement age. The change came about following negotiations between the APT and Inland Revenue. The main reasons for the change were the advent in 1989 of unapproved schemes (see CHAPTER 15) that could exist without prejudicing other tax approved schemes of the employer, the increased costs of purchasing annuities due to unfavourable annuity rates, the reluctance of trustees to disturb successful investments and the cost of annuities for impaired lives. To benefit from this change SSASs had to amend their rules by 4 August 1994 otherwise the five-year rule in 4.95 above will continue to apply. SSASs established after that date may only have the rules deferring the purchase of annuities until age 75 (see 3.42).

4.98   The changed arrangements were effective from 4 February 1994 for all retirements that take place on or after that date. They also applied to members of SSAS who at 4 February 1994 had already retired, but who had not reached the five-year deadline by which time their pension must be purchased and whose pension was or is still being paid from the SSAS. The arrangements do not apply to pensions that should have been purchased prior to 4 February 1994 because the five-year deferral period expired before then.

4.99 In June 1995 the PSO (now IR SPSS) agreed to end its requirement for a surviving spouse's or dependant's pension to be secured immediately following a member's death. The purchase of a pension for any dependant from a SSAS may be deferred until the earlier of the attaining by the dependant of age 75 or the date on which the deceased member would have attained age 75 (see 4.86). In any of these circumstances where the widow or widower is not a trustee of the SSAS or the dependant is aged over 18, their appointment as a trustee should be considered to avoid the self-investment restrictions (see 11.43).

4.100 A member of a SSAS can retire early from age 50 onwards or from the normal retirement of 60 *et seq.* and be paid a pension from the scheme for a period of up to 25 years before it is purchased from a LO. For SSASs established before 5 August 1994 the trustees do not have to make an immediate decision on adopting the age 75 deferral rule unless the current five-year deadline is imminent for a particular member. Adopting the rule amendment can pose difficult questions because once adopted it applies to all members — one-member cannot have the five-year rule and another the age 75 deferral rule. For instance, if a controlling director has a normal retirement age between 70 and 75, or has passed normal retirement age and does not intend to retire and take retirement benefits until between ages 70 and 75, it would be preferable to retain the five-year rule. That allows anyone retiring at, say, age 72 to have their pension paid from the SSAS until age 77. This would suit a one-member SSAS, but where there is more than one member the five-year rule may not suit the other member(s) and a choice has to be made because once the rule change is made its provisions apply to all members. Fortunately for one-member SSASs the trustees' options can be left open (this was confirmed by the PSO (now IR SPSS) on 11 January 1999) and a choice made later.

4.101 IR SPSS stresses (PN 20.40) that the deferral to purchase pensions until age 75 is intended to provide trustees with more flexibility in deciding the most opportune time to effect the purchase rather than an automatic deferral to purchase until age 75. It expects practitioners to keep the desirability of purchasing pensions under constant review and for trustees to consider the position at annual trustees' meetings and whenever changes occur in interest rates or inflation, which have a material impact on the suitability of purchasing pensions. IR SPSS intends to review these latest arrangements periodically to ensure they are not being abused and expects its guidelines on actuarial certificates (see 4.102 and 9.42), on lending and share purchases (see 4.103 and 5.28) and on borrowings (see 4.105 and 7.62) to be complied with otherwise it will require pensions to be purchased immediately. It is important to note that for a SSAS established prior to 5 August 1994, IR SPSS's guidelines as set out in 4.106 to 4.110 do not have to be adhered to if there is no rule deferring pension purchases to age 75.

4.102 IR SPSS (PN 20.41) requires the actuary to certify that the amount of pension that can be maintained when it comes into payment for a member takes into account any contingent dependants' pension and the scheme's income and assets, particularly that part of the fund notionally earmarked to provide the members' benefits. Where a pension comes into payment for a dependant the actuary needs to take into account only the scheme's investments and the assets underpinning the provision of the dependant's benefits. The certificate must compare the pension with the level of pension that could be secured contemporaneously on the open market with the funds available and in the case of a dependant's pension, the initial certificate should compare the pension with an annuity that could have been purchased at the date of death of the member. A divergence greater than 10 per cent between these two figures has to be explained. A copy of this initial certificate has to be provided to IR SPSS with the next triennial actuarial valuation following commencement of the pension or earlier, if requested. At each subsequent triennial valuation a further certificate should be incorporated with the valuation reviewing the amount of pension payable. A renewal certificate confirming the outcome of the actuary's review has to be supplied to the PSO with the triennial valuation.

4.103 On the liquidity front there are restrictions to loans and shares in the principal company or associated companies. Where all scheme members and any dependants are receiving a pension, no loans to or share purchases in such companies or share purchase in any other unquoted company are allowed after the first payment of the final retiring member's pension. Existing loans and shares have to be repaid or sold within five years of the commencement of pension payments. Where there are other members who are not yet drawing pensions, loans are allowed. For these SSASs, the portion of the fund notionally earmarked to provide retired members' benefits or dependants' benefits in payment has to be excluded from the value of the whole fund when determining the maximum amount to be lent to the principal company or associated companies, or used to buy shares therein, i.e. the 50 per cent limit (see 5.8) or 25% limit for a SSAS less than two years old (see 5.10). In addition, for these SSASs, when the final member retires loans and shares have to be repaid or sold including shares in any other unquoted company within five years of that retirement and commencement of pension, or on attainment by a pensioner of age 70 if earlier. If a pensioner is already 70 when payment of pension commences, repayment of any loans and sale of unquoted shares must take place immediately. In the event that no member reaches retirement so that only dependants' pensions come into payment, the restriction will apply on the first payment to the final dependant.

4.104 The trustees may continue to invest in land and buildings during the period of deferral. This must be consistent with the scheme having sufficient readily realisable assets in addition to the real property to secure a pension from age 70 onwards. This requirement ensures the trustees are in a position to secure a pension between the ages of 70 and 75 without getting involved in a forced sale of property.

4.105 The level of any new borrowings by a SSAS during the period of deferral is restricted by excluding the retired members' and dependants' portions of the fund from the value of the scheme assets for the purposes of the 45% limit (see 7.57). The additional calculation of the borrowing limit based on contributions (see 7.58 and 7.59) is unaffected. To provide an element of transitional relief the same five-year and pensioner's age of 70 deadlines as for loans and shares (see 4.103) apply for reducing borrowings already in existence to acceptable levels when a member retires, or if earlier when the last dependant's benefits come into payment. If a pensioner is already 70 when payment of pension commences any reductions in borrowing to comply with the 45% limit must take place immediately.

4.106 The deferment of the pensions purchase would no longer be coupled with a restriction of the pension guarantee period to five years (see 4.94). A ten-year guarantee would be acceptable subject to normal IR SPSS practice. If pensions secured under these arrangements are not secured until after age 75 it can be expected that the SSAS concerned will lose its tax approval.

4.107 Whilst the five-year deferral period has been most useful to SSASs since 1979 the latest rule changes have offered distinct advantages until very recently to SSASs compared with insured schemes, particularly where annuity rates are unfavourable. Also many trustees have a dislike of handing over funds to a LO, funds which they have assiduously administered for many years and will be only too pleased to continue administering. Transfers from insured schemes to SSASs of controlling directors' benefits may well be more attractive. Where a transfer to a SSAS is to be made just prior to a retirement, provided a written request is made to IR SPSS for approval at least one month before the retirement and the SSAS has been formally approved, the transfer may be made after the retirement date if the delay is caused by the need to await IR SPSS approval (see 10.18). Processing by IR SPSS will be speeded up if the information set out in PSO Update No 17 Appendix 2 is supplied at the time of the request. The deferment to age 75 for the pension purchase gives added flexibility and important improvements to SSASs which insured schemes had difficulty matching until a few years ago when IR SPSS provisionally permitted insured schemes to have a similar income withdrawal facility to that which applies to personal pension schemes. PN, App XII contains the current wording, and Pensions Update No 105 introduced model rules for flexible pension provision that may be adopted by the trustees by way of a grandfather clause.

4.108 Following retirement, a member of a SSAS may receive the pension payable direct from the fund for a period of up to five years if the SSAS was established before 5 August 1994 or until age 75. At some time during this period the pension should be secured from a LO (see 4.94). The trustees may increase the pension during this period up to the level of the Index and when the pension is secured the level of pension then in payment must be secured. It is possible if the SSAS continues to exist for further increases to be secured later still subject to the level of the Index. PSO Update No 25 announced that increases and a year-on-year basis may be the greater of 3 per cent or Index.

4.109 If the SSAS has not been funded to a level sufficient to provide the member with the maximum pension allowable and it is desired when the pension is purchased to make some provision for future increases, a decision will be needed at the time of retirement to pitch the level of the pension that can be maintained. It may have to be set at a lower level to secure future increases, which can be costly.

4.110 Pensions are liable to income tax under Schedule E, even if they are paid before a scheme receives formal tax approval. In the case of *Esselmont v Marshall [1994] STI 1005*, the pension scheme was established in 1976, but not approved until much later. Meanwhile a pension was paid and it was claimed the pension was not taxable because it was an illegal payment from a pension scheme that was not approved. It was ruled that the pension was taxable under *section 597*. Whilst the pension is paid from the scheme's resources the trustees should operate PAYE on the pension being paid and account to the Inland Revenue for the tax deducted. If arrears of pension are paid that are attributable to previous tax years the recipient can claim under *FA 1989, s 41(2)* to have the amounts assessed to tax under Schedule E for the years concerned. This can be advantageous where the recipient's rate of tax was less in previous years.

Data capture of PSO records

4.111 The PSO announced in PSO Update No 39 that it was converting some 1.15 million insured scheme and individual arrangement files to computer records over the next four years. Correspondence will be put on a temporary file until closed, when the file will be destroyed. Any material decisions will be recorded on the computerised record.

SSASs, self-managed funds and insured schemes which are subject to the surplus regulations (see 9.45) will be retained in paper copy.

4.112 This chapter has covered the main benefits and limitations thereto that apply to SSASs. The actuary will take into account the benefits that are to be provided and have been communicated to the members in their announcement letters in preparing the initial and subsequent actuarial reports on the scheme and in recommending the funding rates for the scheme. The main actuarial considerations are explained in CHAPTER 9.

A new tax regime

4.113 A simplified tax system for defined contribution schemes and arrangements, including occupational pension schemes, personal pension schemes and stakeholder schemes, came into effect on 6 April 2001. It is possible for schemes to be set up either under the old tax regime (as described in this chapter) or the new tax regime. It is also permitted for existing schemes to elect to adopt the new tax regime with effect from 1 October 2001 under supplementary documentation. However, the main features of the new regime closely resemble personal pension scheme provisions, and it is unlikely that SSASs will wish to opt into the new regime. There is a tight control on contributions and investment activity that would dissuade this from happening, and the earnings cap shall apply. Details on how to convert a scheme from *ICTA 1988, Ch I Pt XIV approval* to *ICTA 1988, Ch IV Pt XIV approval* are given in Pensions Update No 96 and IR 76, Pt 23.

Chapter 5

Investments — Loans

General

5.1   Until 29 August 2000 it was not necessary to include in the trust deed any special restrictions on the investment powers of the trustees apart from the inclusion of those provisions in the regulations banning or limiting certain investments (see 3.21). However, following several years of negotiations with the Association of Pensioneer Trustees (APT), on 29 August 2000 IR SPSS issued PSO Update No 69 requiring pensioneer trustees to be both co-signatories to scheme bank accounts and co-owners of scheme assets. This was part of a package of measures to ensure that SSASs are used to provide only genuine relevant benefits within the normal tax approval rules (see 2.57). SSASs submitted for approval on or after 30 August 2000 must comply from that date and SSASs approved or submitted for approval before that date had to meet the co-signatory requirements by the end of February 2001 and the co-ownership requirements by 29 August 2001. Failure to meet these requirements will lead to IR SPSS refusing to approve a SSAS submitted for approval or in the case of a SSAS approved before 29 August 2000, reviewing and possibly withdrawing approval. Despite these requirements, PN 20.51 states that it is not for IR SPSS to interfere in the way trustees invest scheme funds unless tax avoidance, the *bona fide* sole purposes test, i.e. member use of benefits, or liquidity is involved. This means the trust deed is usually drawn up giving the trustees wide powers of investment.

5.2   It also means that apart from specific areas of investment to which the *Regulations* apply, the trustees may put their funds into a very wide range of investments. Specific types of investments such as loans and property, to which the regulations and IR SPSS discretionary guidelines apply, which are major subjects in themselves, are covered in detail in CHAPTERS 5 and 6 respectively. Unquoted shares and other investments to which the regulations and guidelines also apply are covered in CHAPTER 7. Investments such as equities, gilts, deposit accounts, building society accounts, insurance policies, unit trusts, managed funds etc. do not give rise to problems with IR SPSS. If trustees are investing in these, they need only have regard to IR SPSS liquidity requirements i.e. are the investments easily realisable to purchase annuities when the latter are due, and the statement of investment principles that may be required by virtue of the *Pensions Act 1995* (see 11.98)

Loans to employers

5.3   The ability of the trustees to invest for themselves is one of the major selling points of SSASs. One of the great attractions of SSASs is the facility to lend money back to the employer, so much so that it is a common feature of SSASs. So what can and cannot be done with such loans?

5.4   The *Regulations* and PN 20 set the parameters. Prior to the *Regulations* IR SPSS policy was fleshed out from time to time at meetings with the APT. Broadly, loans may be made from a SSAS to an employer on commercially reasonable terms provided they do not amount to more than half the value of the assets of the scheme, that they are not too frequent, that they are not injudicious and that the scheme's future liquidity requirements are able to be met.

Which employer?

5.5   In the regulations the definition of employer for the purposes of loans includes any company which participates in the SSAS or which is associated in any way with such a company either as a subsidiary or holding company, or if the associated company and the participating company are controlled by the same person. It should be noted that where loans are made to companies in these categories various restrictions apply to the loans.

5.6   The regulations specifically ban loans to scheme members and their relatives, both directly and indirectly. PN 20.52 explains that the reason for this ban is because such a loan would become in reality a charge on the retirement benefit. This would contravene the 'sole provision of retirement benefits' requirement in *s 590(2)(a)* and is why linked pension mortgages are banned (see 7.64). Another reason for the ban is that the SSAS could be used in this way to avoid the tax liability arising on loans direct from a close company to its participators (*s 419*). PN 20.61 mentions that any attempt to circumvent the ban on loans to members by means of back-to-back loans whereby a loan to an unconnected party is lent on to a scheme member, will lose the SSAS concerned its tax approval. This aspect is highlighted in Case 12 of the National Audit Office Survey, Appendix 2.

5.7   The trustees may lend to totally unassociated companies. Whilst this would be a perfectly legitimate investment for the trustees and the *Regulations* would not in their terms apply, IR SPSS, in some instances, still looks at such loans quite critically and they may need to be defended as *bona fide* investments. IR SPSS will enquire about loans to unconnected companies or individuals particularly to establish whether arrangements have been made to circumvent the ban on loans to scheme members or to exceed the limit on loans to companies by means of reciprocal loans to the members or companies by the unconnected companies or individuals. In addition, IR SPSS expects such loans to be for a fixed term, at a commercial rate of interest (SSAS GN 4.36), and evidenced in writing, the terms of which provide for immediate repayment if the conditions are breached, the borrower ceases to trade or becomes insolvent or the trustees require repayment to pay benefits. Further requirements are expected to be introduced by IR SPSS in the future (see 5.53).

The amount

5.8 This is quite straightforward although the formulae contained in the regulations, as amended by *SI 1998 No 728* and *SI 1998 No 1315* (see 2.24), are somewhat complicated. No more than 50% of the value of the scheme's assets may be lent at any one time once the SSAS is two years old. For this purpose the amount of the loan plus the value of any shares in the employer must be aggregated and no more than 50% in total can be lent to or be invested in the employer. The limit is applied at the date the money is loaned. The point about the aggregation of shareholdings arose shortly after JOM 58 was published and was confirmed as an earlier change in IR SPSS practice following the PQ relating to SSASs raised in July 1984. This is confirmed in the regulations.

5.9 It is possible for the trustees to make more than one loan to an employer or to make loans to more than one associated employer at the same time provided that they do not amount in aggregate to more than half of the value of the assets. Where more than one loan is made to an employer, separate loan documentation must be used (see 5.48) and separate reports made to IR SPSS (see 5.49). The same applies to successive loans from SSASs to an employer under a single loan facility. PSO Update No 48 mentions that loans made under a loan facility are in some cases not being separately reported and documented. Every payment under the facility constitutes a separate loan at the time of payment. The documentation for each tranche may consist of the facility agreement and an abbreviated loan agreement provided together they both indicate all the terms of the loan.

5.10 In establishing the value of the assets for the purpose of the 50% limit on loans transfer payments received and policies assigned to the scheme may be included. The value of an insurance policy is its surrender value (SSAS GN 4.34) and the value of a unit-linked policy is its bid value. However, SSASs established from 5 August 1991 cannot make loans exceeding 25% of the value of the assets in their first two years including any shares in the employer and the value of the assets for this purpose is that derived from employer and member contributions only i.e. transfer payments are excluded.

Furthermore, where a SSAS has adopted a rule allowing the purchase of annuities to be deferred (see 3.42), the market value of assets excludes any portion of the assets notionally underpinning any retired member's, ex-spouse's, widow's/widower's or dependant's benefits in payment from the fund and any other liabilities of the trustees, including borrowings taken out to purchase assets (but not borrowings taken out to assist in paying out retirement or death benefits). PN 20.53 refers.

5.11   PN 20.54 explains that IR SPSS applies the 25% and 50% limits to the aggregate of not only all loans made to and shares held in the employers participating in a SSAS and associated employers but also of both loans to individuals and companies who are connected with the SSAS, through a member, trustee or a participating employer, (but are not "connected persons" for the purposes of the regulations) and shares held in such companies. Examples of such connected individuals and companies are:

(a)   an individual who is a business associate of a member, or of a trustee or employer in relation to the scheme, or who is a relative of a trustee or employer;

(b)   a partnership where one of the partners is connected as in (a) with a member, trustee or employer; and

(c)   a company in which a director or influential shareholder (i.e. one who controls 20% or more of the voting shares in the company) is connected as in (a) above.

An individual is connected with a corporate trustee or employer if he or she is a relative or business associate of any director or influential shareholder of the trustee or employer company. Examples of a business associate are: a partner in a partnership; a fellow director in a company; or a fellow influential director in a company. A director of a company is regarded as a business associate of an influential shareholder of the same company and vice versa.

5.12   Many employers may find it extremely useful and financially efficient when setting up a SSAS to obtain a loan from the trustees. They can after all make a payment of an initial contribution of say £100,000 and obtain corporation tax relief on it and on the same day get back £25,000 as a loan for genuine business purposes and obtain further tax relief on the interest paid on the loan. The 25% restriction may not be too popular, but the full 50% can be borrowed after two years.

5.13 There are two other points to be aware of regarding the value of loans. The first being that the value of the assets may go down either fortuitously or by design and as a result the value of the loan may exceed half or a quarter of the value of the fund. The trustees clearly have no direct control over the value of the assets if they fall as a result of stock market fluctuations. In these circumstances IR SPSS takes a lenient view and does not require a reduction in the loan to bring it within the required limit as a result of the fall in value (SSAS GN 4.32). The second point is not likely to find favour with IR SPSS. If one member has left taking a transfer value or another has retired and taken retirement benefits, both of them being from that part of the fund invested other than in a loan to an employer, then if because of the reduced value of the assets, the loan now exceeds the 50% limit, the trustees will have no option but to reduce the loan (see 5.29 however where the securing of pensions are deferred until age 75).

Frequency

5.14 In this area IR SPSS discretionary practice applies and not the regulations. PN 20.57 and SSAS GN 4.22 mention that employer's contributions should not be lent back with such frequency as to suggest that a SSAS which is being presented as funded is in reality an unfunded or partly unfunded scheme. This does not mean that the trustees may not go on lending to the employer on a regular basis each year, making a repeat loan for the same amount every time a contribution is paid, although care is needed here because PN 20.57 contains a warning that funds should not lodge with the employer for longer than is necessary. What IR SPSS is looking to stop is a succession of loans made at the full 50% value of the assets.

5.15 The following simple illustration of loans made on the same day as each contribution should help to clarify matters. The SSAS was established prior to 1 January 1996:

			Example A		*Example B*	
Date of Contri-bution	*Amount of Contri-bution*	*Value of Fund*	*Loan to Employer*	*Repaid*	*Loan to Employer*	*Repaid*
1.1.98	£20,000	£50,000	£25,000	31.12.98	£25,000	31.12.98
1.1.99	£20,000	£75,000	£25,000	31.12.99	£37,500	31.12.99
1.1.00	£20,000	£100,000	£25,000	31.12.00	£50,000	31.12.00
1.1.01	£20,000	£130,000	£25,000	31.12.01	£65,000	31.12.01

In Example A there should be no objection by IR SPSS to the series of loans provided they meet all the usual criteria. However, in Example B 50% of the fund is being lent every year and IR SPSS would maintain the SSAS is partly unfunded and such loans should cease. It is also likely to lay down the condition that no future loans can be made unless IR SPSS is approached first with proposals for another loan. It is not likely that an objection would be made by IR SPSS in Example B until at least three loans at 50% had been made as there would be no pattern of regularity established until that time. If there are also unpaid debts due to the trustees or other loans to totally unconnected persons, the SSAS could be more than 50% unfunded, resulting in further problems with IR SPSS.

Purpose

5.16   The purpose of a loan to an employer can lead to contention with IR SPSS. JOM 58 did not spell out what was an acceptable purpose other than loans must be 'commercially reasonable'. However it was established early on that loans must be for proper business purposes i.e. the money must be used by the company for the furtherance of its trade. In fact the regulations use the phrase 'utilised for the purposes of the employer's business' and PN 20.59 makes the general point that loans should not be made unless the trustees would be prepared to lend the same amount on the same terms to an unconnected party of comparable standing. Utilisation of a loan for purchasing fixed assets, stock, buildings, or developing land by a building company are all acceptable purposes. IR SPSS has made it plain that using a loan to purchase luxury items, e.g. yachts, or assets which a scheme member may use, e.g. residential property, or to lend on to scheme members or to purchase assets which if owned by the trustees themselves would be unacceptable is not acceptable. Loans should not be used for purely speculative purposes such as the purchase of shares or other investments, although a holding company may use a loan to make or manage investments of its trading subsidiaries where it owns 51% or more of the shares (PN 20.56 and SSAS GN 4.23). There is a very wide area of acceptable and unacceptable purposes, plus a grey area of ambiguity, despite the regulations, PN 20 and SSAS GN.

5.17   One would think cars would be acceptable, but if they involve private use at all the loan is likely to be objected to by IR SPSS (see Case 7 National Audit Office Survey Appendix 2 and SSAS GN 9.68). Commercial vehicles would be all right. Re-scheduling the company's finances often means taking out a loan to rationalise or re-organise the company's existing financial commitments. IR SPSS is likely to ask what those existing commitments are and, if they include a loan whose purpose is unacceptable, then the further loan would be unacceptable too.

5.18   It is no good recording the purpose of the loan in the loan document as 'business purposes', 'operating capital', 'cash flow' or informing IR SPSS that it is for such general purposes. IR SPSS wishes to know the precise purpose of the loan or on what it was specifically expended. IR SPSS is aware that companies have cash flow problems which are either seasonal because of the nature of their trade or perennial, but it is most likely to look at the cash flow problem critically perhaps after consulting the company's tax district. It is no good maintaining the company has a cash flow problem if its accounts show otherwise or if the loan was made in January to a retailing company whose main profits are derived from the Christmas trade! A succession of loans for cash flow purposes is also likely to meet with resistance from IR SPSS on the lines that the company should by now have sorted out its cash flow problems and not be relying on its pension scheme to keep bailing it out. If the company is short of funds from which to pay its directors, then a loan from the trustees to enable them to pay the directors will not be acceptable.

5.19   If the trustees make a loan whose purpose IR SPSS finds unacceptable, then it is most likely to have to be repaid if the scheme's continued approval is not to be prejudiced or if approval is to be granted.

5.20   It is always open to IR SPSS to check later with the inspector of taxes how the loan was actually expended. If the inspector of taxes is aware of how the loan was spent and IR SPSS finds out that it is different to what it has been told, then the trustees would be in trouble unless there is a very good reason for spending the loan differently. PSO Update No 32 (4–5) mentions that during compliance audit visits it had found that the whole or part of a loan had been used for purposes other than that given to IR SPSS. If for some reason a company changes its mind as to how it uses the loan, then IR SPSS should be informed at the time. It is the intention of IR SPSS to make trustees responsible for ensuring that loans are used by the borrower for the purpose stated (see 5.53).

Rate of interest

5.21   The regulations require loans to be at a commercial rate of interest. PN 20.58 expects the commercial rate of interest to be at least 3% above the Clearing Bank Base Rate (CBBR) at the time the loan was made. This is widely known as CBBR + 3% and has been in operation since 1980. The rate was confirmed in July 1984 following the PQ raised about IR SPSS changes in practice on SSASs.

5.22   The rate of interest can be expressed as a straight percentage or as the lending rate of a particular lender, but it should be ensured that whatever this rate is, it is equivalent to or greater than CBBR + 3%.

5.23   It is possible for loans to be made to employers at less than CBBR + 3%, but IR SPSS will require evidence that such a rate, for example CBBR +

2%, would be generally available to the employer for the same purpose from other lending sources. The trustees will need to produce something in writing from a bank or other lending source to this effect. However, this may not be possible in the future (see 5.53).

5.24   It is almost self-evident that loans cannot be made interest-free to employers, but there are good reasons for IR SPSS finding this unacceptable. First, the employer would be enjoying a commercial advantage which could not be obtained elsewhere. Secondly, the trustees would not be acting in the best interest of the beneficiaries in not securing a reasonable rate of return on their investment. PN 20.58 emphasises the point that interest on loans must be charged and paid.

5.25   If IR SPSS finds the rate of interest on a loan below its guidelines it will almost certainly seek an amendment to the rate of interest to increase it to an acceptable level. If the loan has been made interest-free, IR SPSS line is likely to be harsher and could involve refusal to approve the scheme or withdrawal of approval.

Deduction of tax

5.26   When the employer pays interest on the loan to the trustees it would normally deduct tax and account for it to the Inland Revenue (*s 348, ICTA 1988*). The trustees being exempt from tax may then claim repayment of the tax suffered if the SSAS has been approved. However, if the loan is for less than a year the interest may be paid gross by the employer. This saves the trustees the trouble of reclaiming tax and it is also very useful to them when tax cannot be reclaimed until approval has been granted if loans are made in the meantime. The interest on loans of one year or more in duration must, however, be paid under deduction of tax.

5.27   The advantages of loans of less than one year have to be carefully considered, however, because there is legislation in force to frustrate the advantage of a series of loans being made with interest paid gross for periods of less than one year. This is a matter mainly for inspectors of taxes, but it should not be overlooked that the scheme's approval may be prejudiced if a series of short loans can be shown to be a device to get round the deduction of tax from interest using the pension scheme as a vehicle to achieve it. It would have to be shown that the series of short loans do not amount to an overall contract for a long period for lending to the employer. Renewals of the same loan after 364 days or less therefore need to be considered with care, particularly in the light of PN 20.57. This explains that it is not acceptable to make a series of 364 day loans just to enable interest thereon to be paid gross when in reality there is no intention of repaying the loan for a number of years.

Liquidity

5.28   As with any other type of investment the trustees need to take their imminent cash needs into account when making a loan. The regulations specify that loans shall become immediately repayable if monies are required by the trustees to purchase annuities. The trustees are limited to lending no more than 50% or 25% of the fund to an employer, so in setting the date for repayment of a loan they need to look at when the SSAS will need to pay any benefits and whether those benefits can be paid from the remainder of the fund if the loan continues beyond then. If there is only one member in the scheme or the other assets are fixed and not readily realisable for cash, IR SPSS generally expects the loan to end about a year before retirement benefits are due to be paid. This would allow a reasonable period for any action to be taken to recover the loan should there be any default.

5.29   If a SSAS has a rule or adopts a rule allowing the purchase of annuities to be deferred until age 75 (see 3.42) and all scheme members and any dependants are in receipt of a pension, no loans to the principal or associated company are allowed following the later of the first payment of the final retiring member's pension or, where a pensions sharing order applies and the ex-spouse is a member of the scheme (see 3.95), the final ex-spouse taking a pension and the first payment of the final widow's/widower's or dependant's pension (PN 20.54). Existing loans should be repaid within five years of the commencement of pension payments, or on attainment of age 70 by a pensioner if earlier. If the pensioner is already 70 when payment of pension commences, the funds necessary to secure the whole pension must be regarded as required immediately. Loans are allowed however where a SSAS has other members not yet drawing benefits. In these cases the portion of the fund representing the retired member's benefits or dependant's benefits in payment has to be excluded when calculating the maximum amount which may be lent to the principal or associated company (see 5.10).

Under PSO Update No 63 issued in June 2000, IR SPSS also imposed these restrictions on SSASs that have retained the facility to defer the purchase of annuities for 5 years (see 3.42) but only in relation to new loans made on or after 1 August 2000, not roll overs of loans made before that date.

5.30   Open-ended loans to employers, for example repayable on demand, will not find favour with IR SPSS because the regulations state loans must be for a fixed period. There is not only the possibility that such loans may never be repaid, but IR SPSS is likely to seek a definite repayment date sometime before retirement benefits are due to be paid.

5.31   There must be no fetter which prevents the immediate repayment of the loan. PSO Update No 31 (4–6) drew attention to this in connection with subordinated loans. For example, a SSAS may make a loan to a corporate member of a self-regulating authority. The corporate member may be a financial adviser who in turn is a member of and regulated by the PIA (see 11.61 to 11.65) who may need to meet the financial resource requirements of the self-regulatory authority. Consequently, a loan to such a corporate member may be subject to a deed of subordination or special agreement to ensure that financial resource requirements are not prejudiced. Any arrangements in a deed, or in writing, must not however prevent the immediate repayment of such a loan made from a SSAS.

5.32 Loans can be made for short periods of a few months or for much longer. There is no specific limit, only the liquidity consideration will eventually limit the length of a loan and funds should not lodge with the employer for a longer period than is necessary (see 5.14). Therefore they can be for several years. A longer loan may well be useful to an employer to enable the repayments to be spread over the whole period or, if it is more convenient, to repay the whole loan at the end of the period. The employer's cash flow circumstances will clearly dictate when and how the repayments are made.

Security and default

5.33 IR SPSS currently has no requirement as to security and it appears that this will continue to be the case in the future (see 5.53). This is a matter for the trustees of the SSAS.

5.34 The minimum rate of interest CBBR + 3% applies to both secured and unsecured loans. IR SPSS has never sought a differing rate of interest on either type of loan and this is confirmed in PN 20.58. However, if the trustees make a secured loan to the employer at less than CBBR + 3%, then the evidence from a bank required by IR SPSS (see 5.23) should make it clear that the bank's terms are based on a similar secured loan being made to the employer. However, this will not be acceptable in the future if current IR SPSS proposals come into force (see 5.53).

5.35 It has become increasingly apparent over the years that IR SPSS has tightened its attitude to loans made to employers in financial difficulties particularly where later the employer goes into liquidation or receivership and there is no prospect of the repayment of the loan. There is probably no other area of loans to employers which leads to more contention with IR SPSS than injudicious loans. The starting point is that the trustees in their fiduciary capacity are expected to act in the best interests of the members of the scheme, a point made in PN 20.59 and SSAS GN 4.38. The fact that the trustees are the directors of the company which needs money to keep it afloat has to be put on one side. The trustees should not lend money in the first place to keep an ailing business afloat or to an employer who is technically insolvent or fail to take all legal steps to enforce repayment. In fact, loans should not be made to an employer or associated employer unless the trustees would be prepared to lend the same amount on the same terms to someone at arm's length of comparable standing (see 5.16). If such injudicious loans are made, and IR SPSS learns of them either because they remain unpaid, are written off or it becomes aware the employer is in financial difficulty, it is likely to take the view that the scheme is not being properly administered and withdraw approval or refuse to approve the scheme. Not only does Case 14 of the National Audit Office Survey Appendix 2 confirm this, but SSAS practitioners will be aware of many cases where this has happened.

5.36   It is apparent from PSO Update No 43 that some SSASs have been involved with injudicious loans, and insured loan back arrangements have tooWith regard to the latter, this led to IR SPSS publishing changes to PN in August 1999 in PSO Update No 55 for all insured loanbacks made on or after 1 December 1999. Details are now contained in PN 16.58 to 16.89. At the same time IR SPSS made it clear to the APT that it wished to implement similar rules for loans from SSASs, but would consider them separately. In October 2000 IR SPSS wrote to the APT outlining proposals for a draft Update to introduce new requirements for loans from SSASs. At the time of writing the proposals were still under discussion between IR SPSS and the APT. For details of the proposals see 5.53 .The advice given in PSO Update No 43 regarding foreclosure, waiver and the imposition of a 35% tax charge under *s 601* is also relevant to SSASs. The tax charge was reduced from 40% by insertion of a new subsection *(2A)* to *s 601* by *FA 2001, s 74*. This advice is given generally in 5.37 to 5.40.

5.37   There may well be instances where a loan had been made injudiciously to the company which later faced liquidation. To reduce its debts and obtain bank borrowings a company may want the trustees to write off the loan before repayment is due as there is no prospect of its repayment, but IR SPSS would take the view that the fact that the SSAS had been prepared to lend money to help prop up an ailing company is an aspect of the SSAS administration it regards as prejudicial to continuing approval. IR SPSS could further insist that should the loan be written-off, the release of the debt would be a payment to the employer liable to tax under *ss 601(1)* and *(2)* by virtue of the *Pension Schemes Surpluses (Administration) Regulations 1987 (SI 1987 No 352)*. This is a tricky area for advisers who may not be aware of the financial position of the company at the time even if they are kept informed by the other trustees regarding scheme investments. As a result some pensioneer trustees are seeking confirmation from third parties, e.g. accountants, that the company's financial position is sound before a loan is made. Such action is likely to become an IR SPSS requirement (see 5.53).

5.38 What if the liquidation or receivership of a company before the due date of repayment of a loan precipitates the period of the loan? The loan then becomes repayable from the date of appointment of the liquidator/receiver subject to there being sufficient funds available to the liquidator/receiver to repay the loan as a secured or unsecured creditor as determined by the legal priorities for repayment. The action taken by IR SPSS will depend on whether or not the loan was made judiciously in the first place. If it was made judiciously and the loan cannot be paid in full or part because insufficient funds are available to the liquidator/receiver to make the repayment and the company is finally wound-up, IR SPSS should have no grounds for raising a tax charge on the value of the loan then written-off, always provided the trustees lodged a legal claim for the debt when the liquidator/receiver was appointed, i.e. they made a proper attempt to recover the capital outstanding and interest accrued thereon. If the loan was made injudiciously and the company cannot repay the debt, withdrawal of approval can be expected but no charge will arise under *s 601*. If the company was capable of repaying the debt, however, IR SPSS action would depend on whether the trustees had endeavoured to enforce their claim. If they did, then only approval would be withdrawn. If they did not then approval would be withdrawn and a charge raised under *s 601, ICTA 1988*.

5.39 The same criteria should apply when a company ceases trading and is struck-off at Companies House as there is no prospect in these circumstances of the company repaying the loan to the trustees if it has no resources from which to make the repayment.

5.40 Problems are likely to arise however where the company continues to trade even on a limited basis because its financial position is not good. In these circumstances, experience of IR SPSS's position shows that if a loan debt is written-off or waived, the tax charge will be raised on the value of the debt involved. It appears that the reasoning behind this is that a loan to a trading company is not irrecoverable whilst the company continues to trade. Irrecoverability involves consideration not just of funds currently available to a company but of funds potentially available. This is why IR SPSS is apparently prepared to consider proposals for repayments of debts generally over periods not exceeding five years, but makes warning noises regarding the application of the surplus legislation if any write-off or waiver is proposed. Thus a commercial arrangement, as envisaged in PSO Update No 43(9) whereby the outstanding capital together with interest will be repaid within a reasonable period of time, should be acceptable to IR SPSS. A proposal to convert the loan into shares in the company would not be acceptable as this would increase the scheme's exposure to possible bad debts (SSAS GN 9.82).

5.41 The majority of loans to employers are unsecured and it is not uncommon for the employer to get into difficulties in meeting the repayments, especially in timesof recession. One way round this is to renew the loan for a further period, but the trustees have to watch that they are acting in the best interests of the members and that benefit payments are not imminent. There is nothing in principle to prevent loans being renewed. Indeed a renewal will be acceptable to IR SPSS after the interest due on the original loan has been repaid, but as stated in PN 20.60, IR SPSS will not agree to a loan being rolled over more than twice. It is not acceptable to include unpaid interest in the capital of a new loan. Some unsecured loans do in fact have guarantors, so if the repayment cannot be met the trustees should ask for the guarantee to be honoured.

5.42 PSO Update No 32(6 and 7) mentions that compliance audit visits have discovered instances of interest being paid late or remaining unpaid after repayment of the loan capital. Subsequently IR SPSS has been using the surplus legislation in *SI 1987 No 352* to enforce payment of interest by threatening to raise a 35% tax charge on the company debtor if the interest is not paid because under *Regulation 4(a)(iii)* a loan must show a reasonable commercial return. So, if interest is not paid, the loan is not showing a reasonable commercial return. Threatening a 35% tax charge which is not available for set off against losses is likely to lead to payment of the outstanding interest, but SSAS practitioners should be aware of the apparent inequitable approach by IR SPSS in this area in respect of huge loans made interest-free by the trustees of the pension scheme behind the case of *Macniven v Westmoreland Investments Ltd 1997 STC 1103* (see 5.46). The possibility of using the circumstances of this case to counter a demand under *Regulation 4(a)(iii)* of *SI 1987 No 352* should not be overlooked.

5.43 Great care is obviously needed in all these circumstances if the 35% tax charge and possible loss of tax approval are to be avoided. It should not be assumed that because the company has no funds to pay the 35% tax charge that the charge will not be raised or in the absence of a charge that is the end of the matter. The possibility may still arise of IR SPSS seeking to limit benefit payments in respect of the amount written-off or waived. This area is fraught with problems for trustees and solutions acceptable to IR SPSS may not necessarily be the same for each SSAS.

5.44 With regard to 5.35 to 5.43 above, IR SPSS intends to introduce new requirements for SSAS trustees to notify IR SPSS of any defaults on payment of interest and repayment of capital in a timely manner (see 5.53).

5.45 The measures announced on 2 November 1994 (see 10.3) are also relevant here. It will be noted that the 40% tax charge in respect of loss of tax approval will be applied to the market value of the scheme's assets at the effective date from which approval ceases, less any debt due from the employer or any connected person. This clearly means that any loan which is subsequently written-off or waived could still involve the imposition of the 35% tax charge under the surplus legislation even though a scheme has lost its tax approval.

5.46   Some advice has been provided in 5.35 to 5.45 as to how problems with loan defaults or injudicious loans may be avoided or overcome or how to counter IR SPSS contentions in this area. A reading of the case reports of *Macniven v Westmoreland Investments Ltd* in the High Court, the Court of Appeal and the House of Lords, may provide practitioners with useful arguments on injudicious interest-free loans. The case reports reveal that a large self-administered pension scheme made huge loans to a captive company to prop it up financially both because it was ailing and to repay earlier loans. Interest was not fully serviced, and some loans were made interest free. Despite these features, which IR SPSS would undoubtedly see as unacceptable in a SSAS, the Court of Appeal judgment, which was upheld in the House of Lords in February 2001, states that the trustees of the large scheme acted properly in their own and the company's commercial interest. A full transcript of the case is available on the House of Lords website (*www.parliament.the-stationery-office.co.uk/pa/ld200001/ldjudgmt/jd010208/ macniv-1.htm*). In addition a technical note on the case and its relevance to SSASs was produced for the APT by the former author of this handbook, John Hayward, and appended to the APT's Newsletter No 146.

5.47   There is one other limited area where SSAS practitioners may be able to find some protection from the 35% tax charge on the waiving of a loan after 31 May 1996. This is the corporate debt legislation in *FA 1996, s 87*. The trustees of a SSAS may be a corporate lender within the definition of *FA 1996, s 87(3)(c)* if they were a participator in the company concerned, which they would be under *s 417(1), ICTA 1988* if they have a share or interest in the capital of the company including any loan creditor of the company, i.e. a debt due to the trustees. The trustees are by definition a participator in the company concerned because they hold shares therein and they have made a loan and that company owed them a debt. They are apparently, therefore, within the corporate debt legislation and no 35% tax charge would arise on waiving the loan.

Documentation

5.48   The regulations lay down that all loans must be documented and they prescribe what conditions must be included, although there is no set format for the documentation. Many practitioners nonetheless have their own standard form for loans incorporating the basic details required by the regulations. The loan document must record all the conditions on which the loan is to be made and these must include provisions for earlier repayment of the loan if the conditions are breached, the borrower ceases business or becomes insolvent and to enable benefits which have become due to be paid. The *Regulations* provide detailed definitions of the circumstances in which the borrower is deemed to have become insolvent. These circumstances include where the borrower has been adjudged bankrupt, or has died and the estate is being administered in accordance with an order under *IA 1986, s 421*, or, where the borrower is a company, a winding-up order or administration order has been made, a voluntary winding-up resolution has been passed or a receiver appointed. Because of the differences in the legal systems of Northern Ireland and Scotland compared with England and Wales, the regulations provide separate definitions for insolvency in Northern Ireland and Scotland as appropriate. It should be noted that loans should not be made in advance of a loan agreement being drawn up.

PSO Update No 69 (24 and 25) and PN 20.22 also require the pensioneer trustee to be a party to the loan document for all loans made on or after 1 October 2000.

5.49 A specimen loan agreement may be found at APPENDIX 30. Renewals may also be documented in this manner. The purpose of the loan does not have to be recorded in the loan agreement provided IR SPSS is informed of the purpose when the documentation is sent in. *SI 1995 No 3103* (see 3.75) requires that loans to participating companies and associated companies must be reported to IR SPSS at the time they are made. There is a prescribed form PS 7013 for this purpose (APPENDIX 31) which asks for full details of the loan. The completed form and a copy of the loan agreement should be sent to IR SPSS within 90 days of the loan being made under the reporting requirements (see 3.75). Late reporting or failure to report may lead to penalties being sought under *TMA 1970, s 98* (see 10.56 to 10.70).

Although not subject to the requirements of *SI 1995 No 3103*, loans to individuals and companies mentioned in 5.11 should be reported in a similar manner.

The position prior to 5 August 1991

5.50 Although it is most unlikely that IR SPSS may still be enquiring into the position of loans made before 5 August 1991 it is important to know in these circumstances what IR SPSS discretionary requirements are for loans made before 5 August 1991. The main point to note is that they were not reportable at the time they were made unless IR SPSS had specifically asked to be informed of all loans at the time. It was therefore possible for short term loans to be made and repaid between actuarial valuations and to escape IR SPSS's notice.

5.51 The loan document itself could be kept relatively simple. A trustee's resolution would suffice. It should show the date of the loan, the amount, the borrower, the rate of interest and the date of repayment. IR SPSS will find the circumstances unacceptable if there is no loan document at all or no repayment date and these in turn will cause approval problems. It would be difficult to argue for the acceptability of a loan without a repayment date and such a condition may have to be accepted to preserve the scheme's approval.

5.52   In the main, the general IR SPSS requirements as to loans as set out in 5.3 to 5.46 apply to all loans made prior to 5 August 1991 except of course that the regulatory requirements were then discretionary. There are some important aspects to bear in mind though. The ban on loans to members (see 5.7) was even then a mandatory rule requirement. The 25% restriction (see 5.10) only came into effect on 5 August 1991. Finally, the *bona fide* establishment of a SSAS prior to 5 August 1991 could be called into question if initially a small contribution was made and a large transfer value received from which a 50% loanback was immediately made. In such a case IR SPSS may question that the employer's intention was not to establish the SSAS, but to obtain the loan via the transfer value.

Current developments

5.53   As mentioned in 5.36 and elsewhere in this chapter, IR SPSS intends to issue an Update implementing further requirements for loans from SSASs, most likely before the end of 2001. The main changes proposed are as follows:

• SSAS trustees will be required to obtain a credit reference report (CRR) from a commercial checking agency, relating to the borrower's financial position. The CRR must be obtained no earlier than 4 weeks before the loan is to be made and a copy must be submitted to IR SPSS with the completed PS 7013 on which the trustees must certify that they are satisfied that the borrower's financial circumstances are healthy. IR SPSS may consider accepting a certificate from an accountant instead of a CRR, provided the accountant is completely independent from any accountant or firm of accountants who act for the borrower or for any member of the SSAS.

• Trustees will be expected to ensure that the borrowed money is used by the borrower for the purpose stated on the PS 7013.

• Loan agreements for any new loans made after the Update has been issued must make it clear that:

— they must be on an ongoing repayment basis with capital and interest being paid at least quarterly;

— the rate of interest is at least CBBR + 3% for both secured and unsecured loans and no lower rate will be accepted as being commercial, i.e. the practice mentioned in 5.23 and 5.34 will no longer be possible; and

— if loan repayments fall into arrears, trustees should ensure any subsequent payments of interest or capital must be set off firstly against outstanding interest with any balance being set against capital.

● New loans will not be possible where the borrower is in arrears on a previous loan from the SSAS or where the borrower has at any time defaulted on an earlier loan.

● Trustees will have to notify IR SPSS within a specified period of any loan default where such default is not rectified within 30 days of the default. They will also have to confirm and provide evidence of what steps are being taken to recover the debt.

● From the date of the Update all new loans, even those to unassociated companies and unconnected persons, will have to be reported to IR SPSS within 90 days.

Chapter 6

Investment in Property and Land

Introduction

6.1   The facility for trustees to invest in property and land, very often purchased from and leased back to the employer, is another major selling point and common feature of SSASs. Property and land are not, however, without problems so far as IR SPSS is concerned and investments therein have led to considerable contention with that office. Within this chapter reference will be made in the main to 'property', and 'land' is only mentioned where considerations are quite different. At the end of this chapter, although they could have been included under loans in CHAPTER 5 or shares in CHAPTER 7, are some general matters concerning clearance in advance with IR SPSS.

Property

6.2   The regulations and PN 20.67–20.74 and 20.76 set out the rules and guidelines. There are specific bans in the regulations relating to certain vendors and purchasers, the type of property and lettings, each of which is covered in detail in CHAPTER 6 with the reasons for the Inland Revenue's bans.

6.3   The regulations ban purchases from and sales to scheme members or their relatives, including partnerships of which the members are partners, of all types of property except for property already owned before 15 July 1991 which may be sold to such persons (see 2.22, 2.23 and SSAS GN 2.23). The reason for this is that such transactions may be undertaken at artificial prices or involve leakage of scheme funds to members. It also brings SSASs into line with self-invested personal pension schemes (see 14.29). The ban on purchases from members includes property owned by the member in the previous three years and sold prior to the acquisition by the trustees. Similarly the ban extends three years beyond the sale by the trustees during which period the property must not be sold to a scheme member etc.

6.4   The purchase of property from and sales to the principal company or associated companies, even if they are not participating in the scheme, are permitted. Purchases or sales are not permitted however if the purchaser or vendor is a company which, though not associated with the principal company, is connected with scheme members or their relatives, i.e. the scheme member controls that company or together with relatives or associates controls that company. However, if such a company participates in a SSAS the company will be treated as associated and transactions may take place with it. Purchases from and sales to totally independent third parties are acceptable of course, but provided the nature of the property is also acceptable (see 6.24).

6.5   There had been substantial confusion between the interpretation of connected persons by IR SPSS examiners and practitioners regarding purchases and sales of property. This was due to the complicated definitions in the regulations and the use of the word 'connected' instead of 'associated' on the reporting form (see 6.6). Some transactions may have taken place between SSAS and connected persons that are companies where the company is controlled by a member or his relations or associates on the basis that the transaction was between associated persons and IR SPSS did not object to them when the report was made. If any of these cases subsequently come to light IR SPSS has agreed to consider them against their own facts. The problem of interpretation should have been removed with the rewording of all the reporting forms on several occasions after 1 January 1996 to make the definition of 'connected' clear and further clarification in PN 20.54.

6.6   If the purchaser and vendor are permitted by the regulations, then subject to the nature of the property being acceptable (see 6.24) the transaction may proceed. The purchase or sale of all property has to be reported to IR SPSS under the 90 day reporting requirements (see 3.75) in part A on the form PS 7012 (APPENDIX 32). This form provides basic information regarding the transaction, e.g. date of purchase or sale, address of the property and its description, purchase or sale price, whether the property is freehold or leasehold, name of the vendor or purchaser and their connection, if any, with the members or principal company, details of any associated agreements. Leasing the property is a separately reportable transaction under *The Retirement Benefits Schemes (Information Powers) Regulations 1995 (SI 1995 No 3103)* and details of the leasing terms must be given in Part B of PS 7012. The reasons for this information being supplied to IR SPSS are looked at in this chapter under the relevant aspect of property involved.

6.7   The date of acquisition or disposal for reporting purposes is the date of completion not the date of exchange of contracts. The date of purchase is required to ascertain whether the trustees had sufficient assets in the fund at that time to enable them to make the purchase. It may also be required to establish if the property was acquired before or after the scheme was set up and sometimes evidence of purchase may be required in the form of the transfer document or conveyance itself.

6.8   The name and address of the vendor is all important in establishing whether the property was purchased at arm's length. An acquisition from someone or an organisation not at arm's length is going to be looked at by IR SPSS more closely to establish whether it is in fact a proscribed transaction, and if not, that an open market value was actually paid. This is where an independent professional valuation becomes relevant. If a property is purchased from a totally independent third party or at an auction then a valuation is not required by IR SPSS. The price paid, in these circumstances, is clearly its open market value. However, if the vendor and the trustees are connected in any way at all, an independent professional valuation is required under the regulations to substantiate the price paid as being the open market value. The trustees and the vendor are connected for these purposes if the vendor is the principal company or an associated company. A copy of the valuation must be sent to IR SPSS with the form PS 7012 and the transaction must take place at the price shown in the valuation.

Valuations

6.9   The reason for establishing the open market value of a property is basically to demonstrate that tax avoidance, e.g. especially CGT, is not involved. The temptation to a connected vendor may be to sell to the trustees at an undervalue and thus avoid CGT on the disposal. IR SPSS would see this as using the SSAS to achieve tax avoidance and obviously such a transaction would put the scheme's approval in jeopardy. An independent professional valuation is therefore necessary. Even where valuations have been produced, it is well known that IR SPSS has recourse to the district valuer to check the value or the rent. It may be possible for the trustees to pay the difference in value to the vendor if the district valuer maintains the open market value is more, but this will very much depend on the circumstances of the case and on major negotiations with IR SPSS.

6.10   Similar problems may be experienced where an overvalue has been paid. Here IR SPSS is likely to maintain there has been a leakage of scheme funds by the trustees to a connected party. This may be a very prejudicial transaction if the vendor happens to be the principal or an associated company. Furthermore, by paying over the odds the trustees could hardly have acted in the best interests of the beneficiaries. The trustees may be able to get their money back, but would IR SPSS see this act by itself as a cleaning up of the scheme? Each case is likely to be contentious and treated on its merits by IR SPSS.

6.11   It is important that the valuation supports the price paid by the trustees at the time of the acquisition. Sometimes, trustees obtain valuations in advance of the acquisition and for various reasons the purchase is delayed. The longer the gap between the valuation and the date of purchase the more likely the open market value may have changed and such a situation is likely to prompt IR SPSS to request a more up to date valuation.

Title document

6.12   As already mentioned in 2.57 and 5.1, it is an IR SPSS requirement that the pensioneer trustee is a registered owner of scheme assets along with the other trustees. The law in England and Wales does not allow more than four names to appear on the title document relating to land. So, SSASs with four or more individual trustees must ensure that the pensioner trustee is included. Alternatively, in the case of registered land, IR SPSS will accept the exclusion of the pensioner trustee from the title document provided a "restriction" is registered at HM Land Registry that the land cannot be sold without the consent of the pensioner trustee. For land in Northern Ireland an "inhibition" (but not a "caution") registered at the Land Registers of Northern Ireland will suffice. It is not possible to register a "restriction" or an "inhibition" in respect of land in Scotland. There is however no limit to the number of names appearing on the title document. Where a scheme owns land in Scotland or Northern Ireland which has been charged as security for borrowings taken out before 29 August 2000, the pensioner trustee need not become a co-owner of that land until the land ceases to be so charged.

The terms of occupancy

6.13   There are several reasons for IR SPSS wanting to know who is occupying or will occupy the property and the rent payable. It needs to be demonstrated that the occupier or tenant is someone other than a scheme member or a relative of a scheme member as a letting to such persons is banned by the regulations. Having established the occupier or tenant is not a member or relative, then IR SPSS is interested in establishing the length of the lease and what rent is payable by the occupant whether it is an independent third party or the principal or an associated company. The rent payable in both circumstances should be commercial, but IR SPSS accepts that where the occupant is totally at arm's length the terms of any lease/rental arrangement between the trustees and the occupant are bound to be commercial and on open market terms. In such situations IR SPSS does not usually require a copy of the lease and an independent valuation of the rent. However, where property is occupied by a participating company, as leasebacks are an especially attractive feature of SSASs, as well as by any other associated company, IR SPSS looks more closely to establish that a commercial rent is being paid as it would had the acquisition been from someone not at arm's length. In such cases an independent valuation of the rent is also required under the regulations. It may, however, be possible where the company has taken over the lease from a previous arm's length tenant at the same rent to avoid a valuation of the rent, as the rent being paid in this situation can be shown to be commercial. In addition IR SPSS requires a copy of the lease possibly to check that the rent payable thereunder is at least that substantiated by the independent valuation. IR SPSS is also likely to check the length of the lease, any premiums paid for it (which again must be supported by an independent valuation if the parties are not at arm's length) and the date from which the rent commences. The latter point is quite important as IR SPSS will wish to ascertain, where a property was occupied some time ago but where the lease is currently dated, that arrears of rent are accounted for to the trustees and that any valuation of the rent applies at the date the rent commenced to be payable. Any rent-free period at the beginning of a lease must be commercially justifiable, e.g. as a set off against the cost of repairs undertaken by the lessee, and where the lessee is connected the valuation should support this.

6.14 As the legal process of completing leases could take some time, a concession beyond the 90 day reporting period was allowed until 26 November 1997 for the production of a lease to IR SPSS. However, IR SPSS indicated in PSO Updates No 29 and 32 that it was not satisfied with the unreasonable delays it had come across in preparing leases for SSAS properties, particularly where the employer was the lessee. As a result, from 27 November 1997, copies of all leases where the property is leased to a connected party have to be produced to IR SPSS within 90 days.

6.15 Problems are going to arise with IR SPSS if no formal lease/tenancy agreement exists (as highlighted in PSO Update No 32 (8)) or the rent being paid in IR SPSS's view is less than a commercial one particularly where the parties are not at arm's length. Indeed problems may arise with the company's inspector of taxes if the rent is in excess of a commercial rent as the excess rental may be disallowed as a deduction under *s 779*. It is always best to get these arrangements formalised at the time to avoid problems with IR SPSS. There will, however, be circumstances where this cannot be done, for instance where the trustees have purchased property which they wish to renovate or refurbish before letting, but IR SPSS may still be looking to see if the trustees are getting a reasonable return on their investment as of course they should, in their fiduciary capacity, act in the best interests of the scheme members. However, if the trustees invested in undeveloped land in the belief that capital appreciation would outweigh the absence of income, this should be acceptable to IR SPSS (SSAS GN 9.54). A low return in terms of rent payable may mean the rent is less than commercial or even if it can be justified, IR SPSS may suspect that the situation is contrived. If in IR SPSS's view the rent is less than the commercial rent, it may make the point that the company, if it is the tenant, is enjoying a commercial advantage. Such an argument could be difficult to counter and it may be best to agree to a higher rent to preserve or obtain the scheme's approval. If no rent is being paid it may be possible to pay any arrears due at a commercial rate, but each case is likely to be looked at on its merits. If rent is in arrears because the tenant is in financial difficulties, particularly if the tenant is the principal or an associated company, IR SPSS will adopt a sympathetic approach to late payment of rent if the financial problems are due to a recession. It will for instance consider requests for time to pay off rent arrears over a period not exceeding five years. If on the other hand the lessee is dilatory in paying rent, particularly if it is the principal or an associated company, IR SPSS will expect the trustees as landlords to enforce payment.

6.16   Where a lease provides for rent reviews, the trustees should obtain an independent valuation of the rent at the date of the review if the lease is to the principal or associated companies. A copy of the valuation does not have to be sent to IR SPSS under the reporting requirements, but should be produced if IR SPSS requests it. Where a property is reported to IR SPSS on form PS 7012 before it is leased, a further form PS 7012 has to be submitted to IR SPSS when the property is leased, (again within 90 days). This should report details of the lease to be accompanied by a copy of the lease and rental valuation, where appropriate. Where a new lease is granted this must also be reported to IR SPSS on form PS 7012.

Liquidity

6.17   Another reason for IR SPSS wanting to know the name of the occupant of property is the question of liquidity. PN 20.51 states that 'investments in land and buildings may be a good long-term investment where the members are many years from retirement, but questions would need to be asked if the property appeared to be an important part of the employer's own commercial premises and thus potentially difficult to realise'. Thus IR SPSS may see problems where the major asset of a SSAS is a property leased to the principal or an associated company or the property is jointly owned.

6.18   There is no basic objection to the trustees investing 100% of the fund in property and that property being leased back to the participating company, provided the lease is on commercial terms. However, the trustees need to take into account the date when they will be required to realise their assets to provide retirement benefits for the members. If a member, or perhaps the sole member, is due to retire in two to three years' time, the trustees must have cash available at that time at least to provide any cash lump sum and to pay a pension, and also to provide the cash to purchase an annuity to secure the pension, although the latter can be deferred for up to five years or to age 75. It is unlikely that in such a time span there will be sufficient cash resources to do this, so the trustees are faced with the problem of realising their major asset which may take time and if occupied by the company as its main trading base could create further problems. IR SPSS will enquire into such situations and it needs to be assured that there will be sufficient cash in the fund at the appropriate time to provide benefits. It may be that the members do not actually propose to retire on reaching their normal retirement ages as controlling directors often continue in service after that age. However, IR SPSS is still likely in these circumstances to regard the appropriate time to provide benefits as being the normal retirement age because cash may still be needed from that date onwards to pay benefits.

6.19   The trustees should also not overlook Opra's requirements where a member asks for a transfer value to be paid to another pension scheme. As explained in 11.4 there is a 6–month time limit for making a transfer payment once it has been requested and, if the transfer value cannot be paid from the liquid assets of the scheme, property may have to be sold within this period to satisfy Opra.

6.20   Over the years IR SPSS has applied a general rule of thumb of five years i.e. if scheme members are due to retire within five years of a property purchase, IR SPSS may find the purchase unacceptable if there are no other assets or other assets are not likely to be sufficient in quantity to meet the needs of an imminent retirement. It is therefore always best to acquire property many years before retirement and to ensure that when benefits become due there are sufficient easily realisable assets in the scheme or that there will be no protracted problems with realising the property itself.

6.21   If a SSAS has or adopts the rule allowing the purchase of annuities to be deferred until age 75 (see 3.42) it is allowed to invest in property during the period of deferral. This must be consistent with the scheme having sufficient readily realisable assets in addition to the property to enable an annuity to be purchased from age 70 onwards. This is to ensure that the scheme is in a position to buy an annuity between the ages of 70 and 75 without getting involved in a forced sale of property.

6.22   Joint ownership of property by trustees with another party may give rise to liquidity problems. There should be no basic objections from IR SPSS to the trustees owning property jointly, either with the participating company or a third party provided IR SPSS's usual requirements are met (SSAS GN 4.47). However, joint ownership with the members or partnerships of which the members are partners is not acceptable (SSAS GN 4.48). It may be that the trustees do not have sufficient funds at present to purchase the whole, so they purchase a half now and the remaining half later or effect the acquisition in a series of tranches. However, where the trustees' interest is a joint one at the time when they come to realise the property, problems may arise. It could be that delay will occur in selling because it is more difficult to sell property in joint ownership. In addition the price the trustees get for the property could be less than the proportionate value of the whole property. The reduced price will reflect the difficulties of joint ownership. These are aspects the trustees will need to take into account and may have to defend if IR SPSS questions the acceptability of jointly owned property. There must be no fetter on the trustees' ability to dispose of jointly owned property (SSAS GN 4.49).

6.23 Another aspect which touches on liquidity is whether scheme property is subject to a mortgage or legal charge. Clearly, if the trustees have borrowed money and secured it on the property by a mortgage or legal charge, they need to make arrangements to pay off the borrowings to release the property from the mortgage or legal charge before they sell it. This is not to say that they cannot sell a property subject to a mortgage or legal charge, but where they do problems may arise with the sale and it may affect the price.

Type of property

6.24 The trustees may invest in land or buildings, both freehold and leasehold, as they see fit, provided tax avoidance is not the objective and provided it is not of a type which is specifically banned, e.g. residential property (see 6.28 to 6.30). Thus they may invest in all commercial premises such as offices, shops and land and industrial premises such as factories, warehouses, etc., in agricultural property and land, forestry and woodlands. All these will be covered in turn.

Commercial property

6.25 This type of property is by far the most common and is a popular investment of SSASs particularly as it allows participating companies to rent scheme property, albeit on a commercial basis, and to obtain tax relief on payments of rent and allows the trustees to receive the rent tax free. Provided all the transactions relating to the property are undertaken on an arm's length basis and there is no residential accommodation involved there should be no problems with IR SPSS.

6.26 There are matters, however, which can arise over the change of use of the property which can create problems with IR SPSS and which the trustees therefore need to consider carefully. If a property has some residential element currently unoccupied and which is being changed to office or some other commercial use, IR SPSS will object to its acquisition (SSAS GN 4.18).

This is because it is residential at the time of purchase and prohibited by the regulations. The trustees may however see a particular investment in property or land currently unoccupied as a good one for the scheme especially if they can obtain planning permission for change of use or development as this could increase the value of their investment considerably. Having obtained planning permission the trustees could refurbish the property or develop the land from scheme funds, but there are several aspects they need to bear in mind if difficulties with IR SPSS and HM Customs and Excise (see 13.22) are to be avoided. Straight refurbishment should be acceptable if the nature of the property remains commercial. Development of the trustees' land to build (say) a factory or warehouse which is leased to a third party or the company (on a commercial basis) should also be acceptable apart from industrial units qualifying for industrial buildings allowance (see 6.35 to 6.38), but the questions of who pays for the development and whether the development is residential may attract IR SPSS attention. If the principal company or an associated company is a building company and it develops the land or it borrows from the trustees to finance the development costs difficulties can arise. IR SPSS may find these aspects unacceptable particularly if they are not done at arm's length and it may deem the company and/or the trustees are enjoying a commercial advantage. To avoid any problem in this area it may be best to clear the arrangement with IR SPSS in advance. Land which is to be developed by building residential property is unlikely to be acceptable to IR SPSS, even if the property is to be sold , on completion of the development, on the open market, because residential property is banned (see 6.28). Indeed, repeated transactions involving the development of commercial property, or frequent purchases and sales of property by the trustees may attract the attention of the inspector of taxes and whilst not prejudicing the scheme's approval may involve the trustees in trading (which is dealt with in CHAPTER 8) and may result in them having to pay tax on such activities.

6.27   Finally, the increase in value of property and land brought about by obtaining planning permission and development can lead to serious overfunding problems. This will not necessarily entail the application of the surplus legislation to a SSAS, but if the scheme is approved and the actuary recommends a refund to the employer then the 35% tax charge would apply to any refund.

Residential property

6.28   The regulations ban residential accommodation with two specific exceptions (see 6.29) as in those cases the accommodation is never going to be used by the members or their relatives. This ban includes long leasehold interests until 6 April 1998 where ground rents would be payable to the trustees as the leaseholder of residential premises even though the premises are occupied by totally independent third parties. There is an exception though for residential property held indirectly by the trustees as investment units in a unit trust scheme, provided the trustees of the unit trust scheme hold such property subject to the trusts of the SSAS.

The APT made several representations to the Inland Revenue for ground rents from long leasehold interests in residential property to be allowable. Eventually the *Regulations* were amended by *The Retirement Benefits Schemes (Restriction on Discretion to Approve) (Small Self-administered Schemes) (Amendment) Regulations 1998 (SI 1998 No 728)* (see 2.24) to allow SSASs to own long leasehold interests in residential property, provided the property is not occupied by a scheme member or a person connected with him.

6.29   The two specific exceptions are residential accommodation occupied by an employee who is not connected with his employer and who is required to live there as a condition of employment and residential accommodation that forms an integral part of business premises both occupied by the same totally independent third party on commercial terms. Thus a caretaker's flat or a flat above a shop are acceptable. The caretaker's flat would need to be an integral part of the whole commercial premises and the employee concerned would be required to live there to carry out the duties of the job. A good example is a builder's yard with accommodation for a caretaker or night watchman where the yard is leased to the principal company. The trustees may invest in a retail shop which is tenanted by a third party. The third party also rents the residential accommodation above the shop which is indivisible from the shop. Provided both rentals are on a commercial basis this is acceptable to IR SPSS.

6.30   A public house with living accommodation above will be acceptable if the tenant is at arm's length and runs the public house (SSAS GN 4.16b). Nursing homes and hotels consist of both residential and commercial accommodation, but if the residential parts are occupied by paying customers and members or their relatives do not reside there, both types of accommodation are acceptable (SSAS GN 4.19).

Agricultural property and land

6.31   The considerations regarding property generally already covered earlier in this chapter apply equally to agricultural property and land, but there are other aspects, particularly as regards agricultural land problems that can arise with IR SPSS. The acquisition by the trustees of agricultural property and land and its leaseback to a third party or to the principal company at a commercial rent is usually acceptable to IR SPSS. However, leasing back the property and/or land, even at a fully commercial rent, to a partnership of which a member is a partner or to a member's unincorporated business is banned under the *Regulations* (see 6.13). The reason for this is the same as for IR SPSS's objection to residential accommodation as the sole provision of relevant benefits test is not met because the scheme is providing a benefit to the member other than a retirement benefit. Another contentious area may be where the farmhouse is part of the scheme assets or the member's residence is adjacent to the agricultural land. If a farmhouse or cottage is occupied by an arm's length employee this is acceptable (see 6.29 and 6.30). IR SPSS may pick this up from any valuation or location map supplied on the acquisition and commence to ask various questions. If the trustees have purchased the farmhouse then it cannot be occupied by a member or relative. The farmhouse needs to be occupied by a third party on an arm's length tenancy to be acceptable. It is not unusual for the land to be leased back to the principal company and for the member to occupy the adjacent farmhouse either owned by the member or the company. This ought to be perfectly acceptable, but IR SPSS may take the view that the member in one way or another has the use of the scheme asset, perhaps as an amenity. It is not unknown for agricultural land to consist of rough grazing, coppices etc. which could be used by a member to keep horses or on which to entertain friends to a rough shoot. Amenity rights are covered in more detail in 6.32 and 6.33, but suffice it to say there is a need to be aware that the acquisition of agricultural land is not always straightforward and personal use by members in all its varieties needs constantly to be borne in mind to avoid the pitfalls. Thus riding stables, which do not have any residential element and provided there is no member use of the investment, will be acceptable (SSAS GN 9.53).

Forestry and woodlands

6.32   Once again investment in these areas is usually acceptable, although it is possible in certain circumstances for the trustees to be considered as trading. The aspects of this type of investment which will attract the attention of IR SPSS are any amenity rights which attach to the land e.g. hunting, shooting and fishing. Rivers, lakes and bothies are bound to show up on location maps submitted to IR SPSS either with valuations or leases. IR SPSS will wish to establish if any hunting, shooting or fishing rights exist, who has them and what the trustees receive for them (SSAS GN 9.52). The point to bear in mind is that these rights cannot be held by a member or a relative even if a fully commercial price is paid for them as all leasing of assets to members and their relatives is banned by the regulations.

6.33   It is as well to remember with regard to amenity rights that other types of property and land may attract such rights or they may provide recreational or leisure facilities, e.g. a golf course. Also, a commercial property with a river frontage may have mooring facilities. It will need to be demonstrated to

IR SPSS that there is no use by a member of the scheme assets in this connection or at least that use by a member is incidental with that of the public at large and that the member pays for any such use on the same basis as the public (SSAS GN 9.52).

Property abroad

6.34   In view of the specific ban in the regulations, any type of residential property abroad will not be an acceptable investment of a SSAS. Villas on the Mediterranean are totally unacceptable and so too will be a flat abroad, leased to the company and used by the company director on business trips abroad. But what about commercial and industrial property abroad? These are acceptable to IR SPSS, but practitioners may need to justify them in the first place. However, since 1 January 1993 there should be no objection to investment in commercial and industrial property at least in the European Union (SSAS GN 4.45).

Industrial buildings allowances

6.35   Investment in industrial property and units can be particularly tax efficient because of the industrial buildings allowances (IBAs) that are available to the owner of the freehold of such property. IBAs have been phased out in recent years, but they are still available in development zones, so whilst the opportunities to invest in this area have diminished there are nonetheless still substantial tax savings available. However, before describing the arrangements that would involve the trustees of SSASs it is well known that IR SPSS is aware of the tax avoidance device underlying the arrangements and this can create serious problems.

6.36   There have been several articles in accountancy magazines over the years describing how the involvement of a SSAS can achieve large tax savings using IBAs. This is how it works. The company purchases an industrial building or a site on which it constructs an industrial building. The company could claim tax relief in respect of the IBAs available up to 100%. The trustees purchase the leasehold interest in the building from the company. The company would not then suffer a clawback of the tax relief it has obtained. This effectively avoids a corporation tax balancing charge. There are variations on this which still achieve the same results. The industrial building is let on a long lease to the trustees with a further sub-letting running almost concurrently to the company. If a claim for IBAs were then made by the freeholder no corporation tax balancing charge would arise in respect of a subsequent disposal of the lesser interest by virtue of *Capital Allowances Act 1990, s 20(3)* because that lesser interest would not be the company's freehold interest. The tax case of *Woods v RM Mallen (Engineering) Ltd 45 TC 619* confirmed the avoidance of tax on a balancing charge in such circumstances. However, the avoidance of tax on balancing charges was curtailed from 13 January 1994 by the provisions of *Finance Act 1994, s 120(3)*. This provides that a balancing charge will be imposed when a long lease is disposed of within seven years. The fact that the trustees of a SSAS would be able to benefit by paying a reduced rent for their leasehold interest because the freeholder could claim the IBA, which the trustees cannot as non-taxpayers, would not assist the trustees' case. The further measures introduced on 24 July 1996 (see 8.39) to curtail the use of accelerated capital allowances will also affect the avoidance of tax on balancing charges.

6.37 In the normal commercial world such an arrangement without using a pension scheme as the intermediary would be generally acceptable to the Inland Revenue, but problems arise with IR SPSS if a pension scheme is involved in the arrangement. The nub of the issue is that the scheme is being used as a vehicle to achieve the tax avoidance. IR SPSS would therefore find the arrangements objectionable and not consistent with approval under *s 590(2)(a) ICTA 1988*, as the pension scheme could not be said to be *bona fide* established for the sole provision of relevant benefits. Thus the arrangements would not only fail to pass the '*bona fide* established' test, but would also fall foul of the guidelines in PN 20.51 regarding tax avoidance. Any SSAS with such a feature would almost certainly fail to obtain approval or, if it was already approved, have its approval withdrawn from the date the claim for IBAs was made provided it was not made before 17 March 1987 (*s 591B(1) ICTA 1988*). If the claim for IBAs was made before 17 March 1987 and the trustees acquired their interest before then, approval could not be withdrawn before 17 March 1987.

6.38 It may be possible to negotiate a way out of the problem with IR SPSS in conjunction with the local inspector of taxes. Possibilities are for the IBA claim to be withdrawn, for the company to pay the tax on the balancing charge which has been avoided or for the trustees to sell their leasehold interest at an open market value. This is however a rather complicated subject and close liaison with clients' tax advisers is needed if a satisfactory result is to be achieved.

Sales

6.39 The trustees of a SSAS are usually empowered to buy and sell property and during the course of a scheme's existence they may do this on a number of occasions. They will need to watch that the frequency of property transactions or the development of land in their ownership does not lead to these transactions being treated as trading by the Inland Revenue (see

CHAPTER 8). Whilst such a situation would not necessarily lead to the loss of the scheme's tax exempt status, nonetheless it could mean that property transactions within the scheme are taxable which is a distinct loss of the tax advantage an approved scheme enjoys. It is not possible to have hard and fast rules on the circumstances that will attract the Inland Revenue's attention and lead to a taxable trading situation. The Inland Revenue will not at present pronounce on a situation in advance, but only after it has happened. It is therefore best to be aware that frequent purchases and sales of property at a profit could cause problems in this area. Furthermore, whilst it is laudable for the trustees to acquire derelict land, spend time and money obtaining planning permission to develop it, then carry out the development and sell it at a substantial profit, they should avoid the possibility that they may be trading and at the same time allay any suspicion on the part of IR SPSS that there is no duality of purpose in their motives for the development.

6.40 Another aspect of sales of property relevant to its development is where a sale at a substantial profit can lead to a surplus within the scheme. The surplus may also be fortuitous in that the value of land may have risen considerably during the period of its ownership, perhaps because of the removal of a planning blight in the area. At the next triennial valuation when the actuary considers the land's current value, even if it is not to be sold, he may consider that such an increase may well have outstripped the previous assumptions for increases in the value of the scheme's assets. The trustees will need to be guided by actuarial advice in these circumstances, but it must be borne in mind that if any surplus is to be repaid to the employer it will be subject to the 35% tax charge if the SSAS is approved or IR SPSS will insist on approving the scheme before a refund is made.

6.41 The details of the sale of a property have to be reported to IR SPSS on the form PS 7012 (APPENDIX 32) under the 90 day reporting requirements. These are unlikely to prompt questions from IR SPSS if the sale is to an unconnected third party. However, if the sale is to a scheme member or relative of a member, which is permitted if the property had been acquired by the trustees before 15 July 1991 (see 2.22, 2.23 and SSAS GN 2.23), or to the principal or an associated company, an independent valuation of the sale price is required and must be sent to IR SPSS. This is clearly to establish that the price being paid to the trustees is the open market value and to guard against a member or the company perhaps acquiring the property at less than its true value. It may be that the company originally sold the property to the trustees and the leaseback arrangement is accompanied by the grant of an option by the trustees to the company to call for the transfer back of the freehold. In such cases the company may have the right to re-acquire the freehold at a price less than the price paid by the trustees and the difference would be chargeable to tax on the company under Schedule D Case VI rather than as a capital gain. On the other hand if the property is sold at a price in excess of its open market value it would not only have avoided CGT on the disposal by the trustees, but established a higher acquisition value for the purchaser. Both instances could lead to problems with IR SPSS and prejudice the scheme's approval, although it ought to be possible to remedy the situation by the purchaser paying the trustees or the trustees repaying the purchaser the difference between the open market value and the purchase price.

6.42 The disposal of a property by the trustees may not necessarily be a cash transaction, but it is nonetheless reportable. For instance the property may be included in a transfer value paid between a SSAS which is winding-up and another newly established SSAS or SIPP for the same member. Such a property may be transferred in this manner in specie, but the disposal and acquisition by the separate trustees must be reported on the form PS 7012 backed up by an independent valuation of its value included in the transfer value. This is not a transaction which is banned by the *Regulations* even though the two sets of trustees may include the member. However, if the property was of a type banned since 5 August 1991, but acceptable before then, it cannot be so transferred. It would have to be sold and the cash realised transferred instead. In specie transfers of property between two approved pension schemes does not constitute consideration within the *Stamp Act 1891, s 57*, and therefore only attract stamp duty of £5 (increased from 50p in Autumn 1999). Transfers of loans to companies in specie from one SSAS to another are not permitted.

6.43 Late reporting or failure to report property purchases and sales or new leases from or to the principal company or an associated company, may lead to penalties being sought under *TMA 1970, s 98* (see 10.56 to 10.70).

'Contrived' situations

6.44 This heading covers a wide variety of situations which can occur with property and which to IR SPSS appear to be contrived and which suggest that the scheme has a duality of purpose. By way of illustration suppose a SSAS is established by deed on Day 1 with an ordinary contribution of £100,000 and a special contribution of £100,000. Also on Day 1 the trustees lend back £50,000 to the company to develop land and with the remaining £150,000 they purchase a piece of land to be leased to the company and which it will develop with the loan. Even if all the necessary back-up information was supplied to IR SPSS at the outset, e.g. actuarial report, loan document, property and rent valuations, one would expect IR SPSS to have doubts about the overall position, particularly the intention behind the establishment of the scheme, and some pretty searching questions could be expected. For instance, how did a piece of land come to be worth exactly £150,000 to fit in with the contribution and loanback position? Furthermore, the purpose of the loan is going to cause problems with IR SPSS. This shows that in setting up a SSAS one needs to avoid the suspicion that the whole thing has been contrived to achieve something other than a *bona fide* pension scheme. Long and convoluted investment arrangements involving property are bound to attract IR SPSS's attention and it must always be borne in mind that it does have the last word under its discretionary powers. In the end no amount of reasoning with IR SPSS may prevent a refusal to approve a scheme unless a particular investment is got rid of.

6.45 Another example is a scheme which has been established for some years and the last actuarial valuation was done almost three years ago. It recommended annual contributions of £50,000 p.a. The trustees wish to buy a commercial property for £500,000 and do not want to use their other assets to finance the purchase. Therefore they borrow £180,000, the company pays an annual contribution of £70,000 to the scheme, and the trustees buy a half share of the property for £250,000. There is nothing wrong with this superficially, but can the contribution of £70,000 be justified and is a half share of the property actually worth £250,000? It all looks very simple, but is there something contrived about it? Would IR SPSS see a duality of purpose behind the arrangements?

6.46 The trouble with many situations is that arguments can develop with IR SPSS well after the event because until 5 August 1991 there were no formal reporting arrangements regarding investments and the triennial actuarial valuation may be the starting point for a purchase prior to 5 August 1991. There is a paramount need for care and to demonstrate that the prime motive for any arrangement is the provision of retirement benefits.

Remedies

6.47 There are some situations where it should be possible to come to an agreement with IR SPSS over a property and avoid prejudicing the scheme's approval. Difficulties in this area are, however, more likely to arise where the scheme has already been approved rather than where it is still to be approved. Advisers should also bear in mind the date when the property was acquired and what if anything IR SPSS had said about it on previous occasions. For instance, was the 'offending' property owned by the trustees prior to the issue of JOM 58 or the *Regulations*? The case can then clearly be made that at the time the investment was made it did not offend IR SPSS guidelines and should therefore remain an asset of the scheme. Similarly, if a property was included in a previous actuarial report sent to IR SPSS and accepted by that office either in writing or tacitly, then a case can be made for its retention. The case of *R v Commissioners of Inland Revenue ex parte Matrix Securities Limited [1994] STC 272* supports such a line if a full picture was given previously and accepted in writing. PSO Update No 37(4) endorses this view and any request by IR SPSS for disposal of the property or threat to withdraw approval from the scheme should be vigorously resisted.

6.48   Other situations may necessitate disposing of a lease to a third party instead of a member, but with residential or holiday accommodation acquired before 5 August 1991 (see 6.51 to 6.57) it is almost certainly going to mean its disposal to maintain the scheme's approval. Fortunately IR SPSS is not so harsh as to insist on an immediate sale in every case. There will be difficulties in selling certain types of property and property in certain areas, and the trustees should be able to secure a reasonable time in which to sell them to get a decent price. General Section Examiners do have discretion in this area (SSAS GN 9.43). It would be as well from the outset to agree the timescale with IR SPSS.

The position prior to 5 August 1991

6.49   IR SPSS guidelines on property investments were set out in JOM 58 in very broad terms. These guidelines were further delineated in the early 1980s at meetings with the APT and reiterated as IR SPSS policy following the PQ on SSASs raised in July 1984. With regard to JOM 58, there was no hard and fast 'no go' area laid down regarding property. The question of the use by members of such investments was hardly alluded to in JOM 58, but it soon became clear that IR SPSS was opposed to SSASs owning residential and holiday accommodation because of its potential use by members and their relatives.

6.50   There was no requirement to notify IR SPSS of the acquisition of property before 5 August 1991. When IR SPSS learned of a property acquired either by production of a list of investments or disclosure via an actuarial valuation, it would ask for some basic information, e.g. date of purchase, the name and address of the vendor, the price, the name and address of the tenant or occupant, and for a valuation of the property and the rent payable if the vendor or tenant were connected. IR SPSS discretionary practice applied to such property and there was no ban on purchases from or sales to scheme members and their relatives. Members were however not allowed to use or occupy scheme property because this would have been contrary to the sole provision of relevant benefits. With the exception of the regulatory requirements introduced from 5 August 1991 all the various aspects in 6.6 to 6.40 applied to property acquired prior to 5 August 1991 and indeed if it has been held since then. There are additional aspects regarding residential property however that are still relevant even now if correspondence is continuing with IR SPSS as to its acceptability and which may be found in 6.51 to 6.57.

Residential property acquired prior to 5 August 1991

6.51   For convenience, holiday accommodation is included in this paragraph because IR SPSS requirements are similar for both types of property. Right from the issue of JOM 58 IR SPSS made it clear that residential property and holiday accommodation were unacceptable investments for SSASs. The reason for this was that such property could be used by the members or their relatives and therefore the scheme would not be solely providing relevant benefits. It mattered not that the residential accommodation may be let to a member at a fully commercial rent or to a totally independent third party and was never likely to be occupied by a scheme member. The potential exists for abuse. This policy has been adhered to quite rigidly by IR SPSS. It was reiterated in reply to the PQ in July 1984 and the consultative document in 1987 made it clear the ban would appear eventually in the regulations.

6.52   It is probably worthwhile repeating what was published following the PQ in July 1984 (Appendix 2).

'The purchase of residential property for leasing to a director/shareholder or to the employer will not normally be regarded as consistent with scheme approval because of the likelihood of beneficial use by or for the benefit of members.

The investment of scheme monies in the purchase of holiday cottages and the like is normally regarded as inconsistent with approval.'

6.53   It can be seen that leasing residential accommodation to the company would not escape the prohibition. Thus if the company wished to make available a flat in London for the directors to use on business trips to the capital and the flat was leased by the trustees, the flat was an unacceptable investment. The same applied to a flat overseas even if the company required its directors to undertake frequent foreign trips for business reasons and they used a flat owned by the trustees.

6.54   It was possible for the trustees to give IR SPSS a written undertaking that accommodation acquired before 5 August 1991 would never be made available to scheme members or their relatives, although this was likely to be met with resistance by IR SPSS. However, if the property concerned was (say) terraced property in a poor condition or in a run-down area and occupied by third parties on fixed tenancies it was unlikely that a member or his family would have considered using the property.

6.55   Ground rents received from long leasehold commercial and residential premises occupied by third parties also should have been acceptable investments.

6.56   What aspects would IR SPSS look for regarding residential/holiday accommodation? Obviously the location, any valuation, plan and lease would be looked at. Residential accommodation at the seaside or well-known inland holiday areas or in large cities was unacceptable. There were other features of holiday accommodation too that attracted IR SPSS attention. Short lettings are prevalent in the holiday trade although they could equally be features of student occupation. The valuation and any accompanying plan often describe the property in detail and even if part of the property contains residential accommodation IR SPSS's interest would be aroused.

6.57   Finally, as regards residential accommodation, there are taxation implications for the members quite apart from the implications to the scheme's tax exempt status should IR SPSS find such accommodation to be an asset of a SSAS. Tax liability under Schedule E may arise on a member in respect of the residential accommodation occupied by the member. The sale of the property to preserve the scheme's tax exempt status will not obviate any previous Schedule E liability.

6.58   It is not possible to cover every conceivable form of property investment in this chapter. Of necessity only the main ones have been referred to. Those areas not covered will be few and far between and of a very specialised nature and would have to be tackled on a one-off basis with IR SPSS if they give rise to problems.

Clearance in advance

6.59   It has always been possible to approach IR SPSS in advance of a particular investment being made to ascertain if it would be acceptable. Indeed PN 20.68 advises this in relation to assets of any kind being acquired from the principal company. Such an approach regarding property can be very useful where there are doubts about certain aspects and in the event it can save much time and cost later if the investment has to be disposed of on the instruction of IR SPSS because it is unacceptable. There are drawbacks however in making this approach which are mainly time constraints. A quick answer to a proposal on the phone is unlikely unless the circumstances are clear cut. It is much more likely that such an approach will meet with a request for the proposal to be put in writing with the result that a delay will occur in getting a reply because of IR SPSS's workload. Experience has shown that it may take up to two months to obtain a written reply to a property proposal. This is borne out in PSO Update No 46 which mentions that IR SPSS's target is to reply to 90% of general correspondence within one month. A property proposal is likely to be more complex and take more than a month to be answered. That may be too long if an offer must be made quickly for a good property investment. However, if there are doubts about a particular investment the only sure way of avoiding problems, particularly in obtaining approval for a SSAS, is to seek IR SPSS clearance in advance. Detailed information should be given as failure to do so will probably lead to a request for further details before a decision can be given causing additional delays.

6.60   In November 1992, however, IR SPSS informed the APT that it would not in future be prepared to answer general enquiries regarding the suitability of investments on the basis that now the regulations were in place these were matters for the scheme's advisers. It would continue to help on interpretation of the legislation if this was unclear. Apparently IR SPSS was being asked too many questions about the suitability of investments. The APT expressed its concern in 1993 at this development which cut across IR SPSS's helpful policy of clearing proposed transactions in advance, and because of the remaining grey areas surrounding the regulations and discretionary practice that still existed. IR SPSS did propose, however, to publish some general clarification on the way in which it believes the regulations apply. This was done in a letter of 21 September 1993 to the APT and subsequently published by the APT to its membership. The contents of this letter of 21 September 1993 have been incorporated in the relevant paragraphs in CHAPTERS 5, 6, and 7. In December 1997, in PSO Update No 37, IR SPSS reiterated its view that it was receiving too many enquires, particularly about the suitability of certain investments by SSAS where the answer was readily available from published IR SPSS guidance. An approach to IR SPSS on the lines suggested in 6.59 should be viewed in this light. The SSAS GN should also now assist in areas that require clarification.

Complaints on contentious cases

6.61   In relation to general or specific enquiries of PSO Update No 37(2) also warns that IR SPSS is unable to help with tax planning or advise on transactions which are designed to avoid or reduce a tax charge that might otherwise arise. IR SPSS is not prepared to respond to enquiries which involve any suggestion of tax planning or of a possible attempt to achieve tax avoidance.

Chapter 7

Unquoted Shares, Other Investments and Borrowings

Introduction

7.1   This chapter covers the various aspects which concern IR SPSS with ownership of shares in participating and associated companies and in unconnected unquoted companies. It also covers non-income producing assets, commodities, futures, options and trustees' borrowings.

Shares in participating and associated companies

7.2   The regulations and PN 20.53 to 20.55 and 20.67 to 20.69 contain the rules and guidelines relating to the acquisition and disposal of shares in the employer company, but these have to be considered together with general taxation principles, particularly in the area of tax avoidance. All these aspects will be covered in turn, but it is sufficient to be said at the moment that there are several hurdles to overcome before shares in the employer company can become acceptable investments of a SSAS. As with any other shares held by a SSAS these must also be held in accordance with the pensioneer trustee requirements introduced in PSO Update No 69 (see 2.57 and 5.1) i.e. they are registered to show the pensioner trustee is a co-owner by including the name of the pensioner trustee on the certificate. If the shares are held for the trustees in the name of an investment manager's or stockbroker's nominee company the pensioner trustee must be a party to the agreement between the trustees and the investment manager/stockbroker and the agreement must ensure that any proceeds paid from the portfolio is only paid to a scheme bank account of which the pensioner trustee is a mandatory co-signatory.

7.3   The aspect of the regulations which has the greatest effect on the number of SSASs holding shares in the company is the ban on transactions between trustees and scheme members and their relatives (see 6.3). Holdings in the company are particularly affected as the vendors or purchasers are a restricted group and will almost certainly include the members and their relatives who are connected persons for the purposes of the regulations, or who together control the company and who are therefore banned from making sales to and from the trustees. The scope for a SSAS to own shares in the company is severely limited and for those acquiring such shares, after 14 July 1991 (see 2.22, 2.23 and SSAS GN 2.23), the only future purchaser may be the company itself, provided the requirements in *s 219* are met.

Value of the shareholding

7.4   The value of the holding itself or when taken together with any loans to the employer and any other relevant shareholdings and loans (see 5.8 to 5.11) should not be more than 50%, or 25% for a new SSAS, of the value of the assets of the scheme (see 5.10) at the date the holding is acquired. Thus, if a loan to the employer currently exists, then the size of the shareholding being purchased may need trimming to fit within these limits whereas the value of a shareholding in an unquoted company that is not connected in any way with the scheme members and their relatives or associated with the participating companies does not have to be taken into account for these limits. In addition, SSAS GN 9.103 warns of acquiring shares in an ailing company in order to provide the company with funds. This is no more acceptable than making a loan to an ailing company (see 5.35).

Size of shareholding

7.5   The regulations state that shareholdings in any unquoted company are limited to those carrying no more than 30% of the voting power or that would entitle the trustees to no more than 30% of any dividends declared in respect of shares of the class held *The Retirement Benefits Schemes (Restriction on Discretion to Approve) (Small Self-administered Schemes) (Amendment) Regulations 1998 (SI 1998 No 728)*. The latter restriction is most relevant where unquoted preference shares are acquired. Whilst ordinary shares may not pay a dividend, preference shares usually do, so a holding of more than 30% of a particular class of issued preference shares would be unacceptable. Any attempt to circumvent the 30% limit by means of dividend waivers will prejudice the approval of the scheme. The point to note is that any private company's shares will be included, not just the employing company or its subsidiaries/associates. The reasons for this limitation stem from SSASs being used to give directors effective control of companies at no cost to themselves and thereafter to strip companies of profit by converting them into tax exempt dividends (SSAS GN 4.12).

Section 703

7.6   If the limitation to the vendor and the value and size of the shareholding can be met, the question arises as to whether the purchase of the shareholding involves tax avoidance and is part and parcel of a transaction to which *s 703* may apply. If so then the SSAS may lose its tax exempt status or may not be approved.

7.7   *ICTA 1988, Pt XVII*, which includes *s 703 et seq*, is concerned with countering tax avoidance. It is not intended to explain its scope in full. Trustees should discuss this with their professional advisers. How the subject concerns IR SPSS is, however, covered in detail. Any purchase of preference or ordinary shares by the trustees which would fall or has fallen foul of this legislation will not be an acceptable investment of a SSAS. To avoid withdrawal of approval or a refusal to approve, it may be possible to seek the sale of the shares, if already purchased, but this will depend on the circumstances of the case and it may be difficult to find a buyer because of the restrictions on the sale of shares in unquoted companies.

7.8   There is an arrangement whereby such share transactions, either proposed or actual disposals, can be cleared with the Inland Revenue. This is very useful because it can cover transactions at the proposal stage relatively quickly and avoid later problems with IR SPSS if the acquisition by the trustees has gone ahead. If full details of the transaction are given to the Inland Revenue, technical division, for clearance under *s 707*, then the technical division is obliged to pronounce on the transaction within 30 days. The technical division will notify that it is satisfied that *s 703* does not apply or that it is not satisfied that *s 703* does not apply. It is important to note that only the Inland Revenue, technical division, gives a clearance under *s 707*. Neither IR SPSS nor local inspectors of taxes can do so and approaches to them will only result in applicants being advised to make their application to the technical division.

7.9   When IR SPSS becomes aware of a holding of unquoted shares or it is asked if such a holding will be acceptable, it may ask if a *s 707* clearance has been obtained. If a clearance has been obtained, then this particular hurdle has been overcome subject to any IHT implications or other objections IR SPSS may have. If on the other hand a clearance has been refused then the shareholding will not be acceptable to IR SPSS even if it satisfies IR SPSS on the IHT requirements of IR SPSS, unless it can be shown that the tax advantage has been counteracted under *s 703(3)*. It is sound advice therefore to obtain a clearance beforehand under *s 707*, otherwise IR SPSS is likely to investigate the transaction itself.

7.10   Issue 4 of the Inland Revenue's own Tax Bulletin contains an interesting example of a SSAS acquiring shares in the company from its four directors. Clearance under *s 707* was applied for retrospectively and refused on the grounds that the directors had obtained income tax advantages by receiving cash from the company in capital form which, if they had not first arranged for it to be paid to the pension scheme, could have reached them as dividends. Technical division apparently was not satisfied that the share transactions should not be subject to *s 703* counteraction. Indeed, clearance under *s 707* would not be withheld unless, on the information available, counteraction, if the transactions were effected, could be expected. In this case as the transactions had already taken place counteraction proceedings under *s 703* were commenced.

7.11 Counteraction by the Inland Revenue under *s 703* as mentioned in 7.9 and 7.10, remains a distinct possibility for pension schemes along with other tax exempt bodies, such as charities. The Board of Inland Revenue let it be known in 1993 following the case of *Sheppard and Sheppard (Trustees of the Woodland Trust) v CIR [1993] STC 240*, that it would continue to take proceedings under *s 703* in appropriate cases on the footing that such tax exempt bodies obtain tax advantages whenever they receive abnormal dividends.

7.12 There is in fact a tax case involving counteraction under *section 703(3)* against an alleged abnormal dividend received by a pension scheme – *Universities Superannuation Scheme Ltd v Commissioners of Inland Revenue (SC000020)*. Here the pension scheme subscribed for shares in a property development company; the shares were subject to a first option which the pension scheme could exercise in order to dispose of them. Later, instead of exercising the option, the shares were repurchased by the property company thus enabling the pension scheme to recover advance corporation tax in relation to the distribution on the buy-back. A counter-notice under *s 703(3)* was made, together with a Schedule F tax charge on the trustees. On appeal it was held that the buy-back did not give rise to an abnormal amount by way of dividend. The notice under *s 703(3)* was quashed and the Schedule F assessment discharged. This was because the Special Commissioner was bound by the *Sheppard* decision (see 7.11) to find that the pension scheme could not obtain a tax advantage within the meaning of *s 703* by taking steps which resulted in it recovering the tax credit. This decision was reversed however in the High Court where it was held that it was possible for a tax exempt body to secure a tax advantage within *s 703*. This effectively prevented reliance on the *Sheppard* decision in future cases.

7.13 Whilst the case of *Universities Superannuation Scheme* was being considered in the High Court changes in legislation were announced regarding the payment of special dividends. The Chancellor was concerned with companies buying their own shares or paying special dividends so that the proceeds end up almost entirely in the hands of those entitled to payment of a tax credit. *FA 1997, Sch 7* brought in legislation effective from 8 October 1996 to remove payable tax credits in relation to certain types of company distributions and to make it clear that a tax advantage includes a repayment of tax credit. The following types of distribution are within the scope of the legislation:

(a) a redemption, repayment or purchase by a company of its own shares;

(b) where there are arrangements by virtue of which the amount, timing or form of the distribution is referable to a transaction in shares or securities.

Taxpayers receiving such distributions since 8 October 1996 are not affected, but shareholders who would formerly have been able to claim repayment of the credits on the distribution, e.g. charities and pension schemes, can no longer do so.

7.14 *Section 709* was amended by *FA 1997, Sch 7* to include the obtaining of a payable tax credit as a tax advantage as one more of various transactions in securities preventing shareholders from obtaining a tax advantage. However, the treatment of special dividends that are not linked to transactions in shares or securities remains unchanged. Other types of dividend, such as payment of cash as an alternative to a stock dividend, or ordinary pre-sale dividends, are not caught by the amended provisions. SSASs that buy shares anticipating a special dividend not caught by the provisions of *FA 1997, Sch 7* may however be liable to counteraction under *s 703*.

7.15 Large self-administered schemes are more likely to be vulnerable to attack than SSASs, especially since 8 October 1996, as the Inland Revenue is far less likely to consider them as mainly tax exempt bodies but more a potential source of additional revenue. With the advent of self-assessment for pension schemes, their advisers need to be on their guard in this connection (see 8.63).

7.16 Fortunately not all transactions in unquoted shares are within the scope of *s 703*. For example, it does not usually apply where the company concerned is not associated in any way with the trustees or the directors/members of the SSAS, the vending shareholder is at arm's length, or the shares are an initial allotment at par. This is however a grey area and trustees should consult their tax advisers as to whether or not a clearance should be sought. The technical division is not generally known to be forthcoming about the types of transactions that do not require a clearance. It is therefore safest to assume that the shareholding in question will be looked at in detail by IR SPSS if the company is the principal company or a participating company, or even if it is neither of these but its directors or shareholders are connected in any way with the trustees or members of the SSAS.

Inheritance tax

7.17 JOM 58(14) simply stated in relation to shareholdings in companies the possibility of IHT avoidance may be grounds for withholding a scheme's tax approval. This does not appear at all in PN 20, but it cannot be taken for granted that IR SPSS will not consider the IHT position. It has to be assumed that IR SPSS looks at this aspect regarding all transactions in the shares of unquoted companies, not just in those associated with the principal employer (see SSAS GN 9.99). The reasons for this are not hard to find. There is a very restricted market for transactions in such shares, transactions are usually between parties not at arm's length and the price paid for them may not necessarily be their open market value.

7.18   IR SPSS has access to the shares valuation division of the Capital Taxes Office, which values shares in unquoted companies, to check the price paid. This is acknowledged in SSAS GN 9.99, where it mentions that, in appropriate cases, share valuation division should be asked for its opinion of value. The appropriate cases are apparently in SSAS GN 9.4, but this paragraph is missing from the version published publicly. So IR SPSS usually asks for full details of the share transaction, even if it is only at the proposal stage. The details requested on the reporting form (see 7.24) PS 7014 (APPENDIX 33) are the company whose shares are being acquired, date of purchase or sale, purchase price, class and number of shares concerned, dividend and voting rights of the shares, name of the vendor and/or purchaser and the relationship if any of the vendor to the trustees/company, total issued share capital, vendor's beneficial interest prior to sale, trustees' reasons for acquiring the shares, total amount invested in loans to and shares in the company, the calculations used in valuing the shares and a copy of any professional valuation or advice obtained, the company's accounts for the last three years and its articles of association if it has more than one class of shares in issue, and details of any associated agreements with any scheme member or connected person. Interestingly, the details of any *s 707* clearance have been omitted from the latest form PS 7014, but were included in all previous printings. It should not be assumed though that a *s 707* clearance no longer need be obtained or that IR SPSS will not check this aspect. Late reporting or failure to report may lead to penalties being sought under *TMA 1970, s 98* (see 10.56 to 10.70).

7.19   If IR SPSS, after consulting the shares valuation division, is satisfied that the price paid for the shares is an open market one then the shareholding should be an acceptable investment of the SSAS having already got over the *s 703* hurdle. The trouble for trustees and their advisers begins if the shares are purchased by the trustees at an over or under-value. For instance, if a shareholding is purchased by the trustees at £1 per share and the shares valuation division is of the view that they are worth £2 per share in the open market, then IHT and/or CGT may be involved in the acquisition at a lower value by the trustees. Or the trustees may be acquiring or have acquired a shareholding at more than its open market value in the opinion of the shares valuation division. In this instance IR SPSS could maintain that by purchasing the shares for more than they are worth, particularly if the vendor is the principal or an associated company , there has been a leakage of scheme funds which is unacceptable. Both instances will give rise to withholding approval or possibly withdrawing approval. It may be possible to negotiate with IR SPSS for the trustees to pay the difference in value to the vendor or for the vendor to refund the difference in value to the trustees to make the investment acceptable to IR SPSS. It will very much depend upon the circumstances of the case whether IR SPSS will adopt this route. It may simply demand that the shares be sold to preserve the scheme's approval or to obtain its approval. If the value of the shares according to shares valuation division is disagreed it may be possible to negotiate the value direct with shares valuation division (SSAS GN 9.40) It is therefore doubly important to ensure the purchase price placed on the shares in an unquoted company represents their open market value.

Sales

7.20   The sale of shares in all unquoted companies will be of interest to IR SPSS because they are unlikely to be made at arm's length. Transactions in such holdings are not only restricted because of the nature of unquoted companies, but also because of IR SPSS restrictions in the regulations for holdings acquired after 5 August 1991. The prospective purchasers are probably going to be connected parties, e.g. the members or their relatives, who may only purchase shareholdings acquired by the scheme prior to 15 July 1991 (see 2.22, 2.23 and SSAS GN 2.23), unless the unquoted company is not associated in the first place. However, the principal company or associated companies can purchase shares from the trustees regardless of when they were acquired by the trustees.

7.21   *Section 703* may or may not be relevant as the case may be, so the trustees would need to discuss this aspect with their professional advisers. The trustees will also need to be careful that they do not fall foul on the sale of their shareholding of the provisions relating to share buy-backs and special dividends (see 7.13 to 7.14). IR SPSS will require the sale details on the form PS 7014 under the reporting procedures (see 7.24). This includes a transfer of unquoted shares in specie. The object is clearly to establish that the price being paid is the open market value of the shares and to ensure the purchaser is not acquiring the shares at less than their proper value.

7.22   Obviously IHT and CGT considerations come into this and IR SPSS may have recourse to shares valuation division to check the value attributed to the sale price. Problems can arise if an under or over-value has been paid for the shares. However, it may be possible as mentioned in 7.19 to negotiate with IR SPSS for the purchaser to pay the difference in value to the trustees or for the trustees to refund the difference in value to the purchaser to preserve the continued approval of the SSAS.

Liquidity

7.23   If a SSAS has or adopts the rule allowing the purchase of annuities to be deferred to age 75 (see 3.42 and 3.43) and all members and any dependants are in receipt of a pension, no shares in the principal or any associated company or in any other unquoted company may be purchased following the later of the first payment of the final retiring member's pension, or, where a pensions order applies and the ex-spouse is a member of the scheme (see 11.95), the final ex-spouse taking a pension and the first payment of the final widow's/widower's or dependant's pension (PN 20.54). Existing shareholdings in these companies have to be sold within five years of the commencement of pension payments, or the attainment of age 70 by a pensioner if earlier. If the pensioner is already 70 when payment of pension commences, all unquoted shares must be sold immediately. Share purchases are allowed, however, where a SSAS has other members not yet drawing benefits. In these cases the portion of the fund representing the retired member's benefits or dependants' benefits in payment has to be excluded when calculating the maximum amount that may be invested in shares in the principal or associated company, together with loans to these companies (see 5.29).

7.24   The form PS 7014 (APPENDIX 33) has to be completed by the administrator under the 90 day reporting requirements (see 3.75) in respect of any acquisition or disposal of shares in the principal company, associated company or unlisted company. An unlisted company includes a company whose shares are traded on the Alternative Investment Market (AIM) or OFEX. APT newsletter 131 drew attention to an apparent requirement to report an investment in OEICs to IR SPSS. This was resolved when the Inland Revenue confirmed to the Association of Unit Trusts and Investment Funds (AUTIF) in July 1999 that it was not necessary for SSASs to report transactions in OEICs. A copy of the Inland Revenue's letter to AUTIF was attached to APT newsletter 134. It is anticipated that changes will be made to *The Retirement Benefits Schemes (Information Powers) Regulations 1995 (SI 1995 No 3103)* in April 2002 making it clear that OEICs do not need to be reported. The information to be supplied on the form PS 7014 is covered in 7.18. If the company whose shares are being bought or sold is in fact quoted although associated, the transaction still has to be reported but the ancillary information at Note 6 on form PS 7014 does not have to be sent to IR SPSS.

7.25   Finally, the Department for Work and Pensions' restriction on self-investment to 5% of scheme assets can cause further problems for SSASs which hold shares in the principal or an associated company. These restrictions and exemptions are covered in 11.33 to 11.35.

The position prior to 5 August 1991

7.26 In the unlikely event of IR SPSS enquiring into the position of shares in unquoted companies acquired before 5 August 1991 either because of protracted correspondence on the size or value of shareholdings or a recent audit has disclosed such investments for the first time, it is still necessary to know what IR SPSS discretionary requirements are for unquoted shares acquired before 5 August 1991 and for such holdings continuing to be held thereafter subject to IR SPSS discretionary practice and the regulations. Acquisitions and disposals were not reportable at the time unless specifically requested by IR SPSS. It was also possible for such shares to be bought and sold between actuarial valuations and escape IR SPSS attention.

7.27 IR SPSS guidelines were set out in JOM 58(14) and need updating for subsequent legislation, e.g. *s 703*. Subsequent pronouncements in this area were made via the APT, on individual schemes or following the PQ raised in July 1984. For example, the overall limit of 50% of the value of the assets of the scheme of loans to and shares in the employer was not contained in JOM 58. IR SPSS practice in this area developed in 1980 and 1981 and was published in 1984 following the PQ.

7.28 In the main the general IR SPSS requirements as to shares in unquoted companies as set out in 7.2 to 7.19 apply to all such shareholdings acquired prior to 5 August 1991 with some important exceptions that do not apply, e.g. the ban on certain vendors (see 7.3), the 25% restriction (see 7.4), the size of the holding (see 7.5) and reporting (see 7.24). There are, however, some important additional aspects to bear in mind on the size of shareholdings.

7.29 The actual size of the holding acquired in terms of the issued share capital in any unquoted company, whether connected or not, has always been a minority holding to satisfy IR SPSS. If a majority holding was being acquired IR SPSS was unlikely to find this acceptable as the trustees would be in a position to control the company and manipulate its profits and dividends. IR SPSS maintained in these circumstances that the scheme was being used as a vehicle to achieve a tax advantage and the scheme's approval would be prejudiced. Such a claim would be very difficult to counter and only a very good case would satisfy IR SPSS. Reduction of the holding to a minority one or its complete disposal were the only way to preserve the scheme's approval. However, it might be possible to make a good case if IR SPSS was aware of the transaction previously and accepted it as satisfactory or acquiesced in the situation without commenting at all for a considerable time (see 6.47).

7.30   Advisers have been aware from individual cases since 1989 that IR SPSS was paying particular attention to the size of holdings in unquoted companies. Considerable pressure was being applied to reduce holdings to around 25–30% of the issued share capital. Following representations to IR SPSS that it appeared to have changed its practice in this area without any widespread publicity through the APT etc., IR SPSS stated it was undertaking a review of the acquisition of shares in employing or associated companies by SSASs. Meanwhile, each case was being treated on its merits, but the APT would be informed once the review had been completed. One development in this area was the publication of the draft regulations in July 1990. These stated that shareholdings in private companies would be limited to those carrying no more than 30% of the voting power or that would entitle the trustees to no more than 30% of any dividends declared and these restrictions were included in the *Regulations*. So for shareholdings acquired between 1989 and 5 August 1991 to be acceptable to IR SPSS they would need to be no more than 30% of the issued share capital.

Continuing investments in shares

7.31   For those shareholdings in unquoted companies held before 5 August 1991 and acceptable under IR SPSS discretionary practice and that continue to be held thereafter, the main provisions of the *Regulations* that apply to them are the ban increasing them to more than 30% of the issued share capital and the reporting of their sale. Shareholdings acquired before 15 July 1991 may be sold to scheme members or their relatives (see 7.20).

Non-income producing assets

7.32   The following paragraphs cover those investments which do not specifically produce income in the hands of the trustees, but which are made because of the capital appreciation they produce. They also cover the problems arising therefrom which concern IR SPSS. Land held for capital appreciation is not regarded as a non-income producing asset in this respect. Just as for any other scheme assets, the documentation evidencing title to non-income producing assets must include the name of the pensioneer trustee (see 2.57(j), 5.1, 6.12 and 7.2).

7.33   Prior to the coming into force of the *Regulations*, works of art and other valuable chattels or non-income producing assets were permitted to a certain level, but they created considerable difficulties for IR SPSS not least in the areas of member use and size in relation to the value of the fund. So, with the coming into force of the regulations on 5 August 1991 the position of non-income producing assets changed substantially. Personal chattels other than choses in action are banned. PN 20.75 and SSAS GN 4.10 provide a list of assets which are personal chattels that are not choses in action and therefore are prohibited from 5 August 1991. These include antiques, works of art, rare books and stamps, furniture, fine wines, vintage cars, yachts, jewellery, gem stones, gold bullion, oriental rugs and Krugerrands.

7.34   PN 20.75 and SSAS GN 4.9 describe a chose in action as something which is not corporeal, tangible, moveable or visible and of which someone has not the present enjoyment, but merely a right to recover it. They provide a list of choses in action which includes company shares, copyrights, traded options, deposit accounts and financial and commodity futures that are permitted investments. To these can be added factoring, milk quotas, second-hand endowment policies, etc. Some of these are looked at in more detail in 7.36 to 7.38, 7.53 and 7.54 and in CHAPTER 8 which covers trading as they may be taxable in the hands of trustees.

7.35   The lists in PN 20.75 are not exhaustive. Foreign currency deposit accounts for instance are apparently choses in action and therefore permissible. Plant and machinery is neither a chose in action nor a personal chattel, but may be an acceptable investment nonetheless. Its leasing by the trustees will however constitute trading (see 8.37). The *Regulations* and PN 20.75 do not mention the former restriction introduced in JOM 58 limiting non-income producing investments to no more than 5% of the value of the fund (see 7.46). This requirement appears to have been dropped, but it would be unwise to make such an assumption when investing in this area.

7.36   Milk quotas are available for purchase on the open market and may be acquired by the trustees of a SSAS with or without the farmland attached, provided they are not acquired from connected persons. The trustees, as owners, would receive a rental income tax-free, although there is some suggestion it could be treated as trading income. The lessee must not be a connected person.

7.37   An investment in a theatrical production is also a chose in action. The backer, or theatrical 'angel', puts up a stake in units ranging from £500 to £10,000 in the expectation that the production will be a success. A return is paid on the original stake, dependent on the financial success of the production. The stake may be lost if the production is unsuccessful, but it is repaid once the show produces sufficient profits. IR SPSS may feel such an investment is speculative, but it should nonetheless be acceptable. Such an investment in a production of the principal company or of a scheme member is not likely to be acceptable though. IR SPSS however does not regard an investment in films as a chose in action (SSAS GN 4.10) and investment in this area is to be avoided.

7.38 Second-hand endowment policies are freely available on the open market and are acceptable investments of SSAS provided they are not purchased from a member or someone connected with a member. Whilst *TCGA 1992, s 210* imposes a CGT liability on the disposal of endowment policies where the person making the disposal is not the original beneficial owner of the policy, CGT does not arise on the trustees of a tax approved pension scheme on such a disposal because of the exemption contained in *TCGA 1992, s 271(1)(g)*. The maturity date of the policy must be consistent with the normal retirement age of members, and premium payments by the trustees should not commit a substantial amount of the scheme funds (SSAS GN 4.46).

However, some doubt existed as to whether the provisions of *section 547(1)(b)* brought the disposal within Case VI of Schedule D in respect of the sponsoring company of the pension scheme for policies made after 14 March 1989. This legislation deems any gain arising on the disposal of a policy by the trustees of a trust established by a company to be part of that company's tax liability. This apparent inequitable treatment of policies on disposal, death or maturity, was the subject of representations by the APT to the Inland Revenue Financial Institutions Division. The latter has since confirmed that *s 592(2)* does have the effect of exempting the company from tax in respect of gains which would otherwise be deemed to be part of its income because they are income derived from investments held for the purposes of a tax exempt pension scheme.

7.39 Not only have the *Regulations* reduced the number of different non-income producing investments that can now be made, they have also significantly reduced the field of vendors. The ban on sales of any asset by scheme members and their relatives to the trustees (see 6.3) together with the ban on the acquisition of personal chattels, severely limits the investment opportunities in this area. There is also a ban on leasing any non-income producing asset to scheme members or their relatives. Such assets can still be purchased from and leased to the employer, subject to an independent valuation of the purchase price and rental. Assets held before 15 July 1991 may be sold to members and their relatives at an independent valuation, but those acquired on or after that date cannot (see 2.22, 2.23 and SSAS GN 2.23).

7.40 Whilst there is now much less scope for investment in this area, nonetheless there is a form PS 7016 (APPENDIX 34) which must be completed by the administrator under the 90 day reporting requirements (see 3.75) in respect of any acquisitions or disposals of this type of investment from or to connected parties and of any lease of the investment to the principal or any associated company. The details required are a description of the asset, date of purchase or sale, purchase or sale price, name of the vendor or purchaser and whether connected to the trustees, employer or members and details of any leasing of the investment. If the purchaser or vendor is connected a copy of an independent valuation must also be provided. If the investment is to be leased or was leased to a connected person copies of the lease and of an independent valuation of the rental must be provided as well. IR SPSS has access to share valuations division and the district valuer to check values of assets and rental valuations respectively (SSAS GN 9.115). Late reporting or failure to report may lead to penalties being sought under *TMA, s 98* (see 10.56 to 10.70).

The position prior to 5 August 1991

7.41   In the unlikely event of IR SPSS enquiring into the position on non-income producing assets made before 5 August 1991 it is still necessary to know what IR SPSS discretionary requirements are for non-income producing assets made before 5 August 1991 and for those continuing to be held after that date subject to IR SPSS discretionary practice and the regulations. Acquisitions and disposals were not reportable at the time unless specifically requested by IR SPSS. It was therefore possible for such investments to be bought and sold between actuarial valuations and be unknown to IR SPSS.

7.42   Advisers may be aware from their own experience of IR SPSS's attitude towards specific investments of this type and what IR SPSS would and would not allow in this area for investments acquired prior to 5 August 1991. Until publication of JOM 109 (now incorporated in PN 20.75) there was no list of acceptable and unacceptable non-income producing assets.

7.43   JOM 58(15) said IR SPSS is unlikely to approve a SSAS which invests a significant amount of its funds in works of art or other valuable chattels or non-income producing assets which could be made available for the personal use of scheme members and lead to transactions between trustees and members being otherwise than on a purely commercial basis. So not only is the size of such investments likely to cause problems, but use of the assets by members certainly will. The sole purpose test in *s 590(2)(a)* is most apposite here regarding the provision of 'relevant benefits'. IR SPSS may not appear to be so concerned with the possibility of tax avoidance with non-income producing assets, although this aspect should never be disregarded, but rather with their use by scheme members. It is their potential use which needs to be considered, not just their actual use, as IR SPSS objections are frequently based on the argument that even if the member does not currently use the asset, the potential exists for the member to do so in future and it does not have the resources to police such use.

Types of assets

7.44 There appeared to be two general categories of non-income producing assets as far as IR SPSS is concerned. These were 'pride in possession' assets, which appeared to be barred (the consultative document actually said in no case will such pride in possession assets be approved), and 'others' in the absence of any definition, which were apparently acceptable if acquired before 5 August 1991. However, the acceptability and unacceptability cannot be taken for granted as will be gathered from later comments. Generally, pride in possession assets such as fine wines, vintage and veteran cars, yachts, stamps, jewellery, stallions etc. were unacceptable. Paintings, antiques, porcelain, in fact all sorts of *objets d'art*, foreign currency and industrial diamonds were acceptable subject to certain limitations which are mentioned later.

7.45 It can be seen from the first group of assets that the potential exists for them to be used by scheme members. Even where a vintage car or yacht was leased on a commercial basis to an independent third party the asset was still likely to be unacceptable to IR SPSS. The second group of assets is somewhat different. There is no possibility of industrial diamonds being used personally by a scheme member and foreign currency similarly, although someone could 'borrow' the latter for a foreign trip! All works of art can however create problems. If they are kept, for instance, in the company's boardroom or at the member's residence then the member would be enjoying their use and the SSAS would be providing a non-relevant benefit. Paintings, antiques and their like should therefore be kept either in a public gallery where they are available for everybody to enjoy or stored in a bank vault.

'Significant amounts'

7.46 It was mentioned earlier that IR SPSS guidelines limit acceptable non-income producing assets to a 'significant amount' of the scheme funds. A significant amount was never quantified after JOM 58 was published until the emergence of the consultative document. Until then it was known through individual SSASs or IR SPSS meetings with the APT that a 'significant amount' was taken to be about 5 per cent of the value of the fund. This was confirmed in the consultative document. So works of art, foreign currency, industrial diamonds etc. should be limited prior to 5 August 1991 to 5 per cent of the value of the fund to be acceptable. This means a SSAS is hardly likely to own a Picasso unless its assets exceed £20 million!

Problems

7.47 Non-income producing assets are often by their very nature highly speculative and constitute very much a grey area because they appear to have

been looked at individually by IR SPSS. In some SSASs such an asset may
have been found unacceptable whereas in another it is acceptable. Fine wines
seem to come into this category. It cannot therefore be said that any such
investments are 100% acceptable to IR SPSS apart from industrial diamonds
and foreign currency.

7.48   It was quite possible that the trustees proposed to purchase a
non-income producing asset from the members or their company or to sell it to
one of these parties. JOM 58(15) warned that such transactions, unless
conducted on a proper commercial basis, may prejudice the scheme's
approval. So, just as for property transactions between the trustees and
connected persons, so in these cases the same procedure of obtaining
independent professional valuations of purchase or sale prices was a necessity.
IR SPSS needs to see that an open market price has been paid in this situation,
just as it does for property transactions that are not wholly at arm's length and
for the same reasons that were explained on property investment in 6.10.

7.49   The most common difficulties to arise with this type of asset with IR
SPSS, leaving aside an outright refusal to accept the investment, are in the
areas of member use, potential member use or where the asset is nonetheless
acceptable, but worth more than 5% of the value of the fund. It should be
possible to overcome the claim of potential member use by the trustees
ensuring the asset is locked away in a bank vault or placed on view to the
public at a gallery. There is no harm in quoting previous cases where this has
been accepted by IR SPSS in defence of the position, although it may be met
with the counter-argument that all cases are looked at individually on their
merits. The acceptance by IR SPSS would have to have been since JOM 58
was published. If IR SPSS insists that the level of the investment must be
reduced to make it acceptable, then there is probably no alternative other than
to reduce the investment if that is possible to around 5% of the value of the
assets otherwise the investment should be sold.

7.50   It may be that in objecting to a particular investment of this type IR
SPSS is doing so for the first time albeit somewhat belatedly. There would be
good grounds for its retention as mentioned in 6.47 if it can be shown that the
investment was acquired pre-JOM 58, or, even if acquired later, that the PSO
has been aware of it and either accepted or acquiesced in its ownership by the
trustees due to the absence of comments in the past by IR SPSS. The case of
Matrix Securities (see 6.47) supports such a line if a full picture was given
previously and accepted in writing. PSO Update No 37(4) endorses this view
and any request by IR SPSS for disposal of the assets or threat to withdraw
approval from the scheme ought to be resisted.

Schedule E tax

7.51   The second part of JOM 58(15) contained a nasty sting in the tail. It
mentioned the possibility of Schedule E liability arising if a non-income

producing asset was placed at the disposal of a member, or a member's family or household under *s 156(5)(6)* (derived from *FA 1976, s 63(4)(5)*). In essence this could mean income tax being charged on the member on 20 per cent of the market value of the asset. The fact that a member may be assessed to tax on such a benefit will not make the investment itself acceptable to IR SPSS. Its ownership by the trustees would still prejudice the scheme's approval even if the Schedule E tax was paid if for instance a painting owned by the trustees remained on the wall of a member's living room. The Schedule E liability in these circumstances is a matter for the member's local inspector of taxes to determine and not IR SPSS, so practitioners should not be surprised if IR SPSS makes no mention of the Schedule E liability whilst objecting to member use of the investment. It is as well therefore to be aware of this and to warn scheme members of the taxation consequences as well as of the implications for the investment concerned.

Continuing investments

7.52   For those non-income producing assets held before 5 August 1991 and acceptable under IR SPSS discretionary practice and that continue to be held after that date, e.g. works of art, industrial diamonds, etc., the only provisions of the regulations that apply are the ban on their leasing to members and their relatives and the reporting of their sale. Those assets acquired before 15 July 1991 may be sold to scheme members or their relatives (see 2.22, 2.23 and SSAS GN 2.23).

Commodities, futures and options

7.53   Until 1984 if the trustees held this type of investment it could have resulted in them being assessable to tax on trading profits. However, with the enactment of *s 659* (derived from *FA 1984, s 45*) gains realised from dealing in financial futures or traded options by approved pension schemes were exempted from tax. Then in 1990 *s 659A* derived from *FA 1990, s 81(2)(4)* replaced *s 659* and exempted from tax all trading income from futures and options owned by pension schemes. PN 20.75 should be read in the light of these changes, so apparently commodities held by SSASs remain taxable although very few invest in this area.

7.54   If the trustees invest in plant, machinery or equipment for hiring out they may become assessable to tax on trading profits (see 8.37 to 8.40). This may involve leasing of some sort and if used as a tax avoidance device in conjunction with a SSAS it is likely to prejudice the scheme's approval. In the case of *Wisdom v Chamberlain 45 TC 92* the Inland Revenue maintained that dealing in platinum bars was taxable. The trustees of a SSAS are now unlikely to invest in this kind of medium or gold or silver, but if they do they need to be aware that they may be deemed to be trading and thereby lose tax exemptions on this activity. Even if they escape this penalty they are still likely to be subject to an overall investment in this area of 5% of the scheme's funds as mentioned in 7.46.

7.55 Whilst PN 17.11 and PN 20.77 give some examples of which features constitute or do not constitute trading by trustees, they do not state this is the preserve of the inspector of taxes and not IR SPSS and that the inspector will pronounce only after the transaction has been carried out. The inspector of taxes will not normally comment on a transaction's taxability in advance. Thus, as mentioned in 6.39 on property, it is best to be aware of the possibility of trading by the trustees in this area and to seek professional advice before proceeding with an investment of this type. Trading by trustees is covered in more detail in CHAPTER 8.

Borrowings

7.56 The final paragraphs of this chapter deal with a common feature of SSASs which is a liability of the trustees rather than an asset.

7.57 The regulations allow the trustees after 5 August 1991 to borrow up to three times the ordinary annual contribution (OAC) paid to the scheme plus 45% of the value of the scheme's net assets, i.e. where a property already held is valued at £150,000 and with a £25,000 mortgage the 45% would relate to £125,000 net asset value for the property plus the value of other investments, a point which was clarified by *SI 1998 No 1315*. The OAC includes both the employer's and the members' contributions (see 7.59). The limit on borrowings applies at the time they are undertaken by the trustees and will not be re-tested at a later date by IR SPSS where the value of the assets changes (SSAS GN 4.7).

7.58 For the purpose of calculating the ceiling on borrowings, the regulations as amended by *SI 1998 No 728* define the employer's OAC and provide for it to be restricted. Thus the employer's OAC is the average of the contributions paid in the three years ended at the end of the previous accounting period of the SSAS or the amount of the annual contributions within the period of the three years prior to the date of the borrowings recommended in writing by the scheme actuary, whichever is the lesser. Whilst this formula could include special contributions it is obviously aimed at schemes where the company's contributions fluctuate substantially. For SSASs that have been established after 7 April 1998 for less than three years at the time borrowings are undertaken, the total amount of the contributions paid to the SSAS by the company in the period since the scheme was

Unquoted Shares, Other Inve... and then divided by the
... year being counted as one
...91 and 6 April 1998 for less
...dertaken, the total amount of
established up to the date of borrowi... pany up to the end of the last
number of years falling within that... by the number of complete
year. For SSAS, established betw... f the trustees wished to borrow
than three years at the time bo... he employer's contribution paid
the contributions paid to th... not be taken into account in the
accounting period was ... 45% of the value of the fund could
years since the end of ... o get round this problem by changing
before the end of ... g it forward, so that the contributions
before any borr...
contribution ...used to determine the borrowings ceiling
be used in ...butions, but include contributions paid as a
the sche... riod to be used is the tax year ended before
could ...

...g from 5 August 1991 is much more generous
...be of considerable assistance to mature SSASs or
...riencing difficulties in maintaining contributions at

...s should help clarify the amount the trustees may
... SSAS has been established for more than three years.

Example A

At 10 March 2001 the trustees wish to borrow £500,000 to acquire a
commercial property. The value of the scheme's investments at that date was
£800,000.

Scheme year ended	Contribution paid by employer	Annual contribution recommended by actuary
31 December 1998	£100,000	£100,000
31 December 1999	£75,000	£100,000
31 December 2000	£125,000	£125,000
	£300,000	

Total employer's contribution divided by three equals £100,000, which is the
same or less than the annual contribution recommended by the actuary in the
last three years.

7.60 *Un*~~q~~*uoted Shares,*

Borrowings ceiling is therefor~~ments and Borrowings~~

   $3 \times £100,000$

   plus 45% of £800,000

Example B

At 10 March 2001 the trustees wish to
commercial property. The value of the scheme
£175,000.

£300,000
£360,000
~~60,000~~

Scheme year ended	Contribution paid by employer	Contribution paid by member	
31 December 1998	£20,000	£1,000	
31 December 1999	Nil	£1,250	£5~~~~
31 December 2000	£25,000	£1,500	£50,00~~~~

Total employer's and employee's contributions divided by three equa~~~~
£16,250 which is less than the annual contribution recommended by the
actuary in the last three years. This is provided the member's contributions in
the calendar years are the same for the three tax years ended 5 April 2000.

Borrowings ceiling is therefore:

$3 \times £16,250$	=	£48,750
plus 45% of £175,000	=	£78,750
		£127,500

In Example A the trustees may borrow the full £500,000 they require, but in
Example B they are restricted to £127,500 instead of £150,000.

The following examples should help clarify the amount the trustees may
borrow where the SSAS has been established for less than a year.

Example C

The SSAS was established on 1 May 2000. At 10 March 2001 the trustees
wish to borrow £375,000 to acquire a commercial property. The value of the
scheme's investments at that date was £108,000.

Scheme year ended	Contribution paid by employer	Annual contribution recommended by actuary
30 April 2001	£100,000	£100,000

Total employer's contribution divided by one equals £100,000, which is the same as the annual contribution recommended by the actuary.

Borrowings ceiling is therefore:

3 × £100,000	=	£300,000
plus 45% of £108,000	=	£48,600
		£348,600

In Example C, the trustees may borrow only £348,600 so they will have to wait until 1 May 1999 when the second annual contribution can be paid to the scheme to borrow the full £375,000 they require.

Example D

The SSAS was established on 1 January 2001 with a contribution of £170,000 of which £100,000 was a special contribution (see 9.32 to 9.38). At 2 January 2001 the trustees wish to borrow £300,000 to acquire commercial property. The value of the scheme's investments at that date was £170,000.

Scheme year ended	Contribution paid by employer	Contribution recommended by actuary	
		Annual only or	Special + Reduced
31 December 2001	£170,000	£100,000 or	£100,000 + £70,000

Total employer's contribution divided by one equals £170,000, which is greater than the annual contribution recommended by the actuary (i.e. £80,000).

Borrowings ceiling is therefore:

3 x £80,000	=	£240,000
plus 45% of £170,000	=	£76,500
		£316,500

In Example D, the trustees may borrow the full £300,000 they require.

It is important to remember that the costs associated with an investment in commercial property by the trustees must also be taken into account when ascertaining whether or not an acquisition can be made and the borrowings ceiling not exceeded. Associated costs will usually include stamp duty, registration charges, solicitor's and surveyor's fees, mortgage arrangement fee etc., and possibly VAT (see 13.20 to 13.54).

7.61   PN 20.65 and SSAS GN 4.6 mention that any borrowings should be used for the purpose of the SSAS. If the borrowings are in turn lent to the employer or an associated company the trustees need to ensure they receive a higher rate of interest on the lendings than they have to pay on the borrowings.

7.62   Borrowings are permissible after one member has retired and before other members retire. However, where the scheme rules allow or are amended to allow the deferral of the purchase of pensions until age 75 (see 3.42 and 3.43), the level of any further borrowing during the period of deferral is restricted by excluding from the value of the scheme assets for the purpose of the 45% limit any retired members', widows'/widowers' and dependants' shares of the fund and any borrowings used to purchase scheme assets which are outstanding at that time and any other liabilities of the trustees which are outstanding at the time other than liabilities to pay benefits (PN 20.62). In addition, within five years of a member's, ex-spouse's, widow's/widower's or dependant's pension coming into payment or the pensioner attaining age 70 if earlier, existing borrowings must be reduced in accordance with these limits. If the person due to receive a pension is already 70 when payment of their pension commences, the borrowings must be reduced immediately (PN 20.63).

Under PSO Update No 63 issued in June 2000, IR SPSS also imposed these restrictions on SSASs that have retained the facility to defer the purchase of annuities for 5 years (see 3.42), but only in respect of borrowings taken out on or after 1 August 2000.

7.63   Trustees' borrowings may be secured or unsecured. They must however be on commercial terms and for the purposes of the scheme. In other words if they are used to finance an investment, that investment must be one which is acceptable to IR SPSS. There is no set period over which the trustees may borrow, but borrowings should be repaid prior to the retirement of a single member SSAS, although trustees may borrow in the short term to finance the payment of benefits. Very often they may use an overdraft facility for this while assets are being realised. It should not be overlooked though that IR SPSS may ask why the trustees do not have liquid funds available (SSAS GN 9.108) to evaluate whether or not the *bona fides* of the SSAS are in doubt (see 7.68). So it is possible for the trustees to take on a mortgage or a legal charge, or a straight bank loan or overdraft, or borrow from another third party or even a connected party. In the last case mentioned, it is most important to ensure the terms of the loan are at a commercial rate, especially the rate of interest, otherwise the scheme's approval may be prejudiced (SSAS GN 9.109). If the principal or any associated company lends to a SSAS it is to the trustees as curators of the pension scheme and not as participators, i.e. shareholders or loan creditors of the company, within the provisions of *s 419*. This legislation does not expressly address participators handling loans in a fiduciary capacity so it can be argued that only transactions for members' use in their own right are caught and that *s 419* does not apply to the trustees.

7.64   The trustees may only mortgage or charge trust property in respect of their own borrowings. They must on no account charge scheme assets in respect of a loan taken out by a third party e.g. a member of the scheme or another joint owner. Charging scheme assets in this way would prejudice the scheme's approval as the scheme would not be *bona fide* established for the sole provision of relevant benefits. Thus a pension mortgage granted by a third party to a scheme member must in no way be linked directly to the assets of the scheme.

7.65   If the trustees acquire a property already subject to a mortgage, then in taking on board the mortgage the trustees still need to have regard to their borrowings ceiling. If the trustees take on further borrowings any previous borrowings not then repaid have to be aggregated for the purposes of the ceiling.

7.66   It should be borne in mind that after 1 June 1996 when the revised funding basis for SSAS came into effect (see 9.22 to 9.47), the trustees' ability to repay borrowings from contributions may be affected. In addition once lesser contributions commence to be paid less monies may be borrowed and therefore borrowings may need to be taken before the new funding basis applies in full.

7.67   Borrowings like other features of SSASs are to be reported to IR SPSS under the *Regulations* whether they are used to finance investments or expenses. Temporary borrowings not exceeding six months and which do not exceed the lesser of 10 per cent of the market value of the fund or £50,000 and the borrowing is repaid at or before the due date do not have to be reported (PN 20.66 and SSAS GN 4.8). Thus if borrowing is rolled over into a further term it has to be reported. Problems are likely to arise with trustees' overdrafts as it will probably not be known in advance when the overdraft facility will end.

7.68   The form PS 7015 (APPENDIX 35) is to be used by the administrator under the reporting requirements (see 3.75) to report trustees' borrowings within 90 days of their commencement. A separate report is required of each borrowing by the trustees, particularly if a borrowing facility is used in tranches unless it is covered by the concession in 7.67. The form incorporates the date of borrowing, the amount, rate of interest, repayment date, purpose, name and address of the lender, value of the fund at the time, the amounts of the employer's contributions in the last three years or lesser period from commencement, the total amount of employee contributions, the amount of borrowing outstanding following the transaction and if the borrowing is a rolling-over of previous borrowings covered by the non-reporting concession (see 7.67). It is clear IR SPSS will pay some attention to these details, not just to check the amount borrowed is within the permitted ceiling. For instance if the lender is a connected person a copy of the loan agreement has to be sent to IR SPSS with form PS 7015. Whilst there can be no objection to the employer or a scheme member making a loan to the trustees, clearly IR SPSS will be concerned to establish that the loan is on fully commercial terms. In addition the purpose of a loan may come in for close scrutiny by IR SPSS. For example, if the trustees borrow to finance the payment of retirement benefits to a member, this would only be acceptable in certain circumstances as retirement dates are generally well known to the trustees in advance and steps should have been taken to realise assets in good time to pay benefits. However, if a property is proving difficult to sell or an unexpected early retirement occurs such borrowings may be acceptable to IR SPSS. Late reporting or failure to report borrowings may lead to penalties being sought under *TMA 1970, s 98* (see 10.56 to 10.70).

7.69   As part of the pensioner trustee requirements introduced by IR SPSS in PSO Update No 69 (see 5.1), the pensioner trustee must be a party to all scheme borrowings taken out on or after 1 October 2000 (see 2.57(c)).

The position prior to 5 August 1991

7.70   It is unlikely that IR SPSS may still be enquiring into the position of borrowings made before 5 August 1991, but if it is then it is necessary to know in these circumstances what its discretionary requirements are for borrowings made before 5 August 1991. Once again, they were not reportable at the time they were made.

7.71   Until January 1983 there were no specific guidelines laid down by IR SPSS regarding the amount the trustees of a SSAS could borrow. The situation on each scheme was considered on its merits. IR SPSS then pronounced through the APT its revised practice in this area. This was to set a ceiling on trustees' borrowings of three times the ordinary annual contribution (OAC) paid to the scheme. The significance of 'three times' is wholly arbitrary and IR SPSS made it clear that it would consider larger borrowings provided the circumstances were satisfactorily explained. The guidelines were again mentioned in 1984 following the PQ about changes in IR SPSS practice since JOM 58 was published. IR SPSS stated that each case would be considered on its own merits, but excessive borrowing by trustees might give rise to doubts as to the 'sole purpose' of the arrangements and lead to difficulty over approval. Any significant proposed borrowing had to be cleared in advance.

7.72 The important point to note is that the three times OAC guideline was missing from the answer to the PQ and, whilst it was understood that it still applied, cases could be made to IR SPSS for 'significant' borrowings, i.e. above the three times OAC, to be arranged. It needed a good case though to justify such a level of borrowings, for example it would probably be no use stressing the good potential of the investment to be made with the finance raised by the trustees, rather the emphasis should have been on the lack of any need for some years to realise scheme assets to provide benefits.

7.73 It is necessary to understand what IR SPSS meant by OAC in the context of borrowings. Firstly, it is the employer's contribution that determines the level of borrowing. Any member's personal contributions cannot be taken into account at all for this purpose. If more than one employer participates in the scheme, then their total contributions can be counted. Secondly, the contribution must be that paid to the scheme at the time the borrowings were arranged. This can cause problems if the borrowings were arranged well into the scheme year and the last contribution was paid at the end of the previous scheme year. Here the borrowings should be based on the last contribution or the trustees could wait a while until the current year's contribution was paid and then take the finance on board based on the latest contribution. Thirdly, and this is the area which has probably lead to most problems with IR SPSS, the contribution on which the borrowing is calculated must be the regular ordinary annual contribution. This is easy enough if contributions were being paid in full in line with the actuary's recommendations, whether they were at a flat rate or a percentage of salaries. However, if contributions have been paid at less than the rate recommended then the regular ordinary annual contribution needs to be established to calculate the ceiling for borrowings and that could be difficult. The position becomes worse if, say, no contribution was paid in the year prior to the borrowings, because then a contribution had to be paid to justify any borrowings at all. Finally, special contributions and transfer values received cannot be taken into account as part of this exercise. Where a regular pattern of ordinary annual contributions has not been established, IR SPSS may already have deemed some contributions as special and this too will affect the ceiling on borrowings.

7.74 The only further general IR SPSS requirements for borrowings undertaken by trustees prior to 5 August 1991 are those set out in 7.63 to 7.65 regarding their commercial terms, charging trust property and additional borrowings.

Chapter 8

Trading and Self-Assessment

Introduction

8.1   There are various references in the earlier part of this book to areas of activity by trustees that may be construed by the Inland Revenue as trading. The circumstances that apply are explained in greater detail in this chapter, extending beyond dealings with investments and including the requirement for SSASs to complete self-assessment tax returns.

8.2   It should be borne in mind that the scope for trading is rather limited in a SSAS particularly when compared with a large self-administered scheme, but trustees and their tax advisers need to be alert nonetheless to the problems such activities can create with the Inland Revenue and not just with IR SSPS. It is important to bear in mind that, even if it trustees have been deemed to be trading, that activity will not necessarily result in the loss of tax approval or a refusal to approve a SSAS. It is only where the trading activity has deliberately involved a SSAS in order to achieve tax avoidance that its approval may be prejudiced e.g. bond washing or dividend stripping (see 8.8). In other circumstances, the trustees would only have to pay tax on the transaction concerned.

IR SPSS guidelines

8.3   PN 17.10 and 20.44 cover trading generally to the extent that if the trustees receive profits from 'an adventure in the nature of trade' they may be assessable to tax. As mentioned in 7.55 IR SSPS is not prepared to give advance ruling as to whether a specific activity is liable to tax. That is a matter for the inspector of taxes to decide, and he will not give an opinion on an activity until it has taken place. It is therefore appropriate to look at the criteria by which the inspector will be guided in making his decision, and then to look at various investment and transaction areas that apply.

PN 20.78 and 20.79 explain the restrictions on investments when no member is actively accruing benefits.

174

The badges of trade

8.4   The question of whether a transaction has given rise to a profit and is to be treated as a trading transaction has been considered before the various appellate bodies. A series of six tests is listed in the final report of the 1954 Royal Commission (Command 9474 paragraph 116) as constituting the relevant considerations in deciding if a transaction involved trading. These are known as the badges of trade, not one of which nor all of which are necessarily conclusive that the activity amounted to trading. They remain, however, the most useful pointers on trading to the present day.

The subject of the transaction

8.5   To be regarded as a trading activity, it must be possible to trade in the subject matter of the transaction. If an asset does not produce income or cannot be actively enjoyed personally it is unlikely to be regarded as an investment. This test is particularly relevant to works of art. A non-income producing asset such as this may not be regarded as an investment, depending on the use to which it was put whilst owned. A work of art could, for instance, be leased at a commercial rent so as to generate income.

8.6   Securities usually produce income and consequently do not give rise to such a problem. However, securities are not always held as an investment and there are cases where it has been established that in certain situations they can be the subject matter of trading. Commodities are normally the subject of trading (see 7.53 and 8.35) and only exceptionally may be the subject of investment.

The length of the period of ownership

8.7   The length of ownership of an asset has a bearing on the establishment of a trading activity. An asset that is sold shortly after acquisition is more likely to be considered a trading transaction than an investment. It would be necessary to demonstrate that circumstances changed materially between the purchase and sale of an asset, which was held for a short period if the trustees are to avoid the transaction being treated as trading.

8.8   The length of ownership of an asset is an area where bond washing and dividend stripping are prone to be attacked. These activities involve the transfer and re-transfer of securities on dates spanning an interest or dividend payment either to avoid tax by selling or to benefit from a tax exemption in receiving it. The use of an approved pension scheme to receive a dividend would free it from tax, but if there is tax avoidance present the likelihood is that the scheme's approval would be prejudiced. However, any action regarding the scheme's approval by IR SSPS would need to be considered in the light of any action taken by the inspector of taxes under *ss 732, 734, 735, ICTA 1988*. If some tax reliefs are lost as a result of the inspector of taxes action, it is reasonable to maintain that the approval of the scheme is no longer prejudiced.

8.9   In relation to dividends paid from UK companies the opportunity for dividend stripping was effectively curtailed from 2 July 1997 with the abolition of repayable tax credits *(F(No2)A 1997, s 19)*. In addition the transfer of dividends to those who can still benefit from a tax credit to avoid the abolition of payment of tax credits was circumvented by *F(No 2)A 1977 s 28* which introduced *s 231B, ICTA 1988*.

The frequency or number of similar transactions

8.10   It is unlikely that a single transaction would be taxed as trading. In most cases, for an isolated transaction to be treated as taxable it would have to be shown to be an adventure in the nature of a trade. There is a useful precedent here in the case of *Marson v Morton and Others [1986] STC 463*, where a profit on the purchase and resale of land made by persons whose normal business was that of potato dealers was held not to be an adventure in the nature of trade assessable under Schedule D Case I. However, where the same type of transaction is repeated frequently then the volume of transactions involved may be sufficient to establish trading. The large volume of underwriting transactions in the *BT* case (see 8.26) was one of several factors in determining that commission received from the transactions was taxable as trading income. As mentioned in 6.25 and 6.38 frequent purchases and sales of property by a SSAS may attract the attention of the inspector of taxes who may consider such activities to be trading, but there never has been a general or specific rule on how many transactions would constitute trading.

Supplementary work on, or in connection with, the property realised

8.11   Supplementary work on, or in connection with, property, is of course is relevant to sales of land, particularly its development by the trustees (see 6.38). The inspector of taxes will determine whether the land was purchased and resold as it stood or whether work was done on it to facilitate a resale. If it was worked on or developed before sale this could suggest an intention to sell by way of trading. When there is an organised effort to obtain profit there is a source of taxable income. It is most important that the trustees seek specialist tax advice on these matters before development is undertaken to ensure an SSAS is not taxed on the 'profit' realised.

The circumstances that were responsible for the realisation

8.12 There may be a very good commercial reason for selling an investment shortly after its acquisition. For instance, there could have been a sudden change in market conditions or a situation or opportunity may have arisen which called for ready money. In such circumstances the trustees should minute the reason for the sale at the time it occurred. This should give weight to the non-trading case and effectively scotch any idea that the original purchase was prompted by a plan to deal.

8.13 In circumstances where an investment has fallen in value due to a fall in the market, the trustees could point out that the investment was no longer prudent and to retain it would have meant that the trustees were not acting in the best interests of the members i.e. the trustees would have been in breach of trust if they did not sell.

Motive

8.14 The intention of the trustees in making transactions is a most important factor in determining whether such transactions will be regarded as trading. The intention extends to the trustees' tax advisers who may have given advice on the purchase and/or sale of an investment. Whilst it would assist any case to record that the trustees were purchasing on investment grounds care should be taken not to provide evidence of the motive in reselling. The motive behind the *BT* case (see 8.26) was to make money for the pension scheme, and therefore the underwriting commission received was taxable as trading income.

8.15 The badges of trade are very general tests so it may be relevant for the trustees' tax advisers to consider what the courts have decided in cases where it has been argued that a taxpayer was trading. There were, however, until 1998 (see 8.26) no leading cases where the Inland Revenue has argued that the trustees of a pension scheme were trading. The previous leading cases all concern taxpayers who made losses on the sale of securities and therefore claimed the losses against other taxable income on the grounds they were trading losses. If a pension scheme was held to be trading the trustees' profit would be taxable, but if they made a net trading loss it would go unrelieved as there would be no other income against which to set the loss. On the other hand if the trustees were not regarded as trading in relation to a transaction the 'profit' would be exempt from CGT. It can therefore be gathered how important it is to the Inland Revenue not to concede that a taxpayer buying and selling securities was trading otherwise it would have to deal with a flood of claims at a time of falling markets.

8.16   For the record, early leading cases are *Salt v Chamberlain*, *Lewis Emanuel & Son Ltd v White* and *Cooper v C and J Clark Ltd*. It is not proposed in this book to go into great detail of these cases. The table of cases at the front of this book provides the appropriate references for those wishing to consider their contents in greater depth. Two of the cases involve companies engaged in buying and selling shares as an ancillary activity to their main business which is unlikely to be the basis for finding a pension scheme to be trading. The primary activity of a pension scheme is not to trade and therefore different considerations ought to apply. This should give rise to a presumption against trading so far as a pension scheme is concerned (see also 8.18).

Forms of trading

8.17   Having looked at the criteria on which the inspector of taxes may base a decision that the trustees are engaged in trading, it is appropriate now to look at specific areas where trading may or indeed does occur. It should also be mentioned that for some years now there have been indications that the Inland Revenue is focusing its attention on the investment practices of some large self-administered schemes with a view to determining whether these schemes may have been trading. There have subsequently been some direct pronouncements by the Inland Revenue which are as relevant to SSASs as they are to large schemes and are therefore mentioned in the paragraphs covering the form of trading concerned.

Trading in shares

8.18   It would be very difficult for the Inland Revenue to argue that shares were sold as part of an organised arrangement to make a profit. The frequent buying and selling of shares or short-term transactions therein are much more likely to be dictated by stock market conditions. Such transactions would also have to be looked at in conjunction with the trustees' other activities as a whole. The question that also has to be asked in connection with a SSAS is would the Inland Revenue consider it a worthwhile target in this area? It seems highly unlikely that the purchase and sale of securities would be shown to be trading in cases where a scheme has been run solely in accordance with normal investment criteria. It is much more likely that any action by the Inland Revenue would only be concentrated in areas of tax avoidance such as bond washing or dividend stripping (see 8.8).

Stock lending

8.19 Stock lending is an activity often undertaken by pension schemes, especially the larger ones, to lend their stock to a market maker who is short of stock due for delivery, together with the right to acquire the same amount of securities within a specified period. The full legal and beneficial ownership of the pension scheme stock that is lent is actually transferred to the borrower. This enables the borrower to transfer the stock free of any encumbrances to a third party with whom he has to settle his own contract. Whilst the stock remains in the trustees' ownership the income received therefrom is exempt from income tax (under *s 592(2)*) as it is income from investments or deposits held for the purposes of the scheme. If the trustees enter into a stock lending arrangement the disposal of the stock to the borrower is also exempt from CGT under *TCGA 1992, s 271(1)* as it is a disposal of investments held by the trustees for the purposes of the scheme. The trustees will obtain security in cash or treasury bills for their lending (see 8.22) and the borrower undertakes eventually to redeliver equivalent stock, although not necessarily the same stock, to the trustees. As a result the trustees will receive a stock lending fee which was taxable under *s 727(1)* until 1 January 1996.

8.20 With the start of the open gilt repo market on 2 January 1996, stock lending fees received by tax approved pension schemes are exempt from tax (*FA 1996, s 129B*) from this date. This brings the treatment of stock lending into line with the sale and repurchase arrangements ('repos') which are commercially equivalent mechanisms. As part of these arrangements the interest on gilts was payable gross to approved pension schemes from 2 January 1996.

8.21 There was, however, some uncertainty previously regarding the position of dividends or interest received had the stock not been lent. This was clarified by the issue of Extra-Statutory Concession C19 on 9 October 1991. This made it clear that where manufactured payments are received by an approved pension scheme under the terms of a stock lending arrangement approved within *s 129, ICTA 1988*, those manufactured payments will be exempt from tax to the extent that had the transfer not taken place, any dividends or interest arising on the securities concerned would have been exempt under *s 592(2), ICTA 1988*. The concession defines a manufactured payment as a manufactured dividend, interest or overseas dividend as defined in *Sche 23A para 1(1), ICTA 1988*.

8.22 The legal ownership of the cash or securities (see 8.19) provided by the borrower as security to the stock lender passes to the trustees of a pension scheme as part of the stock lending arrangements. Any return on the cash or securities would be returned to the trustees to preserve the economic neutrality of the arrangement. In this way the trustees may manufacture a payment of interest or a dividend to the borrower. The provisions of *Sch 23A para 5, ICTA 1988* apply to the underlying dividend or interest which is treated as taxable income of the recipient of the manufactured payment and not of the payment manufacturer. No tax relief is given to the payment manufacturer in respect of the manufactured payments.

8.23 The position of the cash collateral was unclear until 1995. *FA 1995, Sch 19* clarified this. Where the trustees receive interest on cash collateral transferred to them, they may pay the interest to the borrower without any tax consequences to themselves. There is no need for the trustees to withhold tax on the payment. *FA 1995* required the manufactured payment to be identified separate from any stock-lending fee (this requirement was repealed by *FA 1997, Schs 10* and *18, Pt VI* in respect of post 1 July activities, transfers and arrangements). This prevents pension scheme trustees from reducing the amount of the stock lending fee, which is taxable up to 1 January 1996, by the amount of any manufactured payment made on the collateral received.

8.24 Repo transactions, like manufactured payments, may extend across a dividend or a coupon date and up to 1 January 1996 gave rise to a manufactured payment which is taxable under *s 730A* (inserted by *FA 1995, s 85*). However, to bring the position for pension schemes into line at the start of the open gilt repo market and the tax exemption for stock lending fees, regulations were laid to treat manufactured payments arising from approved stock lending arrangements as exempt from tax from 2 January 1996 where they are received by approved pension schemes. The *Manufactured Payments and Transfer of Securities (Tax Relief) Regulations 1995 (SI 1995 No 3036)* brought in the exemption and rendered Extra-Statutory Concession C19 obsolete.

8.25 As part of the arrangements from 2 January 1996 and to bring the treatment of manufactured payments relating to gilts into line with the treatment of gilts themselves (see 8.20), such manufactured payments are payable gross from 2 January 1996. They are also eligible for relief from tax where they are received by the trustees of tax approved pension schemes (see 8.24). As dividends no longer carry any payable tax credits from 6 April 1999, there is no need for payers of manufactured dividends on UK equities to account for ACT when they make such payments on or after 6 April 1999 – the *Manufactured Dividends (Tax) (Amendment) Regulations 1999 (SI 1999 No 621)*.

Commissions

8.26 Underwriting commissions are exempt from tax under *s 592(3)* (see 1.26) if they are applied for the purposes of the scheme. There has been some degree of doubt as to whether fee income from underwriting new issues of stocks and securities constitutes trading income. This ought not to concern SSASs, but only large self-administered schemes. The Inland Revenue's argument would appear to be that such income is not applied for the purposes of the scheme and indeed it would be difficult to show that such activity was directly linked to investment purposes. Despite the Inland Revenue's past assessments on such income received by pension schemes, and its consideration of the potential trading aspects of large and frequent transactions by trustees, there have been successful appeals against the taxation of some underwriting commissions. In particular, there have been decisions in respect of sub-underwriting commissions in favour of BT and Post Office pension schemes recently.

The Bank of England has described underwriting as being identical to a series of put options, the income from which is exempt from tax. However, the Inland Revenue is still expected to step up its activity in checking for any underwriting commission that is received by pension schemes that is not directly linked to investment purposes.

8.27 PSO Updates Nos 33 and 64 give specific guidance on the rules that apply to rebated underwriting commissions In particular, PSO Update No 33 describes the Inland Revenue's practice regarding rebates from financial advisers and other intermediaries, and PSO Update No 64 makes it clear that the requirement that rebated commissions must remain in the fund of the scheme extends to annuity purchases etc.

8.28 Schemes do receive other commission income, which does not fall within the exemption contained in *s 592(3), ICTA 1988*. For instance, the trustees may insure buildings in their ownership from damage and may as a result obtain commission. Such commission could not be said to arise from investments or deposits held for the purposes of the scheme. It is derived from an insurance contract rather than the property itself and is therefore taxable under Schedule D Case VI.

Options, financial futures and forward contracts

8.29 An option is a right to buy or sell something without any obligation to take it up whereas a forward contract is a firm agreement to buy or sell something in the future. A future is a standardised forward contract traded on an exchange.

8.30 During the 1980s there was considerable uncertainty regarding the taxation of options, futures and forward contracts despite legislation purporting to deal with them. In 1984 pension schemes were exempted from tax on gains arising from transactions in traded options and financial futures (see 7.53). Previous legislation actually defined a traded option as 'an option which is for the time being quoted on a recognised stock exchange or on the London International Financial Futures Exchange' (LIFFE). In addition *FA 1985, s 72* defined a financial future as one which is 'for the time being dealt in on a recognised futures exchange'.

8.31   There was some doubt whether gains from financial futures were exempt from tax in the hands of pension scheme trustees. Indeed this uncertainty of tax treatment was shared by other exempt bodies such as investment and unit trusts, charities etc. Following consultation between the Inland Revenue, LIFFE and other interested bodies the Inland Revenue issued a Statement of Practice (SP4/88) on 22 July 1988 regarding 'The Tax Treatment of Transactions in Financial Futures and Options'.

8.32   SP4/88 made it clear that profits and losses arising from investing in financial futures and options were exempt from CGT subject to the reason for and frequency of such investments. SP4/88 also explained that transactions would not be treated as trading if they were infrequent or used to hedge investments. Hedging in this context would reduce the risk of an underlying investment. The variations in price of the futures and options must correspond with the difference in value of the underlying transaction. Such transactions are not liable to CGT. SP4/88 is also helpful in that it provides examples of when an investment may produce a capital gain or loss.

8.33   In 1990 all trading income of pension schemes from futures and options was exempted from tax (PN 17.10) by virtue of *section 659A* introduced by *FA 1990, s 81(2)(4)* (see 7.53). Similarly the CGT legislation in what is now *TCGA 1992, s 271(10)* extended the meaning of investments to include futures and options contracts and any capital gains made by the trustees of an approved pension scheme from such contracts, are exempt from CGT under *TCGA 1992, s 271(1)(g)*. So the position now is very favourable to approved schemes although somewhat complicated. Indeed, with the merger of LIFFE and the London Traded Options Market in 1991 into the London International Futures and Options Exchange, still known as LIFFE, the Inland Revenue took the opportunity to update and clarify its practice. SP4/88 was replaced by SP14/91 on 21 November 1991. SP14/91 expands on the former SP4/88 in relation to transactions in financial futures and options, but acknowledges that it does not apply to approved pension schemes whose profits from futures and options are generally exempt from tax, i.e. by virtue of *s 659A*.

8.34   It is important to note that the trustees must have the power in the definitive deed to use futures, options and other derivatives and to engage in stock lending. They could be seriously embarrassed if they entered into a derivatives contract or engaged in stock lending without the necessary power as the contract may be unenforceable against the scheme assets.

Commodities

8.35 These were mentioned in JOM 58(16) but not in PN 20. The former warning still applies that income therefrom may be taxable in the hands of the trustees. If the trustees derive profits from purchase and sales of commodities, e.g. metals or foodstuffs, there is not much doubt that they will be taxed (see 7.53 and 8.6).

Other forms of trading

8.36 If the trustees invest in a business venture of any kind, such as a shop or farm and they run it directly rather than let it to a third party, they need to be aware of the taxation implications. They may invest in part or the whole of a business and if they do the profits received will be taxable. Capital gains tax exemptions may still be open to them though some businesses, such as hotels and nursing homes, can cause problems even when the trustees let them on commercial terms to a third party to run them. Sound taxation advice is called for on these matters and indeed on all areas where trading may be involved. If the trustees invest in a successful commercial venture they also need to be aware of the problems that may arise regarding the scheme's funding if the investment generates substantial income which may not only fund the scheme without the need for company contributions, but lead to overfunding and resultant actuarial difficulties with regard to surplus repayments. A too successful investment of this nature may well prejudice the scheme's approval if the provisions of *s 590(2)(d), ICTA 1988* are not met i.e. the employer must be a contributor to the scheme.

8.37 PN 20 makes no mention of the former wording in JOM 58(16) that the acquisition of plant and machinery for hiring out may result in the trustees becoming assessable to tax on trading profits, although SSAS GN 9.136 does. The acquisition and leasing of such assets on commercial terms is not debarred by the *Regulations* and whilst such investments are not met frequently on SSASs, the profits derived therefrom will be taxable.

8.38 There are currently several types of leasing arrangements available whereby a non-taxpayer, such as a pension scheme, could benefit from capital allowances via reduced rental payments. These involve leasing plant, machinery and equipment from or to totally unconnected third parties and the third party claiming the capital allowances due. The benefit of the capital allowances is passed on via reduced rental payments. The question arises as to whether such arrangements would be acceptable within a SSAS. Whilst the trustees would be liable to tax on the rental income as trading receipts, the SSAS would nonetheless be used as a vehicle to achieve tax avoidance on the capital allowances. Certainly, if the principal company was involved the arrangements would be unacceptable, *cf* the similar use of IBAs (see 6.34 to 6.36). However, using an unconnected third party could be argued as totally commercial, but because this is such a contentious area great care is needed and an approach to IR SSPS beforehand would be strongly advised.

8.39   In 1996 the Inland Revenue announced measures aimed at correcting perceived defects in the rules for giving capital allowances on fixtures in buildings, primarily because tax was being avoided by obtaining allowances on more than the cost of the fixture through the acceleration of allowances which was never the intention of the legislation. This is a clear reaction to the decision in *Melluish v BMI (No 3) [1995] STC 964* which gave capital allowances to equipment lessors on fixtures leased to persons not liable to tax. So legislation was introduced with effect from 24 July 1996 in *F(No 2)A 1997, s 46* preventing the use of the sale price for a long-life asset which was sold for less than its written down value and treating the asset as sold for its written down value. However, where it can be shown that such sales are made for good commercial reasons and not as a part of a scheme to avoid tax, these counter-avoidance rules will not be applied. The problem for companies leasing fixtures from pension schemes though will be to show that the sale took place for good commercial reasons because the leasing arrangement itself may have been motivated by tax mitigation in the first place. As the expenditure on long-life assets can qualify for IBAs, which are given at an equivalent rate, claimants can choose whether to segregate expenditure on long-life assets and claim machinery and plant allowances or IBAs. However, the lease and sub-lease arrangements explained in 6.35 enabling capital allowances to be obtained and avoiding tax on any balancing charge are affected by the counter-avoidance rules from 24 July 1996 where the tax written down value is used as the sale value.

8.40   There are some variations of the leasing arrangements relating to equipment mentioned at 8.38. If a lease is entered into from 14 July 1984 the lessor and lessee can elect under *Capital Allowances Act 1990, s 53* that the lessor should be entitled to capital allowances in respect of the expenditure by the lessor since 14 July 1984 on machinery, plant or equipment that has become a fixture on the lessee's land. Such an election must be made within two years of the end of the period in which the expenditure was incurred. The parties cannot elect for a figure, which is higher than original cost or the latest disposal value used by the last claimant. (*F(No 2)A 1997, s 46*). So all changes of ownership of the asset since 24 July 1996 need to be checked before a claim can be pursued. It makes no difference that the lessee, i.e. the trustees, are exempt from tax, but the warnings in 8.38 need very careful consideration. Measures were introduced with effect from 2 July 1997 in *F(No 2)A 1997* also to counter arrangements to sell unused capital allowances through sale and leaseback (*s 45*) and to accelerate the benefit of capital allowances through the use of subsidiaries with different year ends (*s 44*).

Further measures were introduced in *FA 98, s 83(4)* preventing claims for first year capital allowances on expenditure on machinery and plant for leasing. Despite there changes leasing arrangements are still available, particularly where purchasers acquire assets from pension funds, although IR SPSS may not see that the trustees, by paying tax on the rent received on the leasing of such assets, would be effectively cancelling out the tax avoidance on the capital allowances gained by the lessor.

8.41 It may be possible to confine all taxable or trading activities of a scheme in a company totally owned by the scheme itself. This may well be a practical proposition for a large self-administered scheme, but it has clear tax implications for SSASs. Paragraph 7.5, and PN 20.44 and SSAS GN 4.12 mention that a majority holding by a SSAS in a company would not be acceptable to the IR SSPS. The trustees would be able to control the company, including its profits and dividends and not just use it for trading activities. Since 5 August 1991, however, the trustees have been banned from acquiring more than 30% of the issued share capital of a company anyway.

Self-assessment

Introduction

8.42 If the trustees have been involved in trading at all they are required to make a return of their income received from such a source to the inspector of taxes after the end of the tax year in which the income arose. Up until 1995/96 they did this on the normal Inland Revenue tax returns and made separate claims for repayment of tax suffered on their income on the form R63N. Scheme accounts were more often than not submitted with the repayment, but their production was not obligatory. They were not called for in all cases, particularly SSAS, if no repayment claim was made, although the Inland Revenue could invoke the provisions of *s 605(1)(c), ICTA 1988* to produce scheme accounts. There was no consistency of treatment. *Section 605(1)(c)* was amended in 1996 with the commencement of the information powers legislation (see 3.84) and the self-assessment legislation now covers the power to require pension scheme accounts (*TMA 1970, s8A*).

8.43 The trustees of approved occupational pension schemes have been within the scope of self-assessment from 6 April 1996 following criticism from the Public Accounts Committee and National Audit Office of the Inland Revenue that adequate systems were not in place to oversee the substantial tax reliefs afforded to pension schemes. The intention is to allow inspectors of taxes to check that repayments have been correctly claimed and made and that the trustees' liability to tax has been correctly notified and the tax paid where appropriate. In particular, self-assessment assists inspectors of taxes, and presumably the IR SSPS, in establishing that schemes, which neither claim repayment nor notify tax liability, e.g. SSASs, are acting correctly.

8.44   Self-assessment applies to the trustees of tax approved self-administered schemes only, i.e. large self-administered schemes and SSAS, and to trading SIPPs (see 14.108). It does not apply to insured pension schemes. It applies in the same way that it does to other taxpayers. Therefore the same time limits and rules apply, including the application of automatic penalties where trustees fail to file the return by the 31st January deadline following the end of the tax year concerned (*FA 1994, s 178–214* and *Sch 20, FA 1994*).

8.45   It is important to note that self-assessment does not apply to administrators of schemes, who are required under the reporting and penalty regime to notify liability on various chargeable events (see 3.84). These include repayment of member's contributions, commutation of pensions that are trivial or in circumstances of serious ill-health and refunds of surpluses to the employer. These should continue to be reported on the form 1(SF) (APPENDIX 25) within the appropriate time limits, and the tax due paid on receipt of an assessment. The tax payable should not be netted off against repayments due to the trustees. General guidance was provided in Appendix 1 to PSO Update No 30 regarding the different responsibilities of the trustees under self-assessment and of the administrator for reporting tax liabilities and this may be found in the notes attached to APT Newsletter III.

8.46   Tax returns for the tax year 1996/97 were issued to the trustees of schemes who had notified the Inland Revenue that the scheme had a tax liability. Trustees who were liable to tax or CGT for 1996/97 who had not received a self-assessment return were encouraged in PSO Update No 30 (10) to notify their inspectors of taxes by 5 October 1997 that they were liable and a return would be sent to them. PSO Update No 30(11) pointed out that the trustees need not notify chargeability for 1996/97 if sufficient tax was deducted at source or tax credits were available to cover any tax chargeable on the trustees' total taxable income and gains—provided that tax deducted or tax credits had not already been repaid.

8.47   For 1997/98 tax returns were issued on a limited basis to around 20% of schemes. As the returns were issued in August and September 1998, trustees had 2 months within which to complete the return and send it in if they wished to calculate the tax or repayment due. Returns sent back after the 31 January 1999 deadline attracted an automatic penalty and payment of tax due after that date was subject to interest and a surcharge. The return had to be completed even if the scheme had no tax liability or repayment due. Trustees who were liable to tax or CGT for 1997/98 who did not receive a self-assessment return were once again encouraged by PSO Update No 49(5) to notify their tax office by 5 October 1998 that they were liable and a return would be sent to them.

The full regime

8.48 From the year 1998/99 the trustees of all self-administered schemes should have received self-assessment tax return forms headed 'Tax Return for Trustees of approved self-administered Pensions Scheme' (APPENDIX 37). In practice, many inspectors of taxes ran out of forms or failed to issue them. However, a nil tax liability was not accepted as an excuse for the non-production of a return, and trustees were advised by the APT to write to the scheme district, or the employer corporation tax district where the scheme district was unknown, to request a return. A set off of tax due against the other liabilities of the trustees or administrator is not permitted. It remains a requirement that, if the trustees of a SSAS do not receive a tax return, they must contact their inspector of taxes. The tax returns and explanatory/accompanying forms are:

(a)   SA 900, for trusts and estates (see Appendix 60);

(b)   SA 970, for approved self-administered schemes (see Appendix 37);

(c)   SA 975, the tax return guide (see Appendix 38);

(d)   SA 976, the tax calculation guide (see Appendix 39).

If the scheme is split approved (see 8.58) the trustees will have to complete form SA 973 showing details of income and gains from the approved and unapproved parts of the scheme.

The same rules for completion of the self-assessment return apply to the trustees as apply for other taxpayers. Completion of particular aspects of the return is covered in 8.52 to 8.60. Of general relevance are the time limits that apply and interest and penalties that can be charged for late completion.

Time limits and interests

8.49 If trustees wish the inspector of taxes to calculate their liability or repayment the return has to be completed and returned by 30 September following the end of the tax year concerned or 2 months from the date of the return if this was after 31 July (*FA 1994, s179*). The form SA 976 does not have to be completed. Otherwise the return has to be completed and sent to the inspector of taxes by 31 January in the year following the end of the tax year concerned together with the completed form SA 976. If, however, the tax return was issued after 31 October then the return and form SA 976 must be completed and sent to the inspector of taxes within 3 months of the date of issue of the return (*FA 1994, s178(1)*).

8.50   If the trustees have any tax to pay in relation to trading income, it is payable on 31 January in respect of any liability for the previous tax year and as a first payment on account for the following tax year (*FA 1994, s 192*). A second payment on account is also payable on 31 July for the following tax year. For example:

31 January 2002	Tax is payable for 2000/2001, and the first payment on account for 2001/2002
31 July 2002	Second payment on account for 2001/2002
31 January 2003	Balance of tax payable for 2001/2002 and first payment on account for 2003

8.51   The interest payable on late payment of tax accrues from the due date to the actual date of payment, and a surcharge is due on tax paid more than one month after it is due. The surcharge increases from 5% to 10% on a sliding scale over one to six months (*FA 1994, s 194*). An automatic penalty of £100 is incurred if a completed return is not received by 31 January, or within 3 months of its issue if issued after 31 October, under *TMA, s93(2)*. Persistent delays may result in loss of approval.

Accounts

8.52   Pension scheme accounts are required to accompany the completed tax return. These do not have to be audited unless the provisions of the *Pensions Act 1995* (see 12.2) or the scheme's trust deed and rules apply (see 12.20). The accounting period covered by the accounts will not necessarily end on 5 April, however, but the inspector of taxes will accept accounts for the scheme accounting period ending in the tax year concerned. Thus accounts for the year ended 31 December 1999 will be acceptable for the tax return for the year ended 5 April 2000 . This means that the scheme income for the year ended 31 December 1999 will be treated as the income for the tax year 1999/2000 and should be included in the tax return as such.

8.53   Where accounts are not produced the return should be completed on the strict basis of the tax year. In these cases, which could well include SSASs, statements of income and outgoings, assets and liabilities for the beginning and end of the tax year will be required.

8.54   Some SSASs, particularly those with scheme years ending on 31 March or 5 April, may have some difficulty obtaining completed accounts before the 30 September deadline for calculating their own tax, especially where the scheme auditor has more than 7 months in which to complete the accounts. This may not matter so much as far as the 30 September deadline is concerned if they have no tax liabilities or repayment due as no calculation would be necessary and the 31 January deadline can be met. However, some SSASs will as a result have to supply the statement of income and outgoings, assets and liabilities (see 8.53) in the absence of accounts by the requisite deadlines.

Problem areas

8.55 There should be few problems, apart from the time involved, in completing the appropriate sections of the self-assessment return in relation to the normal tax exempt income and gains of the trustees eg. dividends, interest, rent etc., especially as the return is designed to lead trustees to complete only those questions appropriate to them. Indeed, the repayment claim section of the return may no longer apply to SSASs with the withdrawal of repayable tax credits on UK dividends from 2 July 1997 unless they have other income from which tax has been deducted at source. Problems are more likely to occur in completing the form if the trustees are trading.

8.56 An initial question in the return asks if the assets were held exclusively for the purposes of the scheme. This is clearly aimed at trading, as income received from assets not held for the purposes of the scheme is taxable. If the trustees are uncertain where to include particular types of income in this connection, it is advisable to enter the income where it appears to them to be most appropriate. In particular, in relation to underwriting commission received (see 8.26 and 8.27), it may be prudent to provide details of the income and the trustees' decisions thereon in the additional information space on the return.

8.57 Another question in the return that may cause problems concerns the receipt of income from UK equities, foreign income dividend scheme dividends and distributions that are treated as foreign income dividends. This includes deemed distributions from all share buy-backs. This is the area of activity that was curtailed by *FA 1997, Sch 7* (see 7.13 and 7.14) from 8 October 1996 to remove payable tax credits in relation to certain types of company distributions and prevent tax advantages where a repayment of tax credits arose. Care is therefore needed in completing this part of the return as tax credits from such income are not repayable. The dividend vouchers concerned will provide the income to be shown in the return.

8.58 It is possible for a SSAS to be part-approved, and part unapproved, in two circumstances. Firstly, IR SPSS (formerly the PSO) may have withdrawn approval under *Sch 22(7)* where a SSAS is over-funded from that part of the fund representing more than 105% of the scheme's liabilities (see 9.50). Secondly, IR SSPS may have approved the scheme under *s 611(3)*, granting approval to the UK part of a scheme in respect of an overseas employer with

UK employees. In both instances the trustees will have to complete form SA 973 showing details of income and gains from the approved and unapproved parts of the scheme.

8.59   It should be noted that one question on form SA 970 asks is whether the scheme is a SSAS. The Tax Return Guide, form SA 975, merely comments that this is necessary for the inspector of taxes to keep his records up to date. Presumably the inspector of taxes keeps a record of large and small self-administered schemes. One is left wondering for what purpose?

Repayments

8.60   The self-assessment return now forms the basic repayment claim for the tax year. However, the trustees or their nominees continue to be entitled to make provisional in-year repayment claims on form R63N (see 3.84 and APPENDIX 24).

8.61   Inspectors of taxes will follow the normal rules governing all self-assessment enquires. The return has to be checked after processing and any enquiry commenced within 2 years of 31 January following the year of assessment. (*FA 1994, s 180*) The selection for enquiry may be at random or as a result of aspects of the return giving rise to suspicion or from information received from elsewhere, e.g. the IR SSPS . Local inspectors are likely to liaise with the IR SSPS and ensure that all aspects of the return are covered. Whilst inspectors of taxes can be expected to concentrate on the repayment and liability aspects, the IR SSPS will monitor ongoing compliance with approval terms. The inspector of taxes can ask for records and check any other information available before commencing or during his enquiries.

8.62   The trustees may make corrections to the tax return within 9 months of filing (*FA 1994, s188*). If the correction results in more tax becoming payable and it is paid after the due payment dates (see 8.50), interest will be chargeable. Penalties will only be sought after a correction if negligence or fraud caused the error. Penalties may be mitigated if the circumstances warrant it.

8.63   It will be interesting to see the approach of the Inland Revenue to self-assessment by pension schemes over the next few years, now that the trustees have to sign off somewhat complicated returns claiming exemptions within strict time limits or face penalties. Further evidence of changes in the Inland Revenue's attitude is all too apparent. The great fear amongst pensions practitioners is that the Inland Revenue will step up its activity in looking into pensions schemes, particularly SSASs which have never had to make returns before (unless they were trading), even though the compliance audit function is available. As mentioned in 7.15, the Inland Revenue is now far less likely to consider pension schemes as mainly tax exempt bodies but more as a potential source of additional revenue. Advisers need to be on their guard in this new scenario to the implications of self-assessment enquiries.

Administration

8.64 Whilst the trustees have the ultimate responsibility of signing the self-assessment tax returns, there is a considerable amount of work for administrators to undertake even for SSAS from 6 April 1999 when the regime started . The production of accounts, which may already be an additional task following the *Pensions Act 1995* (see 12.2 to 12.30), in good time or provision of income and outgoings, assets and liabilities at 6 April in the preceding year and 5 April the next will need to be co-ordinated and ready in time. Clients and their advisers will need assistance with the new procedures. Administrators may choose to fill in the return themselves, to keep close control or arrange for the trustees' accountant to do so. Administrators will also have to field enquiries from inspectors of taxes. All these tasks involve additional work. Some pensioneer trustees will be able to fulfil this role if their systems are designed to provide the appropriate information. Others may wish to outsource it. Self-assessment of pensions schemes is here to stay, however, and even though most SSASs will be making a 'nil return' in the sense that they have to return all their income and gains with nothing to pay thereon or to reclaim, it will have to be accommodated by all the SSAS trustees and their advisers.

Chapter 9

Funding and Actuarial Matters

Introduction

9.1   It is an IR SPSS requirement for both large and small self-administered schemes to have actuarial valuation reports (AVRs) prepared on the establishment of the scheme, and to submit a copy to IR SPSS together with the application for approval (PN 18.4 and see 3.59). If a full AVR was not prepared at the time the scheme was established, then IR SPSS will expect to receive it later, but meanwhile the informal actuarial advice given on the establishment of the scheme must be provided at the time of application for approval (Section [M] of APPENDIX 17). The reason for this is that IR SPSS wishes to see that the scheme is established properly based on actuarial recommendations for its future funding. The absence of any actuarial advice will mean that the application for approval will not be accepted (see 3.55 and 3.59).

9.2   The company will need to commission an initial AVR from a qualified actuary that sets out the likely cost of establishing the SSAS and recommends the initial contribution rate. In some cases this service may be provided by an in-house actuary. In other cases an actuary may be independently commissioned and may also be the pensioneer trustee. Subsequently triennial AVRs will be needed showing what has happened to the scheme since the last valuation and the actuary's recommendations for future contributions. Mention was made at 2.31 of small schemes administered by LOs where the documentation permits self-administration but where the scheme monies are wholly invested in insurance policies. IR SPSS has given a dispensation to such schemes from submitting full-scale AVRs provided that their only investments are insurance policies taken out with one LO.

Both the Institute of Actuaries and Faculty of Actuaries have guidelines for their members setting out how actuarial reports should be generally prepared (APPENDIX 40), and the aspects IR SPSS will expect to see in initial and subsequent AVRs are explained throughout the rest of this chapter.

Basic details

9.3   In a large scheme the initial AVR usually groups the membership into different classes by age, remuneration etc. and makes an allowance for early leavers. In a SSAS because of the small number of members and their position in the company it is not viable to make an allowance for early leavers, so IR SPSS will expect to see full details of each individual member including name , date of birth, sex, date of commencement of service with the company, normal retirement age and current remuneration. It must be borne in mind that it is open to IR SPSS to check service and remuneration details with the relevant inspectors of taxes, and also with the details given to IR SPSS in respect of other approved schemes of the same employer.

9.4 Further details should be provided in the initial AVR of all benefits under other pension arrangements relating to the members' current employment, and any retained benefits in relation to schemes of previous employers and/or personal pensions and retirement annuity contracts relating to previous employment or periods of self-employment that have to be taken into account in the funding of the scheme. Once again IR SPSS should be in a position to check these benefits or it may be aware of others not mentioned in the initial actuarial report and may enquire about them.

In the case of subsequent AVRs (see 9.56) the actuary will also need to take account of the effects of any earmarking order or pension sharing order that may have been made in respect of a member's benefits following divorce (see 3.95).

Benefits

9.5 IR SPSS is interested in what benefits are being provided for each member of a SSAS. This will be gathered from the initial AVR, the members' announcement letters and the scheme's trust deed and rules. There are two basic reasons why IR SPSS is interested. One is to see if the aim is to provide all members with similar levels of benefits and the other is concerned with the level of funding (i.e. the amounts of contributions to be paid).

9.6 It is important that the levels of retirement and death benefits to be provided for each member are similar. The reason for this is to demonstrate that there is only one class of member in a SSAS and that there is not a second class of members who have been brought in with derisory benefits in comparison to the others to make up the membership to more than eleven to avoid the application of the *SSAS Regulations* to the scheme (e.g. the appointment of a pensioneer trustee, restrictions on loans and other investments etc.).

Actuarial assumptions

9.7 IR SPSS will be looking to see what assumptions the actuary has made regarding the long-term rate of return on scheme investments and increases in remuneration levels and pensions in payment, in determining the contribution levels to the scheme for the future. As a result of the *Pensions Act 1995* requirements, pensions derived from contributions received after 6 April 1997 must increase by 5 per cent per annum or RPI if less (see 11.98, under Limited Price Indexation). What IR SPSS is interested in is the difference between the rate of return on investments and the assumed rate of future increases in remuneration (the 'pre-retirement net yield'), and the difference between the rate of return on investments and the assumed increases to pensions in payment (the 'post-retirement net yield').

9.8 It should also be noted that funding for a surviving spouse's pension payable on the death of a member is not permitted unless the member is already married. From 1 June 1996 funding for a dependant's pension is permitted provided the member has a financial dependant. Where the husband and wife are both members, which is very often the case in a SSAS, only one surviving spouse's pension should be funded based on the entitlement of the member who, from an actuarial point of view, is likely to die first.

Mortality assumptions

9.9 Tables showing life expectation at various ages are compiled from information gathered by LOs and the Government Actuary's Department (GAD). These are used by the actuary to estimate the proportion of members who are likely to die in service and the average length of time that pensions will be paid. The most commonly used table for SSASs is the PA(90) table, rated down by the number of years the actuary believes to be appropriate, which is based on experience of scheme members. IR SPSS considered this to be the most appropriate table in relation to funding SSASs, particularly where it was rated down by no more than two years. However, prior to the introduction of the new method of funding for SSASs in 1996 (see 9.10), actuaries could and did use other mortality tables such as the a(90) and a(55), with adjustments, provided that they could convince IR SPSS that these tables were more appropriate (PSI 20.1.20 to 20.1.23). Under the new method introduced in 1996, actuaries no longer have any choice but to use the PA(90) table rated down two years (see 9.27).

9.10 On 30 May 1996, in Update No 16, IR SPSS introduced new requirements for the funding of SSASs, with effect from 1 June 1996. 'The SSAS 1996 Method', as it is known, applied immediately to SSASs established on or after 1 June 1996. It included transitional arrangements for schemes established before that date which will bring all SSASs under the SSAS 1996 Method by 31 May 2002. Details of all aspects of the SSAS 1996 Method are provided in 9.22 to 9.47 and APPENDIX 41 (as updated in Appendix IX to PN).

9.11 As the vast majority of SSASs are now subject to the SSAS 1996 Method, and all will be by 31 May 2002, details of the funding requirements prior to 1 June 1996 will not be covered in as much detail as in the last edition of this book. A summary of the main aspects is provided in 9.12 to 9.21.

The position prior to 1 June 1996

Actuarial assumptions

9.12 The pre- and post-retirement net yields (see 9.7) that were generally accepted by IR SPSS were at least 0.5% and 2% respectively (SSAS GN 3.10 and 3.12), although IR SPSS would accept other net yields (e.g. 0 per cent and 3 per cent respectively) where it was clear that they would not give rise to an excessive funding rate. Where the assumed rate of post-retirement pension increases was 5% or less, the assumed yield on investments could not be less than 8% i.e. a net yield of no less than 3% (SSAS GN 9.18).

Mortality assumptions

9.13 As with pre- and post-retirement net yields it was up to the actuary to decide which mortality table to use and the appropriate rating down factor, subject to IR SPSS agreement, but in the main the PA(90) table rated down 2 years was used, as already mentioned in 9.9.

Contributions

9.14 The actuary uses the assumptions along with the basic details of the members (see 9.3 and 9.4) and the benefits to be provided (see 9.6), to calculate the present value of those future benefits (i.e. the amount of capital needed now which, with future growth, will be sufficient to provide those benefits at retirement). This present value, less the current value of the assets (if it is a triennial AVR), is the present value of the future contributions required. In most cases this cost would be spread over the life of the scheme as a series of level annual contributions. Because this allows for higher contributions in earlier years when members may have achieved only a few years service, it could lead to excessively high funding levels early on, effectively funding future service in advance. It was to avoid this situation that IR SPSS introduced the SSAS 1996 Method in which annual contributions are calculated as a percentage of the member's remuneration (see 9.25) and are at a much lower level in the earlier years.

9.15 Contributions over and above those recommended by the actuary may be paid to a scheme to enable the trustees to pay premiums towards insurance of death-in-service benefits. Such insured benefits are limited to the capital amount which, when added to the value of scheme assets, is sufficient to provide maximum death-in-service benefits.

9.16 Valuing scheme assets at the date of a triennial AVR is fairly straightforward where the AVR date coincides with the scheme's accounting year-end, as the values from the accounts can be used. Where the two dates do not coincide, the actuary will use the asset values in the most recent accounts and adjust them for interest where appropriate. Alternatively, the scheme year can be changed to coincide with the date of the AVR, subject to IR SPSS agreement.

9.17 The actuary could also make allowances in the calculations for scheme expenses (e.g. administration charges) but not for those relating to investment of the scheme's assets.

Special contributions

9.18 A special contribution (SC) is a payment by the employer, which is not an ordinary annual contribution (OAC). However, because there was no definition of an OAC and because it is quite common in the case of SSASs for contributions to vary year by year (e.g. at certain times the employer may be unable to maintain the same level of contribution, particularly during a recession), it was not always easy to establish whether or not a contribution was an SC or an OAC. It was a commonly held misconception that an SC could be paid to a SSAS on its establishment, or later, equal to the level of the recommended OAC, to be held as a general reserve without it being justified. This was never the case because all SCs must be justified by the actuary. The main reasons for which an SC can be justified are to provide back service benefits, which have not yet been funded for, and to augment benefits already funded for (e.g. to provide cost of living increases to pensions in payment).

9.19 OACs are normally allowable in full for corporation tax purposes for the employer's accounting year in which they are paid. SCs were normally only allowable in full in the year of payment where they, together with all other SCs paid by the employer to all its other exempt approved pension schemes for its employees in that year, did not exceed the greater of:

(a)   a *de minimis* of £25,000; and

(b)   the aggregate of all OACs paid by the employer to all its schemes in that year.

Where the aggregate SC exceeded the greater of (a) and (b) above, the tax relief was spread forward over a number of years (to a maximum of 4 years), unless the SC was to provide cost of living increases to pensions in payment in which case it would be allowed in full in the year of payment. The period of spread was determined solely by the size of the aggregate SC, viz.:

£25,001 to £50,000	2 years
£50,001 to £100,000	3 years
Over £100,000	4 years

9.20   As mentioned in 9.18 and 9.19, the main problem for SSASs was where there was no regular pattern of OACs over at least a three-year period. In such circumstances, any contribution in excess of £25,000 in any year, even if within the level of OAC recommended by the actuary, could have been considered by IR SPSS as an SC and tax relief spread forward.

The High Court judgment in the tax case of *Kelsall v Investment Chartwork Limited [1994] PLR 19* confirmed this by stating that the General Commissioners do not have the power to set aside a direction made by the Inland Revenue under *s 592(6) ICTA 1988* to spread tax relief on a contribution.

9.21   Where the aggregate of SCs to all approved schemes of the employer exceeded both £25,000 and the employer's aggregate OAC to all approved schemes, it had to be notified to IR SPSS, unless the SC was to provide for cost of living increases to pensions in payment. With effect from 1 January 1996 this changed and the payment of SCs is reportable to IR SPSS under *SI 1995 No 3103* (see 3.79).

The position from 1 June 1996

Introduction

9.22   Because of the problems of overfunding that were arising in relation to insured money purchase executive pension plans (EPPs), which were funded on the level annual contribution basis (see 9.14), on 1 September 1994 IR SPSS introduced a new funding basis for EPPs. Under the new requirements contributions must be calculated as an annual percentage of earnings (subject to the earnings cap where relevant) and not the level annual contribution basis. IR SPSS then turned its attention to SSASs.

9.23   The negotiations on the funding of SSASs between the Inland Revenue and the APT were concluded in December 1995 (SSAS GN 3.29). The Inland Revenue had wanted SSASs to be funded on the same revised basis as EPPs. The APT resisted this because of the differences between SSASs and EPPs, i.e. because the members of SSASs are more often that not directors and owners of the company (usually a private company) sponsoring the scheme, for whom remuneration levels and contribution rates can fluctuate in line with fluctuations in company profits. Flexibility was needed to enable companies to catch up on contributions in good years at a higher level than was allowed for by EPPs. The Inland Revenue accepted this, and the APT then accepted the new funding basis with contributions expressed as a percentage of earnings. This greater flexibility was subsequently permitted for EPPs as well (see 9.25).

9.24 The agreement on the future funding of SSASs was published in December 1995 by the APT as an Exposure Draft, setting out the revised basis which was to commence on 1 June 1996. The revised basis (see APPENDIX 41), the 'SSAS 1996 Method', specifies that the percentage of earnings method must be used to determine the maximum permitted contributions for all final salary and money purchase SSASs, instead of the former level annual contribution method. It also changes the actuarial assumptions which can be used (see 9.26) to determine the maximum permitted contributions.

9.25 Under the SSAS 1996 Method the maximum permitted contribution rate is calculated as a percentage of the member's earnings. Although this method and the former level annual contribution method permit similar amounts of contributions to be paid into a SSAS over the whole period of a member's service up to retirement, the SSAS 1996 Method allows much smaller contributions to be paid in the earlier years than the former method and this is only made up for in later years, as illustrated in the table below.

Male, age 30, married, earning £40,000 p.a., no past service

Age	Contribution as % of Current Earnings	Monetary Equivalent
30	31.60	(£12,640)
35	44.12	(£17,650)
40	61.60	(£24,640)
43	75.25	(£30,100)
46	91.90	(£36,760)
49	112.27	(£44,910)
52	137.17	(£54,870)
55	167.55	(£67,020)
58	204.70	(£81,880)

Because the SSAS 1996 Method had a higher target at retirement and the mortality basis was higher than for an EPP, a SSAS could be funded at a level 8% higher than an EPP. IR SPSS announced in PSO Update No 16 that the funding basis introduced for EPPs in 1994 would be revised and brought into line with SSASs as soon as practicable. Broadly similar arrangements to those for SSASs were brought in to effect on 1 June 1996 which can have retrospective effect. The funding assumptions for EPPs can be found in Appendix VIII of PN.

Actuarial assumptions

9.26 The funding assumptions are detailed in APPENDIX 41 (as updated in Appendix IX to PN). These are now on a prescribed basis and the pre- and post-retirement net yields are 1.6% and 3.2% respectively. The post-retirement net yield has created problems because at present inflation-proof annuities cannot be purchased as cheaply as this. For example, if a man retired at 60 and his index-linked pension was purchased immediately from a LO, under the present assumptions, he would fail to maximise his opportunity due to limitations of the funding basis. Representations have been made to the Treasury concerning this denial of the opportunity for a member of a SSAS to fund for the maximum Inland Revenue benefits. Meanwhile, the Inland Revenue has stated the assumptions will be reviewed at the same time as the review of the surplus regulations (see 9.51).

With inflation-proof annuities running at high cost since the SSAS 1996 Method was introduced, and the added impact of the withdrawal of the ability to reclaim credit on advance corporation tax announced in the 1997 Budget, the APT continue to lobby IR SPSS and the GAD for a fairer method to be adopted. At the time of writing it is understood that the GAD will be putting forward its proposals for changes to the surplus regulations early in 2002.

Mortality assumptions

9.27 Under the SSAS 1996 Method, mortality table PA(9∅) rated down two years is to be used.

Contributions

9.28 The actuary carries out the necessary calculations in much the same way as mentioned in 9.14 except that the assumptions and other requirements detailed in APPENDIX 41 (as updated in Appendix IX to PN) must also be taken into account.

Contributions during the three years between each AVR are to be determined by reference to one of the bases described in PN 13.12 (a) or (b). Normally, method (a) will be used (see SSAS GN 3.3 and 3.4) i.e. for specifically targeted benefits based on a proportion of final remuneration.

9.29   Guidance is given in APPENDIX 41 on the current valuation of existing assets and is much the same as mentioned in 9.16.

9.30   As was the case prior to 1 June 1996, where the scheme meets its own expenses the actuary can make an allowance for these in calculating the rate of contributions that can be paid to the scheme (see 9.17).

9.31   Contributions towards insurance of death-in-service benefits may be paid in addition to the contributions being paid to fund retirement benefits. This is the same position as prior to 1 June 1996 (see 9.15).

Special contributions

9.32   The most welcome feature of the SSAS 1996 Method announced in PSO Update No 16 was that, for chargeable periods ending on or after 1 June 1996, any SC of less than £500,000 would not be spread for tax relief purposes.

9.33   All SCs paid to a SSAS for chargeable periods ending on or after 1 June 1996 of £500,000 or more, provided they are actuarially justified, will not be allowed in full as deductions for corporation tax purposes in the chargeable period in which they are paid. They must be calculated in accordance with the formula in APPENDIX 41 (as updated in Appendix IX to PN) and will only be permitted if the value of the fund is less than the maximum permitted value based on service to date. This procedure represents a substantive change from IR SPSS's stance at the time the Exposure Draft was published. At that time it had agreed that all SCs paid to a SSAS from 1 June 1996, regardless of their amount, would be allowed in full as deductions for corporation tax purposes, in the chargeable period in which they were paid, provided SCs of £500,000 or more were cleared in advance with IR SPSS because of possible tax avoidance. It left the position of irregular contributions where the actuary recommends OACs of £500,000 or more still to be clarified (see 9.35).

9.34   SCs of £500,000 or more are to be spread as follows:

£500,000 or over but less than £1,000,000	2 years
£1,000,000 or over but less than £2,000,000	3 years
£2,000,000 or over	4 years

9.35   Although it is unlikely to be a common occurrence, where large contributions of varying amounts are paid to a SSAS, and the actuary has recommended OACs of £500,000 or more, IR SPSS has still to clarify how it will treat such contributions for tax-relief purposes. By way of illustration, it is pertinent to ask what IR SPSS practice will be in the following example, bearing in mind its stated commitment that under the SSAS 1996 Method contributions to make up shortfalls in funding will be allowed in full for tax relief purposes in the periods in which they are paid?:

Year End	Contributions Paid	OAC Recommended by Actuary
31 July 1997	£800,000	£800,000
31 July 1998	£700,000	£800,000
31 July 1999	£700,000	£800,000
31 July 2000	£515,000	£515,000*
31 July 2001	£350,000	£535,000
31 July 2002	£600,000	£535,000

*Funding changed to the SSAS 1996 Method.

Will IR SPSS treat the contributions paid in the three years to 31 July 2002 as SCs because no regular pattern of OACs has been established, and spread the contribution of £600,000 paid in the year to 31 July 2002 over two years? The position should be watched closely until IR SPSS clarifies how it will treat irregular contributions in these circumstances.

9.36 Whilst dealing with IR SPSS's power of spreading under *s 592(6)*, it should be noted that *FA 1993, s 112(5)* makes it clear that for accounting purposes any payment treated under *s 592(6), ICTA 1988* as spread over a period of years, is to be treated as actually paid at the time when it is treated as paid in accordance with *subsection 6.*

9.37 As part of the initial application for approval of a SSAS, PN 18.4 mentions that IR SPSS will want to know how the contributions paid to the scheme have been invested (see 3.59).

9.38 The reporting requirements for SCs are as detailed in 3.79.

Transitional arrangements

9.39 For SSASs established before 1 June 1996 there are transitional arrangements set out in APPENDIX 41 (as updated in Appendix IX to PN) to phase in the 1996 method of funding. Such SSASs have until 1 June 2001 or, if later, the effective date of the second actuarial valuation after 31 May 1996. All SSASs will therefore be phased in by 31 May 2002 at the latest. SSASs established after 31 May 1996 have to adopt the new basis of funding from their establishment. However, there is nothing to prevent an existing SSAS after 31 May 1996 adopting the SSAS 1996 Method at any time thereafter.

9.40   During the transitional period the following events will trigger a full move to the SSAS 1996 Method:

(a)   new members join the SSAS;

(b)   SCs are paid after 31 May 1996 which were recommended by an actuary after 1 December 1995 (the date of announcement of the SSAS 1996 Method);

(c)   higher contributions are made than the limit in the last actuarial valuation; or

(d)   undisclosed retained benefits come to light.

At (a) above, the funding of any current members' benefits may remain on the former funding basis as long as (c) above does not apply.

At (b) above, a SC recommended prior to 1 December 1995 may be paid after 31 May 1996 without triggering a move to the SSAS 1996 Method.

The higher contributions at (c) above are likely to be where members' remuneration has increased substantially.

At (d) above, trivial retained benefits which do not exceed £260 in aggregate when expressed in terms of pension, or lump sums of £2,500 in aggregate for Pre–1987 members, need not be taken into account.

9.41   A replacement SSAS can have the benefits of the transitional arrangements only if one of the reasons for continued rights set out in PN Appendix III applies. The transitional arrangements are also available where an employer converts an existing insured money purchase scheme (e.g. an EPP) to, or replaces such a scheme by, a SSAS before 1 June 1996. If someone becomes a member of a SSAS who was a member of an insured scheme before 1 September 1994 he or she may be able to benefit from the transitional arrangements until 1 September 1999.

9.42   PSO Update No 16 explains the application of the transitional arrangements to insured money purchase schemes converting to or being replaced by a SSAS on or after 1 June 1996. If the insured money purchase scheme was established prior to 1 September 1994 it must bring its funding level fully into line with the funding basis for EPPs by 1 September 1999. When it converts to or is replaced by a SSAS on or after 1 June 1996, because it would not have the benefit of the full SSAS transitional basis, it must bring its funding fully into line with the SSAS 1996 Method by 1 September 1999 or an earlier triggering event.

Where the insured money purchase scheme was established on or after 1 September 1994 it will already be subject to the funding basis for EPPs. On its conversion to or replacement by a SSAS it should move straightaway to the SSAS 1996 Method.

9.43   Originally, no check against the SSAS 1996 Method was required where the total annual contributions to all schemes, excluding contributions for death-in-service benefits, for the same employment did not exceed the higher of:

(a)   15% of remuneration up to the earnings cap; and

(b)   6% of the earnings cap rounded up to the next £1,000 (but not exceeding 100 per cent of remuneration for the same period);

subject to contributions, including SCs, not having been at a higher amount than the figure determined from this limit in any earlier year.

There was no corresponding *de minimis* limit for SCs.

9.44   Following an Inland Revenue ruling, this *de minimis* rule was withdrawn with effect from 31 March 1998 (for insured schemes) and 31 July 1998 (for SSASs) on the grounds that it had been abused. The Inland Revenue had previously contended that the rule had been used to promote artificially high levels of contributions, and felt that its warnings had been ignored.

9.45   The following new *de minimis* limit was announced in PSO Update No 42 (as amended by PSO Update No 48):

'No check against the maximum funding rate is required where the annual aggregate contributions to all schemes, excluding contributions for death-in- service benefits, for the same employment do not exceed 17.5% of remuneration (within the earnings cap), subject to contributions (including special contributions) not having been at a higher amount than the figures determined from the limit in any earlier year.

There is no corresponding *de minimis* limit for special contributions.'

9.46   The same *de minimis* limit applies to SSASs from 31 July 1998 (PSO Update No 47, Part III), with the following rider:

'(Contributions to free-standing AVC schemes must be taken into account for this purpose).'

However, this rider does not appear in Appendix IX to PN.

9.47   Compliance with the SSAS 1996 Method is monitored under IR SPSS's compliance audit function. Schemes will be chosen for checking partly on a selective and partly on a random basis.

Triennial AVRs – investments

9.48   Most AVRs provide details of the value of the investments at the valuation date. If only a total value is provided or a total is provided under a particular heading, e.g. property, IR SPSS is likely to request a breakdown or schedule of the investments concerned if it is not aware via the reporting procedures of what comprises this total. The reasons for this are clearly to see if the investments themselves are acceptable and also if there have been any changes as the absence of an asset probably indicates its sale, and IR SPSS may request details. It is only possible between triennial AVRs for assets to be acquired and disposed of without IR SPSS's knowledge in respect of assets that do not have to be reported. However, IR SPSS has been asking for some time now for details of investments at intervals of less than three years particularly since PSO Update No 9 confirmed that enquiries into the affairs of SSASs, including AVRs, would be more selective with greater in-depth examination in some cases.

The time limit within which these enquiries would be made was set at 12 months from receipt of the AVR or other notification of an investment. However, with the introduction of self assessment for SSASs (see 12.2), IR SPSS has brought this time limit into line with those under self assessment legislation, i.e. 12 months from the filing date for the return for the tax year in which the effective date of the AVR falls (Pensions Update No 98).

Triennial AVRs – funding

9.49 Having checked that the actuary's net yield assumptions meet its guidelines, IR SPSS will look at the overall funding position including whether other schemes of the employer, retained benefits and transfers into the scheme have been taken into account. It is particularly interested in whether the scheme has been under- or over-funded and what the actuary's recommendations are for dealing with such situations. It is also interested in those cases where the purchase of a member's and/or dependant's annuity has been deferred until age 75 where the actuary's review of the pension payable must form part of the triennial AVR. This must take the form of a renewal certificate confirming the outcome of the review.

9.50 As regards under-funding, the reasons for the deficiency ought not to create problems with IR SPSS unless there has been a lack of contributions which may involve spreading, or a substantial increase in salaries the level of which IR SPSS can always check with the inspector of taxes. The actuary's recommendations to eliminate the deficiency will attract IR SPSS's attention and it will probably ask if the recommendations have been implemented. A shortfall may well be made up by an increase in contributions, but if this involves a special contribution it needs to be justified.

9.51 It is the over-funded position that attracts greater attention from IR SPSS. This is because in any self-administered scheme the Inland Revenue does not approve of the tax-free build up of assets in excess of the scheme's liabilities. Fortunately, most SSASs are unlikely to become over-funded because of their nature and the introduction of the SSAS 1996 Method. They have been exempted from the requirement to submit a certificate or AVR on the prescribed basis contained in the surplus legislation enacted in 1986. The exemption is contained in *Regulation 3(2)(a)* of the *Pension Schemes Surpluses (Valuation) Regulations 1987 (SI 1987 No 412)*. However, some SSASs do become over-funded during their lifetime or on winding-up and several aspects related to these situations will be considered in detail.

Surpluses

9.52   As the prescribed basis of valuation is not normally used for SSASs (see SSAS GN 3.6), IR SPSS adopts the criteria it has always used for this type of scheme if an over-funded situation is disclosed in a triennial AVR. These criteria may be summarised as follows.

(a)   Is the over-funding substantial?

(b)   How has it arisen?

(c)   What recommendations has the actuary made to reduce it?

(d)   Have those recommendations been adopted?

9.53   IR SPSS's rule of thumb regarding the level at which a SSAS is over-funded appears to be 5% in excess of the liabilities, which coincides with the 105% level on the prescribed basis under the *surplus Regulations* (see also PSO Update No 50). If the surplus is not substantial IR SPSS may simply ask if the actuary's recommendations have been adopted. If there is more than one member in the scheme and members have individual contribution credits (i.e. 'notional' shares of the scheme assets), calculated by the actuary, some of which are in surplus and others which disclose deficiencies, then the overall funding position should be taken into account by IR SPSS in determining the level of any over-funding.

9.54   Much depends on the reason for any substantial over-funding as to whether IR SPSS will pursue this aspect. A drop in salary or a member leaving service are unlikely to give rise to searching enquiries. However, an increase in the value of the fund in excess of the actuarial assumptions may generate questions from IR SPSS. In 6.27 mention was made of a surplus arising because a property had increased appreciably in value or been sold following the granting of planning permission. Such a gain would be protected from taxation because of a scheme's approved status and IR SPSS is likely to accept the surplus has been properly dealt with if the actuary's recommendations meet its requirements (see 9.55). Frequent sales of property at a substantial profit could attract the attention of the inspector of taxes who may deem the trustees to be engaged in trading activities which would be taxable (see 8.10).

Reduction of surpluses

9.55 The actuary's recommendations for reducing a surplus should be acceptable to IR SPSS. The following recommendations would be acceptable to IR SPSS (see *Sch 22 para 3(3), ICTA 1988*):

(a)   suspension or reduction of company contributions for up to five years;

(b)   suspension or reduction of members' contributions for up to five years;

(c)   improving existing benefits;

(d)   providing new benefits;

(e)   a repayment to the company;

(f)   such other ways as may be prescribed by regulations made by the Inland Revenue.

So far as a repayment to the company is concerned the trustees have been given specific obligations by the *Pensions Act 1995, s 37* (see 11.89) although these are unlikely to have much impact on SSASs.

Opra published a booklet ('Opra NOTE 3') in June 1998 which addresses the matter of surpluses. It is entitled the 'Pensions Act 1995. Payment of surplus—Opra's role' and it details the procedures, notices and the use of modification orders when considering the payment of surplus monies to employers from an ongoing scheme and from a scheme which is winding-up.

9.56 Improving existing benefits or providing new ones may involve increases in pensions or additional benefits. Rule changes may be needed before they are implemented. New members could of course be introduced. Where a SSAS has more than one member it should be possible, subject to scheme rules, to reallocate the surplus in respect of a member's 'notional' share of the assets to that of another member whose 'notional' share is insufficient to provide maximum benefits. If increases to pensions in payment are to be awarded from a surplus, the building up of funds for the purpose of increasing pensions in payment must be restricted to schemes where the rules provide for reviews of pensions in payment and for increases. If there are no such rules, a general augmentation provision may not be sufficient in these circumstances.

9.57 In a SSAS the most common actuarial recommendation for an ongoing scheme is to reduce or suspend company contributions. It would be rare for a refund to be recommended as a first resort. Having satisfied itself on the recommendations to reduce any substantial surplus, IR SPSS will ask if the recommendations have been adopted. IR SPSS holds the trump card here because, as PN 13.25 mentions, if large surpluses are held approval may be withdrawn from the scheme unless acceptable proposals are forthcoming for dealing with the situation. This could mean approval being withdrawn from the part of the fund which is over-funded or any surplus being returned to the company and taxed. This is one of the few instances where the surplus legislation applies to SSASs and it would involve a valuation on the basis prescribed in *Sch 22(2), ICTA 1988* and possibly part approval under *Sch 22(7)*.

Winding-up

9.58 A refund of a surplus to the company from a SSAS is more likely to occur where the scheme is being wound-up rather than in an on-going situation. If a surplus is left over in this situation after all benefits up to the maximum permitted are paid out and no prospect exists of new members joining, then repayment must be made to the company and tax deducted at 35% (*s 601(1)* as amended by *FA 2001*). As with all schemes where refunds are to be made, IR SPSS must be approached first so arrangements for remittance of the tax involved can be made. If a final salary SSAS is involved the provisions of the *Pensions Act 1995, s 76* will also apply (see 11.98). Provided a scheme is not being replaced, a valuation on the prescribed basis is not required (PN 13.35) because the amount involved is what remains in the scheme and is ascertained.

9.59 It is uncommon for refunds to be made from schemes which have not yet been approved unless they are being wound-up because IR SPSS has refused to approve them or their approval has been withdrawn. IR SPSS refuses to allow refunds from schemes which have applied for approval, but have not yet been approved. This is in line with PN 13.20 which requires notification to IR SPSS in advance of any refunds.

9.60 Finally, on the tax charge of 35% itself, this is totally free-standing and cannot be set off against losses. It is deducted at source and accounted for by the trustees to the Inland Revenue.

Submission of AVRs to IR SPSS

9.61 In recent years there has been a considerable tightening up in IR SPSS's attitude to delays in submitting triennial AVRs and details of current investments. Procedures were tightened up following the issue of *SI 1995 No 3103* (see 9.64).

9.62   In the past IR SPSS sent reminders for triennial AVRs six months after their effective date and asked for investment details. There would follow reminders depending upon whether investment details were provided or the reason for the delay was explained. Twelve months after the effective date 30 days notice would be given that IR SPSS would write to the managing trustees if the AVR was not forthcoming. Failure to respond would entail the managing trustees being requested to provide the outstanding AVR and a list of assets. If these details were not submitted within 30 days the scheme's approval would be seriously prejudiced or, if it was not approved, IR SPSS would assume the application for approval had been withdrawn. If that deadline was reached without response, approval could be expected to be withdrawn or the application for approval would be assumed to be withdrawn.

9.63   A tightening up of the procedures was introduced in November 1992 following the report of the National Audit Office in 1991 and the Public Accounts Committee's view that delays in obtaining AVRs were unacceptably long. AVRs were still expected to be produced within one year of their due date and to include a full list of the assets of the scheme. However, IR SPSS no longer required a list of assets in advance of the AVR, except in exceptional cases. It sent reminders for triennial AVRs nine months after their effective date. If an AVR was still outstanding one year from its due date, IR SPSS then wrote to the practitioner and trustees warning them that if the AVR was not produced within one month withdrawal of the scheme's approval would be considered or, if the scheme was not yet approved, the application for approval would be considered as withdrawn.

9.64   A further tightening up of the procedures occurred with the issue of PSO Update No 9 and *SI 1995 No 3103*. These latter regulations make it mandatory to provide AVRs for SSASs to IR SPSS without notice or request no more than one year after their effective date, where the effective date is 1 January 1996 or later. IR SPSS can charge penalties for not submitting AVRs at the prescribed time under *TMA 1970, s 98*. Nevertheless, this power does not preclude the possibility of withdrawing tax approval whenever the circumstances warrant it.

9.65   In the interest of customer service IR SPSS has been prepared to issue reminders to the practitioner and to the administrator before an AVR becomes overdue. The first formal notification to the administrator will be sent nine months after the effective date, followed by a reminder to the administrator one month before the due date (see PSO Update No 22). A week or so after the due date a warning is sent to the administrator that unless the AVR is received within 30 days, withdrawal of approval will be considered, or in the case of a scheme not yet approved that the application for approval has been withdrawn. Finally, if the AVR is still not received, a final warning is issued to the administrator that if the AVR is not received within 30 days, approval will be withdrawn from a stated date.

9.66　In November 2000 IR SPSS reduced the reminding process from the four stages mentioned in 9.65 to three, as a work saving measure (PSO Update No 79). The stage that was removed was the one a week or so after the due date for submission of the AVR. In addition the final warning is now issued to the administrator and the trustees (and a copy to practitioners), one month after the due date.

9.67　At the time of writing IR SPSS is proposing to reduce the reminders for AVRs even further, possibly to a single reminder or possibly to scrap it all together, The APT has been asked for comments and it is hoped that the reminder system will be retained in some form.

9.68　If approval is withdrawn because of the delay it can be expected to be effective from a date one year after the due date of the AVR. However, withdrawal of approval could precede the date of the warning letter and may be from any earlier date if justified by other features of the scheme unacceptable to IR SPSS. Once approval has been withdrawn it will not be re-instated even if the AVR is eventually produced.

9.69　If a SSAS that has not yet been approved is involved and tax approval is still required, a fresh application for approval will be required. Tax approval in these cases will not pre-date the beginning of the year in which the fresh application is made, nor will it be forthcoming until all information is received and all facts relating to the scheme are satisfactory for IR SPSS purposes.

9.70　Another point to note is that from 29 August 1995 IR SPSS no longer acknowledges the receipt of an AVR. This has been reiterated on 30 June 2000 in PSO Update No 67. In PSO Update No 9 IR SPSS explained that the absence of such an acknowledgement does not denote acceptance of the AVR. IR SPSS reserves the right to open enquiries within the time limit mentioned in 9.48 and to call for supporting evidence in such cases. This means that if no enquiries are commenced within the time limit practitioners are entitled to take it that IR SPSS has accepted the AVR. If IR SPSS makes enquiries after the time limit has elapsed IR SPSS should be politely and firmly reminded of its statements in PSO Update No 9 and PSO Update No 98.

9.71　Fortunately, the situation need not get so serious, although actuaries are well aware of the delays that can occur in obtaining information from trustees, companies and their accountants to enable triennial AVRs to be prepared. IR SPSS has made it plain to the APT that it is in the interests of both advisers and trustees, where delay is likely in producing and submitting

AVRs, to inform IR SPSS of the reasons and at least to provide details of the current investments in the meantime if they have been requested, and not to wait until the AVR is prepared before doing so. IR SPSS has further stated that its actions will depend on the particular circumstances of a scheme. Where good reasons for delays have been provided, for instance where a scheme's future is uncertain because of the receivership or liquidation of the company, IR SPSS will hopefully accept the situation. IR SPSS would expect to be informed of such circumstances so it can then consider varying its usual procedures. IR SPSS is also prepared to accept AVRs based on unaudited accounts and to consider an AVR after four or five years if the triennial AVR is long overdue.

9.72   In PSO Update No 53(2), IR SPSS granted a concession to SSASs that are winding up. If the SSAS completes winding up within 12 months of the effective date of the AVR, IR SPSS will be prepared to dispense with the need to produce the AVR.

Chapter 10

Withdrawal of Approval and Penalties

Introduction

10.1 IR SPSS's power to withdraw a scheme's tax exempt approval has been mentioned in several places in this book. This chapter explains what withdrawal of approval entails for SSASs and covers the most important aspects of withdrawal of approval. It also covers *FA 1994, ss 105, 106* which introduced penalties for failing to produce or preserve information and for false statements. It should be borne in mind that any type of exempt approved scheme may have its approval withdrawn, therefore the following points concerning withdrawal of approval do not apply solely to SSASs unless specifically mentioned.

Legislation

10.2 The Inland Revenue has discretionary powers not only to approve pension schemes, but also to withdraw that approval. The authority to withdraw approval was first contained in *FA 1970, s 19(3)*. Withdrawal may be made on such grounds and from such date as may be specified in the notice that is issued pursuant to that Act. In the past there had been some doubts as to IR SPSS's (then the PSO's) power to withdraw approval retrospectively. An amendment was contained in *F(No 2)A 1987, Sch 3 (2)*. This legislation gave the Inland Revenue the power to withdraw approval from a date not earlier than 17 March 1987 (the date of the Chancellor's Budget speech) or the date when approval ceased to be justified (whichever fell later). These provisions were incorporated in *s 590(5), ICTA 1988*. However, as there were apparently still some doubts regarding the Inland Revenue's power to withdraw approval, *s 590(5)* was replaced by a new provision, *s 591(B)(1) (FA 1991, s 36(2))* which is the current authority for withdrawing approval for offences committed up to 1 November 1994 relating to SSAS. It means that if the offence giving rise to the Inland Revenue's decision to withdraw a scheme's approval occurred prior to 17 March 1987, the effective date of withdrawal would be 17 March 1987 and no earlier. It should also be noted that a scheme's approval cannot be withdrawn from a date earlier than the effective date of approval.

10.3 On 2 November 1994 the Inland Revenue announced further legislative changes to counter 'trust-busting' of approved pension schemes. An explanation of trust-busting and the background to the legislation may be found in 10.11 and the Press Release (APPENDIX 42). *FA 1995, s 61* amended *s 591, ICTA 1988* by inserting *ss 591C* and *591D* covering the power to withdraw tax approval from 2 November 1994 for offences committed on or after that date. *S 591C* imposes a tax charge on withdrawal of approval of 40% of the value of the fund on the scheme administrator. This tax charge is explained in detail in 10.34 to 10.36. It applies before all the other taxation implications of withdrawal apply (see 10.37 to 10.52), so its effects are much more draconian than the legislation applicable up to 1 November 1994.

10.4 Because of further attempts at trust-busting *s 591C* and *D* was amended by *FA 1998, s 92* with effect from 17 March 1998. Attempts were made to circumvent the 40% tax charge under *s 591C* (see 10.23 to 10.27 for an example). PSO Update No 41 (2) explained that loss of approval might be engineered to allow the scheme assets to be transferred offshore and taken outside the normal pension rules. As this undermines the purpose for which tax reliefs are given the tax charge in *s 591C* has been extended for schemes losing their approval from 17 March 1998 to circumstances where the scheme that has ceased to be approved (not necessarily a SSAS) has received a transfer from another approved occupational or personal pension scheme, or RAC, for a controlling director or a person whose earnings are chargeable to tax under Schedule D.

10.5 The provisions of *s 591C, ICTA 1988* do not extend to all approved pension schemes however. It encompasses schemes which either:

(a) immediately before the date of cessation of approval had less than 12 members; or

(b) in the year before approval ceased had as a member someone who was in that year, or had been, a controlling director of a company that had at any time paid contributions to the scheme.

A member for this purpose includes someone with benefits that have accrued under the scheme and have not been secured or transferred, those persons currently in service or with benefits in payment.

It can be seen that this legislation is aimed mainly at SSAS, but it also encompasses insured schemes either with less than 12 members or with controlling director members. Occupational schemes which are outside the categories of membership at (a) and (b) above that lose their tax approval will not be subject to the 40% tax charge, but will be liable to the tax implications ensuing from withdrawal of approval by virtue of *s 591B(1)*.

Reasons for withdrawal

10.6   *Section 591B(1)* states that the notice of withdrawal of approval should be sent to the administrator and that the grounds for withdrawal may be specified in the notice. It would be most unusual for IR SPSS not to state the reasons for withdrawing approval of a particular scheme unless they were obvious. If the reasons are not stated IR SPSS should be asked to justify its decision. If withdrawal of approval is on the grounds that the circumstances no longer warrant the scheme's tax exempt status details of the circumstances should be requested.

10.7   Withdrawal of approval is a serious step and one not met with too frequently. For instance the National Audit Office Survey of 1991 mentioned that approval was withdrawn from only 64 schemes in the five years to 1991. SSAS GN 6.1 however mentions that the majority of schemes that have their approval withdrawn are SSAS. Until 1 January 1996 (see 10.56 to 10.69) it was the only punitive measure available to the PSO (now IR SPSS) to counter unacceptable features. There is no exhaustive list of 'offences' that warrant withdrawal of approval, but PN 19.2, and the National Audit Office Survey at Appendix 2, PSI 19 and SSAS GN 6.1 give an indication of the circumstances that may cause a scheme's approval to be withdrawn. These are serious breaches of the rules, substantial over-funding, persistent failure by the administrator to furnish information or meet the scheme's tax liabilities and the use of the scheme for tax avoidance (see 10.9). Breaches of the rules could include payment of excessive or unauthorised benefits. Failure to furnish information on a SSAS could embrace details of the investments or non-production of an actuarial report (SSAS GN 6.1(b)), although such misdemeanours are more likely after 1 January 1996 to precipitate a penalty rather than withdrawal of approval. SSAS GN6.1(a) and (c) also mentions that failure to comply with the regulatory requirements concerning loans or to appoint or re-appoint a pensioneer trustee are the most common reasons for withdrawal of approval from a SSAS. Failure to appoint a pensioneer trustee immediately on the resignation of the former pensioneer trustee (see 2.38) after 6 April 1998 will also lead to loss of tax approval. Failure to comply with the *Regulations* after 5 August 1991 may also lead to the loss of approval, as would failure to secure a pension by age 75 if the rule allowing the securing of pensions to that age has been adopted (see 4.95). PN 20.58 also states that failure by the trustees to act in the best interests of the members regarding loans (see 5.34 and Case 14 National Audit Office Survey Appendix 2) and back-to-back loans (see PN 20.61, 5.6 and Case 12 National Audit Office Survey Appendix 2) may also be grounds for the withdrawal of approval. Tax approval also lapsed if a SSAS approved prior to 5 August 1991 did not incorporate the provisions of the *Regulations* into its definitive documentation by 5 August 1994 (see 3.21).

10.8   In 9.57 it was mentioned that failure to reduce a substantial surplus could lead to loss of approval and that following tightening up by IR SPSS over production of investment details and triennial valuations such precipitate action might be taken, even though the imposition of penalties may also be appropriate. The unauthorised winding-up of a SSAS colloquially known as 'trust-busting' (see 10.3 AND 10.11), will also result in removal of its tax exempt status. If a SSAS deliberately seeks unapproved status, e.g. by going offshore, it may entail the pensioneer trustee losing its status also (see 2.35).

10.9   PN 19.2 does not specifically mention that approval would be withdrawn if the scheme's *bona fides* or the sole provision of relevant benefits test were not met. However, as IR SPSS would not exercise its discretionary power to approve a scheme in these circumstances then it must be taken that approval would be withdrawn. This area is most relevant to a SSAS, because if it is used deliberately as a vehicle to achieve tax avoidance (see 10.7 and 10.10) or non-relevant benefits are provided, e.g. loans to members (see 5.6) or directly linked pension mortgages (see 7.64), approval is likely to be withdrawn. IR SPSS is also very concerned about the making of injudicious loans by SSASs. They have written to the APT at length about this practice, and will be publishing tough new guidelines on loans to employer companies and associated companies. The Compliance Section of IR SPSS spends over 50% of its time investigating loans by SSASs, and over 90% of such loans are made on an unsecured basis. Loans must be prudent at the time they are made, and should not be made to companies that are not in a position to repay them. Clearly the trustees must be satisfied that a company's trading accounts demonstrate that it is in a sound position to repay monies, should a loan be made. Subordinated loan agreements are also prohibited, as announced in PSO Update No 31.

10.10   Mention is made in 2.3 that the continuation of approval would be dependent on the sole purpose test in *s 590(2)(a), ICTA 1988* being maintained. Not only do PN 1.1 and 1.4 mention that where a scheme is involved or used for the purpose of tax avoidance will its approval be prejudiced, but PSI 2.2.2 to 2.2.7 do so as well. They mention that establishing a pension scheme provides the opportunity for reducing tax liabilities, but if contributions are not excessive in relation to the emerging benefits and the scheme is not otherwise used to obtain an unacceptable tax advantage this will be accepted as legitimate tax avoidance. PSI also warns that pension schemes may be used to obtain tax advantages that Parliament did not intend to give. It highlights IR SPSS's concern about scheme investments and that SSAS are looked at more closely in this connection because the trustees and indirectly the company control the investments. Finally on tax avoidance, PSI warns that its guidance cannot be comprehensive and that techniques can be very sophisticated, often involving the exploitation of novel or unique situations to avoid, reduce or delay the taxation of profits, gains or earnings. IR SPSS examiners and inspectors of taxes are clearly on the lookout in this area, a fact reinforced by the wider review of the Inland Revenue, announced during the Budget speech of 2 July 1997, of the whole area of leakage and avoidance of direct taxes. In view of the absence of a definition of unacceptable tax avoidance by IR SPSS (see 2.45), the definition provided in 2.46 of acceptable and unacceptable tax avoidance is recommended to practitioners where loss of approval is threatened on the grounds of tax avoidance.

Trust-Busting

10.11 During 1994 some financial advisers were actively encouraging the trustees of SSAS to amend their scheme rules in a way that would force the loss of tax approval. Others were advising SSAS to encash scheme investments and take them offshore so the members could have access to the funds and wind-up the scheme contrary to the rules. APPENDIX 42 adds that the Inland Revenue was encountering arrangements which initially involved taking advantage of the tax reliefs, but later engineering loss of tax approval when access to the scheme funds was desired by the members or the sponsoring company. Any one of these arrangements, if carried through, would be unauthorised winding-up of the scheme, hence the name 'trust-busting'.

10.12 Sadly, trust-busting is still with us, and some pensioneer trustees appear to be complicit in taking business off those who refuse to get involved in the matter. However, the Inland Revenue has identified some of the miscreants, and the APT has disassociated itself from such activities. It is the view of the APT that it would be helpful if the activity were to be regulated by the PIA/FSA. Any such undertaking would then be unlawful and perpetrators could be prosecuted. The Inland Revenue and the APT are awaiting developments.

10.13 Two recent developments are PATs and PLTAs. PATs are private annuity trusts, and advertisers have promised excessive tax-free lump sum payments to investors. IR SPSS does not accept that PATs are acceptable investments and have not approved them for use by SSASs. PLTAs are purpose loan trust arrangements. They are trust-busting schemes and care should be taken if they are encountered.

10.14 The tax approval system for pension schemes is clearly not intended to be used in this manner. It offends the *bona fide* principle of pension schemes. If a scheme wishes to take advantage of the tax reliefs, it must accept all the conditions on which approval is granted. A pensioneer trustees' status with IR SPSS would also be at risk if he or she were to agree to winding-up a scheme contrary to the rules. Any pensioneer trustee must therefore resist such moves and advise against them. If the other trustees nonetheless go ahead with any trust-busting the pensioneer trustee has no option since 7 April 1998 (see 2.38) but to inform IR SPSS.

10.15   In view of the increase in trust-busting by pension schemes where the members were predominantly directors with controlling interests in the sponsoring company and were also the scheme trustees, the Inland Revenue introduced *s 591C, ICTA 1988* and the 40% tax charge to discourage such practices.

10.16   In PSO Update No 6(7) the following reasons were given as causes for withdrawal of a scheme's tax approval:

(a)   where the rules fail to comply with regulations; or

(b)   by exercise of the PSO's (now IR SPSS's) discretion; or

(c)   because an alteration to the scheme which requires IR SPSS's agreement is made without such approval.

The reasons at (*a*) to (*c*) are covered by the examples given in 10.7 to 10.10.

10.17   The winding-up of a SSAS in accordance with its rules will not of itself cause loss of tax approval and imposition of the 40% tax charge. This is provided it is agreed unanimously by all the trustees to wind-up in accordance with the rules. There will be problems though if the trustees, other than the pensioneer trustee, wind-up the scheme in accordance with the rules and there is no doubt that if all the trustees, including the pensioneer trustee, agree to terminate a SSAS contrary to its rules, the SSAS will lose its approval, the 40% tax charge will be raised and the pensioneer trustee's status will be forfeit (see 10.12).

10.18   It was felt that the legislation effective from 2 November 1994 had done enough to deter trust-busting, but during 1995 trust-busting arrangements were being promoted which purported to avoid the 40% tax charge. PSO Update No 10 mentions these arrangements involved paying a transfer value from an existing approved scheme to a new scheme established by a newly incorporated or pre-existing company, the latter occasionally being dormant. After the transfer had been paid the new scheme was transferred offshore immediately and operated as a FURBS. These arrangements appeared to circumvent the 40% tax charge. As a result, where such arrangements are considered by IR SPSS to be artificially contrived, taking or having taken part in them is likely to lead to withdrawal of tax approval from the originating scheme with effect from the date on which the transfer payment was made to the new scheme. This will entail the 40% tax charge being raised on the value of the assets of the originating scheme immediately prior to the transfer.

10.19 As a result of these trust-busting arrangements the PSO (now IR SPSS) introduced an administrative measure from 1 November 1995 as a further deterrent. In fact the PSO Deputy Controller at the time was on record as saying that the PSO wishes 'to tell people that it will come down like a ton of bricks on anyone involved in this sort of thing. They will have all their other tax affairs investigated much more closely'.

10.20 The administrative measure has become firm practice: the prior written consent of IR SPSS must be obtained before making any transfer payment to a SSAS from any tax approved occupational or personal pension schemes, including those awaiting approval, from any FSAVCs, from any RAC or statutory scheme.

10.21 In an endeavour to speed up the processing of transfer payment requests, transfer forms for SSASs were introduced by PSO Update No 93 with effect from 6 April 2001, coded PS 7050F and PS 7050T. Details are given in 4.62.

Effects of withdrawal

10.22 In April 1997 it became apparent from the report of the hearing in the High Court of *R v IRC ex parte Roux Waterside Inn [1997] STC 781,* the *Roux* case, that the trust-busting arrangements described in 10.18 and the measures taken by the PSO (referred to later as IR SPSS) to counter such cases in 10.19 to 10.21 were respectively connected with the result of the *Roux* case.

The Roux case

10.23 Mr and Mrs Roux's company established an insured pension scheme for them which by 1995 was worth around £1.3m. Mr Roux did not want to secure his pension from a LO when he retired and pay tax on his pension. He also wished to avoid the 40% tax charge under *s 591C, ICTA 1988* on the value of the pension fund should approval be withdrawn if his pension was not secured from a LO. So a tax planning exercise was put into operation whereby a SSAS was set up for another of his companies for which approval was sought from the Inland Revenue. He then requested a transfer of his benefits of around £900,000 from the insured scheme to the SSAS. On 1 August 1995 he ceased to be a paid director of the applicant company and to be in pensionable employment for the purpose of the insured scheme. Three weeks later his benefits in the insured scheme were transferred to the SSAS, but at the same time the trustees of the SSAS, including the pensioneer trustee, were removed and replaced by Guernsey-based trustees who amended the SSAS rules to make it incapable of approval.

10.24 When the Inland Revenue became aware of these arrangements it concluded they were an artificial device to extract the value of Mr Roux's benefits from the insured scheme to avoid the restrictions imposed on it as a condition of approval and to invest the benefits in the new scheme where they could be made available to the member without restrictions. So the Inland Revenue exercised its discretion under *s 591B, ICTA 1988* and withdrew approval from the insured scheme from the date of transfer and refused to approve the SSAS. This gave rise to a 40% tax charge under *s 591C* on the value of the funds of the insured scheme immediately prior to the transfer, which included Mrs Roux's share of the fund too. The tax charge fell on Mr Roux's company as the sole trustee of the scheme that would have to pay the 40% tax, although £900,000 had been removed from its trusteeship.

10.25 Mr Roux had apparently been advised that no occupational pension scheme would lose its tax approval if the trustee acted in accordance with its trust deed and rules as this was Inland Revenue practice. So the applicant company applied for judicial review to quash the Inland Revenue's decision to withdraw approval from the insured scheme on the grounds that the Inland Revenue's exercise of discretion to withdraw approval was an abuse of its power. In the High Court judgment, however, it was stated this was not a case purely of administration, but that the Inland Revenue was entitled to look at the overall effects of the tax avoidance scheme, i.e. the avoidance of the 40% tax charge on the whole funds and the tax on the eventual annuity. The tax avoidance principles laid down in *Furniss v Dawson [1981] STC 276* and *Ramsay (WT) Ltd v IRC [1982] AC 300* were adopted in deciding the *Roux* case on the basis that the arrangements were artificially contrived with the object of avoiding payment of tax (but see 10.30). The Inland Revenue was therefore justified in withdrawing approval from the insured scheme. A claim that the Inland Revenue had acted unreasonably in relation to Mrs Roux, who was only a member and not a trustee of the insured scheme and whose fund had been left behind to suffer the 40% tax charge, was dismissed.

10.26 Two relevant side issues of the *Roux* case are worthy of mention. At the time the offending transfer and rule amendment were made the Inland Revenue's statement of practice was not that a pension scheme would not lose its approval if the trustees acted in accordance with the terms of the scheme's trust deed and rules. All pension schemes must meet the requirements of *s 590(2)(a), ICTA 1988* to obtain and retain approval. This is the *bona fide* test acknowledged by the Inland Revenue in its statement of practice. So, if a pension scheme has a duality of purpose, e.g. tax avoidance, it would lose its tax approval even if the trustees complied with the provisions of its trust deed and rules. So the tightening up of the Inland Revenue's statement of practice on 1 November 1995 (see 10.17 to 10.18) although relevant to the *Roux* case, is nevertheless over-ridden by the provisions of *s 590(2)(a)*.

10.27 The other side issue concerns the submission to the High Court that the Inland Revenue had not allowed the trustee of the insured scheme the opportunity to put matters right in accordance with its stated policy where a scheme's approved status is in jeopardy (see 10.29 and 10.48). This states that where the Inland Revenue is considering withdrawing approval it will provide a full and clear warning of what the consequences would be and an opportunity to put matters right. It adds that loss of approval should only occur where a pension scheme, despite being warned, chose not comply with the conditions of approval. The High Court judge dismissed this argument as the primary beneficiary of the pension scheme was in a position to implement a pre-planned and commercially marketed tax avoidance scheme. The parties involved must have known or be presumed to have known the risks of loss of approval. Generally the opportunity to put matters right is afforded to those schemes which have breached the Inland Revenue's guidelines in a less culpable manner, not where the scheme and its advisers have deliberately set out to circumvent the sole purpose test.

10.28 It is clear that as a result of the *Roux* case the opportunity was taken in the Budget of 17 March 1998 to limit trust-busting even further. The measures include amending *s 591C, ICTA 1988* to extend the circumstances in which the 40% tax charge can be raised (see 10.4), amending the default provisions for recovery of the 40% tax charge (see 10.34), amending *s 591D* regarding the value of a scheme's assets at the date of loss of approval (see 10.36), preventing the pensioneer trustee from being removed or resigning without an immediate replacement (see 2.38) and introducing a 40% tax charge on personal pension schemes which lose tax approval (see 14.157).

10.29 The result of the *Roux* case has also given rise to changes in the Inland Revenue's discretionary practice, as described in 4.62. Also, PSO Update No 36(5) stated that transfers are not permitted to occupational or personal pension schemes for which a formal application for tax approval has not been received. PSO Update No 41(20) announced that with effect from 31 March 1998 transfers to pension schemes seeking approval would not be permitted unless exceptionally a genuine need to make such a transfer could be demonstrated to the satisfaction of, and agreed in writing by, the Inland Revenue . In addition PSO Update No 41(22) mentions that schemes involved in tax avoidance of the trust-busting variety should not expect the normal procedures for withdrawal of approval to apply to them, i.e. to be afforded the opportunity to put matters right (see 10.27 and 10.48).

10.30 It is to be hoped that all the measures now in place via statute and IR SPSS discretionary practice will discourage any more attempts at trust-busting or moves to circumvent the 40% tax charge although some are apparently still being marketed. One such proposal would appear to be merging several small schemes into a larger one with 12 or more members as the 40% tax charge would not then apply (*s 591C(5)*). That pre-supposes a centralised scheme for non-associated employers would be acceptable to the IR SPSS in the first place, or even if one common employer was the merged scheme's principal employer there could be controlling director members and make-weights which would still render the scheme a SSAS (see 2.26). The principles of the *Furniss v Dawson* and *Ramsay* cases adopted in the *Roux case* (see 10.25) would nevertheless still apply by seeing the arrangements as pre-ordained steps to circumvent the sole purpose test. Those principles are revisited in the following paragraph.

10.31 The House of Lords judgment in the case of *Macniven v Westmoreland Investments [2001] STC 237* does, however, readdress some of the principles that were established by the *Furniss v Dawson* and the *Ramsay* cases. The principle appears to be narrowed by its application to a legislative provision once a commercial concept , such as a disposal, is involved (rather than a legal concept, such as a payment). However, the principle may also be widened if, in the same circumstances, it is no longer a pre-requisite for the tests in *Furniss v Dawson* to be met. The case of *Citibank Investments v Griffin [2000] STC 1010* shows that the taxpayer would have lost if the relevant transaction had been a commercial concept.

10.32 IR SPSS is nonetheless overly concerned with transfers as they have led not only to abuses involving trust-busting, but with commission payments related thereto (see 3.24 as well. IR SPSS's stock reply when it accepts a transfer payment may be made is apparently to say that it is acceptable provided it is not part of a plan one of whose objects is to render the 40% tax charge in *s 591C, ICTA 1988* ineffective. In consequence it asks to be informed when the transfer is made of the amount paid by any insurer in respect of any commission/reward granted by the transfer payment.

Effects of withdrawal

10.33 The loss of the various tax reliefs, if a scheme loses its approval, can be very severe, and have been in cases where approval was withdrawn on or after 2 November 1994. They are described in PN, Pt 19, and they are looked at in turn below. It should be borne in mind that with the passage of time the significance of 17 March 1987 has diminished. Even though IR SPSS has power to withdraw approval more than six years after the event, in effect the taxation time limits for recovery of tax mean that no more than six tax years to date could be affected, unless fraud was involved. 10.34 to 10.47 should be read accordingly.

10.34 The 40% tax charge is covered first because if it applies it is applicable before all the other tax implications have effect (see 10.37 to 10.47). The tax is chargeable under Case VI of Schedule D on the administrator of the scheme concerned. This will normally be the trustees of the scheme, unless they have appointed someone else to be responsible for the statutory duties of the administrator. In the event of default by the administrator, responsibility for paying the charge reverts to the trustees or ultimately to the sponsoring company. As the Inland Revenue had apparently had difficulty in recovering the tax, *s 606, ICTA 1988* has been amended by *FA 1998, s 92* to deal with instances where the trustees are beyond the jurisdiction for recovery and the employer becomes liable to pay the tax. From 17 March 1998 the ultimate responsibility for paying the tax due, particularly where the employer is a shell with no funds, will fall on the scheme members who were controlling directors of the employer or whose earnings were chargeable to tax under Schedule D.

10.35 The 40% tax charge is calculated on the market value of the scheme's assets for CGT purposes held on the day before it ceases to be tax approved. This avoids a double charge to tax on the scheme's assets under *TCGA, s 239A*. Market value is to be ascertained in accordance with *TCGA, s 272*. Where there is no open market value in an asset the valuation should reflect the price that could be expected on an open market for a transaction between a willing seller and a willing buyer. This could clearly lead to a reference to shares valuation division or the district valuer, where unquoted shares or property are respectively involved.

10.36 Where the scheme's investments include loans to the principal or any associated company or to members or to a person who has at any time been a member or to anyone connected with a member, under *s 591D(2)* the value of the loan capital outstanding and any unpaid interest must form part of the value on which the 40% tax charge is calculated. It is somewhat odd that the legislation should mention loans to members and anyone connected with them as these are banned in a SSAS and if they had been made, approval is likely to have been withdrawn from the date they were made and not from a later date of another offence, unless the loans were part of the trust-busting arrangement.

10.37 There would be loss of corporation tax or income tax relief under *s 592(4)* on any contributions paid between 17 March 1987 and 27 July 1989 in respect of a scheme whose approval was withdrawn from a date falling between these dates. It is possible, though unlikely, that the inspector of taxes could allow such contributions as deductions under the normal rules of Schedule D. For any contribution paid after the 27 July 1989 (the date when *FA 1989* was enacted), *FA 1989, s 76* disallows such contributions unless the benefits payable from the scheme are taxable or the contributions are taxed under Schedule E on the member by virtue of *s 595(1) ICTA 1988* (see 10.38).

10.38   Liability under Schedule E will arise on scheme members in respect of their share of any subsequent employer's contributions under *s 595(1)*. However, this should depend on how the inspector of taxes has treated the employer's contribution for schemes which have had their approval withdrawn from a date between 17 March 1987 and 27 July 1989. If the latter has been allowed as a deduction under the normal rules of Schedule D, Schedule E liability will arise. If the employer's contribution has been disallowed then any liability on the member should not arise.

10.39   If the scheme is contributory then the members would be penalised as they would not qualify for income tax relief on their personal contributions paid after approval was withdrawn except on the first £100 p.a. of contributions paid to secure annuities for a widow and dependants (*s 273*). Personal contributions to a FSAVCS should still qualify for tax relief unless that too has lost its approval.

10.40   Any pensions paid subsequently to members would be liable to tax under Schedule E as they are for any approved or unapproved scheme. The position is different for lump sum payments. Prior to the passing of the *Finance Act 1989* on 27 July 1989 lump sum payments made in commutation of a pension from an unapproved scheme were free from tax. This position applied following the decision of *Wales v Tilley (1942) 1 All ER 455*. However, *FA 1989, Sch 6 para 9* introduced *section 596A, ICTA 1988* which provides for cash lump sum payments from unapproved schemes or from schemes which were formerly approved to be taxed under Schedule E on the recipient. If a scheme's approval is withdrawn from a date between 17 March 1987 and 27 July 1989 then a cash lump sum paid from the scheme in that period in commutation of a pension would not be liable to tax. Also, under *s 189(b), ICTA 1988* a cash lump sum paid to a member would not be taxable if the member had already been taxed under Schedule E in respect of contributions paid by the employer.

10.41   Lump sum death benefits payable to any individuals, bodies or organisations should escape IHT if they are paid under a discretion exercised by the trustees by virtue of *Inheritance Tax Act 1984, s 151*. If a member's estate is included as a possible beneficiary under a discretionary power, an IHT gift with a reservation charge may arise. Lump sum death benefits payable to individuals are exempt from income tax under Schedule E under *s 596A(8)(c), ICTA 1988*. However, lump sum death benefits payable to bodies or organisations are liable to income tax under Schedule D Case VI under *s 596A(3)*.

10.42 Any income of the scheme would no longer enjoy relief from tax. This means that income received without deduction of tax would be taxable in the hands of the trustees e.g. rent from property. The trustees would not be able to claim any refund of tax deducted at source from income received. They would not have been able to do so anyway from 2 July 1997 in respect of tax deducted from a UK dividend distribution. This means that the trustees will effectively be paying tax on such income at basic rate from 2 July 1997 to 5 April 1999 and at 10% from 6 April 1999 with the reduction in the rate of tax credits to 10% depending on the effective date of withdrawal of approval. The scheme's income will, however, be exempt from any additional rate tax by virtue of *s 686(2)(c)(i), ICTA 1988*. If any exempt unit trusts were held they would have to be sold because they may only be held by bodies which are wholly exempt from CGT.

10.43 CGT would arise on the disposal of assets by the trustees. The gain would arise over the whole of the period of ownership by the trustees and not from the effective date of withdrawal of approval although roll-over relief may be available until 5 April 1998 and taper relief thereafter. However, as the disposal would take place after 6 April 1988 that part of any gain which arose before April 1982 would be exempt altogether from CGT, except that if approval is withdrawn from 2 November 1994 or later, under *s 591D(2)*, the value of an asset on which the 40% tax charged is based is deemed under *TCGA 1992, s 239A* to be its acquisition value for CGT purposes in respect of a later disposal and is not deemed to be disposed of by any person at the date from which approval was withdrawn. Under the *FA 1988, s 100* the rate of CGT was restricted to basic rate income tax for disposals up to 5 April 1992. The basic rate continues to apply to disposals thereafter under *TCGA 1992, s 4* until 5 April 1998. From 6 April 1998 *TCGA 1992, s 4* has been amended by *FA 1998, s 120(1)* and gains arising to the trustees from that date are liable to CGT.

10.44 If the scheme is insured, subsequent contributions cannot be referred to exempt pensions business. They would have to be transferred to general annuity business or the remainder of the life fund, as would the funds in which contributions have been placed. The exemption in PN 19.4 is not available for schemes that have had approval withdrawn.

10.45 Prior to the *FA 1989* and the advent of unapproved schemes as a result of the earnings cap, if the employer had another approved scheme then by virtue of the former *s 590(7)* the approval of any other schemes could have been prejudiced whilst the scheme from which approval had been withdrawn remained in existence. This problem should have diminished after 27 July 1989 with the enactment of *ss 590(7)–(11)*, which was introduced by *Finance Act 1989, Sch 6 para 3(4)*, as unapproved schemes no longer have to be considered alongside approved schemes of the employer.

10.46 Any refunds to the employer would be taxed at 35% under the surplus legislation. This is because *s 601, ICTA 1988* brings the free standing charge into effect on the refund to the employer of any funds which were held in a scheme which was formerly approved.

10.47 Finally, tax continues to be chargeable in respect of refunds to members and commutation payments made before the scheme ceased to be exempt approved or in accordance with the rules when the scheme was last an exempt approved scheme. Tax is also chargeable on payments not authorised by the rules during the period of approval even if the assessment is raised after approval has been withdrawn.

Redress

10.48 The effects are very severe and a scheme would have got into severe difficulties with IR SPSS to have lost its approval. It should come as no surprise to the trustees and their advisers that approval is to be withdrawn. PSO Update No 6(9) states that the Inland Revenue will provide the trustees with a full and clear warning of what the consequence will be and an opportunity to put matters right except in cases of trust-busting (see 10.29). This would have to be done rather quickly because once approval has been withdrawn it cannot be re-instated. For instance, if an actuarial valuation is late in being submitted, its submission later than one year after the effective date will not procure re-instatement of approval back to the date of withdrawal. As in any other case that is remedied too late it will be treated as a fresh application for approval from the date of its submission and approval will have lapsed for the interim period.

10.49 Loss of approval should occur only where a SSAS, despite being warned, chooses not to comply with the conditions for tax approval or has deliberately set out to circumvent the sole purpose test. Is there any action that can be taken to reverse or mitigate IR SPSS's action once the notification is received that approval has been withdrawn? One reaction may be to wind-up the scheme as quickly as possible, but the position should be reviewed carefully, particularly the financial implications. A trust still exists with a set of rules and there may be a reason for its continuance despite the loss of tax reliefs. Some of the advantages available to FURBS (see CHAPTER 15) should be carefully considered at this stage but it should not be assumed that FURBS status will be accorded automatically on loss of approval as is inferred by PN 18.10 and PSO Update No 29(1). It is a matter for the inspector of taxes to confer FURBS status if the trustees apply for it (see 3.9) and the scheme meets the relevant requirements. The granting of FURBS status is not within the PSO's jurisdiction despite what is said in PN 18.10 and PSO Update No 29(1).

10.50 There is no provision in the legislation for an appeal against IR SPSS's decision. The removal of the scheme's approval would be taken under IR SPSS's discretionary powers against which there is no formal appeal even if the reason for withdrawal was due to non-compliance with the regulations. It may be possible to rectify the position that has caused the withdrawal of approval, but representations would have to be made to IR SPSS at a high level. If redress were sought solely to reverse IR SPSS's decision without any rectification, then a very good case would be needed. Representations would have to be made to the director at IR SPSS or to the Inland Revenue. If, after writing to the director, a complainant is not satisfied, then a written complaint can be made to the Revenue Adjudicator (see 2.13), as explained in leaflet IR120. Appeals against tax assessments are described in leaflet IR 37. Complaints can be made to the parliamentary ombudsman in cases if maladministration is thought to be appropriate. The only course of action open through the courts to reverse IR SPSS's decision because it was an abuse of its discretion, would be by way of judicial review where the court would look to see that the proper procedures had been followed and that the SSAS had been fairly treated.

Taxation consequences

10.51 It is most important to have a fairly accurate idea of the amount of tax which will become payable following loss of approval and even in cases of refusal to grant approval (see 3.9 and 3.67) as the circumstances will be similar.

This may not only influence the decision on whether or not to challenge IR SPSS's decisions but also whether winding-up or continuation as a FURBS is viable. For instance, if no 40% tax charge is payable because approval has been withdrawn from a date earlier than 2 November 1994 or no company contributions have been paid in the last 6 years and no benefits paid in that period the overall tax bill may not be that great. The question of recovering these costs from advisers for bad advice or negligence should also form part of this informed decision. It should not be overlooked that assessments for out of date tax years or accounting periods cannot be made on the trustees, members or company, unless assessments are already under appeal for such years to which adjustments can be made, provided of course that fraud was not involved.

10.52 Unscrambling the scheme straight away and paying everything back to the employer and or members does not have to follow loss of approval (see 10.49). The position of certain investments will have to be considered, e.g. policies or managed units in a LO, exempt unit trusts, banks and building society account where arrangements have been made to pay interest gross. An annuity purchased from a LO cannot be repaid, but it will have to come out of the LO's exempt pensions business into its general annuity business and in consequence be reduced (see 10.44).

10.53 The position regarding making tax returns will also have to be considered from the date of loss of approval for the trust or FURBS if it is decided to go down that route, although after 5 April 1999 this has not been so relevant for SSASs as they have to complete a self-assessment return anyway, This will eventually result in demands for tax with interest thereon and possibly penalties, if the Inland Revenue has not already commenced on this path following notification from IR SPSS. It is here that the presence of the Special Compliance Office (SCO) may be felt.

10.54 One of the SCO roles is to co-ordinate the collection of tax from various sources. So in cases where tax approval is withdrawn or refused and tax liabilities arise on the company in respect of contributions disallowed, on the members in respect of company contributions paid on their behalf or on cash lump sum benefits paid and on the trustees in respect of their income or capital gains, the SCO may seek to collect all the tax due in a total contract settlement. The settlement would include interest and penalties. This may be a convenient way of settling matter if the trustees, company or members do not want the bother of calculating their liability too accurately or completing returns. However, they are not obliged to go down this route with the SCO. They can insist, and they should do so if it is in their interests, on all parties being assessed to tax separately by their respective inspectors of taxes.

10.55 Points to watch with any contract settlement or demand for tax by direct assessment is assessment of tax for out of date years and the imposition of interest and penalties. Demands for payment of tax for out of date years should be resisted unless fraud is involved (see 10.30) particularly as IR SPSS is likely to have been aware and failed to make time limit assessments in good time. Interest will be payable if the tax was due and payable at an earlier date. Penalties can only be sought for fraud or negligence and they can be mitigated depending on the degree of culpability involved. Penalties should be resisted if IR SPSS was aware of the position or had details in its possession. For instance if the Inland Revenue had information on 1 March 1994 of an unacceptable feature of a SSAS about which it made enquiries but did not threaten to withdraw approval until later, finally withdrawing approval on 31 August 1997 with effect from 1 January 1994, then a good case for no penalty being charged in respect of the tax due between 1 March 1994 and 31 August 1997 could be made because the Inland Revenue was aware of the situation.

Penalties

10.56 One of the recommendations of the National Audit Office Survey was that further sanctions were needed to deter non-compliance, short of withdrawing a scheme's approval. It recognised that withdrawal of approval may sometimes be too severe a sanction, for instance it may penalise innocent scheme members. An intermediate sanction was foreseen between warning administrators to comply with the rules and withdrawal of tax approval. The first steps in this direction were taken in 1993 with the threat to withdraw provisional tax reliefs prior to granting approval if executed definitive documentation was not in place within two years of establishing a scheme (see 3.4 and 3.67). The interim period, however, will shortly be phased out for all but exceptional cases. These intermediate sanctions were taken a stage further with the *Finance Act 1994*, which applied to all occupational pension schemes.

10.57 *Finance Act 1994, s 105(2)* introduced a penalty for failure to provide certain scheme details. It amended *s 605* by adding new *ss (1A)* and *(1C)* enabling regulations to be made later to cover the provision of scheme information, allow for notices to be served to obtain information and documents, to make available records for inspection, require certain records to be kept and provided for a penalty for failure to comply with those regulations of up to £3,000.

10.58 *FA 1994, s 105(4)* amended *TMA 1970, s 98* bringing the regulations envisaged by *s 605(1A) ICTA 1988* within the scope of *TMA 1970, s 98* and providing for an initial penalty of up to £300 and an ongoing penalty of up to £60 per day for non-compliance with a penalty of up to £3,000 where fraud or negligence is involved.

10.59 The penalty legislation was brought into effect on 1 January 1996 by the *Finance Act 1994, s 105 (Appointed Day) Order 1995 (SI 1995 No 3125)* and at the same time *SI 1995 No 3103* was promulgated containing the detailed legislation on the future reporting requirements, serving of notices to obtain information, making records available for inspection and retention of records. Full details of the requirements of *SI 1995 No 3103* may be found in 3.74 to 3.91 and also regarding loans in 5.47, property in 6.6, unquoted shares in 7.24, non-income producing assets in 7.39, borrowings in 7.68 and actuarial valuations in 9.57. PSO Update No 48(16) mentions that any of the reports required by *SI 1995 No 3103* on or after 1 October 1998 must include all the information specified on the latest print of the report forms (Appendices 20 to 25 and 31 to 35) otherwise they will be rejected. So if they are submitted again after the relevant deadline penalties may be sought.

10.60 IR SPSS is able to seek penalties for failing to comply with the requirements of *SI 1995 No 3103* that occur from 1 January 1996 onwards. This entails failing to comply by the due date and total failure to comply. The penalty can be sought from the administrator, the trustees (one or more of them), or a participating company, including a former participating company, depending upon whom is responsible for the failure.

10.61 It is important to note that the penalty regime does not cover IR SPSS's discretionary requirements for SSAS. Penalties can only be sought in relation to late reporting or failure to report or to comply with *SI 1995 No 3103*. If a reported SSAS transaction breaches the prohibition in the 1991 regulations, penalties cannot be imposed, but tax approval could be withdrawn.

10.62 Persistent failures to report or late reports or to comply may not only attract penalties, but could also lead to loss of the scheme's tax approval (see 10.7).

10.63 *Finance Act 1994, s 106(1)* introduced *s 605A, ICTA 1988* which provides with effect from 3 May 1994 for a penalty of up to £3,000 on any person for making false statements to gain approval for an occupational pension scheme or an alteration to such a scheme. The penalty also applies where false statements result in relief or repayment of tax being obtained. An example of the circumstances that may lead to the imposition of a penalty under this provision is given in 4.92. Another example could be higher remuneration than was actually paid to a director being used as the basis for funding the SSAS.

10.64 With the passage of time considerable experience of how IR SPSS implements the penalty regime after 1 January 1996 has been gained. Warnings of the possible imposition of a penalty are likely to be given in advance. Penalties in the taxation field are however imposed by the Board of Inland Revenue so representations to mitigate penalties or have them expunged, even if taken up with the senior officers of IR SPSS, have to be made to the Board. It is also possible to lodge an appeal against a penalty.

10.65 The Inland Revenue provided an early indication of how it intended to administer the penalty regime in PSO Update No 12(1). It was expected to continue its policy of allowing trustees and their advisers to put matters right where a transgression takes place (see 10.48). This happens apparently in 90 per cent of cases, but some of these transgressions may still give rise to a penalty. In relation to the production of actuarial valuations (see 9.57) IR SPSS has stated that it intends making full use of the penalties available to ensure valuations are received by the appropriate date.

10.66 More information emerged in PSO Update No 32 of the Inland Revenue's experience of late reporting and the procedures it would adopt for seeking penalties. This announced that by 31 July 1997 it had identified approximately 600 breaches of the reporting regulations justifying penalty action, but no breakdown was provided between SSAS, insured and large self-administered schemes. No later figures have been produced, but full use is made of penalties in order to try to bring about a behavioural change and to ensure the timely submission of information for the proper monitoring of the administration of pension schemes.

10.67 Initially, on receipt of the documents or information outside the statutory deadline of 90 days or otherwise, IR SPSS will seek the reasons for the delay. If a reasonable excuse for the delay is provided the matter may go no further. A reasonable excuse though would involve very exceptional circumstances, e.g. death or unforeseen illness of the scheme administrator. Failure by an adviser to provide information in time to the administrator to make the report would not be a reasonable excuse. If penalties are to be pursued IR SPSS sends all the relevant documentation to the inspector of taxes to take proceedings for a penalty before the administrator's local General Commissioners of Taxes. This intention is conveyed to the administrator by means of an IR SPSS stock letter PS80E.

10.68 The General Commissioners will issue a summons to the administrator notifying the time and place of the hearing to be held before them, and of their powers to award a penalty of up to £300 for each breach of the reporting regulations. It is then up to the administrator to decide whether to attend the hearing or not. If a decision is made not to attend the hearing IR SPSS is not prepared to enter into negotiations on the penalty. It will only accept informal offers of £300 for each breach of the *Reporting regulations*, which effectively ends the matter. If it is decided to attend the hearing a case to mitigate the penalty can be presented to the General Commissioners who are permitted under *TMA 1970, s 100C(5)* to reduce a penalty if it appears to be excessive. Mitigating circumstances could possibly include some of the information being supplied to IR SPSS before the statutory deadline or where a scheme adviser despite warnings from the administrator, failed to provide the administrator with information on time. It has to be borne in mind however that the costs of attending a hearing may be greater than the penalty especially if a professional adviser is involved, so settling for a penalty of £300 with IR SPSS may be preferable financially.

10.69 Penalties are payable by the administrator or trustees and cannot be met from the scheme funds (see 14.171). If paid by the employer it is not deductible as an expense for corporation tax purposes. The administrator may however be able to recover the penalty under professional indemnity cover, particularly if a third party was responsible for failing to provide information or documents in time and was warned of the possibility of penalties beforehand. If such a claim is made, the insurer is likely to expect all reasonable steps to have been taken by the administrator to limit the liability and this would necessarily include pleading mitigating circumstances at a hearing before the General Commissioners. So the administrator should not dismiss the option of attending a hearing on grounds of cost alone. Nonetheless the professional costs of attending a hearing may be recoverable under indemnity insurance or alternatively financial redress may be sought.

10.70   For the great majority of administrators, practitioners and trustees concerned with SSAS the question of penalties arising from the information requirements after 31 December 1995 does not arise. Most of these were formerly dealt with in undertakings, discretionary practice and the *1991 Regulations* 90–day reporting procedures to which the persons involved have become well accustomed. So long as the deadlines are met and the relevant records retained the overwhelming majority of SSAS will meet the obligations and penalties will not concern them. The increasing IR SPSS compliance audit function is also likely to act as a deterrent to misdemeanours that would otherwise attract penalties. It is advisable for all SSAS practitioners nonetheless, especially where they are acting as an administrator or trustee, not to lay themselves open to a penalty in fulfilling these roles. PSO Update No 32(16) observes that frequently poor communication between the practitioner and trustees is a cause of late reporting, and that where the practitioner acts as a trustee and is a co-signatory to the scheme bank account there have been far fewer problems with late reporting. If a deadline cannot be met IR SPSS should be informed before it expires, together with the reason and any information that is available. When the report is eventually made outside the statutory deadline the reason for the delay should again be given as advised in the notes on completion of all the report forms. Practitioners should also give suitable and timely warnings to their clients as and when deadlines approach, so that penalties can be avoided and also to prevent themselves from being sued in the event that a penalty is sought.

10.71   It should not be overlooked that penalties may also be imposed in relation to the self-assessment regime that commenced for SSASs for 1998/99 (see 8.51 and 8.62). Mitigation is not possible so far as the automatic penalty for late submission of the self-assessment tax return is concerned, but the advice in 10.68 on mitigating penalties may be relevant where an incorrect return leading to an additional tax liability is concerned.

Chapter 11

Requirements of the DWP, Opra etc

Introduction

11.1   As a result of the specific attention which has been paid to SSASs by the Inland Revenue since their inception, they are very highly regulated both by legislation and by the working practice which has been developed in discussion between the Inland Revenue and the SSAS representative bodies over many years. This form of regulation has a beneficial side effect in that it meets many of the recent requirements of the DWP and the *Pensions Act 1995*. As a result SSASs are exempt from most of the arduous procedural and compliance regulations which apply to other occupational pension schemes, including the tight restrictions on self-investment and much of the role of Opra. This chapter deals with those aspects of SSASs that fall within the ambit of the DWP, such as preservation, authorisation under *FSA 1986*, disclosure, winding-up requirements, and the pension schemes' register. It also covers self-investment and other legislation designed to protect occupational pensions, including the appointment of a pensions ombudsman, which impinge on SSASs. In addition to the foregoing, equal treatment, part-time workers, human rights, data protection, maternity rights, parental leave, divorce provisions and the *Pensions Act 1995* and other legislation are covered in so far as they affect SSASs.

An alphabetical checklist of the main provisions of the *Pensions Act 1995* and related legislation, and the exemptions that apply to different types of SSASs and other schemes, appears in 11.98 for ease of reference. Greater detail of the specific requirements of the Act is given in 11.2 to 11.97.

Preservation

The preservation regulations govern all approved pension schemes.

11.2   Almost without exception SSASs are not contracted-out and therefore in relation to the *Pension Schemes Act 1993* the benefits they provide need only be the minimum required for preservation purposes for early leavers. Broadly, this means that those members who leave service before normal retirement age should be entitled to 'short service benefits' or to the permitted alternative benefits (see 3.44). Also, where a member left service on or after 1 January 1986 and there was at least a year between the date of leaving and normal retirement age, benefits must be revalued from the date of leaving to normal retirement age under *PSA 1993, s 84*. The reason for this is to ensure that early leavers are treated no less favourably as far as their benefits are concerned than those members who retire at normal retirement age. See 11.4 for the effect of the *Pensions Act 1995*.

11.3   To qualify for preservation benefits the leaver must have at least two years service (prior to 1 April 1988 this was five years). The period includes any service with a previous pension scheme from which a transfer payment was made to a SSAS.

11.4   Where a member qualifies for preservation benefits he or she has a right on leaving service to request a transfer value (cash equivalent) to be paid to another pension scheme. New requirements to the *Preservation Regulations* were introduced by the *Pensions Act 1995*. Leavers before 1 January 1986 were given a right to a cash equivalent unless their deferred benefits were inflation-proofed. The actuary shall determine whether discretionary benefits will be taken into consideration. The option must be exercised in writing to the trustees and effected within six months of receipt of the member's request for SSASs. Sometimes the trustees are unable to make payment of the cash equivalent within the statutory period. It is not too difficult to imagine this happening in a SSAS where the investments are represented by a property let to the principal company and a loan to the same. Where this situation occurs the trustees may approach Opra for an extension of the time limit. The trustees would need a strong case for any extension and they must abide by Opra's decision.

11.5   A particular case where a delay occurred in making a transfer payment was referred to the Pensions Ombudsman. The principal asset was a property let to the company. One of the two members left requested a transfer value. Some two years after the member left the pensioneer trustee wrote to him with a number of reasons why the transfer could not be paid, none of which over-rode the cash equivalent legislation. As a result the member complained to the Pensions Ombudsman, who initially ruled that the trustees must sell the property expeditiously and pay the transfer value (see 11.80).

Where a transfer has not been effected within six months the trustees must notify Opra. Individual and corporate trustees may be fined if they fail to take all such steps as are reasonable to:

(i)   provide a member with a statement of entitlement; or

(ii)   ensure that a transfer is paid within the time permitted.

Authorisation under the Financial Services Act 1986, and self-investment

11.6 Investor protection legislation came into force on 20 February 1988 and affected the trustees of self-administered schemes who wish to manage their own investments. Everyone who advises on, or manages, investments must seek authorisation by applying for membership of one of the regulatory organisations. The exceptions this general rule (e.g. for certain SSASs) are described in 11.98.

11.7 The DWP requirements on investment were defined in the *Pensions Act 1995*. With the exception of the exemptions previously mentioned, there is a requirement to provide a written statement of investment principles and to appoint an individual or firm as a fund manager if the scheme holds assets which are covered by the *FSA 1986*. The trustees shall have the power of investment, and may delegate that power to a fund manager authorised under the *FSA 1986* (or one exempted under that Act) if the investments are governed by it, or to any other fund manager if they are not. They shall not be liable if the fund manager is suitably experienced and has acted competently and in accordance with the statement of investment principles, and they may authorise a sub-group of two or more trustees to exercise investment decisions.

11.8 Trustees may be subjected to fines or prohibition orders if they fail to comply with the requirements to obtain advice in certain matters and to act in accordance with the specific requirements of the *FSA 1986* and the *Pensions Act 1995*. A breach of the self-investment restrictions (see 11.33 to 11.39) by a trustee is a criminal offence and will result in a fine or imprisonment, or both. Additionally, the *Trustee Act 2000* widens the investment powers of trustees and imposes a statutory duty of care on them.

Disclosure

11.9 Subject to the exemptions described in 11.98; the *Occupational Pension Schemes (Disclosure of Information) Regulations 1986 (SI 1986 No 1046)* were revoked with effect from 6 April 1997, and the *Pensions Act 1995* made several changes to the requirements which had governed the supply of information to scheme members. The main changes were to the timescales involved and the introduction of penalties for non-compliance. Fines not exceeding either £1,000 or £200 in the case of an individual trustee, or not exceeding £10,000 or £1,000 in the case of a corporate trustee, can be imposed by Opra, depending on the particular item not disclosed (see 11.98). The main requirements are described in 11.13 to 11.15, and the original requirements are contained in 11.10 to 11.12. The format of accounts for a SSAS are dealt with in the Statement of Recommended Practice SORP 1 and these details are in 12.2 to 12.7.

11.10   The trustees must obtain audited accounts each year and make them available on request to scheme members and former members who retain an entitlement to a benefit. It should be noted that the PSO's information powers require scheme accounts to be made available (*SI 1995 No 3103*). The format of accounts for a SSAS is dealt with in the SORP 1 issued by the Accounting Standards Board (ASB). These details are stated in 12.2 to 12.7. The auditor has to state that contributions payable to the scheme have been in accordance with the rules and the recommendations of the actuary. Alternatively the auditor must state why such a statement cannot be made. For instance, if the company pays a smaller amount than recommended by the actuary, the auditor would need to amend or qualify his statement and give a brief explanation of the reasons why the recommended rate has not been paid. Accounting and auditing requirements for companies having a SSAS are covered in CHAPTER 12.

11.11   There is an exemption from the need to provide an actuarial statement for money purchase schemes (see APPENDIX 43).

11.12   Members of the scheme, including former members with a retained benefit entitlement, had in certain instances to be provided with information and benefit statements under *Regulation 6(4)* of *SI 1986 No 1046*. Under *Regulation 6(11)*, where a scheme was being wound-up, the trustees must also have provided members and beneficiaries with specified information and details of benefits payable.

Scheme details

11.13   The most significant changes are summarised in this paragraph and 11.14 and 11.15.

For scheme documents, copies must now be provided or be made available for inspection within two months of receipt of request, rather than just within a reasonable time. The charge (if any) must be limited to the photocopying cost plus postage and packing, rather than based on what is deemed to be a reasonable fee.

—The main new requirements

Other new requirements concerning scheme details are (subject to the exemptions described in 11.98):

(a)   whether scheme membership is subject to the employer's consent;

(b)   information must be provided about Opra;

(c)   details must be given of the internal dispute procedures, and who to contact;

(d)   early leavers have a right to a guaranteed statement of cash equivalent;

(e)   details of AVC arrangements must be given;

(f)   the conditions for payment of survivors' benefits must be stated;

(g)   information must be made available, if practicable, to prospective members before joining, or in any case within two months of joining (previously within 13 weeks of joining);

(h)   a statement must be provided showing how transfer values are calculated;

(i)   if a material change is proposed to the scheme; details must be disclosed, all members and beneficiaries must be informed as soon as practicable and in any case within three months (previously within one month) except for deferred pensioners who cannot be traced;

(j)   a statement must show how benefits are calculated, what are the accrual rates and what is the definition of pensionable earnings;

(k)   for contracted-out schemes, it must be stated whether the scheme is salary-related, money purchase or mixed benefit (if, in the latter two cases, the scheme uses a notional return on protected rights, the method and the reason for its use must be stated);

(l)   for contracted-out money purchase schemes, details must be provided of any potential changes in a member's accrual of benefits as a result of a change in scheme status;

(m)   it must be stated that an annual report is available on request;

(n)   it must be stated that further information is available, together with an address for enquiries.

—The requirements that were removed were:

(o)   details of any benefits under earmarked policies;

(p)   identification of which benefits are, and which are not, funded;

(q)   details of discretionary pension increases granted over last ten years;

(r)   a statement of whether the employer had undertaken to pay benefits should the scheme have insufficient assets to do so.

Benefit statements

11.14 The following changes have occurred:

—The main new requirements

New requirements concerning individual benefit statements are:

(a)   if a scheme has a money purchase element, it must automatically provide each member with an annual benefit statement relating to those rights, including deferred pensioners (previously this applied only to pure money purchase schemes or those with salary related death-in-service benefits only). The first statement (for a new scheme) must be provided within nine months of the end of the first scheme year;

(b)   schemes will no longer be able to provide only sufficient information so that individuals can calculate their own benefits;

(c)   details must be given of options under money purchase arrangements at least six months before normal pension age or the earlier agreed date of retirement where the trustees are aware of such a date. If this is not possible, the trustees must give details of the options within seven days of learning of the agreed date of retirement;

(d)   details must be given of benefits to members retiring before normal pension age within two months after retirement (previously one month);

(e)   details must be given of age-related rebates credited during the preceding scheme year, and the date of birth used (with a name and address for correspondence if this should be found to be incorrectly stated);

(f)   deferred pensioners of salary-related schemes are entitled to a statement of benefits within two months of receipt of a request, except within twelve months of a previous request (previously entitled only to a statement of estimated transfer value or contribution refund);

(g)   details of benefits available on a transfer-in are to be provided to members or prospective members within two months of a request (previously as soon as practicable). Prospective members are entitled to a statement of options on leaving pensionable service, within two months of a request;

(h)   if a member of a contracted-out mixed benefits scheme moves from the salary-related section to the money purchase section (or vice versa), the trustees must automatically inform him within two months of the change.

—Winding-up

In the event of the scheme winding up:

(i)   members must be notified automatically within one month; reasons for the winding-up must be given; it must be stated whether death-in-service benefits will continue for active members and whether an independent trustee is required, and a name and address must be given for further enquiries;

(j)   details of the action taken to establish scheme liabilities and to recover assets must be provided, together with an indication of when final details will be known, and the extent to which the value of accrued benefits is likely to be reduced (if trustees have sufficient information), to be provided within one month of the commencement of winding-up, and thereafter at least once every twelve months.

Trustees' report and miscellaneous changes

11.15 The following changes have occurred:

New requirements concerning the annual trustees' report are:

(a)   the number of active, deferred and pensioner members, and of beneficiaries, at any one date in the year must be shown (previously the number of members and beneficiaries);

(b)   the latest actuarial ongoing valuation statement must be presented (previous practice applies under transitional provisions until the first funding valuation under the minimum funding requirements and actuarial valuations regulations);

(c)   to show the names of investment/fund managers and custodians, and of any changes during the year;

(d)   the latest actuarial statement as to the adequacy of the contributions shown on the schedule of contributions for meeting the minimum funding requirement must be provided, where relevant;

(e)   it must be stated if cash equivalents are not determined in accordance with statutory requirements (previously a statement of whether or not so determined);

(f)   the trustees' practice on including discretionary benefits in transfer values must be shown;

(g)   spouses of members and of prospective members are entitled to receive on request a copy of the annual report;

(h)   the trustees' annual report must be made available within seven months of the end of the scheme year;

(i)   it must be stated whether the trustees have produced a statement of investment principles, and if so, that a copy is available on request;

(j)   there must be included a statement by the trustees on their policy on the custody of the scheme's assets;

(k)   if any investments made fall outside the statement of investment principles, a description of those investments and an explanation of why they were made must be given, together with a statement of action proposed or taken to remedy the situation;

(l)   a three or five yearly review must be undertaken of investment performance (in addition to the present one year review);

(m)   a copy of any statement made in accordance with regulations by the scheme actuary where he or she resigned or was removed during the year must be provided.

—The requirements that were removed were:

(n)   to draw to the attention of members and trade unions the availability of the trustees' report and accounts;

(o)   an explanation and proposed remedy where the auditor's statement shows that contributions have not been paid at the correct rate;

(p)   a statement on the availability of the OPB booklet 'Pension Trust Principles';

(q)   the part of the investment report stating the investment strategy pursued during the year;

(r)   any changes in scheme details since the previous year.

—Miscellaneous changes and extensions

(s)   the latest minimum funding requirement valuation, schedule of contributions, and the scheme's statement of investment principles are to be made available to members and prospective members, their spouses, scheme beneficiaries and recognised trade unions within two months of the request;

(t)   spouses of members and of prospective members are entitled to inspect or to receive on request (for a payment to cover the costs of copying and sending) a copy of the latest actuarial valuation within two months of the request;

(u)   a guaranteed statement of cash equivalent must be produced within three months of receipt of a written request by a member of a salary-related scheme (extended to six months if reasons for delay are beyond the trustees' control) and passed to the member within ten days (excluding weekends, New Year's Day, Good Friday and Christmas Day) of production;

(v)   if relevant, a copy of the actuary's report concerning the exclusion of discretionary benefits from transfer value calculations must be produced within one month of request (where it has been necessary to obtain such a report, its availability must be notified to members whenever a cash equivalent statement is provided);

(w)   if an independent trustee is appointed on employer insolvency (see 11.16), details must be passed to the members and any recognised trades unions within two months of appointment. Additionally, details of the past twelve months fees and scale of fees must be provided to any such person or any prospective member within two months of request unless already supplied within the preceding twelve months.

Insolvency and the appointment of an independent trustee

11.16 The *Pensions Act 1995, s 22* provides that, if an insolvency practitioner 'commences to act' in relation to an employer who has employees in an occupational pension scheme (or if the official receiver is appointed as liquidator or provisional liquidator), one of the trustees of the scheme is 'independent'. The *Pensions Act 1995, s 23(1)* gives an insolvency practitioner or the official receiver the power to appoint or secure the appointment of an independent trustee if he is not satisfied that there is such a person among the existing trustees.

11.17 To be classed as 'independent' a person (or company) must not:

(a)   be connected with an associate of the employer, the insolvency practitioner or the official receiver; or

(b)   have any interest in the assets of the employer or the scheme (other than as trustee).

11.18 Certain types of schemes are excluded from the provisions of the *Pensions Act 1995, s 22*.

A brief summary is given in 11.98.

11.19 There is no requirement to have an independent trustee where the insolvency practitioner or official receiver started to act prior to 12 November 1990, as the legislation prescribing the circumstances in which an independent trustee should be appointed came into force on that date.

11.20 Where the scheme is a centralised scheme, the requirement to appoint an independent trustee only applies if the employer who is in receivership or liquidation has the power to appoint and remove trustees or is itself a trustee.

11.21 In the case of a paid-up scheme with no members in pensionable service, an independent trustee has to be appointed only if the power of appointment and removal rests with the employer or the employer is a trustee.

11.22 Whilst the *Pensions Act 1995, ss 22–26* govern the appointment of an independent trustee they are modified from time to time by regulations. The responsibility for seeing that the regulations are complied with rests essentially with the insolvency practitioner or official receiver.

11.23 Most SSAS will not need to appoint an independent trustee as they will either be money purchase schemes or all the members will be trustees. For those few SSAS where an independent trustee is required the pensioneer trustee may fulfil this role as the former prohibition on the pensioneer trustee so acting was repealed.

Opra Note 5 is also of significance here. Paragraph 65(c) states that, in circumstances where Opra need to appoint a trustee for SSAS from its panel of trustees, it is essential that the person appointed has experience of SSAS.

Register of occupational and personal pension schemes

11.24 *PSA 1993, s 6* makes provision for the maintenance of a register of occupational and personal pension schemes and for payment of a general levy based on the number of scheme members. The main aspects are covered in 11.25 to 11.32, and the persons who are entitled to obtain information from the Registry are listed in 11.78.

11.25 The regulations relating to the register and the levy first came into effect on the 1 January 1991 except for the regulation that relates to the inspection of the register that was effective from 1 April 1991. The purpose of the register is to have an up-to-date central records system to enable individuals to trace their preserved pension rights. The general levy is designed to be collected by the Secretary of State to cover the costs of Opra, OPAS, the Pension Schemes Registry and the Pensions Ombudsman.

11.26 The trustees of all 'registrable schemes' are required to provide certain information about the scheme and, unless the scheme is frozen or paid-up, to pay the general, and where applicable the compensation, levy. The information has to be provided on a form PR1 (APPENDIX 44). The compensation levy is determined by the Pensions Compensation Board.

11.27 New schemes must register within three months of commencement date.

11.28 The responsibility for providing the registrar with the relevant information rests with the trustees of the scheme. They are also liable for the levy though this may be paid from the resources of the scheme or by the employer. For SSASs with two to eleven members the general levy is £11. The compensation levy is zero.

11.29 The information on the register will be regularly checked. The levies will be combined for collection purposes and the registrar will send out annual demands.

11.30 The trustees are also responsible for notifying any changes in the relevant information within six months of the change.

11.31 Both levies run from 1 April to 31 March and are based on scheme membership (actives, deferreds and pensioners; but not dependants nor death in service only members). Receipts from fines received by Opra will be taken into account in setting the levy.

11.32 If a scheme is frozen or paid-up it may escape the levies if there is no employer (or the employer is insolvent) and either:

- if it is subject to the minimum funding requirement, the funding level is below 100% (or in the absence of such a valuation the disclosure valuation showed a surplus of less than the levies' liabilities); or

- if it is money purchase, there are insufficient surplus or unallocated assets to pay the levies without affecting benefits.

Self-investment and the *Pensions Act 1995*

11.33 The main requirements are:

—Background

There should normally be a maximum of self-investment of 5% of the market value of scheme assets, with provision for dispensation in appropriate cases.

This limit was unchanged by the *Pensions Act 1995* but self-investment was extended to include delayed payment of employer contributions, and investment in employer-related investments must be on arms length terms. No employer-related investment is permitted whilst self-investment exceeds 5%. The exemptions that apply to most SSASs and certain other types of scheme are described in 11.98.

—Employer-related investments:

Loans

(a) loans to the employer, unpaid contributions due and other sums payable (with the exception of the exemptions in 11.34;

(b)   debentures, loan stock, bonds and related certificates issued by the employer that are not listed on a recognised stock exchange;

(c)   guarantees given to secure obligations of the employer;

(d)   third party loans, the repayment of which depends on the employer's actions or situation (except where this was not the trustees' purpose);

(e)   employer-related loans.

Other

(f)   employer-related shares (quoted or unquoted); and securities (including debentures, loan stock, bonds and related certificates issued by the employer which are listed on a recognised stock exchange);

(g)   property for the purpose of carrying on the business of the employer;

(h)   those assets which are held in a collective investment scheme (including a common investment fund) which would count as employer-related investments; and those assets held in an insurance policy which would count as employer-related investments (where the fund was created solely for the purposes of the policy, or, otherwise, if the trustees or employer can direct investment of the funds in employer-related investments);

(i)   land occupied by, used by or leased to the employer.

Employer

'Employer' includes any associate of, or person connected with, the employer of scheme members ('connected' does not include simply having a common director). Associated or connected persons include:

 (i)   directors, their families and company employees;

 (ii)   companies with one third or more of the voting power under common control,

and so the restriction on self-investment extends to loans to employees.

11.34   The exemptions referred to in 11.38 disapply the 5 per cent limit on employer-related loans and investments in respect of the following:

(a)   earmarked insurance policies where the member has agreed in writing to investment in any employer-related investments to the extent permitted by the Inland Revenue;

(b)   self-invested AVCs where the member has agreed in writing to the investment;

(c)   bank or building society accounts where the employer is the bank or building society;

(d)   any contributions that remain unpaid under the contributions or payments schedule;

(e)   any shortfall below the 90% minimum funding requirement level if provision for payment has not been made within the permitted time;

(f)   any debt on the employer on a winding-up;

(g)   any debt on the employer resulting from payments to a trustee who has been appointed by Opra;

(h)   collective investment schemes where:

    (i)   the scheme is operated by a person permitted to carry on investment business within the meaning of *FSA 1986, s 1(3)*, including the operation of collective investment schemes;

    (ii)   there are at least ten participants in the scheme;

    (iii)   not more than 10% of the assets of the collective investment scheme are attributable (either directly or through any intervening collective investment scheme) to the pension scheme's resources;

    (iv)   not more than 10% of scheme investments are invested in shares or stock in the company's share capital and issued by one issuer;

Participants which are schemes relating to employers within the same group of companies shall be treated as a single participant, and all issuers within a group of companies shall be treated as a single issuer.

(i)   insurance policies issued by the employer which is an insurance company or friendly society authorised to carry on long term business, other than policies invested in a fund created only for the purposes of that policy.

11.35   Transitional regulations under *SI 1992 No 246* permitted the retention of certain employer-related investments that exceeded 5% of the value of scheme assets. These are:

(a)   existing loans as at 17 February 1992, if repayment cannot have been enforced by 18 December 1996 (these may continue until such time as repayment can be enforced);

(b)   unlisted securities, other than loans, held on 9 March 1992 (these may be held indefinitely). If they become listed on a recognised stock exchange they must be disposed of no more than six months after the date of listing;

(c)   property held on 9 March 1992 (this may be held indefinitely);

(d)   other employer-related loans, which should be within the existing 5% limit, may be retained until 6 April 2002 or until such later time as repayment can be enforced.

Additionally, the valuation of assets under the minimum funding requirement from 6 April 2002 must disregard any employer-related investment in excess of the 5% limit, and any employer-related investment held in contravention of the legislation must be disregarded at all times.

11.36 A loan or security which becomes an employer-related loan after 6 April 1997 (e.g. as a result of a change in ownership of the employer or the person to whom the loan was made) may be retained until the latest of:

• two years from that event;

• 6 April 2002; and

• the earliest date on which repayment can be enforced.

11.37 Multi-employer schemes which contain distinct sections relating to each employer or group of employers, with no cross-subsidy between the different sections, have each section treated as a different scheme for the purposes of the restriction on employer-related investments. If a scheme is not so divided or cross-subsidy occurs between sections, no more than 5% of its resources may be employer-related investments in relation to any particular employer and no more than 20% of its resources may be employer-related investments in relation to all employers.

11.38 Property leased to the employing company or to connected or associated companies can continue to be held indefinitely even if it represents more than 5% of the value of the fund if held on or before 8 March 1992.

11.39 It is open to scheme members and their representatives, having obtained scheme accounts to which they are entitled under the disclosure provisions, to ensure the trustees have complied with the regulations. Any redress for investing above the 5 per cent limit or failing to reduce to 5 per cent in time would have to be pursued by any aggrieved party through the courts or the Pensions Ombudsman. NICO may withdraw a scheme's Contracting-out certificate for failure to comply with the regulations.

Documentation

11.40 It should be possible with most SSASs to incorporate in their model definitive documentation an agreed rule that allows the trustees to self-invest and for each scheme member to agree to any future self-investment in writing. Otherwise a deed of amendment will be needed adopting a clause to this effect if exemption from the 5% limit is required.

11.41 For a SSAS operating on interim documentation wishing to obtain exemption from the 5% limit and where a deed of amendment would be inappropriate, a trustees' resolution to the effect that the rule requirement will be incorporated in the definitive deed when it is executed should be acceptable.

11.42 The form of the agreement in writing by the members (see 11.39) can be kept in simple terms. A Members' Agreement Form for this purpose may be found at APPENDIX 47. It does not have to be sent to the IR SPSS. Neither does it have to be completed where there is only one member of a SSAS who is also a trustee because that member will invariably be a signatory to the relevant loan agreement or property lease.

Some problem areas

11.43 There will be some SSAS where it is not possible to appoint all members as trustees to obtain exemption from the 5% limit. This may be where a member has left the company's service and whose deferred benefits remain in the SSAS or a dependant's pension for someone aged under 18 has not yet been purchased or a trustee becomes bankrupt and their trustee appointment ceases.

Additionally, the Opra is able to prohibit the appointment of persons as trustees or remove them from office under the provisions of the *Pensions Act 1995, s 3* or suspend a trustee under the provisions of the *Pensions Act 1995, s 4.*

A member who has left service may have resigned as a trustee at the time and re-appointment may not be possible. If exemption from the 5% restriction on self-investment is required such members should be persuaded as far as possible to take a transfer value or that a deferred annuity be purchased in their name. Where a member is about to retire they should be advised to remain as a trustee so as to preserve the self-investment exemptions. This also applies to retired members whose benefits have been secured by way of an annuity purchase from an insurance company in the name of the SSAS trustees rather than in the member's name, which is an IR SPSS requirement (PN 20.38).

11.44 The trustees may wish to repair, refurbish or redevelop their property leased to the employing company and the question arises if any of these improvements constitute new self-investment as they would add to the value of the investment. The DWP has confirmed that it is not the intention of the self-investment regulations to prevent trustees from improving their property. Thus repairs and maintenance may be carried out without infringing the DWP regulations. However, the trustees should distinguish between repairs and development, as a reconstruction or development will have a greater bearing on the value of the property and be liable to the 5% limit if the value of the property is increased by such undertakings and is let to the employing company or is to be let to it.

11.45 It is always possible for the value of the fund to fluctuate after self-investment has been made and also for the value of the self-investment to fluctuate. The DWP has indicated that it is not unduly concerned about breaches of its regulations caused by fluctuations in asset values if the trustees are taking steps to remedy the situation. The trustees are not expected to monitor values closely, but to keep an eye on the position and to take remedial action if they become aware that the 5% limit is being exceeded.

Other DWP legislation

Pensions Ombudsman

11.46 The Pensions Ombudsman was established by the *Personal and Occupational Pension Schemes (Pensions Ombudsman) Regulations 1991 (SI 1991 No 588)* from 1 April 1991 which, as subsequently amended, set out the guidelines within which he operates.

11.47 The Ombudsman's role is that of a watchdog for people with rights under occupational or personal pension schemes. He is able to adjudicate between a member of a scheme and its trustees, manager or administrator where there is a complaint about injustice caused by maladministration or a dispute of fact or law and will look at intra-trustee disputes. The service is free of charge.

11.48 It is expected that complainants will first raise their complaint with the trustees, managers or administrator. If they fail to get satisfaction the next step should be to ask OPAS for help. Where OPAS is unsuccessful or if the complainant is still not satisfied or where a judgment and determination are required particularly in matters of fact or law the ombudsman should be approached to resolve the issue.

11.49 In seeking the Ombudsman's assistance, a complainant must apply in writing within three years from the time when the matter of the complaint or dispute arose. The Ombudsman's decisions will be binding on the parties concerned subject to a right of appeal on a point of law to the High Court.

11.50 The Ombudsman's remit does not extend to a complaint or a dispute appropriate to another ombudsman, e.g. the insurance ombudsman, or to a complaint or a dispute regarding a State social security benefit. It is important not to confuse the Ombudsman's role with that of the parliamentary ombudsman in the field of pension schemes. The Ombudsman deals with disputes between scheme members and the trustees. The Parliamentary Ombudsman, in dealing with complaints arising from pension schemes, would be concerned with the application by IR SPSS or Inland Revenue or DWP of the legislation which they supervise e.g. a dispute regarding the withdrawal of tax approval by IR SPSS. A description of the recently extended role of the Ombudsman is given in 11.79.

Increases to pensions

11.51 The *Pensions Act 1995, s 51* consolidated earlier legislation regarding pensions increases. The impact of limited price indexing is described in 11.98.

Equal treatment

11.52 The *Barber* case concerned increases to pensions from an occupational pension scheme and the equalisation of benefits for male and female members.

11.53 The European Court judgment confirmed that pensions in respect of service before 17 May 1990 (the relevant date of the *Barber* case) may be unequal and that pensions in respect of service after 17 May 1990 must be equal. Where members of the same sex have different normal retirement ages in respect of service after 17 May 1990 the principles of the *Barber* case must be applied to equalise benefit accrued. Different normal retirement ages for men and women after 17 May 1990 are not allowed and the disadvantaged must be treated in the more favourable way until benefits are equalised.

11.54 The principle of equality of treatment for men and women within an occupational pension scheme is particularly important in relation to part-time employment.

11.55 Even if part-time employees are reinstated into scheme membership the employer must bear the cost of reinstatement and where members' personal contributions are a condition of membership the reinstated member will have to pay retrospective contributions. PSO Updates Nos 27 and 68 explain the PSO approach to this matter.

Part-Time Work Directive

11.56 The *Part-Time Work Directive* came into effect on 15 December 1997. The UK was not included (being a non-adherent to the Social Charter) but agreed on 7 April 1998 to extend the Directive to the UK.

The Directive requires the removal of discrimination against part-time workers, and that part-time workers shall not be treated less favourably in their employment conditions solely because they work part time. Nonetheless Member States can, for objective reasons, exclude from their legislation part-time workers who work on a casual basis, and limit their legislation to part-time workers who satisfy a qualifying condition based on service, hours worked or earnings (subject to periodic review).

Discrimination against part-time workers is only unlawful in the UK if it can be shown to be indirect sex discrimination. Significantly, following the European Court of Justice judgment on the *Preston v Wolverhampton Healthcare NHS Trust [2000] PLR 171* and the *Fletcher v Midland Bank* cases, the House of Lords gave its ruling on 8 February 2001. The ruling states that membership can be backdated to 8 April 1976 if sex discrimination can be proven, and a claim is made within 6 months of leaving service. Members must make up any contributions that are owed. The meaning of part-time service, changes to and from part-time service, and the rights and the entitlements of part-time workers are described in the *Part-time Workers (Prevention of Less Favourable Treatment) Regulations 2000 (SI 2000 No 1551)*.

Parental and maternity leave

11.57   The *EU Parental Leave Directive*, which makes provision for a parent to be able to take three months' (unpaid) leave to care for a child, is being adopted, and the two-year service criterion for maternity leave will in future be met after one year for an extended period of maternity absence. The contract of employment continues during these periods, and terms and conditions (other than remuneration) 'continue to apply to any extent set out in the regulations'. However, the extent of the continuation of pension rights is still far from clear. Additionally:

(a)   the statutory minimum period of maternity leave under the *Employment Rights Act 1996* is extended from 18 weeks to 26 weeks with effect from April 2003 (at which time the level of payment will be £100 per week). Pension accrual must continue in full throughout, based on notional unreduced pay. Any employee contributions will be based on actual pay.

(b)   adoption leave will be at the same rate and for the same period as maternity leave.

(c)   paid paternity leave will be at the same rate, for two weeks, and from the same date.

Quality in Pensions

11.58   The (then) DSS published its consultation document on quality in pensions (QiP) on 11 March 1999 in order to raise standards, reward and spread best practice in occupational pension schemes. QiP covered four main areas: namely scheme governance, administration, communication and individual information.

A simplification of procedures was looked for, whilst addressing the various types of products available. There were to be certain minimum benefit criteria to be met, and general access for all employees, if a scheme was to be capable of accreditation. On attaining the required standard, a logo would be available to put on communications for the following three years, subject to any major changes or problems before the end of that period (e.g. being sanctioned by Opra).

11.59 In the main schemes would have had to appoint competent advisers, review their performance, have informed trustees who act responsibly and have had adequate places for member trustees, provided clear information to members and have given automatic annual benefit statements.

The intended minimum benefits were:

- 80ths of annual pensionable pay, reviewed on a contribution basis for money purchase schemes. The rate could be lower for contracted-in schemes or schemes with less than 4% member contributions; or greater if they have certain benefit design features (e.g. 'integrated more than one times the basic state pension');

- a provision for ancillary benefits, such as death in service pensions and/or lump sum and death in retirement benefits.

11.60 It was envisaged that the establishment cost of QiP would be borne by the (then) DSS, and future costs met by schemes seeking accreditation. The PMI had been considered as a possible independent operator, and costs were provisionally thought to be in the region of £1,200 for schemes with less than 500 members rising up to £2,500 for schemes with over 5,000 members. In the event, the outline for this new accreditation scheme was dropped in favour of the publication of best practice guidelines.

EU Investment Services Directive

11.61 The *Investment Services Directive* (ISD) of the EU came into effect on 1 January 1996 and is applicable to pensioneer trustees. The PIA issued an explanatory document in November 1995 which included new categories of permitted business that change 'Permitted Business 10', the category which covered SSAS, from the definition of 'Old Permitted Business 10' – acting as trustee or managing the assets of a 'small' occupational pension scheme (being a scheme of a kind) specified in an order made under *Financial Services Act 1986, s 191(3)*. There are proposals by the European Parliament to update the ISD on capital adequacy and investment services to create a Securities Committee.

Until the EU Commission re-forms the status of the Directive is not certain.

11.62 The new Permitted Business 10 was sub-divided into three categories. These were:

(a)   acting as trustee of a small occupational pension scheme without taking part in investment decisions or managing investments held in the scheme or dealing on the trustees' behalf or advising on or arranging deals in those investments;

(b)   acting as a trustee of a small occupational pension scheme without taking part in investment decisions or managing investments held in the scheme or dealing on the trustees' behalf but where advising on or arranging deals in those investments;

(c)   acting as a trustee of a small occupational pension scheme where taking part in investment decisions as a trustee or managing investments held in the scheme at discretion or dealing on the trustees' behalf; managing at discretion on behalf of the trustees' investments held in a small occupational pension scheme; and dealing in such investments on behalf of the trustees.

11.63 Amongst examples set out in the explanatory document (see 11.61) of activities which would be caught by the ISD is the following:

'permitted activity 10 is only relevant where trustee activity is carried on by the member itself or one of its partners, directors or employees. (It would not apply to the member simply as a result of there being a corporate trustee in the same group.)'

Prior to the issue of the explanatory document it became clear from PIA members specialising in SSAS that the PIA appeared to be suggesting that pensioneer trustees were subject to the *Financial Services Act* despite *section 191(3)* indicating that trustees of SSAS would not need to be authorised to manage the scheme assets (see 11.6).

11.64 The APT arranged a meeting with the PIA to ascertain the position. Following the meeting the situation appeared as follows:

(a)   where the pensioneer trustee is regulated under the *Financial Services Act*, then irrespective of whether it provides discretionary or non-discretionary investment management services it is subject to the ISD;

(b)   where the pensioneer trustee only provides trusteeship to SSAS where all the members are trustees it is not subject to the *Financial Services Act* and the ISD does not apply;

(c)   where there is an associated company that is regulated under the *Financial Services Act* that company should only have current Permitted Business 10 if it manages assets of SSAS on a discretionary basis. If it provides non-discretionary investment advice and does not have client assets it is not subject to the ISD and should not have current Permitted Business 10. If however clients' assets are held, then irrespective of whether the investment services are discretionary or non-discretionary the member is subject to the ISD;

(d)   a non-regulated pensioneer trustee may hold trust assets without becoming subject to the *Financial Services Act.*

11.65   There is some doubt however as to whether this is the full story. The PIA make the distinction that consideration should be given as to whether a trustee's activity would fall to be regulated as investment business and if so whether that business is within or outside of the scope of the ISD. At present there is not a clear line between those pensioneer trustees who are caught by the ISD and those who are not. The practical line would seem to be that where the pensioneer trustee is an individual who is employed by a regulated firm then that firm appears to be subject to the ISD. However, if the pensioneer trustee is a non-regulated bare trustee company that is associated to a regulated company, then the regulated company is not necessarily subject to the ISD purely because of the activity of its associated company. It is likely that the regulated company would not require Permitted Business 10 as it is not acting as trustee. If however the regulated company offered discretionary fund management services or held client money or assets then it would in any event be an ISD company.

Pensions and divorce

11.66   During 1992 the Pensions Management Institute (PMI) with the agreement of the Law Society established a working party to consider pensions and divorce. The background to this move was the particularly unsatisfactory position of divorced women who have few or no pension rights of their own yet their ex-husbands may have substantial pension rights. Additionally, in divorce settlements in the UK outside Scotland the courts have discretion only to make an award at the time of the financial settlement of the divorce to compensate the wife for the forfeited widow's pension. Whereas in Scotland there is an automatic right to compensation for the ex-wife in respect of the husband's pension benefits.

11.67   The PMI published its report *'Pensions and Divorce'* in May 1993. Its main recommendation was that the law should be changed empowering matrimonial courts to direct a pension scheme authority to split pension scheme assets (measured as the early leaver transfer value, not the past service reserve) following a couple's divorce, with the proportions of the split left to the court's discretion. The report was published whilst the Pension Law Review Committee was deliberating on Pension Law Reform. Subsequently, in that Committee's recommendations it was recommended that further detailed work should proceed on the basis of the PMI's report. The results of that detailed work and recommendations flowing from it were still that pensions should be split on divorce rather than earmarked until the divorced scheme member retires and then brought into payment. Under pressure the Government amended *sections 166* and *167* of the *Pensions Act 1995* to avoid defeat on more radical amendments and in the light of a substantial decrease in tax revenues should splitting pensions on divorce become law.

11.68 The *Pensions Act 1995, s 166* amended the *Matrimonial Causes Act 1973* and the *Pensions Act 1995, s 167* amended the *Family Law (Scotland) Act 1985*. The changes, described in 11.70, are expected to any petitions for divorce filed on or after 1 June 1996 and to pension payments due on or after 6 April 1997 and to one-off lump sum payments payable on or after 1 July 1996.

Prior to the new legislation described below, pension entitlements were normally taken into account by the Courts by means of 'set-off' (i.e. by a reallocation of other assets of the marriage to take account of the value of such entitlements). This is still a fairly common form of settlement on divorce. The reasons for this approach were mainly because:

- an order against pension scheme assets could often be frustrated by an extant 'forfeiture' rule under the scheme provisions;

- Inland Revenue rules require a beneficiary to be a dependent person.

11.69 Under the *Matrimonial Causes Act 1973* it is permitted for a divorce settlement to be made by distributing other assets so that pensions rights are kept intact. Alternatively, financial provision orders may require a scheme to pay part or all of any lump sum or pension payments directly to a member's former spouse at the time they come into payment. In other words, pensions can be earmarked or paid in part or whole as ongoing maintenance (periodical payments), but need not be included in a divorce settlement if the matrimonial assets in full are sufficient for a settlement to be reached without disturbing them. Entitlements to periodical payments under set-off arrangements cease on re-marriage and could effect the cessation of an order. In all cases, the Petitioner's financial resources, earning capacity and age will need to be considered. The *Welfare Reform and Pensions Act 1999* extends these extant earmarking and attachment provisions to overseas divorcees.

11.70 Under the *Welfare Reform and Pensions Act 1999*, and the *Finance Act 1999*, there is a sharing (previously known as splitting) concept, similar to that described in 11.71 below. The *Finance Act 1999* contains details of the changes made to Inland Revenue discretionary practice in order to accommodate the introduction of family law and social security law that is intended to enable such a clean break to made between parties in a pension sharing divorce settlement.

Trustees must use the cash equivalent transfer value, which is based on the amount a member would receive by way of a transfer payment on a request to join another scheme or arrangement. A pension credit may normally be retained in the scheme unless the ex-spouse requests an external transfer. However, the trustees will need to decide whether an alternative provider is to be selected to receive a transfer out in the event of a pension sharing order, and should a default option become necessary in the absence of full details (or on grounds of impracticality) from the spouse.

The trustees will have to obtain a schedule of charges to give to the divorcing couple before the order is made so that they may recover their costs. The National Association of Pension Funds has published a recommended scale of charges for this purpose.

Brooks v Brooks [1996] AC 375 (House of Lords, 29/6/95)

11.71 This case concerned a SSAS, and pensions 'splitting' at divorce. The Courts were deemed to have power to vary the scheme, which was considered to be a post nuptial settlement. There were precise circumstances in play, mainly:

(a) the agreement of IR SPSS to a deed of variation was required in order that the Court Order shall have effect and ensure that the variation would not prejudice approval (and diminish the rights of other members);

(b) the divorced spouse had been an employee of the sponsoring company of the SSAS, but was not a member. She therefore could have an 'own right' pension under the scheme;

(c) an allocated sum was set aside for the provision of a pension for the spouse under the Court Order, and reflected in a deed of variation;

(d) there was power under the scheme for the husband to surrender benefits for the spouse, and there was an adequate amendment power to achieve this above under the scheme's trust;

(e) an actuarial calculation of the maximum benefits that could be provided for the petitioner in respect of her own income and years of service was provided for the purpose of calculating the allocated sum;

(f) the scheme was in surplus and had a sole member—therefore it is important, if relying on it for a precedent, not to diminish the interest of any other scheme members ('third parties');

253

(g)   the scheme was looked at 'in the round';

(h)   the petitioner was given an own right pension, and a pension in the event of the respondent's death, and the case is regarded as relevant only to SSASs and personal pension schemes.

The Pensions Act 1995

11.72   The *Pensions Act 1995* addressed the issue of financial provision out of assets on divorce in respect of a pension scheme. Although there are limitations on the Court's power with regard to future entitlements, these can be overcome to a large extent by earmarking orders. *Section 166* of the Act effectively gives power to make an attachment of earnings order on benefits, from when they become due, by means of earmarking.

There is power to make regulations to amend the provisions of the *Matrimonial Causes Act 1973 (MCA)* under the *Pensions Act 1995*. The Courts must take a respondent's pension into account, and a cash equivalent transfer value of his/her interest in the scheme must be obtained (but not necessarily used to determine the settlement amount).

Regulations under the *Matrimonial Causes Act 1973* govern the way in which a value is placed on the pensions rights for the purpose of divorce proceedings. For SSASs (money purchase schemes) this transfer value is represented by accumulated contributions with interest, and includes any contingent pension payable to the member's spouse.

It is prudent to obtain the scheme accounts, the deed and rules, an actuarial report and benefit statements. The *Disclosure Regulations* entitle members to scheme information that will also be available to a spouse on divorce.

The Inland Revenue position

11.73   IR SPSS has published various guidelines explaining its approach to divorce and pension matters. These are described in 3.95.

The role of Opra

11.74   Opra monitors occupational pension schemes, and took over some of the functions of the OPB from April 1997. There are 'whistle-blowing' requirements for actuaries and auditors to report breaches of the law of a material significance concerning the administration of a scheme. In practice, Opra seeks to encourage schemes to be run on a proper footing, and reports of maladministration are treated far more leniently if the cause of the problem has been removed or corrected by the time that the matter is reported.

Opra publishes regular bulletins that describe its actions, reasons for taking them and any penalties that it has imposed. It makes decisions by its committee of board members through a determination committee or, where a criminal offence is involved, through a prosecution committee. The penalties that apply are listed in 11.98.

First criminal prosecution

11.75 Opra's first criminal prosecution was concluded at Staffordshire Magistrates' Court on 21 December 1998. The case concerned an individual who had been imprisoned following a conviction in November 1995 on a count of eight criminal offences involving dishonesty and deception.

The *Pensions Act 1995, s 29(1)* disqualifies such a person from acting as a trustee of an occupational pension scheme. Despite this, the individual concerned continued to act as a trustee of two schemes, and there was no evidence that the professional advisers to those schemes had informed him at any time that he was disqualified from acting. When Opra notified him of this transgression, he continued to act (despite having given an assurance that he would not do so).

The individual was fined by the Magistrate for continuing to act. The Magistrate stated that any one who acts or wishes to act as a trustee must acquaint himself with, and act in compliance with, the terms of the *Pensions Act 1995*.

Other significant cases

11.76 Three further Opra cases that also concerned SSASs, and one of general application, are summarised here for interest. They are:

(a)   A SSAS had four trustees, including the pensioneer trustee who was considering resigning. One of two former trustees had a criminal conviction for dishonesty and another had entered into an arrangement with his creditors, both being automatically disqualified from acting under the *Pensions Act 1995, ss 29(1)(a)* and *29(1)(e)* respectively. The former of these two trustees was still involved in the administration of the scheme.

The board may appoint a trustee under the *Pensions Act 1995, ss 7(3)(a)* and *(c)* if it thinks it appropriate to do so. As the board considered that the remaining trustees lacked the expertise to continue the scheme, or to apply the assets, it appointed a person from its panel of professional trustees, ordering that his expenses and fees be paid out of the scheme's resources. It further ordered that the appointed trustee's powers be exercised to the exclusion of the other trustees (Opra Bulletin No 2, summary 11). The pensioneer trustee subsequently asked for this appointment to be reviewed. The board's decision was upheld and it was further ordered that the appointed trustee's fees should be treated as a debt due from the company to the trustee. The level of fees was assessed and were considered to be fair and reasonable (Opra Bulletin No 5, summary 12).

(b)   The board appointed a trustee from its panel of professional trustees as the SSAS had only one remaining trustee. The pensioneer trustee had previously resigned prior to the requirement that an immediate replacement must be found. Additionally, a former trustee had a criminal conviction involving dishonesty and was automatically disqualified from acting. The scheme assets were considered to be at risk. Amongst other things, the existing trustee had endeavoured to operate a scheme bank account against the authorised signature mandate.

The board's appointed trustee could operate in certain circumstances to the exclusion of existing trustees (Opra Bulletin No 1, summary 11). This was upheld on review, and the appointed trustee's power was extended to the exclusion of all other trustees (Opra Bulletin No 2, summary 1).

(c)   The SSAS had fourteen deferred pensioner members. The scheme trustees were the managing director and the pensioneer trustee. The managing director relied on the advice and professional judgement of the pensioneer trustee. There were three breaches:

- failure to prepare a statement of investment principles *(Pensions Act 1995, s 35(6)(a))*;

- failure to appoint an auditor *(Pensions Act 1995, s 47(1)(a))*; and

- non-implementation of an internal disputes procedure *(Pensions Act 1995, s 50)*.

The pensioneer trustee was fined £1,000 for each of the first two breaches, and £100 for the third breach. Additionally, the board prohibited him from being a trustee of the scheme and disqualified him from being a trustee of any other scheme (under the *Pensions Act 1995, s 29(3)*). Prior notice of suspension had been given.

(d)   Although initially involving a FURBS, the following case has general application. One trustee was an actuary who gave actuarial advice whilst prohibited from doing so by virtue of his trustee status. This is a criminal offence under the *Pensions Act 1995, s 27(4)*. Additionally, the other trustees relied on the actuary for advice and no internal dispute resolution procedures were in place. The board imposed a sanction of £100 on the actuary for the latter offence, and prohibited him from being a trustee of the scheme and disqualified him from being a trustee of any other scheme (under the *Pensions Act 1995, s 29(3)*). Prior notice of suspension had been given.

Summary of the main issues dealt with by Opra

11.77 Opra fines tend to range from £100 to £1,000 (occasionally £2,500), but are normally reasonably low in amount. A brief list of the main issues that have been dealt with by Opra, in addition to the detailed cases above, is given below:

- Failure to prepare a statement of investment principles;
- Failure to appoint an auditor;
- Failure to appoint a scheme actuary;
- Failure to implement an internal disputes procedure;
- Non-implementation of an internal disputes procedure;
- A trustee who was an actuary giving actuarial advice whilst prohibited from doing so by virtue of his trustee status;
- Failures to pay contributions on time;
- Failure to obtain audited accounts.

Opra will supply a prescribed form for completion where there has been a late payment of contributions. Trustees can help their own case by providing evidence of prior consideration, planning, alternative actions and the correction of past misdemeanours.

Opra Registry

11.78 On 1 April 1997, Opra became the registrar of occupational and personal pension schemes in the UK and assumed responsibility for compiling and maintaining the register of every registrable scheme. The following is a list of persons who are entitled to obtain information from the registry, on written request:

(a) a person who is currently, prospectively, or contingently entitled to benefit under the scheme (or any agent acting for such a person);

(b) the trustees, but only once in a twelve month period;

(c) Opra;

(d) the Pensions Ombudsman;

(e) the Pensions Compensation Board;

(f) the Official Receiver or insolvency practitioner who acts in relation to a participating employer; and

(g)   any person who agrees in writing not to use the information for the purposes of marketing a product or service, subject to a fee and to the registrar's discretion (such persons will not be entitled to information about the names of the trustees and scheme administrator, and the names and addresses of past and present participating employers).

Failure to register or to provide information constitutes a civil offence.

The role of the Ombudsman

11.79   The Ombudsman deals with disputes about pension entitlement and maladministration. His or her powers have recently been extended by the *Child Support, Pensions & Social Security Act 2000*. The various considerations that concern the Ombudsman are:

(a)   disputes between trustees of the same scheme, where the matter is raised by at least half of the trustees;

(b)   complaints against, or disputes with, the trustees (or former trustees) of a scheme by an independent trustee;

(c)   requests for a direction by a sole trustee on how it should carry out trustee business under a scheme;

(d)   referrals by trustees of disputes between employers or administrators and trustees;

(e)   referrals by employees of disputes, or complaints against employers, in connection with personal pension schemes;

(f)   referrals by persons entitled to a pension credit of disputes or complaints against a scheme; and

(g)   referrals of disputes or complaints which have already been to a tribunal or court but which remain unresolved.

Appeals may be made against a determination by the Ombudsman. Additionally, it is likely that the Ombudsman will be empowered to investigate cases that may affect other members, by permitting them to make representations and for them to be bound by a decision.

A significant early case

11.80   The following Ombudsman's case, which was overturned on appeal, is also of interest because of the hard line taken by the Court. The High Court overturned the Ombudsman's decision on the grounds that the Ombudsman was not thinking beyond his statutory duty. The assets of the SSAS concerned had been invested in a property held by the company sponsoring the scheme, and the Ombudsman had ruled that the failure to diversify investment had resulted in a failure to pay a cash equivalent in respect of a member.

However, it was held by the Court that the member had not indicated where he required the cash equivalent to be paid (e.g. to a named scheme or arrangement), and that the trustees' obligation to provide information and relevant documentation did not extend to providing additional explanation.

Compensation payments

11.81 PSO Update No 59 addressed the issue of compensation payments directed by the Ombudsman to be made by the trustees of pension schemes. IR SPSS had maintained that such payments would not constitute relevant benefits and would breach the sole purpose test required by *ICTA 1988*. The Update states that such payments will now be classified as administration expenses of the scheme. The inspector of taxes will deal with the individual's taxation according to the circumstances of the case. Exemption will only be possible if the payment is by way of an augmentation within Inland Revenue limits.

Member-nominated trustees

11.82 There is provision for at least one-third of the trustee body to be appointed from members of the scheme. All SSASs have been exempted from appointing nominated trustees (see 11.98).

Trustees generally

11.83 The legislation lays down who can and cannot be a trustee. The *Pensions Act 1995, s 27* prohibits an auditor or actuary of the scheme from being a trustee. However, for SSASs there is a specific exemption for actuaries who may be both a trustee, i.e. the pensioneer trustee, and the actuary to the SSAS.

11.84 The responsibilities of trustees are reinforced by the *Pensions Act* and substantial further duties are placed upon them (see 11.74). Provision has now been made for them to proceed by majority decision unless the scheme's rules provide otherwise. Clearly the unanimous decision to wind-up a SSAS required by IR SPSS over-rides this (see 3.20). They may in most cases be indemnified by the employer in respect of fines imposed on them.

Investment

11.85 The trustees have the same power to make investments as if they were investing their own funds. They must take care and exercise skill in performing investment functions. They will not be able to delegate any discretion to make investment decisions except to an authorised fund manager or to two or more of themselves or to a non-authorised fund manager in respect of non-FSA investments. Under the *Pensions Act 1995, s 35(1)* the trustees will be obliged to produce a written statement of investment principles (see 11.98 for exemptions).

11.86   The trustees are obliged under the *Pensions Act 1995, s 49* to keep money received by them in a separate bank account authorised under the *Banking Act 1987*. A building society account qualifies as such if a SSAS has no bank account.

Advisers

11.87   The trustees are required by the *Pensions Act 1995, s 47* to appoint the scheme's actuary and auditor and, if required by *FSA 1986*, a fund manager. This is to ensure that, because the trustees are responsible for the proper running of the scheme, any advice on which they act comes from advisers whom they have appointed. The trustees will need to keep records of their meetings to show that they have made appointments of advisers as required, be able to produce a formal letter of engagement and demonstrate they have satisfied themselves that the appointments they have made are suitable and proper (see 11.98 for exemptions).

11.88   Both actuaries and accountants, but not solicitors, have an obligation under the *Pensions Act 1995, s 48* to inform Opra (whistle-blowing) if they have any reason to believe that any statutory obligation of the trustees has not been complied with and that the breach is likely to be of material significance in the exercise of Opra's functions. Exemptions have been sought for SSASs.

Disputes

11.89   The trustees are required by the *Pensions Act 1995, s 50* to put in place a procedure for resolving disagreements between themselves and all members of the scheme including deferred members, pensioners, and dependants. Some SSASs will have to comply with this requirement. Failure to do so may lead to a fine being imposed by Opra (see 11.98). The dispute procedure will not apply to a disagreement where proceedings have begun in a court or tribunal, or where the Pensions Ombudsman has commenced investigations.

The Myners Report

11.90   The Chancellor announced, at the time of the Budget last year, that Paul Myners (the Chairman of Gartmore Investment Management plc) would conduct a review into institutional investment. The report set out almost 50 areas where it was perceived that barriers to investment growth and innovation could be removed from the UK economy. Most of these concerned pension schemes. Amongst other things, the minimum funding requirement, as described in 11.91, came under fire The main areas of interest in the report were:

(a) funding tests;

(b) stakeholders governance;

(c) accounting standards;

(d) individual involvement in investments;

(e) the incentive system for investment managers, their accountability and the concentration of the consulting industry; and

(f) trust law, and the unacceptable lack of trustee experience in investment matters.

The Minimum Funding Requirement (MFR)

11.91 Most schemes are required to ensure the value of their assets equals their liabilities at least every three years (see 11.98 for the main MFR details which apply to final salary schemes, and the exemptions). The existing MFR test of solvency is to be abandoned with an, as yet, unspecified run-off period. New measures were announced in the Budget 2001. The new measures are fairly draconian. However, there are some good principles in the measures that are worthy of consideration. The full list is as follows:

(a) a recovery plan for underfunded schemes – a scheme must have a plan in place, which is available to members and monitored by Opra, for recovery of a deficit over (say) 3 years;

(b) a long-term scheme-specific accounting standard – requiring the scheme trustees and advisers to look at scheme-specific needs;

(c) transparency and disclosure – a publicly available scheme funding statement, showing potential growth and future liabilities;

(d) a statutory (that is, legislative) duty of care for members by the actuary – meaning the actuary will have to give members clear guidance on acceptable funding methods;

(e) full benefit provision on scheme wind-ups – meaning more legislation, and employers paying full liabilities immediately, or as they fall due; and

(f) a consideration of an extension to the payments due under the fraud compensation scheme beyond MFR deficits to the cost of securing the members' benefits (or the actual loss, if less).

Additionally, the Government:

• is likely to make it a legal requirement that trustees are familiar with the investment issues on which they are taking decisions;

• will legislate on institutional decision-making, if it thinks it necessary to do so; and

• will endeavour to determine whether a change in the law would resolve uncertainties about the ownership of surpluses.

11.92   The *Pensions Act 1995, s 87(2)* requires the trustees of money purchase schemes to maintain a payment schedule showing the amounts of contributions due to be paid to the scheme by the employer and members and the dates on or by which such contributions are to be paid. If contributions are not paid over by the appropriate dates the trustees will have to inform Opra and the members and if the trustees failed to take all such steps as are reasonable to secure compliance with payment they may be liable to a fine.

11.93   For those final salary SSAS that pay contributions to meet an MFR shortfall including any SC the Inland Revenue has accepted that such contributions will be allowed in full as deductions for corporation tax purposes in the company's accounting period in which they are paid.

Winding-up

11.94   The *Pensions Act 1995, s 75* provides that where a scheme's liabilities exceed the value of its assets the amount of the deficiency is to be treated as a debt due from the company to the trustees. This does not apply to money purchase schemes. The value of a scheme's liabilities and assets are to be calculated in accordance with the valuation method set out in Guidance Note GN19 published by the Institute and the Faculty of Actuaries. IR SPSS must be notified on form PS199 (see APPENDIX 13).

11.95   The *Pensions Act 1995, ss 73, 74, 76* and *77* make further changes to the winding-up requirements for final salary schemes that are subject to the MFR (see 11.98).

11.96   Generally, if on winding-up a final salary SSAS there is a surplus, such surplus may not be repaid to the employer until:

(a)   liabilities have been fully discharged;

(b)   a decision on whether to exercise any power of augmentation has been taken;

(c)   limited price indexation has been awarded where necessary; and

(d)   the members have been informed of the proposed repayment.

11.97 Where an ongoing scheme authorises a repayment of surplus to an employer, the *Pensions Act 1995, s 37* provides that in future this power must be exercised by the trustees regardless of what the rules contain and can only be exercised if:

(a)   the proposals have been agreed by the IR SPSS;

(b)   the trustees are satisfied the repayment is in the members' interests;

(c)   pensions in payment have been indexed as required; and

(d)   notice has been given to the members of the proposals and they have had an opportunity to make representations.

SSASs will generally be unaffected by these provisions.

The main provisions of the *Pensions Act 1995*, related matters and the exemptions which apply

11.98 The following alphabetical list describes the *Pensions Act 1995* requirements and exemptions for occupational pension schemes. It will be seen that the exemptions that apply to SSASs, money purchase schemes and unapproved schemes give rise to significant administrative savings over large self-administered final salary schemes. Indeed, the Green Paper in 1998 promised more exemptions for SSASs, although these are still awaited. On a transfer of monies to or from large self-administered final salary schemes, or a change of scheme status, the wider aspects of the *Act* must be considered. Accordingly, it is hoped that the comprehensive nature of the list will be appreciated by those practitioners who administer large schemes, and who are purchasers of this book primarily for assistance with their in-house SSAS portfolios.

References below to sections are to the sections of the *Pensions Act 1995*, and to the *Act* are to that Act.

—Administration and trustee business

The main provisions are:

(a)   a reasonable period of written notice must be given for general trustees meetings unless an emergency meeting is required;

(b)   trustee decisions must be by majority vote;

(c)   employees must be allowed time off with pay for training and trustee duties;

(d)   written minutes to be kept of all trustee meetings;

(e) scheme assets to be segregated from the employer unless the employer is acting as a paying agent, and then specific time limits apply;

(f) trustees must maintain detailed records of the scheme and obtain audited accounts.

Exemptions

- unapproved schemes and one-member schemes are not required to maintain formal records or to regularly audit accounts, to conduct trustee meetings in accordance with the *Act* or to take minutes;

- unapproved schemes are generally exempt from the other administration provisions;

- money purchase SSASs in which all members are trustees and all decisions are made by unanimous agreement of all the trustees (other than the pensioneer trustee) are not required to comply with the accounts procedures or to obtain audited accounts;

- schemes providing only death benefits, and under the provisions of which no member has accrued rights;

- schemes with fewer than two members;

- schemes established under trust in the UK to provide benefits for service wholly outside the UK;

- Local Government schemes and certain schemes under statute;

- earmarked schemes in which all members are trustees and all decisions have to be made unanimously (disregarding, for this purpose, any trustees who are not members);

- schemes established by the *Salvation Army Act 1963*;

- the Devonport Royal Dockyard Pension Scheme, the Rosyth Royal Dockyard Pension Scheme, the Rosyth Royal Dockyard Pension Scheme for Senior Executives, the Atomic Weapons Establishment Scheme, and the BR Shared Cost Section of the Railways Pension Scheme;

- independent trusteeship does not apply to a SSAS, or a scheme for which each member is a trustee, or a money purchase scheme, or a death in service only scheme, or an insured scheme or a pre–1997 contracted-out money purchase scheme.

—Amendments

The requirements are:

(a) trustees are responsible for deciding whether any scheme amendment affecting entitlements or accrued rights may proceed. Any such amendment will only be allowed if the scheme actuary (or, where the scheme is exempted from the requirement to appoint a scheme actuary, an actuary) has certified that it does not have an adverse affect on any member's entitlement or accrued rights, or where the members affected have given their individual written consent. Where a package of benefit changes is proposed which is beneficial overall but includes an element that represents a worsening in a benefit, member consents may nevertheless be required;

(b) for a scheme which is not established under trust, amendments which might adversely affect the entitlement or accrued rights of a member may only be made with the member's consent;

(c) Opra may modify a scheme on receipt of an application by the trustees to achieve certain purposes, such as to enable the reduction of an excessive surplus, to allow a scheme being wound-up to make a payment of surplus assets to the employer or to enable a scheme to be treated as contracted-out during a prescribed period;

(d) the trustees may modify the scheme by resolution in order to comply with certain requirements of the *Act*, including equal treatment, MNT's, assignment and forfeiture of benefits (where they would otherwise be unable to comply).

Exemptions

• the limitation on the use of powers does not apply to unapproved schemes.

—Assignment and forfeiture

Benefits may only be assigned, surrendered, commuted or charged in accordance with the *Act*. Employers' lien and any set offs are subject to the legislative requirements. The following exceptions apply to prohibition:

(a) assignment of pension for a spouse or dependant;

(b) surrender of pension for a spouse or dependant, or a different benefit for a member;

(c) commutation at retirement, or on triviality grounds/in exceptional circumstances of ill-health or when the scheme winds up;

(d) where an attachment order is made by the Court.

Contracting-out rights benefits may not be charged or assigned, and forfeiture is only permitted when:

(e) a member attempts to assign, commute or surrender rights other than in accordance with legislative provisions, or where his rights would otherwise pass automatically to another party, e.g. on bankruptcy (such benefit shall be payable to the beneficiaries or withheld);

(f)   no pension is claimed within six years;

(g)   the member has been convicted of treason or offences under the *Official Secrets Act* and sentenced to at least ten years' imprisonment before the benefit has come into payment;

(h)   the member caused loss by criminal, negligent or fraudulent act or omission, or by a breach of trust if the member is a trustee;

(i)   the purpose is to recover criminal losses suffered by the scheme or the employer, extended in the case of a public sector scheme to include loss not arising from a criminal act;

(j)   the member's spouse or other dependant is convicted of an offence involving the unlawful killing of the member.

Exemptions

• the inalienability and forfeiture provisions do not apply to unapproved schemes;

• legislation appeared in the *Welfare Reform and Pensions Act 1999, s17,* to protect pension rights in bankruptcy, and forfeiture provisions on bankruptcy are to be prohibited;

• personal pension schemes, subject to certain restrictions.

—Compensation Scheme

The Compensation Scheme is funded by a levy on occupational pension schemes. If an employer becomes insolvent, compensation may be claimed from the Pensions Compensation Board for any assets that have been lost through offences such as theft or fraud. The amount of compensation will not exceed 90% of the lost assets, plus interest, and shall not increase the Fund to greater than 90% of its liabilities. The Green Paper in 1998 outlined a 100% compensation rate for pensioners and for members within ten years of retirement. This came into force by virtue of the *Welfare Reform and Pensions Act 1999, s17,* with effect from 23 April 2001 together with some minor changes for money purchase schemes.

Exemptions

• unapproved schemes are exempt from the general requirements of the scheme;

• one member SSASs and schemes with less than twelve members all of whom are trustees and decisions are by unanimous agreement (other than a pensioneer trustee);

- public service schemes and schemes with a Government guarantee;

- scheme established under trust in the UK to provide benefits for service totally outside of the UK;

- centralised schemes for non-associated employers which are not contracted-out and under which the only benefits provided on or after retirement (other than money purchase AVC benefits) are lump sum benefits which are not linked to salary levels;

- schemes which provide benefits only on death in service and under the provisions of which no member has accrued rights;

- schemes which have fewer than two members and no beneficiaries.

—Contracting-out

Contracted-out salary-related schemes no longer provide GMPs from 6 April 1997. Most schemes that were contracted-out on a GMP basis remain contracted-out on the reference scheme basis. There are age-related rebates and a minimum standard which must be met in order to contract-out money purchase schemes and appropriate personal pension schemes. Protected rights can be discharged on a winding-up by means of a buy-out, accrued GMPs are preserved, and buying back into SERPS is restricted.

Hybrid contracting-out is possible from 1997. Existing defined benefit schemes are permitted to retain GMP liabilities whilst contracting-out on a money purchase basis for future service. Two sections of a single scheme can contract-out concurrently on different basis.

Exemptions

- unapproved schemes are not contracted-out;

- SSASs are not normally contracted-out.

—Disclosure

The main provisions are in the amended *Occupational Pension Schemes (Disclosure of information) Regulations 1996 (SI 1996 No 1655)*:

(a) notification to members within specified time limits where a scheme is to be wound-up, and details of action being taken to establish scheme liabilities and to recover assets;

(b) an annual trustees' report is to be issued and made available;

(c) actuarial and investment documents are to be made available on request;

(d)   a guaranteed statement of cash equivalent entitlement is to be supplied, within a specified time limit, on a transfer;

(e)   details of the appointment of an independent trustee on insolvency are to be given within a specified time limit;

(f)   time limits on disclosure of scheme documents;

(g)   time limits on disclosure of scheme details;

(h)   the provision of individual benefit statements within specific time limits, either automatically or on request.

Exemptions

- unapproved schemes (from most of the requirements);
- limited requirements for public service schemes;
- schemes with less than two members;
- death benefit only schemes, with no accrued rights;
- schemes which are neither established in the UK nor have one or more trustees resident in the UK;
- unfunded schemes.

—Disputes

Trustees must appoint an individual to make decisions on disputes in accordance with the *Occupational Pension Schemes (Internal Dispute Resolution Procedures) Regulations 1996 (SI 1996 No 1270)*. The regulations under *PA 1995* impose specific time limits within which a complainant must receive a response, and trustees are liable to a fine by Opra if they fail to operate a disputes procedure.

The following people may make a complaint:

(a)   all scheme members whether actives, deferreds or pensioners, widows, widowers and surviving dependants of deceased members;

(b)   those who have the option to become members, or will have the option if they remain in the same employment for a sufficiently long period;

(c)   those who will become members automatically unless they choose otherwise;

(d)   those who may be admitted to membership subject to the consent of their employer;

(e)   those who ceased to be in any of the above categories within the six months immediately preceding the date of making a complaint;

(f)   those who have a disagreement relating to their claim to be in one of the above categories.

Exemptions

• schemes with less than 2 members;

• schemes where all the members are trustees.

The dispute procedure will not apply where proceedings have commenced in a Court or tribunal, or where the Pensions Ombudsman has commenced an investigation or where a notice of appeal has been issued under certain regulations which govern the Fireman's Pension Scheme or Police Pension Scheme.

—Divorce

Pension rights on divorce will normally be calculated as the cash equivalent, including the value of the death in service cover. In cases of late and post retirement and SERPS the calculation may be determined by the Court. An order requiring the trustees or managers to pay part of the scheme benefits to a divorced spouse may be effected by transferring or buying-out benefits or paying the benefits out of the scheme.

—Equal treatment

Trustees must ensure that the scheme complies with the equal treatment requirements with effect from 17 May 1990 in respect of service commencing no later than that date. Claims by members and prospective members may be made against the trustees via employment tribunals.

Exemptions

• schemes with less than 2 members.

—Investment

The main requirements:

(a)   the trustees must appoint an individual or a firm as investment manager if the scheme's investments are covered by the *Financial Services Act 1986*;

(b)   the trustees must comply with the restrictions on employer-related investments;

(c) the trustees must ensure that the investment managers have appropriate knowledge and experience and are acting in accordance with a statement of investment principles;

(d) failure to comply with the legislative requirements is a criminal offence that could lead to the trustees being imprisoned.

Exemptions

- schemes with fewer than twelve members all of whom are trustees and all of whom must consent in writing to any decision to invest in employer-related investments;

- wholly insured schemes, unapproved schemes, unfunded schemes, SSASs, public service schemes, death benefit only schemes with no accrued rights and schemes with less than two members do not require an investment manager;

- statutory schemes;

- overseas schemes where there are no members resident in the UK and the schemes are neither established in the UK nor have a UK resident trustee.

—Levies

The levy provisions took effect from 1 April 1997, and Opra is funded by the general levy.

Exemptions

- unapproved schemes;

- schemes with less than two members;

- death in service only schemes;

- money purchase schemes are not subject to the MFR;

- SSASs where all members are trustees and trustee decisions are unanimous.

—Limited Price Indexation

LPI applies to benefits accrued in occupational pension schemes after 5 April 1997, at a level of 5% per annum or the rise in the Index if less. The Secretary of State's annual revaluation order under *PSA 1993, Sch 3* is deemed to meet the LPI requirements. Excess increases for one year can be offset against the following year at the trustees' discretion.

Exemptions

- statutory schemes;

- AVCs and FSAVCs;

- members aged under 55, except on incapacity retirement, but there will be 'catching up' on attaining that age;

- unapproved schemes.

—Member-nominated trustees

Members may appoint one-third of the trustees, with a minimum of two (one, if membership if less than one hundred) unless the employer puts forward alternative proposals for member agreement after an appropriate period of consultation.

Exemptions

- schemes where all the members are trustees, death in service only schemes;

- schemes which are neither approved nor relevant statutory schemes;

- where an independent trustee is appointed on insolvency;

- schemes with fewer than two members;

- SSASs, or schemes that would be SSASs if not insured;

- centralised schemes for non-associated employers which are not contracted out and under which the only benefits provided on or after retirement (other than money purchase AVC benefits) are lump sum benefits which are not linked to salary levels;

- certain paid up insured schemes;

- schemes established under trust in the UK to provide benefits for service wholly outside the UK.

—MFR and schedule of contributions

Trustees of salary-related schemes must maintain a schedule of contributions payable by the employer and the members, and show the due dates for payment. Contributions must be certified by the actuary as meeting the MFR requirements.

The requirements are:

(a) actuarial valuations will be required triennially, and an annual certificate of solvency provided and made available to members;

(b) if funding falls below 90% on the prescribed basis, it must be restored to that figure within twelve months, and the employee must provide to restore 100% funding within five years. Unpaid contributions are a debt on the employer;

(c) the trustees of money purchase schemes must prepare a scheme of payments concerning the due date of contributions.

Exemptions

• unapproved schemes and public service schemes;

• money purchase schemes escape most of the above requirements but must provide a schedule of payments;

• the debt on the employer regulations do not apply to unapproved schemes except salary-related schemes;

• one member schemes are exempt from schedules of contributions and money purchase schedules of payments, as are money purchase SSASs under which all members are trustees and all decisions are unanimous;

• schemes providing only death benefits, and under the provisions of which no member has accrued rights;

• schemes with fewer than two members;

• schemes established under trust in the UK to provide benefits for service wholly outside the UK;

• earmarked schemes in which all members are trustees and all decisions have to be made unanimously (disregarding, for this purpose, any trustees who are not members).

—Ombudsman

The Ombudsman is concerned with complaints by:

(a) members or employers against the scheme trustees or the scheme manager;

(b) the trustees or manager against employers;

(c) the trustees or manager against another scheme.

Exemptions

• complaints applying to IMRO, PIA, SIB, FSA or their successors, except for the management of a personal pension scheme;

• statutory schemes disputes other than the NHS Superannuation Scheme for England and Wales;

- armed forces schemes complaints where there is a right to make a complaint to the Defence Council;

- cases of complaint or disputes in which Court proceedings have begun unless the Ombudsman is already acting.

—Opra

Opra monitors occupational pension schemes. Scheme actuaries and auditors must report breaches of the law of a material significance concerning the administration of a scheme under 'whistle-blowing' requirements. Opra has issued comprehensive notes, and reports should be made under *section 48(I)*. Such reports extend to APPSs.

The following carry a criminal penalty:

- a conviction in a Magistrates Court (incurring fines up to the statutory maximum);

- a conviction in a Crown Court on indictment (possible imprisonment for up to two years, unlimited fines;

- the prohibition of trustees from acting, under *section 3*;

- a civil penalty for other misdemeanours.

Criminal sanctions may be imposed on trustees, managers or administrators for failure to provide prescribed information, or for the provision of false or misleading information. Trustees, managers, professional advisers and others may also attract criminal sanctions for serious breaches.

The maximum penalties are:

High: £5,000 for individuals, £50,000 for corporate bodies
Medium: £1,000 for individuals, £10,000 for corporate bodies
Low: £200 for individuals, £1,000 for corporate bodies.

Exemptions

- unapproved schemes are exempt from the whistle-blowing requirements, and the jurisdiction of Opra, except where statutory obligations are placed on them by legislation;

- Opra is likely to have limited application to SSASs, as they are exempt from many of the *Act*'s provisions.

—Preservation

The main requirements on leaving service, etc. are contained in the *Preservation Regulations*. Most schemes will still be subject to preservation.

Exemptions

- unapproved schemes, in part only;
- lump sum benefits, other than separate lump sums or lump sum only schemes.

—Professional advisers

The trustees must appoint a scheme actuary and an auditor, and Opra may require advisers to produce documents that concern their services and duties to the scheme. Lawyers must be appointed by formal letters of appointment. Actuaries and auditors have whistle-blowing responsibilities.

Exemptions

- schemes with less than two members do not need a scheme actuary or an auditor;
- money purchase schemes and SSASs where all members are trustees and decisions are by unanimous agreement (except by any pensioneer trustee) do not need a scheme auditor. A SSAS will need an actuary to meet PSO requirements—and any appointment by the trustees must be in accordance with the Act and scheme administration regulations;
- money purchase schemes, and centralised schemes which provide lump sums (other than from AVC's) which are not contracted-out or salary-related do not require a scheme actuary;
- unapproved schemes, unfunded schemes, death in service only schemes with no member accrued rights, public service schemes and schemes with a Government guarantee, Local Government schemes and certain other statutory schemes, UK trust schemes for service wholly outside the UK and the scheme established by the *Salvation Army Act 1963*;
- the Devonport Royal Dockyard Pension Scheme the Rosyth Royal Dockyard Pension Scheme, the Rosyth Royal Dockyard Pension Scheme for Senior Executives, the Atomic Weapons Establishment Scheme, and the BR Shared Cost Section for the Railways Pension Scheme.

—Statement of investment principles

Trustees of schemes must prepare and maintain a statement of investment principles and seek advice from an investment adviser with experience of the management of pension schemes, and there must be compliance with self-investment regulations. The employer may not influence investment decisions directly, but before preparing or revising the statement of investment principles the trustees must also consult the employer and may take his views into account.

The statement should indicate:

(a)   the intended investments;

(b)   the balance of investments;

(c)   the anticipated investment return;

(d)   the realisation of investments;

(e)   any matters of a prescribed nature.

Exemptions

• unapproved schemes;

• schemes with less than twelve members all of whom are trustees and must agree the investment decisions in writing;

• schemes under Government guarantee, UK schemes that provide overseas benefits and non-discretionary money purchase schemes;

• SSASs are exempt from the self-investment restrictions, but have separate regulatory controls.

—Surpluses

Limited Price Indexation increases on pensions in payment must be paid before a refund of surplus monies may be made to an employer. The trustees have power to make the refund, and they may ask Opra for a modification order if the rules do not permit such payments. Members shall receive two written notices within specified time-scales and the trustees must obtain clearance from Opra before a refund is made. Opra may seek a restitution order under *PA 1995, s 14* if the requirements of the *Act* are not complied with. The *Act* lays down priorities on winding-up, dependent on any augmentation powers in the rules and whether or not a refund to the employer is permitted (if a refund is not permitted, benefits must be augmented).

Exemptions

• unapproved schemes;

• unlikely to have much impact on SSASs;

• money purchase schemes escape the strict notification requirements on refunds.

275

—Transfers

A member of a salary-related scheme shall, on requesting a transfer, be issued with a Statement of Entitlement that will show a guaranteed amount of value. Transfer valuations and quotations must be in accordance with the requirements and the time-scales under the *Act*, and transfers must be paid within six months of the date of request.

Exemptions

- money-purchase schemes do not need to guarantee cash equivalents;
- transfer requirements for unapproved schemes are under review by the DWP.

—Winding-up

(a) Deficiency provisions

There will be a debt on the employer if there is a deficiency calculated on the MFR basis.

Exemptions

- unapproved schemes;
- schemes with less than two members;
- death benefit only schemes, with no accrued rights;
- non contracted-out centralised schemes for non-associated employers that do not provide a salary-linked lump sum;
- statutory schemes or schemes with a Government guarantee;
- the scheme established by the *Salvation Army Act 1963*;
- only relevant to money purchase if misappropriation applies;
- UK schemes providing only overseas benefits.

(b) Deferral of winding-up

Trustees may defer winding-up the scheme if it is in the best interests of the members to do so (even if the employer is insolvent). Opra may order a scheme to wind-up.

Exemptions

- unapproved schemes;
- money purchase schemes.

(c) Priorities

There are statutory priority orders for schemes which wind-up before 6 April 2007 and those which wind-up after 5 April 2007. If the liabilities of the scheme are not fully met on winding-up the deficit is a debt on the employer.

Exemptions

- schemes not subject to the MFR;
- unapproved schemes;
- SSASs and money purchase schemes;
- the Green Paper in 1998 envisaged that money purchase schemes will be exempt from the requirement for a schedule of payments.

(d) Independent trustees

An independent trustee shall be appointed on the winding-up of a scheme in the circumstances described in the *Act*.

Exemptions

- unapproved schemes;
- various public sector schemes;
- scheme where every member is a trustee;
- money purchase schemes, including SSAS;
- death in service only schemes;
- insured schemes.

(e) Augmentation

The trustees shall have power to augment.

Exemptions

- unapproved schemes.

(f) Discharge of liabilities

For schemes subject to the MFR, the trustees are discharged from liability on transfers or buy-outs if the prescribed arrangements are met.

Flexible pension payments

11.99   Members of personal pension schemes have the income withdrawal facility (see 14.118 to 14.148) whereby in retirement they may withdraw variable amounts within certain limits from their pension scheme up to age 75 before securing an annuity from a LO. The Inland Revenue has now published model rules for money purchase schemes, buy-out policies and AVCs under cover of Pensions Update No 105. These form part of amended PN, App XII.

Data Protection Act 1998

11.100 With the increasing accessibility of private and sensitive information on computers, it is essential that a system of accountability and control be put in place. The UK issued replacement data protection legislation in 1998. The *Data Protection Act 1998* requires data controllers to notify the Data Protection Commissioner of what personal data they are processing, and for what purposes. The information will be entered on a central register. This replaces the previous requirement, which involved a formal registration procedure, and also introduced new security measures. Any exchange of personal data with an employer must be restricted to the minimum necessary unless the member's consent has been obtained.

The Commissioner specifies the form of the notification, which contains the following registrable particulars:

- the name and address of the data controller;

- if the data controller has nominated a representative for the purposes of the *Act* (which he or she must have done, if he or she is outside the EEA (the European Economic Area, which comprises the European Union, Norway, Iceland and Liechtenstein) but uses equipment in the UK for processing), the name and address of that representative;

- a description of the personal data that is being processed, or is to be processed, and the category of the data subject to which they relate;

- a broad description of the purposes for which the data are to be processed (for example, pension fund administration);

- a description of anyone to whom the data controller may disclose the data;

- the names of any countries outside the EEA to which the data controller may wish to transfer the data;

- if data are excluded on the grounds that they are manually processed, a statement of that fact.

It is also necessary for the data controller to submit a general description of the measures to be taken to ensure compliance with the principle of security against unlawful or unauthorised processing of data. Any changes to the particulars or security issues must be notified within 28 days. There can be exemptions, for example because the data is manually processed.

Application to SSASs

11.101 For the time being, the extent of the application of the *Act* to SSASs is still uncertain. The APT is endeavouring to find out more details, in particular:

- who must notify;

- what exemptions are available;

- how notification can be made most easily;

- what the penalties are for failing to comply; and

- whether APT members can make a bulk notification in respect of all cases where they act as pensioneer trustee.

The Human Rights Act

11.102 The *Human Rights Act* came into force in the UK on 2 October 2000. It will have ongoing impact on taxpayers and the Inland Revenue and its commissioners, and it will mean that it will be possible to take into account the *Convention for the Protection of Human Rights and Fundamental Freedoms* without taking proceedings to the European Court of Human Rights. As the convention relies on community law, it is also clear that VAT and HM Customs and Excise rulings can be affected. However, the appropriateness of decisions will need to be considered when applying them to individual cases.

Compliance with the *Act* will require some UK legislative changes to be brought into effect, together with some changes of practice. In particular, from the tax perspective, it will be necessary to ensure that there is not unreasonable selectivity in:

- tax assessment and the imposition of interest and penalties;

- the granting of tax concessions;

- the conduct of tax investigations;
- prosecutions, by way of sexual or racial discrimination;
- the ability to appeal against decisions;
- the requirement to produce documents; and
- the future and retrospective application of taxation.

The Accounting Standards Board

11.103 The UK Accounting Standards Board published a rule in November 2000 requiring companies to disclose more about their employee pension schemes. This disclosure will force companies to reveal gains and losses on the bond and equity markets that concern the investments that make up their employer funds. The deadline for compliance is the year 2003 but there has been marked reluctance, particularly among the FTSE–100 companies, to implement the requirement for their own schemes. There has been much debate, and several sitting committees, on the openness of companies and directors in pension matters in the UK in recent years. Accounting standards are also recommended by the Myners report and the Government (see 11.90 and 11.91).

Chapter 12

Accounting and Auditing Requirements

Introduction

12.1 There are a number of accounting and auditing requirements relating to pension schemes. Firstly, in the circumstances outlined below, trustees must obtain audited annual accounts. Secondly, sponsoring employers are required to account for the cost of pensions in their own accounts in accordance with Statement of Standard Accounting Practice number 24 (SSAP 24), 'Accounting for Pension Costs': this is in the process of being replaced by Financial Reporting Standard 17 (FRS 17), 'Retirement Benefits'. Finally, there are *Companies Act 1985* (CA) requirements specifying matters to be disclosed relating to directors' pensions in corporate accounts and additional Stock Exchange requirements for listed companies. This chapter examines each of these in turn.

Scheme accounts

12.2 The need for SSAS trustees to produce scheme accounts and the statutory requirements depend on the nature of the SSAS and its trust deed and rules. The statutory requirements are discussed in 12.14 as they are directly related to audits under the *Pensions Act 1995*. Some SSASs have a requirement to produce annual accounts in the deed and rules but this is by no means invariable. However, it is clearly advisable to produce scheme accounts on a timely basis at least once a year so that the trustees can monitor contributions and investments. With the introduction of self-assessment, schemes have to submit scheme accounts with their tax returns (see 8.52). If accounts have not been prepared, the Inland Revenue is asking for a statement of assets and liabilities at the beginning and end of the tax year, i.e. as at 6 April 2001 and 5 April 2002 for the 2001/02 return. In addition, actuaries generally ask for scheme accounts at the time of the valuation.

12.3 The form and content of scheme accounts intended to provide a 'true and fair view' are set out in the Statement of Recommended Practice (SORP) 'Financial reports of pension schemes' issued by the Pensions Research Accountants Group in September 1996. The accounts comprise two statements, a fund account and a net assets statement, and the format as set out in the SORP for money purchase schemes (as SSASs are almost invariably of this type) is given below:

Defined contribution scheme fund account

	1996	**1997**
	£,000s	*£,000s*
Contributions and benefits		
Contributions receivable	276	302
Transfers in	33	34
Other income	11	180
	320	516
Benefits payable	–	177
Leavers	63	55
Other payments	47	44
Administrative expenses	18	22
	128	298
Net additions from dealings withmembers	192	218
Returns on investments		
Investment income	13	10
Change in market value of investments	805	(210)
Investment management expenses	(7)	(5)
Net returns on investments	811	(205)
Net increase in the fund during the year	1,003	13
Net assets of the scheme		
At 1 January 1997	4,461	4,448
At 31 December 1997	5,464	4,461

Defined contribution scheme Net Assets Statement

	1997	*1996*
	£,000s	*£,000s*
Assets not designated to members		
Investments		
Managed funds	239	204
Current assets and liabilities		
Bank balances	5	4
Debtors and prepayments	2	3
Creditors and accruals	(6)	(8)
	240	203

Assets designated to members
Investments

Managed funds	5,205	4,240
Debtors and prepayments	19	18
	5,224	4,258
Net assets of the scheme at 31 December 1997	5,464	4,461

12.4   There are a number of disclosures required by the SORP which generally closely match those required by the *Occupational Pension Schemes (Requirement to Obtain Audited Accounts and a Statement from the Auditor) Regulations 1996 (SI 1996 No 1975)*, the *Audited Accounts Regulations* issued under the *Pensions Act* which prescribe the content of scheme accounts where these are required by legislation. The significant disclosures relating to analysis of investments are as follows:

(a)   Insurance policies;

(b)   Public sector fixed interest investments;

(c)   Other fixed interest investments;

(d)   Index linked securities;

(e)   Equities (including convertible shares);

(f)   Property (freehold and leasehold land and buildings);

(g)   Unit trusts invested in property;

(h)   Other unit trusts;

(i)   Managed funds invested in property;

(j)   Other managed funds.

Accounting issues

Money purchase arrangements

12.5   In a money purchase scheme contributions are designated for the purchase of investments for the member on whose behalf the contributions are paid. There is no general pool of assets from which pensions are paid as there is in a final salary scheme. On retirement, the member's investments are applied to buy an annuity for that individual. Thus although the trustees are responsible for the assets, in accounting terms they are already notionally allocated. For this reason, the SORP recommends that the net assets statement shows 'assets allocated to members'. The notes to the accounts normally amplify the rationale for this presentation by referring to the fact that members receive an annual statement confirming the contributions paid on their behalf and the value of their money purchase rights.

Insurance policies

12.6 The *Audited Accounts Regulations (SI 1996 No 1975)* state that, where the assets include insurance policies

> 'which are specifically allocated for the provision of benefits for, and which provide all the benefits payable under the scheme to, particular members or other persons in respect of particular members or both, those policies must be included in the [net assets] statement and there must be a note of the existence of such policies, but that entry need not include their market value or an estimate'.

This means that annuities purchased at retirement are excluded from the net assets of the scheme, and as a corollary, the associated pension payments are also excluded.

12.7 This statutory requirement may be interpreted as extending to money purchase insurance policies which provide all scheme benefits. This may lead to the apparently anomalous situation where a member's designated assets which are spread across different types of investments, including insurance policies, are included in the net assets statement, and another member's assets which comprise only such policies are omitted. Since there should be consistency of treatment of similar assets in scheme accounts, trustees should discuss problems of this nature with their accountants and auditors.

Valuation of assets

12.8 All investments of a pension scheme should be included in the net assets statement at market value, with the exception of certain insurance policies (see 12.6). The SORP recommends the following bases be adopted:

(a) quoted securities should be included at mid-market value;

(b) unquoted securities should be included at the market value estimated by the trustees, based on the advice of the investment managers or other appropriate professional adviser;

(c) unitised securities should be included at the average of the bid and offer prices, or if the bid is not available, by an adjustment to the offer price;

(d) properties should be included at open market value or other appropriate basis of valuation determined in accordance with the Royal Institution of Chartered Surveyors' Appraisal and Valuation Manual and the Practice Statements contained therein. The SORP notes that detailed guidance on valuation of assets owned by pension schemes is contained in Practice Statement 20. It also states:

> 'The valuation of properties may involve additional expense in professional fees and the frequency of valuation is therefore a matter of

judgement for the trustees, subject to any specific requirements in the scheme documentation. Where property comprises a significant proportion of total investments, it is recommended that property valuations should be carried out by independent valuers at least at the same frequency as actuarial valuations of the fund'.

As actuarial valuations are carried out every three years for a SSAS (see 3.19) a professional valuation of property holdings is often undertaken at that time.

12.9   Insurance policies should also be valued at market value. This is a difficult area, and the SORP points out that there is no single generally accepted method of valuation and the usual methods are surrender value, premium value, modified premium value and actuarial value.

The SORP emphasises that the choice of method depends on the circumstances and is a matter of judgement; in general, the surrender value may be more appropriate for unit-linked policies while premium value or actuarial value may be used for policies where there is an underlying guarantee.

Self-investment disclosure

12.10   Most SSASs are exempt from the *Pensions Act 1995* requirements restricting self-investment to 5% of scheme assets (see 11.40). However, the SORP requires disclosure of all self-investment. The Audited Accounts Regulations also require disclosure of the percentage of self-investment, and where it exceeds 5% of scheme assets, the percentage of scheme assets which are permitted as self-investments under the exemptions in the *Occupational Pension Schemes (Investment) Regulations 1996 (SI 1996 No 3127)*.

Investment income

12.11   Interest and rents receivable should be accounted for on an accruals basis. Rents may be shown gross or net of property outgoings, but the basis should be made clear in the notes to the accounts and consistently applied.

Income from shares should be accounted for on an 'ex-div' basis. Some unitised funds do not distinguish investment income from capital growth/ decreases in value, such income being reflected in the value of the units. In such cases, changes in value will appear as change in the market value of investments, and there will be no investment income shown in the accounts.

Actuarial position

12.12   The vast majority of SSASs are money purchase arrangements. Under *SI 1996 No 1655* (the *Disclosure Regulations*), there is no need for an actuarial statement in such a scheme's annual report and thus there need be no reference to such a statement in the scheme's accounts (see 12.3).

12.13   However, it is important to indicate that the accounts do not include liabilities to pay future benefits, and the first two sentences in the example wording below may be used to convey this. Where a scheme provides final salary benefits the *Disclosure Regulations* require an actuarial statement in the scheme's annual report. In these circumstances, the SORP states that the accounts should refer to the actuary's statement by way of a note.

> 'The financial statements summarise the transactions and net assets of the scheme. They do not take account of obligations to pay pensions and benefits which fall due after the end of the scheme year. The actuarial position of the fund, which does take account of such obligations, is dealt with in the statement(s) by the actuary on pages 00 to 00 of the annual report and these accounts should be read in conjunction with it (them).'

If the actuary's report is not recent and the actuary's statement has not been updated by an interim or supplementary statement, the above wording may need to be amended.

The legal requirements for the audit of a SSAS

12.14   The statutory audit requirement was introduced in the *Occupational Pension Schemes (Disclosure of Information) Regulations 1986 (SI 1986 No 1046)* and it included SSASs with more than one member. The *Occupational Pension Schemes (Scheme Administration) Regulations 1996* (the *Scheme Administration Regulations*), which apply for accounting periods ending on or after 6 April 1997, contain a number of exemptions, including certain SSASs. Single member SSASs are exempt from the requirement to appoint an auditor like all other schemes with only one member. Certain other SSASs are exempt from the requirement to appoint a scheme auditor under the *Pensions Act* if:

(a)   they fall within the definition of a SSAS as set out in *Regulation 2(1)* of the *1991 SSAS Regulations*;

(b)   they are money purchase (as SSASs are almost invariably); and

(c)   all members are trustees; and

(d)   all decisions are made only by the trustees who are members (excluding the pensioner trustee) by unanimous agreement.

12.15   The exemption from the need to appoint an auditor brings with it the exemption from a statutory audit under the *Pensions Act*. This means that audited accounts are not required to be prepared within the seven-month deadline for their completion imposed by the *Audited Accounts Regulations*.

If these conditions are not met and sometimes, for example, decisions may not be made unanimously, then the scheme must appoint a statutory scheme auditor and the trustees must obtain audited accounts within seven months of the scheme year end.

12.16 Funded unapproved retirement benefit schemes (FURBS) are exempt from the requirement to appoint an auditor and thus from the requirement to obtain audited accounts (see 15.22(*b*)).

Appointment, resignation and removal of auditor

12.17 The *Scheme Administration Regulations (SI 1996 No 1715)* require trustees to provide the auditor with a written notice of appointment specifying:

(a)   the date the appointment is to take effect; and

(b)   from whom the auditor is to take instructions.

The auditor is required to acknowledge the appointment within one month and to confirm in writing that he will notify the trustees immediately he becomes aware of any conflict of interest. Model statutory appointment and acceptance letters are included at Appendices 48 and 49.

12.18 Professional standards require scheme auditors to issue a formal letter of engagement to the trustees (or other appointing body) which sets out the responsibilities of the trustees and the auditor. The letter covers such matters as:

(a)   the responsibility for producing accounts;

(b)   the statutory and professional duties of the auditor;

(c)   the trustees' statutory duties in relation to the audit;

(d)   the trustees' responsibilities for the maintenance of records and safeguarding assets; and

(e)   other services, staffing, timetable and fees.

12.19 An auditor must resign in writing or may be removed by written notice from the trustees. In each case, the auditor must provide:

(a)   either a statement which specifies any circumstances connected with his resignation or removal which in his opinion significantly affect the interest of the members, prospective members or beneficiaries; or

(b)   a declaration that he knows of no such circumstances.

A statement must be included in the statutory annual report where one is prepared.

Appointment of an auditor in the capacity of professional adviser

12.20 Where the conditions for exemption are met, but the SSAS's deed and rules require an audit, or the trustees decide to have one, then the auditor should be appointed not as statutory scheme auditor but as a professional adviser. This means undertaking the formal appointment procedures under *PA 1995, section 47(3)*. (The statutory appointment procedures do not apply to a FURBS). However, because the scheme accounts are not statutory accounts, the seven-month deadline for the completion of audited accounts does not apply. Some SSASs only obtain audited accounts for the triennial actuarial valuation, which is required by the PSO (now IR SPSS). Provided that the scheme is exempt from the statutory audit requirements, this is not a regulatory problem.

Duty to provide the auditor with information

12.21 If an auditor is appointed, whether in the capacity of statutory auditor or professional adviser, the *Scheme Administration Regulations (SI 1996 No 1715)* impose a duty on the employer and employer's auditor to disclose on request to the trustees such information as is reasonably required for the audit. The trustees have a similar duty towards the scheme's auditor, and have to make available to the auditor any books and records.

These rules are a change from the 1987 requirements, for the scheme auditor now has to seek information and explanation from the trustees and no longer has a statutory right of direct access to the employer and employer's auditor.

Eligibility to act as auditor

12.22 The scheme auditor must be independent of any trustee and may not be:

(a)   a scheme member;

(b)   employed by the trustees or managers;

(c)   a participating employer;

(d)   ineligible to audit the accounts of a scheme employer under *CA s 27*.

There is no requirement for a scheme auditor to be a different person or firm from the auditor of the sponsoring employer.

Pension scheme audit reports

12.23 Where the *Audited Accounts Regulations (SI 1996 No 1975)* apply, they require the auditor to report on three fronts:

(a) firstly, whether the accounts contain the information required to be disclosed by the *Regulations*;

(b) secondly, whether the accounts show a true and fair view of the transactions of the scheme during the year and of the disposition of the assets at the year end;

(c) thirdly, whether the contributions to the scheme during the year have been paid in accordance with the schedule of contributions (defined benefit scheme) or payment schedule (money purchase scheme) (see 11.89).

12.24 Auditors' reports are drafted in accordance with Statement of Auditing Standard 600 (SAS 600), and explain the respective responsibilities of trustees and auditors as well as providing the opinion required by the *Disclosure Regulations (SI 1996 No 1655)*. An example is included at APPENDIX 50. Many SSASs have a non-statutory audit report, and such a report, where the deed and rules require audited accounts, is shown as APPENDIX 51.

12.25 SAS 600 also requires that the trustees include with the audited accounts a statement of trustees' responsibilities in relation to the accounts. Examples of such statements to accompany statutory and non-statutory accounts are included as Appendices 52 and 53.

Pension costs in the accounts of the employer

12.26 The procedure for dealing with pension costs in the accounts of sponsoring employers is currently in a period of transition from that set out in Statement of Standard Accounting Practice 24 (SSAP 24) 'Accounting for pension costs' to that in Financial Reporting Standard 17, 'Retirement benefits'. The latter should be regarded as standard for accounting periods ending on or after 22 June 2003.

The objective of SSAP 24 is that 'the employer should recognise the expected cost of providing pensions on a systematic and rational basis over the period during which he derives benefit from the employees' services'.

Defined contribution schemes

12.27 For a defined contribution scheme, the charge against profits should be the amount of contributions payable to the pension scheme in respect of the accounting period (SSAP 24, para 78). FRS 17 adopts a similar approach. The following disclosures are required:

(a) the nature of the scheme (i.e. defined contribution);

(b)   the accounting policy;

(c)   the pension cost charge for the period; and

(d)   any outstanding or prepaid contributions at the balance sheet date (SSAP 24, para 87).

Nearly all SSASs fall into this category, and the accounting disclosures required are thus straightforward. SSAP 24, Appendix 1(a), gives an example of disclosure for a defined contribution scheme as:

'The company operates a defined contribution pension scheme. The assets of the scheme are held separately from those of the company in an independently administered fund. The pension cost charge represents contributions payable by the company to the fund and amounted to £500,000 (1986 £450,000). Contributions totalling £25,000 (1986 £15,000) were payable to the fund at the year-end and are included in creditors.'

12.28   However, it should be noted that only contributions actually paid in the accounting period are allowed as a charge against profits for corporation tax (s 592(4)). Some doubt existed about this, particularly following the introduction of SSAP 24. It was possible to argue that a tax deduction was permissible on an accruals basis although the Inland Revenue has consistently refused to accept that this is so. However, such an argument was ended by the enactment of *FA 1993, s 112*. This makes it clear that for periods of account ending after 5 April 1993 only sums paid, and not provisions for such payments, will be allowed in computing profits for tax purposes. Note that the Inland Revenue may arrange for special contributions to be allocated over several chargeable accounting periods. This is reinforced in *FA 1993, s 112(5)* which confirms that for tax accounting purposes any contribution spread over a period of years is still to be treated as actually paid at the time it is treated as paid in accordance with *s 592(6), ICTA 1988* (see 9.39). This may also have deferred tax consequences in the company's accounts to allow for the timing differences between the contributions being paid and the tax allowances being given.

Defined benefit schemes

12.29   Accounting for pension costs under SSAP 24 is more complex for defined benefit schemes. SSAP 24 requires that the pension cost should be calculated using actuarial valuation methods which meet the objectives of the standard, and that the actuarial method and assumptions used should lead to the actuary's best estimate of providing the promised pension benefits. The standard adds that the method of providing for expected pension costs over the service lives of employees in the scheme should be such that the regular pension cost is a substantially level percentage of the current and expected future pensionable payroll in the light of current actuarial assumptions.

12.30 SSAP 24 costs are generally calculated by the actuary at the time of the actuarial valuation. Sometimes, but not always, the best estimate for SSAP 24 purposes may lead to the actuary using different assumptions from those used for funding purposes, leading to the build-up of a prepayment in the employer's balance sheet.

The Accounting Standards Board has now issued the new standard, FRS 17 'Retirement benefits', which will be fully effective for accounting periods ending on or after 22 June 2003, with transitional arrangements in place for periods ending on or after 22 June 2001 and 2002. Its main features are as follows:

(a)   pension assets and liabilities must now be measured at market value. This means discounting liabilities at corporate bond rates;

(b)   the resulting surplus or deficit, subject to some restrictions, must be immediately recognised on the balance sheet;

(c)   the profit and loss account charge will consist of the cost of the benefits accruing in the year plus interest on the liabilities less the expected return on assets, together with the cost of any benefit improvements granted during the year and the effect of certain specified events (know as settlements and curtailments);

(d)   other gains and losses will be shown in the statement of recognised gains and losses (STRGL) and will not be recycled through the profit and loss account.

The main changes from SSAP 24 are the use of market values and the immediate recognition of surpluses and deficits on the balance sheet. The disclosures required under FRS 17 are much more comprehensive and informative, but rather more complex. Copies of FRS 17 are available from ASB Publications and directors may wish to consult their actuary and auditors about the implications of the new standard.

Statutory disclosure of pension costs in company accounts

12.31 *CA 85 Schedule 6* requires the disclosure in company accounts of details of emoluments and other benefits received by directors. These disclosure requirements, which include those relating to directors' pensions, were changed in 1997 by the *Company Accounts (Disclosure of Directors' Emoluments) Regulations 1997, SI 1997 No 570*, which came into effect on 31 March 1997 for companies' financial years ending on or after that date. As a result of the changes *SI 1997 No 570* made to *Sch 6*, the term 'emoluments' now does not include pension scheme contributions paid or treated as paid in respect of a director, nor pension benefits to which he is entitled. Instead, there is a requirement to show the aggregate value of any 'company contributions' paid or treated as paid to a money purchase pension scheme in respect of directors' qualifying services. There is also a requirement to disclose the number of directors to whom retirement benefits are accruing in respect of service under both money purchase and final salary pension schemes. The general disclosure rules are set out in 12.32 to 12.38. Directors should consult their auditors for specific advice on their particular circumstances.

Disclosure of highest paid directors' remuneration and other particulars

12.32 For listed companies, where the total of the aggregate amounts disclosed under directors' emoluments, gains on the exercise of share options and amounts receivable under long-term incentive schemes amounts to £200,000 or more, and for unlisted companies where the same threshold applies, except that the amount of any gains on the exercise of share options or of any shares receivable under long-term incentive schemes are not taken into account, the accounts must disclose:

(a)   the amount of that total which is attributable to the 'highest paid director'; and

(b)   the amount of company contributions to a money purchase pension scheme which is attributable to the highest paid director.

Where the scheme is a defined benefit scheme, the accounts must show for that director:

(1)   the amount of his accrued pension at the end of the financial year; and

(2)   the amount at the end of the financial year of his 'accrued lump sum',

accrued pension and accrued lump sum being the amount of the annual pension and the amount of the lump sum which would be payable when he attained normal pension age if

(i)   he had left the company's service at the end of the financial year;

(ii)   there were no increases in the general level of prices in the UK during the period beginning with the end of that year ending with his attaining normal retirement age;

(iii)   no question arose of any commutation of the pension or inverse commutation of the lump sum; and

(v)   director's additional voluntary contributions and any money purchase benefits which would be payable under the scheme were disregarded.

Pension 'top-ups' instead of a bonus (or other emoluments foregone)

12.33 A director may make a bonus sacrifice or forgo some other benefit and have an equivalent amount paid into the pension scheme. The issue then arises of whether this is a company pension contribution or is part of directors' emoluments or long-term incentive payments. In practice, the matter should be established by determining whether the director is choosing to have as a top-up an amount which would otherwise be paid to him as a salary or bonus and if this is the case, the payment should be included within directors' emoluments or long-term incentive payments, notwithstanding the fact that the treatment might be different.

12.34 Where payments are made in connection with a director's ceasing to hold office, there will be a similar need to exercise judgment as to whether a particular amount falls to be included as compensation for loss of office or as a company contribution to a pension scheme. In a final salary scheme, this amount could be an actuarial value for any pension enhancement.

London Stock Exchange Requirements

12.35 In May 1997, the Stock Exchange introduced a requirement for most listed companies to disclose particulars concerning the pensions benefits of each director. For money purchase schemes, disclosure of the contribution or allowance made by the company in respect of each director during the period under review is required.

12.36 For final salary schemes, disclosure is required of the amount of the increase in the period under review (excluding inflation) and the accumulated total amount at the end of the period, in respect of the accrued benefit to which each director would be entitled on leaving service or is entitled having left service during the period and

(a)   either the transfer value (less the director's contributions) of the relevant increase in accrued benefit as at the end of the period; or

(b)   as much of a list of prescribed information as is necessary to make a reasonable assessment of the transfer value in respect of each director.

12.37 Note that the scope of the auditor's report on the financial statements is required to cover these disclosures. The auditors are required to state in their report if, in their opinion, the company has not complied with any of these requirements and, in such a case, to include in their report, so far as they are reasonably able to do so, a statement giving the required particulars.

Small and medium sized companies

12.38   If a company meets the size criteria for a small company, there are exemptions which allow the company to produce modified accounts. In such cases, instead of showing separately the aggregate amounts of directors' emoluments, long-term incentive schemes and company contributions to a money purchase scheme, the modified accounts may disclose only the aggregate of these three amounts. Details of the highest paid director's emoluments and of any excess retirement benefits (see 12.40) need also not be given.

FURBS

12.39   Contributions payable to a money purchase FURBS are disclosable as contributions paid to a money purchase pension scheme. If the company or group operates more than one money purchase scheme, there is no requirement to sub-analyse the contributions made to the different schemes. Listed companies are required to show the contribution or allowance payable made by the company or any other person in respect of each director during the period under review. Remuneration reports of the board usually disclose the existence of any directors' FURBS, the nature of those FURBS and the amounts paid to them in respect of each director during the year.

Excess Retirement Benefits

12.40   There is also a requirement for disclosure of increases during the financial year in retirement benefits paid to or receivable by directors and past directors except where the increase was (or could have been) paid without recourse to additional contributions **and** the increase was given to all pensioner members of the scheme on the same basis.

Chapter 13

Value Added Tax and Insurance Premium Tax

Introduction

13.1 The Value Added Tax (VAT) implications for a SSAS are often overlooked either because pension schemes are generally not liable for direct tax or a SSAS's turnover is relatively small. However, VAT can have an impact on the income of a SSAS particularly in respect of rental income and it may therefore be possible to offset VAT incurred by a SSAS on its administration costs against the VAT received in rent from property it leases. These aspects and others, including whether a SSAS should register for VAT purposes, are covered in this chapter, together with the Insurance Premium Tax (IPT) which came into effect on 1 October 1994. The VAT position relating to SIPPS is covered in 14.248 to 14.257.

Administration costs

13.2 The question of whether the company or trustees pay the administration costs of a SSAS is most relevant. It may be that the company pays the administration costs of its SSASs in order to claim relief from corporation tax on such expenditure and also to recover VAT incurred (Input Tax) from VAT it receives on its income (Output Tax), unless it is partially or fully exempt. Partial exemption entails making some supplies which carry the right to recovery of Input Tax and some which do not. Full exemption applies to the sale of securities or a solicitor's fee for the lease of a property where no option to tax has been exercised (see 13.22). Sales of securities to a purchaser outside the EU are zero-rated. This is acceptable if the expenses incurred are legitimately those of the company and it has Output Tax available for such a set-off.

13.3 HM Customs and Excise takes the view that the establishment and administration of a pension fund is a business activity of the company and therefore any Input Tax incurred by the company in connection with this activity is recoverable. In that Department's VAT Leaflet 700/17/April 1996 '*Value Added Tax Funded Pension Schemes*', those services rendered to the trustees of a pension scheme by the company which constitute the Input Tax of the company are given as:

(a)   making of arrangements for setting up a pension fund;

(b)   management of the scheme, e.g. collection of contributions and payment of pensions;

(c)   advice on a review of the scheme, and implementing any change to the scheme;

(d)   accounting and auditing, insofar as they relate to the management of the scheme, e.g. preparation of annual accounts;

(e)   actuarial valuations of the assets of the fund;

(f)   general actuarial advice connected with the fund's administration;

(g)   providing general statistics in connection with the performance of a fund's investments, properties etc;

(h)   legal instructions and general legal advice including drafting of trust deeds insofar as they relate to the management of the scheme.

If the company pays any of the above costs on behalf of the trustees of a SSAS it will be able to claim Input Tax in respect of the VAT incurred provided it holds a tax invoice made out in the company's name unless it is partially or fully exempt. This is at odds with the provisions of the *Pensions Act 1995* (see 11.89) where the trustees are required to appoint the scheme auditor, actuary and legal adviser and it could have been expected that input tax incurred on their fees would have been the Input Tax of the trustees. The VAT leaflet nonetheless makes no comment on this. If the company recharges any of these costs to the trustees, the recharge is not subject to VAT. This follows from *National Coal Board v Commissioners of Customs and Excise [1982] STC 863*, where it was decided that there was no consideration for any supplies to the trustees by the employer so therefore there could be no supply of services.

13.4   The VAT leaflet goes on to explain that the trustees are responsible for investing and dealing in the assets of the fund and in the Department's view these aspects are business activities of the pension fund and not of the company. Thus, any VAT incurred on costs related to the trustees' investment activities in respect of a SSAS is not recoverable by the company. It may, however, be recovered by the trustees as Input Tax if the SSAS is registered for VAT, unless it is partially exempt. The following are examples of costs related to investment activity:

(a)   advice in connection with making investments;

(b)   brokerage charges;

(c)   rent and service charge collection for property holdings;

(d)   producing records and accounts in connection with property purchases, lettings and disposals, investments etc.;

(e)   trustees services, ie. scrvices of a professional trustee in managing the assets of the fund;

(f)   legal fees paid on behalf of representative beneficiaries in connection with changes in pension fund arrangements;

(g)   custodian charges.

13.5   In the case of the *Wellcome Trust Ltd v C & E Commissioners LON/93/1491 No 12206* heard before the European Court of Justice the question was considered of whether brokerage, agents' charges and all other services relating to the acquisition of assets are a business activity or not of a non-taxable body. HM Customs and Excise contended that the shares and other securities held by the Wellcome Trust were held for charitable purposes and the disposals thereof had not been made in the course or furtherance of any business carried on by the trust, but in pursuance of the normal management of investments in order to fund charitable activities. So the VAT charged on the provision of the professional services of which the trust had availed itself in connection with sales of shares did not constitute Input Tax that was recoverable. The trust appealed to the VAT Tribunal which deferred to the European Court of Justice for a ruling. That body concluded that irrespective of whether the activities in question are similar to those of an investment trust or a pension fund, the Wellcome Trust must be regarded as confining its activities to managing an investment portfolio in the same way as a private investor. It ruled that the business carried on by the Wellcome Trust was not within the VAT concept of economic activities. The purchase and sale of shares and other securities by a trustee in the course of management of the assets of a charitable trust was not within the common system of VAT and therefore Input Tax incurred on fees paid in these circumstances was not recoverable.

13.6   The ruling in the *Wellcome Trust* case has clear implications for self-administered pension schemes. It was widely feared that HM Customs and Excise would use this ruling to restrict the recovery of Input Tax payable on brokers' fees on share sales and possibly on solicitors' and valuers' fees on property sales. In the event this has not happened and it can only be assumed that HM Customs and Excise is treating the disposal of shares by pensions schemes and the advice given thereon by brokers etc. to be an economic activity. However, if the company pays such fees the Input Tax is not recoverable (see 13.7 and 13.8). Also if a management or administration company charges these fees to the trustees then Input Tax attributable would not be recoverable (see 13.10 and 13.13).

13.7   If the company pays any of the costs in 13.4 on behalf of the trustees, it cannot reclaim the Input Tax paid thereon. This was one of the points at issue in *Ultimate Advisory Services Ltd v Commissioners of Customs and Excise [1993] PLR 273*, where the company had a SSAS. The case concerned *inter alia* whether certain payments made to legal advisers were of such a nature that the company was entitled to treat its payment of the VAT thereon as Input Tax. The payments were made by the company as the scheme trust deed provided for all costs, charges and expenses of the administration and management of the SSAS to be paid by the company. The payments were, however, in respect of solicitors' fees for legal services supplied to the trustees, not to the company. Despite the trust deed providing for such costs to be met by the company it was held that this did not mean such expenses are necessarily incurred for the company's business. The VAT Tribunal concluded that events which affect the scheme as a total entity can properly be regarded as being within the business activities of the company, whereas the deployment of the fund within the SSAS is the responsibility of the trustees. The company's claim to recover Input Tax therefore failed because the VAT was not its liability. The findings on this case are most important when considering whether the trustees of a SSAS should register for VAT if they wish to recover Input Tax.

13.8 A similar decision was reached by the VAT Tribunal in *Plessey Company Limited (LON/94/254 No 12814)* where the VAT legal costs incurred by the company on behalf of the beneficiaries of its pension schemes were at issue. The company wanted to wind-up three pension schemes, but the trustees insisted on court approval. This could not be effected without the court being advised of the position of the beneficiaries. The beneficiaries in turn were not prepared to join the proceedings unless their costs were met and the trustees were advised that the court was most likely to award costs against the pension schemes' funds. The Input Tax on the costs was disallowed because the advice was given to the beneficiaries, who were the clients, not to the trustees, let alone the company, which sought the reclaim. The invoices were addressed to the beneficiaries. Even though satisfied that the trustees had to meet the costs and that the services could be said to have been used for the purposes of the company's business, the VAT Tribunal found the costs had not been supplied to the company, but to the beneficiaries.

Financial services

13.9 There are certain VAT exemptions available to banks and other financial services providers for services bought in. Banks and other financial services providers are more likely to be involved in SIPPs than SSASs (see 14.194), but the Budget 1999 changes in this area are nonetheless mentioned here as some pensioneer trustees are in this category. The *Value Added Tax (Finance) Order 1999 (SI 1999 No 594)* clarifies the VAT exemptions for financial services by providing an exemption for intermediary services supplied in respect of an exempt financial transaction. This replaces the former exemption for the making of arrangements. Intermediary services are defined as bringing together persons wishing to buy financial services with persons providing such services, e.g. banks, financial institutions, together with the work preparatory to the conclusion of a contract for the provision of financial services. This brings SSASs within the scope of the exemption when the service is being supplied to a bank, LO or financial institution administering the SSAS portfolio. Intermediary services in relation to a transaction in securities remain exempt also. This has obvious VAT benefits for SSASs and includes the service of introducing clients wishing to buy or sell securities to a person effecting transactions in securities.

Management charges

13.10 In 13.2 it was mentioned that the company or the trustees could pay the running costs of the pension scheme. If the trustees pay these costs they can recover them by making a management charge to the sponsoring company for those costs. The company would obtain corporation tax relief on payment of the management charge and the trustees, by charging Output Tax, would then be able to set-off any Input Tax against it, unless they are partially exempt. Some care is needed, however, as only Input Tax attributable to the taxable outputs covered in the management charge may be set-off. For instance, if the management charge includes any of the costs for which the trustees are responsible (see 13.4) VAT thereon cannot be set-off by the trustees.

13.11 If more than one company participates in the pension scheme it may be preferable for the trustees to make a management charge on each company, particularly if the companies concerned wish to obtain relief for corporation tax on the management charge. It may, however, be difficult to establish which part of the scheme's administration is attributable to a particular participating company. The reverse situation is acceptable, whereby each company, instead of the trustees, pays its share of the administration costs, including the VAT thereon.

13.12 The VAT leaflet sets out in detail the services provided in relation to the investment activities of a pension scheme (see 13.4). It provides advice on whether each activity should be regarded as an 'investment' or 'management' function and concludes that where it is not possible to segregate the services in this way HM Customs and Excise will be prepared to allow an apportionment of 70% to the trustees ('investment') and 30% to the employer ('management'). Some pension schemes may however have special arrangements agreed with HM Customs and Excise prior to April 1996 when the VAT leaflet was published. Subsequent moves by HM Customs and Excise to terminate such special arrangements should be resisted if the Department is not using its powers to secure a fair and reasonable attribution if the decision to terminate results in the use of a method which is less fair and reasonable (*Merchant Navy Officers Pension Fund Trustees Ltd*; *Merchant Navy Ratings Pension Fund Trustees Ltd LON/95/2944 (14262).*)

Administration companies

13.13   It is not uncommon for both administration and investment-related services to be supplied by a professional trustee or administration company. Sometimes with a SSAS appointing the pensioneer trustee itself, or a company associated with the pensioneer trustee or the LO concerned supplies these services. Their overall charge will include VAT for both services provided to the company in the general administration of the scheme and for investment services provided to the trustees. The company is not, however, entitled to claim Input Tax in respect of investment services provided to the trustees (see 13.4) even if they are invoiced together with general administration services.

13.14   If the company holds one VAT invoice for both types of supplies in its own name it can make a deduction for Input Tax provided the invoice shows the details separately relating to the services for which it is entitled to make a claim. It is preferable though for the professional trustee or administration company to separate the charges so that one invoice is made out to the company for administration costs and another is made out to the trustees for investment-related costs. If they prefer, the trustees may pay the professional trustee or administration company for administration related services and the company itself will still be able to recover Input Tax thereon, provided the invoice is made out to the company.

Pensioneer trustee liability for VAT

13.15   It is apparent that HM Customs and Excise has been pursuing some pensioneer trustees for VAT liabilities relating to SSASs of which they are a trustee. The Department has apparently based its claim on an extension of the rules applicable to group registrations for VAT. Under such registrations (by a corporate trustee and the principal company) the parties to the registration are jointly and severally liable for VAT due from the representative member and in the event of that member failing to meet the VAT debt of the registered group, the Department holds each member of the group registration liable for the amount of the debt. HM Customs and Excise advised that this liability extends to all assets of the group members including the assets of any pension scheme whose trustee is, or was, within the group registration. Thus, HM

Customs and Excise were seeking to recover VAT liabilities from the assets of a SSAS of which a pensioneer trustee was a trustee in respect of the VAT debts due by another SSAS of which the pensioneer trustee was also a trustee.

13.16 This inequitable claim was successfully challenged by the APT as group registrations do not apply to pensioneer trustees. How could the assets of a pension scheme that is totally unassociated with another pension scheme be at risk from a claim for VAT liabilities in respect of another pension scheme simply because one of the trustees of both schemes is the same? Fortunately, the Department accepted it had no right of recourse against another pension scheme of which the pensioneer trustee (or any other trustee for that matter) is a trustee. Furthermore, the Department has given an assurance that a representative member will not be held liable for the debts of other members of the group in the VAT Leaflet at paragraph 15.

13.17 Unfortunately, the problems outlined in 13.15 and 13.16 have not totally gone away. HM Customs and Excise published a discussion document in late 1995 in connection with businesses carried out by trustees. One of the areas on which it invited comments was trustees' liability for VAT debts. The document proposes trustees should be jointly and severally liable for compliance of all VAT requirements including VAT debts. Under this proposal trustees could be personally liable for VAT debts where they exceed the amounts of assets in the pension fund. Once again this proposal will result in an unfair burden falling this time on non-professional and family trustees. It is to be hoped that representations to make it more equitable that trustees should not be liable over and above the assets of a pension scheme unless there is evidence of fraud and/or dishonesty, will be taken on board before the Department announces new arrangements.

13.18 As between the trustee and the pension scheme the trustee is entitled to have VAT borne by the pension scheme, but if its funds are insufficient for any reason the trustee would have to pay HM Customs and Excise from his own pocket. So where pensioneer trustees are being asked to consent to a SSAS being registered for VAT (see 13.48 to 13.53) it is worth considering obtaining indemnities from co-trustees at the same time.

13.19 Group registration for VAT was reviewed by HM Customs and Excise during 1998 and 1999 and resulted in HM Customs and Excise having power to remove from groups companies that that are no longer eligible to be grouped or whose membership of a group poses a threat to the revenue. The intention was to make the grouping provisions more flexible for business whilst at the same time tidying up on the prevention of abuse. However, many corporate pensioneer trustees act not just as trustees, but also as scheme administrators. Most of them are subsidiaries of a parent company which provides a range of financial services one of which is pension administration.

Some are simply trustees and do not trade at all. Corporate trustees are however registered as part of an employer's group for VAT purposes so they set off VAT more easily.

It is not totally clear from the Budget notice 56/99 whether such companies will be no longer eligible to be grouped or pose a threat to the revenue. It is clear though that HM Customs and Excise will use its powers to remove a company from a group if it is not established in the UK, where avoidance is suspected. There is a risk that revenue due may not be collectible or the revenue loss goes beyond that arising as a natural consequence of grouping. Corporate pensioneer trustees that were not exempt from the changes had until 1 January 2000 to restructure their arrangements or will have had to leave their group or appeal against their removal by HM Customs and Excise on eligibility or revenue protection grounds.

Property

13.20   The trustees of a SSAS have, since 5 August 1991, only been able to own residential property, with two exceptions (see 6.28), and in one instance commercial property would also be involved anyway. Paragraphs 13.21 to 13.47 are therefore concerned with VAT chargeable on the acquisition or sale of commercial property and the rent payable to the trustees therefrom.

13.21   Dealing in property may be exempt, zero-rated or standard rated in respect of property situated in the United Kingdom. Zero-rating applies to the grant of a major interest, meaning the freehold or a lease, etc., exceeding 21 years, in a qualifying building by the person constructing. Zero-rating is also available for a qualifying building which is Grade 1 or Grade 2 listed (or the equivalent in Scotland and Northern Ireland) if it has been a substantial reconstruction by the trustees. The trustees must grant a major interest following the substantial reconstruction. A 'substantial reconstruction' is either, that at least 60% of the costs undertaken relate to approved alterations or, the reconstructed building incorporates no more of the original building than the external walls and any external features of architectural or historical interest. The definition of approved alterations can cause difficulties and, in applying this part of the rules, professional advice is recommended. This is also recommended when the trustees undertake the construction of a building on their land as the developer's self-supply charge must be taken into account (see 13.25 and 13.26) and trader registration may be desirable.

13.22   The grant of a short lease is exempt from VAT. However, the landlord has the option to waive this exemption and charge the tenant VAT on the rent on a short lease. If the trustees decide to exercise their option and charge VAT on the rent, they must notify their local VAT office in writing. The sale of a long lease from 21 July 1994 of a new dwelling is also exempt from VAT provided it was created by the conversion of non-residential buildings. It is understood in this connection that a public house with living accommodation or a shop with a flat would not be exempt from VAT on conversion. If the trustees own more than one property and decide to charge VAT on the rent on them all, they must elect to tax each property. They cannot be covered by a general election for all properties.

13.23 Where the trustees are the landlord of a property and they intend to carry out building work on that property, if the rent they receive has previously been exempt from VAT, they must obtain permission from HM Customs and Excise if they intend to recover future Input Tax on the building works and day-to-day overheads.

13.24 Since 1 April 1989 all new commercial properties have been subject to VAT at the standard rate. So if the trustees sell the freehold of their commercial property they have to account for the Output Tax they receive. If they buy freehold commercial property they are likely to incur Input Tax which will not be recoverable unless they receive Output Tax against which it may be set-off. From a practical point of view the solicitor acting for the trustees should ask at the pre-contract stage if the vendor will be charging VAT. If VAT is not to be charged the contract for sale should include a clause whereby the vendor agrees not to exercise the option to charge VAT in the period between contract date and completion. The trustees have also to account for the Output Tax on any rents received where they have elected to charge VAT. It can therefore be seen that the trustees have an important decision to take as to whether or not to register for VAT purposes so they can recover any Input Tax against Output Tax. That decision will depend on whether the annual rents on which they can charge VAT exceed the VAT registration threshold or they sell a property worth more than the threshold. Unfortunately, this decision was further complicated by legislation with effect from 30 November 1994 (see 13.27 to 13.35) and from 26 November 1996 (see 13.37 to 13.44).

13.25 Mention is made at 6.26 that the trustees may develop their property or land from scheme funds and 13.21 warns in this connection that if they construct a building on their land the developer's self-supply charge must be taken into account. In the case of *C & E Commissioners v R & R Pension Fund Trustees LON/95/2274A (13733)*, the trustees constructed a commercial building and recovered Input Tax incurred during the course of the work. They then granted a lease of the building from 1 August 1993 for 15 years, which triggered the self-supply charge whereby the trustees were assessed to VAT as if they had made a fully taxable supply of the building itself. To recover VAT on that supply the trustees sought to elect to waive exemption on the supply of the building under the lease, thus making taxable all subsequent rental payments. However, the date the election was to take effect (1 August

1993 when the lease commenced) required the prior written consent of HM Customs and Excise. This was refused and the trustees appealed. They were successful before the VAT Tribunal, but the Department appealed and the case was heard in the High Court. There it was held HM Customs and Excise should only give permission for an election where there would be a fair and reasonable attribution of the Input Tax concerned as was the case here, otherwise it would lead to the trustees being subject to assessment for VAT under the self-supply charge with no means of recovering Input Tax as there would be no taxable outward supply of the property. The trustees' appeal was therefore upheld and their election to waive exemption granted. Subsequently HM Customs and Excise published Business Brief 17/96 clarifying the position of the recovery of Input Tax following an election to waive exemption.

13.26   Fortunately, the self-supply charge is being gradually abolished. Any development where construction commenced after 1 March 1995 will not be liable to a taxable self-supply charge. It is no longer the case that a taxable supply will always be made of commercial property. It will only be so if the developer intends to make a taxable sale of the freehold of a new property or has opted to tax the property and intends to let it. This change means it is essential for HM Customs and Excise to establish the developer's intentions at an early stage. Trustees are therefore recommended to seek good accountancy advice in these areas so that the written consent of HM Customs and Excise will be given.

The *VAT Buildings and Land Order*

13.27   Following the case of *Commissioners of Customs and Excise v Robert Gordons College [1994] STC 698*, the Chancellor in his 1994 November Budget announced an anti-avoidance measure relating to property leasebacks between connected parties. The measure was introduced with effect from 30 November 1994 by the *Value Added Tax (Buildings and Land) Order (SI 1994 No 3013))* (APPENDIX 55) and referred to as the *VAT Buildings and Land Order*. This prevents the option to tax (see 13.22) from applying to grants of interest in property and land between connected persons.

13.28   The *VAT Buildings and Land Order* amends *VAT Act 1994 Sch 10* and applies to new leases with effect from 30 November 1994. Leases in existence at that date are not affected. The landlord's option to charge VAT on a new lease from 30 November 1994 does not apply if the landlord and the lessee in relation to the new lease are connected persons and either of them is not a fully taxable person. The question of whether a person is connected is determined by the provisions of *section 839* which are somewhat different to the criteria in *sections 416(a)* and *840,* used by the PSO (now the IR SPSS) regarding connected party transactions in the *1991 Regulations*. The provisions of *section 839* in relation to two or more persons acting together to secure or exercise control of a company were considered in the case of *Steele v EVC International NV [1996] STC 785* and may be relevant here. A fully taxable person, for VAT purposes, is either the landlord or tenant who at the end of the VAT accounting period in which the new lease is granted is entitled to credit for Input Tax on all supplies to and acquisitions or importations by him or her in that period.

13.29 If the circumstances in 13.28 apply, then in respect of the rent payable on a new lease to the landlord no Output Tax is chargeable. If a property is purchased and Input Tax paid on the purchase price, the landlord is prevented from reclaiming such Input Tax against Output Tax attributable to the same property. The Input Tax also paid by the landlord on expenditure relating to the property cannot be reclaimed against Output Tax.

13.30 If the trustees of a SSAS as the landlords grant a new lease on property or land to a connected person, they are prevented from opting to charge VAT on the rent payable under the lease if they or the tenant would be entitled to credit for Input Tax. Because SSASs frequently lease property to the company or its associates, connected persons per the provisions of *section 839*, they are caught by the legislation.

13.31 It was widely felt that it was not HM Customs and Excise's intention to penalise SSAS and other pension schemes with this anti-avoidance legislation. However, SSAS lose out financially because they are unable to reclaim Input Tax against Output Tax as there is no Output Tax payable on the rent received by the trustees. The simple example below illustrates how a SSAS that grants a new lease to its principal company after 30 November 1994 is affected financially compared with the position had it granted the lease before then:

(*a*) New lease before 30 November 1994

Rent £6,500 p.a. plus VAT £1,137.50 =	£7,637.50
Output Tax payable to HM Customs and Excise	£1,137.50
Less Input Tax on pension scheme activities	£1,000.00
Net VAT payable to HM Customs and Excise	£137.50

(*b*) New lease after 30 November 1994

Rent £6,500 p.a. but no Output Tax chargeable

Input Tax on pension scheme activities £1,000, but not available for set-off.

The SSAS loses £862.50 (£1,000 – £137.50) compared with previously. It would be substantially worse off financially if it bought a property and incurred Input Tax thereon as there would be nothing against which to set the Input Tax.

13.32   There were widespread representations against the *VAT Buildings and Land Order* because of its application to non-tax paying bodies. Some extra-statutory concessions were given, but not to SSAS, despite strong representations from the APT. HM Customs and Excise maintained the legislation was intended to combat the increasing and aggressively marketed lease and lease-back schemes aimed at VAT avoidance. The APT on the other hand made the point that pension schemes had never been in the van of such avoidance schemes and that the Inland Revenue had approved leaseback arrangements in SSAS for many years.

13.33   Eventually HM Customs and Excise conceded the legislation had been too wide ranging and subsequently announced two extra-statutory concessions. The first was announced on 21 December 1995 whereby for the purposes of *VAT Act 1984, Sch 10 para 3(8)(A)* a person may be treated as fully taxable if at the end of the accounting period in which the grant of a new lease is made that person is entitled to recover 80% or more of the VAT he incurs or would be able to recover 80% or more of the tax he incurred were it not for other supplies falling within group 1 of *VAT Act 1994, Sch 9*. The aim of this concession was to restore the option to tax for persons connected with each other who make supplies of commercial property to each other which are not motivated or characterised by tax avoidance. The concession was retrospective to 30 November 1994.

13.34   This first concession was not particularly helpful to SSAS although HM Customs and Excise undertook to consider individual cases which were not able to take advantage of it, but which were not motivated by tax avoidance and for which there is a clearly demonstrable ordinary commercial motivation and justification.

13.35   The second extra-statutory concession announced on 28 February 1996 was much more helpful to SSAS though not to SIPPS (see 14.199). In its News Release 11/96 (APPENDIX 56) HM Customs and Excise stated it had granted an extra-statutory concession specifically for SSAS because the leaseback arrangements caught by the *VAT Buildings and Land Order (SI 1994 No 3013)* were not the avoidance the Order sought to prevent. Under the concession for the purposes of *VAT Act 1994, Sch 10 para 3(8)(A)*, a SSAS may be treated as a fully taxable person. The effect of the concession is that where a grant of a new lease is made between a SSAS and a connected person, the taxable status of the SSAS is essentially ignored and the *VAT Buildings and Land Order* will disapply an election only if the other party is not fully taxable. The other party may take advantage of the earlier 80% concession (see 13.33) in determining whether he is fully taxable. This concession is also retrospective to 30 November 1994 and SSAS have subsequently been encouraged to apply to their local VAT offices to reclaim Input Tax that could not be reclaimed after 30 November 1994.

13.36 The extra-statutory concession at 13.35 should assist most SSAS caught by the *VAT Buildings and Land Order*. It should be noted nonetheless that if HM Customs and Excise do not exercise their discretion to operate the extra-statutory concessions mentioned in 13.33 and 13.35 an appeal to the VAT Tribunal may not assist. This is because VAT Tribunals do not have jurisdiction to consider the operation of an extra-statutory concession by HM Customs and Excise. Representations may have to be made to the Revenue Adjudicator, who also handles HM Customs and Excise matters, or judicial review sought to remedy the problem. The nature of the concession is different however to that expected by the APT as HM Customs and Excise had been considering the definition of 'connected person' might not apply insofar as the trustee body of a pension scheme was concerned if at least one of the trustees was an independent person, i.e. not a scheme member nor connected to the principal company. Such a definition would have exempted SSAS and SIPPS from the *VAT Buildings and Land Order (SI 1994 No 3013)* because they are both obliged by the Inland Revenue to appoint an independent trustee. However, the definition of 'connected person' is widely used by the Inland Revenue quite apart from pension schemes and it is suspected that if HM Customs and Excise had treated the trustee body as unconnected because one of its constituents was independent, this would have caused widespread problems for the Inland Revenue.

Land and buildings supplied to non-taxable persons

13.37 HM Customs and Excise continued to be concerned at the position of banks and insurance companies, which are substantially exempt from VAT and which were exploiting the option to tax through the use of associated leasing companies so as to increase their Input Tax recovery significantly. The connected persons provisions of the *VAT Buildings and Land Order (SI 1994 No 3013)* were apparently ineffective to counter this. So the *VAT Buildings and Land Order* was repealed with effect from 26 November 1996 by *FA 97, s 37* and replaced from 19 March 1997 by more comprehensive anti-avoidance provisions which do not apply to transactions between unconnected persons.

13.38 The repeal of the *Buildings and Land Order (SI 1994 No 3013)* effectively removes the restrictions on the option to charge VAT for connected persons who are not fully taxable. For SSASs, the period between 30 November 1994 and 26 November 1996 is covered by the extra-statutory concessions (see 13.35), but thereafter they are in the same position as all self-administered pension schemes. From 19 March 1997 the option to tax land and buildings by the trustees or a developer or someone who finances a development or a person connected with any of them is not available for supplies made to persons who do not use the property wholly or mainly for taxable purposes. This applies to the rent or sale of property to an exempt person. This prevents a SSAS from electing to charge VAT on a commercial property lease or sale to a tenant or purchaser whose business is VAT exempt. The trustees are also unable to reclaim Input Tax attributable to such a property.

13.39   VAT exempt businesses include banks, building societies, insurance companies and brokers, providers of private education (schools) and private health. Fortunately, certain types of premises are excluded from the type of commercial property being leased or sold, e.g. shops, public houses, hotels, small workshops, markets and exhibition centres. SSASs do lease high street premises to banks, building societies, insurance companies and brokers and will be subject to these measures from 26 November 1996, but they only apply if the property is potentially within the capital goods scheme (see 13.46) and cost more than £250,000 or major alterations to the building cost more than that amount. Moreover if the parties entered into an agreement for lease before 26 November 1996, the lease will be excepted from the requirements provided the actual lease is granted before 30 November 1999 *(FA 1997, s 37(5))*. A further restriction is to be imposed by the *Value Added Tax (Buildings and Land) Order 1999 (SI 1999 No 593)* with effect from 10 March 1999. This is where, at the time of the grant of the lease, the development was not a capital item within the capital goods scheme but it was nonetheless the intention that it would become so either for the business or any one to whom the property is sold or transferred.

13.40   The trustees as landlords may be faced with significant financial implications. They cannot charge VAT on the rent receivable nor can they set off Input Tax they incur attributable to the property. The Input Tax could be irrecoverable if it relates to legal or agents' costs in setting up the lease although it may be possible to invoice the lessee for irrecoverable VAT as part of any service charge. The trustees may be reluctant to lease a property in these circumstances except at an increased rent or with a covenant from the lessee to compensate for the VAT drawbacks. The increased rent would also have to be justified to the PSO with an independent valuation because the lease would be connected. Some trustees may decide it is not worth proceeding with VAT exempt tenants and seek a letting to a VATable business instead.

13.41   It was foreseen in the legislation that the trustees would need to protect themselves in some areas, for instance if the tenant at a later stage uses the premises wholly or mainly for taxable purposes (see 13.38) or assigns the lease to an exempt tenant. *FA 1997, s 37* requires tenants to notify landlords of any relevant change in their use of the property. It may also be worth while ensuring the tenant indemnifies the trustees against any adverse Input Tax consequences.

Sales

13.42   The sale of a freehold commercial property less than three years old remains standard rated for VAT purposes. The sale of other freehold commercial property by a SSAS to a VAT exempt business is however caught by the provisions of *FA 1997, s 37* from 19 March 1997 as are assignments or surrenders of leases. The trustees as vendors will need to ascertain at the outset the VAT status of the prospective purchaser and the extent of the use of the property before they can decide whether or not to charge VAT on the sale price. The criteria for the purchaser's status and for the extent of the use of the property are as set out in 13.38 and 13.39.

13.43   There are transitional provisions similar to leases (see 13.39) where the trustees sell property pursuant to a written agreement entered into before 26 November 1996 which fixed the terms of the sale, but allow the option to tax to continue up to 30 November 1999 regardless of the prospective purchaser's intended use of the property.

13.44   Where the trustees sell property to a VAT exempt business which will not use the property wholly or mainly for taxable purposes, they will not be able to charge VAT on the sale and will have to consider the financial implications of not being able to recover Input Tax attributable to the property. They may as a result decide not to sell to this type of purchaser and look elsewhere for a buyer. They could increase the sale price to compensate themselves for Input Tax drawbacks. It is important to note that if the purchaser claims to be an exempt purchaser and therefore that the sale is exempt, it is incumbent on the trustees to require proof of the same. If the purchaser misleads the trustees and they do not in consequence collect any VAT on completion, the trustees as the vendor remain liable for Output Tax to HM Customs and Excise.

'Going Concern' Principles

13.45   Where a property is owned by a third party and purchased by the trustees with vacant possession 'going concern' does not apply. However, where the third party owned the property and continued as the tenant after the property was purchased by the trustees, 'going concern' provisions may apply. The vendor and subsequent tenant may often be the principal company of the SSAS.

These arrangements would mean that the purchasing trustees, who would have opted to tax in respect of the rent, although registered for VAT, would not be able to reclaim VAT if it has already been paid. This could result in potential action against the vendor – embarrassing if it is the principal company – who should not have charged VAT. Both parties should be registered for VAT for the 'going concern' provisions to apply. The VAT leaflet 700/9/94 is available from local VAT offices to assist trustees in this connection, together with PSO Update 1 thereto of 1 January 1996.

Capital goods scheme

13.46 The scheme operates to ensure that the correct amount of VAT is reclaimed on higher value business purchases of land and property and computer equipment by requiring the tax reclaimed to be adjusted over a period of years if the use to which the asset is put changes. The scheme was changed with effect from 3 July 1997 to prevent abuse and make it more equitable. Under the *Value Added Tax (Amendment) (No 3) Regulations 1997 (SI 1997 No 1614)* the capital goods scheme has been extended to cover refurbishment and fitting out costs for existing properties, including civil engineering works carried out by the owner, subject to a minimum value and an adjustment period of up to 10 years. Rent will also be included in the scheme if it is paid, due or invoiced more than 12 months in advance. It will be included in the value of the taxable interest supplied to the owner when determining whether it exceeds the minimum value. These changes did not however cater for cases where the owner's initial deduction on the asset reflects accurately use in the first year of the capital goods scheme. So the 1999 Budget proposals contained in the *Value Added Tax (Amendment) (No 2) 1999 Regulations (SI 1999 No 599)* provided for capital goods scheme adjustments from 10 March 1999 to compare the later use of the asset with the initial deduction of Input Tax. Because of the amount involved large self-administered schemes are more likely to be within the capital goods scheme than SSASs.

Nominee Ownership

13.47 Finally, regarding property, HM Customs and Excise issued a Statement of Practice on 1 June 1996 covering the situation where the legal title in land is held by a nominee for a named beneficial owner which is often the case where the legal title is held on trust for a pension scheme. The named beneficial owner of the land, and not the nominee, will be considered as the transferee for the purpose of establishing the transfer of a property letting business as a going concern provided both parties agree to such treatment. Persons transferring an interest in land to a person who is a nominee for a named beneficial owner are expected to check the VAT registration and where necessary the VAT elections made by the beneficial owner.

Registration

13.48 It is most advisable that the trustees seek their accountant's advice on whether or not they should register for VAT purposes with HM Customs and Excise. So far as a SSAS is concerned the decision to register will very much depend on the scheme's property transactions and rents the trustees receive on which they can charge VAT. A person is required to register for VAT if the value of the taxable supplies in a twelve-month period has exceeded the registration threshold (see 13.54). If he is making taxable supplies, but the value of such supplies has not exceeded the threshold, he is entitled to register if he wishes to, but he is not required to do so. One sale only of a property worth over the threshold will put a SSAS above the threshold, so that the question of registration should be considered whenever a property is sold. On the other hand, the level of the trustees' Input Tax must be considered and who pays it – the trustees or the employer – as only the Input Tax attributable to the trustees can be recovered against their Output Tax (see 13.4).

13.49 The trustees may apply for voluntary registration if their taxable turnover does not exceed the threshold. They can then claim Input Tax provided they are making taxable supplies, i.e. their supplies are zero-rated at least for VAT purposes. Input Tax cannot otherwise be reclaimed. Should the trustees' Input Tax exceed their Output Tax they may claim a repayment.

13.50 Registration must be in the name of the trustees of the pension scheme. A separate registration is required for each funded pension scheme as the trustees as individuals or corporate bodies may be registered for VAT in their own right or as trustees of other schemes. A pensioneer trustee may be a corporate body anyway and the problems in paragraphs 13.15 and 13.16 above will be avoided. So the SSAS is treated as a separate business carried on by the trustees and they will account for VAT to HM Customs and Excise monthly or quarterly under the usual arrangements.

13.51 The decision to register for the trustees of a pension scheme is further complicated where they jointly own property and let it to one tenant. At present all joint owners must register separately for VAT if Output Tax is to be charged on the rent receivable. This cannot be done if only one joint owner registers for VAT. Each joint owner cannot opt individually to tax their own share of the rent. This situation can create confusion where one of a number of owners wishes to opt to tax and the other co-owners do not. Difficulties may also arise where some of the owners are registered and some are not.

13.52 These problems have been addressed by *FA 1995, s 26* which introduced *VAT Act 1994, s 51A*. This legislation envisages that where the co-owners propose to exercise the option to waive exemption, tax rents, etc., they must act unanimously. By unanimous decision the co-owners, including the trustees of a pension scheme, will choose to register for VAT. Such registration will cover all co-owners as a single person and the co-owners will be jointly and severally liable for the VAT consequences. *Section 51A* does not come into force though until enacted by regulations. Meanwhile, it should be noted that this legislation will not effectively deal with the position of professional trustees (see 13.50). This is because co-owners will be treated as the same taxable person for the supply in question and any other supplies. So where there are professional trustees, such as the pensioneer trustee, who will act for a numbers of schemes, they would appear to be treated as the same taxable person for all supplies of land and buildings owned by any of these schemes.

13.53 In connection with the discussion document issued in 1995 (see 13.17), it is proposed that individual trusts, i.e. pension schemes, should be registered separately in the name of the trust and should be supported with the details of the trustees. It is also proposed that registration should be continuous and not take account of changes in trustees. It is to be hoped that these administratively efficient arrangements are adopted.

13.54 The registration threshold for VAT after 31 March 2001 is £54,000 (£52,000 for the previous year). The standard rate remains at 17.5%.

Insurance premium tax

13.55 This was introduced by *FA 1994, s 48* and came into operation on 1 October 1994. Insurance companies are to pay IPT at a net rate of 5% with effect from 1 July 1999 (previously 4%) on most general insurance to HM Customs and Excise. Insurance companies are required to register and make quarterly returns to the Department. The tax will not apply to long term insurance including pensions. Long term insurance is defined in *Insurance Companies Act 1982, Sch 1* and this includes life and pensions.

13.56 So far as SSASs are concerned, premiums paid by the employer to a LO operating a SSAS that are invested in policies will be exempt from IPT, as will premiums paid by the trustees towards a policy investment of a SSAS. Term assurance is, however, not within *Insurance Companies Act 1982, Sch 1*, but it is understood that premiums paid by the trustees or the employer to provide death-in-service cover for a member (see 4.83 and 14.90 below) should not attract IPT. Exemption should be confirmed by reference to the actual wording of the insurance contract.

13.57 If the trustees of a SSAS own property or any other fixed asset and insure it, they will pay IPT on the insurance premium from 1 October 1994.

Chapter 14

Self-Invested Personal Pensions — SIPPs

Introduction

14.1   Before 1988 there was no real opportunity for the great majority of employees who were not members of occupational pension schemes to provide themselves with a pension in respect of their employment. Until then only directors, the self-employed or partners were able to take advantage of the tax system by establishing retirement annuity contracts (see 1.3) for themselves to provide pensions when they retired. Membership of occupational schemes was very often compulsory and therefore many employees could not choose the type of pension scheme to which they wished to belong.

14.2   At the same time the escalating costs of the State Earnings Related Pension Scheme (SERPS) were causing concern. The Government decided to reduce the level of SERPS over a period of years and to encourage employees to contract-out of SERPS. In 1988 personal pensions were created to assist in this process. Personal pensions gave the opportunity to all those employees not in occupational schemes to have a pension together with the self-employed. Members of occupational schemes were also given a choice of the type of pension scheme to which they wished to belong as compulsory membership was abolished.

14.3   The first personal pensions were wholly insured, i.e. their funds were invested with LOs, but in 1989 the Chancellor's Budget statement directed that it should be made easier for individuals to control their own pension fund investment. It was therefore made easier for individuals to choose how they wished their contributions to be invested. This brought them into line with retirement annuity contracts where there had been a facility for several years prior to 1988 for individuals to direct into which type of investment managed by a LO their contributions should be paid, e.g. unit trusts, property, equities, etc. Such personal pensions are the equivalent of self-managed funds (see 2.33). Later in 1989 the fully self-invested personal pension (SIPP) came into being with the publication of Memorandum No 101 (APPENDIX 57), effectively sanctioning control over the investment portfolio by the member.

14.4   *Self-Invested Personal Pensions — SIPPs*

14.4   As SIPPs developed and became more numerous during the 1990s, particularly with the advent of the income withdrawal facility in 1995 (see 14.182), providers, trustees and administrators of SIPPs made more and more representations to the Inland Revenue requesting agreement to different types of investments, where it was unclear whether or not they fell within one of the categories in the range of permitted investments in Memorandum 101. This culminated in the SIPP Provider Group (SPG) – the representative body for providers, trustees and administrators of SIPPs – publishing to their members on 10 March 1998 a 'list of permitted investments' (APPENDIX 62), which had been agreed with the Inland Revenue at a meeting on 15 January 1998.

14.5   It was anticipated that this list would be incorporated into the Inland Revenue's then current guidance notes for personal pensions, IR 76 (1991) the equivalent of PN for retirement benefits schemes, but it never was. So, despite the publication of an updated version of the guidance notes in 1999 (which omitted parts 11 and 12 on SIPPs and transfers respectively), Memorandum 101 and parts 4.39 and 8.9 – 8.15 of IR76 (1991), remained the only practice relevant to investments actually published by the Inland Revenue until regulations came into force in April 2001 (see 14.151), and part 11 was inserted into the latest edition of their guidance notes IR76 (2000), (see 14.153).

14.6   There has always been a tendency for a SIPP to be regarded as a very different type of pension scheme to a more traditional insured personal pension, and this tendency is likely to continue now there is a statutory definition of a SIPP (see 14.155). However, it should always be remembered that although there are additional requirements imposed on SIPPs because of the member's ability to control how the fund is invested (hence the term 'self-invested'), a SIPP is a personal pension and subject to the legislative requirements and Inland Revenue discretionary practice that apply to personal pensions.

14.7   With the advent of stakeholder pension schemes a new tax regime was introduced with effect from 6 April 2001 by changes to *ICTA 1988, Pt XIV, Ch I and Ch IV* introduced under *FA 2000, s 61* and *Sch 13*, to apply not only to stakeholder schemes but also any defined contribution (i.e, money purchase) occupational pension scheme wishing to be approved under the new regime and all personal pension schemes, including SIPPs (see 14.23 and 14.24).

14.8   The remainder of CHAPTER 14 concentrates on SIPPs, the requirements of IR SPSS and the DWP in relation to SIPPs and VAT aspects.

14.9   There had always been, and indeed currently continue to be, Friendly Society based plans available to seven or more partners in a partnership.

These are however specialised by nature and specifically targeted, and therefore excluded from this book.

The advantages of SIPPs

14.10 It is not the intention here to advise where a SIPP will be more advantageous than a SSAS as it will depend on the particular circumstances of each case. Comparisons can be made in certain areas, e.g. investments, contributions, income withdrawal, etc. The advantages of establishing a SIPP will be explored, but it must always be borne in mind that a big disadvantage compared with any type of occupational scheme is that a SIPP is mainly funded by personal contributions by the member (in the absence of an employer's contribution for self-employed taxpayers) and the general reluctance of employers to make contributions on behalf of their employees to personal pensions.

14.11 For the company director, self-employed partner, or sole proprietor, a SIPP can provide the opportunity to purchase commercial property, such as offices, which can be let on arm's-length terms to the member's business. The purchase could be funded not just from the fund itself, but from borrowings or a transfer payment brought in from previous pension arrangements.

14.12 The ability of the member to decide on his/her own investments, subject to IR SPSS requirements, either as a trustee of his/her own SIPP fund or by instructing the trustee, is most compelling for those who wish to control the investments personally. Such control is not available with an insured personal pension unless it is of the self-managed variety (see 2.33). Even if the member is a trustee and makes all the investment decisions, an administrator (see 14.73) must be appointed. SIPPs should appeal strongly to directors of private companies and the self-employed who are used to running their own company or business and who require flexibility.

This flexibility also allows members to adjust the investment policy to suit their attitude to risk, the spread of investments and ethical investment, to their working lifestyle and eventually to retirement. There is nothing to prevent a cautious member selecting cash, gilts or LO with profits and managed funds. If a greater element of risk is acceptable then the full range of permitted investments is available under (*SI 2001 No 117*) (Appendix 66).

14.13 The benefit structure of a SIPP may appeal to some individuals. For instance a normal retirement age of 50 can apply. There is no maximum limit on the pension payable, although the tax- free lump sum cannot exceed 25% of the fund. (These and other aspects of benefits from a SIPP are covered in 14.108 to 14.132).

14.14   The carrying forward of unused tax relief from previous years and the carrying back of personal contributions to previous years to obtain tax relief have been very attractive, not only where an individual's income fluctuates over the years, but also where an individual has the ability to pay additional contributions in later years from other sources. Unfortunately, as part of the new tax regime, the carry forward facility has been abolished. Nevertheless, for historical purposes, because the abolition does not apply to retirement annuity contracts and because in certain cases it will still be possible to utilise carry forward until 31 January 2002, aspects of the operation of carry forward and carry back up to 6 April 2001 are explained in 14.37 to 14.48.

14.15   Although the position from 6 April 2001 does not provide any facility for making one-off contributions to catch up on previous tax years where the maximum tax relief was not used up, it does break the link with 'net relevant earnings' in a number of ways. This allows for contributions to be made up to a certain level known as the 'earnings threshold', without reference to earnings and, in certain circumstances, where the individual is also a member of a retirement benefits scheme. It also allows for higher level contributions above the 'earnings threshold' (currently £3,600) to be based on 'net relevant earnings' for a particular tax year and then continue at the same rate for each of the following five years even if earnings decrease or cease altogether (see 14.49 to 14.52). There are, however, strict eligibility requirements that need to be satisfied in each case (see 14.68 and 14.69)

14.16   Under the new tax regime all personal contributions, must be paid net of basic rate income tax, which may be of some advantage for the self-employed from a cash flow perspective.

14.17   The facility to take income withdrawals from a SIPP after retirement and up to age 75 within certain parameters (see 14.188 and 14.189) is undoubtedly a distinct advantage. It is more flexible than either the more common facility under a SSAS to defer the purchase of annuities to age 75 (see 4.97 to 4.106). Where the level of pension must be maintained, (subject to sufficiency of funds) or the less used facility introduced in PSO Update No 54 (see 3.42 and 3.43) which is also available to all types of money purchase retirement benefits schemes, the main areas of greater flexibility are those in relation to 'phased' income withdrawals (see 14.208) and death benefits (see 14.199). It is also advantageous to director members of retirement benefits schemes who wish to continue in an executive capacity but also draw retirement benefits (see 14.113).

14.18   SIPPs are not covered by the majority of the *Pensions Act 1995* provisions (see 14.235). As a result they are usually much less complex administratively than occupational schemes.

14.19 SIPPs are the pensions success story of the last ten years, much assisted by their simplicity, the income drawdown facility and their flexibility with various options available on the approach of retirement and in the event of death. The potential market for SIPPs is much greater than SSASs and it is not likely to diminish even with the recent introduction of regulations relating to investments (see 14.151 to 14.175), keeping records, providing information and permitting a compliance audit function (see 14.102 to 14.107).

Legislation and guidelines

14.20 The Inland Revenue legislation and guidelines governing SIPPs are covered generally in 14.21 to 14.30 and in greater detail later in the chapter, together with DWP legislation, VAT aspects, the *Data Protection Act 1998* and the *Trustee Act 2000*. The effects of Data Protection legislation are covered in CHAPTER 11, and EU law in CHAPTER 16.

14.21 SIPPs are subject to the following legislation and guidelines:

(a)   *ICTA 1988* and successive *Finance Acts*;

(b)   Statutory Instruments;

(c)   Personal Pension Schemes Guidance Notes IR 76;

(d)   Pensions Updates (formerly PSO Updates and Memoranda);

(e)   Changes in practice announced via the SIPP Provider Group (SPG).

14.22 *Chapter IV Part XIV ICTA 1988* contains the main legislation relating to personal pensions in *sections 630–655* and which therefore apply to SIPPs. Some subsequent Finance Acts have introduced legislation which applies generally to all pension schemes, e.g. *FA 1989* and the earnings cap and *FA 1998* with the 40% tax charge on loss of approval. Some include specific application for personal pensions. So SIPPs eg. *FA 1995* and the income withdrawal facility, and *FA 1998* empower the Inland Revenue to make regulations to limit their discretion to approve a personal pension scheme by reference to the benefits the scheme provides, the investments held etc, (*section 638A*) and regulations requiring the provision to the Inland Revenue of information and documents, record keeping, and for inspections (*section 651A*).

14.23 In December 1998 the Secretary of State for Social Security published a Green Paper 'A New Contract for Welfare: Partnership In Pensions' setting out a framework for the new Labour Government's stakeholder pensions. This included proposals for a simplified tax regime not just for stakeholder pensions but for all defined contribution (i.e. money purchase) pension schemes, irrespective of whether they are set up as occupational or personal pension schemes, and was to be broadly based on the existing regime for personal pensions.

14.24 The framework for stakeholder pensions was put in place under the *Welfare Reform and Pensions Act 1999* which also introduced the framework for the new rules relating to pensions sharing on divorce (see 3.95) and protection of a member's benefits in the event of bankruptcy. The new tax regime was introduced under *FA 2000, s 61* and *Sch 13*, by making amendments to the rules for approval of, and tax relief on, contributions to pension schemes, in *ICTA 1988, Part XIV, Chapters I* and *IV*. The main changes relevant to SIPPs came into force on 6 April 2001 and are as follows:

• money purchase occupational pension schemes, including SSASs, can convert to personal pension schemes (see 14.76). From 6 April 2001, new money purchase occupational pension schemes, including SSASs may apply for approval as retirement benefits schemes under *Chapter I* or as personal pension schemes under *Chapter IV*, or even have separate parts approved under each. In addition such schemes that are already approved under *Chapter I* may convert to personal pensions under *Chapter IV*. However, it will not be possible to convert back from *Chapter IV* to *Chapter* I approval;

• personal pension schemes may be established under trust without the need for an authorised provider (see 14.74);

• new eligibility rules for membership (see 14.68 to 14.72) and payment of contributions (see 14.49 TO 14.57);

• all contributions by individuals must be paid net of basic rate income tax;

• carrying forward tax relief will no longer be possible after 6 April 2001, with one exception (see 14.55).

Throughout the rest of this chapter occupational pension schemes that are approved as retirement benefits schemes under *Chapter I* will be referred to as '*Chapter I* schemes' and those that opt for approval under *Chapter IV* as '*Chapter IV* schemes'.

14.25 As part of the process of introducing details of how the new tax regime is to operate, a variety of regulations have been introduced under the relevant powers in the primary legislation mentioned in 14.21 The main regulations affecting SIPPs are contained in the following Statutory Instruments:

• the *Personal Pension Schemes (Restriction or Discretion to Approve) (Establishment of Schemes under Trusts) Regulations 2000 (SI 2000 No 2314)*, from the Inland Revenue which came into force on 1 October 2000. See 14.74.

- the *Personal Pension Schemes (Information Powers) Regulations 2000 (SI 2000 No 2316)* (APPENDIX 63), from the Inland Revenue, which came into force on 1 October 2000 (see 14.105).

- the *Personal Pension Schemes (Relief at Source) (Amendment) Regulations 2000 (SI 2000 No 2315)*, from the Inland Revenue which came into force on 6 April 2001. See 14.50.

- the *Personal Pension Schemes (Establishment of Schemes) Order 2000 (SI 2000 No 2317)*, (APPENDIX 64) from the Treasury which came into force on 1 October 2000. See 14.74.

- the *Personal Pension Schemes (Concurrent Membership) Order 2000 (SI 2000 No 2318)*, from the Treasury which came into force on 6 April 2001. See 14.69.

- the *Personal Pension Schemes (Payments by Employers) Regulations 2000 (SI 2000 No 2692)* (APPENDIX 65), from the Secretary of State for Social Security, which came into force on 6 April 2001. See 14.243.

- the *Personal Pension Schemes (Restriction on Discretion to Approve) (Permitted Investments) Regulations 2001 (SI 2001 No 117)* (APPENDIX 66), from the Inland Revenue, which came into force on 6 April 2001. See 14.151 to 14.175.

- the *Personal Pension Schemes (Conversion of Retirement Benefits Schemes) Regulations 2001 (SI 2001 No 118)* (APPENDIX 67), from the Inland Revenue, and came into force on 6 April 2001. See 14.76.

- the *Personal Pension Schemes (Transfer Payments) Regulations 2001 (SI 2001 No 119)* (APPENDIX 68), from the Inland Revenue, part of which came into force on 14 February 2001 (see 14.125) and the rest on 6 April 2001(see 14.191).

14.26 IR SPSS guidelines setting out its discretionary practice for personal pensions were first published in Memorandum No 99 in March 1989. These guidelines were very basic, but Memorandum No 99(59) promised further details including safeguards required by the Inland Revenue as soon as possible. Memorandum No 101 (APPENDIX 57) followed in October 1989 and the first version of Personal Pension Schemes Guidance Notes IR76 was published in March 1988. Updated versions were issued in 1991, 1999 and 2000. The latest version IR76 (2000) is available on the Inland Revenue's website (*www.inlandrevenue.gov.uk*) and has already been updated on several occasions, particularly when Statutory Instruments have been issued.

14.27 Memorandum No 101 referred to the Chancellor's Budget statement (see 14.3) and to members of personal pension schemes having the opportunity to become more involved in decisions about how their contributions are invested. It set out the guidance applicable to all personal pension schemes wishing to give members a degree of investment choice. The guidance covered the investment of members' contributions and the use of scheme funds. It made it clear that the extent of choice which members of a SIPP have are matters for each scheme to decide and that there were no Inland Revenue requirements in this respect. Thus, some SIPPs have limited individual involvement to selecting the parameters of the investment portfolio and leave the selection of particular investments to a fund manager. Alternatively, other SIPPs have given members a direct say regarding specific investments to be held and when they should be acquired and disposed. Memorandum 101 has been superseded by *SI 2000 No 117*, which limits IR SPSS discretionary powers in prescribed circumstances, and Part 11 of IR 76 (2000).

14.28   Booklet IR76 (2000) is the equivalent of PN for personal pension schemes. This sets out in detail IR SPSS discretionary practice relating to all personal pension schemes and therefore encompasses SIPPs including in Part 11 and Appendices 24 and 25, the range of acceptable and unacceptable investments and the use of scheme funds. See 14.29

14.29   Memorandum No 101(9) first mentioned primary legislation in the shape of *section 839* in relation to connected transactions and it is as well to mention this here because of its importance to SIPPs and investment transactions they undertake (see 14.134 to 14.175). The trustees of a SIPP are not allowed to purchase from or sell to a person who is connected with a member if that person is within the definition of connected person in *section 839*, any of the permitted investments. *Section 839* defines a connected person as a:

- scheme member or their relatives;

- partner of a partnership of which the member or his relatives are also partners;

- trustee of a settlement where the trustee or the settlor is the scheme member or his relatives;

- company controlled by a member of the scheme personally or together with his relatives.

This definition is very much in line with the definition of proscribed vendors and purchasers for SSASs (see 6.3 and 6.4). The same three-year time limit applies as for SSASs in that if a member sold a property to a third party three years must elapse before it can be acquired by the member's SIPP. It is the administrator's duty to ensure that any transaction is not one with a connected person. This is now enshrined in regulation 9 of *SI 2001 No 117*, but with one exception in respect of joint property investments. (See 14.166).

14.30   Changes in practice have occurred over the years with the growth in IR SPSS's experience of SIPPs. These have usually been promulgated through IR SPSS Updates, but sometimes the representative body, the SPG, has been informed and indeed used through the publication of joint meeting minutes. Probably the most important aspects to be published via the SPG have been the minutes of the joint meeting of 15 January 1998 and the resultant list of permitted investments and the minutes of a joint meeting on 14 March 2001 which resulted in the addition of Part 11 to IR76 (2000) on the Inland Revenue website. This then led to further representations by the SPG for further clarification of certain aspects of *SI 2001 No 117* and Part 11 IR76 (2000), largely in connection with property transactions (see 14.164 to 14.175). It is anticipated that IR SPSS will provide such clarification in the form of a greatly expanded Part 11 to IR76 (2000) before the end of 2001.

In August 2001 IR SPSS also produced a useful summary of the main aspects of personal pensions and stakeholder pensions under the new tax regime in the booklet PSO 2 entitled 'Personal Pension Schemes (including Stakeholder Pension Schemes) A Guide for Members of Tax Approved Schemes', which is available from the Inland Revenue website (*www.inlandrevenue.gov.uk*) or from IR SPSS stationery order line on 0115 974 1670.

Tax advantages and funding

14.31 SIPPs like all other types of approved pension schemes enjoy tax advantages of various kinds. It is still important to bear in mind though that the use of a SIPP as a vehicle to achieve tax avoidance will not satisfy the test in *section 630* (1)'whose sole purpose is the provision of annuities or lump sums'. The tax reliefs available to SIPPs are those generally available to other approved pension schemes with some differences.

14.32 The new tax regime, which came into force on 6 April 2001, has introduced many changes particularly relating to funding and created additional differences not only with other approved pension schemes but also with the situation for personal pensions prior to 6 April. Therefore, the position before 6 April 2001 is explained in 14.33 to 14.48 and the position from 6 April 2001 in 14.49 to 14.57.

The position prior to 6 April 2001

14.33 There was no obligation for an employer to contribute to a SIPP, but where an employer did contribute the aggregate contributions paid by the member and to all personal pensions and retirement annuity contracts could not exceed 17.5% of the member's net relevant earnings for the year in which the contributions were paid (*section 640(4)*) subject to the earnings cap (APPENDIX 26) for that year (*section 640A*). This percentage was more generous for older members (*section 640(2)*) because of the shorter time available before retirement and could be very attractive to higher rate taxpayers.

Age at beginning of tax year	% age of net relevant earnings
36–45	20
46–50	25
51–55	30
56–60	35
61–74	40

The above table also applies from 6 April 2001 and still relates to 'gross' contributions (i.e. including any basic rate tax to be reclaimed).

14.35 All contributions had to be cash payments, not in the form of assets.

14.36 Section *640(3)* limited contributions that could be applied to secure a lump sum death benefit under a term assurance contract to no more than 5% of a member's net relevant earnings.

(*a*) Employer contributions–allowable as deductions for corporation tax purposes under section 640(4). Such contributions are not liable to tax under Schedule E in the hands of members by virtue of section 643(1).

(*b*) Personal contributions paid by members subject to the limits in 14.33 – deductible from, or set off against, any relevant earnings for the year of assessment in which paid under section 639(1).

(*c*) The income of a SIPP–exempt from income tax at the basic and additional rate under section 643(2).

(*d*) Any gains realised on the disposal of an asset–exempt from Capital Gains Tax under *TCGA 1992, s 271(1)(h)(j)*.

Carry back of contributions and carry forward of tax relief

14.37 Prior to the introduction of the new tax regime these were two very attractive facilities applicable to all personal pension schemes, particularly for higher rate taxpayers or where members could afford to pay contributions in one year greater than the percentage on which tax relief was allowed. Personal contributions could be paid in the current tax year and carried back to the previous year for tax relief purposes if there were earnings in that year (*section 641(1)*). Additionally, if the personal contributions in any year were less than the maximum allowable the balance of unused tax relief could be carried forward to any of the following six tax years (*section 642 (1)*).

14.38 If a member so elected, a contribution paid in a given tax year could be treated as having been paid in the preceding tax year and tax relief given thereon subject to the contribution limit applicable to the member's age (see 14.33). Employer's contributions could not and still cannot be carried back. If there were no relevant earnings against which to set the contribution carried back then it was possible to carry back the contribution to the year before that. For 1996/97 and subsequent years the election had to be made on or before 31 January next following the end of the tax year in which the contribution to be carried back was actually paid (*FA 1996, Sch 21 para 18*). Thus, for a contribution paid in 1998/99, the election had to be made by 31 January 2000. Elections for 1995/96 and previous years had to be made not later than three months after the end of the tax year in which the contribution to be carried back was paid. Elections were made on the prescribed form PP43 and the amount to be carried back had to be stated thereon in monetary terms. The election could not cover contributions relating to more than one year and it could not be made until the first contribution in the year of assessment had been paid.

14.39 If a further tax assessment was made on income of the year to which the election related then *TMA 1970, s 43A* allowed an election to be made or amended within one year from the end of the tax year in which further assessment was made. This extension did not apply however, where the further assessment was made to recover tax lost through fraud or negligence. Once an election had been made to carry back contributions it could not be amended or withdrawn after the period for making the election had expired.

14.40 With the move to self-assessment from 6 April 1996 and the change from previous year to current year basis of assessment for Schedule D taxpayers, some legislative changes were made regarding carry-back relief. *TMA 1970, s 8(1)* was amended by *FA 1996, s 121* to allow personal pension contributions paid in 1996/97 that were carried back for relief purposes to 1995/96 to be taken into account when setting the level of any payments on account required for 1996/97. This meant that contributions made to a personal pension scheme in 1996/97 and carried back to 1995/96 would not affect Schedule D assessments made for 1995/96 for members who were sole traders. It stated that the different procedures for partnerships in the transitional year would not result in any benefit for partners who were members. However, claims to relate back contributions paid in 1997/98 or later years to the previous tax year would not reduce payments on account due for 1997/98 onwards but would be given by repayment of tax. For 1997/98 and later years carry-back claims might not have been ideal under self-assessment and provide improved cash flow in any situation. Members needed advice, particularly sole traders whose accounting period ended on or shortly before 5 April who might have had difficulty in establishing a pattern of paying their maximum contributions in the tax year itself. The Inland Revenue's 26th *Tax Bulletin* of 31 December 1996 provided several useful examples of how carried back contributions were dealt with for tax relief purposes.

14. 41 When a contribution was paid that was to be carried back, if the member was employed tax had to be deducted at the basic rate and the net amount paid to the administrator. If the member was self-employed the contribution was paid gross. In both instances this was in line with the arrangement for claiming tax relief. For self-employed members liable to the basic or higher rate of tax form PP43 had to be sent to the scheme administrator, who reclaimed the basic rate of tax. For employed members liable to the higher rate of tax, PP43 and PP120 had to be sent to the member's inspector of taxes to claim the higher rate relief. A copy of PP43 had to be provided to the administrator as it might ultimately have been required by FICO (Repayments) (see 14.42).

Carry back of contributions worked very simply and allowed a member to pay contributions in a current year that they could not have afforded the previous year. For example, a member received Schedule E remuneration in 1997/98 of £40,000 from an employer who had no occupational scheme. In 1998/99 this remuneration was £45,000 and the member decided, before 5 April 1999, to pay contributions to a personal pension scheme at the maximum rate for his age, of 20%. A contribution of £17,000 was paid on 31 March 1999 and an election made before 31 January 2000 to carry back £8,000 of this contribution to 1997/98. Thus the maximum tax relief would have been given on £8,000 for 1997/98 and £9,000 for 1998/99.

14.43   A member could elect to carry forward unused tax relief to any of the following six tax years in which contributions had been paid that exceeded the amount relievable in the year in which they were paid. The time limit for making such an election was by 5 April of the tax year that ended six years after the end of the year for which unused relief was to be carried forward. Carry-forward of relief was not available for an individual source of income from a period of employment when the member was also a member of an occupational pension scheme, or for contributions paid by an employer or to a tax year falling after a member had attained the age of 75.

14.44   If a member had unused tax relief available from previous years to carry forward there was a limit on the additional contributions that could be paid in later years to use up the unused relief. Thus, total contributions paid in a later year could not exceed the member's relevant earnings for that year. For example, if an employed member was paid £20,000 in 1998/99 and unused relief from previous in-date years that exceeded £20,000, total contributions of £20,000 only could have been paid to a personal pension scheme in 1998/99 and could then be allocated against the unused relief in the earliest years first. Any balance of unused relief could be carried forward and possibly used up by paying further contributions in 1999/00 not exceeding the member's relevant earnings. For employed members liable to the basic or higher rate of tax an application to carry forward relief was made on PP42 and this plus PP120 was sent to the member's inspector of taxes. For self-employed members liable to the basic rate of tax, PP42 was sent to the scheme administrator who would reclaim the basic rate of tax. For employed members liable to the higher rate of tax the administrator had to give the original PP42 and PP120 for onward transmission to the member's own tax office to claim the higher rate tax relief. The administrator had to retain a copy of PP42 before releasing the original to the member as it might ultimately be required by FICO (Repayments).

Interaction of relief

14.45 The facility to carry-forward unused relief for up to six years was a most useful one and its interaction with the facility to carry back contributions could be used to good effect in tax planning. Care was needed to ensure that each election was made by the appropriate 31 January and, for tax years that were going out of date, contributions were paid by the end of the sixth year to use up unused relief that would otherwise be lost. The following example illustrates how this interaction worked in practice.

Example

A taxpayer was born on 30 April 1939 and established a personal pension scheme on 1 October 1995 in respect of Schedule E remuneration by paying regular monthly contributions of £50 per month from that date. During 1999/00 sufficient income from other sources became available from which the taxpayer wished to pay further contributions to use up unused relief from previous years. Remuneration assessable to Schedule E was:

1993/94	£4,852
1994/95	£5,120
1995/96	£5,822
1996/97	£6,028
1997/98	£5,434
1998/99	£5,434

and continuing at that level for the purpose of this example. What additional contributions could have been paid in 1999/00 and in later years to eliminate relief?

(a) Contributions actually paid were £350 for 1995/96 and £600 for 1996/97 onwards.

(b)   Maximum reliefs due were:

Year	Remuneration	Rate of Relief	Maximum Relief	Relief on Contributions	Unused Relief
1993/94	£4,852	at 20% = £1,970.40 less		NIL	£1,970.40
1994/95	£5,120	at 20% = £1,024.00 less		NIL	£1,024.00
1995/96	£5,822	at 25% = £1,455.50 less		£350	£1,105.00
1996/97	£6,028	at 25% = £1,507.00 less		£600	£1,907.00
1997/98	£5,434	at 25% = £1,358.50 less		£600	£1,758.50
1998/99	£5,434	at 25% = £1,358.50 less		£600	£1,758.50

(*c*)   Allocation of unused relief

Year	Remuneration	Maximum Contributions Payable	Allocation to Unused Reliefs
1999/00	£5,434	£5,434	£970.40 (1993/94)
			£1,024.00 (1994/95)
			£1,105.50 (1995/96)
			£907.00 (1996/97)
			£758.50 (1997/98)
			£668.60 (1998/99)
			£5,434.00
2000/01	£5,434	£5,434	£89.90 (1998/99)
			£1,358.50 (1999/00)
			£1,448.40

The taxpayer could pay contributions of £5,434 in 1999/00 and £1,448.40 in 2000/01 that would include the payments of £50 per month and eliminate the unused relief. It was essential that by 5 April 2000 the election to carry forward the unused relief for 1993/94 had been exercised and that by 31 January 2001 the election to carry back the contribution of £1,358.50 to the year 1999/00 had also been exercised.

14.46   The carry forward and carry back facility was also available in respect of premiums paid to retirement annuity contracts. Where membership of a retirement annuity contract and personal pension scheme overlap there were special rules for dealing with the interaction of the carry forward and carry back relief between the two types of pension arrangements. Form PP/RA43A was available from IR SPSS and inspectors of taxes giving guidance on the calculations required. There is also an example in Appendix 12 to IR76 (2000).

14.47   Form PP/RA43A could be difficult to understand and the split between the two types of arrangements might be more easily understood from the table below which sets out the figures in the case of *Brock v O'Connor (SC000118)* heard before the Special Commissioners in 1997. The case concerned the practical application of the tax statutes regarding the transitional provisions for self-employed taxpayers who continued to pay both retirement annuity premiums and personal pension contributions. The appellant paid retirement annuity premiums in 1990/91 and 1991/92 and both retirement annuity premiums and personal pension contributions in 1992/93 and 1993/94. She contended that both retirement annuity premiums of £4,100 and personal pension contributions of £3,000 paid in 1993/94 should be allowed based on unused relief brought forward. The inspector of taxes allowed the personal pension relief of £3,000 for 1993/94, but only £3,312 for retirement annuity relief. Net relevant earnings in 1993/94 were £16,499 producing potential retirement annuity relief of £3,300 and personal pension relief of £4,950. The dispute concerned the unused retirement annuity relief brought forward which the inspector calculated as £12 and the appellant as £1,636, in which case the whole of her retirement annuity pension payment of £4,100 would have been allowable. :

Year	Net relevant earnings	Relief	% age Arising	Actual contributions		
		RAC	PP	RAC	PP	Total
1990/91	£21,448	£4,290	£6,435	£4,200	Nil	£4,200
1991/92	£22,727	£4,546	£6,818	£3,000	Nil	£3,000
1992/93	£17,631	£3,526	£5,289	£3,150	£2,000	£5,150
1993/94	£16,499	£3,300	£4,950	£4,100	£3,000	£7,100

Relief allowed			Unused relief arising		
RAC	PP	Total	RAC	PP	Year
£4,200	Nil	£4,200	£90	£2,235	1990/91
£3,000	Nil	£3,000	£1,546	£3,818	1991/92
£3,150	£2,000	£5,150	Nil	£139	1992/93
£3,312	£3,000	£6,312	Nil	Nil	1993/94

The inspector's case was that unused retirement relief brought forward to be reduced by a personal pension contribution paid in the later year even when there was sufficient entitlement to personal pension relief to cover the contribution of that type paid in that later year. The appellant however argued that in these circumstances the personal pension contribution reduced the personal pension relief available for that year and also any unused retirement annuity relief for that year alone, but did not have any impact on the retirement annuity relief brought forward.

The purpose of the legislation was to ensure that double relief was not available to a taxpayer that paid both types of premiums in any one tax year. The Special Commissioner considered that the inspector's interpretation of the law was more consistent with the language of the statutes than the appellant's submission and decided for the Inland Revenue.

14.48 In October 1996 the Inland Revenue published an extra-statutory concession to help members of small lump sum retirement benefits schemes who were inadvertently also contributing to a personal pension scheme or RAC. They were able to maintain their pensions provided they waived their entitlement to lump sum benefits under the occupational scheme subject to the lump sum not exceeding £400 for each year of pensionable service. The tax relief given on contributions paid to the RAC or personal pension scheme would not be withdrawn.

The position from 6 April 2001

14.49 Contributions can only be paid provided the member satisfies the relevant eligibility criteria (see 14.68 and 14.69) and all personal contributions must be paid net of basic rate tax.

14.50   There is still no obligation for an employer to contribute to a SIPP, but where an employer does contribute, the aggregate gross contributions paid by the member and the employer to all personal pensions, retirement annuity contracts and stakeholder schemes, must not exceed either:

(a)   the 'earnings threshold' (*section 630(1)(c)*) for the tax year in which the contributions are paid, or where higher level contributions are to be paid;

(b)   the relevant percentage (from the table in 14.33) of net relevant earnings either for the tax year of payment or for one of the previous five tax years, known as the 'basis year' (*section 646B*), subject to the earnings cap relevant to the basis year chosen (*SI 2000 No 2315*).

As mentioned earlier, the earnings threshold has been set at £3,600 for each tax year but may be amended by Treasury order (*section 630 (1A)*). Anyone who satisfies the eligibility criteria in 14.66 may pay contributions up to the earnings threshold whether or not they have relevant earnings (see 14.62 and 14.63).

14.51 For contributions exceeding the earnings threshold the net relevant earnings for the basis year may be used not only for the year of payment but also for each of the tax years falling within the five year period from the end of the basis year. A new basis year may be chosen when required (e.g. when net relevant earnings have increased), and contributions can be made in respect of net relevant earnings for the new basis year, in that basis year itself, if it is the year of payment, and in each of the five years following the new basis year, subject to production of appropriate evidence of earnings (see 14.97 to 14.99).

Example

A taxpayer is 44 on 6 April 2001 and has net relevant earnings (NRE) as follows:

Year	NRE £
1996/97	32,000
1997/98	34,000
1998/99	44,000
1999/00	36,000
2000/01	38,000
2001/02	40,000

The taxpayer chooses 1998/99 as the basis year, i.e., net relevant earnings of £44,000. Contributions can be paid as follows:

Year	Age	% of NRE	NRE (for basis year) £	Maximum Contribution £
2001/02	44	20	44,000	8,800
2002/03	45	20	44,000	8,800
2003/04	46	25	44,000	11,000

The taxpayer would need to choose a new basis year for contributions in 2004/05 and subsequent years falling within five years of the end of the new basis year. This could be the year 2004/05 or one of the five years preceding it.

14.52 If the member ceases earning during a tax year ('cessation year') and has no relevant earnings in the following tax year ('break year'), higher level contributions may continue for the rest of the cessation year and the next five years ('qualifying post-cessation years') until the member either has relevant earnings again or becomes a member of a retirement benefits scheme throughout the tax year.

The maximum contribution in any qualifying post cessation year will be based on net relevant earnings for either the cessation year or one of the five tax years immediately before it ('reference years').

Example

A taxpayer is 38 on 6 April 2001 and chooses 2001/02 as the basis year.

Year	Age	% of NRE	NRE	NRE for basis year	Maximum contributions
2001/02 (basis year)	38	20	60,000	60,000	12,000
2002/03	39	20	58,000	60,000	12,000
2003/04	40	20	58,000	60,000	12,000
2004/05	41	20	55,000	60,000	12,000
2005/06	42	20	52,000	60,000	12,000
2006/07	43	20	50,000	60,000	12,000

Earnings cease in March 2007 and do not recommence in the future. The taxpayer does not become a member of an occupational pension scheme. 2006/07 will be the 'cessation year', 2007/08 the 'break year' and 2001/02 to 2006/07 will be the 'reference years'. So NRE for 2001/02 could still be used for further contributions in each of the 'qualifying post-cessation years', i.e., 2007/08 to 2011/12 as follows:

Year	Age	% of NRE	NRE	NRE for reference year	Maximum contributions
2007/08	44	20	0	60,000	12,000
2008/09	45	20	0	60,000	12,000
2009/10	46	25	0	60,000	15,000
2010/11	47	25	0	60,000	15,000
2011/12	48	25	0	60,000	15,000

For years 2012/13 onwards contributions up to the 'earnings threshold' could still be made.

Should a member recommence earning or become a member of a retirement benefits scheme during the qualifying post cessation period it will be necessary to start all over again by choosing a new 'basis year' as in 14.51.

14.53 *Section 640(3)* has been amended by *FA 2000, Sch 13* and now limits the proportion of total contributions paid in any tax year that can be taken from those contributions and applied as a premium to secure a lump sum death benefit under a term assurance contract to 10%. Term assurance contracts already in force by 5 April 2001 may continue on the pre–6 April 2001 basis (see 14.34). This includes a member's arrangements under a SIPP which commenced before 6 April 2001 and which included an option to apply for term assurance, even if the option is not exercised until 6 April 2001 or later. In such cases, the SIPP administrator should obtain a declaration that the amount applied to such term assurance contracts will not exceed 5% of net relevant earnings for the year in question.

Carry back

14.54

A simplified form of the facility to carry back contributions (see 14.37 to 14.41) has been retained under the new tax regime (*section 641A*). The main principles (other than those relating to procedures for obtaining tax relief – see 14.95 to 14.97) are:

- elections to carry back to the previous tax year can be made if the contribution was paid between 6 April and 31 January, and the election was made at or before the time of payment;

- contributions must have been paid before age 75;

- elections can be made for future payments up to 31 January;

- employer contributions cannot be carried back;

- contributions paid on or after 6 April 2000 must be paid net of basic rate income tax.

14.55 As a result of the abolition of the carry forward facility from 6 April 2001, it will no longer be possible for carry back to be combined with it (see 14.37 to 14.48) after 31 January 2002. Until that date it will still be possible, but only where the member pays a contribution before 31 January 2002, elects to carry it back to 2000/01, or an earlier year, provided the maximum contribution for that year has not already been paid, and the member has some unused relief available from the preceding six years. The amount carried back may exceed the relevant percentage of net relevant earnings (see 14.61 to 14.64) for the previous or earlier year, but must not exceed the relevant earnings (see 14.62 and 14.63) for that year (as in 14.44).

Example

A taxpayer born on 1 May 1960 with earnings of £40,000 for the tax year 2000/01 and paid a personal pension contribution of £2,000 in that year. Unused relief of £10,000 is available from previous tax years. He pays a personal contribution of £14,000 on 1 December 2001 and elects to carry it back to 2000/01. The position for the year 2000/01 will be as follows:

Contribution actually paid	£ 2,000
Contribution paid December 2001 and carried back	£14,000
Total paid for 2000/01	£16,000
less	
Maximum contribution possible	(£40,000 × 20%) = £ 8,000
Excess contributions	£ 8,000

The excess of £8,000 can be met from the unused relief of £10,000 leaving £2,000 of unused relief from previous tax years that will be lost after 31 January 2002.

14.56   The tax reliefs mentioned in 14.36 are still available although changes were made by *FA 2000, Sch 13* to *section 639* (member's contributions), *section 640* (employer's contributions), and *section 646* (meaning of net relevant earnings), to accommodate the new rules relating to contributions up to the earnings threshold (see 14.50), and to higher level contributions by reference to net relevant earnings in a basis year (see 14.51) or in a reference year (see 14.52).

14.57   Before 6 April 2001, it was only possible, under IR SPSS's discretionary practice for contributions to a SIPP to be in the form of cash (see 14.35). *FA 2000, Sch 13* made amendments to *section 638* confirming this with effect from 6 April 2001 with the exception of contributions by members in the form of 'eligible shares'. These are shares which the member has exercised the right to acquire, or which have been appropriated by the member in accordance with the rules of a savings-related share option scheme, approved profit-sharing scheme or employee share ownership plan. The market value of the shares at the time of transfer to a SIPP will represent a contribution net of basic rate tax (which will be reclaimed by the SIPP administrator as in 14.97). However, the gross value must be taken into account when calculating the maximum contributions payable in a tax year (see 14.34). The transfer of the shares must take place no later than 90 days from the date the member exercised the right to acquire or appropriated the shares.

14.58   The tax relief explained in 14.34 and 14.36 may be affected in future if the Scottish Parliament exercises its tax varying powers (see 1.30). Careful consideration would then need to be given to the advantages and disadvantages of any differences in the tax rates in Scotland and the remainder of the UK.

14.59   The tax relief on personal contributions may be even more attractive to members liable to tax at the higher rate where they have investment income as well as net relevant earnings, particularly where a claim to carry back contributions is concerned (see 14.54). Here it may be possible to obtain relief at an effective marginal rate of 42 per cent instead of 40%. The amount of the relief given on the contribution carried back is the difference between:

(a)   the amount in which the member is chargeable to tax for the earlier year; and

(b)   the amount on which the member would be chargeable if the contribution had been included in the tax return for that year.

If the member is on the margin between 22% and 40% and the affect of carrying back the contribution is to take investment income down from higher to basic rate this will give an effective marginal rate of relief on the contribution of 42%. Any claims by inspectors of taxes that relief has already been given at 22% and therefore the member is only entitled to a further 18 per cent should be resisted and the statutory basis in *TMA 1970, Sch 1B para 2(4)* correctly adopted, to afford the correct tax relief.

14.60 There are various tax exemptions that apply to payments made from a SIPP. These are covered later in this chapter together with the taxation of some payments made.

Net relevant earnings

14.61 Mention is made in 14.33, 14.50 and 14.55 of the maximum contributions that can be made to a SIPP in relation to a member's net relevant earnings for any particular year. So it is important to understand what actually constitutes net relevant earnings especially as members can be self-employed or employed.

14.62 For self-employed members relevant earnings comprise all earned income assessable to tax under Schedule D Cases I and II whether as a sole trader or partner. Net earnings are those after deduction of allowable expenses but before personal allowances. These are defined in *sections 644(2)(c)* and *646*.

14.63 For employed members net relevant earnings comprise all remuneration assessable to tax under Schedule E. These are defined in *section 646* and are in line with the definition of pensionable remuneration for occupational schemes mentioned in 4.21 to 4.27 with the same exceptions. Net relevant earnings are those after allowable expenses but before personal allowances. Remuneration as a controlling director of an investment company (*sections 644(5)* and *644(6)*) does not constitute net relevant earnings. Nor does remuneration as a controlling director of a trading company where the controlling director is in receipt of benefits from either a *Chapter I* scheme of that company or a personal pension which had received a transfer payment from such a *Chapter I* scheme (*section 644(6A)*).

14.64 The earnings cap (see 4.28 to 4.30) applies to all personal pension schemes and restricts net relevant earnings for both self-employed and employed members of SIPPs for the years 1989/90 onwards. The maximum contributions payable for each age band are limited to the earnings cap for the appropriate year (APPENDIX 26) which can cause some practical problems under the new tax regime, particularly for the self-employed (see 14.99).

14.65 Having looked at the advantages of establishing a SIPP, the legislation and guidelines under which it operates and how it can be funded, the potential members and their advisers can decide on how the SIPP is to provide the level of benefits within Inland Revenue limits in the most tax efficient way for the members. The remainder of the chapter is devoted to these aspects, including:

- their documentation (14.77 to 14.89);
- their benefit structure (14.109 to 14.116);
- their investments (14.134 to 14.175);
- the income withdrawal facility (14.179 to 14.216);
- withdrawal of approval (14.217 to 14.229);
- the requirements of the DWP (14.235 to 14.243); and
- VAT aspects (14.244 to 14.257).

Membership

The position prior to 6 April 2001

14.66 Any individual could be a member of a SIPP provided they:

(a) had not reached the age of 75;

(b) were in receipt of remuneration liable to tax under Schedule E; or

(c) earned income liable to tax under Schedule D.

Thus, membership was open to company directors and ordinary employees, together with self-employed sole traders and partners. However, controlling directors of investment companies could not be members of SIPPs. Even where an individual had no earnings a SIPP could have been established to receive a transfer payment including a pension credit from a pension sharing order (see 3.95).

14.67 However, an individual could not be a member of an occupational scheme and a SIPP concurrently for the same source of income, unless the occupational scheme was only providing death in service benefits or the SIPP was only receiving the SERPS rebate. For an employed member this generally meant voluntary cessation of membership of the occupational scheme or not joining it in the first place.

The position from 6 April 2001

14.68 Before 6 April 2001, individuals in receipt of remuneration liable to tax under Schedule E (including non-UK residents receiving foreign emoluments within the meaning of *section 192*) may be members of SIPPs and pay contributions within the constraints mentioned in 14.49 to 14.57. However, there is no longer a requirement for an individual to be in receipt of such remuneration. Provided the individual is under 75, resident or ordinarily resident in the UK (or a Crown Servant or the spouse of a Crown Servant) the individual may be a member of a SIPP and contribute up to the earnings threshold (see 14.50) in any tax year. For the first time it is possible for controlling directors of investment companies to be members of SIPPs and contribute up to the earnings threshold.

14.69 Under *section 632B* and *SI 2000 No 2318* it is also possible for an individual who is accruing pension benefits (as well as for an individual who has only death in service benefits) in a 'Chapter I scheme' to be a member of a SIPP at the same time and contribute up to the earnings threshold in each tax year, provided the individual:

(a)   satisfies the residency criteria above;

(b)   is not a controlling director; and

(c)   had remuneration in at least one of the preceding five tax years (years prior to 2001/02 do not count) of no more than £30,000. IR SPSS have confirmed that remuneration for these purposes relates to the total amount(s) shown for the year on the member's P60(s) (see definition of 'Remuneration Limit' in the Glossary to IR76 (2000)) for each office and each employment held on 5 April in that year.

14.70 Before 6 April 2001, any individual who is under 75 may become a member of a SIPP solely for the purpose of receiving a transfer payment from another approved pension scheme (see 14.66). This also applies to an ex-spouse who has pension credit rights from a pension sharing order (see 3.95), subject to the agreement of the SIPP administrator. In the case of prospective members under 16, or 18 if not in employment, the legal guardian may only enter into a contract for membership of a SIPP.

14.71 While it was possible prior to 6 April 2001 (and is still possible from 6 April 2001) to establish a SIPP solely to receive a SERPS rebate or a transfer payment consisting of, or including, benefits relating to contracted-out employment (see 14.115 and 14.116), such a SIPP must meet the conditions in *PSA 1993, s 9(5)* for an 'appropriate personal pension scheme' (APPS). These are broadly that it must be an arrangement for the issue of insurance policies or annuity contracts; a unit trust; or a deposit account, effectively excluding it from the definition of a SIPP in *SI 2001 No 117* (see 14.155). There are also investment restrictions on *Chapter IV* schemes that are contracted-out under *PSA 1993, s 9(3)*. For instance, it would not be possible to lease a property held by the scheme to the member's employer unless the value of the property represented no more than 5% of the value of the fund. There are also other considerations when contemplating a transfer from a contracted-out final salary scheme to a SIPP (see 14.115).

14.72 There is no limit to the number of SIPPs an individual may have, a distinct advantage over SSASs, which are limited to one per company. In addition, there can be more than one member in a SIPP, which is particularly useful for partnerships and for pooling investments.

Authorised provider

14.73 Prior to 1 October 2000, to obtain tax approval a SIPP could only be established by an authorised provider, e.g. a LO, unit trust company, building society or bank. It also had to be established under irrevocable trust to allow the freedom of investment permitted. The members could be appointed as trustees depending on what role they were to play in investment decisions (see 14.27). The authorised provider could play an active role also as a trustee and as the administrator. If an administrator were appointed who was not an authorised provider, e.g. a pension consultant or actuary, the authorised provider's overall role had to be made clear and the administrator, sometimes a custodian trustee, would become a trustee of the SIPP.

14.74 Since 1 October 2000, it has been possible to do without the type of provider mentioned above and for anyone to establish a SIPP under trust (*SI 2000 No 2317*). However, the Inland Revenue can restrict approval for certain trust based schemes (*SI 2000 No 2314*). For instance, the trust deed of an occupational pension scheme applying for approval under, or conversion to, the new tax regime (see 14.24), must contain a provision that if there are less than 12 members, an independent trustee must be appointed in a similar manner to a pensioneer trustee for a SSAS.

14.75 At the time of writing there is little evidence of a significant move from SIPPs with an authorised provider to trust based SIPPs without a provider or conversions of *Chapter I* schemes to *Chapter IV* schemes. It is very early days and developments, particularly regarding the conversion of both insured executive pension plans (EPPs) and SSASs, are expected shortly. Despite the possible advantage of a greater tax free lump sum on retirement for certain individuals as a result of a conversion (see 14.76) rather than a transfer (see 14.121 and 14.123). The main problems with conversions from SSAS to SIPP are that no conversion can take place for a member who is in receipt of benefits. As a converted SSAS or EPP will still be an occupational pension scheme for the purposes of the *Pension Schemes Act 1993*, it will remain subject to the *Pensions Act 1995*, unless it satisfies the relevant exemption criteria for such schemes (see 11.98).

14.76 Details of the requirements for converting part or all of a *Chapter I* scheme to a *Chapter IV* scheme, including a SIPP, are contained in *Schedule 23ZA* to *ICTA 1988* (inserted by *FA 2000, sch 13*), SI 2001 No 118, and Part 23 of IR76 (2000). The main points are:

(a) the trust must be suitably amended to ensure that the assets that relate to each member are clearly identifiable;

(b) the affected employees must be identified and their assets valued;

(c) an application must be made for approval on form PSPP101 (APPENDIX 58) accompanied by a copy of the deed of conversion and the scheme rules (if the model rules have not been adopted);

(d) as a conversion is effectively a transfer to a personal pension scheme, specific regulatory valuations will be required for those who are/have been controlling directors within the last ten years or have had earners in excess of the earnings cap within the last six years in the same way as is required under *SI 2001 No 119* for the currently more common method of transfer for such employees (see 14.121);

(e) it may be necessary to reduce a member's fund to a permitted value;

(f) the maximum tax free retirement lump sum must be certified in a similar manner to that required for transfers (see 14.121 and 14.123) but only for controlling directors. Somewhat surprisingly, it does not apply to individuals who are 45 or over and have earned in excess of the earnings cap in one of the last six years as it does in respect of transfers for such individuals under *SI 2001 No 119* (see *14.123*)

Documentation

14.77 The establishment of a SIPP under irrevocable trusts is relatively simple, as it requires only one deed encompassing its establishment, the trustees' power, and IR SPSS rules. This makes the approval process that much quicker compared with an occupational scheme. It is usual for the member to join by completing a contract in the form of the SIPP provider's application form or by executing a supplemental deed, particularly if the member is to become a trustee. There is certain other documentation required and this is covered under application for approval (see 14.90 to 14.96).

Contents of the deed and rules

14.78 The deed should include all the usual clauses and rules that IR SPSS expects for a SIPP established under irrevocable trusts seeking discretionary approval. In 14.79 to 14.88 the essential requirements that must appear in the deed so far as IR SPSS is concerned are covered to the extent that they are not already mentioned in 3.17 to 3.45.

14.79 In the preamble to the deed IR SPSS will expect to see the appointment of the authorised provider and/or the administrator and any custodian trustee if there is to be one.

14.80 There will need to be appropriate limitations on members' contributions that may be paid (see 14.33 and 14.49 to 14.57). In view of the possibility that contribution limits may be exceeded there should be provision for repayment of excess contributions together with the procedure for the administrator to adopt.

14.81 *The Personal Pensions Schemes Restriction on Discretion to Approve) (Permitted Investments) Regulations (SI 2001 No 117)* (APPENDIX 66) came into force on 6 April 2001. Before this, IR SPSS specifically required a rule containing provisions expressly prohibiting investments that are banned, e.g. loans to members, residential property and personal chattels, and transactions with connected persons. The rules also had to include a provision that any lease of commercial property to a business or partnership connected with a member is on commercial terms determined by a professional valuation. It is unclear at the time of writing whether or not SIPPs that are set up on or after 6 April 2001, or not approved by that date, must include the requirements of *SI 2001 No 117* in their rules. SIPPs approved before 6 April 2001 need to insert them into their scheme rules, as the regulations are silent on this point.

14. 82 The retirement age for a member of a SIPP can be at any time between age 50 and 75 so there is no need for any early retirement rule. It is possible for some members of a SIPP to have a lower retirement age than 50 if they are in certain occupations, e.g. sportsmen (see IR 76 (2000 Appendix 10). In these instances the rules must ensure the special provisions relating to members with low retirement ages are included.

14.83 The lifetime benefits payable from a SIPP may be taken totally as an annuity or up to 25% of the member's share of the fund taken as a cash lump sum and the balance as an annuity. The latter option if it is available must be written into the rules with the 25% limitation. Provisions should also be included as to when the annuity is payable, at any time between ages 50 and 75 and for its immediate purchase from a LO from whom it will be paid, unless the income withdrawal facility is adopted. The LO from whom the annuity is purchased may be one established within any country situated in the EU (see 4.96) with a presence in the UK to ensure tax is deducted therefrom (see 4.96 and 14.209).

14. 84 If death benefits are to be provided the rules must include the type of benefits, e.g. dependants' annuities and lump sums, and how they are to be secured and paid. It is important with lump sum death in service benefits and lump sum guarantee payments to ensure the rules are so worded that they are distributable by the administrator at the trustees' discretion (see 3.29) so they are not liable to IHT. However, if the death benefits are passed within two years of the member's death to a discretionary trust in which there is no beneficial interest, the payment could be a gift with reservation of benefit and IHT payable.

14.85 *Section 638(2)* specifically requires a rule for 'the making, acceptance and application of transfer payments as satisfies any requirements imposed by or under regulations . . .'. This rule is particularly important in relation to transfer's receivable (see 14.118 to 14.125) because of the restrictions that apply under *SI 2001 No 119*.

14.86 A SIPP may operate as a closed scheme if the rules so allow. IR SPSS requirements for winding-up a SIPP are different from a *Chapter IV* scheme and the rules will need to encompass the following points. The authorised provider or trustee must give notice to the administrator of the winding-up who in turn must notify the members of their rights, e.g. to draw benefits or take a transfer value to another pension scheme.

14.87 If the income withdrawal facility is to be adopted (see 14.179 to 14.215) then the rules must include the appropriate provisions (see 14.89).

14.88 DWP requirements are not normally included in the rules of a SIPP except in relation to pension sharing on divorce (see 3.95). Transfer payments from the SIPP where the preservation requirements of *PSA 1993, s 84* must be met, because they are not involved in providing early retirement benefits on leaving service and they are not contracted-out. In the rare event of a SIPP being established solely for the purpose of receiving a SERPS rebate then JOM 78 and 82 should be consulted. The equal treatment requirements of the *Pensions Act 1995, ss 62* to *66* will however need to be met by the rules (see 3.45).

Model rules

14.89 It is possible to agree model rules with IR SPSS for SIPPs in the same manner as for SSASs (see 3.47 to 3.50). IR SPSS has published a set of Integrated Model Rules coded (IMR 2000), for use by contracted-out and non-contracted out schemes and stakeholder schemes which is available on the Inland Revenue website (*www.inlandrevenue.gov.uk/stakepension*). If a SIPP adopts these without amendment it should ensure the SIPP is approved for tax purposes.

Application for approval

14.90 IR SPSS requirements for all personal pension schemes (including *Chapter IV* schemes) are set out in Part 13 of IR 76 (2000) Applications for approval of SIPPs must be made to IR SPSS in writing using the prescribed form PSPP101 (APPENDIX 58) and PSPP103 giving details of the trustee(s) (APPENDIX 58A), and must be accompanied by certain documents. The same strict procedures as to full completion of the form PSPP101 apply (see 3.55 and IR 76 (2000)(13.2)) as for *Chapter I* schemes. However, the timing of the application is not as crucial because of the tax position of the trustee or administrator who will be able to obtain tax relief on the income on the investments and of the member who obtains tax relief as explained in 14.95 to 14.101.

Applications for approval of conversions of Chapter I schemes to Chapter IV schemes must follow the procedures and satisfy the requirements detailed in Part 23 IR 76 (2000).

14.91 Form PSPP101 requires considerable information, most of which is self evident and therefore the parts most relevant to SIPPs or those requiring further explanation will be looked at more closely. Details of the authorised provider and the administrator are required, but not of the membership except in the accompanying documentation. If model rules are not used then the main features of the scheme must be listed at Part 3 of the form.

14.92 Among the accompanying documentation must be a deed limiting withdrawals from the trust fund to the provision of benefits. This entails the member entering into a binding agreement with the administrator not to require withdrawal of the trust funds or income therefrom other than for the payment of benefits from the SIPP at the time they are due.

14.93 An application form must be completed by all prospective members, but a copy need not be sent with the application for approval. Members who are employees and who make contributions to a SIPP on or after 6 April 2001 do not have to provide a completed certificate of eligibility (the employer's certificate) on the lines prescribed in Appendix 8 to IR76 (2000). Instead, the application form must contain all the information listed in Appendix 19 to IR76 (2000). For all members for whom contributions are to be made this includes:

(a) appropriate declarations in respect of eligibility and concurrent membership of a Chapter I scheme (see 14.68 to 14.72);

(b) ensuring contribution limits are not exceeded (see 14.34 and 14.50 to 14.57)

(c) ensuring payments are based on qualifying earnings where necessary (see 14.61 to 14.64),

(d)   informing the administrator when earnings cease or recommence (see 14.51 and 14.52) or when the member becomes or ceases to be a controlling director (see 14.69) etc.

14.94   Formal notification of approval is sent by IR SPSS to the provider, trustee or administrator. IR SPSS will also send notification of approval to those tax offices and other offices concerned with the tax consequences of approval.

Obtaining tax relief

14.95   From 6 April 2001, all members pay the net amount of the contribution after deduction of tax at the basic rate to the personal pension scheme and gain the appropriate tax relief under *section 639(1)*. If a member is liable to tax at the higher rate a claim for additional tax relief must be made to the inspector of taxes on the annual tax return or using form PP120 (APPENDIX 69). Evidence of membership and payment may be required by the inspector and should be in the form of Appendix 6 to IR76 (2000).

14.96   Self-employed members can no longer pay gross contributions to personal pensions.

14.97   The administrator is left with the task of reclaiming tax deducted at the basic rate from contributions paid by members. The administrator does this on application to the repayment division of the Inland Revenue Financial Intermediaries and Claims Office (FICO Repayments). The procedures and requirements are laid down in the *Personal Pension Schemes (Relief at Source) Regulations 1988 (SI 1988 No 1013)*, as amended by *SI 2000 No 2315*, and Part 15 of IR76 (2000). To enable a claim to be made the member must have provided the appropriate declarations as in 14.93. Where contributions in excess of the earnings threshold are to be made, evidence of earnings as prescribed by SI 1988 No 1013 as amended by *SI 2000 No 2315* will be required. Details of acceptable forms of evidence are contained in IR76 (2000) (14.39 to 14.49).

14.98   Estimates of earnings are no longer acceptable, which could prove a problem for self-employed members who wish to use anticipated current year earnings on which to base contributions, ie chose the current year as the 'basis year' (see 14.50), unless they can obtain a written statement from their accountant, solicitor or auditor showing the net relevant earnings for the current year.

14.99   For employees, evidence may be in the form of a declaration from the employer stipulating the amount of remuneration paid or to be paid for the 'basis year', which could be for the current year.

14.100 As mentioned in 14.80, if the member's contributions have exceeded the statutory limits, repayment of excess contributions is applicable. The procedures are laid down in SI 1988 No 1013 as amended by *SI 2000 No 2315* and in Part 18 of IR76 (2000). The excess is treated as arising from a member's contribution and repaid to the member. The administrator repays the net amount to the member and accounts for the tax to either by set-off against a claim for other members or by repayment. Where full contributions were paid, (e.g. prior to 6 April 2001) by a self-employed member, the full amount of the excess is repaid to the member. Any tax relief obtained by the administrator on the original amount of the excess must also be repaid to FICO (Repayments).

14.101 The administrator is also responsible for reclaiming any tax deducted from the income received by a SIPP. This is done on application to the administrator's own inspector of taxes and may be done annually or more frequently depending on the flow of income and its size.

Reporting requirements

14.102 Until 1 October 2000, *sections 630–655* placed very few reporting requirements on the administrator of a SIPP apart from making applications for approval, tax reclaims and repayments of excess contributions. There was a statutory requirement in *SI 1988 No 1013* for the administrator to keep certain records for inspection by the Inland Revenue and to provide certain information when called upon to do so by that Department. Part 17 of IR76 (2000) also requires the administrator at the end of each tax year to provide the Inland Revenue with certain information to enable compliance checks to be undertaken. These compliance checks are undertaken by FICO (Audit & Compliance) from time to time and have involved checking of Schedule E income tax reclaims in respect of employed member's contributions.

14.103 From 6 April 2001, such checks will also encompass the self-employed. FICO (Audit & Compliance) have published a Code of Practice entitled 'Inspection of Schemes operated by Financial Intermediaries' explaining how the Inland Revenue carry out inspections which is available on request from them. Details of the objectives and procedures of an inspection are also contained in Part 16 of IR76 (2000).

14.104 Well before the introduction of regulations contained in SI 2001 No 117 limiting Inland Revenue discretion in relation to investments by SIPPs, IR SPSS had indicated to the SPG that it wished to bring its discretionary requirements for SIPP transactions and investments and the associated reporting requirements into line with those for SSAS. *Section 651A* provided for regulations to be introduced imposing such reporting requirements and these are now in force (see 14.105).

14.105 Like SSASs, there are now statutory requirements for SIPPs to report purchases and sales of investments and scheme borrowings, These are contained in *The Personal Pension Schemes (Information Powers) Regulations 2000 (SI 2000 No 2316)* which came into force on 1 October 2000. As for SSASs, the report must be made on the prescribed form within 90 days of the transaction. However, at the time of writing forms have not been issued by IR SPSS and the SPG has been advised that until such forms have been issued, transactions do not need to be reported. IR SPSS has also advised the SPG that, to start with, only purchases and sales of property and associated borrowings will need to be reported.

14.106 IR SPSS commenced a compliance audit of SIPPs on a voluntary basis a few years ago. However, *SI 2000 No 2316* also requires the administrator, authorised provider, trustee or anyone who has provided administration services to a personal pension scheme to produce certain information, make it available for inspection and retain certain records. If the Inland Revenue serves notice, the information, including any supporting documents, that must be supplied within 28 days, is virtually identical to that required in respect of a SSAS under *SI 1996 No 1715* (see 3.87 – 3.89 and 3.91).

14.107 The aim of the legislation in 14.105 and 14.106 is to improve the monitoring of personal pension schemes

Self Assessment

14.108 In an addendum to the agreed minutes of the meeting between IR SPSS and the SPG on 14 March 2001, IR SPSS confirmed that self assessment will not normally apply to SIPPs but it will apply to SIPPs which trade. IR SPSS also confirmed that it is putting together an audit package that will replace self-assessment for non-trading SIPPs. Before implementation it will be discussed with the SPG.

Benefit structure

14.109 The maximum benefits that may be paid will as always depend upon the rules and once again it cannot be stressed enough how important it is when drafting the deed and rules of a SIPP to allow for the maximum benefits in all circumstances. Amendments can be made subsequently, but these may be costly and take time and possibly delay payment of benefits.

14.110 A SIPP is a money purchase scheme. The benefits it can provide are determined by the level of contributions paid to it and the amount of growth of those contributions once invested. The only control on contributions is the level at which they may be paid (see 14.33 and 14.50 to 14.52). No actuarial calculations and recommendations as to the funding of a SIPP are therefore required. The value of what is invested at the time of payment of benefits, provided the contributions have not been excessive, determines the level of benefits to be paid.

14.111 The only benefits that may be paid are:

(a)   an annuity payable to a member;

(b)   a lump sum payable at the time the annuity commences;

(c)   an annuity payable on a member's death to the spouse or dependants;

(d)   a lump sum payable on a member's death before age 75 under a term assurance contract; and

(e)   if no annuity is payable on the member's death, a lump sum not exceeding the contributions paid by the member and employer.

A SIPP can provide for all of these benefits or for some of them only.

14.112 The lump sum payable at the time the annuity commences is an option and can only be paid if provided for in the rules as such (see 14.83). The amount payable is limited to 25% of the member's share of the fund and is tax free like a lump sum commutation payment from a *Chapter I* scheme. The balance left after paying the lump sum is available to purchase an annuity from any LO which is payable for life and can be guaranteed for up to ten years or from which to take income withdrawals up to age 75 before purchasing an annuity.

14.113 The annuity and lump sum may be paid to a member at any time between ages 50 and 75 of the member's choosing. There is no requirement for the member to retire. The benefits do not have to be paid at the same time as a member receives retirement benefits from an occupational scheme where he has paid up benefits, from a different employer's scheme, from another personal pension scheme or a retirement annuity contract. It is possible to be paid benefits before 50 if the member is incapacitated. In such instances the administrator needs to be satisfied that the member is incapable through infirmity of body or mind from carrying out his occupation or any occupation of a similar nature on the basis of suitable medical evidence. The annuity payable on incapacity grounds may be enhanced to an extent acceptable to IR SPSS.

14.114 Before 6 April 2001, members could elect in writing to the administrator that up to 25% of their contributions paid to a SIPP were applied as a premium under a contract of insurance. This would provide for their share of the fund to be increased if they were eligible for benefits on the grounds of incapacity. From 6 April 2001, this is no longer possible, although contracts in existence before that date may continue.

14.115 Up to 5 April 1997, transfer values were permitted from contracted-out final salary schemes to personal pension schemes. In these cases that part of the transfer value relating to the GMP (see 4.62 and PN 10.21) is identified and subject to special restrictions, e.g. it cannot be taken before age 60 nor exchanged for a tax-free cash sum. Only the balance of the transfer value is subject to the normal pension provisions within a personal pension scheme. Under the contracting-out rules from 6 April 1997, there are no GMPs so it is not possible to identify that part of the transfer value that is a substitute for SERPS benefits. Consequently, *PSA 1993, s 42A(3)* inserted by *PA 1995, s 137(5)* provides for the whole of that part of a transfer value to a personal pension scheme which relates to benefits earned from 6 April 1997 to be subject to the special provisions applicable to the GMP component. This means benefit cannot be taken before age 60 and no tax-free cash sum can be taken. Full details are contained in the *Personal and Occupational Pension Schemes (Protected Rights) Regulations 1996 (SI 1996 No 1537)*.

14.116 As SIPPs are not contracted-out (see 14.71), neither the GMP element nor the post–5 April 1997 element can be accepted as part of a transfer from a contracted-out final salary scheme., This would have to be left behind in the final salary scheme, where possible, or transferred to an arrangement capable of receiving these elements, e.g. as an APPS (see 14.71).

Transfer payments

14.117 While transfer payments may be received in two stages in some instances by a SIPP from various types of approved pension schemes, including retirement annuity contracts, they may carry with them certain protected rights which will need to be taken into account when benefits are actually paid (see 14.115). Transfers cannot be received from schemes only receiving the SERPS rebate. In addition, transfers from *Chapter I* schemes are not permitted to a personal pension scheme where benefits are in payment nor from a SSAS without the prior written agreement of IR SPSS (see 4.63). Transfers of members' benefits, including an ex spouse's rights from a pension sharing order (see 3.95) can be made to all types of approved pension schemes, including FSAVCS from 19 March 1997, but not to retirement annuity contracts. Transfers to FSAVCS should be made in the form of an assignment if a policy is involved, but if the benefits are secured under a master policy then the transfer payment should be made in cash and not the assets.

14.118 *Self-Invested Personal Pensions — SIPPs*

14.118 There are limitations on transfer payments and certification requirements which have been laid down by *SI 2001 No 119* with further details in Part 12 of IR 76 (2000). In connection with SIPPs, there is one area of transfer payments receivable which is of particular relevance to a controlling director or an individual whose earnings exceed the earnings cap are concerned.

14.119 Until 6 April 2001, transfers between Chapter I schemes and personal pensions were governed by *The Personal Pension Schemes (Transfer Payments) Regulations 1988 (SI 1988 No 1014)* as amended by *The Personal Pension Schemes (Transfer Payment) (Amendment) Regulations 1989 (SI 1989 No 1115)*. The main restriction under these regulations was that a controlling director or an individual earning in excess of the earnings cap could only transfer to a personal pension provided their transfer value did not exceed the maximum amount. This is calculated by an actuary in accordance with the regulations and actuarial guidance notes GN11 (commonly known as the 'GN11 test'), and the transferring scheme administrator certified this to the receiving scheme. If the individual's transfer value was greater than the maximum permitted under the GN11 test, the individual could not transfer.

14.120 In addition, for the same individuals and anyone else aged 45 or over, the maximum tax-free lump sum available under the transferring scheme at the time of the transfer had to be certified to the administrator of the receiving personal pension scheme. The administrator then had to ensure that the individual received the lower of the certified amount, increased in line with the retail price index to the date of payment, and 25% of the accumulated transfer value. So, if the tax-free lump sum under the transferring scheme was greater than 25% of the transfer value, it might not be worthwhile making the transfer.

14.121 From 6 April 2001, the position has become even worse for controlling directors and individuals who are both earning in excess of the earnings cap and aged 45 or over ('regulated individuals' — see Glossary to IR76 (2000)). *The Personal Pension Schemes (Transfer Payments) Regulations 2001 (SI 2001 No 119)* replaced *SI 1988 No 1014*, (as amended by *SI 1989 No 1115*), except in the case of certain deferred annuity contracts (e.g. section 32 contracts) (see 14.124). They have brought in a more restrictive test to establish the 'maximum transferable fund' (the MTF test), which produces a lower maximum permitted amount in almost all cases, thus making it much more difficult for regulated individuals to transfer at all. Details of the new MTF test are contained in Appendix XI of PN.

14.122 However, there is one concession that also extends to regulated individuals. The value of an individual's minimum cash equivalent may be transferred from a final salary Chapter I scheme which is subject to the

Minimum Funding Requirement (MFR) (see Appendix XI of PN), even if it exceeds the maximum permitted under the new MTF test

14.123 The maximum tax-free lump sum certification procedure mentioned in 14.120 above has been retained, but only for regulated individuals. For all other individuals wishing to transfer from retirement benefit schemes to personal pension schemes their maximum tax free lump sum will be 25% of the accumulated transfer value unless subject to a nil certificate. This can be particularly attractive where the lump sum under the transferring scheme would have been considerably lower.

14.124 *SI 2001 No 119* does not apply to *section 32* contracts taken out before 6 April 2001, which remain subject to the restrictions mentioned in 14.119 and 14.120. A transfer will only be possible if the certificate mentioned in 14.119 was completed at the time the contract was taken out or is now completed by the administrator of the original retirement benefit scheme as at the date of the transfer to the *section 32* contract, and is passed on to the SIPP administrator with the transfer payment. This also applies to other types of deferred annuity contracts such as individual policies assigned to the member after leaving service (e.g. the policy earmarked for an individual under an executive pension plan), and policies bought by trustees on winding up a *Chapter I* scheme.

14.125 *SI 2001 No 119* also provides, with effect from 14 February 2001, for transfers to take place between personal pension schemes where the member or widow(er) or dependant is receiving income withdrawals (see 14.194 AND 14.195) subject to the following:

(*a*)   both the transferring scheme and the receiving scheme have amended their rules to allow such transfers;

(*b*)   the transfer payment comprises the whole of the funds under the relevant arrangement(s) (see 14.208) being transferred;

(*c*)   a subsequent transfer of the same funds to another personal pension scheme cannot take place for at least a year;

(*d*)   the arrangement(s) in the receiving scheme to which the transfer is to be made cannot receive contributions, but can receive further transfers;

(*e*)   the member, widow(er) or dependant must elect for income withdrawals under the receiving scheme at the same time as the transfer.

14.126 There is also another area of concern for IR SPSS in relation to transfer payments to SIPPs. This is its concern with commission payments as explained not only in PSO Updates No 33, and No. 64 but also implied in PSO Update No 31 regarding other abuses (see 3.24 and 10.32). Of particular relevance may be a transfer made between personal pension schemes which results in commission being paid for a purpose that is not the provision of retirement benefits under the scheme. Here, IR SPSS may consider that the receiving scheme was established other than for the sole purpose of providing relevant benefits and withdraw its tax approval from commencement. The transfer payment too could be treated as an unauthorised payment and taxed on the member who made the personal pension arrangement under *section 647*. Another area of concern is where investment and financial advisers pass on to their clients some of the commission received from insurers on the introduction of new business relating to personal pension schemes. If these rebates are the result of commission generated by movements of funds between investment vehicles and are not used to enhance the value of pension scheme funds, IR SPSS is likely to conclude the scheme's tax approval has been prejudiced.

Death benefits

14.127 If a member dies before benefits become payable the whole of the member's share of the fund may be used to purchase an immediate annuity for the member's spouse and/or dependants. The total annuities payable must not exceed the highest annuity that would have been payable to the member. The surviving spouse's annuity is payable for life or may cease on re-marriage. The dependants' annuities cease when they attain the age of 18 or cease to be in full time education or vocational training. If a member or dependant dies while receiving payments under the income withdrawal facility, 14.194 to 14.215 should be consulted regarding the procedures that must be adopted.

14.128 In the early years of a SIPP the member's share of the fund will not be sufficient to provide surviving spouse's and dependants' annuities at a substantial level so contributions may be used to buy term assurance to provide such annuities should the member die before drawing benefits. This arrangement, it may be recalled, is the same as for SSASs (see 4.81). A lump sum payable on a member's death before age 75 can also be funded by term assurance (see 14.53).

14.129 The lump sum is not liable to IHT provided the rules are worded so that the exercise of discretion is vested in the trustees to pay benefits among a wide class of beneficiaries (see 14.84) unless at the same time term assurance is taken out the member was not in reasonably good health. Provision should be made for members to complete an expression of wish as to whom the lump sum benefit should be paid in the event of their death (APPENDIX 29). However, if the death benefits are passed within two years of the member's death to a discretionary trust in which there is no beneficial interest IHT may be payable (see 14.84).

14.130 If a member's benefits comprise a transfer from an insured scheme which was established by deed poll as opposed to irrevocable trusts, the death benefit in relation to the underlying policy concerned will be liable to IHT because the policy will not be subject to a trust. The SIPP administrator should check this point when accepting transfers from insured schemes.

14.131 If no surviving spouse's or dependants' annuities are payable on a member's death, then the member's share of the fund less an amount to cover expenses is payable as a lump sum as in 14.129, free from IHT, provided the trustees have discretion as to its disposal. It is important therefore for scheme members to complete an expression of wish or take steps during their lifetime to establish a trust to receive the lump sum death benefit. The benefit must be paid out from the trust within 2 years to avoid IHT. Some personal pension schemes established by LOs give members power to nominate death benefits. If there is such a legally binding power under which the member can direct death benefits to his estate, whether or not it is exercised, IHT will apply to the lump sum benefit because of the reservation of benefit rules.

14.132 Prior to 6 April 2001, the maximum proportion of the benefits transferred into a personal pension which originated in a retirement benefit scheme that could be paid as a lump sum on any member's death before vesting was 25%. If no surviving spouse's or dependants' annuities were payable, the whole amount could be paid as a lump sum. As part of the changes relating to transfer payments introduced by *SI 2001 No 119* from 6 April 2001, this restriction now only applies to regulated individuals (see 14.121). For all others, including those who transferred before 6 April 2001 and who are not regulated individuals, the whole of the accumulated transfer may be paid as a lump sum as in 14.127.

Investments

The position prior to 6 April 2001

14.133 Prior to 6 April 2001, It was not necessary to include in the trust deed any special restrictions on the investment powers of the trustees apart from the inclusion of those provisions set out in IR 76 (1991)(8.10–8.13) banning certain transactions and investments. This meant that apart from specific areas of investment that were banned, flexibility (see 14.12).

Permitted investments

14.134 A list of permitted investments for SIPPs was first published in Memorandum No 99(58) and repeated in Memorandum No 101(4) (APPENDIX 57) with the addition of commercial property.

14.135 *Self-Invested Personal Pensions — SIPPs*

This was eventually updated after discussions between IR SPSS and SPG by the publication by the SPG on 10 March 1998 (see 14.30) of an agreed list of permitted investments (APPENDIX 62). This is summarised as follows:

- stocks and shares (e.g. equities, gilts, debentures, etc) quoted on the UK Stock Exchange including securities traded on the Unlisted Securities Market, including the AIM but not OFEX, and in Open Ended Investment Companies (OEICs);

- stocks and shares traded on a recognised overseas stock exchange;

- unit trusts and investment trusts;

- policies or funds of UK insurance companies (or UK branches);

- deposit accounts;

- commercial property;

- currency and equity bond futures and options traded through a relevant exchange;

- foreign currency (only for the purposes of other investment);

- second hand endowment policies.

It should be noted that the list agreed between IR SPSS and the SPG was never incorporated into IR76.

14.135 Building society and bank accounts were included under deposit accounts. US mutual funds were included under stocks and shares traded on a recognised overseas stock exchange provided such investments were recognised by the FSA. OEICs were not permitted to be a SIPP provider (see 14.73), but shares in OEICs were permitted investments of SIPPs established by other providers subject to the latter being empowered to invest therein by virtue of their own regulatory frameworks and investment limitations. Commercial property is looked at in more detail in 14.143 to 14.148 because there were specific requirements in this connection. However, there was a considerable grey area between the list of permitted investments and those that were specifically proscribed in Memorandum No 101(6–8). This grey area was looked at in the light of omissions from the permitted and proscribed investments and from experience gained of IR SPSS practice in this area since 1989 and from the SPG.

14.136 The specifically proscribed investments were:

(*a*)   loans to members and their relatives;

(*b*)   residential property or land connected with such property;

(*c*)   personal chattels capable of private use.

To this list can be added unquoted company shares because quoted company shares were permitted. Certificates of deposit were also not permitted because there was no specific tax exemption for them in *ICTA* in relation to personal pension schemes.

14.137 The grey area between permitted and proscribed investments for SIPPs existed because since Memorandum No 101 was issued in October 1989 by IR SPSS, no further guidance had emerged except on individual SIPPs. When the SPG was formally established in 1996 it provided a clearer channel of communication with IR SPSS and more definitive guidance. So it appeared that secured and unsecured loans to third parties, provided they were not members or their relatives and made on commercial terms were permitted. However, IR SPSS indicated it was not satisfied that loans to third parties should be made, particularly if the SIPP member selected the borrower. Secured loans, particularly commercial mortgages, appeared to be acceptable but IR SPSS was not entirely happy with this investment area and an approach to IR SPSS beforehand would have been advisable (see 14.140). It should be noted though that Memorandum No 101(6) states that no loan from another source to a scheme member should in any way affect the return on the investments representing that member's interest in the scheme. Ordinary insurance policies were acceptable as were second-hand endowment policies, provided they were not held directly in the member's own name and were transacted through a recognised market maker. The CGT and income exemptions mentioned in 7.38 apply to the disposal of these policies by SIPPs.

14.138 The holding of foreign currency bank accounts was acceptable for settling overseas share purchases, but not for other purposes. Deposit accounts held other than in sterling were acceptable. Traded options and futures were acceptable, but commodities were not. Authorised unit trusts could be held. Non-exempt unauthorised unit trusts were not permitted. Tax-exempt unauthorised unit trusts had to be within the UK.

14.139 Another area of doubt was liquidity. There was no mention in Memorandum No 101 that in making investments the trustees had to be mindful of their liquidity requirements when members' benefits were due for payment. It can only be assumed they were left to their own judgment on this because a member could receive benefits at any age after 50. PSO Update No 8 which set out the requirements for income withdrawal, also mentioned nothing about liquidity during the period of withdrawal, although this was clearly an aspect to watch (see 14.206). During 1997 however, IR SPSS began to express concern over liquidity in relation to property ownership and trustee borrowings during income withdrawal. At the joint IR SPSS/SPG meeting of 15 January 1998 it was agreed that no commercial property could be purchased after the later of commencement of income withdrawals and a member's 65th birthday (see 14.168) and no borrowings were permitted once income withdrawal commenced (see 14.149).

14.140 Because there were a number of indeterminate areas of investment still left open, advice was clearly necessary before making some investments and an approach to IR SPSS beforehand was to be recommended particularly regarding loans to unconnected persons see (14.137). IR SPSS indicated though that member choice of investments was limited to the acceptable list (see 14.135 and APPENDIX 62) and only the administrator should approach IR SPSS regarding the acceptability of other investments that the administrator and not the member wished to make.

14.141 It was as well to bear in mind the ban in *section 839* on transactions taking place between a SIPP and certain persons (see 14.29). This applied to the acquisition and disposal of all permitted investments. In particular it could be very tempting to acquire equities from a member or to sell them to a member. Such direct transactions were not permitted. All transactions in quoted UK or overseas securities had to take place through a recognised stock exchange.

14.142 Transfers of assets in specie from say a SSAS to a SIPP were also a case in point (see 6.42). These were permitted in principle even though the trustees of both schemes and the members were connected persons within *section 839*. An approach to IR SPSS first for its agreement should have been made. Where a commercial property was involved an independent valuation was needed. IR SPSS would not agree to any transfer that included an investment that a SIPP was banned from making. If a transfer was being made to a FSAVCS of underlying policies PSO Update No 34(5) and 14.117 should have been followed.

Commercial property

14.143 Memorandum No 101(4) and (8) referred simply to commercial property being an acceptable investment and that residential property or land connected with such a property was not acceptable. So with an attractive investment of this nature it was important to establish the type of property a SIPP could acquire and then to whom it may be let and on what terms.

14.144 The trustees could acquire the freehold or leasehold of commercial property such as offices, shops, industrial premises, factories and warehouses, etc. They were not permitted to receive ground rents from residential property even when the SPG made representations to permit them once they could be received by SSASs (see 6.27). They could also acquire land for development, agricultural land and forestry. Some providers believed land capable of development would remain an acceptable investment until developed when it should be sold if it comprised residential property. Others understood the position to be that if planning permission for residential development was obtained, the land must be sold before any such development commenced. The writer's own experience is that IR SPSS exercised its discretion in accordance with the latter.

14.145 Residential property was not a permitted investment of a SIPP except in the following instances that were broadly in line with the exemptions for SSASs:

(*a*)   commercial property with a flat used solely by a caretaker;

(*b*)   a shop with an integral flat occupied by the same unconnected person who runs the shop;

(*c*)   commercial property such as a public house or hotel where the residential element is occupied by the proprietor or staff and who are unconnected persons or the paying public;

(*d*)   a nursing home or residential care centre where the residents and live-in staff are unconnected persons.

Farmland with a farm cottage occupied by an unconnected farmhand would come within the exceptions, but any other farm dwelling would not.

14.146 Any permitted property could be leased to a business or partnership of which the member or a person connected with the member, was the proprietor or a partner, unlike a SSAS, as well as to any other unconnected persons. Where property was let to a business or partnership of which the member or person connected with the member, was the proprietor or partner there had to be a commercial lease between the trustees and the occupant drawn up on commercial terms and determined by a professional valuation. Most importantly the rent payable under the lease had to be evidenced by the valuation. This was in fact a rule requirement of a SIPP (see 14.81). There was no such requirement where the trustees and lessee were totally unconnected as it was expected that because they are at arm's-length from each other a fully commercial lease with an open market rent would be operated.

14.147 Because all purchases and sales of property could only take place between unconnected persons, it was also assumed an arm's-length price would be paid and there was therefore no IR SPSS requirement for a supporting price valuation.

14.148 The eventual sales of all investments, including property, did not have to be reported to IR SPSS, but they cannot be made to connected persons.

Borrowings

14.149 Memorandum No 101 made no reference at all to a SIPP being able to borrow monies for a purpose of the scheme, e.g. to finance a property purchase or imminent benefits, where assets may take some time to realise. Borrowings were permitted, though there was no limit on the amount the trustees could borrow as there is for SSASs (see 7.57). It is understood that IR SPSS had expressed concern over the extent of any borrowing not distorting the taxation treatment of SIPPs. This eventually led to no borrowings being permitted (see 14.139) from the commencement of income withdrawal although if part of the fund had not been taken as income withdrawal, borrowings could be secured on the assets represented by that part of the fund not subject to income withdrawal.

14.150 It has never been entirely clear whether or not borrowings could be made from the member or someone connected with the member. Clearly they would have had to be made on commercial and prudent terms so that the trustees fulfilled their fiduciary role in acting in the best interests of the members of the scheme. A mortgage or legal charge would usually be the vehicle for borrowing with security over the trustees' property or other investments. The period of borrowings would need to fit in with members' intended retirements as far as possible. A member could not provide personal security for any borrowing and the trustees could only charge trust property in respect of their own borrowings (see 7.64).

The position from 6 April 2001

14.151 In Autumn 2000, the Inland Revenue put forward for consultation draft regulations with the aim of limiting their discretion to approve a personal pension scheme by restricting the investments in which the scheme may invest. During the consultation period there was a meeting between IR SPSS and the SPG on 24 October 2000. Following this meeting the SPG made a further submission to IR SPSS. On 14 January 2001 *The Personal Pension Schemes (Restriction on Discretion to Approve) (Permitted Investments) Regulations (SI 2001 No 117)* were laid before the House of Commons and came into force on 6 April 2001.

14.152 Regulations on investments had been expected for several years to bring SIPPs more into line with SASSs. It was widely anticipated that they would reflect the existing Inland Revenue discretionary practices and, hopefully, clarify some of the grey areas (see 14.137 and 14.139). However, the speed with which they were rushed through in order to coincide with the introduction of stakeholder schemes and the new tax regime (see 14.23) created considerable confusion and consternation amongst SIPP providers, as they struggled to interpret exactly how the *Regulations* applied to real situations. There were also some in the legal profession who challenged the validity of some of the *Regulations* as not being within the Inland Revenue's powers under *section 638A*.

14.153 A further meeting between IR SPSS and the SPG was held on 14 March 2001 in an attempt to clarify a whole range of points, including transitional provisions for investments held in schemes approved before 6 April 2001, but which are no longer permitted under the *Regulations*. The *Regulations* are silent both on this point, and whether or not it is necessary for such schemes to incorporate the requirements of SI 2000 No 117 into their rules. At the time of writing, the Inland Revenue's integrated model rules (see 14.89) did not include these requirements, yet IR SPSS has confirmed that schemes seeking approval after 6 April 2001 must adopt provisions mirroring the requirements of the *Regulations*.

14.154 On 26 March 2001 IR SPSS inserted Part 11 into IR 76 (2000) on the Inland Revenue website. IR 76(2000) (see IR76(2000), 11.36 to 11.39) contains details of the transitional provisions relating to investments held prior to 6 April 2001 (see 14.174). Part 11 and Appendix 25 to IR76 (2000) include further restrictions on investments not contained in SI 2001 No 117 and other inconsistencies with the regulations. This gave rise to further submissions from the SPG requesting clarification. At the time of writing, the SPG is still awaiting a full response from IR SPSS. Most of the points requiring clarification relate to investment in commercial property and borrowings that are covered in 14.164 to 14.173 and 14.175.

Definition of a SIPP

14.155 *Regulation 3* of SI 2001 No 117 defines a 'self-invested personal pension scheme' broadly as a member's arrangement(s) within a personal pension scheme in which the member has the power to direct how the funds are invested. So, this includes both SIPPs as they were already understood and such arrangements under an insured personal pension with a self managed facility (see 14.3).

14.156 *Regulation 4* includes a definition of an individual pension account (see APPENDIX 66). This kind of product is merely a 'wrapper' for certain types of investments, all of which a SIPP can invest directly in, it is not intended to provide further details in this chapter.

Permitted investments

14.157 *Regulations 6* to *10* impose the relevant restrictions on the Inland Revenue's discretion. It is, therefore, very important to remember that the regulations are paramount and IR SPSS have no discretion not to apply them.

14.158 *Regulation 6* states that no investments may be held directly or indirectly for the purposes of a SIPP other than those listed in the Schedule to the *Regulations* (APPENDIX 66). The list of permitted investments in the Schedule is similar to the one agreed between IR SPSS and the SPG in 1998 (see 14.134 and APPENDIX 62) but there are some differences in relation to stocks and shares (see 14.159) and in relation to commercial property and borrowings (see 14.164 to 14.173 and 14.175).

14.159 There is no longer any mention of shares listed on the Alternative Investment Market (AIM) with regard to stocks and shares listed or dealt in on a recognised stock exchange. However, IR SPSS has confirmed that AIM shares are covered by the words 'or dealt in' and are still permitted investments. OFEX and unquoted shares are not permitted, although the purchase of shares in a site maintenance company as part of a commercial property purchase is acceptable as the shares are treated as part of the property transaction and not a separate transaction in shares. A list of stock exchanges recognised by the Inland Revenue is available on their website (*www.inlandrevenue.gov.uk/fid/rse.htm*).

In the schedule of permitted investments forming part of *SI 2001 No 117* (APPENDIX 66), futures and options are only allowed where they relate to stocks or shares, not currency as was the case prior to 6 April 2001 (see 14.134 and APPENDIX 62). However, in Appendix 24 to IR 76(2000) (APPENDIX 70) currency futures and options are included as permitted investments. The SPG has asked IR SPSS to clarify the position.

14.160 *Regulation 7* imposes restrictions on investments that personal pension schemes other than SIPPs are permitted to hold.

14.161 *Regulation 8* bans a SIPP from lending money to any person including members and persons connected with the member, but does allow a personal pension scheme that is not a SIPP, to lend to persons other than the member or persons connected with the member.

14.162 *Regulation 9* sets out the restrictions on transactions with members and connected persons including the three year rule (see 14.39) effectively confirming the pre 6 April 2001 position except in respect of the following:

• eligible shares (see 14.57), which are excluded;

• certain transactions relating to pooled property investments, which are excluded (see 14.166); and

• leasing of property to connected persons, which is now more restrictive (see 14.165).

IR SPSS has also confirmed that *Regulation 9* does not apply to in specie transfers from a SSAS to a SIPP (see 14.142) nor between SIPPs (IR76 (2000) (11.21)).

14.163 *Regulation 10* confirms the pre- April 2001 position relating to the dates beyond which a property may be purchased (see 14.139) and any new borrowing taken out (see 14.149).

Commercial property

14.164 The types of property that may be purchased on or after 6 April 2001 are still those described in 14.144. In addition, ground rents from residential property not occupied by the member or anyone connected with the member are now permitted.

14.165 The SIPP trustee(s) may still lease property to the member's business subject to normal commercial terms and an independent professional valuation of the rent payable. However, it is no longer possible for property to be leased to the business of a person connected with the member (see 14.174). This aspect has been taken up with IR SPSS by the SPG, as situations beyond the trustee(s) control could arise in future that result in the property being let to a connected person's business. For instance, if the member subsequently retires from his company and his children succeed him, the tenant-company then becomes a connected person. One would hope that IR SPSS will confirm that the contractual obligations of the lease override the connected person requirements.

There is also the possibility that the purchase of the freehold interest in a property which is already let to the member's business, i.e it has a leasehold interest, has been unintentionally prohibited by the wording of *Regulation 9(1)* (see APPENDIX 66). The SPG is awaiting clarification from IR SPSS.

14.166 Where a number of members' funds are pooled together to invest in property and they are connected with each other by virtue of being in the same partnership or company, *Regulation 9(3)* allows the purchase and sale on commercial terms and subject to an independent professional valuation, of each member fund's share of the property to any other member fund holding a share in the property. Provided, however, that the property is leased to the member's partnership or company and, in the case of the latter, provided the company is a trading company and not an investment company.

14.167 Although this exemption from the restrictions on transactions with connected persons is welcome, it has thrown up a number of uncertainties that the SPG has raised with the IR SPSS. For example, are pooled property investments by connected members permitted where the tenant is not the business of the members i.e., the tenant is a totally unconnected third party? IR 76 (2000) (11.19) suggests that they are not. Even if this is not the case and it is possible, it still suggests that it would then not be acceptable for connected members' funds to buy and sell their shares in the property from/to each others funds in the same way as described in 14.168.

14.168 The ownership by a SIPP of a member's business premises or a partnership's offices can be an extremely attractive investment and carries various advantages with it. A shelter from CGT is provided on its ultimate disposal. The rent while still being a legitimate business expense is not taxable in the hands of the trustees. If rent payable to the trustees falls into arrears they should take the appropriate steps under the lease to recover it. The property itself is divorced from the business or partnership and its position remains so even if the business or partnership encounter financial difficulties or cease to operate. There is a disadvantage, however, in that such property cannot be purchased in the first place from the members nor sold later to them because of the ban on purchases from and sales to connected persons. Furthermore, no commercial property may be purchased after the later of the member attaining age 65 and commencing income withdrawals from that part of the fund from which the purchase is to be made. Consideration will therefore have to be given as to the appropriate time to sell the property when an annuity is purchased or a member takes income withdrawals, particularly if a partnership is involved. In the latter instance realising the property to pay the benefits of one partner while the other partners remain members of the SIPP should be avoided by building up sufficient other assets in the funds for such an eventuality. The untimely death of a member could create problems over selling a jointly owned share of the property to pay death benefits (see 14.173).

14.169 The trustees will need to consider the position of VAT in relation to rent receivable and on the sale of property. In particular, if a property is sold for over £54,000 the question of registration for VAT should be considered. These aspects are covered in greater detail in 14.246 to 14.259.

Borrowings

14.170 *Regulation 6* bans borrowing by a SIPP for any purpose other than purchasing a freehold or leasehold interest in commercial property or for the development of such property. Commercial property is defined in the regulations as including land. Development of a property can only be carried out by someone who is not connected to the member(s) (IR 76(2000) (11.30)).

14.171 The amount borrowed must be secured only on that property or on any other asset of the member's fund. It must not exceed 75% of the purchase price or the costs of development. For these purposes purchase price includes legal and other costs incidental to the purchase price and development includes refurbishment or renovation of, or any other improvements to, buildings. Additional borrowing is also permitted to defray any liability for VAT arising in connection with the purchase price or development costs.

Borrowings in respect of the VAT element must be repaid when the VAT is received from HM Customs and Excise and this must be not later than 12 weeks from the date of purchase or completion of the development. This is another matter on which the SPG has made representations to IR SPSS because the usual quarterly returns system for VAT will not always enable administrators to reclaim VAT within this 12–week period.

14.172 Replacement borrowings are permitted but only to the value of the amount outstanding on the original borrowing.

14.173 *Regulation 10* prohibits any new investment in property after the later of the member's 65th birthday and the date on which income withdrawals commence in relation to that part of the fund from which the purchase is to be made. It also prohibits any borrowing in relation to any part of the fund from which income withdrawals have commenced. These conditions mirror the position prior to 6 April 2001 (see 14.139).

Liquidity problems generally should always be kept under scrutiny by the trustees in case of a retirement at any time after age 50. While joint ownership of property by a SIPP is acceptable in principle (see 14.166), its ultimate realisation by the trustees should not be unduly fettered. Prior to 6 April 2001, any re-allocation of jointly owned property on the death of a member should have been structured to avoid the connected transaction provisions being breached.

Unfortunately, the *Regulations* have exacerbated potential liquidity problems in the event of a member's death as described in 14.16. The *Regulations* permit borrowing only for the purposes of purchasing and/or developing land and property (see 14.170). At the time of writing the SPG was gathering information from its members to assess how seriously this will affect schemes in the future, and then, if necessary, to make representations to IR SPSS for changes to be made to the *Regulations*.

Transitional Provisions

14.174 IR SPSS has confirmed (IR 76 (2000), 11.36 to 11.38) that investments held or transactions made before 6 April 2001 which are no longer allowed under the regulations but were acceptable under the then current guidelines, may be retained and continue. For example, borrowing in excess of 75%, leasing of property to the business of a person connected with the member, and loans to unconnected parties.

Prohibited Investments

14.175 In Appendix 25 to IR76 (2000) (APPENDIX 71), IR SPSS have provided a list of prohibited investments for SIPPs. The majority of these are not contestable. However, there are two entries relating to commercial property which are not explicitly prohibited by the regulations viz:

(a)   leisure property (e.g. golf courses), or property with an affiliated leisure interest such as sporting rights; and

(b)   any land or property directly adjacent to any land or property owned by the member or anyone connected with the member.

The SPG has made further representations to IR SPSS, as pubs, hotels etc (see 14.145), which IR SPSS has confirmed as acceptable both prior to and after 6 April 2001, will often have leisure facilities. In addition, there seems no reason to prohibit commercial property merely because it is adjacent to a member's property except perhaps for land next to the member's residence where there is potential for private use.

Payment of Annuities

14.176 When a scheme member or dependant who has not opted for the income withdrawal facility, has an annuity purchased from a LO, the latter becomes responsible for payment of the annuity to the member or dependant and for deducting tax therefrom. Up to 5 April 1995, all such annuities were liable to tax under Schedule D. The LO deducted tax at the basic rate (*section 349(1)*) and the annuitant claimed a repayment if not liable to tax or paid any higher rate tax. The position changed with effect from 6 April 1995 as *section 648A* inserted by *FA 1994, s 109* brought all annuities from personal pension schemes within the PAYE system, along with all pensions. LOs must therefore operate a PAYE code for each annuitant in these circumstances, which ensures the correct amount of tax is deducted from each payment.

14.177 Prior to the payment of any lump sum benefit and where income withdrawal is not adopted, there may be insufficient funds to purchase an annuity for a scheme member. In such circumstances IR SPSS allow, as an administrative procedure from 6 April 1996, repayment of the fund to the member. The procedures are set out in PSO Update No 15.

They are only applicable to a SIPP where the member:

(a)   has either attained age 50 or has retired early on grounds of incapacity;

(b)   is not a member of another personal pension scheme or in receipt of an annuity from any personal pension scheme;

(c)   whose fund under the SIPP is insufficient to provide an annuity of £260 p.a. or more, or does not exceed £2,500; and

(d)   is aware that part of any repayment is chargeable to tax, has consented to the repayment and in consideration waived all rights under the SIPP.

PSO Update No 34(12) amended these procedures to allow members with low customary retirement ages (see 14.82) to be included.

14.178 Where the conditions at 14.177 are met the repayment may be made without consulting IR SPSS. The procedures to be adopted by the administrator are set out in PSO Update No 41(29) and IR76 (2000) 9.54 with regard to the deduction of tax under PAYE from the payment. The administrator should send a list annually to IR SPSS with details of all such repayments. Members should be advised by the administrator to enter details of the payment on their tax returns. Until 17 March 1998 IR SPSS withdrew tax approval from the relevant arrangements because the main purpose of the arrangement was frustrated by the inability to secure an annuity. However, changes in *FA 1998, s 95(1)* introducing a 40% tax charge on loss of tax approval would have involved a double tax charge on trivial repayments of this nature because the provisions of *section 647* would also have taxed the repayment as an unauthorised payment. Tax approval is not withdrawn in these cases arising after 17 March 1998. SIPP model rules should not be amended in consequence to encompass this procedure as that would trigger withdrawal of approval.

Any administration expenses incurred in operating these procedures may be recouped out of the member's fund before repayment. The amount reported to IR SPSS will, accordingly, be that after deduction of such administration expenses.

Income Withdrawal Facility

Background

14.179 From the advent of SIPPs, when members retired, they had to take a cash lump sum and/or buy an annuity from a LO (see 14.176). Often the annuity purchased would be level with no increases rather than a lesser amount with built-in annual increases to allow for inflation. Once purchased the annuity could not be changed. This inflexible approach had obvious disadvantages if annuity rates were low at the time the annuity was purchased and there was no flexibility to take cash when it was needed. Initially staggered vesting was developed by some LOs to circumvent these problems by allowing policies to be cashed in a few at a time to buy annuities. This would leave some policies to be encashed before age 75 when annuity rates were better, or the member's circumstances changed.

14.180 In late 1993 a few LOs developed managed annuities allowing members to control the underlying investments of the policies and to provide a measure of flexibility over the income taken annually. Assets would be transferred from a personal pension policy after taking a cash lump sum to a managed annuity contract backed by fixed interest investments or equities and unit linked or with profits. Members could then withdraw cash, subject to tax, whenever required by encashing assets and leave the remaining assets to grow in the managed annuity contract. Some contracts were even structured to allow payments to continue on the member's death to dependants and then on their death the residue would be paid to the deceased's estate, whereas with staggered vesting the underlying investments would be lost in such circumstances.

14.181 However, in 1994, managed annuities were brought to an abrupt end by IR SPSS on a legal technicality. This precipitated intensive lobbying by the LOs for more flexible arrangements for paying annuities from all personal pension schemes and led to a White Paper in June 1994 regarding annuity purchase deferral prospectively to be introduced by 1997. In the event, things moved more rapidly with the Chancellor's Budget announcement in November 1994.

14.182 The Chancellor proposed that the *Finance Act 1995* when enacted, would allow members of personal pension schemes to defer the purchase of an annuity when they retired to age 75 and to withdraw amounts during the period of deferral broadly equivalent to the annuity the member's fund could have provided. The proposals did not include retirement annuity contracts despite some later lobbying. The Chancellor's intention was to give members of personal pension schemes greater flexibility in the way they use their funds. This applies particularly when they retire when annuity rates are low and have to buy a smaller annuity than if they had been permitted to defer the purchase of the annuity until rates were more favourable. The proposals very much mirrored the thinking behind the deferral of purchase of pensions for members of SSAS announced in February 1994 (see 4.97 to 4.108).

14.183 It was made clear that members of personal pension schemes who choose in future to defer purchasing an annuity would be allowed to make income withdrawals in the period of deferral whether or not they elected to take a cash lump sum. The income withdrawals would still be subject to tax, but from 1995/96 *et seq* would be liable to income tax under Schedule E. Withdrawals would be reviewed every three years to ensure the pension fund was not depleted too rapidly. The fund investment income and capital gains would continue to build up tax-free during the period of deferral.

14.184 Between the Chancellor's announcement and the enactment of the *Finance Act 1995* on 1 May 1995 various conditions and checks to ensure the new arrangements met the Inland Revenue's requirements were considered in consultation with the pensions industry. These included the maximum and minimum income that could be taken each year, the nature of the three-year review and options following the death of a member in the deferral period. *FA 1995, s 58* and *Sch 11* and PSO Update No 8 contained the detailed legislation and guidance on the operation of the income withdrawal facility until changes made by *FA 1996* (see 14.193), the publication by the ABI of a guidance note agreed with CTO on inheritance tax issues on the death of a member or survivor while making income withdrawals, and certain changes introduced under *FA 2000, Sch 13* to give even greater flexibility in respect of the three year review (see 14.191).

Legislation and guidance

14.185 *FA 1995, s 58* provided for the enabling legislation in *Sch 11* thereof to be brought into effect for income withdrawals to be made under a personal pension scheme where the purchase of an annuity is deferred. *Sch 11* amended *ss 630–655* where appropriate and set out the broad parameters for income withdrawals including what should happen when a member dies while taking income withdrawals. *Sch 11* also provided for regulations to be promulgated subsequently with details of the annuity tables to be used and how they are to be applied, but in the event such regulations were not necessary (see 14.188).

14.186 Definitions of 'income withdrawal' and 'pension date' were added to *s 630*. Income withdrawal is defined as payment of income from a personal pension scheme otherwise than by way of an annuity and pension date is the date an annuity is first payable. The latter is between age 50 and 75 so the existing legislation is unchanged (except for the administrative easements introduced under *FA 2000* – see 14.191), but the link between the cash lump sum and commencement of the annuity is totally severed, enabling the lump sum to be taken, but the purchase of the annuity to be deferred. Thus, the cash lump sum is payable on the date on which the election to defer the purchase of the annuity takes effect (the pension date) and it cannot be taken later, particularly if no lump sum was taken at all at pension date. The restrictions which apply to cash lump sums derived from transfer payments received (see 14.114) must still be observed though particularly where benefits cannot be taken before age 50 or no tax free cash sum can be taken.

14.187 Under the income withdrawal facility members must withdraw income from their funds during the period of deferral except in the year the annuity is purchased or in which the member dies. All amounts withdrawn are assessable to income tax under *Schedule E* by virtue of *section 203* and the scheme administrator should operate PAYE thereon. Income withdrawals are accepted by the CTO as not providing an interest in possession and therefore outside the scope of IHT. Regular income withdrawal payments may also generate commission payments. If such commission is paid to a financial adviser or SIPP member from the fund then the tax approval of the SIPP may be prejudiced (see 14.126).

14.188 *Section 634A* provides for a maximum and minimum limit on the amount of annual income withdrawal. The maximum is roughly equivalent to a level single-life annuity and is calculated by reference to tables provided by the Government Actuary's Department (GAD). These were expected to be made available in regulations, but were issued in May 1995 by the GAD as annexes to its consultation paper, 'Income Withdrawals from Personal Pension Funds during Annuity Deferral'. Revised versions are available from IR SPSS Supplies Section. The tables also contain instructions on their usage. The calculations also take into account the amount of the member's fund available for annuity purchase at pension date. There is a minimum level of income withdrawal of 35% of the maximum permitted. In the first year of payment the value of the fund to be used will be after any lump sum benefit has been paid or is to be paid.

14.189 Within the 100% and 35% limits explained in 14.188, members are free to choose the level of income withdrawal and vary the amounts from year to year. Scheme administrators are responsible for ensuring withdrawals remain within the limits each year. The initial maximum and minimum withdrawal limits apply for the first three years when a fresh calculation must be made at the first day of each subsequent three-year period, again using the GAD tables and the balance of the member's remaining fund.

14.190 The first triennial reviews of income withdrawal took place in 1998 and have continued since. The fall in the value of gilts and shares and of annuity rates since 1995 will have affected many members who have taken the maximum level of withdrawals. This underlines the fact that income withdrawal is usually more suitable for high net worth members with other financial resources which enable them to cushion these adverse trends until investment conditions improve. Members of SIPPs who have taken income withdrawals close to the minimum level are unlikely to have their income reduced as a result of a triennial review however.

14.191 With the experience of triennial reviews in 1998 and subsequent years, it became apparent that improvements were needed to the review process as it only allowed for the recalculation of the amounts that a member can withdraw over the next three years on one particular fixed day. Furthermore, where the member's income withdrawals were being phased in from different 'arrangements' within the fund (see 14.208) on different dates, there are an ever-increasing number of review dates (i.e. one for each 'arrangement' or group of 'arrangements' as and when they are 'phased in') giving rise to serious administrative problems. After consultation with the pensions industry, changes were made by *FA 2000, Sch 13*, to sections *634A* and *636A* (to allow a 60–day window for calculating the new amounts of withdrawals in respect of a review date and to combine all review dates into a single date relevant to all arrangements from which income withdrawals are being made, both with effect from 1 October 2000). A new section *638ZA* was inserted to allow multiple pension dates in a single arrangement within a member's fund with effect from 6 April 2000. Full details and worked examples of how these facilities operate in practice can be found in IR 76 (2000) (9.18 to 9.49).

14.192 Further contributions and transfer payments to a member's 'arrangements' within a personal pension scheme are precluded under *section 638* after the member's pension date, i.e. after the member has opted for income withdrawals from those 'arrangements', except in the case of transfers that qualify as exceptions from *section 638(7A), see* 14.125.

Death of a member

14.193 Until the substitution of *section 637A* with a new *section 637A* under *FA 1996, s 172*, there were restrictions which prevented the member's surviving spouse and/or dependants from passing on the remaining pension fund to their heirs in certain circumstances (e.g. where the survivor had chosen to defer the purchase of an annuity and then died, while receiving income withdrawals, more than two years after the member died). 14.194 to 14.202 set out the position from 29 April 1996.

14.194 If a member dies during the period of income withdrawal the payment of a lump sum death benefit of the whole of the member's fund may be made within two years of death. While the lump sum may not be liable to IHT if paid under discretionary powers by the trustees, it is nonetheless liable in the first place to a tax charge of 35% under *section 648B* and which is payable by the administrator. The advice given in 14.129 and 14.131 for members either to complete an expression of wish or establish a trust to receive the lump sum death benefit is most relevant here. In the latter case, the benefit must be paid within two years of the member's death and the trust must provide for a beneficial interest to avoid IHT liability. If an annuity is to be provided for a surviving spouse and/or dependant, they may each choose to defer the purchase of an annuity and take income withdrawals instead. This option is not available though to surviving spouses who elect to defer the annuity until they reach some age not later than 60. A surviving spouse or dependant cannot defer the purchase of an annuity beyond their 75th birthday or the 75th birthday of the deceased member, if earlier.

14.195 The same maximum and minimum limits apply to a surviving spouse or dependant who opts for income withdrawal (see 14.190 and 14.191) using the GAD tables, but in this instance taking into account the amount available for that survivor's annuity at the death of the member. The amount available may have to be restricted by reference to the annuity it would buy but for the deferral. The withdrawal limits apply for the first three years from the member's death when a fresh calculation must be made at the first day of each subsequent three-year period using the GAD tables and the balance of the survivor's remaining fund.

14.196 If under the rules a surviving spouse's entitlement ceases on remarriage or a dependant's entitlement ceases at age 18 or on cessation of full-time education, the person concerned may still opt for income withdrawal during the intervening period. If an annuity has not been purchased at the date entitlement ceases, however, the remaining annuity fund is forfeit and must be used to meet administration expenses of the personal pension scheme generally.

14.197 Instead of opting for income deferral a surviving spouse and/or dependants may choose to take the deceased member's fund as a cash lump sum. This option has to be made within two years of the member's death even if the survivor has taken income withdrawals in that time. If the member was not in income withdrawal at his/her date of death the lump sum is not taxable under section 648B, otherwise the lump sum is chargeable to tax at 35% (see 14.194) and the balance may also be liable to IHT depending on the exemptions available.

14.198 Where a surviving spouse or dependant in receipt of income withdrawals dies within two years of the member's death and no annuity has been purchased, the balance of the survivor's fund must be paid as a lump sum (subject to the 35% tax charge) under *section 648B* to a wide range of beneficiaries in accordance with the scheme rules. However, in the guidance note agreed between the ABI and CTO in 1999 (see 14.184) it is explained that even if paid under discretionary powers, the lump sum may still be liable to IHT under the *Inheritance Tax Act 1984, s 5(2)*, as amended, because the deceased had a 'general power' to dispose of the benefits (ie, elect to take the balance of the fund as a lump sum during those two years). Where the survivor dies more than two years after the member and the annuity has not been purchased, the balance in the annuity fund will be paid as a lump sum under discretionary powers and should not be liable to IHT. It will be subject to the 35% tax charge under *section 648B*.

14.199 If a member dies before taking any benefit or electing to defer the purchase of an annuity, any surviving spouse and/or dependant entitled to an annuity may choose to defer its purchase and take income withdrawals. The same restrictions as described in 14.194 to 14.196 will apply. The option to take the lump sum (see 14.197) is available also, and it would not be subject to the 35% tax charge under *section 648B*. If the surviving spouse or dependant dies and the annuity has not been purchased, the balance of the fund will be paid, as a lump sum in accordance with the scheme rules. If paid under discretionary powers there should be no IHT liability, and no 35% tax charge under *section 648B*.

14.200 *Section 636(3)(b)* provides that the income continuing to a beneficiary under income withdrawal shall not be greater than the pension that could have been bought for the deceased member the day before death. However, this can have the adverse affect of cutting back the benefits and the excess becomes a windfall profit for the provider or trustee to cover general administrative expenses. This could happen where the older children of the deceased member are still in full time education and income withdrawal would cease at the end of full time education or an annuity could only be purchased to cover that limited period. In IR76 (2000) (10.25) it is confirmed that the fund should be reduced, if necessary, at the outset to take account of the restriction in *section 636(3)(b)* and no further restriction will be required during the period of annuity deferral. It is also confirmed that the restriction does not apply if the beneficiary opts for the lump sum.

14.201 Anyone who wishes to defer annuity purchase knowing that they are seriously ill with the intention of boosting death benefits for dependants may not prevent exemption from IHT for any consequent cash lump sum. The lump sum may be liable to IHT under the *Inheritance Tax Act 1984, s 3(3)* if it can be shown that the intention of the member was not to make provision for his or her retirement, given the prospect of an early death, but to maximise the lump sum passing on death.

Model rules

14.202 The Integrated Model Rules (IMR 2000) (see 14.89) incorporate the provisions relating to annuity purchase deferral and income withdrawals mentioned in 14.185 to 14.192.

SIPPs established on or after 1 October 2000, may therefore adopt such rules from outset and SIPPs approved before that date may amend their rules accordingly. Clearly because of the benefits the income withdrawal facility offers, SIPPs will wish to incorporate it into their rules. The Integrated Model Rules IMR (2000) prohibit an assignment to a trust under which the policy-holder or his estate can benefit. If life assurance policies are held by a SIPP at the member's death they are not treated as part of the member's estate for IHT purposes.

14.203 The PSO (now IR SPSS) has introduced a certificate procedure similar to that adopted for SSAS (see 3.58) whereby it will accept amendments to the model rules without detailed examination. The form PS6 (APPENDIX 19) should be used in these circumstances.

Advantages and disadvantages

14.204 There is no doubt that the income withdrawal facility has given members of personal pension schemes increased flexibility in how they use their pension fund. They are able to escape from being forced to buy annuities when rates are low and buy at a time of their choosing before age 75. This puts them on a par with members of SSAS who can defer pension purchase until age 75. They can choose the level of income they need annually between the maximum and 35% thereof, whereas SSAS members can only vary the level of their pensions once in payment provided the scheme rules have been amended to allow the facility introduced by PSO Update No. 54 (see 3.42). If members are prudent, their fund performs well and administration costs are reasonable, there should be sufficient capital available to purchase their annuity later from a LO.

14.205 Income withdrawal should not be seen however as a direct replacement for an immediate annuity. It should be seen as a mechanism that permits annuity purchase deferral until the member wishes to receive a steady level of income for life. Nevertheless, this facility does have the advantage to the member of retaining access to the capital sum both during lifetime and death if that occurs before the annuity has been purchased. So the member has the added advantage of continuing to be involved in the investment advice and strategy of the SIPP.

14.206 There are some restrictions on the nature or level of investments during the period of income withdrawal regarding further property acquisitions and borrowings (see 14.173). The administrator of a SIPP will however need to keep an eye on liquidity though at least to ensure the 35% limit can be met from easily realisable assets to start with. As the member or survivor gets nearer to age 75 even more careful consideration should be given to selecting appropriate investments for the member's fund, taking the necessary professional advice as required. The member though will need to take into account several factors when deciding on income withdrawal or securing an annuity. The following list, which is not exhaustive, is offered as a basis for such a decision:

- size of the fund;
- spouse's and dependants' position;
- state of health of the member, spouse and dependants;

- any restrictions to the cash lump sum payable;
- ages of the various people concerned;
- other income and capital;
- present and future tax rates;
- IHT position;
- interest and annuity rate prospects;
- investment choices and current yields; and
- costs.

14.207 There is an element of risk in income withdrawal that should be taken into account by members and their advisers. The risks include:

(a) high income withdrawals may not be suitable during deferral;

(b) withdrawals may erode the capital value of a fund particularly if investment returns are poor and high levels of income are taken. This may result in a lower income when the annuity is eventually purchased;

(c) investment returns may be less than those anticipated or shown in illustrations; and

(d) annuity rates may be worse when annuity purchase takes place.

So, if the income withdrawn is more than any increase in the value of the SIPP after charges in any year the potential to reduce income withdrawal exists. This could arise through poor investment performance, poor investment decisions, neglect, or over-confidence. Income withdrawals at a cautious level should avoid these problems, but the level of future annuity rates cannot always be predicted. It is not possible to guarantee a particular level of income either from income withdrawal or annuity purchase for the future, so regular monitoring of the fund and level of income withdrawal should reduce the risks. SIPP members must be made fully aware of the risks. Failure by the provider or trustee or any appointed manager to point out these risks may give rise to potential financial liability on their part.

14.208 Annuity rates move in line with changes in yield on medium-term gilts. People retiring in 2001 face an income of approximately 30% less than those retiring 10 years ago with the same size of fund. To minimise these problems it is possible to write a personal pension as being divided into a number of arrangements (most commonly 100 or 1000) or in the case of insured personal pension schemes, as a cluster of policies, colloquially known as clustering or segmentation. Here segments of the pension policy or arrangements within a member's fund in a SIPP may be encashed each year to provide a tax-free cash lump sum and income withdrawals while leaving the remainder to roll-up gross eventually free from IHT should the member die. Using clustering in this way to 'phase' in a member's benefits, hence the now more commonly used term 'phased income withdrawals', increases the tax efficiency of the whole arrangement and the potential return of capital on death of the member. However, there are some IHT problems with clustering policies and phased income withdrawals, (see 14.215). Nonetheless, the member can take full account of the income from 'arrangements' vested in earlier years, whether via an annuity or income withdrawal, and regard the tax-free cash from 'arrangements' vested in the current year as part of this year's income requirement and not particularly as a windfall.

14.209 As mentioned in 14.187 all withdrawals of income by scheme members, their surviving spouses and dependants are liable to income tax under Schedule E and the scheme administrator must operate PAYE thereon. Eventually, when any of these persons attain age 75 or earlier if they so decide or the rules dictate, the fund must be used to purchase an annuity from a LO. The choice of LO is the same as for SSAS (see 4.96) and once purchased the LO becomes responsible for payment of the annuity and for deducting tax therefrom under the PAYE system (see 14.176).

14.210 The advantage of the income withdrawal facility for personal pension schemes may not be permanent. The Chancellor announced in his November 1995 Budget the possibility of extending the option to take a variable pension on their retirement to members of occupational schemes. These proposals were overtaken by the Inland Revenue's discussion paper of 2 February 1998 (see 4.109) on enhanced flexibility for occupational pension schemes. Discussions then took place with the pensions industry about options which would give similar flexibility to members of money purchase occupational schemes including SSAS and the possibility of paying retirement benefits between ages 50 to 75 regardless of whether a member actually retires. Members of insured money purchase schemes were given the opportunity to make income withdrawals on a provisional basis on similar lines to personal pension schemes until it was replaced by the 'improved flexibility in pension provision' for all money purchase occupational pension schemes, introduced under PSO Update No. 54 (see 3.42) on 30 June 1999. PSO Update 54 did not include any provisions for paying retirement benefits between ages 50 and 75 regardless of whether a member actually retires.

Remaining IHT problems

14.211 PSO Update No 8 (27–29) mentioned that the model rules available at that time had been amended to minimise the possibility of the lump sum death benefit forming part of the member's estate for IHT purposes. This is also reflected in the Integrated Model Rules (IMR 2000). The rules exclude trusts under which a beneficial interest in a benefit can be payable to a member, his estate or legal personal representatives. However, doubts still exist over the avoidance of IHT where a personal pension scheme adopts model rules stemming from fundamental flaws in the documentation of some insurance companies (see 14.202). The problems should not apply directly to SIPPs which are invariably established by a master trust arrangement whereby any benefits that become payable on the death of a member before benefits vest would be subject to an overriding discretionary trust. However, SIPPs may be indirectly affected at a later stage.

14.212 It is possible to avoid IHT on the lump sum death benefit if there is no interest in possession by holding the lump sum on a discretionary trust (see 14.194), and the property is held for the purposes of an approved personal pension scheme. To come within the statutory exemption though any lump sum payable on death must be properly alienated before the member's death. Some LOs may not have created a trust in the first place effectively separating the death benefit from the member's estate. This can occur with personal pension schemes established by deed poll or indeed insured arrangements established in the same manner.

14.213 Some LOs adopt an alternative approach and encourage each member to decide whether or not to place their lump sum death benefit under trust. Unfortunately, this comes up against the statutory bar to assignment of an annuity. Some LOs take the view that the death benefit element alone of a personal pension policy cannot be placed on trust and so the whole of the policy must be placed on trust, but this constitutes an assignment, which is prohibited. So how can the administrator of a personal pension scheme be satisfied that there is a valid trust as required by the model rules?

14.214 Additionally, not all individual trusts established previously will pass the tests set out in the model rules. For example, there can be no reversion to the member or the member's estate or legal personal representatives.

14.215 The problems at 14.211 to 14.213 have been the subject of discussion between IR SPSS, Capital Taxes Office and ABI for some time, but it is hoped eventually clear guidance will be published on the IHT position. Meanwhile, there can be IHT problems for SIPPs. If a transfer or assignment is arranged from an insured personal pension scheme or arrangement with shortcomings in its documentation or an assignment is made from an arrangement established by deed poll there will be a charge to IHT for the value of the transfer or assignment unless the deceased member's estate is below the exemption limit or the spouse exemption applies. The documentation of the SIPP even if properly drawn up will not be sufficient to protect it. To avoid these problems, all policies brought into a SIPP to benefit from clustering for phased-income withdrawals, should be looked at before they are accepted.

14.216 There was an additional problem with the amount of the lump sum death benefit. The lump sum benefit at pension date is limited to 25% of the value of the member's fund at that date (see 14.83). If a member died during income withdrawal, the death benefit could have been restricted if the member's fund consisted of transfer values or assignments from other schemes or arrangements. Following the *FA 1995*, the *Transfer Regulations* were not amended to take account of the income withdrawal facility due to an oversight. Thus, if the balance in the fund consisted of transfers or assignments from elsewhere, only 25% of that part of the fund relating to the transfers and assignments could have been paid as part of any lump sum death benefit until *SI 1988 No 1014* had been amended. IR SPSS recognised an inconsistency existed and wrote to the ABI on 30 October 1997 saying that it was not the intention that the 25% restriction would apply on death during income withdrawal. It would amend the transfer regulations in due course and the model rules at the earliest opportunity to correct this. Meanwhile, IR SPSS would not regard a personal pension scheme as being in breach of the conditions for tax approval if on death during income withdrawal the whole of the fund, apart from protected rights, was paid out as a lump sum subject to the 35% tax charge under *section 648B*. This position is now reflected in the SI 2001 No 119 and the Integrated Model Rules (IMR 2000).

Withdrawal of approval

14.217 IR SPSS's power to withdraw the tax approval of a personal pension scheme is contained in *section 650*. Approval can be withdrawn if the circumstances warrant it from the date when the facts were such as not to warrant the continuance of approval and this cannot be earlier than the date the scheme was established.

14.218 *Section 650(2)* states that notice of withdrawal of approval should be sent to the administrator and, if appropriate, to the member who established the scheme. *Section 650(4)* requires the notice of withdrawal to state the grounds on which and the date from which approval is withdrawn.

14.219 *FA 1998, s 95(1)* introduced *section 650A, ICTA 1988* with effect from 17 March 1998. This provides for a tax charge at 40% on the value of the assets of a personal pension scheme at the date of withdrawal of tax approval if it is on 17 March 1998 or later. The tax is chargeable under Schedule D Case VI and payable by the scheme administrator. If there is no administrator, the administrator cannot be traced or fails to meet his obligations, then the person who made the personal pension arrangement, i.e. the member, will be responsible for payment, provided an assessment is raised on him within three years of the date the administrator was due to pay the tax charge.

14.220 The provisions of *section 650A,* are aimed at offending members only and therefore where withdrawal of tax approval takes place from 17 March 1998 it will be withdrawn from the particular arrangements and not the entire personal pension scheme. It is not clear what has led to this particular charge although it must be surmised it reflects the criteria for withdrawal of tax approval from occupational pension schemes where a similar tax charge applies (see 10.3) and the amended provisions of *section 591C* involving transfers from personal pension schemes. The inference of the legislation must be it is aimed at trust-busting, but the 40% tax charge imposed on occupational pension schemes that lose their approval from 2 November 1994 only applies where controlling directors are involved (see 10.5). All other occupational pension schemes with 12 or more members are not subject to the 40% tax charge on loss of tax approval. There is clearly no level playing field on loss of approval for personal pension schemes.

14.221 There is no exhaustive list of 'offences' that warrant withdrawal of approval, but they will clearly be serious breaches of legislation or IR SPSS guidelines. There are some indications, however, of the circumstances that could lead to loss of tax approval. *Section 650(3)* mentions where securing the provision of benefits under the scheme was not the sole purpose of the individual making them. IR76 (2000) (21.10) mentions unacceptable amendments will lead to loss of approval. Other 'offences' may be breaches of the rules, e.g. payment of excessive lump sum benefits, the acquisition of banned investments, transactions with connected persons, etc., the failure to furnish information or to secure a pension by age 75, or trust-busting.

14.222 Where the 40% tax charge is applicable, it applies before all the other tax implications have effect (see 14.223 and 14.229). It is calculated on the market value of the scheme's assets held on the day before it ceases to be tax approved. Market value is to be ascertained in accordance with *TCGA, s 272.* Where the scheme's investments include loans made to the member or his employer if the company has made contributions to the scheme to anyone connected with the member or his employer, under *section 650A(8)* the value of the loan capital outstanding and any unpaid interest must form part of the value on which the 40% tax charge is calculated. It is odd once again (see 10.36) that the legislation should mention loans to members and anyone connected with them as they are banned in a SIPP. If they had been made approval is likely to have been withdrawn from the date they were made and not from a later date of another offence.

14.223 Other tax exemptions and relief will be lost from the effective date of withdrawal of approval after the deduction of the 40% tax charge where applicable. Thus, any employer's contribution paid subsequently would not be allowable as a deduction for corporation tax or income tax purposes under *section 640(4).* In consequence the members would be liable to tax under

Schedule E in respect of the contributions paid on their behalf as the exemption in *section 643(1), ICTA 1988* would no longer apply. The members would in addition not qualify for income tax relief on their personal contributions under *section 639(1)* after approval is withdrawn except on the first £100 p.a. of contributions paid to secure annuities for a widow and dependants as mentioned in 10.39.

14.224 Any pensions payable to members subsequently would be liable to tax as they are from any approved or unapproved occupational scheme. Any payments to or for the benefit of members which would not have been expressly authorised by the scheme's rules before disapproval will be liable to income tax. Lump sum benefit payments up to 25% of the member's share of the fund made subsequently will not be taxable on the member to the extent that they have already been taxed under Schedule E in respect of contributions paid by the employer (*section 189*).

14.225 Lump sum death benefits paid subsequently should still escape IHT if paid by a discretion exercised by the trustees (see 10.38), but they are liable to tax under Schedule E subject to their not already having been taxed in respect of contributions made by the employer.

14.226 Any income of the scheme will no longer qualify for tax relief under *section 643(2)*. The income should however be exempt from additional rate tax under *section 686(2)(c)(i)*. So far as a SIPP is concerned income received without deduction of tax, e.g. rent from property, will be taxable in the hands of the trustees.

14.227 CGT will arise on the disposal of assets by the trustees, the gain arising over the whole period of ownership (see 10.44) and not from the effective date of withdrawal of tax approval. Thus no disposal takes place at the date of withdrawal of tax approval and the trustees will pay CGT on the eventual disposal of the assets on any gain arising between the date of their acquisition and disposal. Under *FA 1988, s 100* the rate of CGT was restricted to the basic rate of income tax for disposals up to 5 April 1992. The basic rate continued to apply to disposals thereafter under *TCGA 1992, s 4* until 5 April 1998. From 6 April 1998, *section 4* was amended by *FA 1998, s 120(1)* and gains arising to the trustees of SIPPs from that date are liable to CGT at 34%.

14.228 If the scheme is established by a LO or Friendly Society, subsequent contributions cannot be referred to exempt pensions business. They must be transferred to general annuity business or the remainder of the life fund, as would the funds in which the contributions have been placed (see 10.44).

14.229 The administrator still remains liable for the repayment of excess contributions, in particular any tax reclaimed erroneously as a result of excess contributions (see 14.98). *SI 1988 No 1013* provides for the administrator after loss of tax approval to account for such tax to the Inland Revenue.

Refusal to approve

14.230 IR SPSS may refuse to approve a personal pension scheme possibly for the reasons already given in 14.221. In such instances, IR SPSS issues a formal notice stating the grounds for refusal.

Redress

14.231 The position is totally different from withdrawal of tax approval of any occupational pension scheme where representations can only be made and ultimately judicial review sought. For personal pension schemes *section 651(1)* provides that where either approval is refused or withdrawn an appeal can be made in writing within 30 days to the Board of Inland Revenue, in effect IR SPSS, stating the grounds for the appeal. If the matter cannot subsequently be resolved with IR SPSS then the appeal may be heard before the Special Commissioners of Income Tax. They have the power under *section 651(3)* to allow or dismiss the appeal or to order that withdrawal of approval shall have effect from a date other than that determined by IR SPSS.

14.232 The appeal procedure may not be relevant to other adverse decisions by IR SPSS. In those cases representations along the lines suggested in 10.50 should be pursued with staff at a senior level in IR SPSS. Alternatively, an unresolved complaint can be taken up with the Revenue Adjudicator or the parliamentary ombudsman, as explained in leaflet IR120.

Penalties

14.233 *Section 653* provides for a penalty not exceeding £3,000 where any person knowingly makes a false statement on making an application for approval under *section 631* or for the purpose of obtaining relief from or repayment of tax. This is very much in line, with *FA 1994, s 106* for occupational pension schemes (see 10.60). The penalty cannot be paid from scheme funds.

14.234 *Section 651A(3)* introduced by *FA 1998, s 96(1)* provides for a penalty not exceeding £3,000 to be imposed for failing to comply with the requirements of *SI 2000 No 2316* (see 14.105)

Requirements of the DWP (formerly the DSS)

14.235 The main social security legislation governing personal pension schemes may be found in *PSA 1993*, as modified where appropriate by regulations issued under the *Pensions Act 1995* and *WRPA 1999*. The original guidelines were set out in Memorandum No 92. It is not proposed here to cover every aspect of personal pension schemes dealt with by the DWP, particularly those that contract-out of SERPS. These will be few in numbers so far as SIPPs are concerned because they are not financially viable as vehicles to receive the SERPS rebate. If an individual is contemplating such a move, then some general considerations also have to be taken into account, such as age, job mobility, reduced incentive payments from 6 April 1993, age-related rebates from 6 April 1997, restrictions to cash lump sums derived from transfer payments after 5 April 1997 following the abolition of GMPs (see 14.114 and 14.115) and sound financial advice is required before reaching a decision. The DWP does however provide a number of guides relating to pensions including State pensions, stakeholder pensions and personal pensions. These are available on the internet (*www.pensionguide.gov.uk*) or from the Pensions Info-Line on 0845 7313233.

14.236 The remaining paragraphs deal with those aspects of SIPPs that fall within the ambit of the DWP, such as preservation, equal treatment, authorisation under the *FSA 1986*, disclosure, the pension scheme's register, the pensions ombudsman, pensions and divorce, and the *Pensions Act 1995*.

14.237 Preservation and equal access have already been covered at 14.88. The position regarding authorisation under the *FSA 1986* is as set out in 11.6 to 11.8 for SSAS.

14.238 The disclosure provisions applicable to SIPPs are found in the *Personal Pension Schemes (Disclosure of Information) Regulations 1987 (SI 1987 No 1110)* as amended by the *Personal and Occupational Pension Schemes (Tax Approval and Miscellaneous Provisions) Regulations 1988 (SI 1988 No 474)* and by the *Occupational and Personal Pension Schemes (Miscellaneous Amendments) Regulations 1992 (SI 1992 No 1531)*, by the *Occupational and Personal Pension Schemes (Consequential Amendments) Regulations 1994 (SI 1994 No 1062)*, by the *Occupational and Personal Pension Schemes (Miscellaneous Amendments) (No 2) Regulations 1995 (SI 1995 No 3067)* and by the *Personal and Occupational Pension Schemes (Miscellaneous Amendments) Regulations 1997 (SI 1997 No 786)*. These regulations place the onus on the trustees to supply members with certain documentation and information. Some of that documentation has already been mentioned at 14.92 and 14.93 in connection with applications for approval. The trustees also have to provide details of the amount of contribution credited in the previous twelve months, including the value of protected rights and any other rights. Members must be informed if the scheme is tax approved or an application for approval is pending and how tax relief on contributions is effected. This information has to be supplied at least once every twelve months. Similar information is required when a member leaves a SIPP or it is wound-up. Within 13 weeks of joining a SIPP a member must receive basic information regarding the scheme. The requirement where an employer contributes to a SIPP but subsequently ceases to pay contributions, that members must be informed in writing if their contributions are not received on or before the date on which payment was expected was revoked by *SI 2000 No 2692*, which introduced more stringent requirements (see 14.243).

14.239 A SIPP must provide an annual Financial Statement containing information prescribed in the regulations and has to be available to members on request within one year after the end of the scheme year.

14.240 The register of occupational and personal pension schemes is explained in 11.24 to 11.32. Its requirements with regard to SIPPs are as set out in those paragraphs, except that the form PR2 is used to provide information to the registrar.

14.241 The position of the Pensions Ombudsman is explained in 11.46 to 11.50 and his jurisdiction extends to all forms of personal pension schemes. There is one area, however, in relation to a SIPP where the insurance ombudsman may be the appropriate person to approach rather than the pensions ombudsman. This relates to investments in insurance policies and if a dispute arises in this connection.

14.242 On pensions and divorce, what is said in paragraphs 3.95 and 11.66 to 11.71 relates equally to all personal pension schemes, including SIPPs

14.243 Regarding the *Pensions Act 1995*, personal pension schemes are not generally encompassed by its provisions nor the subsequent secondary legislation. Although SIPPs were not within the remit of Opra, this changed when, as part of the introduction of stakeholder pensions and the new tax regime (see 14.24), the Government felt it necessary to regulate the monitoring and control of employer payments (i.e. employer contributions and employee contributions deducted from pay and paid by employers to stakeholder pensions and personal pensions) in a similar manner to the requirements under the *Pensions Act 1995* for money purchase occupational pension schemes. *The Personal Pension Schemes (Payments by Employers) Regulations 2000 (SI 2000 No 2692)* made under the provisions of *WRPA 1999, s 9*, came into force on 6 April 2001 and include the following requirements:

(a) rates of contributions by the employer and employee must be shown separately on the employer's record of payments;

(b) deductions from earnings must reach the scheme by the 19th day of the following month;

(c) late payments must be reported within 30 days to Opra;

(d) if payment is 60 days late, both the employee and Opra must be notified;

(e) notifications of late payments of Opra can be suspended where Opra sees fit; and

(f) members must receive an annual statement setting out the amounts of payments and dates they were made.

These regulations apply to all stakeholder and personal pension schemes including SIPPs.

VAT Aspects

14.244 The various aspects of VAT as they apply to occupational pension schemes which are explained in CHAPTER 13 apply in general to SIPPs. Wherever mention is made in CHAPTER 13 of a pensioner trustee for SSASs this should be read as the trustee for SIPPs. There are two areas however regarding financial services and regarding property and registration where SIPPs are somewhat differently affected and which are covered here.

Financial Services

14.245 In 13.13 mention is made of both administration and investment-related services being supplied by a professional trustee or administration company to the principal company and trustees of a SSAS. Their overall charges include VAT for services provided to the company in the general administration of the scheme and for investment services provided to the trustees. The situation is similar to some degree with a SIPP with overall charges including VAT though provided to the member in general administration of the SIPP and for investment services provided to the trustees and the member if he appoints an investment manager. However, some of the administration and investment services are provided by LOs who are exempt from VAT in relation to some of the costs involved, e.g. provision of insurance or dealing with money.

14.246 The question of whether these charges were exempt from VAT or standard-rated was decided before a VAT Tribunal in 1997 in relation to two SIPPs, the *Winterthur Life Self-administered Personal Pension Scheme* and the *Personal Pension Management Scheme, in* the case of *Winterthur Life UK Ltd (formerly Provident Life Association Ltd) (LON/1787)(14935)*—the *Winterthur* case. The provider of both SIPPs was Winterthur Life (UK) Ltd and two of its wholly owned subsidiaries provided services by or through their agency to both SIPPs, Winterthur Life (UK) Ltd being the representative member of a VAT group which included the two subsidiaries. Both SIPPs authorised members to control the management and investment of the funds and the subsidiaries were entitled to recover administrative expenses from the funds for investment costs, remuneration of investment managers and advisers, and other professional fees and disbursements. HM Customs and Excise claimed that the charges were standard rated as trust administration. The Tribunal held however that the two SIPPs embodied contracts of insurance between the provider, a LO, and the members even if this was operated through the agency of subsidiaries. This meant the administration services incidental to the implementation of those contracts were part of the provision of insurance by a permitted insurer and exempt from VAT under the *VAT Act 1994, sch 9.*

14.247 The ruling in the *Winterthur* case means quite simply that where a LO or its subsidiary acts as trustee and administrator to a SIPP, VAT is not chargeable for administrative fees. The exemption also applies to non-insured SIPP business where a LO brands a SIPP through, say, a stockbroker. The ruling in the *Winterthur* case is not only helpful to LOs operating SIPP. The Tribunal chairman also provided views that may be relevant where the provider is not a permitted insurer which a good number of SIPP providers are not. The Chairman's views were restricted to considering whether the VAT exemption for dealing with money might apply in any event to the following charges:

(a) exempt — *VAT Act 1994, Sch 9 Group 5 Item 1.* 'The issue, transfer or receipt of, or any dealing with money, any security for money or any note or order for the payment of money,' e.g. charge on contributions received.

(b) exempt — *VAT Act 1994, Sch 9 Group 5 Item 5.* 'The making of arrangements for any transaction comprised Item 1,' e.g. charge for installation or variation of direct debit.

(c) may be exempt depending on nature of services provided—*VAT Act 1994, Sch 9 Group 5 Item 6.* 'The issue, transfer or receipt of, or any dealing with any security, or secondary security,' e.g. charge for assets action.

(d) may be exempt depending on the nature of transaction and type of service supplied—*VAT Act 1994, Sch 9 Group 5 Item 6,* e.g. transaction charge.

He also concluded that a charge for the appointment of an investment manager would not be exempt. While the VAT Tribunal Chairman's views must be taken as *obiter*, and not therefore binding, they provide very useful pointers for non-LO providers of SIPPs and should be read together with the Budget 1999 proposals (see 13.9) regarding VAT exemptions for intermediary financial services.

Property

14.248 SIPPs are allowed to lease commercial property to members or partnerships of which the partners are members or to a company which is controlled by the members (see 14.165) on arm's-length terms. Such arrangements may have been caught by the *VAT Buildings and Land Order* from 30 November 1994 until 26 November 1996 when it was repealed by *FA 1997, s 37.* This discusses whether or not the member is a trustee of the SIPPS because in all these instances the lease would be between connected persons by virtue of the provisions of *section 839(3).* This states that any 'person in his capacity as a trustee of a settlement is connected with any individual who in relation to the settlement is a settlor, any person who is connected with such an individual and any body corporate which is connected with that settlement'. Thus, a member of a SIPP is connected with the trustees of the SIPP even if he or she is not a trustee because the member is a settlor of the trust scheme itself by reason of the personal contributions paid to the trustees.

14.249 SIPPs were not caught by the *Buildings and Land Order* if either of the parties to a lease is a fully taxable person. If the administration company operating the SIPP registered for VAT (see 14.254 the problem should be obviated, but if each individual member's fund within the SIPP registered (see 14.256) there may still be a problem. For instance the trustees, as landlord, may be unable to reclaim Input Tax against Output Tax as they are prevented from opting to charge VAT on the rent they receive on a new lease (see 13.29 and 13.30).

14.250 Unfortunately, the extra statutory concession announced on 28 February 1996 (see 13.35) did not specifically assist SIPPs because it was granted exclusively to SSAS. However, HM Customs and Excise News Release 11/96 (APPENDIX 56) did state that the Department would consider individual cases where businesses were not able to take advantage of the concession, especially if they were not motivated by tax avoidance and for which there was a clearly demonstrable ordinary commercial motivation and justification, and encouraged applications to be made to local VAT Enquiry Offices in this connection. SIPPs appear to be such 'businesses' and should have approached HM Customs and Excise for the concession if at all possible, although the caution expressed in 13.36 should be noted about the operation of concessions by HM Customs and Excise and that further representations may have to be made to the Adjudicator.

14.251 If SIPPs were not able to take advantage of the extra-statutory concession of 28 February 1996 it was possible to reduce some of the losses in respect of irrecoverable Input Tax. For instance as the property is let to a connected person it may be relatively easy for expenditure normally incurred by the landlord to be paid by the lessee under the lease. Alternatively, it was worth looking at reversing the option to tax. This meant a VAT loss for the trustee of the SIPPs as vendor or landlord, but the sum involved would be far less.

14.252 When the *VAT Buildings and Land Order* was repealed on 26 November 1996 (see 14.248) the extra-statutory concession of 28 February 1996 was also repealed. The VAT position for SIPPs then reverted to that available to 29 November 1994 except in relation to sales and leases after 19 March 1997 (see 14.253). SIPPs gained a small advantage from the repeal of the *Buildings and Land Order* as leases to connected persons from 26 November 1996 are no longer caught (see 13.37). So if the trustees of a SIPP are registered for VAT and sell commercial property they charge Output Tax on the sale and account for it to HM Customs and Excise. If they buy commercial property and pay Input Tax thereon, the Input Tax may be reclaimed against any attributable Output Tax, e.g. on the rent receivable. The grant of a short lease on commercial property from 26 November 1996 is exempt from VAT unless the landlord opts to waive the exemption and charge VAT on the rent. If the trustees of a SIPP are registered for VAT and opt to charge VAT on the rent they receive (Output Tax), they must also account for it to HM Customs and Excise less any Input Tax attributable to expenses incurred in respect of the property concerned.

14.253 From 19 March 1997 the provisions of *FA 1997, s 37* restrict the amount of Input Tax recoverable on leases and sales of property. The circumstances that apply should not generally involve SIPPs because the VAT avoidance 14.254 and 14.255. The point to watch is that land is not being developed by the trustees and the member's business or company or buildings are not being refurbished even on arm's-length terms via a contract, which would have to be the case anyway to satisfy IR SPSS (see 14.170). If this is the case, and the ultimate letting is to a VAT exempt business, eg a bank, insurance company, building society etc., the provisions of *FA 1997, s 37* are likely to apply and the trustees of the SIPP and the member should seek specific VAT advice from their accountancy advisers.

14.254 In fact there has been a SIPPs case where the provisions of *FA 1997 s 37* apply — *Winterthur Life (UK) Ltd (No 2) LON/98/127 (15785)*, the second *Winterthur* case. A company in the Winterthur group, Personal Pension Management Ltd (PPM), was the trustee of a number of SIPPs and a member of a VAT group. It purchased a long leasehold interest in a newly built property for £270,000 plus VAT as the vendor had elected to waive the exemption. PPM then granted a lease of the property to three SIPP members whose personal contributions had been used to fund the property acquisition together with a bank mortgage. The three SIPP members occupied the property for an exempt insurance business. PPM needed to opt to tax the rent receivable to recover the Input Tax incurred on the lease premium so it elected to waive the exemption to charge Input Tax on the rent. HM Customs and Excise ruled that the election by PPM was ineffective and that the lease to the three SIPP members remained exempt. The representative member of PPM's VAT group (see 13.15) appealed to the VAT Tribunal on the grounds that the legislation in *VAT Act 1994 Sch 10 para 2(3AA)* introduced by *FA 1997 s 37* was intended to counter tax avoidance whereas the transaction at issue was a legitimate commercial transaction.

14.255 The VAT tribunal dismissed the appeal and upheld the ruling of Customs and Excise. The SIPP members had provided the finance for the acquisition of the property even though this was done indirectly through the pension scheme. Thus a person who had financed the development was connected with the tenant and at the same time the tenant was using the building other than for a taxable purpose, i.e. an exempt insurance business. The conditions of *VAT Act 1994 Sch 10 para 2(3AA)* were satisfied and the election to waive the exemption to charge Input Tax on the rent was ineffective. The facts that the transactions were not for the avoidance of tax and the terms of the lease were fully commercial were not conclusive. There was no ambiguity in the legislation to permit a different decision. The anti-avoidance rules designed to prevent businesses which make exempt supplies from planning to recover VAT on the full cost of standard-rated property at the cost of paying much smaller amounts on rent. So the reprieve obtained by SIPPs on leases to connected persons following the repeal of the *Buildings and Land Order* (see 14.252) lasted only until 19 March 1997 where ultimate letting is to a VAT exempt business.

Registration

14.256 The trustees of a SIPP should seek their accountant's advice on whether or not they should register for VAT purposes, particularly because of the manner in which a SIPP is administered. The decision to register will depend on the criteria set out in 13.48 to 13.53 for SSAS to a great extent. However, the structure of a SIPP and the ease of administration must also be considered.

14.257 It is possible for the whole of the SIPP to be registered for VAT purposes, usually by the administration or trustee company operating the SIPP. That may give rise to administration difficulties in allocating Input Tax recovered to the correct member's fund within the SIPP. On the other hand, if a SIPP is established under a master trust, it is also possible to register each individual part of the SIPP whether or not the member is a trustee in respect of that part. This obviously means multiple registrations, but the allocation of recovered Input Tax is greatly simplified. If a property is not registered for VAT, for instance if the tenants do not wish to pay VAT on the rent, the member's fund will have to pay the VAT.

Chapter 15

Funded Unapproved Retirement Benefit Schemes (FURBS)

Introduction

15.1 This chapter primarily concerns funded unapproved retirement benefit schemes (FURBS). For reasons of tax efficiency these schemes are normally set up under trust for individual members. Under FURBS it is possible to provide a wide range of benefits on a very flexible funding basis. These benefits can include the payment of a large tax-free lump sum. Furthermore, FURBS enjoy a refreshing lack of formal control over their investments and administration and they are a particularly attractive form of benefit provision for directors (see 3.9 concerning the possible automatic treatment of a scheme as a FURBS by the PSO (now the IR SPSS)).

15.2 Prior to 1989 the generally disadvantageous tax treatment of FURBS meant that they were relatively few in number. The majority which were set up provided benefits for those persons who were prevented by the PSO at the time from joining tax advantaged, i.e. approved pension schemes. Those persons included directors and their families of investment or property companies (see 2.8). Clearly something significant must have taken place in 1989 as the popularity of FURBS has increased greatly since that time, and it is continuing to do so. That event was the enactment, on 27 July 1989, of *FA 1989*. This put into effect the announcement of intent by the Chancellor in his Budget Speech on 14 March 1989 to encourage wider pension provision. A description of the major (and largely unexpected) changes which were introduced by that Act which have added to the attractiveness of FURBS as a means of modern benefit provision for directors and executives, together with a summary of the subsequent developments, is given in 15.3 to 15.8.

Background

15.3 Before the enactment of *FA 1989* pensions tax legislation in the UK did not permit the provision of retirement benefits through an unapproved retirement benefits scheme (e.g. a scheme which provided benefits which were in excess of the normal Inland Revenue limits which applied to approved schemes) for, or in respect of, any employees who were concurrently accruing benefits under an approved scheme in relation to the same employment. This restriction was removed in its entirety on 27 July 1989 by *FA 1989, Sch 6 para 3(4)* which amended *section 590(7)* of *ICTA 1988*.

15.4 Significantly, for aggregate Inland Revenue limits purposes, the extended *ss 590(7)–(11)* required approved schemes to take into account only benefits that are from other approved schemes. As a consequence, FURBS rapidly became an attractive product for companies to offer as part or all of their benefit packages for new and existing senior employees. This was in keeping with the Chancellor's statement that his intent was to enable companies 'to provide whatever pensions package they believe necessary to recruit and reward their employees'.

15.5 In particular, employees whose incomes exceeded, or seemed likely to exceed, the earnings cap under *s 590C* (see 4.29) found FURBS to be a means of providing additional benefits in respect of their excess income over the earnings cap and its successors in a beneficial and secure manner.

The effect of the earnings cap on approved schemes is described in more detail in 4.28 to 4.32. The level of the cap is shown in APPENDIX 26. Additionally, the cap can be imposed on members who were previously treated as Continued Rights Members in cases where future transfers are involved. It should be noted that increases in the salary packages of directors and senior executives traditionally outstrip the rate of RPI increases over the same period. Not only is the earnings cap increase limited to the rate of the Index, but it was frozen for the year 1993/94. It is not surprising, therefore, that FURBS are taking an increasingly bigger slice of the executive retirement benefits cake because the cap is catching more executives.

15.6 Two further relaxations under *FA 1989* had a stimulating effect on the provision of unapproved benefits. The first was the allowance of company contributions to FURBS as an expense against company profits. Previously such an allowance relied solely on the decision of the relevant inspector of taxes under the ordinary rules of Schedule D. The second was to permit the payment of unrestricted tax-free lump sums. Furthermore, the additional tax charge on scheme income does not apply to FURBS. 15.18 to 15.20 below contain comprehensive details of the current tax position of FURBS.

15.7 As a result of the above changes it continues to be popular for directors and senior executives to accrue benefits up to the maximum permissible level under an approved scheme, and to accumulate additional benefits under a FURBS on their other income from the same employment. A description of the main types of benefit provision that may also be used alongside a FURBS is given in 15.9 to 15.12.

15.8 The Pensions industry's expertise in the field of FURBS has increased greatly since 1989, although it must be said that the general understanding of the tax position for unapproved schemes was a little uncertain in the early days which followed *FA 1989*. However, in August 1991, the Inland Revenue published a booklet entitled *The Tax Treatment of Top-up Pension Schemes* (APPENDIX 59). Despite its title this booklet deals with all types of unapproved pension schemes, an indication in itself that the Inland Revenue was aware of the increasing popularity, yet need for guidance, in the area of unapproved retirement benefit provision. It is a very helpful publication and it is written in an easy to digest style.

Alternative arrangements for directors and executives

15.9 It is appropriate at this point in the chapter to describe the main alternative forms of retirement and death benefit provision for directors and executives that have not been referred to specifically elsewhere in this book.

These may be found in 15.10 to 15.12.

15.10 'Group Unapproved Funded Final Salary Plans' (sometimes referred to as GUFFSAPS) are group FURBS with multiple membership. The benefits under such schemes are related to salary, rather than accumulated on a money purchase basis, which is more favourable for FURBS for reasons given later. With careful monitoring and accounting they can be an efficient benefit vehicle, although administration will be appreciably more complex and so more costly than it is for FURBS.

Group FURBS like individual FURBS, will normally pay all member benefits in tax-free lump sum form for reasons of tax advantage. These payments should escape any tax charge if the Inland Revenue is satisfied that the administration of the scheme meets its expectations of prudent funding and fund allocation for members. Without such monitoring tax would be chargeable on the emergent benefits to the extent that they exceed the contributions paid, and so it is important to find an adviser who can give firm guidance in this area.

If GUFFSAPS are to hold insurance policies, they are best held for individual members (see APPENDIX 59, paragraphs 3.2.3 and 3.2.4). This will simplify the application of *s 596A(8)* when calculating any relevant tax on gains under *s 547(1)* on the payment of any benefits which are in excess of the cost of the premiums charged on the member under *s 595(1)*. Generally, however, it is preferable not to hold policies of the description contained in 15.19(h) and 15.31(b) for the reasons contained therein.

Section 595(4) apportions the tax payable in proportion to the members' benefits. In the event that a member does not receive such benefits, the tax may be reclaimed by virtue of *s 596(3)*.

A further administrative consideration is that contributions that are made by the company must be calculated separately for each member in order to determine his or her tax liability under *s 595(1)* (see 15.29).

Otherwise the remaining tax position for group FURBS is similar to that which applies to individual FURBS.

15.11 'Unfunded Unapproved Retirement Benefits Schemes' (UURBS), if properly established, will effectively defer a member's tax liability until his or her benefits come into payment (at which time the company will be able to claim tax relief against its profits on the benefit cost). Like FURBS they are lightly regulated in comparison with approved schemes. UURBS provide member benefits by means of an advance promise, on the date the employee retires or dies, without any pre-funding by the company. In connection with the last point it is inadvisable to maintain any form of reserve account for an UURBS. This is because, since the enactment of *FA 1989*, it has been virtually impossible to obtain tax relief for corporation tax purposes on company contributions at any time in advance of the payment of the unfunded benefit promise out of the scheme. Before that Act, a reserve which was held on an acceptable actuarial basis under the principles established in the case of *Owen v Southern Railway of Peru [1957] AC 234* could be tax relievable, but mainly for approved schemes only. A charge to income tax under Schedule E on the member may well be incurred under the provisions of *s 595(1)* in respect of funds that are held in reserve, and any insurance premiums paid shall be assessed on the member. Otherwise, tax relief is normally given to the company at the time the benefits are paid (see APPENDIX 59, paragraphs 3.1.1 to 3.1.3). All benefits payable under UURBS are assessable to income tax under Schedule E on the recipient by virtue of *s 596A* (see APPENDIX 59, paragraphs 2.3.5 and 2.3.6).

The initial popularity of UURBS, which followed the enactment of *FA 1989*, was mainly because of the relatively simple procedure involved in establishing them. This was often achieved, with proper legal advice, by means of a letter of promise or a variation in a contract of employment. However, schemes must be established for a *bona fide* reason. UURBS are not subject to the preservation regulations. For various reasons, the most significant of which are listed below, UURBS appear to be in decline:

(a) lack of security for the member;

(b) all the benefits are taxable;

(c) difficulty in avoiding IHT without a discretionary trust;

(d) problems with annuity purchase (see APPENDIX 59, paragraphs 2.3.7 to 2.3.8); and

(e) problems with transferring the entitlements arising from an unfunded promise out of the scheme.

UURBS documentation can be in the form of a service agreement, letter of promise or deed poll. It is important to obtain legal advice, as requirements will vary according to existing employment rights and the memorandum and articles of association of the employing company.

Since 1989 there have been various attempts to arrange 'arm's length' security for UURBS, including USA style unfunded arrangements, which rely with varying degrees of effectiveness on set-aside monies or insurances. However, such arrangements do not sit comfortably with UK tax and pensions law and care should be taken before embarking on such forms of benefit provision.

15.12 '*Section 590* schemes' are exempt approved schemes, normally funded on a money purchase basis but occasionally on a final salary basis, which provide benefits strictly in accordance with the terms for mandatory approval that are laid down in *s 590*. This means that pension accrual is restricted to a basic rate of 60ths of the last three years' average final remuneration for each year of service; the earnings cap applies to post–31 May 1989 joiners; lump sums are restricted to 3/80ths of final remuneration calculated on the basis described above; benefits may only be paid on retirement at a specified age; and the only permissible death benefit is a pension to a spouse on death after retirement not exceeding two-thirds of the member's maximum pension. In view of the restrictive level and form of these benefits such schemes are, in practice, only favoured by those persons who are directors of investment or property companies and members of their families (see 2.8 and 15.2).

The documentation, administration and permitted investments for such schemes generally follow similar lines to those that apply to SSASs.

Advantages of FURBS

15.13 The main advantages of FURBS that are of a general nature are described in 15.14 to 15.17. Specific tax advantages are described in 15.20.

15.14 FURBS enable a company to continue an established policy for its directors and/or senior executives to receive a pension of two-thirds of final remuneration at normal retirement age. This was possible regardless of income level for pre–1987 members under an approved scheme if the member had ten or more years potential service to normal retirement age, a period which, for other members, has been extended to twenty or more years (see 4.12). The restrictions which have been imposed on benefit accrual and pensionable remuneration levels since that date have severely curtailed such benefit provision under approved schemes, resulting in an unequal treatment of new and existing employees. Furthermore, the earnings cap in all cases restricts the amounts which can be paid into personal pension schemes for such persons' benefit provision (see 14.22).

Following the worrying development in 1993, when the Chancellor froze the earnings cap at a level of £75,000 for the oncoming year (see 15.5), approved schemes are becoming less able to meet the full benefit expectations of an increasing number of senior employees.

15.15 The Inland Revenue do not impose limits on benefits payable under FURBS (unless they are so excessive in amount that they may bring into question the *bona fides* of the scheme as a retirement benefits scheme), not even on tax-free lump sums nor, in the main, on the level of funding (see 15.25). Some further advantages of FURBS are:

(a) contributions may be paid when tax rates are low and/or when cash is most readily available, and are allowable against profit;

(b) there is no requirement to appoint a pensioneer trustee, or to comply with the tight Inland Revenue and *Pensions Act 1995* controls over investments that apply to approved schemes in general;

(c) the member can be sure that his benefits are being funded and are safely invested;

(d) the member has control of his personal wealth, the yield on which is taxed at the lower or basic rate of tax (see 15.19(g));

(e) because all benefits may be paid in the form of a tax-free lump sum there is no requirement to secure an annuity, which may decrease in real terms and will, ultimately, cease;

(f) FURBS benefit from the annual CGT exemption (see 15.19(h)) and tapering relief;

(g) the scheme assets can remain after 'approved' funds will normally have ceased, so that the capital remains in the member's family and may be paid out in the form of tax-free lump sums;

(h) there are major exemptions from the requirements of the *Pensions Act 1995* (see 15.22 and 11.89);

(i) FURBS are particularly attractive to private companies. The small companies' rate of corporation tax is described in Appendix 61. Small companies form by far the majority of taxable companies. The lower and upper limits to qualify are also described in Appendix 61;

(j) administration costs are low due to the lack of stringent statutory controls;

(k) FURBS are not affected by the Inland Revenue information powers (see Appendix 5) which govern all approved and relevant statutory schemes, although schemes formerly approved are;

(l) IHT is easily avoidable (see 15.20(d)).

15.16   *Funded Unapproved Retirement Benefit Schemes (FURBS)*

15.16   The considerations listed in 15.13 to 15.15 otherwise apply also to schemes that were previously approved but have ceased to be approved (see APPENDIX 59, 2.4.1, and 10.30 to 10.44).

15.17   A FURBS can be an efficient means of increasing benefits in the later years of an employee's service, subject to consideration being given to the Greenbury Committee Report's recommendation that benefit levels should not be unrealistically disproportionate to the company's performance and costs to the scheme. Because increased company contribution levels will be assessable on the member to income tax under Schedule E (see 15.19(e)), there is scope at present for the payment of additional contributions on behalf of a member to any approved scheme to which the employee belongs, thereby securing increased benefits including the lump sum where there is room to do so. Benefits under a scheme in respect of the same employment may, of course, be based on pensionable salary that includes the additional remuneration available. An example, which covers the main tax regimes and based on an earnings cap of £95,400 for the tax year year 2001–2002, is given below:

Example

Member's current age : 50
Member's normal retirement age : 60
Service to date : 5 years
Current Salary : £110,000

So, using current figures and the tax rates throughout for the purpose of the example, the maximum tax-free lump sum at age 60 for the tax regimes will be:

Approved Scheme

Member A (a pre–1987 Member)	72/80 (uplifted scale) × final remuneration = £99,000 [initial pension 2/3 × £110,000 = £73,334]
Member B (a 1987 Member)	72/80 (uplifted scale) × final remuneration (IR maximum remuneration is £100,000) = £90,000 [initial pension 15/30 × £110,000 = £55,000]
Member C (a Full 1989 Member)	2.25 × initial capped pension below = £107,325 [initial pension 15/30 × £95,4000 (the earnings cap) = 47,700]

390

If a FURBS is set up now, with an annual contribution of (say) £20,000, the FURBS fund would accumulate in 10 years' time (less 40% marginal rate tax) to 10 × £20,000 @ 60% = £120,000.

The pensionable remuneration under the approved scheme will have increased by £20,000. This means that further tax relievable contributions can be paid into the approved scheme and, for Members A and B, final remuneration will increase to £130,000 . If Member C's income was below the earnings cap, the extra remuneration can increase his or her final remuneration up to that level.

So, the total package will then look like this:

	Approved Scheme	*FURBS*
Member A	Lump sum = £117,000	£120,000
	[new initial pension = £86,667]	
Member B	Lump sum (IR maximum	£120,000
	remuneration is £100,000) = £90,000	
	[new initial pension = £65,000]	
Member C	Lump sum = £107,325 (as before)	£120,000
	[new initial pension = £47,700]	

Result: the total tax-free lump sums for members A, B and C therefore have increased by £138,000£120,000 and £120,000 respectively.

Allowing for a factor of 12.1 for converting lump sums to pension, the net pensions would now be £76,917 , £57,500 and £38,756 respectively. This represents a net change of plus £11,833, plus £10,000 and NIL respectively.

If desired, it would be possible to secure further separate pensions by investing some of the increase in lump sum benefit in, say, a purchased life annuity where only the income element is taxable (see 15.20(*a*)).

Tax position

15.18 Despite being 'unapproved schemes', FURBS enjoy significant tax benefits by virtue of their status as 'retirement benefits schemes'. These are schemes that provide 'relevant benefits' (see 15.32 for the purpose of both of these definitions).

It is important that such schemes do not offend the 'sole purpose' test of providing relevant benefits as laid down in *s 686(2)(c)(i)* if they are to avoid the higher rate of income tax that applies to trusts. Inspectors of taxes report FURBS to FICO on receipt of a notification described under 15.14. FICO is reviewing FURBS with regard to any need to keep the investment and funding activities of trustees under closer scrutiny.

The taxable payments that are incurred by FURBS are described in 15.19 and the tax reliefs which they enjoy are described in 15.20. VAT is dealt with separately in 15.45 to 15.47.

15.19   *Funded Unapproved Retirement Benefit Schemes (FURBS)*

15.19   The taxable items, and their charging sections, are:

(a)   pensions and annuities payable to members, or in respect of members on their death, are assessable to income tax under Schedule E by virtue of *ss 19(1)(2)* or *(3)*. The person making the payment under the PAYE system should deduct the tax. Such tax can be avoided by paying benefits in lump sum only form, rather than in pension form. The Inland Revenue (see Appendix 59, paragraphs 2.3.2 to 2.3.4) points out this alternative;

(b)   benefits in kind may be assessable to income tax under Schedule E tax by virtue of *s 596A(1)*. If the benefits are not in cash form, the tax charge will be levied on the cash equivalent calculated as laid down in *s 596B*. The recipient must declare the benefit in his or her return of income. As *s 154* also imposes a tax charge on benefits in kind, *s 155(4)* exempts lump sums and other retirement benefits from a double tax charge. If the benefit continues into retirement the cash equivalent can be chargeable to income tax under Schedule E by virtue of *section 596A* (APPENDIX 59, paragraph 2.3.12) However, the charge is not applicable, by virtue of extra statutory concession A72, for payments 'for a member of the employee's family or household' which fall to be assessed to income tax under Schedule E by virtue of *s 595(1)*. With effect from the tax year 1998/99, *s 566A(4)(b)* charges non-cash benefits at the greater amount of Schedule E tax under *s 19* and the cash equivalent described above;

(c)   annual payments are taxed under Schedule D, Case III and the person making the payment should deduct the tax due;

(d)   payments made to a body other than an individual or his or her family, e.g. to a charitable organisation or a club or an association, will normally be assessed to income tax under Schedule D, Case VI by virtue of *section 596A(3)*. The tax charge is payable by the trustees/administrator on the cash equivalent described in 15.19(*b*) at the 40% rate;

(e)   company contributions are assessable to income tax under Schedule E on the member by virtue of *s 595(1)* except to the extent that they represent scheme establishment and management expenses. Under *s 596(3)* it may be possible to obtain repayment of all or part of the tax paid under *s 595* if the member does not ultimately derive any benefit from the scheme.

Arrangements can be made to gross up the tax chargeable on the member under *s 595(1)*. The tax will be payable through the PAYE system and the additional payment will attract NICs. However, as directors cannot receive tax-free income (*Companies Act 1985, s 311(1)*), a further taxable payment to the director to make good the tax may be necessary to enable such a payment to operate;

(f)   the determination of any tax chargeable on the scheme investment yield, whether as income or gains, is for the relevant inspector of taxes to decide (see paragraphs 15.19(g) and (h));

(g)   tax on income (for example, from dividends and bank interest) will be charged at the lower rate if the trustees have discretion over the level of benefits or can accumulate surplus monies (*s 686(2)(a),(c)(i)*), and income from trade and land will be taxed at basic rate. Non-UK equity dividends will be taxable at the overseas withholding tax rate, if higher;

(h)   the CGT indexation allowance is available, together with half the small annual capital gain exemption (see APPENDIX 61) for sponsored superannuation schemes. There has been an increase in the CGT rate that applies to FURBS. The current rate, and the earlier lower rate that applies to gains realised before 6 April 1998, are described in 15.20(h). The company may also be taxable on gains made on life policies and annuity contracts etc. (see APPENDIX 59, paragraphs 3.2.1 to 3.2.4, 7.61 and 15.31(b) in this chapter);

(i)   subject to any double taxation agreement which may be in place, income from overseas property is taxable under Schedule D Case IV or V as if it were from a UK source;

(j)   the tax position of unapproved death benefit schemes is described in detail in Chapter 6 of Tolley's Taxation of Pension Benefits. In summary:

- it can be efficient to insure benefits, but a charge may be incurred by the sponsoring employer to corporation tax. Term life assurance, or individual policies, should avoid such a charge. For group cover, any charge will depend chiefly on the amount of any excess of the surrender value of the policy over the amount of the premiums paid;

- if the scheme is established under trust, the trust may make provision for the sponsoring company to be reimbursed out of the fund for any charges incurred. The charge described in the preceding point can be avoided with proper planning and by agreeing the position in advance with the inspector of taxes;

- a sponsored superannuation scheme with discretionary powers of distribution will fall within the *Inheritance Act 1984, s 151*, and IHT charges on settled property will not apply. Close companies should expend contributions wholly and exclusively on company business if this status is not to be prejudiced;

- benefits should be distributed at the trustees' discretion to persons other than the member's estate;

- if the member is taxed on the employer's contributions under *s 595(1)*, lump sum benefits will be tax-free and the company's contributions will be allowable against corporation tax;

- the trust documentation must be compatible with any policy conditions;
- the effective date of the establishing document, and the commencement date, must be no later than the date on which the benefit cover begins;
- it is usual for a full deed and rules to be executed at inception; and

(k) ex-gratia payments (see APPENDIX 59, paragraph 1.2) which fall to be treated as non-approved relevant benefits, rather than redundancy/genuine loss of office payments, are treated in the same way for tax purposes as unapproved schemes (see 4.41 to 4.45).

15.20 Tax reliefs are available as follows:

(a) lump sum payments, regardless of the type or amount, are wholly exempt from any tax charge under *section 596A, s 19(1)* and *s 148* by virtue of *s 189(b)* for members and *s 596A(8)* in respect of other individuals. However, if final salary benefits are being provided, benefits should relate to the contributions paid for the member plus the rate of the fund's investment growth (see 15.29) if a tax charge is to be avoided. If desired a member may buy an annuity, e.g. a purchased life annuity, with the lump sum. Only the income element will be taxable. The capital element (*s 656*) will be exempt from tax. This is preferable to the scheme purchasing the annuity as the tax exemption will be lost (*s 657(2)(d)*);

(b) the disallowance of a company's costs, under *FA 1989, s 76*, in providing unapproved benefits does not apply to FURBS by virtue of *s 76(3)(b)* thereof. This is because the company's contributions are assessable on the member under *s 595(1)*. The company's contributions, whether made on a regular basis or as lump sums, are allowable against corporation tax in full under either Schedule D, Case I or II or under *FA 1989, s 76*;

(c) relief in respect of the costs of scheme establishment and management is determined by the relevant inspector of taxes under the ordinary rules of Schedule D. Such costs are not chargeable on the member under *s 595(1)*. Note that it is strongly recommended that members do not contribute to FURBS. Such contributions are not normally allowable against the member's assessable income under Schedule E nor does the tax exemption for lump sums apply to benefits secured by such contributions (see 15.29). The monies would be more beneficially applied as contributions to any concurrent approved scheme to which the employee belongs;

(d) there are clear advantages in establishing the scheme under discretionary trust. No IHT is payable on settled property if the scheme pays death benefits under discretionary powers of distribution (*IHTA 1984, s 151*). This is the same exemption that applies to approved schemes (see 3.29). Properly established FURBS qualify as 'sponsored superannuation schemes' and it is important that this status is preserved (see APPENDIX 59, paragraph 2.5.2) if a charge to IHT above the current threshold (see APPENDIX 61) is to be avoided. However, care should be taken when listing the potential beneficiaries in the deed, rules or in a nomination form. If the member's estate is included as a potential beneficiary a tax charge may be incurred under *section 596(A)(8)* (unlike for approved schemes) on 'gifts with reservation' (see APPENDIX 59, paragraph 2.5.5);

(e)   there is a minor tax exception which permits the allowance of a small contribution paid by a member in respect of a payment to secure an annuity under *s 273* (see APPENDIX 59, paragraph 2.2.2.);

(f)   until 6 April 1998 no employer or employee NICs arose in respect of company contributions which were chargeable as income of the member, nor on the benefit payments which were made out of the scheme, as these were payments which were made out of an occupational pension scheme. However:

- With effect from 6 April 1998 NICs were imposed on employer contributions made to some FURBS, whether or not through a third party, and in some cases the Contributions Agency had sought to charge retrospectively if there had been evidence of earlier abuse of the use of FURBS (that is, where the trust fund has not been used solely for the purpose of providing retirement pension or other permitted relevant benefits).

- It had previously been announced that the charge would have effect from a year later, and the first formal announcement of change was in a Press Release on 17 November 1997. The charge affects employer contributions and employee contributions (although the latter will probably already exceed the chargeable ceiling). Responsibility for NICs passed to the Inland Revenue on 6 April 1999.

- The following is taken from the text of a Contributions Agency letter. It gives some guidance on the in–house charging intent of the relevant authority:

'I would advise you that where an individual person is given a beneficial interest in a FURB............NIC liability arises on payments made by an employer into a trust fund. The legislation will encompass other collective or discretionary schemes............the collection will not be enforced on the FURB scheme set up prior to the date of this letter [sic: early in 1998] on condition that the............trust fund [is] used solely for the purpose of providing retirement pension or other relevant benefits as are permitted.

If used in whole or in part for any other purpose..........we will assess and collect [NICs] on the whole amount of the fund, not just the amount taken on that occasion.

Should any further payments be made into the FURB..........we will also..........make relevant assessment and collection of the contributions..........

If you are not satisfied with the decision or ruling, please let us know in writing within 28 days..........we will consider what you have told us and tell you if we can change the ruling.

Full details of our complaints system are given in leaflet CA62 'Unhappy with our service?' available from...........any.....Social Security office'.

- However, in a later development the Contributions Agency announced in a Press Release dated 15 March 1999 that new regulations *SI 1999 No 568* (see 3.9) come into effect on 6 April 1999. The DWP wanted to ensure that a number of FURBS are not subject to NICs, and the regulations exclude most payments to schemes where the employer's payment is not taxed under *Schedule E* on the employee. There is also provision for apportionment of a payment to a discretionary scheme, such as a GUFFSAPS as described in 15.10, but payment of earnings prior to 6 April 1999 will continue to be scrutinised carefully to determine whether a payment of earnings was made.

The operational and policy operations of the Contributions Agency transferred to the Inland Revenue with effect from 1 April 1999. From 6 April 1999 new employers have been able to register for tax through a special helpline that is part of NESI, and receive a starter pack. As the effective date of the regulations described above is 6 April 1999 there is some uncertainty as to whether the NICO will seek to impose NICs from the earlier date of 6 April 1998. Before its dissolution the CA had stated that it would closely scrutinise discretionary trust arrangements and will seek NICs if it can establish a payment of earnings to or for the benefit of an employee prior to 6 April 1999.

(g)   trustees do not normally incur any tax charge on insurance contracts (see APPENDIX 59, paragraph 2.7.3) but, importantly, see 15.19(h) for the company's position;

(h)   trustees do not incur any additional tax charge under *section 686(2)(c)(i)* on the income of a self-administered FURBS, by virtue of the status of the scheme as one which solely provides 'relevant benefits' (see 15.32). Until the enactment of the *Finance Act 1998*, the additional rate on capital gains under *TCGA 1992, s 4* did not apply, and gains normally benefited from half the personal annual exemption for capital gains (see 15.19(h), and APPENDIX 59 paragraphs 2.7.3 and 2.7.4). By virtue of *FA 1998, s 120* gains realised on or after 6 April 1998 are taxed at the rate applicable to trusts, but taper relief may apply as described in APPENDIX 61. In short, indexation was withdrawn from April 1998 (and is proportionate to that date) and chargeable gains reduce according to the period for which assets are held and offer a bigger reduction for business assets than for other gains;

(j)   the 'benefit to settlor' rules, which can give rise to tax charge on the member in respect of gains, do not apply to properly constituted FURBSs which provide a similar style of benefits to those which are provided by approved schemes (see APPENDIX 59, paragraph 2.7.5). However, if the trustees move overseas (perhaps to avoid capital gains tax) the tax position will be as described in 15.41 and 15.42; and

(k)   the compensation and general levies on occupational pension schemes do not apply to FURBS and UURBS.

Legislation and official guidelines

15.21   FURBS are often referred to as *s 595(1)* schemes as that is the main charging section for company contributions that are assessable on the member of a FURBS. The main legislation in the guise of *ICTA 1988; Finance Acts; Pension Schemes Act 1993*; Statutory Instruments, together with Memoranda and PSO Updates, is referred to in the appropriate paragraphs in this chapter. Additionally, it is important that the company should ensure that its own Memorandum and Articles enable it to contribute to a FURBS.

FURBS do not include statutory schemes or partially approved schemes.

Ex gratia payments (see 4.41 to 4.45, and APPENDIX 59, paragraph 1.2) which are treated by the inspector of taxes as non-approvable relevant benefits will be treated in the same way for tax purposes as unapproved schemes.

Separate reference is made to those requirements that emanate mainly from the *Pensions Act 1995* in 15.22 and 15.23 and 11.89. FURBS are exempt from many of the provisions of the Act but must comply, on present information, with the points contained in 15.23.

15.22   The following exemptions apply:

(a)   the *Occupational Pension Schemes (Assignment, Forfeiture, Bank-ruptcy etc) Regulations 1997 (SI 1997 No 785)* exempts FURBS from the inalienability and forfeiture provisions of the *Pensions Act 1995, s 91(7)*. Additionally, under the *Welfare Reform and Pensions Act 1999*, the Secretary of State may make regulations to provide for rights under unapproved arrangements to be excluded from a bankrupt's estate by order of court.

(b)   the requirement to: notify the Opra Registry and to pay the levies on pension schemes; meet the minimum funding requirement; index-link benefits; appoint member-nominated trustees professional advisers and fund managers; 'blow the whistle' by the scheme actuary or auditor; maintain formal records and to audit regularly scheme accounts, although this is good practice; meet many of the disclosure requirements (see 15.23) e.g. to provide copies of documentation, solvency certificates, valuations, reports and accounts on request, and to automatically issue booklets and individual member statements; and the requirements of the compensation scheme;

(c)   the administrative constraints on winding-up; schedules of contributions; investments; maintenance of separate bank accounts; keeping minutes of trustee meetings; most restrictions on assignment of benefits; the use of surpluses; the right to pay AVCs; the facility to resolve disputes (exempt for single member schemes); and for trustees to be sanctioned for relying on the skill or judgement of other persons.

Additionally:

(d)   as FURBS will normally qualify as 'occupational pension schemes' most of the restrictive aspects of *FSA 1986* will not apply and, for 'relevant schemes' as described in the *Financial Services Act 1986 (Occupational Pension Schemes) (No 2) Order 1988 (SI 1988 No 724)*, there is exemption for trustees from the need to seek authorisation to carry on investment business (see 11.6, 11.7) by virtue of *FSA 1986, s 191*;

(e)   in the case of *Royal Masonic Hospital v Pensions Ombudsman the High Court* ruled that unfunded schemes are not subject to the preservation regulations, although they apply in the main to funded schemes, as they are schemes without resources (however, the scheme provisions may contain such protection of benefits and their accumulated value).

15.23   There must be compliance as follows:

(a)   with the disclosure requirements in respect of those limited parts of the *Pensions Act 1995* which apply to unapproved schemes; equal treatment; voluntary membership; the jurisdiction of the Pensions Ombudsman over points of law or fact under the *Pension Schemes Act 1993*; the jurisdiction of Opra only to the extent that legislation imposes statutory obligations on unapproved schemes; and some compliance with the *Preservation Regulations* (see (b) below and the relevant paragraphs in CHAPTER 11). Other requirements include a notification to members of the funded status of the scheme; a notification of the exemptions which apply under the *Pensions Act 1995*; the means of securing scheme benefits; the restrictions on some amendment powers (but not, generally, limitation on use) and a point of contact for future information.

The December 1992 Cadbury Report's Code of Best Practice on corporate governance requires a full and clear disclosure of directors' total emoluments and pension contributions in company accounts. Listed companies must state whether or not they comply with the Code. The July 1995 Greenbury Committee Report's proposal for a listing rule for the disclosure of pension costs for directors and for disclosure of details of directors' sources of income and gains, under the *Companies Act 1985* was largely reflected in the *Company Accounts (Disclosure of Directors' Emoluments) Regulations 1997 (SI 1997 No 570)* which requires disclosure of company contributions, the number of directors, emoluments, incentive schemes, compensation for loss of office payments, breach of contract/termination payments, money purchase benefits, additional final salary benefits, accrued pension levels, pension ages, excess pension benefits and small company accounting procedures/contents (see 12.38);

(b)   in the case of funded schemes, the *Preservation Regulations* mean that the early leaver requirements and revaluation requirements must generally be applied in the same way as for approved occupational pension schemes (see 3.44 and 11.2 to 11.5), and that payment of immediate benefits for early leavers must only be made in circumstances which would be permissible under approved schemes. Additionally, see (*a*) above concerning the treatment of transfer payments;

(c)   the debt on the *Employer Regulations* shall not apply for final salary schemes and no independent trustee will be required on the winding-up of a FURBS if it is established by deed;

(d)   although the final impact of the Greenbury Committee Report on directors' pensions is still not certain, it would be good practice for any public company involved to establish a remuneration committee to decide how much pay is pensionable, particularly if bonuses and benefits in kind are to be considered;

(e)   there is no current case law on divorce for unapproved schemes, a Government lead on this matter is awaited, but it is likely that they will be similarly treated to approved schemes;

(f)   unapproved schemes will not be permitted to contract-out.

Membership

15.24 It should be noted, when considering scheme membership, that the meaning of 'employees' in the definition of 'relevant benefits' includes current and past employees and officers and directors, including non-executive directors, of the company. There is no formal restriction in the tax legislation on who may be the recipient of benefits in respect of an employee's unapproved scheme membership, other than in the potential tax charge in the situation described in 15.20(d) concerning death benefits.

Benefits and funding

15.25 It is generally required, in order to satisfy the definition of a 'retirement benefits scheme', that benefits under a FURBS shall come into payment on retirement or on death (see 15.23(b)). In fact, Inspectors of Taxes consider each case on its own merits and the Inland Revenue imposes no formal control over the nature or timing of the benefits payable. However, for certainty, if a member of a FURBS is also a member of an approved scheme in respect of the same employment it is recommended that he or she should 'retire' from both schemes at the same time. Failure to do so may lead the inspector of taxes to conclude that the scheme does not constitute a *bona fide* retirement benefits scheme. This could prejudice all or some of the tax exemptions to the scheme, most significantly those described in 15.20(a) which concerns tax free lump sums and 15.20(b) which concerns company contributions. The word retirement has no formal meaning, but it is generally considered to mean the cessation of the employment to which the benefits relate. Clearly there will be room for flexibility where there is more than one employment/ directorship involved.

15.26 Benefits may be paid in any form within the meaning of 'relevant benefits'. There are considerable advantages in paying benefits in lump sum form. Not only are lump sums normally tax-free (see 15.20(a)) but there is no limit on the amount which may be paid or how the recipient shall expend it.

However, the payment of a tax-free lump sum to a retiring member in respect of whom a large cash sum was paid into the scheme just before his or her retirement could well be taxed under Schedule E on the member, and there may be no relief given against the company's profits.

It is most inadvisable to pay non-relevant benefits, e.g. disability cover, out of a FURBS as such payments can cause the scheme to lose some of the tax advantages which apply to retirement benefit schemes, particularly those described in 15.25, and lead to serious administrative problems. Both pension benefits and death benefits escape the Inland Revenue limits that apply to approved schemes. However, death benefits must be paid to designated beneficiaries along the lines described in *s 595(5)*, in order to avoid a charge to income tax under Schedule E, but preferably omitting the member's estate as a potential beneficiary (see *s 596A(8)* and 15.20(d)).

15.27 There is no requirement that the contributions that are paid by a company to a FURBS must relate directly to the level of remuneration of the scheme member. However, the Inland Revenue do expect the contributions to bear some relationship to earnings, e.g. they are made on a prudent basis which reflects normal commercial considerations for directors. It is possible that a clearly excessive payment, or series of payments, could give rise to a tax charge on 'bounty' (*TCGA 1992, s 77*, and *Part XV*), (*Bulmer v*

Commissioners of Inland Revenue 44 TC1 and Commissioners of Inland Revenue v Plummer [1979] STC 793, and see also 15.41). It is advisable to make contributions regularly or annually if they are to be allowed against profits (*Atherton v British Insulated and Helsby Cables Ltd 10 TC155*).

15.28 Any payments that are made out of the scheme to the company shall be assessed on the company as a trading receipt in the year of payment. However, it is most inadvisable to permit the company to receive any payments out of the scheme. Such payments are not within the meaning of 'relevant benefits' and, in the absence of specific legislation permitting such payments to be made, the advantageous tax rates which apply to the trust monies could be lost. Neither would it be prudent to make a loan to a scheme member on non-commercial terms, as case law indicates that the payments made to the scheme may not, in such circumstances, be deductible under general tax principles.

15.29 Funding of FURBS is much more efficient when undertaken on a money purchase basis rather than a final salary basis. This is not only because of the significant saving in administration costs, or the potential problem that can arise in making good a deficit with a large lump sum contribution at a time when tax rates may be unfavourable. The most important consideration is that it is the view of the Inland Revenue that tax shall be charged on the difference between the benefit payable and the value of accumulated contributions paid to the scheme in respect of the member. As can be seen a money purchase scheme, which operates under an accumulation trust, will avoid such a tax charge.

There is no formal limit on the level of company contributions which may be paid to a FURBS, but it will be necessary for the relevant inspector of taxes to accept them as payments made in the furtherance of the company's trade or undertaking if they are to be wholly allowable against profits. Company contributions do not need to be made on a regular basis, unlike the case for approved schemes, but the company by whom the member is employed must make them. As described in 15.20(c), the payment of member contributions is inadvisable (a tax-free lump sum under *s 596A(8)* is dependent on contributions being assessed on the member under *s 595(1)* — a charging section which does not apply to member contributions). Additionally, a scheme's investments will suffer a backlash if such contributions fall to be regarded as a transfer of money to settled property, in which event they will be assessed at the member's marginal rate.

15.30 Payments made by the company in non-cash form, e.g. in kind or by means of a transfer of an asset, can give rise to a charge to CGT as a chargeable disposal. However, it is possible to avoid or reduce such a charge in respect of a FURBS by virtue of *TCGA 1992, s 77.* The company will need to seek specialist advice before proceeding with any transfer. If the transfer is from an UURBS it is likely that an income tax charge will be made on the member (see 15.35), and DWP guidance is awaited as to whether or not the tax can be deducted from the payment made.

Investments

15.31 The trustees of a FURBS may be given wide powers of investment under the scheme's trust. The self-investment provisions which are contained in the *Pension Schemes Act 1993* as modified by the *Pensions Act 1995* (see 11.33 to 11.39) and associated investment matters in the *Pensions Act 1995* do not apply to FURBS. However, if the company is a close company, as defined in *s 414*, tax advice should be sought before the trustees make any loan out of the scheme assets or acquire shares in the company and, if a corporate trustee is included in the body of trustees, see 11.61 to 11.65 concerning the applicability of the European Union Investment Services Directive. There are no formal constraints on lending and borrowing to and from the company or connected parties other than that difficulties can be experienced with the PSO requirements if such investment activities involve SSAS funds, and in respect of loans made to members as stated in 15.28.

Nevertheless, the Inland Revenue has tightened up on its treatment of FURBS investment activities recently and it should be noted that anything which brings the bona fides of the scheme into question (such as rent-free accommodation in a trustee-held property, interest-free loans without security and/or trustee power to call in, market transactions which do not reflect market value and other activities made on uncommercial terms is likely to lead to the Inland Revenue withdrawing FURBS status.

Although trustees may generally invest the scheme monies wherever and in whatever manner they think fit, it will clearly be prudent for trustees to select investments which are most beneficial to FURBS, e.g. for reason of tax efficiency. In this connection, many trustees of FURBS consider index-linked gilts, and approved unit trusts with their deferral of CGT, to be advantageous investments for this type of scheme. Some further investment considerations are:

(a) investments in offshore pooled investment funds will be taxed at the time of encashment;

(b) life insurance investments can be a potential risk for FURBS. This is not only because there may be tax borne by the underlying investment on its profits and gains under *s 547(1)* (see 15.19(h)), combined with a higher premium cost as monies can only be referred to annuity business not pensions business, but there is likely to be an 'exit charge' on the difference between the premiums paid and the policy yield (see

APPENDIX 59, paragraphs 3.2.1 to 3.2.4, and *s 547(1)(b)*) on all life policies, life annuity contracts and capital redemption policies. Additionally, an insurance premium tax (see APPENDIX 61) was introduced with effect from 1 October 1994 on general insurance business. There is normally no exemption from this tax, as explained in 13.55. It is therefore strongly recommended that trustees seek the advice of the insurance provider before entering into such forms of investment;

(c)   investments in second-hand endowment policies were previously vulnerable to a charge to gains on disposal. Following representations by the APT this has now been relaxed. The Inland Revenue have agreed that *s 547(1)(b)* does not apply and that no tax is chargeable on the sponsoring company on the maturity or sale of second-hand endowment policies;

(d)   if contributions are made to a FURBS in specie, for example in the form of loans from the sponsoring company or transfers of shares, it is for the inspector of taxes to determine whether or not the member should be charged to tax under *s 595(1)* and to determine the assessable amount;

(e)   tax planning through enterprise zones. The inspector of taxes should be consulted before a full commitment is made, but the following is a brief description of the way in which these arrangements have been put forward by some tax advisers in the past.

The company buying enterprise zone trusts and transferring them to the member increases the member's remuneration. The member takes out a private/bank loan, buys more enterprise zone trusts and claims IBAs. Following the issue of the tax certificates, cash bonuses are voted by the company and paid into the member's loan accounts. The inspector of taxes will determine the taxation method and a favourable result can be obtained with specialist tax assistance both for the company and the member. The tax saved can then be invested in the FURBS;

(f)   Pensions Update No 102 prohibits transactions between SSASs and FURBS.

Documentation

15.32 There are no statutory requirements that govern the form of documentation of a FURBS. However, in order to enjoy in full the tax advantages that are described in 15.20, the scheme must be set up as a 'retirement benefit scheme' which provides 'relevant benefits'. APPENDIX 59, paragraphs 1.1.3 and 1.2.1 to 1.2.3 give the full meaning of these terms. In order that the scheme may satisfactorily demonstrate that these conditions are met it is beneficial to document the scheme by means of a formal deed, declaration of trust or resolution with in-built or appended rules. A more straightforward means of establishing a FURBS, e.g. by a right contained in an employment contract or a letter of explanation/exchange sent by the company to the employee, can also be effective if carefully worded, but see 15.20(d) concerning IHT implications). It may be preferable for such methods to be used for the purpose of initial scheme establishment rather than full scheme documentation.

There is no restriction on the persons who may be trustees of a FURBS other than persons who are generally excluded from trusteeship by *Trustee Act 1925, s 54* being persons of unsound mind, or minors or bankrupts.

It is likely that the company or the member, together with a professionally qualified person, will be appointed. The *Pensions Act 1995* does not debar the scheme actuary from trusteeship, unlike approved schemes. However, if any of the trustees are overseas, see 15.36 to 15.44.

An indication of the main points that should be considered when drawing up the formal documentation of a FURBS is given in 15.33. Such documentation should be obtained from a suitable specialist legal adviser or practitioner. It is also strongly recommended that, for the purpose of the security of the member's benefit promise, legal advice is sought when inserting a reference to the existence of a FURBS in the employee's contract of employment.

15.33   The following points should be considered:

(a)   an announcement should be sent to the employee, informing him or her that the scheme has been set up as a retirement benefits scheme to provide certain benefits which are deemed to be relevant benefits under *ICTA 1988*;

(b)   a deed, declaration of trust or a resolution should establish, or confirm the establishment of, the scheme. The document together with any rules appended thereto should normally contain or cover the main points detailed in (c) to (h) below;

(c)   compliance with the *Preservation Regulations*, where applicable, and other relevant legislation (see 15.21 to 15.23);

(d)   power to open a bank account, amend the scheme, and to conduct reviews. Formal actuarial reviews will be required if the scheme is funded on a final salary basis;

(e)   a description of the powers and duties of the parties to the scheme (including annual accounting, reporting and tax deduction, winding-up powers, and expenses);

(f) the form of benefits available, the contributions payable, the transfer powers, the nature of beneficiaries who may receive payments from the scheme, discretionary powers of distribution of death benefits, powers to accumulate monies in the fund and, if it is intended to operate a 'grossing-up' arrangement (see 15.19(e)), the power to do so;

(g) the name of the administrator of the scheme (see 15.34 for the administrator's duties and definition);

(h) a perpetuity period;

(i) the requirements that apply to record-keeping under the scheme;

(j) the amount, and the method of payment, of the contributions to the scheme;

(k) a trustees' indemnity clause, where appropriate;

(l) the scheme's amendment powers;

(m) a provision for the settlement of disputes;

(n) details of any evidence required from members/beneficiaries, and to whom it should be sent;

(o) the availability of the scheme documentation for inspection;

(p) a facility to admit other employers, if required;

(q) any provision for temporary absence cover; and

(r) the classes of beneficiary.

Tax returns, reporting requirements and administration

15.34 Self-assessment has applied to FURBS from 1996/97. The principles are the same as for approved schemes as described in 8.48 to 8.64. As for approved schemes, penalties will be incurred on late returns, and interest and possibly surcharge imposed on payments made after 31 January. The annual return for unapproved trusts is the SA 900 (formerly form 1), and guidance can be obtained from FICO. For the purposes of this paragraph, the administrator shall be the trustees unless they appoint another in their place under *ss 611AA and 612(1)*. The following requirements must be met:

• the employer must notify the inspector of taxes who deals with the company's accounts of scheme establishment within three months from the date on which the scheme is set up (*s 605(3)(a)*). The inspector may call for further information and the requirement to provide this is in *s 605(3)(b)* for the employer and *s 605(4)* for the administrator;

• if a grossing-up arrangement has been set up (see 15.19(e)), the employer shall enter the grossed-up equivalent of the contribution and the amount of tax payable on the pay records on form P11(FOT) for the period in which the payment is made;

- if there is no grossing-up arrangement, the employer shall enter the contributions paid in the appropriate period at the end of the year on form P9D or form P11D;

- the employer shall provide the employee with the P9D or P11D by the 6 July next following the tax year end;

- an annual return form SA 900 (see APPENDIX 60) must be sent to the inspector of taxes by the trustees or the administrator. This form details the member's income as an employee, and lists scheme investment income and gains. Benefits that are not paid in cash form must be reported within three months of the date of payment;

- any payments made to a person or persons who are not the member or the member's family must be reported within three months of the end of the period in which they are paid;

- a member must declare any benefits in kind, including those that continue beyond retirement date, in his or her annual return of income. Payments which are taxed through the PAYE system need not be reported by virtue of *TMA 1970, s 7*. SP 1/96 states that chargeable payments must be notified to the inspector of taxes within six months of year end;

- the member must be notified of the *s 595(1)* charges at the time that they are incurred, and keep them in a safe place. Evidence of payment will probably be needed in future to justify the tax-free payment of lump sums out of the scheme;

- the trustees or the administrator should ensure that the accounting procedures are in accordance with SSAP24, that the company auditor is responsible for compliance, and that as a matter of prudence the scheme's accounts are audited on a regular basis;

- the above requirements also apply to UURBS, where relevant;

- late returns attract a £100 penalty (a return must be completed within 3 months of its date of issue, if later than the 31 January deadline);

The penalty and surcharge regimes are as follows:

(a) penalties are incurred under the *TMA 1970, s 98* (see (b) to (i) below for details) and fall on persons on whom notice has been served to deliver any return or other document or information who fails to comply under that Act;

(b) the normal initial level of penalty is £300 maximum;

(c) subsequent maximum penalties are incurred at £60 per day in the event of a continuing failure to comply;

(d) an upper level of penalty of £3,000 maximum is imposed in cases of fraud and/or negligence;

(e) interest and surcharges can be imposed under *TMA 1970, s59C* on late payments of tax (that is, payments made after 31 January);

(f) surcharges range from 5% (after 28 days from the due date) to 10% (after 6 months from the due date);

(g) interest rates are tabled in *ICTA 1988, Volume I*;

(h) once a surcharge has been imposed it carries interest for late payment at the rates in *FA 1989, s178* (Table L);

The main reporting requirements are contained in PN 16.1. Further guidance on the penalty regime can be obtained from FICO.

Transfer payments

15.35 Transfers may be made freely between FURBS and other unapproved schemes, whether or not previously unfunded, without normally incurring a tax deduction from the payment. However, if a transfer payment is received from an UURBS, the cash equivalent of the benefits transferred must be used to secure transfer credits in the receiving scheme. A tax liability under *s 595(1)* is therefore likely to fall on the member (see APPENDIX 59, paragraphs 2.6.1 to 2.6.4, and 15.30 in this chapter).

Pensions Update No 102 (effective from 2 July 2001) now specifically prohibits all transactions, including transfers, direct and indirect sales of assets, joint investments between a SSAS and a non-approved scheme and direct and indirect loans, between approved and non-approved schemes. Such transactions are not considered to be compatible with tax approval, and non-approved schemes extends in meaning to schemes that were previously approved but have subsequently lost approval.

The treatment of transfer payments in general under the *Pensions Act 1995* is currently being considered (see 15.23(a)). Additionally, PSO Update No 31 extended the requirement to obtain the written consent from IR SSPS before accepting transfers into a SSAS to a similar application before making a transfer out to any of the schemes or arrangements described in PN, 10.23 to a SSAS, namely:

(a) approved schemes under *ICTA 1988, Ch I of Pt XIV*, includung FSAVCs;

(b) personal pension schemes;

(c) relevant statutory schemes;

(d) annuity contracts to which *ICTA, s 431(B)(d) or (e)* applies;

(e)   funds to which *ICTA 1988, s 608* applies;

(f)   approved retirement annuity contracts.

It is possible that IRSSPS will lift the SSAS transfer restrictions in similar fashion to the conditions that apply to other self-administered schemes in the future.

Overseas considerations

15.36   The then Chancellor announced, in the November 1993 Budget, that the previously advantageous position of offshore FURBS over UK FURBS was to be countered by new tax rules. Offshore means schemes which are mainly administered overseas and whose trustees are all resident overseas or the controlling majority of whom are overseas. Until the Budget changes the capital gains and much or all of the income of such schemes was tax-free. The Chancellor stated that the purpose of the new tax rules was to bring into charge benefits that had not previously been assessed to UK tax. This charge extended to insured offshore FURBS. His underlying objective was to ensure that offshore FURBS did not benefit from greater tax advantages than on-shore FURBS. The result was *FA 1994*. With effect from 1 December 1993, *s 108* of that Act imposed tax, at the member's marginal rate, on lump sums payable under FURBS unless all company contributions and income and gains had previously been charged to tax, with the exception of such gains which are not so chargeable e.g. gains from UK gilts. The employee, if he or she is UK taxable, is chargeable to tax by virtue of *s 596A(8)*.

If company contributions have been charged to tax on the employee, but the income and gains have not been wholly so, the lump sum will be taxable net of the company contributions (*s 596A(8)–(11)*) or the invested value thereof. The exemptions and allowances that are described in 15.19 are generally lost.

15.37   FURBS which were set up prior to 1 December 1993, in respect of which the member had paid tax on the company's contributions, do not attract tax on the member's lump sum payments unless the accrual rate for benefits is changed. However, non-cash payments have generally been chargeable to tax by virtue of section 596A with effect from 27 July 1989.

The Inland Revenue's anti-avoidance legislation could be triggered for such schemes (*ss 86* and *87* of *TCGA 1992* for capital gains, and see 'Transfer of Assets Abroad' for transfers under *ss 739* and *740*, and 15.41), particularly in cases where transfers offshore are not deemed to be made for *bona fide* reasons under the provisions of *TCGA 1992, s 86*. The Inland Revenue is becoming increasingly vigilant in this area.

Transfer payments from approved schemes to unapproved overseas schemes are still permitted in the circumstances described in PN, App VI. The Inland

Revenue's practice in this area was modified by PSO Update No 82, which was issued on 22 January 2001. It was decided that most overseas transfer payments no longer needed to be reported to IR SSPS in respect of persons who had gone abroad permanently. Some of the original requirements that remain are:

- the member, the overseas employer and the overseas scheme must be in the same jurisdiction;

- the member must have requested the transfer, or given his or her written consent for it to take place;

- special requirements apply to the transfer of contracted-out rights;

- written details of the benefits and conditions that apply under the overseas scheme must have been sent to, or given to, the member.

With effect from 6 April 2001 prior consent to transfers out of approved schemes and arrangements is only required if the transferee is a controlling director or subject to the earnings cap (although the previous provisions may apply in other cases until that date if so wished). Transfers of contracted-out rights and safeguarded rights under *PSA 1993* must still follow the DWP rules.

The main features of the new procedure are:

- IR SSPS no longer require sight of the overseas rules, but the receiving scheme must be authorised/recognised as a pension scheme in its own jurisdiction or country and be able to accept the transfer;

- a contribution must be made to the receiving scheme before the transfer is effected;

- evidence of compliance must be kept for six years (failure to comply could mean that the transferee is taxed, or the approval of the transferring arrangement is lost).

Transfers may be accepted from overseas schemes and *s 615* schemes with the prior consent of IR SSPS provided that:

- the transferring employee has been in the overseas employment for at least two years;

- any emerging tax-free lumps sums will be subject to the post 1989 limits;

- there are no overriding conditions attached to the payment;

- the transfer payment is paid direct from the overseas scheme;

- the *Preservation Regulations* apply to the benefits being secured.

The Inland Revenue has reciprocal transfer arrangements with the tax authorities of Jersey, Guernsey, the Isle of Man and the Republic of Ireland. These are outlined below.

15.37 *Funded Unapproved Retirement Benefit Schemes (FURBS)*

Jersey:

Pension schemes can be approved under *Article 131* or *131B* of the *Income Tax (Jersey) Law 1961 (as amended)*. Details can be obtained from:

The Comptroller of Income Tax
States of Jersey
PO Box 56
Cyril le Marquand House
The Parade
St Helier
Jersey
Channel Islands.

Approval of the scheme will grant exemption from income tax in respect of income derived from investment or deposits subject to certain conditions. In particular, the scheme must be bona fide; established under irrevocable trusts in connection with a trade or undertaking carried on wholly or partly outside Jersey and has for its sole purpose the provision of retirement benefits within stated limits. Preservation is voluntary, and no income tax will be charged on any pension paid from the scheme to a person who is not tax resident in Jersey.

From the UK perspective, it is not clear that *IHTA 1984, s151* applies to exempt lump sum payments on death and it is also not possible to rule out the application of the anti avoidance provisions of *s 739* and *740*. Therefore there could be disadvantages for members if they intend to retire in the UK.

The reciprocal transfer form is PS119.

Isle of Man:

Pension schemes can be approved under the *Income Tax (Retirement Benefits Scheme) Act 1978* (as amended) or under *Part 1, Income Tax Act 1989*, as amended. Details of their application can be obtained from:

The Assessor of Income Tax
The Treasury
Income Tax Division
Government Offices
Douglas
Isle of Man
IMI 3TX.

The Isle of Man has parallel provisions to preservation and contracting-out, has introduced parts of the *Pensions Act 1995*, and UK transfers are treated in the same way as transfers between schemes in the UK. The reciprocal transfer form is PS120.

Guernsey:

Pension schemes can be approved under *section 150* or *157A* of the *Income Tax (Guernsey) Law 1975 (as amended)*. Details can be obtained from:

The Administrator of Income Tax
States of Guernsey Income Tax Office
PO Box 37
2 Cornet Street
St. Peter Port
Guernsey
Channel Islands.

The criteria are similar to those for Jersey for occupational pension schemes, although preservation is compulsory. The reciprocal transfer form is PS121. Guernsey approve personal pensions schemes and retirement annuity trust schemes (RATS). There is also an informal approval code for flexible schemes under *section 40(o)* of the *Income Tax (Guernsey) law 1975*. Such schemes are not covered by the reciprocal arrangements.

Republic of Ireland:

The arrangements are:

- PSO Update No 11 announced the divergence of pensions legislation in the UK and the ROI, and the withdrawal of the reciprocal approval agreement–the forms SF 117 and SF 118. Schemes approved in Ireland now will only receive UK approval for their UK element if they meet all the requirements of approval in the UK;

- under a protocol, if the tax criteria are satisfied, members will be granted similar tax reliefs to those that apply to approved schemes;

- most existing pension schemes are approved in the Republic of Ireland under the *FA 1972*. Details of its application can obtained from:

  Office of the Inspector of Taxes
  Retirement Benefits District
  Lansdowne House
  Lansdowne Road
  Dublin 4
  Republic of Ireland

The reciprocal transfer form is coded PS 122

15.38 Schemes described in 15.37 should be administered and monitored carefully. In particular, such schemes must constitute a 'retirement benefits scheme' under which members neither contribute nor should they or other potential beneficiaries take over control of the investment decisions.

Additionally payments into the fund must be made on a proper commercial footing and if any member contributions are made they may invoke the 'benefit to settlor' tax rules (APPENDIX 59, paragraph 2.7.5). An overseas scheme may be used for contracting-out provided that:

(a)   contracted-out benefits are secured and terms met;

(b)   there is a UK Administrator;

(c)   there is compliance with equal access and preservation requirements.

15.39   Lump sums which are payable to individuals, other than the member, out of offshore FURBS may be paid free from income tax under Schedule E and IHT (subject to 15.36 to 15.38 and 15.40) only if they are paid to an individual designated by the employee e.g. on an expression of wish form which is not binding on the trustees (*s 596A(8)*). Payments made to persons other than an individual shall be chargeable to income tax under Schedule D, Case VI as described in 15.19(d). Such individuals may include a spouse, child, dependant or other designated individual, generally in keeping with *section 595(5)*. Pensions are assessable to income tax under Schedule E or Schedule D, Case V if the person making the payment is outside the UK. However, if the recipient is not UK tax resident, he or she may be entitled to relief from the tax charge, e.g. under a local double taxation agreement. FICO, or the relevant inspector of taxes, will give advice in each circumstance.

15.40   Under *s 660B* the trustees must deduct tax in respect of the member for all monies paid out of the scheme for or to his or her minor unmarried children. However, by virtue of an Inland Revenue concession dated 25 January 1996, the member can claim a tax credit in respect of such payments for the year 1995/96 onwards. There are specific conditions which must be met for the concession to apply. These mainly concern the prior payment of tax on scheme income as described in 15.36.

15.41   Corporation tax relief, under Schedule D, Case I of II or *FA 1989, s 75*, is only available when the benefit is paid; trustees are not taxed on offshore bank interest or bonds paid gross or subject to UK CGT; UK equities are subject to UK withholding tax at the 20% rate; and overseas equities are chargeable at the overseas withholding tax rate, if any.

Income received by beneficiaries in respect of overseas possessions is generally tax exempt but, if a FURBS is not considered to be a bona fide retirement benefits scheme (see, for example, 15.20(*i*)), UK beneficiaries may be charged under *s 739* or *s 740* (see 15.37) if they have not already been subjected to charge under *s 596A* or elsewhere. In particular, controlling director membership may lead to a FURBS being treated as a settlement under *s 660G* and all the beneficiaries being taxed on the income of the trust where there is deemed to be an element of bounty (see 15.27) or the members treated as transferors of assets abroad if not already taxed on the company's contributions (*Commissioners of Inland Revenue v Mill 49 TC 367,* and *Crossland v Hawkins 39 TC 493*).

Tax Bulletin April 1999 gives detailed notes on the appropriateness and meaning of *s 739* to *749*, and explains the Inland Revenue's interpretation of the legislation based on case law and its general understanding of the principles involved.

15.42 Chargeable gains will normally arise on income which is received from UK insurance policies, under Schedule D, Case VI. However, if the insurance company is based offshore, corporation tax will not normally be charged on policy income although it is possible that the Inland Revenue will impose an income tax charge under *s 739* if the member or beneficiaries directly controls or control the investments under the policy.

The gains on an offshore policy will not normally be chargeable to tax (*TCGA 1992, s 210(2)*).

If the trustees of a UK FURBS go overseas to gain a deliberate tax advantage (see 15.20(j)) the accumulated income of the scheme may attract the tax charge which applies to the disposal of assets provisions contained in *TCGA 1992, s 80*, and future income could fall under *ss 86* and *87* of that Act in respect of settlors who receive benefits from gains on overseas settlements. Additionally the tax charges described in 15.41 may be incurred in appropriate circumstances and lump sum payments made to UK residents will otherwise fall to be taxed under Schedule E by virtue of *s 596A*.

15.43 The administration costs of offshore FURBS can be high compared with the cost of managing a FURBS with UK trustees, because of the tax implications described above. Additionally, it seems inadvisable to include any UK trustees in such a scheme in view of the potential impact of regulations under the *Pensions Act 1995* on such persons.

It should be noted that *s 611AA(4)* requires the trustees to appoint a person resident in the UK to deal with UK tax matters if all the trustees are overseas. It is possible to establish offshore pension funds under trust by using corporate trustees such as a bank, and the available jurisdictions include Bermuda, the Bahamas, the British Virgin Islands, the Channel Islands and the Cayman Islands.

In conclusion, there seems to be less to recommend offshore FURBS following the enactment of *FA 1994*. Although the Government's proposed formal anti-avoidance regulation regime is on hold at the present time, the Chancellor declared his intent at the time of the Budget on 2 July 1997 to curtail unacceptable tax loss. He has commissioned the Inland Revenue to look into areas of concern, with particular emphasis on transferring monies to overseas tax havens or transferring trusteeship overseas in order to gain an unacceptable tax advantage. Nevertheless there will still be circumstances in which they will be an attractive benefit vehicle for some senior employees. In such cases it is strongly recommended that prior consent is obtained from the PSO before establishing a new scheme in the future.

15.44 15.36 to 15.43 above concern members of overseas FURBS who are in UK employment. It is recommended that the advice of IR SSPS is sought before setting up new schemes.

VAT aspects

15.45 The various aspects of VAT as they apply to occupational pension schemes which are explained in CHAPTER 13 apply in general to FURBS. There are two areas however, regarding property and registration, where some further explanation is necessary.

15.46 FURBS can clearly lease commercial property to the sponsoring company or its associated companies and to the members, all of whom will be connected, and therefore the provisions of the *VAT Buildings and Land Order* will apply from 30 November 1994 to 25 November 1996 unless either of the parties to the lease is a fully taxable person. For those FURBS which are caught the trustees as landlord may be unable to reclaim Input Tax against Output Tax as they are prevented from opting to charge VAT on the rent they receive on the grant of a new lease after 30 November 1994 (see 13.27 to 13.30). The extra statutory concession announced on 28 February 1996 (see 13.35) does not assist because it was granted exclusively to SSAS. The news release (APPENDIX 56) issued at the time mentioned that HM Customs and Excise will consider cases where businesses are not able to take advantage of the concession, but only if they were not motivated by tax avoidance and provided there is a clearly demonstrable ordinary commercial motivation and justification to the leasing arrangements. FURBS may have difficulties meeting these criteria, especially dispelling any notions of tax avoidance, but if the case can be made for the concession application should be made to the local VAT Enquiry Office.

15.47 The trustees of a FURBS should seek their accountant's advice on whether or not to register for VAT purposes. If a series of FURBS are established with the same employer for the same member then all the FURBS will be taken together as one for the purposes of the threshold and registration. They will not be able to avoid registration by keeping their individual turnover below the registration threshold.

Chapter 16

European Law and Directives

Introduction

16.1   There have been significant changes to pension and employment rights in Europe in recent years. The UK has followed many of Europe's leads and, where there is already clear practice and/or legislation in place in the UK, cross-references to the relevant subjects are given in this chapter. This chapter also looks at those areas where the UK will need to consider ongoing actions in Europe and how it will adapt appropriate practice domestically as a Member State.

Equal treatment

16.2   The Barber case is referred to in 11.52 to 11.53, and the UK already have in place equal treatment procedures and documentation for pension schemes to accord with the European Court judgment in *Barber v Guardian Royal Exchange [1990] IRLR 240* which confirmed that pensions in respect of service before 17 May 1990 may be unequal and that pensions in respect of service after 17 May 1990 must be equal. This is also relevant to part-time employment, as stated in 11.55.

Part-Time Work Directive

16.3   The *Part-Time Work Directive* came into effect on 15 December 1997, and the UK agreed on 7 April 1998 to extend the Directive to the UK. The effect of the Directive on the UK is described in 11.56. In particular:

(a)   the European Court of Justice has ruled that scheme membership can be backdated to 8 April 1976 if sex discrimination can be proven, and a claim is made within 6 months of leaving service; and

(b)   at present, discrimination against part-time workers is only unlawful in the UK if it can be shown to be indirect sex discrimination.

Working Time Directive

16.4   The European Court of Justice recently gave a decision in the case of *Sindicato de Medicos de Asistencia Publica v Conselleria de Sanidad y Consumo de la Generalidad Valenciana,* which concerned medical staff. This is important, as it is the first ruling on the European Working Time Directive. The UK implemented the Directive in 1998 by the *Working Time Regulations 1998 (SI 1998 No 1833).* Working time is defined in both as time when a worker is *working, at the employer's disposal and carrying out his activity or duties.* These are the three parts of the definition.

The main considerations were:

(a)   are hours when an employee is on-call, but not at work, working time hours? (no, all three parts must be met);

(b)   the *European Working Time Directive* defines a night worker as a person who as *a normal course* works at least three hours of daily working time during night time – so, do on-call hours count towards the limit on hours for night workers? (they could do, depending on their frequency, but each case will be different);

(c)   the *European Working Time Directive* defines a shift worker as a person whose work schedule is part of shift work, being *any method of organising work in shifts whereby workers succeed each other ....according to a certain pattern..........................at different times over a given period........* – so, are doctors shift workers? (yes, in the case in hand, which means that the employer can benefit from the exceptions that apply to the provision of rest periods for such persons);

(d)   the *European Working Time Directive* entitles adult workers to a daily rest period of at least eleven consecutive hours, and a weekly rest period of twenty-four hours (more for young employees) – so, do on-call hours count as rest periods? (yes, if they fall outside the definition of working time).

Whereas it may seem that the *Working Time Directive* does not concern pension provision, the definition of pensionable pay (and, potentially, pensionable service) in a scheme's rules could have an impact on benefit levels.

The European Parental Leave Directive

16.5   The *European Parental Leave Directive* makes provision for a parent to be able to take three months' (unpaid) leave to care for a child, and its impact on the UK is described in 11.57. The forthcoming changes to maternity leave in the UK are described in 11.57 and mainly concern:

(a) an extension of the statutory minimum period of maternity leave to 26 weeks with effect from April 2003;

(b) a continuation of pension accrual based on notional unreduced pay;

(c) any employee contributions to be based on actual pay;

(d) adoption leave will be at the same rate and for the same period as maternity leave;

(e) paid paternity leave will be at the same rate, for two weeks, and from the same date.

Divorce law is also going through major developments in the UK, and this is described in 11.66 to 11.71.

EU Investment Services Directive

16.6   The effect on SSASs, and in particular their pensioneer trustees, of the *Investment Services Directive* of the European Union is described in 11.61 to 11.65. The proposal to create a European Securities Committee was hindered by the dissolution of the European Union Commission a while ago, and further details are still awaited. Also there is a proposed European Directive to impose a five per cent limit on self-investment on pension schemes. There will be an opportunity for member states to disapply the directive for schemes with less than 100 members. The DWP feels that SSASs should remain exempt from the existing UK 5% limit and from the proposed European Directive.

The *Data Protection Act 1998*

16.7   The UK updated its data protection legislation in 1998, as described in 11.91. Included in the registrable particulars is name and address of the representative where a data controller has nominated one for the purposes of the *Act* (that is, if he or she is outside the EEA but uses equipment in the UK for processing).

Additionally, the data controller must give the names of any countries outside the EEA to which he or she may wish to transfer the data.

Human Rights, and the application of European law

16.8   The UK has brought in the *Human Rights Act 1998* to enable it to take into account the *Convention for the Protection of Human Rights and Fundamental Freedoms* without taking proceedings to the European Court of Human Rights (see 11.92 for the impact of the *Act* in the UK). The European

Court of Justice has responsibility for determining the meaning and application of European law (as laid down in the treaty of Rome), so it can be seen that Europe can be involved in the actions of member States in more than one way.

The reason for the UK action on human rights is best explained by taking a look at how the European Convention came about, and the rules that apply to Member States. The European Convention was signed by the members of the Council of Europe on 4 November 1950 and since that time all full membership of the Council has only been available to States who ratify the Convention. The relevance of the Council of Europe is that States must belong to it if they are to join the European Union. The UK ratified the Convention at an early stage, and wishes to avoid being taken directly before the European Court of Human Rights wherever possible. Any challenge to a decision by the European Commission of Human Rights may be determined by a Court or a Tribunal. Additionally, there are anti-discriminatory provisions within the Treaty of Rome.

16.9   European human rights law does not refer directly to pensions, but clearly must impact upon them by giving rights to individuals. The two main subjects that are worthy of note are described below:

(a)   an individual is entitled to a fair and public hearing, within a reasonable time and before an independent and impartial tribunal established by law, in determining his or her civil rights and obligations (for example, pensions matters and disputes) or any criminal charge against that person;

(b)   an individual is entitled to a peaceful enjoyment of his or her possessions, and freedom from discrimination (which means discrimination in respect of the rights and freedoms that are set forth in the Convention, and has clear impact on pension schemes).

16.10   European law, which is dealt with by the European Courts of Justice, requires member States to apply the principle of equal pay for equal work, and pay has been shown by case law to include pension rights. One of the most contentious issues that has arisen in respect of pensions concerns part-time workers (see 11.56). In this area it can be seen that the UK has followed the European lead.

Age discrimination

16.11   The European Council of ministers gave an anti-discrimination Directive on 18 October 2000, which must be implemented by October 2003. The directive forbids, amongst other things, discrimination on the grounds of age. Pension schemes would have needed to be careful not to act in breach of this directive (for instance, in respect of maximum and minimum entry ages, medical evidence for older employees, NI age-related rebates and contributions based on a member's age etc). However, the NAPF lobbied for an amendment and the directive now contains the following text:

> Member States may provide that the fixing for occupational social security schemes of ages for admission or entitlement to retirement or invalidity benefits, including the fixing under those schemes of different ages for employees or groups or categories of employees, and the use, in the context of such schemes, of age criteria in actuarial calculations, does not constitute discrimination on the grounds of age, provided that this does not result in discrimination on the grounds of sex.

Clearly there may still be pitfalls for some schemes (for example, schemes which permit different sex, but not same sex, partners to be beneficiaries and schemes which pay benefits to spouses but not other dependants).

Acquired Rights Directive

16.12 The Council of the European Union adopted a consolidated directive of existing law on the approximation of States laws concerning the safeguard of employee rights on a transfer of undertakings, businesses or parts of the same.

Proposed Directive of the European Parliament and of the Council on the activities of IORPs

16.13 The European Union Commission have proposed a Directive on institutions for occupational retirement provision to accord with the intention of implementing the Commission's Financial Services Action Plan in full by the year 2005. The Economic and Social Committee adopted an Opinion on the proposed Directive on 28 March 2001 which supported the Directive with certain recommendations. The proposed Directive is extensive, and its main aims are:

(a) the establishment of a framework for institutions for occupational retirement provision (IORPs);

(b) Member States to be able to impose their own investment rules on IORPs, but have to permit investment up to 70% in shares and corporate bonds and at least 30% in currencies other than the currency of their future pension liabilities;

(c) a high level of protection for future pensioners and beneficiaries;

(d) freedom to develop effective investment programmes and policy, so that there is greater freedom within prudent guidelines;

419

(e)   greater investment security;

(f)   improved investment management, and the choice of managers approved by the Member State;

(g)   improved investment diversity;

(h)   effective liquidity, as needed;

(i)   a rationalisation of the tax problems encountered in differing States by pension schemes and arrangements;

(j)   to continue to permit Member States to determine the style of pension provision, whether by advance funding or pay-as-you-go schemes;

(k)   the management of pensions schemes across one Member State to another (so as to comply with the principle of a single integrated financial market, and avoid an unnecessary multiplicity of managers around the European Union);

(l)   a control of administration costs;

(m)   a simplification or removal of current restrictions and obstacles to integration.

It is to be hoped that the intent to give much greater freedom and investment opportunities, whilst reducing costs and improving security, can be attained within the intent to allow Member States wide flexibility within their own jurisdictions.

List of Appendices

Appendix

1. Joint Office Memorandum No 58.
2. Notes on Practice by the Inland Revenue issued to the Association of British Insurers and the Association of Pensioneer Trustees.
3. Occupational Pensions: Small Self-Administered Schemes Consultative Document.
4. Statutory Instrument 1991 No 1614.
5. Statutory Instrument 1995 No 3103.
6. Board Minute Resolving to Establish a Small Self-Administered Scheme.
7. Clause for Insertion in the Memorandum of Association of a Company Authorising the Establishment of a Pension Scheme.
8. Specimen Investment Power.
9. Specimen Power of Amendment.
10. Definition of a Controlling Director — Appendix I to PN.
11. Power to Make and Receive Transfer Payments.
12. Specimen Deed of Adherence.
13. Discontinuance — Form PS199(6/01).
14. Trustees Declaration Adopting PSO Model Rules for SSAS Winding-up.
15. Model Rules for Small Self-Administered Pension Schemes.
16. Model SSAS Rules to cover the transitional provisions.
17. Occupational Pension Schemes Application for Approval — Form PS 176 (4/01).
18. Documentation Certificate — PS5 (4/01).
19. Documentation Certificate — PS6 (4/01).
20. Occupational Pension Schemes Centralised Schemes — Participating Employers — Form PS274 (4/01).
21. Participating Employers: Changes — Form PS256 (4/01).
22. Special Contributions — Form PS251 (4/01).
23. Controlling Directors — Form PS255 (4/01).
24. Tax Declaration for Use by Approved Schemes — Form R63N.
25. Chargeable Events — Form 1(SF) (7/98).
26. The 'Earnings Cap' Maximum Pensionable Earnings — Section 590C ICTA 1988.
27. Ex-Gratia Lump Sum — Form PS60 (4/01).
28. Continuous Service Questionnaire — Form PS155 (7/01).
29. Expression of Wish Form.
30. Specimen Loan Agreement.
31. Scheme Investments — Loans to Employer and Associated Companies — Form PS7013 (4/01).
32. Scheme Investments — Land or Buildings — Form PS7012 (4/01).

63. Statutory Instrument 2000 No 22316
64. Statutory Instrument 2000 No 2317
65. Statutory Instrument 2000 No 2692
66. Statutory Instrument 2001 No 117
67. Statutory Instrument 2001 No 118
68. Statutory Instrument 2001 No 119
69. Income Tax — Form PP120
70. Appendix 24 of IR76(2000).
71. Appendix 25 of IR76(2000).

Appendix 1

Joint Office Memorandum No 58

MEMORANDUM NO 58

Joint Office of   **February 1979**
Inland Revenue Superannuation Funds Office and
Occupational Pensions Board

Lynwood Road
Thames Ditton
Surrey KT7 0DP

01-398 4242

SMALL SELF-ADMINISTERED SCHEMES

Issued by the Inland Revenue Superannuation Funds Office

INTRODUCTION

1 Following about 3 years' experience with applications for tax approval of small self-administered schemes, it is now opportune for the Superannuation Funds Office (SFO) to publish more guidance on this subject. As will be seen from what follows, such schemes cannot be treated in the same way as either self-administered schemes catering for large numbers of rank and file employees, or as insured schemes. Employers have been encouraged by press articles referring to "tax havens" and "captive funds" to regard a small self-administered scheme as more than just an arrangement "for the sole purpose of providing relevant benefits" (see section 19(2) Finance Act 1970) and the progressively more critical approach adopted by the SFO in individual cases has followed inevitably from proposals which seem designed either for tax avoidance or to benefit the employer's business financially, rather than as straightforward arrangements for providing financial support for the members in old age.

2 This memorandum, which supersedes the existing short leaflet on form SF 133, outlines the special considerations applicable to small self-administered schemes. In other respects, normal Inland Revenue practice applies to them and benefits for 20% directors should satisfy the conditions described in Memorandum No 25. It has been assumed that such schemes will not be contracted-out under the Social Security Pensions Act 1975, but if, exceptionally, contracting-out is involved, the Occupational Pensions Board guidance on self-investment in Memorandum No 43 will apply.

Meaning of "small" scheme

3 Since it is necessary for practitioners to know which schemes will be subject to this memorandum, "small" generally means "with less than 12 members". But the SFO has taken the view that a scheme primarily for a few family directors, to whom were added some relatively low-paid employees with entitlement only to derisory benefits, included as a make-weight to bring the total membership to 12 or slightly more, was nevertheless "small". Conversely it might not be necessary to apply "small scheme" treatment to one, albeit with fewer than 23 members, where all the members were at arm's length from each other, from the employer and the trustees. No. special action under the memorandum will normally be required in respect of a self-administered scheme already approved under the Finance Act 1970 in the ordinary way, merely because at a later date the membership fortuitously falls below 12. A small insured scheme, which becomes self-administered after approval will of course need to comply with the memorandum, except that the question whether a "pensioner trustee" (see paragraph 4) needs to be appointed in place of, or in addition to, the existing trustee, will be considered in the light of the facts of the case.

Pensioneer trustee

4 It is necessary for the trustee to be, or the trustees to include, an individual or body widely involved with occupational pension schemes, and having dealings with the SFO, who is prepared to give an undertaking to the SFO that he will not consent to any termination of a scheme of which he is trustee, otherwise than in accordance with the approved terms of the winding-up rule. Such a trustee is customarily described as a "pensioneer trustee". For the avoidance of doubt, it is

worth stating that the undertaking has no hidden implications; a pensioneer trustee is not a "watchdog" for the Inland Revenue in any area other than the improper termination of the scheme.

5   If the trust instrument establishing the scheme provides for the trustees to act on majority rather than unanimous decisions, this provision must be qualified so that it does not apply where the question for decision relates to the termination of the scheme.

6   Where a corporate body wishes to act as a pensioneer trustee, it is normally essential that the directors, or a majority of them, should be acceptable as pensioneers in their own right, and that the acceptable directors should have the power to determine how the corporate body will vote in any proceedings of the pension scheme trustees.

7   The object of the Revenue's insistence on the appointment of a pensioneer trustee is that he should be able to block any request from the members of the scheme, or some of them, that the trust should be terminated and the funds distributed among them, subject perhaps to their giving the trustee an indemnity against the contingency of a claim by a remoter beneficiary having an interest on a member's death. It is accepted that the opposition of one trustee, or even of all, would be immaterial if all the persons having an interest under the trust were agreed in requiring the termination of the scheme (cf *Saunders v Vautier, 1841*).But such a consensus is unlikely in the context of a typical pension scheme except where all the members have retired and all interests have vested.

8   It has recently been suggested that as an alliterative to the appointment of a pensioneer trustee, a trustee corporation, qualified by rules made under the Public Trustee Act 1906 to act as a custodian trustee, should be appointed as such. The trust deed would include provisions to prevent any payment out of the trust fund to the managing trustees apart from sums required from time to time to finance benefits as they fall due. Without commitment, the SFO will consider any proposal on these lines.

Investment of funds

9   It is not necessary to include in the trust deed any special restrictions on the investment powers of the trustees, except for a prohibition on loans to members of the scheme or to any other individual (for example, relatives of members) having a contingent interest under the scheme. This restriction is considered necessary in small schemes in particular, because of the possibility (arising from the less than arm's length relationship of all the parties) that such loans would become, in reality, a charge on the retirement benefit, and that the pension scheme would be used in this way so as to avoid the tax liability arising on loans direct from close companies to their "participators".

10   Where schemes have already been approved, or draft documents have been agreed, without any prohibition on loans to members, the matter may remain in abeyance until some other rule charge is being introduced. Meanwhile, however, if the financial information obtained (see paragraph 23 below) shows that such loans have actually been made, the SFO may need to ask about the conditions of the loan, the rate of interest being paid and the arrangements for repayment.

11   On the other hand there is no outright objection to loans out of scheme funds to the employer on commercially reasonable terms, provided that –

      (a)   employer's contributions are not returned to him in this way with such frequency, or

      (b)   the proportion of the total assets lent to the employer is not so great,

as to suggest that a scheme which is being presented as a funded scheme is in reality an unfunded or partly unfunded one.

12   The SFO is unlikely to question the *bona fides* of a scheme on the grounds mentioned in paragraph 11 if the loans to the employer do not exceed one-half of the assets, unless, exceptionally, this situation appears to be inconsistent with the imminent cash needs to the scheme for purchasing annuities (see paragraph 17 below).

13   It does not follow from the reference in paragraph 9 to the terms of the trustees' investment powers, that the SFO will necessarily regard any form of investment, however unconventional, as consistent with approval of the scheme just because it is not *ultra vires*. Obviously it is not for the Inland Revenue to interfere in the way the trustees invest trust monies, except where tax avoidance is in point, or where the investment appears to be irreconcilable with the *bona fides* of the scheme having regard to its cash needs for purchasing annuities. Investment in land or buildings may be a good long-term investment for a scheme where the members are many years from retirement, but even so, questions would need to be asked if the property purchased appeared to be an important part of the employer's own commercial premises, and thus potentially difficult to realise.

14   If assets are acquired from the employer, the SFO will generally need to consult the Inspector of Taxes dealing with the employer's tax affairs to determine whether tax avoidance is involved, and particularly whether the acquisition is part and parcel of a "transaction in securities" to which section 460 Income and Corporation Taxes Act 1970 might apply. It goes without saying that a retirement benefit scheme used in this way will not be approved, and indeed it would probably be appropriate to withdraw any existing approval. Even where section 460 is not in point, similar consultation will be necessary if the scheme is to acquire shares or debentures in the employing company whether by subscription, bonus issue, or by purchase from existing shareholders. The possibility of capital transfer tax avoidance may be grounds for withholding tax approval of the scheme.

15   It is unlikely that the SFO will be prepared to approve a small self-administered scheme which invests a significant amount of its funds in works of art or other valuable chattels or non-income producing assets, which could well be made available for the personal use of scheme members and lead to transactions between the trustees and the members otherwise than on a purely commercial basis. In any event, if such an asset were placed at the disposal of a member or of his family or household, he would be assessable to income tax under Schedule E by virtue of section 63(4) and (5) Finance Act 1976 on an annual sum equal to 10% of the market value of the asset.

16   Purchases of commodities, dealings in commodity futures, or the acquisition of plant and machinery for hiring out, may result in the trustees becoming assessable to tax on trading profits or profits from "an adventure in the nature of trade" (see *Wisdown v Chamberlain 45 TC 92*); such income is not exempt from tax under section 21(2) Finance Act 1970. The SFO is not competent to give any information as to whether the income from specified activities will be regarded as trading income or not, and it is not normally the practice of Inspectors of Taxes to discuss transactions not yet carried out.

17   It was previously Inland Revenue practice to require the rules to provide for any member's pensions to be secured immediately on becoming payable by the purchase of a non-commutable non-assignable annuity from a Life Office, subject to certain exceptions for impaired lives and pension increases. This requirement was intended primarily as a safeguard against a situation in which, under the principle in *Saunders v Vautier*, the members would be able to demand the termination of the scheme in any way they chose, since, as indicated in paragraph 7 above, this situation is more likely to occur where all or most of the members have retired. But it is now accepted that a risk of this kind is no more significant during the first 5 years of retirement than it was during service, if the pension is guaranteed for 5 years minimum and there is a lump sum guarantee payment prospectively distributable to the dependants or legal personal representatives of the deceased pensioner. Thus, in such a case the SFO will be content for the rules to provide for the purchase of an annuity at some time during the first 5 years of a member's retirement. This easement is intended to enable the trustees to choose a financially opportune time for the transaction, and to avoid having to purchase at a moment when Life Office annuity rates may be relatively unfavourable, or the market value of the scheme's investments depressed.

18   Where the rules provide for pension increases linked with prospective increases in the cost of living (but not where the pension increases are to be at a fixed rate of 3% per annum (see PN 7.2(a)) money to finance the increases may be retained in the fund.

19   Where there is a prospective widow's reversionary pension, the rules may provide either that the widow's pension shall be purchased simultaneously with the member's pension, whenever that may be (as may be desirable on grounds of cost) or that the purchase of the widow's pension shall be deferred until the husband dies. If the latter method is adopted the rules should normally provide for the widow's pension to be payable to whichever woman is the member's wife at the time he dies.

20   The newer practice set out in paragraph 17 above makes it inappropriate to continue exempting shares from purchasing annuities for members with impaired lives. The directors of family companies for whom many small self-administered schemes cater, often postpone retirement to an advanced age; if purchase of an annuity is then deferred for 5 more years, the individual will be of an age when the dividing line between an impaired and an unimpaired life is often blurred. A dispensation in those instances where life is considered to be impaired, from the normal requirement to purchase an annuity would, it is feared, often be misused.

Death benefits

21   All death in service benefits should be insured from the outset insofar as they exceed the value from year to year of the employee's interest in the fund based on his accrued pension and other retirement benefits. In order to reduce the risks of the principle in *Saunders v Vautier* applying, the scheme rules should provide that lump sum benefits payable on death in service and lump sum guarantee payments should be distributable at the trustees' discretion among the usual wide range of individuals customarily designated for this purpose in the rules of pension schemes, *except* where general SFO practice precludes discretionary distribution of a benefit payable on death on or after age 75 – see, for example Memorandum No. 41 paragraph 8.

Full commutation of pension

22   Where scheme rules contain a provision for the full commutation of pension where the employee is "in exceptional circumstances of serious ill-health", it has always been Inland Revenue practice to leave the application of the rule in

particular cases to the trustees. In large schemes the arm's length relationship, and in insured schemes the interest of the Life Office, provide a reasonable guarantee that the facility will not be abused. Neither factor is present in the context of small self-administered schemes and the rules should therefore provide for full commutation on serious ill-health grounds to be subject to the agreement of the Inland Revenue. The SFO does not intend to do more than confirm that proper medical evidence has been obtained (see PN 8.11) and that its terms appear to warrant a conclusion that the member's expectation of life is very short.

Funding, actuarial reports and other information

23   As a condition of approval the SFO will expect actuarial reports to be made at intervals not greater than 3 years, and will examine the assumptions that have been used as a basis for funding the scheme. In view also of the significance attaching to the investment policy of the trustees (see paragraphs 11–15 above) the SFO will need to know, when the application for approval is first considered, and in conjunction with the examination of later actuarial reports, how the funds are to be or have been invested.

24   There seems to be a widely-held view that irrespective of the needs of the scheme, SFO general practice allows an employer, when money is available, to make a special contribution equal to one year's ordinary annual contribution, to be held as a general reserve. This is a misconception. The SFO will question the payment of special contributions not justified by the recommendations of the actuary and the liabilities of the scheme.

General enquiries

25   Every effort has been made to make the explanation of practice in this memorandum as informative as any general statement on this subject can be. It is an area where the facts of the particular case are all-important, and the treatment of the scheme from the tax-approved viewpoint cannot be infallibly deduced in advance from abstract propositions and "rules of thumb". It is unlikely therefore that the SFO will be able to enlarge on what is said in paragraphs 9–16, and 23–24, above in reply to hypothetical or general enquiries which do not disclose the title of the scheme to which they relate and other relevant facts and figures.

Notes on Practice by the Inland Revenue issued to the Association of British Insurers and the Association of Pensioneer Trustees

Small self-administered schemes

Application of Memo No 58

1. *Purchase by Trustees of Residential Property*

The purchase of residential property for leasing to a director/shareholder or to the employer will not normally be regarded as consistent with scheme approval because of the likelihood of beneficial use by or for the benefit of members.

2. *Holiday property*

The investment of scheme monies in the purchase of holiday cottages and the like is normally regarded as inconsistent with approval.

3. *Purchase at arm's length of shares in the employer company*

This may be acceptable in principle subject to consideration of all the circumstances but the value of such holdings must be aggregated with loans to the employer for the purpose of the 50% self investment maximum laid down in paragraph 12 of Memorandum No 58.

4. *One man schemes*

In cases where the employer is providing for one employee only we are prepared to approve a one man small self-administered scheme. If, however, more than one employee is to be pensioned all should be included in one self-administered scheme.

5. *Borrowing by Trustees to facilitate purchase of property etc.*

Each case will need consideration on its own merits but excessive borrowing by Trustees may give rise to doubts as to the 'sole purpose' of the arrangements and lead to difficulty over approval. Any significant proposed borrowing should therefore be cleared with the SFO in advance.

6. *Purchase of pension increases*

Where the rules provide for pension increases linked to prospective increases in the cost of living, such increases should be secured with a Life Office as soon as they are awarded unless the guarantee period has not expired and the basic pension has not been so secured at that time. If that is the case then all COL increases awarded since the pension commenced must be secured at the appropriate time along with the basic pension.

7. *Employer going into liquidation without successor*

The scheme documentation should provide that in these circumstances the scheme will be wound up, or partially wound up if appropriate, and the proceeds used in accordance with the documentation to purchase or transfer accrued benefits of members. Any surplus being returned to the employer.

Any other course should be subject to the specific approval of the Board of Inland Revenue.

Appendix 3

Occupational Pensions: Small Self-Administered Schemes

Consultative Document

Introduction

1.　The Inland Revenue press release published on Budget Day (17 March 1987) announced a change in the present tax regime for occupational pensions (*section 19 et seq. Finance Act 1970*). Paragraph 26 of the Background Document which accompanied the press release stated that the purpose of this change was to clarify the scope and extent of the discretionary powers conferred on the Board by *section 20* of that Act. In particular, the amendment to the legislation would enable additional conditions for tax exempt approval to be prescribed in Regulations e.g. in the case of small self-administered pension schemes.

2.　Such an amendment was considered necessary because recently obtained legal advice suggested that the discretionary powers conferred by *section 20* were in practice unfettered. If the Board were to exercise their discretion properly, they must therefore be prepared, in an individual case, to consider *any* request for concessionary treatment in respect of *any* of the conditions for tax approval. This was so even if such a concession had never been allowed in the past. This advice raised the unwelcome prospect of an increase in the already considerable volume of correspondence relating to scheme approvals—particularly where small self-administered schemes were involved.

3.　In consequence, paragraph 3(5) of Schedule 3 to the *Finance (No 2) Act 1987* adds three new subsections (*4*) to (*6*) to *section 20* of the 1970 Act. The substantive change is made by the new *section 20(5)*, which enables the Board to limit its discretion to approve a scheme by Regulations relating to:

'the benefits provided by the scheme, the investments held for the purposes of the scheme, the manner in which the scheme is administered, or any other circumstances whatever'.

430

4. The purpose of this note is to give a broad outline of what these Regulations will contain and to invite written comments by 25 September. It is hoped that draft Regulations will subsequently be available in time to allow further consultations.

Present position

5. The present discretionary practice in relation to small self-administered schemes evolved following the lifting, in 1973, of the statutory ban on membership of an approved scheme by a controlling director. In view of the obvious danger that such schemes might be used for purposes other than *bona fide* provision for retirement, it has always been considered necessary to impose special conditions for tax approval. These were codified in a Joint Office Memorandum (JOM) 58, issued by the Superannuation Funds Office (SFO) in February 1979 (Annex A). Since then practice has developed on a number of minor detailed aspects (Annex B).

6. It must be emphasised that JOM 58 has always been regarded only as a general guide to the tax approval of small self-administered schemes. The Inland Revenue has continually made it clear that, in a particular case, additional conditions might be imposed if the facts warranted this.

Proposed changes in current practice

7. In general, no major changes are envisaged in the general approach underlying the requirements in JOM 58. Many features of the existing rules—for example, the meaning of 'small' scheme—will remain substantially the same as now. But it is proposed to make a few detailed changes, including some changes of emphasis. The main aspects are as follows:

(i) The Regulations will proscribe completely certain types of investment which hitherto have almost invariably been refused under present practice and they will specify the conditions which currently attach to loans by the scheme to the employer, and to self-investment in the employer's company. Two new conditions will be introduced (paragraphs 9 to 15 below).

(ii) The Regulations will require the automatic provision of full information about certain prescribed transactions and investments by the scheme (paragraphs 16 to 20 below).

(iii) The Regulations will set out the conditions applicable to 'pensioneer trustees'. In general, a much wider range of individuals and companies will be able to act in this capacity (paragraph 21 below).

8. At present, these aspects are all areas of current practice which, in a minority of cases, generate considerable work, both for SFO and pensions advisers. The purpose of reducing the degree of flexibility in current practice is to cut out the, frequently protracted, correspondance to which each of these aspects can give rise, while in no way inhibiting the activities of the majority of schemes whose sole purpose is the provision of retirement benefits for their members.

I. Investment of scheme funds

9. No general restriction is proposed on the investment powers of trustees, except for the general prohibition on loans to members of the scheme or to any other persons who have a contingent interest (e.g. relatives of members)—as already applies under paragraph 9 of JOM 58.

10. As regards loans to the employer, the conditions outlined in paragraphs 11 and 12 of JOM 58 will continue to apply. In future, however, those conditions will apply to all loans. Furthermore, two additional conditions will apply:

(i) all loans must be properly secured; and

(ii) in the first two years after the establishment of the scheme, all loans to the employer should not exceed 25 per cent (as opposed to 50 per cent, as now) of the scheme's assets excluding the value of transfer payments and assigned policies.

11. The question of scheme *investment in property* gives rise to a great amount of protracted correspondence between SFO and pension advisers. The effect of the Regulations will be as follows:

(*a*)   *Commercial property*
The conditions outlined in paragraph 13 of JOM 58 will continue to apply.

(*b*)   *Residential property*
Although not expressly covered in JOM 58, practice in recent years has normally been not to approve the purchase of residential property for use by, or leasing to, a director/shareholder or to the employer. The same has applied for investment in holiday homes etc. These

restrictions—which are necessary because of the real danger that such property could be used for the benefit of members before retirement—are frequently the subject of disputes. The Regulations will therefore provide that no such investment will be approved unless the property is occupied by an arm's length employee (such as a caretaker) who is required to live close to the employer's premises.

12. The purchase by a scheme of shares in the employer's company will continue to be subject to the conditions outlined in paragraph 14 of JOM 58, and the further requirement will also continue to apply that the value of such holdings must be aggregated with any loans to the employer for the purpose of the 50 per cent (and the new 25 per cent) rules.

13. Paragraph 15 of JOM 58 states that 'significant' investment in works of art, valuable chattels etc. is unlikely to be acceptable. As a rough rule of thumb, 'significant' has generally been taken to mean 5 per cent of scheme assets. But the reason for the restriction is the same as for the restriction on investment in residential property (see para 11. above). For this reason the Regulations will provide that in no case will such pride in possession assets be approved.

14. It is not uncommon for a scheme to borrow money to help finance the purchase of investments. As a general rule such borrowings have been regarded as acceptable if they did not exceed three times the amount of the employer's ordinary annual contributions to the scheme. This limit on borrowings will be included in the Regulations.

15. As a transitional measure, where a scheme currently holds assets that will be prohibited by the Regulations, those assets may be retained (provided that they were consistent with existing practice). But once such assets are disposed of they should not be replaced by assets of a similar nature.

II Provision of information

16. One of the greatest sources of unproductive work for SFO is the monitoring of the activities of small self-administered schemes after they have received tax approval. Serious difficulties frequently arise in:

— finding out about particular types of transaction and obtaining full details; and

— investigating individual transactions when there is *prima facie* reason to suspect an infringement of current requirements

17.   This often gives rise to lengthy and time-consuming correspondence, even where the scheme trustees are willing to provide all the information requested. But in a minority of cases it is apparent that the trustees are anxious to conceal the true nature or purpose of a given transaction—thereby making even more difficult the task of getting at all the facts.

18.   Paragraph 23 of JOM 58 requires the trustees of small self-administered schemes to provide actuarial valuations every three years at least. The Regulations will include this requirement; and in addition they will require schemes to volunteer certain other information, which will be prescribed in the Regulations. In particular, automatic notification will be required of any transaction in the categories described in paragraphs 9 to 14 above, together with an undertaking that the transaction does not infringe current requirements and any further material to support such an undertaking.

19.   The Regulations will also require the automatic notification of any transaction between the scheme and a connected person. For this purpose the following will be regarded as a connected person:

— the principal employer;

— another participating employer;

— a company associated with the principal employer or participating employer because it is a subsidiary or it shares a common trade, shareholdings or directorships;

— a scheme member, the member's husband or wife, a relative of the member or the relative's spouse.

20.   The Regulations will provide for this information to be furnished at the time of, and preferably before, the date of the transaction. Failure to comply with these requirements is likely to result in withdrawal of tax approval.

III   Pensioneer trustees

21.   The present requirements which SFO impose on 'pensioneer trustees' have been reviewed, and the following changes in emphasis are proposed.

(*a*)   The Regulations will require all small self-administered schemes to appoint a 'pensioneer trustee'. Failure to do so will result in a refusal to approve the scheme, or a withdrawal of approval if already granted.

(*b*) If the 'pensioneer trustee' resigns or is dismissed or has his status withdrawn the Regulations will stipulate that a suitable successor must be appointed within 30 days.

(*c*) The main function of the 'pensioneer trustee' will continue to be the prevention of a premature winding-up of the scheme (paragraph 4 of JOM 58).

(*d*) However, the Regulations will impose a new requirement, which is that the 'pensioneer trustee' must undertake to notify SFO of any transaction undertaken by the scheme which, in his opinion, is likely to infringe the requirements for approval. Failure to do so is likely to lead to withdrawal of 'pensioneer trustee' status.

(*e*) The conditions for SFO approval of an application for 'pensioneer trustee' status will be considerably simplified. In general, any reputable professional person with pensions experience will be regarded as competent to act as a 'pensioneer trustee'.

Appendix 4

1991 No 1614

Retirement Benefits Schemes (Restriction on Discretion to Approve) (Small Self-Administered Schemes) Regulations 1991

Made:15th July 1991

The Commissioners of Inland Revenue in exercise of the powers conferred on them by section 591(6) of the Income and Corporation Taxes Act 1988, hereby make the following Regulations:

Citation and commencement

1   These Regulations may be cited as the Retirement Benefits Schemes (Restriction on Discretion to Approve) (Small Self-Administered Schemes) Regulations 1991 and shall come into force on 5th August 1991.

Interpretation

2—(1) In these Regulations unless the context otherwise requires—
"Act" means the Income and Corporation Taxes Act 1988
"actuary" means—

(a)   a Fellow of the Institute of Actuaries,

(b)   a Fellow of the Faculty of Actuaries, or

(c)   a person with other actuarial qualifications who has been approved as a proper person to act for the purposes of regulation 8 of the Occupational Pension Schemes (Disclosure of Information) Regulations 1986 in connection with the scheme;

. . .

"the Board" means the Commissioners of Inland Revenue;
"business" includes a trade or profession and includes any activity carried on by a body of persons, whether corporate or unincorporate, except the activity of making or managing investments where those investments do not consist of shares in 51 per cent subsidiaries of the body of persons which do not themselves carry on the activity of making or managing investments;
"close company" has the meaning given by sections 414 and 415 of the Act;
"company" means any body corporate or unincorporated association, but does not include a partnership;
"control", in relation to a body corporate or partnership, shall, subject to paragraph (2), be construed in accordance with section 840 of the Act; and the like construction of "control" applies (with the necessary modifications) in relation to an unincorporated association as it applies in relation to a body corporate;
"controlling director" means a director to whom subsection (5)(b) of section 417 of the Act (read with subsections (3), (4) and (6) of that section) applies;
"director" means a director within the meaning of section 612(1) of the Act;
"employer" in relation to a scheme means an employer who, by virtue of the governing instrument, is entitled to pay contributions to the scheme;
"governing instrument" in relation to a scheme means a trust deed, or other document by which the scheme is established, and any other document which contains provisions by which the administration of the scheme is governed;
"pensioneer trustee" means a trustee of a scheme who—

(a)   is approved by the Board to act as such, and

436

(b)   is not connected with—

    (i)   a scheme member,

    (ii)   any other trustee of the scheme, or

    (iii)   a person who is an employer in relation to the scheme.
"relative" means brother, sister, ancestor or lineal descendant;
"residential property" means property normally used, or adapted for use, as one or more dwellings;
"scheme" means a retirement benefits scheme as defined in section 611(1) of the Act;
["small self-administered scheme" means a retirement benefits scheme where—

(a)   some or all of the income and other assets are invested otherwise than in insurance policies;

(b)   a scheme member is connected with—

    (i)   another scheme member, or

    (ii)   a trustee of the scheme, or

    (iii)   a person who is an employer in relation to the scheme; and

(c)   there are fewer than 12 scheme members;]
"scheme member" in relation to a scheme means a member of the scheme to whom benefit is currently accruing as a result of service as an employee;
"shares" includes stock;
"the trustees" in relation to a scheme includes any person having the management of the scheme;
"unlisted company" means a company which is not officially listed on a recognised stock exchange within the meaning of section 841 of the Act;
"51 per cent subsidiary" has the meaning given by section 838 of the Act.

(2)   The interpretation of "control" in paragraph (1) does not apply in relation to a body corporate which is a close company and in relation to such a body corporate "control" shall be construed in accordance with section 416 of the Act.

(3)   For the purposes of these Regulations any question whether a person is connected with another shall be determined in accordance with paragraphs (4) to (8) (any provision that one person is connected with another being taken to mean that they are connected with one another).

(4)   A person is connected with an individual if that person is the individual's husband or wife, or is a relative, or the husband or wife of a relative, of the individual or of the individual's husband or wife.

(5)   Without prejudice to paragraph (4) a person, in his capacity as a scheme member, is connected with an employer in relation to a scheme if—

(a)   where the employer is a partnership, he is connected with a partner in the partnership, or

(b)   where the employer is a company, he or a person connected with him is, or at any time during the preceding 10 years has been, a controlling director of the company.

(6)   A company is connected with another company—

(a)   if the same person has control of both, or a person has control of one and persons connected with him, or he and persons connected with him, have control of the other, or

(b)   if a group of two or more persons has control of each company, and the groups either consist of the same persons or could be regarded as consisting of the same persons by treating (in one or more cases) a member of either group as replaced by a person with whom he is connected.

(7)   A company is connected with another person if that person has control of it or if that person and persons connected with him together have control of it.

(8)   Any two or more persons acting together to secure or exercise control of a company shall be treated in relation to that company as connected one with another and with any person acting on the directions of any of them to secure or exercise control of the company.

(9)   For the purposes of these Regulations a company is associated with an employer if (directly or indirectly) the employer controls that company or that company controls the employer or if both are controlled by a third person.

Restrictions on the Board's discretion

3   The Board shall not exercise their discretion to approve a scheme by virtue of section 591 of the Act in circumstances where the scheme is a small self-administered scheme and—

    (a)   the Board have previously approved such a scheme—

        (i)   of which an employee of any employer in relation to the scheme has at any time been a scheme member, and

        (ii)   to which any such employer was entitled to pay contributions, and

        (iii)   which has not been wound up; or

    (b)   subject to regulation 11, the governing instrument of the scheme does not contain provisions of a description specified in regulations 4 to 10.

Provisions as to borrowing

4—(1) The description of provision specified in this regulation is a provision to the effect that at the time of any borrowing the trustees of the scheme in their capacity as such shall not have borrowed an aggregate amount, including the amount of that borrowing but excluding any amount which has been repaid before that time, in excess of the total of—

    (a)   three times the ordinary annual contribution paid by employers;

    (b)   three times the annual amount of contributions paid by scheme members as a condition of membership in the year of assessment ending immediately before that time;

    [(c)   the amount found by the formula—

$$((A - B) \times 45)/100$$

where—

A is the market value of the assets of the scheme at that time, other than assets franking any pension in payment under the rules of the scheme where the purchase of an annuity has been deferred (including any pension that would be payable to a widow or widower of a member of the scheme following the member's death in a case where the rules of the scheme limit such pension to the person to whom the member was married at retirement), and

B is the aggregate of any sums borrowed to purchase those assets [which are outstanding at that time], and any other liabilities incurred by the trustees which are outstanding at that time, other than liabilities to pay benefits under the scheme.]

    (2)   In this regulation "ordinary annual contribution" means the amount which is the smaller of—

    [(a)   the amount found—

        (i)   where the scheme has been established for three years or more at the time of any borrowing, by dividing the amount of the contributions paid by employers in the period of three years which ended at the end of the previous accounting period of the scheme by three, or

        (ii)   where the scheme has been established for less than three years at the time of any borrowing, by dividing the amount of the contributions paid by employers in the period since the scheme was established ending at the time of that borrowing by the number of years falling within that period (a part of a year being counted as one year), and]

(b)   the amount of the annual contributions which, within the period of three years immediately before the date of any borrowing, an actuary has advised in writing would have to be paid in order to secure the benefits provided under the scheme.

Provisions as to investments

5—(1) The description of provision specified in this regulation is a provision to the effect that the trustees of the scheme in their capacity as such shall not directly or indirectly hold as an investment—

(a)   personal chattels other than choses in action (or, in Scotland, movable property other than incorporeal movable property);

(b)   residential property other than that specified in paragraph (2);

(c)   shares in an unlisted company which—

(i)   carry more than 30 per cent of the voting power in the company, or

(ii)   entitle the holder of them to more than 30 per cent of any dividends declared by the company [in respect of shares of the class held].

(2)   The residential property specified in this paragraph is—

(a)   property which is, or is to be, occupied by an employee who is not connected with his employer and who is required as a condition of his employment to occupy the property; and

(b)   property which is, or is to be, occupied by a person who is neither a scheme member nor connected with a scheme member in connection with the occupation by that person of business premises held by the trustees of the scheme in their capacity as such.

(3)   For the purposes of paragraph (1), trustees shall not be regarded as indirectly holding as an investment residential property other than that specified in paragraph (2) where they hold as an investment units in a unit trust scheme—

(a)   which is an authorised unit trust within the meaning of section 468(6) of the Act, or

(b)   where all the unit holders would be wholly exempt from capital gains tax or corporation tax (otherwise than by reason of residence) if they disposed of their units, and the trustees of the scheme hold such property as an investment subject to the trusts of the scheme.

[(4)   For the purposes of paragraph (1), trustees shall not be regarded as indirectly holding as an investment residential property other than that specified in paragraph (2) where—

(a)   they hold as an investment subject to the trusts of the scheme a right which confers entitlement to receive payment of any rentcharge, ground annual, feu duty or other annual payment reserved in respect of, or charged on or issuing out of, that property, and

(b)   the property is not occupied by a scheme member or a person connected with him.]

Provisions as to lending and the acquistion of shares

6—(1) The description of provision specified in this regulation is a provision to the effect that the trustees of the scheme in their capacity as such shall not directly or indirectly lend money—

(a)   to a member of the scheme or a person connected with him, other than an employer in relation to the scheme or any company associated with that employer, or

(b)   to an employer in relation to the scheme, or any company associated with that employer, unless the lending is within the exception contained in paragraph (2).

(2)   Lending is within the exception contained in this paragraph—

(a)   only if the amount lent is utilised for the purposes of the borrower's business, and

    (b)   if it is—

        (i)   for a fixed term,

        (ii)   at a commercial rate of interest, and

        (iii)   evidenced by an agreement in writing which contains the provisions specified in paragraph (3) and all the conditions on which it is made.

(3)   The provisions specified in this paragraph are provisions to the effect that the amount lent shall be immediately repayable—

    (a)   if the borrower—

        (i)   is in breach of the conditions of the agreement,

        (ii)   ceases to carry on business, or

        (iii)   becomes insolvent; or

    (b)   if it is required to enable the trustees to pay benefits which have already become due under the scheme.

(4)   Subject to paragraphs (5) and (6), for the purposes of this regulation a borrower shall be taken to have become insolvent if—

    (a)   he has been adjudged bankrupt or has made a composition or arrangement with his creditors;

    (b)   he has died and his estate falls to be administered in accordance with an order under section 421 of the Insolvency Act 1986 or Article 365 of the Insolvency (Northern Ireland) Order 1989;

    (c)   where the borrower is a company, a winding-up order or an administration order has been made with respect to it, or a resolution for voluntary winding-up has been passed with respect to it, or a receiver or manager of its undertaking has been duly appointed, or possession has been taken, by or on behalf of the holders of any debentures secured by a floating charge, of any property of the company comprised in or subject to the charge, or a voluntary arrangement is approved under Part I of the Insolvency Act 1986 or Part II of the Insolvency (Northern Ireland) Order 1989.

(5)   Until the coming into operation of Article 365 of the Insolvency (Northern Ireland) Order 1989, paragraph (4) above shall have effect in its application to Northern Ireland subject to the following modifications—

    (a)   in sub-paragraph (b) of that paragraph for the reference to that Article there shall be substituted a reference to section 30(1) of, and Part I of Schedule 1 to, the Administration of Estates Act (Northern Ireland) 1955; and

    (b)   in sub-paragraph (c) of that paragraph the words from "or an administration order" to "it" (where those words first occur) and the words from "or a voluntary arrangement" onwards shall be omitted.

(6)   In the application of this regulation to Scotland, for sub-paragraphs (a), (b) and (c) of paragraph (4) above there shall be substituted the following sub-paragraphs—

    (a)   an award of sequestration has been made on his estate, or he has executed a trust deed for his creditors or has entered into a composition contract;

    (b)   he has died and a judicial factor appointed under section 11A of the Judicial Factors (Scotland) Act 1889 is required by the provisions of that section to divide his insolvent estate among his creditors; or

    (c)   where the borrower is a company, a winding up order or an administration order has been made, or a resolution for voluntary winding-up is passed with respect to it, or a receiver of its undertaking is duly appointed, or a voluntary arrangement for the purposes of Part I of the Insolvency Act 1986 is approved under that part.

(7) For the purposes of this regulation and of regulation 8 a member of a scheme includes—

    (a) a scheme member;

    (b) a person who is in receipt of a pension from the scheme;

    (c) a person who has left the service of the employer but was a scheme member during that service;

    (d) a person who is in the service of the employer but is no longer a scheme member.

7—(1) The description of provision specified in this regulation is a provision to the effect that at the time that any money is lent, or any shares in an employer or any company associated with that employer are acquired, the aggregate of—

    (a) the total amount outstanding of money lent to an employer and any company associated with him in accordance with regulation 6(2) and (3), and

    (b) the market value of shares in an employer and any company associated with him held by the trustees in their capacity as such,

    shall not, where that time is during the period of two years from the date on which the scheme was established, exceed the figure specified in paragraph (2) or, where that time is after the end of that period, exceed the figure specified in paragraph (3).

[(2) The figure specified in this paragraph is the amount found by the formula—

$$((C - D) \times 25)/100$$

where—

C is the market value at the time in question of the assets of the scheme which are derived from contributions made by an employer and by employees since the scheme was established, other than assets franking any pension in payment under the rules of the scheme where the purchase of an annuity has been deferred (including any pension that would be payable to a widow or widower of a member of the scheme following the member's death in a case where the rules of the scheme limit such pension to the person to whom the member was married at retirement), and

D is the aggregate of any sums borrowed to purchase those assets [which are outstanding at that time], and any other liabilities incurred by the trustees which are outstanding at that time, other than liabilities to pay benefits under the scheme.

(3) The figure specified in this paragraph is the amount found by the formula—

$$((E - F) \times 50)/100$$

where—

E is the market value at the time in question of all the assets of the scheme, other than assets franking any pension in payment under the rules of the scheme where the purchase of an annuity has been deferred (including any pension that would be payable to a widow or widower of a member of the scheme following the member's death in a case where the rules of the scheme limit such pension to the person to whom the member was married at retirement), and

F is the aggregate of any sums borrowed to purchase those assets [which are outstanding at that time], and any other liabilities incurred by the trustees which are outstanding at that time, other than liabilities to pay benefits under the scheme.]

Provisions as to transactions with scheme members and others

8—(1) The description of provision specified in this regulation is a provision to the effect that the trustees of the scheme in their capacity as such shall not directly or indirectly purchase, sell or lease any asset—

    (a) from or to a member of the scheme or a person connected with him, other than an employer in relation to the scheme or any company associated with that employer, or

    (b) from or to an employer, or any company associated with that employer, except in accordance with paragraph (2).

(2)   A purchase, sale or lease is in accordance with this paragraph only when it is made—

    (a)   after the trustees have obtained independent professional advice in writing, and

    (b)   in accordance with that advice.

(3)   For the purpose of this regulation—

    (a)   a purchase by the trustees shall not be regarded as a purchase indirectly from a member of the scheme, or a person connected with him, if the purchase by the trustees took place three years or more after the sale by the member or person connected with him; and

    (b)   a sale by the trustees shall not be regarded as a sale indirectly to a member of the scheme, or a person connected with him, if the purchase by the member or person connected with him took place three years or more after the sale by the trustees.

[Provisions as to pensioneer trustees]

[9]—[(1) The description of provision specified in this regulation is a provision to the effect that—

    (a)   one of the trustees of the scheme shall be a pensioneer trustee,

    (b)   the appointment of that trustee as a pensioneer trustee, and his obligation and entitlement to act as such, shall be incapable of termination at any time except—

        (i)   by the death of the trustee,

        (ii)   by an order of the court,

        [(iia)   by virtue of section 3, 4 or 29 of the Pensions Act 1995 or Article 3, 4 or 29 of the Pensions (Northern Ireland) Order 1995 (prohibition, suspension or disqualification),]

        (iii)   by withdrawal by the Board of their approval of the trustee to act as a pensioneer trustee, or

        (iv)   in the circumstances specified in paragraph (2), and

    (c)   where termination occurs by virtue of any of the events specified in paragraph (1)(b)(i) to (iii) or in the circumstances specified in paragraph (2)(b), the appointment of a successor to the former pensioneer trustee of the scheme is made no more than 30 days after the termination.

(2)   The circumstances specified in this paragraph are where—

    (a)   another trustee is appointed to act as pensioneer trustee in place of the trustee, and the appointment of the other trustee takes effect at the same time as the termination;

    (b)   the trustee has committed a fraudulent breach of trust in relation to the scheme and that is the reason for the termination.]

10

[. . .]

Schemes awaiting approval

11—(1)Where at the date of coming into force of these Regulations a scheme which is a small self-administered scheme is in existence and either—

    (a)   has not yet been submitted to the Board for approval, or

    (b)   is before the Board for approval,
the Board shall not be prevented from approving it by virtue of section 591 of the Act by reason only that it contains a provision or provisions of a description specified in any of sub-paragraphs (a), (b) and (c) of paragraph (2).

(2)   The description of provisions specified in this paragraph is—

    (a)   a provision which authorises the trustees of the scheme to retain an investment of a description mentioned in sub-paragraph (a), (b) or (c) of regulation 5(1) which is held by them immediately before the day on which these Regulations were made;

(b)   a provision which authorises the trustees of the scheme to continue to lend money, or retain shares in an employer or any company associated with that employer, which was being lent or held by them immediately before the day on which these Regulations were made, where at the time the money was first lent or the shares were acquired the aggregate referred to in paragraph (1) of regulation 7 exceeded the figure specified in paragraph (2) of that regulation, but did not exceed the figure specified in paragraph (3) of that regulation, notwithstanding that the loan was made or the shares were acquired during the period of two years from the date on which the scheme was established;

(c)   a provision which authorises the trustees of the scheme to sell assets held by them immediately before that day to a member of the scheme or a person connected with him.

Appendix 5

1995 No 3103

Retirement Benefits Schemes (Information Powers) Regulations 1995

Made: 30th November 1995

The Commissioners of Inland Revenue, in exercise of the powers conferred on them by section 605(1A), (1B), (1D) and (1E) of the Income and Corporation Taxes Act 1988, hereby make the following Regulations.

Part I
Introductory

Citation and commencement

1   These Regulations may be cited as the Retirement Benefits Schemes (Information Powers) Regulations 1995 and shall come into force on 1st January 1996.

Interpretation

2   In these Regulations unless the context otherwise requires—

"actuary" means—

(a)   a Fellow of the Institute of Actuaries, or

(b)   a Fellow of the Faculty of Actuaries, or

(c)   person with other actuarial qualifications who has been approved as being a proper person to act for the purposes of regulation 8 of the Occupational Pension Schemes (Disclosure of Information) Regulations 1986 in connection with the scheme;

"approved", in relation to a retirement benefits scheme, means—

(a)   approved by the Board for the purposes of Chapter I, or

(b)   before the Board in order for them to decide whether to give approval for the purposes of that Chapter;

"the Board" means the Commissioners of Inland Revenue;

"Chapter I" means Chapter I of Part XIV of the Taxes Act;

"company" means any body corporate or unincorporated association, but does not include a partnership;

"controlling director" has the meaning given by paragraph 5(5) of Schedule 23 to the Taxes Act;

"exempt approved scheme" means an approved scheme which is for the time being within paragraph (a) or (b) of section 592(1) of the Taxes Act;

"friendly society" has the meaning given by section 116 of the Friendly Societies Act 1992;

"insurance company" has the meaning given by section 659B of the Taxes Act;

"insured scheme" means an approved scheme, the contributions to which, apart from voluntary contributions made by members, are invested wholly by way of insurance premiums, and the policies in respect of which do not provide that levels of contributions require to take account of surpluses, but does not include a scheme—

(a)   the policies in respect of which provide only for lump sum benefits for members on death before the normal retirement date, or

(b)   which is a simplified defined contribution scheme;

444

"large self-administered scheme" means a self-administered scheme which is not a small self-administered scheme and is not a simplified defined contribution scheme;

"member", in relation to a retirement benefits scheme, means a member of the scheme to whom benefit is currently accruing as a result of service as an employee;

"normal retirement date" means the date specified in the rules of a retirement benefits scheme as the date at which an employee will normally retire;

"permitted maximum" has the meaning given by section 590C of the Taxes Act;

"relevant statutory scheme" has the meaning given by section 611A of the Taxes Act;

"retirement benefits scheme" has the meaning given by section 611(1) of the Taxes Act;

"scheme year" means—

(a)   a year specified for the purposes of the scheme in any document comprising the scheme or, if no year is specified, a period of 12 months commencing on 1st April or on such other date as the trustees select; or

(b)   such other period (if any) exceeding 6 months but not exceeding 18 months as is selected by the trustees—

    (i)   in respect of the scheme year in which the scheme commences or terminates, or

    (ii)   in connection with a variation of the date on which the scheme year is to commence;

"self-administered scheme" means an approved scheme some or all of the income and other assets of which are invested otherwise than in insurance policies;

"shares" includes stock;

"simplified defined contribution scheme" means a retirement benefits scheme approved by the Board by reference to limitations on—

(a)   the aggregate amount of the contributions which may be paid by a member and his employer,

(b)   the maximum lump sum which may be provided under the scheme, and

(c)   the benefits payable on death which may be provided under the scheme;

"small self-administered scheme" has the meaning given by regulation 2(1) of the 1991 Regulations;

"special contribution" means any contribution paid to a retirement benefits scheme by an employer which is neither a fixed amount paid annually, whether in instalments or otherwise nor an annual amount, that is payable over a period of three years or more and is calculated on a consistent basis in accordance with actuarial principles by reference to the earnings, contributions or number of members of the scheme;

"Taxes Act" means the Income and Corporation Taxes Act 1988;

"unlisted company" means a company which is not officially listed on a recognised stock exchange within the meaning of section 841(1) of the Taxes Act;

"1991 Regulations" means the Retirement Benefits Schemes (Restriction on Discretion to Approve) (Small Self-administered Schemes) Regulations 1991.

Part II
Information Required Without Notice

Prescribed person

3   For the purposes of this Part of these Regulations, "the prescribed person" in relation to a retirement benefits scheme means—

(a)   the person who is, or the persons who are, for the time being the administrator in relation to the scheme by virtue of section 611AA of the Taxes Act; or

(b)   where section 606(1) of the Taxes Act applies at any time in relation to the scheme, the person who is, or the persons who are, by virtue of that section responsible at that time for

Appendix 5

the discharge of all duties imposed on the administrator under Chapter I (whenever arising) and liable for any tax due from the administrator in the administrator's capacity as such (whenever falling due); or

(c) where section 599(7) of the Taxes Act applies in relation to an insurance company, that insurance company.

Actuarial valuation reports—self-administered schemes and insured schemes

4—(1) The prescribed person in relation to a self-administered scheme or an insured scheme shall furnish to the Board, at the time prescribed by paragraph (2) below, any valuation report of the scheme's assets in relation to its liabilities having an effective date that falls on or after the date of coming into force of these Regulations, where the report—

(a) was commissioned for the purposes of the scheme, and

(b) consists of an actuarial valuation determined and dated and signed by an actuary.

(2) The time prescribed—

(a) where the valuation report relates to a large self-administered scheme or an insured scheme, is any time not later than two years after the date stated to be the effective date in the valuation;

(b) where the valuation report relates to a small self-administered scheme, is any time not later than one year after the date stated to be the effective date in the valuation.

Investment and borrowing transactions of small self-administered schemes

5—(1) The prescribed person in relation to a small self-administered scheme shall furnish to the Board, at the time prescribed by paragraph (2) below, such information (including copies of any relevant books, documents or other records) as—

(a) is specified on the relevant form supplied by the Board, and

(b) relates to any transaction that is—

(i) of a kind specified in paragraph (3) below, and

(ii) entered into by or on behalf of the trustees or the administrator of the scheme on or after the date of coming into force of these Regulations.

(2) The time prescribed is any time not later than 90 days after the date of the transaction in question.

(3) The transactions specified in this paragraph are—

(a) the acquisition or disposal of land;

(b) the lending of money to an employer in relation to the scheme or any company associated with him;

(c) the acquisition or disposal of shares in an employer in relation to the scheme or any company associated with him;

(d) the acquisition or disposal of shares in an unlisted company;

(e) the borrowing of money;

(f) the purchase, sale or lease from or to an employer in relation to the scheme, or any company associated with him, of any asset other than one specified in sub-paragraph (a), (c) or (d).

(4) References in paragraph (3) above to a company associated with an employer shall be construed in accordance with regulation 2(9) of the 1991 Regulations.

Participation of employers in a scheme

6—(1) The prescribed person in relation to an approved scheme shall furnish to the Board, at the time prescribed by paragraph (2) below, such information (including copies of any relevant books, documents or other records) relating to an event specified in paragraph (3) below and occurring on or after the date of

446

coming into force of these Regulations as is specified on the relevant form supplied by the Board.

(2) The time prescribed is any time not later than 180 days after the end of the scheme year in which the event in question occurs.

(3) The events specified in this paragraph are—

    (a) the admission of a new employer as a participant in the scheme;

    (b) in relation to any employer who is a participant in the scheme—

        (i) a change in his name or address;

        (ii) the occasion of his ceasing to carry on a trade or business;

        (iii) a change in his association with any other employer who is a participant in the scheme.

(4) For the purposes of paragraph (3)(b)(iii) above, an employer is associated with another employer if—

    (a) the association falls within the meaning given by subsection (3) of section 590A of the Taxes Act, read with subsection (4) of that section, or

    (b) there exists some other basis of association between the employers which, for the purpose of granting or maintaining approval of the scheme, the Board have accepted as being sufficient to establish a permanent community of interest between the employers, whether by reason of the association falling within any of the situations specified in paragraph (5) below or otherwise.

(5) The situations specified are where—

    (a) all the employees of the employers are the same individuals;

    (b) the operations of the employers are interdependent;

    (c) in the case of employers who are companies, the same individuals comprise the majority of the directors of, or hold the majority of the ordinary share capital in, each of the companies.

Special contributions by employers

7 —(1)The prescribed person in relation to an exempt approved scheme shall furnish to the Board, at the time prescribed by paragraph (2) below, such information (including copies of any relevant books, documents or other records) relating to the special contribution specified in paragraph (3) below as is specified on the relevant form supplied by the Board.

(2) The time prescribed is any time not later than 180 days after the end of the scheme year in which the special contribution was paid to the scheme by the employer.

(3) The special contribution specified in this paragraph is any special contribution paid to the scheme by an employer on or after the date of coming into force of these Regulations, other than a contribution which—

    (a) has been certified by an actuary as made solely to finance cost of living increases for existing pensioners under the scheme; or

    (b) when aggregated with other special contributions paid by that employer to the scheme in the same chargeable period other than a contribution falling within sub-paragraph (a) above, does not result in an amount which exceeds—

        (i) one half of the permitted maximum as at the end of the scheme year referred to in paragraph (2) above, or

        (ii) the total contributions, other than special contributions, made by the employer to the scheme in the same chargeable period,

    whichever is the greater.

Controlling directors as members of schemes

8—(1) The prescribed person in relation to an approved scheme shall furnish to the Board, at the time prescribed by paragraph (2) below, such information (including copies of any relevant books, documents or

Appendix 5

other records) relating to an event specified in paragraph (3) below and occurring on or after the date of coming into force of these Regulations as is specified on the relevant form supplied by the Board.

(2)   The time prescribed is any time not later than 180 days after the end of the scheme year in which the event in question occurs.

(3)   The events specified in this paragraph are—

(a)   the admission of any person to membership of the scheme who is, or has been at any time within the period of 10 years prior to the date of admission, a controlling director of a company which is an employer in relation to the scheme;

(b)   the occasion of an existing member of the scheme becoming a controlling director of a company which is an employer in relation to the scheme.

Controlling directors—benefits on retirement due to incapacity or serious ill-health

9—(1) The prescribed person in relation to an approved scheme shall furnish to the Board, at the time prescribed by paragraph (2) below—

(a)   notification of any proposal such as is specified in paragraph (3) below and is made on or after the date of coming into force of these Regulations, and

(b)   the information specified in paragraph (4) below.

(2)   The time prescribed—

(a)   in the case of the proposal specified in paragraph (3)(a) below, is any time not less than 28 days prior to the proposed payment of the benefits;

(b)   in the case of the proposal specified in paragraph (3)(b) below, is any time not less than 14 days prior to the proposed payment of the benefits.

(3)   The proposals specified in this paragraph are—

(a)   any proposal for the scheme to pay benefits to a person who is a controlling director of a company which is an employer in relation to the scheme in circumstances where that person is to retire on grounds of incapacity prior to the normal retirement date;

(b)   any proposal for the scheme to pay benefits commuted wholly to lump sum form to a person who is a controlling director of a company which is an employer in relation to the scheme in circumstances where that person is to be retired on grounds of serious ill-health.

(4)   The information to be furnished shall be in the form of copies of documents relating to the decision of the administrator of the scheme to permit retirement on grounds of incapacity prior to the normal retirement date or, as the case may be, full commutation of benefits to lump sum form on retirement on grounds of serious ill-health, including copies of medical reports and other documents in the possession or under the control of the prescribed person containing details of the medical evidence which formed the basis of that decision.

(5)   In this regulation—

"incapacity" means physical or mental deterioration which is sufficiently serious to prevent a person from following his normal employment or which seriously impairs his earning capacity;

"serious ill-health" means ill-health which is such as to give rise to a life expectancy of less than one year.

Reporting of chargeable events

10—(1) A person who is a prescribed person within regulation 3(a) or (b) in relation to a retirement benefits scheme which is—

(a)   an approved scheme, or

(b)   a relevant statutory scheme established under a public general Act,

448

shall furnish to the Board, at the time prescribed by paragraph (2) below, such information (including copies of any relevant books, documents or other records) relating to an event specified in paragraph (3) below as is specified on the relevant form supplied by the Board.

(2) The time prescribed is any time not later than 30 days after the end of the year of assessment in which the event in question occurs.

(3) The events specified in this paragraph are—

(a) any repayment under the scheme to which section 598 of the Taxes Act applies (repayment of employee's contributions);

(b) any commutation of an employee's pension under the scheme to which section 599 of the Taxes Act applies;

(c) any payment under the scheme to which section 599A of the Taxes Act applies (payment to or for the benefit of an employee or his personal representatives out of surplus funds);

(d) any payment to an employer to which section 601 of the Taxes Act applies (charge to tax on payments to employer out of funds of an exempt approved scheme).

11—(1) An insurance company which is a prescribed person by virtue of regulation 3(c) in relation to a retirement benefits scheme which is—

(a) an approved scheme, or

(b) a relevant statutory scheme established under a public general Act,

shall furnish to the Board, at the time prescribed by paragraph (2) below, such information (including copies of any relevant books, documents or other records) relating to an event specified in paragraph (3) below as is specified on the relevant form supplied by the Board.

(2) The time prescribed is any time not later than 180 days after the end of the chargeable period of the insurance company in which the event in question occurs.

(3) The events specified in this paragraph are—

(a) any repayment under the scheme to which section 598 of the Taxes Act applies;

(b) any commutation of an employee's pension under the scheme to which section 599 of the Taxes Act applies;

(c) any payment to an employer to which section 601 of the Taxes Act applies.

Part III
Notices Requiring Particulars and Documents

Approved schemes and relevant statutory schemes

12—(1) The Board may by notice require any of the persons prescribed by paragraph (2) below, within the time prescribed by paragraph (3) below, to furnish to the Board such particulars, and to produce to the Board such documents, as they may reasonably require relating to—

(a) any monies received or receivable by an approved scheme or a relevant statutory scheme, or

(b) any investments or other assets held by that scheme, or

(c) any monies paid or payable out of funds held under that scheme.

(2) The persons prescribed are—

(a) the person who is, or the persons who are, for the time being by virtue of section 611AA of the Taxes Act the administrator of the scheme which is the subject of the notice;

(b) any person who was, or any persons who were, at any time prior to the relevant date by virtue of section 611AA of the Taxes Act the administrator of that scheme, other than an excluded person;

(c) the trustee or trustees of that scheme, or any person who was, or any persons who were, at any time prior to the relevant date the trustee or trustees of that scheme, other than an excluded person;

    (d)   any person who is, or has been at any time prior to the relevant date, an employer in relation to that scheme, other than an excluded person;

    (e)   any person who is, or has been at any time prior to the relevant date, a scheme sponsor in relation to that scheme, other than an excluded person;

    (f)   any person who provides, or has at any time prior to the relevant date provided, administrative services to that scheme, other than an excluded person.

(3)   The time prescribed is such time (not being less than 28 days) as may be provided by the notice.

(4)   A notice under paragraph (1) above may require particulars to be furnished, and documents to be produced, relating to more than one scheme.

(5)   In paragraph (2) above—

    (a)   "excluded person" means a person who, on ceasing to act in relation to the scheme or, as the case may be, provide administrative services to the scheme, transferred all documents in his possession or under his control relating to the scheme to another person who succeeded him in acting in relation to the scheme or providing administrative services to the scheme;

    (b)   "the relevant date" means the date on which the time prescribed by regulation 15(3)(f) ends.

Annuity contracts

13—(1) The Board may by notice require any of the persons prescribed by paragraph (2) below, within the time prescribed by paragraph (3) below, to furnish to the Board such particulars, and to produce to the Board such documents, as they may reasonably require relating to any annuity contract issued by that person by means of which benefits provided under an approved scheme or a relevant statutory scheme have been secured.

(2)   The persons prescribed are—

    (a)   the insurance company which issued the annuity contract, where that company is a body corporate;

    (b)   the chief executive and the manager, within the meaning of section 96D of the Insurance Companies Act 1982, of the insurance company which issued the annuity contract;

    (c)   the friendly society which issued the annuity contract, where that friendly society is a society incorporated under the Friendly Societies Act 1992;

    (d)   the chief executive and the secretary, or any assistant or deputy chief executive, or assistant or deputy secretary, of the friendly society which issued the annuity contract.

(3)   The time prescribed is such time (not being less than 28 days) as may be provided by the notice.

(4)   A notice under paragraph (1) above may require particulars and documents relating to more than one annuity contract.

Part IV
Inspection and Retention of Records

Inspection of records

14—(1) The Board may by notice require any of the persons prescribed by paragraph (2) below to make available for inspection by an officer of the Board authorised for that purpose, within the time prescribed by paragraph (3) below, all books, documents and other records in his possession or under his control relating to—

    (a)   any monies received or receivable by an approved scheme or a relevant statutory scheme, or

450

(b)   any investments or other assets held by that scheme, or

(c)   any monies paid or payable out of funds held under that scheme, or

(d)   any annuity contract by means of which benefits provided under that scheme have been secured.

(2)   The persons prescribed are—

    (a)   the person who is, or the persons who are, for the time being by virtue of section 611AA of the Taxes Act the administrator of the scheme which is the subject of the notice;

    (b)   any person who was, or any persons who were, at any time prior to the relevant date, by virtue of section 611AA of the Taxes Act the administrator of that scheme, other than an excluded person;

    (c)   the trustee or trustees of that scheme, or any person who was, or any persons who were, at any time prior to the relevant date the trustee or trustees of that scheme, other than an excluded person;

    (d)   any person who is, or has been at any time prior to the relevant date, an employer in relation to that scheme, other than an excluded person;

    (e)   any person who is, or has been at any time prior to the relevant date, a scheme sponsor in relation to that scheme, other than an excluded person;

    (f)   any person who provides, or has at any time prior to the relevant date provided, administrative services to that scheme, other than an excluded person.

(3)   The time prescribed is such time (not being less than 28 days) as may be provided by the notice.

(4)   A notice under paragraph (1) above may require books, documents and other records relating to more than one scheme to be made available for inspection.

(5)   Where records are maintained by computer the person required to make them available for inspection shall provide the officer making the inspection with all the facilities necessary for obtaining information from them.

(6)   The authorised officer may take copies of, or make extracts from, any books, documents or other records made available for inspection in accordance with paragraph (1) above.

(7)   In paragraph (2) above "excluded person" and "the relevant date" have the meanings given by regulation 12(5).

Retention of records

15—(1)   Each of the persons prescribed by paragraph (2) below shall preserve, for the time prescribed by paragraph (3) below, all books, documents and other records in his possession or under his control relating to—

    (a)   any monies received or receivable by an approved scheme or a relevant statutory scheme, or

    (b)   any investments or other assets held by that scheme, or

    (c)   any monies paid or payable out of funds held under that scheme, or

    (d)   any annuity contract by means of which benefits provided under that scheme have been secured, or

    (e)   any person who is, or has been, a controlling director of a company which is an employer in relation to the scheme.

(2)   The persons prescribed are—

    (a)   the person who is, or the persons who are, for the time being by virtue of section 611AA of the Taxes Act the administrator of the scheme;

    (b)   any person who was, or any persons who were, at any time prior to the relevant date, by virtue of section 611AA of the Taxes Act the administrator of that scheme, other than an excluded person;

451

(c)   the trustee or trustees of that scheme, or any person who was or any persons who were, at any time prior to the relevant date the trustee or trustees of that scheme, other than an excluded person;

(d)   any person who is, or has been at any time prior to the relevant date, an employer in relation to that scheme, other than an excluded person;

(e)   any person who is, or has been at any time prior to the relevant date, a scheme sponsor in relation to that scheme, other than an excluded person;

(f)   any person who provides, or has at any time prior to the relevant date provided, administrative services to that scheme, other than an excluded person.

(3)   The time prescribed—

(a)   in the case of accounts and actuarial valuation reports relating to the scheme, including books, documents and other records on which such accounts or reports are based, is 6 years from the end of the scheme year in which falls the date on which the accounts were signed or, as the case may be, the report was signed;

(b)   in the case of books, documents or other records containing information which is required to be furnished pursuant to regulation 5, is 6 years from the end of the scheme year in which the transaction in question occurred;

(c)   in the case of books, documents or other records containing information which is required to be furnished pursuant to regulation 6, 8, 10 or 11, is 6 years from the end of the scheme year in which the event to which the information relates occurred;

(d)   in the case of books, documents or other records containing information which is required to be furnished pursuant to regulation 7, is 6 years from the end of the scheme year in which the special contribution to which the information relates was paid to the scheme;

(e)   in the case of books, documents or other records containing information which is required to be furnished pursuant to regulation 9, is 6 years from the end of the scheme year in which the benefits to which the information relates began to be paid;

(f)   in the case of books, documents or other records relating to an event specified in paragraph (4) below, is 6 years from the end of the scheme year in which the event occurred.

(4)   The events specified are—

(a)   the provision by the scheme of any benefit to an employee, or to the widow, widower, children, dependants, or personal representatives, of an employee;

(b)   the refund of contributions to a person who left service as an employee without entitlement to benefits under the scheme;

(c)   the payment of contributions to the scheme by an employer or employee;

(d)   the making of payments by the scheme to any employer participating in the scheme;

(e)   the payment of transfer values or the purchase of annuities under the scheme;

(f)   the acquisition or disposal of any asset by the scheme;

(g)   the undertaking of any transaction for the purposes of the scheme;

(h)   the receipt by the scheme of any income resulting from—

(i)   the investment of assets held by the scheme, or

(ii)   any trading activity carried on by the scheme.

(5)   The duty under paragraph (1) above to preserve books, documents and other records may be discharged by the preservation of the information contained in them.

(6)   In paragraph (2) above "excluded person" and "the relevant date" have the meanings given by regulation 12(5).

Appendix 6

Board Minute Resolving to establish a Small Self-Administered Scheme

ABC LIMITED

Minutes of a meeting of the board of directors of the company held on. . . . . at. . . . .

Present   . . . .

                 . . . .

                 . . . .

There was produced to the meeting an initial actuarial costing report from Messrs. . . . . . . .advising of the cost to the company of establishing an occupational pension scheme for the controlling directors.

Directors D, E and F disclosed their interests and it was resolved that the company should proceed to establish such a pension scheme and that the company's advisers be instructed to prepare the requisite documentation and to apply to the inland Revenue for the approval scheme.

It was further resolved that Messrs. D, E and F would be the first trustees of the scheme together with the pensioner trustee.

Chairman

Clause for Insertion in the Memorandum of Association of a Company Authorising the Establishment of a Pension Scheme (paragraph 3.2)

'To establish, maintain, participate in or contribute to or produce the establishment and maintenance of, participation in or contribution to any pension, superannuation, benevolent or life assurance fund, scheme or arrangement (whether contributory or otherwise) for the benefit of, and to give or procure the giving of donations, gratuities, pensions, allowances, benefits, and emoluments to, any persons who are or were at any time in the employment or service of the company or any of its predecessors in business, or of any company which is a subsidiary of the company or is allied to or associated with the company or with any such subsidiary or who may be or have been directors or officers of the company, or of any such other company as foresaid, and the wives, widows, widowers, families and dependants of any such persons'.

Appendix 8

Specimen Investment Power

Subject always to the provisions of the Pensions Act 1995, the trustees shall have the power to invest any monies forming part of the Scheme in the purchase of or at interest upon the security of such stocks funds shares securities annuities or other investments or property of whatsoever nature and wheresoever situate and whether involving liability or not and whether producing income or not or upon such personal credit with or without security and to raise or borrow any sum or sums of money and secure the repayment thereof in such manner and upon such terms as the Trustees think fit and charge the sums so raised or borrowed or any part thereof on all or any investments of the Scheme as the Trustees shall in their absolute discretion without being liable to account think fit to the extent that the Trustees shall have the same full and unrestricted powers of investing and transposing investments in all respects as if they were absolutely and beneficially entitled to the assets of the Scheme and without prejudice to the generality hereof, trust money may (i) be placed or retained upon deposit or current account at such rate of interest (if any) and upon such terms as the Trustees shall think fit with any bank investment company, building society, local authority or finance company or any United Kingdom office or branch of an insurance company established in the European Union (ii) be invested in any type of Unit Trust which is empowered to transact business with the trustees of pension schemes designed to satisfy the provisions of Part XIV Chapter I of the Income and Corporation Taxes Act 1988 be invested in underwriting or sub-underwriting new issues of stocks and shares (iii) be used to pay the premiums on any insurance policy the proceeds of which will fall to meet any benefit payable pursuant to the Rules or part thereof and (iv) be invested in or upon any stocks shares or securities of the Principal Company and Associated Companies (as hereinafter defined) and may be lent to or placed on deposit with any of the said Companies on such normal commercial terms and at such commercial rate of interest as the Trustees may arrange with the said Companies PROVIDED THAT no loan shall be granted to any member or to any individual having a contingent interest under the Scheme.

Appendix 9

Specimen Power of Amendment

(i) The Principal Company may at any time, and subject only to the following Rules of this Section, by deed, alter or repeal this Deed and all or any of the Rules whether retrospectively or otherwise for the time being in force or make any new Rules to the exclusion of or in addition to all or any of the existing Rules, and any Rules so made shall be deemed to be Rules of the same validity as if originally made and shall be subject in the same way to be altered or modified, provided that the approval of the scheme under Part XIV Chapter I of the Income and Corporation Taxes Act 1988 is not thereby prejudiced.

(ii) There shall be no alteration without the consent in writing of the Trustees.

(iii) PROVIDED THAT the trustees shall comply with the requirements of the Pension Act 1995 with regard to the modification of schemes.

Definition of Controlling Director — Appendix I to PN

A Controlling Director is defined in *ICTA 1988, 23 Sch 5(5)* as a person who is a director and within *paragraph (b)* of *section 417(5)* in relation to the employer company. For practical purposes this means a member who, at any time after 16 March 1987 and within ten years of retirement or leaving service or leaving *pensionable service*, has been a director and, either on his or her own or with one or more associates has beneficially owned or been able to control, directly, indirectly or through other companies, 20 per cent or more of the ordinary share capital of the company.

For the purposes of this definition:

(i) 'Associate' means in relation to a director, any relative (i.e. spouse, forebear, issue or sibling) or partner, the trustees of any settlement in relation to which the director is, or any relative of his or her (living or dead) is or was, a settlor and, where the director is interested in any shares or obligations of the company which are subject to any trust, or are part of the estate of a deceased person, the trustees or the settlement concerned, or as the case may be, the personal representatives of the deceased, and

(ii) the expression 'either on his or her own or with one or more associates' requires a person to be treated as owning or, as the case may be, controlling what any associate owns or controls, even if he or she does not own or control share capital on his or her own.

Appendix 11

Power to Make and Receive Transfer Payments

Subject to the provisions of the Pension Schemes Act 1993 and the Pensions Act 1995 and, where required, the prior consent of the Board of Inland Revenue:

[   ] The Trustees may, with the consent of the Principal Company, accept in respect of any Member a transfer from the trustees or administrator of another fund, scheme or arrangement approved under the Act or for the purpose of this Rule [   ] by the Board of Inland Revenue (referred to in this Rule [   ] as 'the other scheme') of all or any of the assets of the other scheme upon the footing that the Member's Credit shall be increased by the amount of value of the assets transferred, provided that:

(*a*)   no such transfer shall be made if the Actuary advises that it would cause any benefit payable under the Scheme to exceed the limits set out in Rule [   ], and

(*b*)   such part of the assets transferred as is derived from the contributions (if any) made to, or treated under it as having been made to, the other scheme (but only such part) shall be treated under the Scheme as having been derived from contributions made by the Member to the Scheme and shall be subject to such restrictions as to refunds and otherwise as are notified to the Trustees by the trustees or administrator of the other scheme on such transfer being made and as is necessary for the purpose of the continued approval of the Scheme under the Act.

[   ] The Trustees may, at the request of a Member, transfer to the trustees or administrator of any fund, scheme or arrangement which is certified by the trustees or administrator thereof to be approved under the Act or which is approved for the purposes of this Rule [   ] by the Board of Inland Revenue and in which the Member's employer participates (any such fund, scheme or arrangement being referred to in this Rule [   ] as 'the other Scheme') assets equal in value to the Member's Credit at the date of transfer upon the footing that such assets shall be applied under the other scheme in providing benefits (consistent with approval of the Scheme under the Act) in respect of the Member. The Trustees shall supply the trustees or administrator of the other scheme with such information relating to the Service of the Member and

458

any contributions made by him as may be requested by them. Upon any such transfer being made, the Member's Credit shall be extinguished with all entitlement relating thereto.

Appendix 12

Specimen Deed of Adherence

DEED OF ADHERENCE

DATED

PARTIES

(1) J BLACK AND SONS LIMITED
     30 The Common
     Anytown
     Blankshire ANl 2ZQ   ('the Principal Company')

(2) JAMES BLACK
     4 London Road
     Anytown
     Blankshire ANl 5PQ

     JESSICA BLACK
     4 London Road
     Anytown
     Blankshire ANl 5PQ

                                                      ('the Trustees')

(3) J BLACK AND SONS (CARDIFF) LIMITED
     34 High Street
     Cardiff CF2 lNS   ('the New Participating Company')

WHEREAS

(A) By an Interim Pension Trust Deed ('the Interim Deed') dated [   ]
     and made between (1) the Principal Company and (2) the Trustees there
     was established with effect from that date the J Black & Sons Ltd
     Pension Scheme ('the Scheme') for providing relevant benefits (as
     defined in *section 612(1)* of *ICTA 1988*) for certain employees of the
     Principal Company and certain other companies which might thereafter
     agree to participate in the Scheme.

(B) There was executed on   by (1) the Principal Company and (2) the Trustees a Definitive Pension Trust Deed ('the Definitive Deed') in accordance with the provisions of which and of the Rules scheduled thereto the Scheme is administered.

(C) The Principal Company pursuant to the provisions of Clause .... of the Definitive Deed may with the consent of the Trustees extend the benefits of the Scheme to companies subsidiary to or associated with the Principal Company.

(D) The Principal Company wishes to extend the benefits of the Scheme to employees of the New Participating Company and the Trustees consent is indicated by their execution hereof.

NOW THIS DEED WITNESSES AS FOLLOWS:-

1. The benefits of the Scheme are hereby extended to the New Participating Company and the participation of the New Participating Company in the Scheme is deemed to be effective from the ....

    .

2. The New Participating Company agrees to comply with the provisions of the Definitive Deed and the said Rules and any amendments thereto.

IN WITNESS WHEREOF etc.

Appendix 13

Inland Revenue

**Audit & Pension Schemes
Services**
Yorke House
PO Box 62
Castle Meadow Road
Nottingham   NG2 1BG

Telephone: 0115 974 0000
Fax: 0115 974 1480

To: Audit & Pension Schemes Services
Yorke House
PO Box 62
Castle Meadow Road
Nottingham
NG2 1BG

Date:

Your ref: SF ..../...................../...............

Our ref:

DISCONTINUANCE

NAME OF PRINCIPAL EMPLOYER ....

NAME OF SCHEME ....

The above scheme has been discontinued. Relevant details are shown below.

Scheme Closed	- Scheme rules have been amended to preclude new members from joining. The scheme still continues for existing members and contributions are still being made in respect of them.	
	- Date Closed to new members.	/ /
	- Date of birth of the youngest member.	/ /
Scheme Paid-Up	- No further contributions are being made but the assets of the scheme continue to be held by the Administrator to be applied in accordance with the scheme rules.	
	- Date paid-up.	/ /
	- Date of birth of the youngest member.	/ /
Scheme Wound-Up	- Scheme has ceased to exist. Assets have been applied to meet liabilities in accordance with the winding-up rules.	
	- Completion date.	/ /
Scheme Abandoned	- Scheme was in existence for only a short time and has been treated as if it never existed.	☐ ✓

See notes overleaf for further information and guidance.

From:

IR (SPSS) use only	
CORA notified	

NOTES

It is important that scheme administrators, or practitioners on their behalf, advise IR (SPSS) when a scheme is discontinued (other than schemes providing solely death-in-service benefits). This is so that we can keep accurate records. The following gives some guidance on our procedures and requirements on discontinuance. Please also see the Practice Notes IR12 (1997).

Scheme Paid-Up   If an employer goes into liquidation without a successor it is possible for a scheme to continue in paid-up form, rather than being wound-up, only with the prior agreement of IR (SPSS).

Scheme Wound-Up   **Normally you should notify IR (SPSS) after completion of winding-up.** This is the date when all benefits have been secured and any surplus funds dealt with.

Benefits for members should be secured in accordance with the rules of the scheme. There is no need to notify particulars to IR (SPSS) however, they reserve the right to call for particulars or to conduct an audit of benefits on selected cases.

Payments which give rise to tax liability should be reported to the local Tax Office dealing with the tax affairs of the scheme, i.e.

- refund of employees' contributions
- refund of employees' surplus AVCs
- commutation of the entire pension on grounds of triviality or serious ill-health. (In the event of serious ill-health commutation for a controlling director prior agreement must be obtained from IR (SPSS).)
- refund to employer(s). Please see note below.

Scheme not yet approved Full definitive documentation or a Documentation Certificate will be needed before exempt approval may be given to a closed or paid-up scheme.

Where a scheme begins winding-up before definitive documentation has been adopted IR (SPSS) will not insist that full definitive documentation is executed for the purposes of Inland Revenue approval in all cases, i.e.:

- Insured schemes which have been in existence for less than 2 years and have 100 or less members may usually be approved on receipt of a signed declaration on form PS 160 that the scheme has been administered in accordance with the requirements for approval. For further information see notes on PS 160.

- Self-administered schemes and those insured schemes not covered by the above paragraph may normally be approved after the execution of a short supplemental deed setting out the events which have occurred. The deed should contain similar wording to that on PS 160 and enabling powers for dealing with the scheme assets and any benefits already in payment. Small self-administered schemes should, in addition, comply with the SSAS Regulations [SI 1991 No 1614]. This entails reporting disposals of investments covered by the Regulations.

Refund to Employer(s)   **No repayment should be made to the employer without the prior written agreement of IR (SPSS).** Where surplus funds arise on winding-up and it is proposed to refund monies to the employer(s) particulars must be provided to IR (SPSS) at the earliest opportunity. The necessary arrangements will then be made for the payment of tax under section 601 ICTA 1988 so that an interest charge can be avoided.

Block transfers   When as part of the winding-up of the scheme groups of employees are joining other schemes, IR (SPSS) must be given full particulars on form PS 295 for **prior agreement** to the transfer of assets or payments from one scheme to another.

Scheme Abandoned   **Scheme not yet approved**
If the scheme is insured, has less than 100 members, and none of the members have completed two years qualifying service, IR (SPSS) will normally accept the request for abandonment of the scheme (PS 14.14 refers).

Scheme approved
As approval will have to be cancelled, you should write to IR (SPSS) before abandoning the scheme (Do not send the PS 199 at this stage). If IR (SPSS) advise that approval can be cancelled, send in a completed form PS 199 when the abandonment has taken place.

Appendix 14

Trustees Declaration Adopting PSO Model Rules for SSAS Winding-up

'We   being the Trustees of   (the Scheme) declare that the attached schedule of rules entitled Model Rules for Small Self-Administered Pension Schemes are hereby adopted and shall stand as part of the governing instrument of the Scheme.

We also declare that the Scheme has since its inception been administered in a manner consistent with approval under Chapter I Part XIV of the Income and Corporation Taxes Act 1988 and the Retirement Benefit Schemes (Restriction on Discretion to Approve) (Small Self-Administered Schemes) Regulations 1991.'

(See 3.58)

Appendix 15

Small Self-Administered Schemes

[1] Notwithstanding anything to the contrary in the Scheme provisions the following rules [2 to 8] shall have full effect except that they may not be construed as conferring powers on the Trustees which they do not otherwise have by virtue of the Trust Deed and Rules.

(1) In these rules the following expression shall have the meanings ascribed to them:

[See Note 2]

(a) "Business" includes:
(i) a trade or profession, or
(ii) any activity other than investment carried on by a body of persons, whether corporate or unincorporate, or
(iii) any activity carried on by a holding company for a trading group.

(b) "Close Company" has the meaning given by sections 414 and 415 of the Act.

(c) "Company" means anybody corporate or unincorporated association, but does not include a partnership.

(d) "Control" in relation to a body corporate (other than a close company) or partnership shall be construed in accordance with section 840 of the Act and in relation to an unincorporated association that section shall be applied as it applies to a body corporate.

In relation to a Close Company "control" shall be construed in accordance with section 416 of the Act.

(e) "Ordinary Annual Contribution" means for the purpose of the Rule [2] the smaller of:
(i) the amount found—

[See Note 7]

(A) where the scheme has been established for three years or more at the time of any borrowing, by dividing the amount of the contributions paid by employers in the period of three years which ended at the end of the previous accounting period of the scheme by three, [or,

(B) where the scheme has been established for less than three years at the time of any borrowing, by dividing the amount of the contributions paid by employers in the period since the scheme was established ending at the time of that borrowing by the number of years falling within that period (a part of a year being counted as one year,] and
(ii) the amount of the annual contributions which, within the period of 3 years immediately preceding the date of the borrowing, an Actuary has advised in writing would be necessary to secure the benefits payable under the Scheme.

(f) "Pensioneer Trusts" means a Trustee of the Scheme who:
(i) is approved by the Board of Inland Revenue to act as such, and
(ii) is not connected with a Scheme Member, another Trustee or an Employer.

(g) "Private Company" means a company which is not officially listed on a recognised stock exchange within the meaning of section 841 of the Act.

(h) "relative" means a brother, sister, ancestor or lineal descendant.

(i) "Residential Property" means property normally used, or adapted for use as one or more dwellings.

465

(j) "Scheme Member" means a member of the Scheme to whom benefit is currently accruing by virtue of service as an employee.

(2) For the purpose of these rules any question of whether a person is connected with another shall be determined as follows:

(a) a person is connected with an individual if that person is the individual's spouse or is a Relative or the spouse of a Relative of the individual or of the individual's spouse;

(b) a Scheme Member is connected with an Employer if:

(i) the Employer is a partnership and the Scheme Member is connected with a partner, or

(ii) the Employer is a Company and the Scheme Member or any person connected with him or her is, or has been during the last 10 years a Controlling Director of the Company;

(c) a Company is connected with another Company if:
(i) the same person has Control of both, or
(ii) a person has Control of one and persons connected with that person have Control of the other, or
(iii) a person has Control of one and that person and persons connected with that person have control over the other;

(d) a Company is connected with another person if that person has Control of it or if that person and a person or persons connected with him or her together have control of it;

(e) any two or more persons acting together to secure or exercise Control of a Company shall be treated in relation to that Company as connected one with another and with any person acting on the directions of any of them to secure or exercise Control of the Company.

(3) For the purpose of these rules a company is associated with an Employer if (directly or indirectly) the Employer controls that company or that company controls the Employer or if both are controlled by a third person.

(4) For the purpose of these rules a member of the Scheme includes:

(a) a Scheme Member,

(b) a person in receipt of a pension from the Scheme, or

(c) a person who has been a Scheme Member.

[2] Provisions as to borrowing

Any power of the Trustees to borrow shall be restricted so that, at the time of any borrowing the Trustees shall not have borrowed and not repaid an aggregate amount including the amount of that borrowing in excess of the total of:

(a) three times the Ordinary Annual Contribution, and

(b) three times the annual amount of contributions paid or payable as a condition of membership by Scheme Members in the year of assessment ending immediately before that time, and

(c) the amount found by the formula—

$$\frac{(A - B) \times 45}{100}$$

where—

A is the market value of the assets of the Scheme at that time, other than assets franking any pension in payment under the rules of the Scheme where the purchase of an annuity has been deferred (including any pension that would be payable to a widow or widower of a member of the scheme following the member's death in a case where the rules of the Scheme limit such pension to the person to whom the member was married at retirement), and

B is the aggregate of any sums borrowed to purchase those assets which are outstanding at that time, and any other liabilities incurred by the trustees which are outstanding at that time, other than liabilities to pay benefits under the Scheme

[3] Provisions as to investment

The Trustees' powers of investment shall be restricted to preclude investment either directly or indirectly in:

[See Note 8]

(a) personal chattels other than [choses in action] [moveable property other than incorporeal moveable property]; or

Residential Property other than that which is, or is to be, occupied:
(i) by an employee who is not connected with his or her Employer and who is required as a condition of employment to occupy that property, or
(ii) by a person other than a Scheme Member or a person connected with a Scheme Member where that person also occupies connected business premises which are also held by the Trustees as an investment of the Scheme; or

(c) Stock or shares in a Private Company which:
(i) carry more than thirty per cent of the voting power in the Company, or
(ii) entitle the holder to more than thirty per cent of any dividends declared by the Company in respect of shares of the class held.

For the purposes of this rule the Trustees are not regarded as

(A) holding a Residential Property where they hold as an investment units in a unit trust scheme
(i) which is an authorised unit trust scheme within the meaning of section 468(6) of the Act, or
(ii) an exempt unit trust within the meaning of section 96 of the Capital Gains Tax Act 1979, and
(iii) that unit trust scheme holds Residential Property as an investment.

(B) indirectly holding as an investment Residential Property other than that specified in paragraph (b) where—
(i) they hold as an investment subject to the trusts of the Scheme a right which confers entitlement to receive payment of any rentcharge, ground annual, feu duty or other annual payment reserved in respect of, or charged on or issuing out of, that property, and
(ii) the property is not occupied by a scheme member or a person connected with him.

[4] The Trustees in the capacity shall not directly or indirectly lend money:

(a) to a member of the Scheme or to a person who is connected with a member of the Scheme other than an Employer or any Company associated with an Employer; or

(b) to an Employer or a Company associated with an Employer unless the loan is:
(i) utilised for the purpose of the borrower's Business, and
(ii) for a fixed term, and
(iii) at a commercial rate of interest, and
(iv) evidenced by an agreement in writing which contains all the conditions on which it is made and, in particular, the provisions specified in paragraph c. below;

(c) the provisions specified in this paragraph are that the lending shall be repaid immediately if:
(i) the borrower is in breach of the conditions of the agreement; or
(ii) the borrower ceases to carry on business; or

(iii) the borrower becomes insolvent within the meaning defined for the purposes of Regulation 6 of the Retirement Benefit Schemes (Restriction on Discretion to Approved) (Small Self-administered Schemes) Regulations 1991; or

(iv) the money is required to enable the Trustees to pay benefits which have already become due under the Scheme.

[5] At the time any money is lent, or any shares in the Employer or any company associated with an Employer are acquired, the aggregate of:

(a) the amount outstanding of any lending to an Employer and/or a Company associated with an Employer made in accordance with Rule[4]b and c above, and

(b) the market value of stock and shares in an Employer and/or a Company associated with an Employer held by the Trustees in that capacity

shall not, where that time is after the end of a period of two years from the date on which the Scheme was established, exceed the amount found by the formula—

$$\frac{(E - F) \times 50}{100}$$

where—

E is the market value at the time in question of all the assets of the Scheme, other than assets franking any pension in payment under the rules of the Scheme where the purchase of an annuity has been deferred (including any pension that would be payable to a widow or widower of a member of the Scheme following the member's death in a case where the rules of the Scheme limit such pension to the person to whom the member was married at retirement), and

F is the aggregate of any sums borrowed to purchase those assets which are outstanding at that time, and any other liabilities incurred by the Trustees which are outstanding at that time, other than liabilities to pay benefits under the Scheme.

[See Note 9] [and shall not, where that time is during the period of two years from the date in which the Scheme was established, exceed the amount found of the formula—

$$\frac{(C - D) \times 25}{100}$$

where—

C is the market value at the time in question of the assets of the Scheme which are derived from contributions made by an Employer and by employees since the Scheme was established, other than assets franking any pension in payment under the rules of the Scheme where the purchase of an annuity has been deferred (including any pension that would be payable to a widow or widower of a member of the Scheme following the member's death in a case where the rules of the Scheme limit such pension to the person to whom the member was married at retirement), and

D is the aggregate of any sums borrowed to purchase those assets which are outstanding at that time, and any other liabilities incurred by the Trustees which are outstanding at that time, other than liabilities to pay benefits under the Scheme.]

[6] Provisions as to transactions with members of the Scheme

The Trustees in that capacity shall not directly or indirectly purchase, sell or lease any investment or asset from or to a member of the Scheme or a person (other than an Employer or a company associated with an Employer) connected with a member. A purchase will not be construed as being an indirect purchase from a member of the Scheme or a connected person if at the time of purchase 3 or more years have elapsed since the investment or asset was owned by the member or connected person. A sale will not be construed as an indirect sale to a member of the Scheme or a connected person if the purchase by the member or connected person takes place 3 years or more after the sale by the Trustees.

[7] Provisions as to transactions with Employers and associated companies

The Trustees in that capacity shall not directly or indirectly purchase, sell or lease any investment or asset from or to an Employer or a Company associated with an Employer except in accordance with independent professional advice obtained in writing.

[8] Provisions as to Pensioneer Trustees

One of the Trustees shall be a Pensioneer Trustee and the appointment of that trustee and his obligation and entitlement to act as a Pensioneer Trustee, shall be incapable of termination at any time except:

(a) by the death of the trustee,

(b) by an order of the court,

(c) by virtue of section 3, 4 or 29 of the Pensions Act 1995 or Article 3, 4 or 29 of the Pensions (Northern Ireland) Order 1995 (prohibition, suspension or disqualification),

(d) by withdrawal by the Board of Inland Revenue of their approval of the trustee to act as a Pensioneer Trustee, or

(e) where termination occurs by virtue of the trustee having committed a fraudulent breach of trust in relation to the scheme

(f) where another trustee is appointed to act as Pensioneer Trustee in place of the trustee, and the appointment of the other trustee takes effect at the same time as the termination.

The appointment of a successor to the former Pensioneer Trustee shall, except where (f) above applies, be made no more than 30 days after the termination.

NOTES

1 All the passages in square brackets are either optional, or indicate permissible alternatives.

2 It is assumed that the rules will contain acceptable definitions of the terms, Actuary, Administrator, Controlling Director, Dependent (this term to include "widow" or "widower"), Incapacity and Trustees. Care is required to ensure that terms defined for the purpose of these rules do not conflict with terms defined for the purposes of the Scheme generally.

3 It is assumed that "Employer" means the current Employer of a Member participating in the Scheme.

4. Paragraphs 1 (c) (ii) and 2 (c) (ii) may not be acceptable if the Scheme's normal retirement age is unusually low.

5 Paragraphs 3 and 4 (c) may be omitted if the Scheme does not permit late retirers to take benefits at Normal Retirement Date under PN 7.43.

6 See paragraph 28 of Memorandum No 108.

7 The words in square brackets may be excluded where this rule is adopted more than 3 years after the establishment of the Scheme.

8 The second alternative should be substituted for the first in schemes subject to the law of Scotland.

9 The words in square brackets may be excluded where this rule is adopted more than 2 years after the establishment of the Scheme.

10   *Where fluctuating emoluments* have not been paid for the full 3 years, they should be averaged over the period from the commencement of their entitlement to payment (or the beginning of the 3 year period, if later) to the end of the relevant basic pay year. Where, however, it is proposed to include in final remuneration a *fluctuating emolument* which was payable in a single year only the agreement of the Pension Schemes Office must be sought.

Appendix 16

Model SSAS Rules to cover the transitional provisions

Example A

Suggested wording for transitional provisions in Model Documentation

Subject to the exception set out below on or after 15 July 1991 the Trustees in that capacity shall not directly purchase, sell or lease any investment or asset to or from a member of the Scheme or a person (other than an Employer or a Subsidiary Company) Connected with him *except that the Trustees may sell to a member of the Scheme any investment or asset which they owned before 15 July 1991.* A purchase will not be construed as being an indirect purchase from a member of the Scheme or a person Connected with him if at the time of purchase three or more years have elapsed since the investment.

(NB The words in italics have been introduced to cover the transitional provisions.)

Example B

The following should be inserted immediately prior to the Model Rules for Small Self-Administered Pension Schemes incorporated within your document.

'The following Inland Revenue [Provisions][Rules][Clauses] shall be operative from the Fifth day of August One thousand nine hundred and ninety-one

(i)   The effect of [sub-rules][sub-clauses][see Note 1], [see Note 2] and [see Note 3] below shall not be to limit or nullify any such transaction proscribed thereunder already undertaken prior to the Fifteenth day of July One thousand nine hundred and ninety-one

(ii) Where a proscribed transaction has been undertaken in relation to [sub-rule][sub-clause][see Note 3] below prior to the Fifteenth day of July One thousand nine hundred and ninety-one the effect of [sub-rule][sub-clause][see Note 3] below shall not be to limit or nullify

471

the Trustees' power to sell to a member of the Scheme or Connected person the specific asset or investment comprising such transaction'.

Notes
1.   Insert the number of the provision relating to Investment.
2.   Insert the number of the provision relating to limits on Loans.
3.   Insert the number of the provision relating to Transactions with members of the Scheme.

Inland Revenue

For official use only		
REJ		INT
ACC		APP
		FUL

OCCUPATIONAL PENSION SCHEMES
APPLICATION FOR APPROVAL

Ref No

SCHEME OPEN TO MORE THAN ONE EMPLOYEE

An application for approval under Chapter I Part XIV Income and Corporation Taxes Act (ICTA) 1988 (as amended) for a scheme open to more than one employee must be made on this form, completed in accordance with the Notes on Completion (PS 176 (Notes)).

PLEASE COMPLETE IN BLOCK CAPITALS

A. PRINCIPAL EMPLOYER INFORMATION   *see note*

Name of employer	1
Employer's address	2
Nature of business	3
Status of employer *(enter code – see key in notes)*	4
Company Registration Number *(if applicable)*	5
Employer's accounting date	6
Employer's Tax District	7
Employer's Tax District reference	8
Employer's PAYE Tax District	9
Employer's PAYE Tax District reference	10
Is the employer carrying on a trade in the UK? (Y/N)	11
Is the employer resident in the UK for tax purposes? (Y/N)	12

B. BASIC SCHEME INFORMATION

Name of scheme	13
Type of scheme *(enter code – see key in notes)*	14
Scheme year end date	15

C. PRACTITIONER INFORMATION

Name of Practitioner No.	16
Address No.	17
Practitioner's reference	18

PS 176 *(4/01)*

Appendix 17

D. SCHEME INFORMATION   see note

Date of commencement ☐☐☐☐☐☐ 19
Date of first premium/contribution ☐☐☐☐☐☐ 20
Total expected contributions to be paid by ALL participating employers to this scheme in first year £ ☐☐☐☐☐☐ 21
Percentage of scheme contributions payable by the principal employer in respect of own employees ☐☐☐ % 22
Employee contributions (as percentage of remuneration) ☐☐☐ % 23
NRA (M) ☐☐   or NRA Range (M) ☐☐.☐☐ 24
(F) ☐☐   (F) ☐☐.☐☐

E. SCHEME DOCUMENTATION

INTERIM *(tick if accompanying application)* ☐
- Date of establishment ☐☐☐☐☐☐ 25
- Is document standard? (Y/N) ☐ 26
- Standard reference number *(if applicable)* ☐☐☐☐☐☐☐☐☐☐☐☐ 1 27
- Amended? *(tick if applicable)* ☐ 2 28
DEFINITIVE *(tick if accompanying application)* ☐
- Date of establishment ☐☐☐☐☐☐ 25
- Is document standard? (Y/N) ☐ 26
- Standard reference number *(if applicable)* ☐☐☐☐☐☐☐☐☐☐☐☐ 2 27
- Amended? *(tick if applicable)* ☐ 2 28
The rules adopted are *appropriate* for this scheme *(tick if applicable)* ☐ 29

F. DIRECTOR INFORMATION

Does the current membership include Controlling Directors of the principal employer? (Y/N) ☐ 30

Details of each Controlling Director 31

	Title	Initials	Surname	Date of birth	Date of joining company
1					
2					
3					
4					
5					

	NI Number	Current pensionable earnings	Retained benefits? (Y/N)
1		£	
2		£	
3		£	
4		£	
5		£	

Appendix 17

G. SCHEME BENEFITS INFORMATION _{see note} 32

Benefits to be provided by the scheme (tick appropriate boxes)

Defined Benefits	1	Pension on Retirement	3	Lump Sum by commutation	5
Money Purchase	2	Death in Service Benefits	4	Separate Lump Sum	6

H. SCHEME ADMINISTRATOR

Is the principal employer the Scheme Administrator? (Y/N)   33

Name of Administrator   34

Address of Administrator
for official correspondence

Please complete and return PS 176 (A/T) in relation to all of the trustees/sponsors of the scheme.

I. SCHEME MEMBERSHIP INFORMATION

Number of members   35

Date first employee notified (see s590(2)(b) ICTA 1988)   36

Is scheme membership discretionary? (Y/N)   37

Pensionable earnings of highest paid scheme member   £   38

J. FUNDING

Nature of scheme investment *(tick one box)*   Insured   1

Self-administered   2   39

Unfunded   3

K. SMALL SELF-ADMINISTERED SCHEMES ONLY

Name of Pensioneer Trustee

Address of Pensioneer Trustee
for official correspondence

Have there been any transactions of the kind described in regulation 5 of the Retirement Benefits Schemes (Information Powers) Regulations 1995 prior to the date of this application? (Y/N)   40

If yes, please ensure that the relevant forms are completed and attached.

At the date of the application is the Pensioneer Trustee (along with other trustees) a co-signatory to all scheme bank/building society accounts and a co-owner of all scheme assets? (Y/N)   41

Appendix 17

L. DECLARATION BY TRUSTEES (OR SCHEME SPONSOR IF NON-TRUST SCHEME) see note

I/We hereby apply for approval of the retirement benefits scheme named in Section B of this form under Chapter I Part XIV ICTA 1988 (as amended). 42

I/We declare that to the best of my/our knowledge and belief the information given in this application is correct and complete and further declare that:-

a) the scheme has been bona fide established for the sole purpose of providing approvable relevant benefits, and

b) there is no intention of taking any action, if approval is granted, other than in accordance with the approved terms of the trust deed and rules, and all statutory and published Inland Revenue conditions for the approval and continued approval of the scheme.

     Signatures(s)   Date(s)   Please print names here

Tick if above are signing as scheme sponsors of a non-trust scheme

This declaration must be signed by <u>all</u> of the scheme trustees/sponsors. Please attach photocopies of this page if further space is required.

M. DOCUMENTS TO ACCOMPANY APPLICATION

A copy of the Interim Deed establishing the scheme, if non-standard. 43

A copy of the Definitive Deed and/or rules governing the scheme, if non-standard.

PS 176(A/T)(s).

If a Self-administered scheme or an insured scheme which falls within the Pension Scheme Surpluses (Valuation) Regulations 1987 [SI 1987 No 412], a copy of the initial valuation report or advice (signed by an Actuary) on which funding is based.

If a Small Self-administered Scheme, a list of current investments of the scheme and transaction notification forms as appropriate (section K refers).

PS 274(s) for participating employers.

N. SUBMITTING THE APPLICATION

Please ensure that all relevant sections have been fully completed. Incomplete applications will be rejected. Send the completed application form together with all relevant documents (see section M) to:-

       Applications Section
       Inland Revenue (Savings, Pensions, Share Schemes)
       Yorke House
       P O Box 62
       Castle Meadow Road
       Nottingham
       NG2 1BG

(Please do not staple this form and keep applications and general correspondence for IR (Savings, Pensions, Share Schemes) in separate mailings.)

Appendix 17

Notes on Completion of Application Form PS 176

General

The Application Form PS 176 should be completed in respect of the principal or only employer. If there are further participating employers, form PS 274 should be completed in respect of each of them and should accompany the application for approval.

All questions should be answered in full: "None" or "Not Applicable" should be entered where appropriate. Blank spaces, or "to be advised" are not acceptable and may result in the application being rejected as incomplete. **This may affect the date of approval granted to the scheme.** Ticks (✓), Yes (Y) or No (N) should be used where indicated. Where there is insufficient space on the form a separate sheet may be used as necessary.

A.	**PRINCIPAL EMPLOYER INFORMATION**

1.   Name of principal or only employer.

2.   Address of principal or only employer - registered office if a company; principal place of business if an individual or partnership.

3.   Nature of business of principal or only employer.

4.   Enter code representing status of employer as appropriate;

    1 - PLC

    2 - Limited Company

    3 - Unlimited Company

    4 - Partnership

    5 - Sole Trader

    6 - Charity   (See notes 7 and 8)

    7 - Friendly Society

    8 - Other   (Please give details)

    9 - Public Sector

5.   Please enter the 9 digit Company Registration Number, if applicable. This can be obtained from Companies House.

6.   Employer's accounting date in DD/MM format.

7.   Enter the name of the employer's Schedule D or corporation tax district. For Charities, please enter FICO in all cases even if there is also a Schedule D district.

8.   Enter the reference number of the employer's Schedule D or corporation tax district. For Charities, please quote FICO reference number in all cases, even if there is also a Schedule D district.

9.   Enter the name of the PAYE tax district.

10. Enter the reference number of the PAYE tax district.

11. Enter N if the Inspector of Taxes regards the company as an investment company for tax purposes.

12. If you do not know this please contact the local Tax Office responsible for the principal employer's registered office/principal place of business address.

[1]   **PS 176 (Notes)** *(4/01)*

477

Appendix 17

B. BASIC SCHEME INFORMATION

13. Name of scheme as in governing document.

14. Enter code representing the type of scheme as appropriate;

    03 - Insured Earmarked Scheme with only one member at outset.

    04 - Insured Earmarked Scheme with more than one member at outset.

    05 - Insured Common Trust Fund.

    06 - Self-Managed Fund - Practice Notes IR12 (1997) (PN) 16.90 refers.

    08 - Small Self-administered Scheme – PN 20.1 refers.

    09 - Large Self-administered Scheme - a self-administered scheme with 12 or more members.

    10 - Unfunded Scheme.

15. Enter the date the scheme year ends in DD/MM format. See definition regulation 2 of the Retirement Benefits Schemes (Information Powers) Regulations 1995.

C. PRACTITIONER INFORMATION

16. Name of Practitioner submitting the application and Practitioner number (if known).

17. Address of Practitioner and Practitioner address number (if known) - address to which correspondence should be sent.

18. Practitioner's reference number to be quoted on correspondence.

D. SCHEME INFORMATION

19. Date of commencement of scheme.

20. Date of payment of first premium or first contribution to the scheme.

21. Total contributions should include ordinary annual contributions and special contributions.

22. Give an indication of the approximate level of contributions to the scheme by the principal or only employer as a percentage of the total contributions paid by the employer and his employees (excluding employees' AVC's). (It is a condition of Inland Revenue approval that the employer makes a significant contribution of not less than 10% of the total).

23. Give an indication of the expected approximate level of employee contributions (including AVC's) as a percentage of the employee's remuneration.

24. State Normal Retirement Age or age range for males and females.

2

478

Appendix 17

E. SCHEME DOCUMENTATION

25. Date of execution of Deed.

26. Indicate (Y/N) whether the documentation is based on standard documentation agreed or under negotiation with Pension Schemes Technical Advice, part of IR (Savings, Pensions, Share Schemes).

27. If standard, enter the SF reference number of the document.

Completion of these boxes and the signing of the application form removes the need for submitting a signed Inland Revenue Documentation Certificate.

28. If, exceptionally, the agreed wording has been added to or amended in any way this should be indicated (✓) and a marked up copy of the standard document should be enclosed identifying all differences.

29. *Appropriate* rules means those used for the purpose designated, as agreed with Pension Schemes Technical Advice, part of IR (Savings, Pensions, Share Schemes).

F. DIRECTOR INFORMATION

30. Indicate (Yes/No) whether current scheme membership includes Controlling Directors of the principal employer (formerly 20% Directors) as defined in PN Glossary.

31. Provide full details of each Controlling Director, continuing on a separate sheet in similar format if necessary. Retained benefits are defined in PN Glossary.

G. SCHEME BENEFITS INFORMATION

32. Indicate type of benefits to be provided by ticking the appropriate boxes.

H. SCHEME ADMINISTRATOR

33. Enter N if the principal employer is not the Scheme Administrator (section 611AA(8) ICTA 1988 refers).

34. Enter details of the person(s) appointed to act as administrator of the scheme. If no such appointment made leave blank as the trustees (or the scheme sponsor(s) in the case of a non-trust scheme) will be the legal administrator under the above legislation.

I. SCHEME MEMBERSHIP INFORMATION

35. Enter the approximate number of employees of ALL participating employers joining the scheme at commencement.

36. Enter the date when members were first notified of their rights to benefit under the scheme.

37. Enter N if the employees (subject to their meeting the scheme eligibility criteria) have an automatic right to join the scheme or Y if entry is at the discretion of the employer or Administrator.

38. Enter current pensionable earnings of highest-paid member.

Appendix 17

J. FUNDING

39.   Tick relevant box to indicate how the scheme funds are invested at the outset

   1 - wholly insured at outset.

   2 - wholly or partly self-administered at outset.

   3 - not funded.

K. SMALL SELF ADMINISTERED SCHEMES ONLY

40.   The relevant forms relating to scheme investments are as follows

   PS 7012 – Land or Buildings
   PS 7013 – Loans to Employers and Associated Companies
   PS 7014 – Shares in Employer, "Associated" or Unlisted Companies
   PS 7015 – Scheme Borrowing
   PS 7016 – Miscellaneous Acquisitions, Sales and Leases

41.   The Pensioneer Trustee is not required to be a co-signatory to a scheme account that only gives rise to a liability, such as loan or overdraft accounts. For land/property, the Pensioneer Trustee may, where possible, register a legally binding "restriction" instead of being a registered co-owner (a "caution" in respect of land registered at the Land Registers of Northern Ireland is not acceptable). The Pensioneer Trustee must be a co-signatory to any management arrangement between the trustees and the fund manager/broker where scheme assets are held under an investment management arrangement.

L. DECLARATION BY TRUSTEES (OR SCHEME SPONSOR IF NON-TRUST SCHEME)

42.   The application/declaration must be signed by **all** scheme trustees in the case of a trust scheme and by the scheme sponsor(s) in the case of a non-trust scheme. Full details of all scheme trustees/sponsors should be shown on form PS 176 (A/T).

   Approvable relevant benefits are relevant benefits (as defined by section 612(1) ICTA 1988) which could be provided by a scheme approved under Chapter 1 Part XIV ICTA 1988.

M. DOCUMENTS TO ACCOMPANY APPLICATION

43.   A Contracted-out Money Purchase Scheme established for less than 12 members and accepting only minimum payments and incentive payments under SSA 1986 need not provide a valuation report or list of investments.

Data Protection

The Inland Revenue is a Data Controller under the Data Protection Act. We hold information for the purposes specified in our notification made to the Data Protection Commissioner, and may use this information for any of them.

We may get information about you from others, or we may give information to them. If we do, it will only be as the law permits to
- check accuracy of information
- prevent or detect crime
- protect public funds.

We may check information we receive about you with what is already in our records. This can include information provided by you as well as others such as other government departments. We will not give information about you to anyone outside the Inland Revenue unless the law permits us to do so.

480

Appendix 18

Audit & Pension Schemes Services
Yorke House
PO Box 62
Castle Meadow Road
Nottingham   NG2 1BG

DOCUMENTATION CERTIFICATE – TO OBTAIN SCHEME APPROVAL

Certificate for the purposes of approval under Chapter I Part XIV ICTA 1988.

Name of Employer ....

Name of Scheme ....

....

Ref No (if already known)   SF ..../.................................

Practitioner Reference ....

I/We certify

    a. that the above Scheme was established by trust deed/exchange* letter dated ..../........./..........., and

    b. has adopted standard/model * rules which accord in **all** respects with standard/model* documents agreed under reference SF ⌊_ _ _⌊_ _ _⌊_ _ _⌊_ _ _⌋ [1], and

    c. that, in my/our opinion, the rules adopted by the Scheme are appropriate [2].

In addition, I/we undertake

    d. to notify IR (SPSS) of any alteration to the Scheme of which I/we become aware.

delete as appropriate

Signature(s)	This certificate must be signed by one of the following:
	(i) the Scheme Administrator
Name(s)	(ii) a director of the Life Office with whom the scheme funds are wholly or partly insured, or an employee of that company who is authorised to sign such a certificate on its behalf
and professional pensions qualification(s) (if any)	
Capacity	
(administrator or practitioner)	(iii) a legal practitioner
	(iv) a Fellow of the Institute or Faculty of Actuaries
Name of Practitioner Company (if appropriate)	(v) a Fellow of the Pensions Management Institute
....	
....	

Date   ..../........./.................

Notes:

1.   Enter SF reference number of standard/model rule document.

2.   Appropriate rules means those used for the purpose designated, as agreed with Pension Schemes Technical Advice, part of IR (Savings, Pensions, Share Schemes).

3.   This certificate must accompany any notification of alteration of the Scheme in lieu of the Scheme rules where those rules accord with agreed standard documentation.

4.   IR (SPSS) reserves the right to call for copies of the documentation of any particular scheme.

5.   A false declaration of facts concerning the Scheme or its administration may result in the non-approval of the Scheme or withdrawal/loss of approval.

Appendix 19

**Audit & Pension Schemes
Services**
Yorke House
PO Box 62
Castle Meadow Road
Nottingham NG2 1BG

DOCUMENTATION CERTIFICATE – TO AMEND A STANDARD ON AN APPROVED SCHEME

Certificate for the purposes of continued approval under Chapter I Part XIV ICTA 1988.

Name of Employer   ....

Name of Scheme   ....

....

Ref No   SF ..../....................................

Practitioner Reference   ....

I/We certify

    a.   that the above Scheme was amended by standard/model* rule amendment dated ...., which accords in **all** respects with the standard/model amendment document agreed under reference number SF |⌴_⌴_⌴_⌴_⌴_⌴_⌴_⌴_⌴_⌴_⌴_⌴_⌴_⌴|[(1)], and

    b.   that, in my/our opinion, the rule amendment adopted by the Scheme is appropriate[(2)].

In addition, I/we undertake

    c.   to notify IR (SPSS) of any alteration to the Scheme of which I/we become aware.

* delete as appropriate

Signature(s)   ....

Name(s)   ....
and professional pensions qualification(s) (if any)

Capacity   ....
(administrator or practitioner)

Name of Practitioner Company (if appropriate)

....

....

Date   ..../........./...................

This certificate must be signed by one of the following:
(i)   the Scheme Administrator
(ii) a director of the Life Office with whom the scheme funds are wholly or partly insured, or an employee of that company who is authorised to sign such a certificate on its behalf
(iii) a legal practitioner
(iv) a Fellow of the Institute or Faculty of Actuaries
(v) a Fellow of the Pensions Management Institute

Notes:

1.   Enter SF reference number of standard/model rule amended.

2.   Amended rules means those used for the purpose designated, as agreed with the Pension Schemes Technical Advice, part of IR (Savings, Pensions, Share Schemes).

3.   This certificate must accompany any notification of alteration of the Scheme in lieu of the Scheme rules where those rules accord with agreed standard documentation.

4.   IR (SPSS) reserves the right to call for copies of the documentation of any particular scheme.

5.   A false declaration of facts concerning the Scheme or its administration may result in the non-approval of the Scheme or withdrawal/loss of approval.

Part of IR Savings, Pensions, Share Schemes   Business Director: Roger Hurcombe   **PS 6** (4/01)

Appendix 20

OCCUPATIONAL PENSION SCHEMES
CENTRALISED SCHEME –

PARTICIPATING EMPLOYERS

Information required under regulation 6 of The Retirement Benefits Schemes (Information Powers) Regulations 1995

The Administrator *(see note 1)* is required to supply the following information **not later than 180 days** after the end of the scheme year in which the participation commences. **Failure to do so may lead to penalties under section 98 Taxes Management Act 1970.**

Each request for IR (SPSS) approval of the participation of an employer in a pension scheme approved or being considered for approval under Chapter I Part XIV Income and Corporation Taxes Act (ICTA) 1988 (as amended) must be made on this form, completed in accordance with the Notes on Completion (PS 274 (Notes)).

PLEASE COMPLETE IN BLOCK CAPITALS

A. PARTICIPATING EMPLOYER INFORMATION	see note
Name of employer	2
Employer's address	3
Nature of business	4
Status of employer *(enter code – see key in notes)*	5
Company Registration Number *(if applicable)*	6
Employer's accounting date	7
Employer's Tax District	8
Employer's Tax District reference	9
Employer's PAYE Tax District	10
Employer's PAYE Tax District reference	11
Is the employer carrying on a trade in the UK? (Y/N)	12
Is the employer resident in the UK for tax purposes?(Y/N)	13

B. BASIC SCHEME INFORMATION	
Reference number	14
Name of scheme	15

PS 274 *(4/01)*

Appendix 20

C. SCHEME INFORMATION ^{see note}

Date participation commenced 16

Scheme year end date 17

Are the principal and participating employers associated? (Y/N) 18

Degree of association 19

Total expected contributions by the participating employer to this scheme in the first year £ 20

Employee contributions (as percentage of remuneration) % 21

Pensionable earnings of highest paid scheme member of this employer £ 22

Percentage of scheme contributions payable by participating employer in respect of own employees % 23

D. PRACTITIONER INFORMATION

Name of Practitioner No. 24

Address No. 25

Practitioner's reference 26

E. DIRECTOR INFORMATION

Does the current membership include Controlling Directors of the participating employer? (Y/N) 27

Details of each Controlling Director 28

	Title	Initials	Surname	Date of birth	Date of joining company
1					
2					
3					
4					
5					

	NI Number	Current pensionable earnings	Retained benefits? (Y/N)
1		£	
2		£	
3		£	
4		£	
5		£	

484

F. DECLARATION BY ADMINISTRATOR

see note

29

I/We hereby apply for IR (SPSS) approval of the participation of the above employer in the retirement benefits scheme named in Section B of this form. I/We declare that to the best of my/our knowledge and belief the information given in this application is correct and complete.

Signatures(s)	Date(s)	Please print names here
....	....	
....	....	
....	....	
....	....	

Please use photocopies of this page if further space is required.

G. DOCUMENTS TO ACCOMPANY APPLICATION

A copy of the Deed of Adherence or other instrument binding the employer in Section A to observe the scheme rules and conditions.

H. SUBMITTING THE APPLICATION

Please ensure that all relevant sections have been fully completed. Incomplete applications will be rejected. Send the completed application form together with all relevant documents (see section G) to:-

Applications Section
Inland Revenue (Savings, Pensions, Share Schemes)
Yorke House
P O Box 62
Castle Meadow Road
Nottingham
NG2 1BG

(Please do not staple this form and keep applications and general correspondence for IR (Savings, Pensions, Share Schemes) in separate mailings.)

485

Appendix 20

General

The Application Form PS 176 should be completed in respect of the principal or only employer. If there are further participating employers, form PS 274 should be completed in respect of each of them.

All questions should be answered in full: "None" or "Not Applicable" should be entered where appropriate. Blank spaces, or "to be advised" are not acceptable and may result in the application being rejected as incomplete. **This may affect the date of approval granted to the scheme.** Ticks (✓), Yes (Y) or No (N) should be used where indicated. Where there is insufficient space on the form a separate sheet may be used as necessary.

A. PARTIPATING EMPLOYER INFORMATION

1. The "Administrator" will be the trustees (or the scheme sponsor(s) in the case of a non-trust scheme) or such persons as are appointed by them (section 611AA ICTA 1988 refers).

2. Name of participating employer.

3. Address of employer - registered office if a company; principal place of business if an individual or partnership.

4. Nature of business of employer.

5. Enter code representing status of employer as appropriate;

   1 - PLC

   2 - Limited Company

   3 - Unlimited Company

   4 - Partnership

   5 - Sole Trader

   6 - Charity   (See notes 8 and 9)

   7 - Friendly Society

   8 - Other   (Please give details)

   9 - Public Sector

6. Please enter the 9 digit Company Registration Number, if applicable. This can be obtained from Companies House.

7. Employer's accounting date in DD/MM format.

8. Enter the name of the employer's Schedule D or corporation tax district. For Charities, please enter FICO in all cases even if there is also a Schedule D district.

9. Enter the reference number of the employer's Schedule D or corporation tax district. For Charities, please quote FICO reference number in all cases, even if there is also a Schedule D district.

10. Enter the name of the PAYE tax district.

11. Enter the reference number of the PAYE tax district.

12. Enter N if the Inspector of Taxes regards the company as an investment company for tax purposes.

13. If you do not know this please contact the local Tax Office responsible for the principal employer's registered office/principal place of business address.

PS 274 (Notes) *(4/01)*

B.	BASIC SCHEME INFORMATION

14. PSO reference number of scheme. Leave blank if form PS 274 is accompanying an application form PS 176 since the scheme reference will not be known.

15. Name of main scheme to which this employer is adhering as in governing documentation

C.	SCHEME INFORMATION

16. Date of commencement of participation in the scheme as stated in the deed of adherence or instrument binding the employer to the scheme rules.

17. Scheme year is as defined in The Retirement Benefits Scheme (Information Powers) Regulations 1995. Please give the scheme year in which the participation commenced.

18. Associated employer is explained in Practice Notes IR12 (1997) (PN) 21.1 and the PN Glossary.

19. Explain how the employers are associated.

20. Total contributions should include ordinary annual contributions and special contributions expected to be paid to the Scheme by the Participating Employer in the first year of participation.

21. Give an indication of the expected approximate level of employee contributions (including AVC's) as a percentage of the employee's remuneration.

22. Enter current pensionable earnings of highest paid member in the service of the participating employer.

23. Give an indication of the approximate level of contributions to the scheme by the participating employer as a percentage of the total contributions paid by the employer and his employees (excluding employees' AVC's). (It is a condition of Inland Revenue approval that the employer makes a significant contribution of not less than 10% of the total).

D.	PRACTITIONER INFORMATION

24. Name of Practitioner submitting the application and Practitioner number (if known).

25. Address of Practitioner and Practitioner address number (if known) - address to which correspondence should be sent.

26. Practitioner's reference number to be quoted on correspondence.

E.	DIRECTOR INFORMATION

27. Indicate (Y/N) whether current scheme membership includes Controlling Directors of the participating employer (formerly 20% Directors) as defined in PN Glossary.

28. Provide full details of each Controlling Director, continuing on a separate sheet in similar format if necessary. Retained benefits are defined in PN Glossary.

Appendix 20

F.   DECLARATION BY ADMINISTRATOR

29.   The application/declaration must be signed by the person(s) appointed to act as Administrator of the scheme (section 611AA (8) ICTA refers). If no such appointment has been made the trustees (or the scheme sponsor(s) in the case of a non-trust scheme) will be the legal Administrator under the above legislation.

By concession IR (SPSS) will accept the signature of a third party on behalf of the Administrator provided all parties making up the Administrator provide written authorisation to IR (SPSS) for the signatory to sign on their behalf. If appropriate, please provide a copy of the authorisation or otherwise confirm that it has previously been submitted.

Data Protection

The Inland Revenue is a Data Controller under the Data Protection Act. We hold information for the purposes specified in our notification made to the Data Protection Commissioner, and may use this information for any of them.

We may get information about you from others, or we may give information to them. If we do, it will only be as the law permits to

- check accuracy of information
- prevent or detect crime
- protect public funds.

We may check information we receive about you with what is already in our records. This can include information provided by you as well as others such as other government departments. We will not give information about you to anyone outside the Inland Revenue unless the law permits us to do so.

Appendix 21

**Audit & Pension Schemes
Services**
Yorke House
PO Box 62
Castle Meadow Road
Nottingham NG2 1BG

Telephone: 0115 974 0000
Fax: 0115 974 1480

To: Audit & Pension Schemes Services   From:
     Yorke House
     PO Box 62
     Castle Meadow Road
     Nottingham
     NG2 1BG

Date:

Your ref: SF ..../...................../...................

Our ref:

PRINCIPAL / PARTICIPATING EMPLOYER CHANGES – ALL SCHEMES
(see note 1 overleaf)

Please read the notes overleaf before completing this form.

**Information required under regulation 6(3)(b) of the Retirement Benefits Schemes (Information Powers)
Regulations 1995 [SI 1995 No 3103].**

The Scheme Administrator *(see note 2)* is required to supply the following information **not later than 180 days
after the end of the scheme year in which the change(s) took place. Failure to do so may lead to penalties
under section 98 Taxes Management Act 1970. If notification is not made within the time limit specified,
please provide the reason for the delay.**

NAME OF EMPLOYER ....

NAME OF SCHEME ....

SCHEME YEAR END DATE *(see note 3)*   ..../............/........................

Please use block capitals

1	New name and/or Registered Office address or principal place of business *(See note 4)*	
	Date of change	............/............/........................
2	Details of ceasing to carry on a trade or business	
	Date of cessation	............/............/........................

(continued overleaf)

Part of IR Savings, Pensions, Share Schemes   Business Director: Roger Hurcombe   **PS 256** *(4/01)*

Appendix 21

<table>
<tr><td>3</td><td>Details of a change of association with any other employer who is a participant in the scheme</td><td></td></tr>
<tr><td></td><td>Date of change</td><td>............/............/........................</td></tr>
</table>

Signed *(by I on behalf of* the Scheme Administrator)* ....

....

*delete as applicable *(see note 7)*

Name(s) ....

NOTES ON COMPLETION

1. "Participating employer" means the principal employer and any other employer participating in the scheme.

2. The "Scheme Administrator" will be the trustees or such persons as are appointed by them (paragraph 2.6 of the Practice Notes IR12 (1997) and section 611AA Income and Corporation Taxes Act 1988 refer).

3. "Scheme year" means a year specified for the purposes of the scheme in the scheme's governing documents. If no year is specified see the definition in regulation 2 of the Retirement Benefits Schemes (Information Powers) Regulations 1995 [SI 1995 No 3103].

4. It is not necessary to submit a copy of the Certificate of Incorporation on Change of Name. We only requires changes of Registered Office for companies, or principal place of business for individuals or partnerships (see also paragraphs 10-12 of PSO Update No 53).

5. Please report on a separate form for each participating employer where a change has occurred.

6. Please ensure that the boxes relevant to the change(s) are completed in their entirety.

7. The scheme administrator must give written authorisation to a third party to sign this form on their behalf. A copy of the authorisation must be sent to the address at the head of this form (see paragraph 9 of PSO Update No 47).

8. A false declaration of facts concerning the above could lead to withdrawal of approval of the scheme.

Appendix 22

Inland Revenue

Awarded for excellence

**Audit & Pension Schemes
Services**
Yorke House
PO Box 02
Castle Meadow Road
Nottingham NG2 1BG

Telephone: 0115 974 0000
Fax: 0115 974 1480

To: Audit & Pension Schemes Services
Yorke House
PO Box 62
Castle Meadow Road
Nottingham
NG2 1BG

From:

Date:

Your ref: SF ..../...................../...................

Our ref:

SPECIAL CONTRIBUTIONS

Please read the notes overleaf before completing this form.

**Information required under regulation 7 of the Retirement Benefits Schemes (Information Powers)
Regulations 1995 [SI 1995 No 3103].**

The Scheme Administrator *(see note 1)* is required to supply the following information **not later than 180 days**
after the end of the scheme year in which the chargeable period ends, during which the special contribution(s)
was made *(see notes 2 and 3)*. **Failure to do so may lead to penalties under section 98 Taxes
Management Act 1970.**

NAME OF EMPLOYER *(see note 4)* ....

NAME OF SCHEME   ....

Please use block capitals

1. Chargeable period to which this report refs *(see note 3)*	Year ending ..../........./...................
2. Scheme year end date *(see note 2)*	........./........./...................
3. The total **reportable** special contribution(s) paid by the employer to the scheme in the above chargeable period *(see notes 5, 6 and 7)*	£...............................

continued overleaf

Appendix 22

4. Reason(s) for the payment of the special contribution(s)	

Signed (by / on behalf of* the Scheme Administrator)

....

*delete as applicable *(see note 10)*

Name(s) ....

NOTES ON COMPLETION

1. The "Administrator" will be the trustees or such persons as are appointed by them (paragraph 2.6 of the Practice Notes IR12 (1997) and section 611AA Income and Corporation Taxes Act 1988 refer).

2. "Scheme year" means a year specified for the purposes of the scheme in the scheme's governing documents. If no year is specified see the definition in regulation 2 of the Retirement Benefits Schemes (Information Powers) Regulations 1995 [SI 1995 No 3103].

3. "Chargeable period" is defined in section 832 ICTA 1988 as "an accounting period of a company or a year of assessment".

4. Where the scheme is a centralised scheme the name of the employer to be entered on the front page is the name of the participating employer making the special contribution.

5. "Special contribution" is defined in Part I of the Regulations (see Glossary to Practice Notes IR12 (1997)) as any contribution paid to a retirement benefits scheme by an employer which is neither a fixed amount paid annually, whether in instalments or otherwise, nor an annual amount that is payable over a period of three years or more and is calculated on a consistent basis in accordance with actuarial principles by reference to the earnings, contributions or number of members of the scheme.

6. You do not need to report special contributions which have been certified by an actuary as made solely to finance cost of living increases for existing pensioners.

7. You do not need to report special contributions which when aggregated with other special contributions (except those described in note 6) paid to the scheme by the employer in the same chargeable period, do not exceed:-

    (i)   one half of the permitted maximum (see Glossary to Practice Notes IR12 (1997)) as at the end of the scheme year in which the chargeable period, during which the special contribution(s) was made, ends, or

    (ii)   the total contributions, other than special contributions, made by the employer to the scheme in the same chargeable period,

    whichever is the greater.

8. A copy of this form should be completed in respect of each employer paying a reportable special contribution to the scheme.

9. Please do not leave blank spaces or enter "to follow" or "to be advised", as this will constitute an incomplete report and may lead to financial penalties.

10. The scheme administrator must give written authorisation to a third party to sign this form on their behalf. A copy of the authorisation must be sent to IR (SPSS) (see paragraph 9 of PSO Update No 47).

11. If notification is not made within the time limit specified, please provide the reason for the delay.

Appendix 23

**Audit & Pension Schemes
Services**
Yorke House
PO Box 62
Castle Meadow Road
Nottingham NG2 1BG

Telephone: 0115 974 0000
Fax: 0115 974 1480

To: Audit & Pension Schemes Services   From:
     Yorke House
     PO Box 62
     Castle Meadow Road
     Nottingham
     NG2 1BG

Date:

Your ref: SF ..../...................../..................

Our ref:

CONTROLLING DIRECTORS

Please read the notes overleaf before completing this form.

Information required under regulation 8 of the Retirement Benefits Schemes (Information Powers) Regulations 1995 [SI 1995 No 3103].

This form should be completed in respect of any Controlling Director *(see note 1)* who joins the scheme after an application for approval has been submitted to the Inland Revenue, or any existing member who becomes a Controlling Director.

The Scheme Administrator *(see note 2)* is required to supply the following information **not later than 180 days** after the end of the scheme year in which the Controlling Director joins or the existing member becomes a Controlling Director. **Failure to do so may lead to penalties under section 98 Taxes Management Act 1970.**

NAME OF EMPLOYER ....

NAME OF SCHEME ....

Please use block capitals

1	Scheme year end date *(see note 3)*	....
2	Name of member	....
3	Date of joining scheme	........./........./...................
4	Date of becoming a Controlling Director	........./........./...................

continued overleaf

Part of IR Savings, Pensions, Share Schemes   Business Director: Roger Hurcombe   **PS 255** *(4/01)*

493

Appendix 23

5 Date of birth	........./........./....................
6 Date of joining company	........./........./....................
7 National Insurance Number	........./........./........./........./......
8 Current pensionable earnings	£................................
9 Have the member's retained benefits been taken into account for funding purposes?	Y / N *

Signed *(by / on behalf of* the Scheme Administrator)*

....

*delete as applicable *(see note 7)*

Name(s) ....

NOTES ON COMPLETION

1. "Controlling Director" means a member who is, or at any time within the last ten years has been, a director of a company which is an employer for the purposes of this scheme, and, either on his or her own or with one or more associates has beneficially owned or been able to control, directly, indirectly or through other companies, 20% or more of the ordinary share capital of the company (the Glossary to the Practice Notes IR12 (1997) refers).

2. The "Administrator" will be the trustees or such persons as are appointed by them (paragraph 2.6 of the Practice Notes IR12 (1997) and section 611AA Income and Corporation Taxes Act 1988 refer).

3. "Scheme year" means a year specified for the purposes of the scheme in the scheme's governing documents. If no year is specified see the definition in regulation 2 of the Retirement Benefits Schemes (Information Powers) Regulations 1995 [SI 1995 No 3103].

4. Where the scheme is a centralised scheme and the Controlling Director joins the scheme as a director of a new participating employer, it is not necessary to submit this form if all the information has been supplied on form PS 274 within the time prescribed by regulation 6.

5. Where the scheme is a centralised scheme and the new Controlling Director is a controlling director of more than one participating employer, a copy of this form should be submitted in respect of each employer *(but see note 4.)*

6. Please do not leave blank spaces or enter "to follow" or "to be advised", as this will constitute an incomplete report and may lead to financial penalties.

7. The scheme administrator must give written authorisation to a third party to sign this form on their behalf. A copy of the authorisation must be sent to IR (SPSS) (see paragraph 9 of PSO Update No 47).

8. If notification is not made within the time limit specified, please provide the reason for the delay.

Appendix 24

Inland Revenue

Tax Claim Exempt Approved Retirement Benefits Scheme

Section 592 Income and Corporation Taxes Act 1988

Name of scheme *if form is issued to agent*

Use this form to claim repayment of UK Income Tax for a retirement benefits scheme which

* is approved by the Board of Inland Revenue and
* is treated as exempt under Section 592 ICTA 1988.

The claim must be made and signed by a trustee of the scheme or a person authorised in writing by the trustees to make claims on their behalf.

If a single scheme is regarded in law (Section 611(3) ICTA 1988) as two separate schemes and only one scheme is an exempt approved scheme, make the claim for the exempt approved scheme's income only.

If there is not enough space on this form to give all the details, please attach a separate sheet and carry the totals to the appropriate place on the form. When this form is completed send it to the Tax Office, whose address is shown aside. You can get help and advice on completing the form from this Tax Office. Do not send the form to Pension Schemes Office.

Scheme for which the claim is being made   *Please use CAPITAL letters*

Full title of pension scheme

Full address of pension scheme

Postcode

Payee details

(if different from pension scheme)

I authorise (Name(s) to be shown on payable order)

of (address)

to receive on my behalf the amount due.

Signature _____ Date _____

Declaration

I as a trustee of the Scheme or a person duly authorised by the trustees declare that the particulars given on this form are correct and complete to the best of my knowledge and belief.

I understand that false statements can lead to prosecution.

I claim the sum of £ _____ for the year ended 5 April 19 _____ .

Signature _____ Date _____

Full name Mr / Mrs / Miss / Ms

Full address

R63N(1998)

Your reference

Tax Office reference

Return completed form to

For official use only

Last claim to	Stats code

Date received by Inspector

Period

_____ year to _____ 19 __

| Instalment ☐ | Provisional ☐ |
| Final ☐ | Supplementary ☐ |

Amount   £

Supplement £

Total   £

Examined   Initials _____

Date _____

Vouchers cancelled	Supplement
	Calculated ☐
	Not due ☐
Initials _____	Initials _____
Date _____	Date _____

Renewal form R63N
to be issued ☐   not to be issued ☐

Checked in detail	Passed for order
	Initials _____
	Date _____

Payable order

No _____

Checked   Initials _____

Appendix 24

Please read the notes before each section carefully. They will tell you what to enter on the form. Attach the vouchers requested. It helps us deal with your claim more quickly if you put the vouchers into the order in which they are listed on this form.

Section 1	Income from which UK Income Tax has been deducted and which is from investments or deposits held for the purposes of the Scheme

UK income

Enter here all income from which UK Income Tax has been deducted, including interest on loans and deposits, bank and building society interest, dividends or interest on UK Government securities (including those held in the form of Bearer Bonds) and interest from Unit Trusts. Do not include UK dividends with tax credits, stock dividends, foreign income dividends or foreign dividends. Give the name and address of the person paying the income to the scheme. Attach a certificate signed by the person who deducted the tax and paid it to the Revenue. Income from Deeds of Covenant is not exempt.

Number of vouchers	Name and address of person paying the income to the Scheme	Gross amount of income before deduction of Income Tax £	Income tax deducted £
1			
2			
3			
4			
5			

Foreign dividends

Enter all foreign dividend income. Attach, in the same order as you list them, the counterfoils or certificates showing the amount of dividends for the period for which the claim is made. Do not include stock dividends because the notional income tax attached to these dividends is **not repayable under any circumstances.**

Number of vouchers	Name of company paying dividend	Amount of dividend £	UK Income tax deducted £
1			
2			
3			
4			
5			
6			
	Totals		

Summary

	Income £	Tax £
Total UK income		
Total foreign dividends		
Totals of income and tax shown in Section 1		

496

Section 2   *Payments made under deduction of tax by the Scheme*

Enter here details of all charges on the Scheme's income which were paid under deduction of tax at the basic rate. If a new charge began during the period of the claim give its starting date. Do not include payments under the Pay As You Earn (PAYE) system.

	Gross amount before deduction of tax £	Tax deducted £
a. Annuities and other annual payments		
b. Interest, rent, etc., paid to anyone who normally lives abroad		
Totals		

Section 3   *Calculation of claim*

Total tax from Section 1 summary	
Less total tax from Section 2	
Amount of claim	

Appendix 25

CHARGEABLE EVENTS

Information required under Regulation 10 of the Retirement Benefits Schemes (Information Powers) Regulations 1995 (SI 1995 No 3103)

The Administrator (see note 1 overleaf) is required to supply the following information **not later than 30 days after the end of the tax year in which the event occurs. Failure to do so may lead to penalties under Section 98 Taxes Management Act 1970. Nil reports are not required.**

This report should be sent direct to HM Inspector of Taxes dealing with the tax affairs of the scheme. Where this is not known it may be sent to the Pension Schemes Office at Yorke House, PO Box 62, Castle Meadow Road, Nottingham, NG2 1BG, who will forward it to the appropriate Tax District.

Please read the notes on the reverse before completing this form

NAME OF EMPLOYER..

NAME OF SCHEME...

Tax year ended 5 April		£	See note	HMIT use only
1	Contributions (including interest thereon, if any) repaid to employees or former employees during their lifetime except surplus voluntary contributions		2, 3 and 6	IM 8130
2	Payments to an employee or their personal representatives out of surplus funds arising from employee's voluntary contributions		7	
3	Lump sums paid in commutation of entire pension in the following special circumstances		2, 4 and 6	IM 8141
	a. on the grounds of triviality	a.		
	b. in exceptional circumstances of serious ill-health	b.		

4	Payments to an employer out of funds held for the purposes of the scheme		5	IM 8121

ADMINISTRATOR INFORMATION (See note 1)

NAME...

ADDRESS..

Signed (*by / on behalf of* * the Administrator) ....
* delete as applicable - see note 8

Person to whom any enquiries may be sent, if not the administrator

NAME...

ADDRESS..
....

NOTES ON COMPLETION

1. The "Administrator" is the trustees or such persons as are appointed by them (Section 611 AA Income and Corporation Taxes Act 1988 refers).

2. Where the rules allow the Administrator to deduct the amount of the tax payable from the refund or lump sum, enter thefull amount available for the employee before any such deduction. But you can ignore any part of the amount available which is withheld to reimburse the employer for:
- a 'payment in lieu of contributions' to the National Insurance Fund,
- a State Scheme premium under the Social Security Pensions Act 1975, or
- any financial loss caused by the employee's fraud or negligence.

3. Enter the total of the gross amounts repaid to employee's during their lifetime (including interest if any).

4. Enter the total of the chargeable amounts. The chargeable amount is normally the amount of the commutation payment less -

   a.   a sum equal to 3/80ths of the employee's average annual remuneration over the last 3 years' service multiplied by the number of years' service (maximum 40) or, if greater,

   b.   the largest sum which could have been received by way of commutation under the rules of the scheme, apart from the special circumstances, on the assumption that any discretion conferred on the Administrator or employer as to the extent to which an employee may commute their pension would have been exercised to give the maximum lump sum consistent with the rules of the scheme.

Attach a computation for each item included in the total where the amount included is less than the full amount payable to the employee in question, ie where a deduction is made under a. or b. above. Where, apart from the special circumstances, the benefits under the scheme take the form of a pension and a separate lump sum, rather than a partially commutable pension, restrict the amount deducted by the amount of the separate lump sum. Where it is known that the employee was also a member of another scheme relating to the same employment, give the name(s) of the other scheme(s) because the law prevents relief being given twice in these circumstances.

5. Enter the total of the sums paid or which became due. Any refunds out of pension scheme surpluses should have been notified already to the Inland Revenue, Pension Schemes Office, but if not already reported enter them in this section. Exclude any amounts which are paid to an employer to reimburse:

- a 'payment in lieu of contributions' to the National Insurance Fund,

- a State Scheme premium under the Social Security Pensions Act 1975, or

- any financial loss caused by the employee's fraud or negligence.

6. Where relief is claimed on the grounds that the employee's employment was carried on outside the United Kingdom give full particulars of all the places where the employment was carried on with dates. Include the amount(s) on which relief is claimed in the totals entered on the return (see notes 2, 3 and 4) and give details separately.

7. Where the total funds available to provide benefits are excessive, the surplus, to the extent that it originates from the member's voluntary contributions, may be repaid to the member or the member's estate. Enter the full amount before any deduction of the tax due under Section 599A Income and Corporation Taxes Act 1988.

8. The scheme administrator must give written authorisation to a third party to sign this form on their behalf. A copy of the authorisation must be sent to the PSO (see paragraph 9 of PSO Update 47).

9. If this notification is not made within the time limit specified, please provide the reason for the delay.

Appendix 26

The 'Earnings Cap'

Maximum Pensionable Earnings — Section 590C ICTA 1988

1989/90	£60,000	
1990/91	£64,800	
1991/92	£71,400	* £5,950
1992/93	£75,000	* £6,250
1993/94	£75,000	* £6,250
1994/95	£76,800	* £6,400
1995/96	£78,600	* £6,550
1996/97	£82,200	* £6,850
1997/98	£84,000	* 7,000
1998/99	£87,600	* 7,300
1999/00	£90,600	* 7,550
2000/01	£91,800	* 7,650
2001/02	£95,400	* 7,950

* PN23.14(b) – one twelfth of the earnings cap below which all single ex-gratia lump sums do not need to be submitted for approval.

Appendix 27

**OCCUPATIONAL PENSION SCHEMES
APPLICATION FOR APPROVAL**

EX GRATIA LUMP SUM BENEFIT ON RETIREMENT OR DEATH
(See Inland Revenue Statement of Practice SP 13/91)

Each application for approval under Chapter I Part XIV Income and Corporation Taxes Act (ICTA) 1988 (as amended) must be
made on this form, completed in accordance with the Notes on Completion (PS 60 (Notes)), within the specified time limit.

see note
1
2

PLEASE COMPLETE IN BLOCK CAPITALS

A. PRINCIPAL EMPLOYER INFORMATION

Name of employer		3
Employer's address		4
Nature of business		5
Status of employer *(enter code – see key in notes)*		6
Company Registration Number *(if applicable)*		7
Employer's accounting date		8
Employer's Tax District		9
Employer's Tax District reference		10
Employer's PAYE Tax District		11
Employer's PAYE Tax District reference		12
Is the employer carrying on a trade in the UK? (Y/N)		13
Is the employer resident in the UK for tax purposes?(Y/N)		14

B. BASIC SCHEME INFORMATION

Name of scheme	EX GRATIA LUMP SUM	15
Type of scheme	1 1	16

C. PRACTITIONER INFORMATION

Name of Practitioner	No.	17
Address	No.	18
Practitioner's reference		19

D. DETAILS OF PAYMENT

Date of payment of lump sum (or intended date of payment)		20
Amount of lump sum paid/payable to employee, or	£	21
Amount of death benefit	£	

PS 60 *(4/01)*

Appendix 27

E.   EMPLOYEE INFORMATION ^{see note}

	Title	Initials	Surname	
Employee name				22

NI Number

Date of birth

Date of joining employer's service   23

Date when employee left service/retired/died

Remuneration   - Basic Pay   £ [ ]   Other emoluments £ [ ]   24

Is/Was the employee a Controlling Director? (Y/N)   25

F.   ANNUITANT OR BENEFICIARY INFORMATION (if not employee)

Title	Initials	Surname	Relationship to employee	
				26

G.   DECLARATION BY SCHEME SPONSOR

I/We hereby apply for approval of the retirement benefits scheme named in Section B of this form under Chapter I Part XIV ICTA 1988 (as amended).   27

I/We declare that to the best of my/our knowledge and belief the information given in this application is correct and complete and further declare that:-

a)   the scheme has been bona fide established for the sole purpose of providing approvable relevant benefits, and

b)   there is no intention of taking any action, if approval is granted, other than in accordance with the approved terms of the trust deed and rules, and all statutory and published Inland Revenue conditions for the approval and continued approval of the scheme.

I/We further certify that the criteria set out in paragraph (7)(a) of the Inland Revenue Statement of Practice 13/91 are satisfied.

Signatures(s)   Date(s)   Please print names here

....   [ ]

....   [ ]

....   [ ]

....   [ ]

This declaration must be signed by all of the scheme trustees/sponsors. Please attach photocopies of this page if further space is required.

H.   SUBMITTING THE APPLICATION

When this form is fully completed, send to:-

      Pension Schemes Office
      Inland Revenue (Savings, Pensions, Share Schemes)
      P O Box 62
      Castle Meadow Road
      Nottingham
      NG2 1BG

Appendix 27

General

All questions should be answered in full: "None" or "Not Applicable" should be entered where appropriate. Blank spaces, or "to be advised" are not acceptable and may result in the application being rejected as incomplete. **This may affect the date of approval granted to the scheme.** Ticks (✓), Yes (Y) or No (N) should be used where indicated. Where there is insufficient space on the form a separate sheet may be used as necessary.

1. In order to gain approval a fully completed form PS 60 should be submitted to the address at Section H of the form to be received by the PSO not later than the relevant date set out in the following table:

	Date or intended date of payment of ex-gratia lump sum		Date by which application must be received by IR (SPSS)
In the 6 months ending	5 October	by the following	5 April
In the month ending	5 November	" " "	5 May
" " " "	5 December	" " "	5 June
" " " "	5 January	" " "	5 July
" " " "	5 February	" " "	5 August
" " " "	5 March	" " "	5 September
" " " "	5 April	" " "	5 October

2. Approval will usually be given to the payment of a lump sum of the amount set out below:

    i. to a former employee aged 50 or more – an amount not exceeding 3/80 times Remuneration (see note 23) for each year of service with the employer, or

    ii. where a lump sum death benefit is to be paid in respect of a former employee – an amount not exceeding 4 times Remuneration (see note 23).

A. EMPLOYER INFORMATION

3   Name of employer.

4   Address of employer - registered office if a company; principal place of business if an individual or partnership.

5   Nature of business of employer.

6   Enter code representing status of employer as appropriate;

    1   -   PLC

    2   -   Limited Company

    3   -   Unlimited Company

    4   -   Partnership

    5   -   Sole Trader

    6   -   Charity   (See notes 9 and 10)

    7   -   Friendly Society

    8   -   Other   (Please give details)

    9   -   Public Sector

7. Please enter the 9 digit Company Registration Number, if applicable. This can be obtained from Companies House.

8. Employer's accounting date in DD/MM format.

9. Enter the name of the employer's Schedule D or corporation tax district. For Charities, please enter FICO in all cases even if there is also a schedule D district.

10. Enter the reference number of the employer's Schedule D or corporation tax district. For Charities, please quote FICO reference number in all cases, even if there is also a Schedule D district.

11. Enter the name of the PAYE tax district.

12. Enter the reference number of the PAYE tax district.

13. Enter N if the Inspector of Taxes regards the company as an investment company for tax purposes.

14. If you do not know this please contact the local Tax Office responsible for the principal employer's registered office/principal place of business address.

PS 60 (Notes) *(4/01)*

B.	BASIC SCHEME INFORMATION

15. This box has been completed for you.

16. This box has been completed for you.

C.	PRACTITIONER INFORMATION

17. Name of Practitioner submitting the application and Practitioner number (if known).

18. Address of Practitioner and Practitioner address number (if known) - address to which correspondence should be sent.

19. Practitioner's reference number, to be quoted on correspondence.

D.	DETAILS OF PAYMENT

20. Indicate date of payment of the ex-gratia lump sum. Where approval is being sought in advance the expected date of payment should be inserted.

21. Indicate in the appropriate boxes the lump sum benefit to be provided.

E.	EMPLOYEE INFORMATION

22. Provide details of the employee in respect of whom the Arrangement has been established.

23. If the answer to the question in Section A, "Is the employer resident in the UK for tax purposes?" is Yes, enter the total period of service with the employer during which the employee was chargeable to tax under UK Schedule E, case I or II, using DD/MM/YYYY format.

24. State the employee's basic pay during the last year of employment and the amount of any other emoluments received in the year. The amounts must be chargeable to tax under Schedule E (case I or II) and must exclude any amounts which

i. Are chargeable under section 148 ICTA 1988, or

ii. Arise from the acquisition or disposal of shares or an interest in shares or from a right to acquire shares.

25. Indicate (Y/N) whether the employee is or was a Controlling Director.

F.	BENEFICIARY INFORMATION (if not employee)

26. Where the benefits are not payable to the employee named in Section E, provide details of the beneficiary.

G.	DECLARATION

27. The application/declaration must be signed by the scheme sponsor(s).

Approvable relevant benefits are relevant benefits (as defined by section 612(1) ICTA 1988) which could be provided by a scheme approved under Chapter 1 Part XIV ICTA 1988.

Your attention is drawn to paragraph 7 of Statement of Practice 13/91, which explains that approval will not be granted to ex-gratia lump sums relevant benefits where the employee concerned is already a member of their employer's occupational pension scheme or of a relevant statutory scheme.

Data Protection

The Inland Revenue is a Data Controller under the Data Protection Act. We hold information for the purposes specified in our notification made to the Data Protection Commissioner, and may use this information for any of them.

We may get information about you from others, or we may give information to them. If we do, it will only be as the law permits to
* Check accuracy of information
* Prevent or detect crime
* Protect public funds

We may check information we receive about you with what is already in our records. This can include information provided by you as well as others such as other government departments. We will not give information about you to anyone outside the Inland Revenue unless the law permits us to do so.

Appendix 28

SCHEME NAME: ....

CONTINUOUS SERVICE QUESTIONNAIRE FOR A *CONTROLLING DIRECTOR*

Words and phrases in *italics* are explained in full in the notes at the end of this form. Where there is insufficient space on this form, please continue on a separate sheet.

ABOUT THIS FORM

- **What is continuous service?**
  When you move from one employer to another (i.e. you stop working for one employer and start working for another employer) your pension benefits from each employer are usually calculated separately. Your pension benefits are based on your service with and your pensionable earnings from each employer. If continuous service is allowed your benefits will be calculated as though your employment with both your old and new employers was a single continuing employment. This means that your benefits will be based on the total length of service with both employers and your pensionable earnings from your new employer and/or in some instances the old employer provided the rules of the new employer's scheme permit benefits to be calculated in this way.

- **When is it necessary to complete this form?**
  If you are a *controlling director* of either or both employers you can have continuous service only with the prior agreement of *IR (SPSS)*. The conditions a *controlling director* must satisfy to qualify for continuous service are explained in the notes at the end of this form. Claims for continuous service should be made only where these conditions are satisfied. Claims should be made on PS 155. A separate PS 155 should be completed for each *controlling director* and sent to *IR (SPSS)*.

- **Does a claim cover more than one pension scheme of the new employer?**
  Yes. This claim covers all of the new employer's schemes which you join. If this claim is agreed you should tell the *administrator/*trustees of all schemes of the new employer that you are entitled to continuous service. You should not make a new claim when you join another scheme of the new employer.

- **Does a claim cover more than one change of employer?**
  No. A separate PS 155 must be completed each time you change employers.

Appendix 28

A. **SIMULTANEOUS/CONCURRENT EMPLOYMENT PRECLUDES CONTINUOUS SERVICE**

Continuous service is not allowable if you were employed simultaneously (concurrently) by both the old and new employers at any time.

For continuous service purposes employment includes:-

- Any period of employment with the employer in any capacity, with remuneration assessable under Schedule E

- Any period as a director of the employer, even if you received no remuneration for these duties

- Any period as an officer of the company e.g. company secretary, even if you received no remuneration for these duties

- Any period in which you took part in the management of the affairs of the employer, even if you received no remuneration for doing so

N.B. Periods when the employer was not trading must be included in the periods above. Periods when the employer was in the hands of a liquidator, administrator, administrative receiver, receiver, must be included above. Periods when the employer was dormant must be included in the periods above.

Were you employed simultaneously (concurrently) at any time by the old and new employers?

No ☐   **Go to Part B**

Yes ☐   **Continuous service is not allowable. Do not complete the rest of this form. Do not send this form to *IR (SPSS)*.**

B. **PERIOD BETWEEN OLD AND NEW EMPLOYMENTS**

Is there a gap of more than three months between the end of the old employment and the start of the new employment? (Employment has the same meaning as in Part A)

No ☐   **Go to Part C**

Yes ☐   **The gap between the two employments is too long: there is no continuity between the employments. Continuous service is not allowable. Do not complete the rest of this form. Do not send this form to *IR (SPSS)*.**

507

Appendix 28

C.	**TIME LIMITS FOR MAKING A CLAIM FOR CONTINUOUS SERVICE**

1.	Did you leave your old employer more than 6 years ago? No ☐ Go to question 2. Yes ☐ **Your claim is too late and cannot be accepted. Please do not complete the rest of this form. Do not submit this form to *IR (SPSS)*.**
2.	Have both the old and new employer forwarded accounts to Companies House for the period in which you moved from one to the other? Yes ☐ Go to question 3. No ☐ **Do not send in this claim yet. We cannot consider your claim until both sets of accounts have been sent to Companies House.**
3.	Have both the old and new employer forwarded their annual returns to Companies House for the made-up date (*) following your move from one employer to the other? Yes ☐ **Go to Part D.** No ☐ **Do not send in this claim yet. We cannot consider your claim until both annual returns have been sent to Companies House.** (*) this is usually the anniversary of the incorporation of the company or of the made-up date of the previous annual return registered at Companies House

D.	**YOUR EMPLOYMENT DETAILS** (Employment has the same meaning as in Part A)

1.	What is the date on which your employment with the old employer started? ..../........./...................
2.	What is the date on which your employment with the old employer ended? ..../........./...................
3	What is the date on which your employment with the new employer started? ..../........./...................
4	Please state the names and *IR (SPSS)* references of all schemes of the new employer of which you are a member ....

508

E. BASIS OF CLAIM

If the old and new employers are *associated* and your employment has changed because of a transfer of business your claim must be based on the transfer of business. You cannot make a claim on the basis that the old and new employers are *associated*. **Go to Part G.**

If the old and new employers are not *associated* and your employment has changed because of a transfer of business, **go to Part G.**

If the old and new employers are *associated* and your employment has not changed because of a transfer of business, **go to Part F.**

If the old and new employers are not *associated* and your employment has not changed because of a transfer of business the connection between the two employers is not sufficiently close to permit continuous service. **As continuous service is not allowable do not complete the rest of this form. Do not send this form to** *IR (SPSS).*

F. MOVE BETWEEN *ASSOCIATED EMPLOYERS*

(NB. If you are completing this part, **do not** complete Part G)

1	Are the employers *associated by a permanent community of interest* only?
	No ☐ Go to question 2
	Yes ☐ **Continuous service is not allowable. Do not complete the rest of this form. Do not send this form to** *IR (SPSS).*
2	Does one employer directly or indirectly *control* the other?
	No ☐ Go to question 3
	Yes ☐ Which employer *controls* the other and how does it do so? Please give full details.
	....
	....
	....
	Go to Part K
3	Were both employers *controlled* by a third person for at least one year before you moved from one employer to the other?
	Yes ☐ Go to question 4.
	No ☐ **Continuous service is not allowable. Do not complete the rest of this form. Do not send this form to** *IR (SPSS).*

Appendix 28

4	Did the period of *control* by the third person continue up to the date you moved from the old employer to the new employer?
	Yes ☐ Go to question 5
	No ☐ **Continuous service is not allowable. Do not complete the rest of this form. Do not send this form to *IR (SPSS)*.**

5	Did both the old employer and the new employer carry on a genuine commercial trading activity for the whole of the 12 month period immediately before you moved to the new employer?
	No ☐ **Continuous service is not allowable. Do not complete the rest of this form. Do not send this form to *IR (SPSS)*.**
	Yes ☐ Please give details of the trading activity carried on by both employers in this period. Please also give details of the person who *controlled* both employers and how that person did so.
	....
	....
	....
	....
	....
	Go to Part K

G. TRANSFER OF BUSINESS

(NB. If you are completing this part, **do not** complete Part F)

1	Were you a director of the old employer immediately before you left that employment and are you a director of the new employer?
	Yes ☐ Go to question 2
	No ☐ You are not performing similar duties for both employers. **Continuous service is not allowable. Do not complete the rest of this form. Do not send this form to *IR (SPSS)*.**

2	Was the whole of the trading activity of the business carried on by the old employer transferred to the new employer?
	No ☐ Go to question 3
	Yes ☐ **Go to Part H**

3	Was the whole of the trading activity of the business carried on by the old employer transferred to two or more undertakings, one of which was the new employer?
	Yes ☐ **Go to Part I**
	No ☐ **Go to Part J**

510

	H. WHOLE OF THE TRADING ACTIVITY OF THE OLD BUSINESS TRANSFERRED TO THE NEW EMPLOYER
1	Please give a full description of the trading activity of the business of the old employer and where it was carried out immediately before the transfer. Please state the date the trading activity was transferred to the new employer. ....
2	Please give a full description of the trading activity of the business of the new employer and where it was carried out immediately after the transfer. ....
3	Is the new employer still carrying on the same trading activity that was formerly carried on by the old employer? Yes ☐ Go to question 4 No ☐ When did the new employer stop doing so and why? Please give full details. .... Go to question 4
4	Did the new employer take over at least 75% of the liabilities of the old employer? Yes ☐ Please give full *supporting evidence* e.g. accounting evidence of 100% of these liabilities and accounting evidence that the new employer took on 75% of these liabilities. Go to question 6 No ☐ Go to question 5
5	If the new employer did not take on at least 75% of the liabilities of the old employer, did the price paid for the business take account of the liabilities that stayed with the old employer? No ☐ **Continuous service is not allowable. Do not complete this form. Do not send this form to *IR (SPSS)*.** Yes ☐ Please forward details together with full *supporting evidence* e.g. a copy of the agreement and related correspondence setting out the details of the price adjustment. .... Go to question 6

Appendix 28

6	Were <u>all</u> the business assets of the old employer transferred to the new employer?
	Yes ☐ Please provide full supporting evidence. Go to question 7
	No ☐ Which assets were transferred and what happened to the rest?.
	....
	....
	....
	Go to question 7
7	Were <u>all</u> the employees of the old employer transferred to the new employer?
	Yes ☐ Go to question 8
	No ☐ Which employees were transferred and what happened to the rest?
	....
	....
	....
	Go to question 8
8	Does the new employer serve the same customers as the old employer?
	Yes ☐ **Go to Part K**
	No ☐ Please give details.
	....
	....
	....
	Go to Part K

I.	**TRANSFER OF THE WHOLE OF THE TRADING ACTIVITY OF THE OLD BUSINESS TO TWO OR MORE UNDERTAKINGS**
1	Please give a full description of the whole of the trading activity of the business of the old employer and where it was carried out immediately before the transfer.
	....
	....
	....

512

2	Please give a full description of the trading activity of the business of the new employer immediately after the transfer and where it was carried out. Please specify which trading activity was transferred from the old employer and state the date the trading activity was transferred to the new employer.
	....
	....
	....
3	Is the new employer still carrying on the same trading activity that was formerly carried on by the old employer?
	Yes ☐ Go to question 4
	No ☐ When did the new employer stop doing so and why? Please give full details.
	....
	....
	....
	Go to question 4
4	Did the old employer transfer at least 75% of its liabilities to the new employer and one or more undertakings?
	No ☐ Go to question 5
	Yes ☐ Go to question 6
5	If the new employer and the other undertakings did not take on at least 75% of the liabilities of the old employer, did the price paid for the business take account of the liabilities that stayed with the old employer?
	No ☐ **Continuous service is not allowable. Do not complete this form. Do not send this form to *IR (SPSS)*.**
	Yes ☐ Please forward details together with full *supporting evidence* e.g. a copy of the agreements and related correspondence setting out the details of the adjustment of the prices paid by the new employer and the other undertakings.
	....
	....
	....
	Go to question 7

6	a) What were the liabilities of the old employer? Please give full details including amounts. b) Which of these liabilities were taken on by the new employer and which were taken on by other undertakings? Please give full details including amounts. Please provide full *supporting evidence* for a) and b) above e.g. accounting evidence of all the liabilities of the old employer, accounting evidence of the percentage of the old employer's liabilities assumed by the new employer and accounting evidence of the percentage of the old employer's liabilities assumed by the other undertakings .... Go to question 7
7	a) What happened to the business assets of the old employer? b) What proportion of these business assets were transferred to the new employer? Please give full details and full *supporting evidence*. .... Go to question 8
8	What happened to the employees of the old employer? Please give full details. .... Go to question 9
9	To what extent does the new employer serve the same customers as the old employer? .... **Go to Part K**

J.	**BUSINESS SPLIT BETWEEN OLD AND NEW EMPLOYERS**
1	Did the split take place in such a way that the legislation on demergers in sections 213 to 218 *ICTA 88* was satisfied? No ☐ Go to question 2 Yes ☐ **Go to Part K**
2	Did the employer carry on more than one trade? Yes ☐ Go to question 3 No ☐ **Continuous service is not allowable. Do not complete this form. Do not send this form to *IR (SPSS)*.**
3	Were the old employer's trades separately identifiable i.e. could the income, expenditure, business assets and business liabilities all be allocated or attributed to the individual trades? Yes ☐ Go to question 4 No ☐ **Continuous service is not allowable. Do not complete this form. Do not send this form to the *IR (SPSS)*.**
4	Did the old employer transfer one or more trades in their entirety to the new employer? Yes ☐ Go to question 5 No ☐ **Continuous service is not allowable. Do not complete this form. Do not send this form to *IR (SPSS)*.**
5	Did the new employer take over at least 75% of the liabilities of the old employer which were attributed to the trade(s) transferred to the new employer or did the price paid to the old employer for the trade(s) take account of the liabilities that stayed with the old employer? Yes ☐ Please give full details and *supporting evidence* of the transfer of the trade(s) to the new employer. These details and evidence should include: • confirmation that the old employer no longer carries on the transferred trade(s) • evidence that the trades formerly carried on by the old employer were separately identifiable • the date the trade(s) was (were) transferred to the new employer • evidence that the new employer carries on the transferred trade(s) • evidence that at least 75% of the old employer's liabilities attributable to the transferred trade(s) were assumed by the new employer or that the price paid for the trade(s) took account of liabilities remaining with the old employer • evidence of the percentage of business assets allocated to the transferred trade(s) which are now owned by the new employer • confirmation that the employees working in the transferred trades have changed employment to the new employer. No ☐ **Continuous service is not allowable. Do not complete this form. Do not send this form to *IR (SPSS)*.** **Go to Part K**

515

Appendix 28

K. CLAIMANT'S DETAILS			
		Old Employer	New Employer
1	Name of Employer	....	....
2	Registered Office Address		
3	Corporation Tax District and reference number	..../................................	..../................................
4	Company Registration Number	....	....
5	Were you a *controlling director*? If "No" what was the nature of your employment?	**Yes/No***	**Yes/No*** ....
6	Your usual residential address	....	
7	Your National Insurance Number	........./........./........./........./......	
8	Your date of birth	........./........./...................	
9	Your pensionable earnings with old employer	£	
10	Your present remuneration from new employer	£	
11	Your normal retirement age in the new employer's scheme(s).	....	

* *delete as applicable*

516

L. PERSON DEALING WITH THIS APPLICATION

Please give the name and address of the individual/organisation* to whom all correspondence about this claim should be sent:-

Name (block capitals)
....

Address (block capitals)
....

....

....

....

Telephone number:- ....

Reference to be quoted in any correspondence:- ....

Signed on behalf of the above:-...

Name (block capitals):- ....

M. DECLARATION BY CLAIMANT

I declare to the best of my knowledge and belief that the information in Parts A to M inclusive is correct and complete and authorise the individual/organisation* named in Part L to act on my behalf in connection with this claim.

Signature   ....   Date ..../........./..................

Full name (block capitals)   ....

* *delete as applicable*

517

Appendix 28

COPY OF PUBLISHED GUIDANCE ON CONTINUOUS SERVICE

The conditions applying to continuous service are set out in paragraphs 7.15 to 7.21 of *IR12(2001)* and *PSO* Updates numbers 42 and 53. These are reproduced below.

Paragraphs 7.15 to 7.21 of *IR12 (2001)*

"7.15 – Subject to Part 21, an employer may only provide benefits in respect of service with that employer. Where, however, a business has been taken over, merged or reconstructed and an employee's position before and after the change is essentially unchanged (typically the employee is doing the same job in the same place) service with both employers may be treated as continuous service for the present employer. Where in these circumstances, the employee in question is a *controlling director* of either or both of the employers concerned, it will be necessary to seek the specific prior approval of the *IR (SPSS)* to continuous service treatment. The *IR (SPSS)* will only accept service being treated as continuous for such individuals where it can be shown that there is a continuity of trade. The main requirements to be satisfied are as follows:-

a. There has been a succession of trade from one employer to another, and

b. At least 75% of the vendor's liabilities have been assumed by the purchaser.

The following will also be taken into account as they will help to establish that true continuity exists.

c. The extent to which the business assets and the employees of the predecessor company have been transferred to the successor company, and

d. The extent to which the successor company serves the same customers as its predecessor.

7.16 – Where the original business is split between two or more new businesses, at least 75% of the liabilities of the old business must be assumed by the new businesses. In these circumstances the fact that less than 75% is assumed by one or other of the new businesses would not in itself necessarily preclude the granting of continuous service. All the relevant facts relating to the transfer would have to be considered before a conclusion is reached.

7.17 – Continuous service will not be accepted where the liabilities of the original company are not taken over by the successor company unless the purchase price for the buy-out of the business takes into account the fact that the liabilities will be retained by the vendor. In such cases a claim for continuous service would have to be supported by a copy of the sale agreement setting out the details.

7.18 – Continuous service for a *controlling director* may be accepted where only part of a trade has been transferred provided that the circumstances are such that the legislation on demergers as set out in sections 213-218 is satisfied.

7.19 – Where a *controlling director* dies in service before a decision on a claim for continuous service has finally been reached then the death in service benefit may be given on the basis of continuous service.

7.20 – Where an employee (including a *controlling director*) moves from one employer to another, (other than in a takeover, merger etc situation where paragraphs 7.15 to 7.18 applies), and those employers are *associated employers*, service may be treated as continuous for the purpose of benefit provision by the second employer. Where, however, in these circumstances the employee is a *controlling director*, it is again necessary to seek the specific prior approval of the Pension Schemes Office to continuous service treatment. In the situation where the employers are associated by common control, the employers must have been so associated and carrying on a genuine commercial trading activity, for at least one year prior to the date on which the *controlling director* moves from one to the other, in order for continuous service treatment to be acceptable. Where the move is between two employers who are associated only by virtue of *permanent community of interest*, service may not be treated as continuous where the individual concerned is a *controlling director* of either or both of the employers concerned.

7.21 – A claim for continuous service in respect of a *controlling director* should be made on a fully completed PS 155 – a specimen is included in Appendix II."

PSO Update No 42

CONTINUOUS SERVICE AND CONCURRENT EMPLOYMENTS

For the provisions of Practice Notes 7.14 to 7.20* to apply there needs to be a **change** of employer i.e. the member ceases employment with the original employer and the new employer is either associated with (as defined in the Appendix I Glossary to *Practice Notes*) or has taken over all or part of the trade of the original company. A form PS 155 is required for *controlling director* members who change employer.

Where the employments are **concurrent** (for example becoming a director of an associated company whilst remaining a director of the original company) the provisions of Practice Notes 16.50 to 16.53** should be applied. **In these circumstances the form PS 155 is not appropriate.**"

*now paragraphs 7.15 to 7.21 of IR 12 (2001)

** now paragraphs 16.52 to 16.56 of IR 12 (2001)

PSO Update No 53

CONTINUOUS SERVICE

Would customers try and ensure that requests for continuous service are made contemporaneously. Revenue records are rarely retained for more than 6 years so it can be very difficult to consider cases which are very old."

DEFINITIONS OF TERMS USED IN THIS FORM

Administrator As defined in section 611AA *ICTA 88*

Associated by a permanent community of interest There are sufficient links between the old and new employers for them to be regarded as associated, for example:-
there is common management in that the same individuals form a majority on the board of directors of each company; or
there are common shareholders but the companies are not *controlled* by the same person or
staff are interchangeable or jointly employed; or
the employers' operations are interdependent, for example, one sells most of its products to the other.

Associated Employers Companies where one is directly or indirectly *controlled* by the other or both or all are *controlled* by a third person.

Control As defined in section 416 *ICTA 88* for close companies or in section 840 for other corporate bodies when used in connection with *associated employers*.

Controlling Director A controlling director is defined in paragraph 5(5) of Schedule 23 *ICTA 1988* as a person who is a director and within paragraph (b) of section 417(5) in relation to the employer company. For practical purposes this means a member who:

- in relation to the old employer
  was at any time after 16 March 1987 and within 10 years of leaving service a director and, either on his or her own or with one or more associates, beneficially owned or was able to *control*, directly, indirectly or through other companies, 20% or more of the ordinary share capital of the company,
  or,
- in relation to the new employer
  is or was a director who either on his or her own or with one or more associates, beneficially owned or was able to *control*, directly, indirectly or through other companies, 20% or more of the ordinary share capital of the company.

For the purposes of this definition:

[i] "associate" means in relation to a director, any relative (i.e. spouse, forbear, issue or sibling) or partner (within the meaning of the Partnership Act 1890), the trustees of any settlement in relation to which the director is, or any relative of his or her (living or dead) is or was, a settlor and, where the

director is interested in any shares or obligations of the company which are subject to any trust, or are part of the estate of a deceased person, the trustees of the settlement concerned or, as the case may be, the personal representatives of the deceased, and

[ii] the expression "either on his or her own or with one or more associates" requires a person to be treated as owning or, as the case may be, *controlling* what any associate owns or *controls*, even if he or she does not own or control share capital on his or her own.

ICTA 88 Income and Corporation Taxes Act 1988.

IR 12 (2001) The Inland Revenue's guidance notes on the tax approval of occupational pension schemes.

IR (SPSS) This stands for Inland Revenue (Savings, Pensions, Share Schemes). With effect from 1 April 2001, the *Pension Schemes Office* became a part of IR (SPSS) which is now responsible for work on pensions.

Pension Schemes Office now part of *IR (SPSS)*

Pensionable service Service for an employer in respect of which benefits (other than benefits payable solely on death before retirement) accrue under an approved scheme.

Practice Notes IR 12 (2001)

PSO *Pension Schemes Office*

Supporting Evidence This is documentary evidence needed in support of some of the statements you have made on this form. Its nature will depend on the circumstances of your claim. Examples are:- accounting evidence, invoices, sale agreements, legally binding agreements, minutes of board meetings, any formal material vouched for or witnessed by a third party (such as audited accounts).

Data Protection

The Inland Revenue is a Data Controller under the Data Protection Act. We hold information for the purposes of taxes, social security contributions, tax credits and certain other statutory functions as assigned by Parliament. The information we hold may be used for any of the Inland Revenue's functions.

We may get information about you from others or we may give information to them. If we do, it will only be as the law permits, to

- check accuracy of information
- prevent or detect crime
- protect public funds

We may check information we receive about you with what is already in our records. This can include information provided by you as well as by others such as other government departments and agencies and overseas tax authorities. We will not give information about you to anyone outside the Inland Revenue unless the law permits us to do so.

Appendix 29

Expression of Wish Form

TO: The Trustees of

Name of Member ....
               (Surname)   **(First Names)**

I understand that under the Rules of the Scheme a lump sum will be payable if I die while still in the service of the Company and, in certain circumstances, on death after retirement. I also understand that the Trustees have discretionary powers to pay the lump sum to such one or more of my relatives and dependants as they shall decide or to my legal personal representatives.

For the guidance of the Trustees in such circumstances I would like the following person or persons to receive the benefits in the proportions shown.

Name   *Relationship with Member*   *Proportion of lump sum*

I understand that this expression of wish does not in any way bind the Trustees or fetter the exercise of their discretionary powers.

Signature.. Date..

NOTES

1.   To ensure confidentiality you may wish to place this Form in a sealed envelope when you return it. The envelope will then only be opened by the Trustees in the event of your death.

521

2. Your 'legal personal representatives' are, if you leave a will, your Executors; if not, the administrators of your estate.

3. If your personal circumstances change and you wish to alter this expression of wish, you should ask for the return of this Form and complete a further form in its place.

Appendix 30

Loan Agreement

1. Name of Pension Scheme ....

2. Name of company to whom loan is granted ....

3. Amount of Loan £ ....

4. Purpose of the Loan ....
   ....

5. The loan is *Secured/*Unsecured   *delete as necessary

6. Date from which loan is to run...

7. Date on which loan is due for repayment ....

8. Interest is due annually on the anniversary of the loan, or on earlier repayment at a rate of 3% above (the Clearing Bank's) base lending rate ruling on the due date.

9. The Trustees and the company have agreed that the loan may be repaid at the option of the company prior to the date due for repayment. The loan may be recalled by the Trustees giving the Company one month's notice.

10. Notwithstanding the provisions of paragraph 9 the loan shall be repayable if;

    (i)   the company is in breach of the conditions of this agreement; or

    (ii) the company ceases to carry on business; or

    (iii) the company becomes insolvent within the meaning defined for the purposes of Regulation 6 of the Retirement Benefit Schemes (Restriction on Discretion to Approve) (Small Self-Administered Schemes) Regulations 1991; or

    (iv) the money is required to enable the Trustees to pay benefits which have already become due under the Pension Scheme.

523

11. Subject to the agreement of the Trustees, this loan may be renewed for a further period on similar terms.

12. The terms and conditions set out above have been accepted by the company.

13. We hereby confirm that the terms of this loan set out above have been approved by a majority of the trustees acting in accordance with their powers of investment as conferred by the Trust Deed.

Signature.................................... Signature....................................
          Trustee   Trustee

Date.................................... Date....................................

Signature.................................... Date....................................
      On Behalf of the Company

14. All the members of the Pension Scheme hereby agree to the loan

Signature.................................... Signature....................................
          Member   Member

Signature.................................... Signature....................................
          Member   Member

Appendix 31

Inland Revenue

**Audit & Pension Schemes
Services**
Yorke House
PO Box 62
Castle Meadow Road
Nottingham NG2 1BG

Telephone: 0115 974 0000
Fax: 0115 974 1480

To: Audit & Pension Schemes Services   From:
      Yorke House
      PO Box 62
      Castle Meadow Road
      Nottingham NG2 1BG

Date:

Your ref: SF ...../.................

Our ref:

**SMALL SELF-ADMINISTERED SCHEME INVESTMENTS: LOANS TO EMPLOYERS AND "ASSOCIATED"
COMPANIES**

Please read the notes overleaf before completing this form.

**Information required under regulation 5 of the Retirement Benefits Schemes (Information Powers)
Regulations 1995 [SI 1995 No 3103].**

The Scheme Administrator *(see note 1)* is required to supply the following information and documentation **not
later than 90 days** after the trustees lend money *(see note 2)* to an employer or an "associated" company *(see
note 3)*. **Failure to do so may lead to penalties under section 98 Taxes Management Act 1970.**

A COPY OF THE LOAN AGREEMENT MUST BE FURNISHED WITH THIS QUESTIONNAIRE *(See note 5)*

NAME OF PRINCIPAL EMPLOYER ....

NAME OF SCHEME ....

Please use block capitals

1 Name of borrower and whether employer or "associated" company *(see note 3)*	
	EMPLOYER / "ASSOCIATED" EMPLOYER *
2 Date of loan	........./........./..................
3 Amount of loan *(see notes 4 and 5)*	£..............................
4 Total market value of the fund at the date of this loan *(see note 6)*	£..............................

continued overleaf

Part of IR Savings, Pensions, Share Schemes   Business Director: Roger Hurcombe   **PS 7013** *(4/01)*

Appendix 31

5	Rate of interest *(see note 7)*	................%
6	Repayment date	........./........./................
7	Purpose of loan *(see note 8)* *(Full details are required; "cash flow" is* **not** *sufficient*	
8	If this is an extension or "roll-over" of an existing loan, confirm that all interest has been paid up to the date of the loan renewal	
9	The total amount invested in loans and shares in the employer and "associated" company at the date of this loan (including the amount of this loan). The 25%/50% limit *(see note 4)* applies to loans and shares combined	

DETAILS OF ALL OTHER OUTSTANDING LOANS TO EMPLOYERS AND "ASSOCIATED" COMPANIES

10	Name of company	Principal, participating or "associated" employer (state which)	Date of loan	Amount of loan	Amount of loan outstanding at the date at 2 above

DETAILS OF SHARES IN EMPLOYERS AND "ASSOCIATED" COMPANIES

11	Name of company	Principal, participating or "associated" employer (state which)	Market value of shares as at date of loan *(see note 9)*

Signed *(by / on behalf of* the Scheme Administrator)*

....

(see note 10)

Name(s)

....

*delete as applicable

NOTES ON COMPLETION

1. The "Scheme Administrator" will be the trustees or such persons as are appointed by them (paragraph 2.6 of the Practice Notes IR12 (1997) (PN) and section 611AA Income and Corporation Taxes Act 1988 refer).

2. You must submit reports of loans that have been made, not proposed loans. The submission of a report of a loan facility before any money has actually changed hands does not satisfy the reporting requirement and will be rejected.

3. For the purposes of this form a company "associated" with an employer in the scheme if it falls within the definition in regulation 2(9) of the Retirement Benefits Schemes (Restriction on Discretion to Approve) (Small Self-administered Schemes) Regulations 1991 [SI 1991 No 1614].

4. The amount of the loan must not exceed the amount specified in regulation 7(2) and (3) of SI 1991 No 1614 as amended by regulation 8 of The Retirement Benefits Schemes (Restriction on Discretion to Approve) (Small Self-administered Schemes) (Amendment) Regulations 1998 [SI 1998 No 728] and regulations 4 and 5 of The Retirement Benefits Schemes (Restriction on Discretion to Approve) (Small Self-administered Schemes) (Amendment No 2) Regulations 1998 [SI 1998 No 1315].

5. If a loan is made in instalments each instalment counts as a separate loan subject to SI 1991 No 1614, as amended by SI 1998 No 728 and SI 1998 No 1315, and SI 1995 No 3103 and must be documented and reported as such. It is acceptable for the separate documentation to consist of an abbreviated loan agreement signed by both parties. The terms and conditions of the agreement need not be fully (re-) stated as long as they are said to be identical to those in the facility agreement. Each instalment must satisfy the requirements of the above Regulations as at the date the money is paid over.

6. The market value of the fund must be calculated in accordance with regulation 7(2) and (3) of SI 1991 No 1614 as amended by regulation 8 of SI 1998 No 728 and regulations 4 and 5 of SI 1998 No 1315.

7. If the rate of interest is lower than the Clearing Bank Base Rate + 3% per annum, you must supply evidence that the borrower could borrow from a bank or other arm's length financial institution on similar terms.

8. **The subsequent forwarding of a loan to members of the scheme or any "connected" person as defined in regulation 2(4) to (8) SI 1991 No 1614 will lead to withdrawal of the scheme's approval (see PN 20.41) or, where approval has not yet been given, to the application being refused.**

9. You must provide details of how the market value of the shares has been calculated.

10. The Scheme Administrator must give written authorisation to a third party to sign the form on their behalf. A copy of the authorisation must be sent to IR (SPSS) (see paragraph 9 of PSO Update No 47).

11. Please do not leave blank spaces or enter "to follow" or "to be advised", as this will constitute an incomplete report and may lead to financial penalties.

12. If notification is not made within the time limit specified, please provide the reason for the delay.

Appendix 32

<table>
<tr><td></td><td>**Audit & Pension Schemes Services**
Yorke House
PO Box 62
Castle Meadow Road
Nottingham NG2 1BG

Telephone: 0115 974 0000
Fax: 0115 974 1480</td></tr>
</table>

┌   ┐   ┌   ┐

To: Audit & Pension Schemes Services   From:
          Yorke House
          PO Box 62
          Castle Meadow Road
          Nottingham NG2 1BG

└   ┘   └   ┘

Date:

Your ref: SF ..../........................

Our ref:

SMALL SELF-ADMINISTERED SCHEME INVESTMENTS: LAND OR BUILDINGS

Please read the notes overleaf before completing this form.

Information required under regulation 5 of the Retirement Benefits Schemes (Information Powers) Regulations 1995 [SI 1995 No 3103].

The Scheme Administrator *(see note 1)* is required to supply the following information and documentation **not later than 90 days** after the trustees acquire, lease or otherwise dispose of any land or buildings (or part thereof) *(see notes 3 and 4)*. **Failure to do so may lead to penalties under section 98 Taxes Management Act 1970. If this notification is not made within the time limits specified, please state the reason for the delay.**

NAME OF PRINCIPAL EMPLOYER ....

NAME OF SCHEME ....

Please use block capitals

PART A (all land or building transactions)

1	Date and manner of transaction	........./........./...............	ACQ. / DIS.*
	(e.g. purchase, transfer, lease, sale)	....	
2	a) Address of property		
	b) Description *(e.g. shop, factory, office)* *(see note 5)*		

(continued overleaf)

3	Scheme's interest in property	FREEHOLD / LEASEHOLD *
4	Name of other party to the transaction and whether "connected" or "associated" *(see notes 2, 6 7 & 8)*	
5	Purchase/sale price at the time of acquisition/disposal *(see note 9)*	£................................
6	If disposal (including leasing), a) Date property acquired by the trustees *(see notes 3 & 6)* b) Purchase price at time of acquisition	........./........./............... £................................
7	If there is any related agreement concerning the property or otherwise involving any member of the scheme or any connected person, please give details	

PART B – LEASE ASSOCIATED WITH PROPERTY NOTIFIED IN PART A *(see note 3)*

8	a) Name of lessee b) "Connected" or "Associated" *(see notes 2 & 8)*	
9	a) Date lease commenced b) Length of lease c) Rent payable d) Date of first rent review	........./........./............... .... £................................ ..../........./...............

All relevant supporting documentation is attached *(see notes 7, 8, & 9)* ☐ ✓

Signed *(by / on behalf of* the Scheme Administrator)* ....
(see note 11)

Name(s) ....

*delete as applicable

Appendix 32

NOTES ON COMPLETION

1. The "Scheme Administrator" will be the trustees or such persons as are appointed by them (paragraph 2.6 of the Practice Notes IR12 (1997) and section 611AA Income and Corporation Taxes Act 1988 refer).

2. "Connected" is as defined in regulation 2(4) to 2(8) of the Retirement Benefits Schemes (Restriction on Discretion to Approve) (Small Self-administered Schemes) Regulations 1991 [SI 1991 No 1614]. Participating employers or companies associated with participating employers are as defined in regulation 2(9) of SI 1991 No 1614.

3. Disposal includes letting of property owned by the scheme. If the property is being let at the same time as the property acquisition is reported, the details should be entered on this form in Part B. Please note that the acquisition of property and the leasing of property are two separate reportable transactions under the Information Powers Regulations 1995. Failure to report both transactions within 90 days will give rise to penalty proceedings for two separate breaches of the Regulations. If however, having acquired the property and leased it at the same time, you find that you are unable to report both transactions with 90 days, please submit a PS 7012 for the property acquisition, within the time limit, and a further PS 7012 for the leasing. If you follow this procedure the Administrator will only be liable for a penalty for the late reporting of the lease if this is received outside the statutory time limit.

4. If the property is let at a later date or the tenant of the property changes at any stage, the Scheme Administrator must submit another PS 7012, together with copies of the appropriate documentation, to IR (SPSS) within 90 days of the commencement of the letting.

5. Pension schemes are prohibited from acquiring, holding or disposing of residential property, unless covered under regulation 5(2) of the Retirement Benefits Schemes (Restriction on Discretion to Approve) (Small Self-administered Schemes) Regulations 1991 [SI 1991 No 1614], as amended by regulation 7 of the Retirement Benefits Schemes (Restriction on Discretion to Approve) (Small Self-administered Schemes) (Amendment) Regulations 1998 [SI 1998 No 728].

6. Assets held by the scheme since before 15 July 1991 may be sold to members of the scheme (including former members) and their relatives and to companies they control (either alone or together with relatives). **All other transactions with such persons are prohibited**, unless they are participating employers or companies associated with participating employers.

7. If the property has been acquired as a contribution, a transfer in specie, a donation or a bequest from a "connected" or "associated" party, or disposed of as a transfer in specie to a "connected" or "associated" party, you must enter the market value of the property, explain how this was established, and provide an independent valuation of the property.

8. If the lessee is "connected" or "associated" you must enclose an independent valuation of the rental value and a copy of the executed lease.

9. Please provide a form PS 7015 giving details of any trustees' borrowing not previously reported.

10. Please do not leave blank spaces or enter "to follow" or "to be advised", as this will constitute an incomplete report and may lead to financial penalties.

11. If a third party is to sign this form, written authorisation must be given by the Scheme Administrator. A copy of the authorisation must be sent to IR (SPSS) (see paragraph 9 of PSO Update No 47).

12. A false declaration of facts concerning this transaction could lead to withdrawal of approval of the scheme.

530

Appendix 33

 **Inland Revenue**

Audit & Pension Schemes
Services
Yorke House
PO Box 62
Castle Meadow Road
Nottingham NG2 1BG

Telephone: 0115 974 0000
Fax: 0115 974 1480

To: Audit & Pension Schemes Services
Yorke House
PO Box 62
Castle Meadow Road
Nottingham NG2 1BG

From:

Date:

Your ref: SF ..../............................

Our ref:

SMALL SELF-ADMINISTERED SCHEME INVESTMENTS: SHARES IN EMPLOYER, "ASSOCIATED" OR UNLISTED COMPANIES

Please read the notes overleaf before completing this form.

Information required under regulation 5 of the Retirement Benefits Schemes (Information Powers) Regulations 1995 [SI 1995 No 3103].

The Scheme Administrator *(see note 1)* is required to supply the following information and documentation **not later than 90 days** after the trustees acquire or dispose of shares in an employer or an "associated" *(see note 2)* or unlisted company (i.e. one which is not officially listed on a recognised stock exchange within the meaning of section 841(1) ICTA 1988 (USM and AIM shares are treated as unlisted)). A separate form is required for each acquisition/disposal. **Failure to do so may lead to penalties under section 98 Taxes Management Act 1970.**

NAME OF PRINCIPAL EMPLOYER ....

NAME OF SCHEME ....

Please use block capitals

1 Name of company and whether an employer, "associated" or unlisted company *(state which)* *(see note 2)*	
2 Date of acquisition/disposal *(state which)*	........./........./..................
3 Name of other party to the transaction and whether "connected" or "associated" *(see notes 2 and 6)*	

531

4	Purchase/sale price or market value at time of acquisition/disposal *(see note 3)*	£................................
5	Class and number of shares concerned	
6	Total issued share capital of the class of share named in 5 above after this transaction	
7	If disposal, date shares acquired by the trustees *(see note 4)*	........./........./..................
8	Dividend and voting rights of shares *(see note 5)*	
9	If acquisition, vendor's beneficial interest (as % of total issued share capital of the class of share named in 5 above) prior to sale	
10	What is the reason for the acquisition?	
11	In the case of an acquisition of shares in an employer or "associated" company a. the total market value of the fund at the date of the transaction *(see note 7)*, and b. the total market value of the amount of the fund invested in loans to and shares in the employer "associated" company at the date of the transaction (including this acquisition). NB the 25%/50% limit applies to loans and shares combined *(see note 7)*	

DETAILS OF SHARES IN EMPLOYERS AND "ASSOCIATED" COMPANIES

12	Name of company	Principal, participating or "associated" employer (state which)	Market value of shares as at date of loan *(see note 9)*

Appendix 33

DETAILS OF ALL OTHER OUTSTANDING LOANS TO EMPLOYERS AND "ASSOCIATED" COMPANIES					
13	Name of company	Principal, participating or "associated" employer (state which)	Date of loan	Amount of loan	Amount of loan outstanding at the date at 2 above

Signed *(by / on behalf of* the Scheme Administrator*...
(see note 10)

Name(s) ....

*delete as applicable

NOTES ON COMPLETION

1. The "Administrator" will be the trustees or such persons as are appointed by them (paragraph 2.6 of the Practice Notes IR12 (1997) (PN) and section 611AA Income and Corporation Taxes Act 1988 refer).

2. For the purpose of this form "connected" has the meaning as defined in regulation 2(4) to (8) of the Retirement Benefits Schemes (Restriction on Discretion to Approve) (Small Self-administered Schemes) Regulations 1991 [SI 1991 No 1614]. "Associated" is defined in regulation 2(9).

3. You must provide details of how the market value of the shares has been calculated. If the shares were acquired or disposed of as an in specie transfer or were acquired as an in specie contribution, bequest or donation, you must enter the market value of the shares at the time of the acquisition and explain how this was established.

4. Assets held by the scheme since before 15 July 1991 may be sold to members of the scheme (including former relatives) and their relatives and to companies they control (either alone or together with their relatives). **All other transactions with such persons are prohibited**, unless they are participating employers or companies "associated" (as defined in regulation 2(9) of SI 1991 No 1614) with participating employers.

5. Regulation 5(1) of SI 1991 No 1614 as amended by regulation 6 of the Retirement Benefits Schemes (Restriction on Discretion to Approve) (Small Self-administered Schemes) (Amendment) Regulations 1998 [SI 1998 No 728] prohibits the scheme from holding shares in any unlisted company which

(i) carry more than 30% of the voting power in the company, or

(ii) entitle the holder of them to more than 30% of any dividends declared by the company in respect of the shares of the class held.

533

Appendix 33

6. If the vendor/purchaser is "connected" or "associated" and the shares were purchased/sold privately, or if the shares were acquired as a contribution or transfer in specie or as a donation or bequest, from a "connected" or "associated" party or disposed of as a transfer in specie to a "connected" or "associated" party, you must provide:

   (a) full details of the calculations used in valuing the shares and a copy of any professional valuation or advice obtained; copies of the last 3 years' accounts of the company;

   (b) a copy of the Articles of Association if the company has more than one class of shares in issue, and;

   (c) details of any related agreement with anyone connected with the scheme to purchase or sell shares in the company.

7. The market value of the fund must be calculated in accordance with regulation 7(2) and (3) of SI 1991 No 1614 as amended by regulation 8 of SI 1998 No 728 and regulations 4 and 5 of the Retirement Benefits Schemes (Restriction on Discretion to Approve) (Small Self-administered Schemes) (Amendment No 2) Regulations [SI 1998 No 1315].

8. You must provide details of how the market value of the shares has been calculated.

9. Please do not leave blank spaces or enter "to follow" or "to be advised", as this will constitute an incomplete report and may lead to financial penalties.

10. The Scheme Administrator must give written authorisation to a third party to sign the form on their behalf. A copy of the authorisation must be sent to IR (SPSS) (see paragraph 9 of PSO Update No 47).

11. If this notification is not made within the time limits specified, please provide the reason for the delay.

Appendix 34

Inland
Revenue

**Audit & Pension Schemes
Services**
Yorke House
PO Box 62
Castle Meadow Road
Nottingham NG2 1BG

Telephone: 0115 974 0000
Fax: 0115 974 1480

To: Audit & Pension Schemes Services   From:
       Yorke House
       PO Box 62
       Castle Meadow Road
       Nottingham NG2 1BG

Date:

PSO ref: SF ..../..............................

Our ref:

**SMALL SELF-ADMINISTERED SCHEME INVESTMENTS IN MISCELLANEOUS ACQUISITIONS, SALES
AND LEASES**

Please read the notes overleaf before completing this form.

Information required under regulation 5 of the Retirement Benefits Schemes (Information Powers)
Regulations 1995 [SI 1995 No 3103].

The Scheme Administrator *(see note 1)* is required to supply the following information and documentation **not
later than 90 days** after the trustees purchase from, sell to, or lease from or to an employer or "associated"
company *(see note 2)* any asset. **If this notification is not made within the time limits specified, please
state the reason for the delay.**

Transactions involving land, including buildings, and shares should not be reported on this form but on forms
PS 7012 and PS 7014 respectively.

NAME OF PRINCIPAL EMPLOYER ....

NAME OF SCHEME ....

Please use block capitals

1	Description of asset	
2	Date of purchase/sale/lease *(state which)*	........./........./................... PURCHASE / SALE / LEASE *
3	Purchase/sale price or rent being charged/paid	£.................................

continued overleaf

Appendix 34

4	Name of vendor/purchaser/lessee/lessor and whether employer or "associated" company *(state which) (see notes 2 and 3)*	
		VENDOR / PURCHASER / LESSEE / LESSOR *
		EMPLOYER / ASSOCIATED EMPLOYER *
5	In the case of a lease please give brief details i.e. term, rent etc *(see note 3)*	

Signed *(by / on behalf of* the Scheme Administrator)*

....

(see note 5)

Name(s)

....

*delete as applicable

NOTES ON COMPLETION

1. The "Administrator" will be the trustees or such persons as are appointed by them (paragraph 2.6 of the Practice Notes IR12 (1997) (PN) and section 611AA Income and Corporation Taxes Act 1988 refer).

2. Assets held by the scheme since before 15 July 1991 may be sold to members of the scheme (including former members) and their relatives and to companies they control (either alone or together with their relatives). **All other transactions with such persons are prohibited**, unless they are participating employers or companies associated (as defined in the Retirement Benefits Schemes (Restriction on Discretion to Approve) (Small Self-administered Schemes) Regulations 1991 [SI 1991 No 1614] with participating employers.

3. In the case of a purchase or sale you must supply a copy of an independent valuation of the asset. In the case of a lease, you must supply a copy of an independent valuation of the rental value and a copy of the lease.

4. Please do not leave blank spaces or enter "to follow" or "to be advised", as this will constitute an incomplete report and may lead to financial penalties.

5. The Scheme Administrator must give written authorisation to a third party to sign the form on their behalf. A copy of the authorisation must be sent to IR (SPSS) (see paragraph 9 of PSO Update No 47).

6. If this notification is not made within the time limit specified, please provide the reason for the delay.

536

Appendix 35

Audit & Pension Schemes Services
Yorke House
PO Box 62
Castle Meadow Road
Nottingham NG2 1BG

Telephone: 0115 974 0000
Fax: 0115 974 1480

To: Audit & Pension Schemes Services
Yorke House
PO Box 62
Castle Meadow Road
Nottingham NG2 1BG

From:

Date:

Your ref: SF ..../.............................

Our ref:

SMALL SELF-ADMINISTERED SCHEME BORROWING

Please read the notes overleaf before completing this form.

Information required under regulation 5 of the Retirement Benefits Schemes (Information Powers) Regulations 1995 [SI 1995 No 3103].

The Scheme Administrator *(see note 1)* is required to supply the following information and documentation **not later than 90 days** after the trustees borrow money *(see note 2)*. **Failure to do so may lead to penalties under section 98 Taxes Management Act 1970.**

NAME OF PRINCIPAL EMPLOYER ....

NAME OF SCHEME ....

Please use block capitals

1	Date of borrowing	
2	Amount borrowed *(see notes 3 and 4)*	£...............................
3	Rate of interest	
4	Repayment date	........./........./.................
5	Purpose of borrowing	

continued overleaf

Appendix 35

6 Name and address of lender *(If the lender is "connected" or "associated" you must supply a copy of the loan agreement – see note 5)*	
7 Total market value of the fund as at the date of this transaction *(see note 6)*	£.................................
8 Total amount of borrowing outstanding following this transaction	£.................................
9 The "ordinary annual contribution" paid by the employer to the scheme *(see note 7)*	£.................................
10 The annual amount of contributions paid by the scheme members (as a condition of membership) in the tax year ending immediately before the date of this transaction	£.................................
11 Is this borrowing a rolling over of a previous borrowing which was not reported to the PSO under the concession mentioned in note 8?	

Signed *(by / on behalf of* the Scheme Administrator)*

....

(see note 10)

Name(s)

....

delete as applicable

538

NOTES ON COMPLETION

1. The "Administrator" will be the trustees or such persons as are appointed by them (paragraph 2.6 of the Practice Notes IR12 (1997) (PN) and section 611AA Income and Corporation Taxes Act 1988 refer).

2. You must submit reports of borrowing that has been made, not proposed borrowing. The submission of a report of a borrowing facility before any money has actually changes hands does not satisfy the reporting requirement and will be rejected.

3. If a scheme borrows money in instalments each instalment counts as a separate borrowing subject to the Retirement Benefits Schemes (Restriction on Discretion to Approve) (Small Self-administered Schemes) Regulations 1991 [SI 1991 No 1614], as amended by the Retirement Benefits Schemes (Restriction on Discretion to Approve) (Small Self-administered Schemes) (Amendment) Regulations 1998 [SI 1998 No 728] and the Retirement Benefits Schemes (Restriction on Discretion to Approve) (Amendment No 2) Regulations 1998 [SI 1998 No 1315], and SI 1995 No 3103 and must be documented and reported as such. It is acceptable for the separate documentation to consist of an abbreviated agreement signed by both parties. The terms and conditions of the agreement need not be fully (re-)stated as long as they are said to be identical to those in the facility agreement. Each instalment must satisfy the requirements of the above Regulations as at the date the money is paid over.

4. The aggregate amount borrowed must not exceed the amount specified in regulation 4(1) of SI 1991 No 1614 as amended by regulation 4 of SI 1998 No 728 and regulation 3 of SI 1998 No 1315.

5. For the purposes of this form "connected" has the meaning as defined in regulation 2(4) to (8) of SI 1991 No 1614. "Associated" is defined in regulation 2(9).

6. The market value of the fund must be calculated in accordance with regulation 4(1)(c) of SI 1991 No 1614 as amended by regulation 4 of SI 1998 No 728 and regulation 3 of SI 1998 No 1315.

7. For the purposes of borrowing limits "ordinary annual contributions" is defined in regulation 4(2) of SI 1991 No 1614 as amended by regulation 5 of SI 1998 No 728.

8. As a concession, no report need be made of temporary borrowings for a period not exceeding 6 months where the aggregate amount borrowed does not exceed the lesser of

   a) 10% of the market value of the fund, and

   b) £50,000,

   and the borrowing is repaid at or before the due date. If a borrowing is rolled over into a further term this concession will not apply.

9. Please do not leave blank spaces or enter "to follow" or "to be advised", as this will constitute an incomplete report and may lead to financial penalties.

10. The Scheme Administrator must give written authorisation to a third party to sign the form on their behalf. A copy of the authorisation must be sent to IR (SPSS) (see paragraph 9 of PSO Update No 47).

11. If this notification is not made within the time limit specified, please provide the reason for the delay.

Appendix 36

Summary of Main Changes Introduced by SI 1991 No 1614

1. SSAS approved by 5 August 1991.

Rule Amendments
— in line with Model Rules to be executed by 5 August 1994 (see 3.21).

Borrowings
— may be undertaken from 5 August 1991 in line with new criteria (see 7.57–7.67).

Non-income producing assets
— acquisition banned from 5 August 1991 except for choses in action (see 7.32–7.34). If acquired before 15 July 1991 may be retained if acceptable under PSO's previous discretionary practice (see 2.22).

Residential property
— acquisition banned from 5 August 1991 with only two exceptions (see 6.28). If acquired before 15 July 1991 may be retained if acceptable under PSO's previous discretionary practice (see 2.22).

Unquoted shares
— acquired from 5 August 1991 limited to 30 per cent of issued share capital (see 7.5). If in the employer or associated company amount limited to 25 per cent of value of fund unless SSAS established for more than two years, otherwise 50 per cent of value of fund. 25 per cent and 50 per cent limits include value of any loans (see 7.4).

Loans (made from 5 August 1991)	—	terms must conform to provisions of Regulations (see 5.46–5.47).
	—	amount limited to 25 per cent of value of fund unless SSAS established for more than two years, otherwise 50 per cent of value of fund may be lent. 25 per cent and 50 per cent limits include value of any shares in the employer or associated company (see 5.8–5.9).
Trustee/member transactions	—	banned from 5 August 1991, but if investment made before 15 July 1991 and acceptable under PSO's previous discretionary practice may be sold later to scheme members at open market value (see 2.23).
Pensioneer trustee	—	provisions as to resignation and appointment of successor from 5 August 1991 (see 2.36).
Reporting requirements	—	transactions from 5 August 1991 that include purchase and sale of property, loans to employers, purchase and sale of unquoted shares, borrowings and purchase from or sale to employer or associated company of any asset other than property to be reported within 90 days (see 5.47, 6.6, 7.24, 7.40 and 7.68).

2.   SSAS not approved by 5 August 1991, but established before that date.

Rule amendments	—	in line with Model Rules to be executed before approval will be granted (see 3.21).
Borrowings	—	may be undertaken from 5 August 1991 in line with new criteria (see 7.57–7.67).
Non-income producing assets	—	acquisition banned from 15 July 1991 except for choses in action (see 7.33–7.34).

If acquired before 15 July 1991 may be retained if acceptable under PSO's previous discretionary practice (see 2.22).

Residential property — acquisition banned from 15 July 1991 with only two exceptions (see 6.28). If acquired before 15 July 1991 may be retained if acceptable under PSO's previous discretionary practice (see 2.23).

Unquoted shares — acquired from 15 July 1991 limited to 30 per cent of issued share capital (see 7.5). If in the employer or associated company amount limited to 25 per cent of value of fund unless SSAS established for more than two years, otherwise 50 per cent of value of fund. 25 per cent and 50 per cent limits include value of any loans (see 7.4).

Loans (made from — terms must conform to provisions of
5 August 1991) Regulations (see 5.46–5.47).

— amount limited to 25 per cent of value of fund unless SSAS established for more than two years, otherwise 50 per cent of value of fund may be lent. 25 per cent and 50 per cent limits include value of any shares in the employer or associated company (see 5.8–5.9).

Trustee/member — banned from 5 August 1991 (see 2.23).
transactions If investment made before 15 July 1991 and acceptable under PSO's previous discretionary practice may be sold later to scheme members at open market value (see 2.23).

Pensioneer trustee — provisions as to resignation and appointment of successor from 5 August 1991 (see 2.36).

Reporting requirements	— transactions from 15 July 1991 that include purchase and sale of property, loans to employers, purchase and sale of unquoted shares, and purchase from and sale to employer or associated company of any asset other than property to be reported within 90 days (see 5.47, 6.6, 7.24 and 7.40).
	— borrowings from 5 August 1991 to be reported within 90 days (see 7.68).

3.   SSAS established from 5 August 1991 et seq.

Rule amendments	— in line with model rules to be executed before approval will be granted (see 3.21).
Borrowings	— to be undertaken in accordance with Regulations (see 7.57–7.67).
Non-income producing assets	— acquisition banned except for choses in action (see 7.33–7.34).
Residential property	— acquisition banned with only two exceptions (see 6.28).
Unquoted shares	— limited to 30 per cent of issued share capital (see 7.5). If in the employer or associated company amount limited to 25 per cent of value of fund for first two years of SSAS, then 50 per cent of value of fund. 25 per cent and 50 per cent limits include value of any loans (see 7.4).
Loans	— terms must conform to provisions of Regulations (see 5.46–5.47).
	— limited to 25 per cent of value of fund for first two years of SSAS then 50 per cent of value of fund may be lent. 25 per cent and 50 per cent limits include value of any shares in the employer or associated company (see 5.8–5.9).

Appendix 36

Trustee/member transactions	—	banned (see 2.23).
Pensioneer trustee	—	provisions as to appointment, resignation and appointment of successor (see 2.36).
Reporting requirements	—	transactions that include purchase and sale of property, loans to employers, purchase and sale of unquoted shares, borrowings and purchase from or sale to employer or associated company of any asset other than property to be reported within 90 days (see 5.47, 6.6, 7.24, 7.40 and 7.68).

Appendix 37

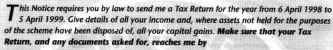

Tax Return for Trustees of approved self-administered Pension Schemes

for the year ended
5 April 1999

*T*his Notice requires you by law to send me a Tax Return for the year from 6 April 1998 to 5 April 1999. Give details of all your income and, where assets not held for the purposes of the scheme have been disposed of, all your capital gains. **Make sure that your Tax Return, and any documents asked for, reaches me by**

- **30 September 1999 if you want me to calculate the tax (or repayment) due,**

OR

- **31 January 2000, at the latest, or you will be liable to an automatic penalty.**

Please send a copy of any accounts for the pension scheme for each period of account ending in the year from 6 April 1998 to 5 April 1999 inclusive. If accounts have been prepared, you may, if you wish, complete the Tax Return based on the accounts for a twelve month period of account ending in the year from 6 April 1998 to 5 April 1999 inclusive.

If no accounts have been drawn up to a date ending in the year to 5 April 1999 then please send Statements of Assets and Liabilities as at 6 April 1998 and 5 April 1999. Please also include a statement of Incomings and Outgoings of the Scheme during the year ended 5 April 1999. To comply with this Notice the Return must be sent with a copy of the Pension Scheme accounts or statements of assets and liabilities, incomings and outgoings by 31 January 2000.

Make sure your payment of any tax the Pension Scheme owes reaches me by 31 January, or you will have to pay interest and perhaps a surcharge.

All Tax Returns will be checked. Please remember that there are penalties for supplying false information.

If you need help refer to the Pension Scheme Tax Return Guide or ring your Tax Office on the telephone number shown above.

SA970

Please turn over

545

Appendix 37

546

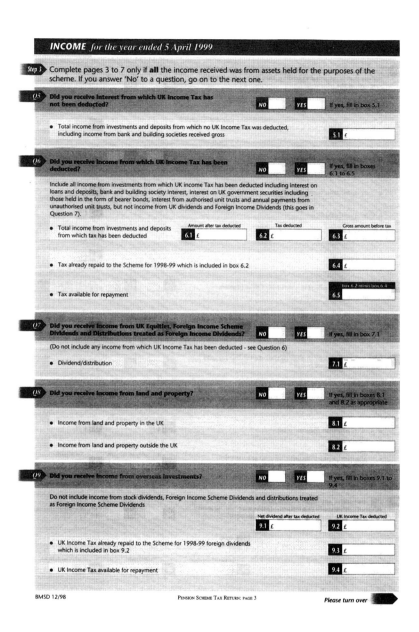

INCOME *for the year ended 5 April 1999*

Step 3 Complete pages 3 to 7 only if **all** the income received was from assets held for the purposes of the scheme. If you answer 'No' to a question, go on to the next one.

Q5 Did you receive interest from which UK Income Tax has not been deducted?

NO [ ] YES [ ] If yes, fill in box 5.1

- Total income from investments and deposits from which no UK Income Tax was deducted, including income from bank and building societies received gross

5.1 £ [ ]

Q6 Did you receive income from which UK Income Tax has been deducted?

NO [ ] YES [ ] If yes, fill in boxes 6.1 to 6.5

Include all income from investments from which UK income Tax has been deducted including interest on loans and deposits, bank and building society interest, interest on UK government securities including those held in the form of bearer bonds, interest from authorised unit trusts and annual payments from unauthorised unit trusts, but not income from UK dividends and Foreign Income Dividends (this goes in Question 7).

	Amount after tax deducted	Tax deducted	Gross amount before tax
• Total income from investments and deposits from which tax has been deducted	6.1 £	6.2 £	6.3 £

- Tax already repaid to the Scheme for 1998-99 which is included in box 6.2

6.4 £ [ ]

- Tax available for repayment

box 6.2 minus box 6.4
6.5 [ ]

Q7 Did you receive income from UK Equities, Foreign Income Scheme Dividends and Distributions treated as Foreign Income Dividends?

NO [ ] YES [ ] If yes, fill in box 7.1

(Do not include any income from which UK Income Tax has been deducted - see Question 6)

- Dividend/distribution

7.1 £ [ ]

Q8 Did you receive income from land and property?

NO [ ] YES [ ] If yes, fill in boxes 8.1 and 8.2 as appropriate

- Income from land and property in the UK

8.1 £ [ ]

- Income from land and property outside the UK

8.2 £ [ ]

Q9 Did you receive income from overseas investments?

NO [ ] YES [ ] If yes, fill in boxes 9.1 to 9.4

Do not include income from stock dividends, Foreign Income Scheme Dividends and distributions treated as Foreign Income Scheme Dividends

	Net dividend after tax deducted	UK Income Tax deducted
	9.1 £	9.2 £

- UK Income Tax already repaid to the Scheme for 1998-99 foreign dividends which is included in box 9.2

9.3 £ [ ]

- UK Income Tax available for repayment

9.4 £ [ ]

Appendix 37

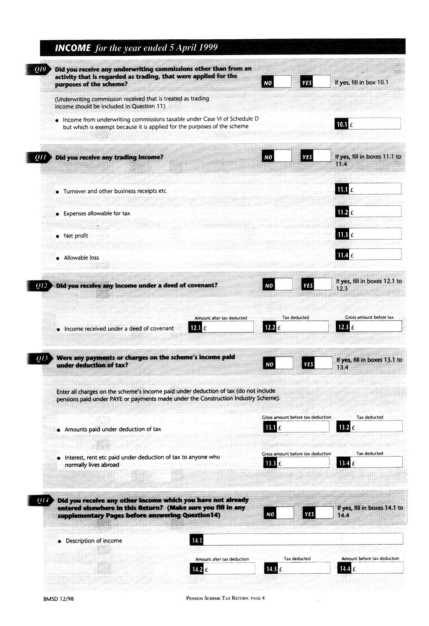

INCOME *for the year ended 5 April 1999*

Q10 Did you receive any underwriting commissions other than from an activity that is regarded as trading, that were applied for the purposes of the scheme?

NO ☐   YES ☐   If yes, fill in box 10.1

(Underwriting commission received that is treated as trading income should be included in Question 11)

• Income from underwriting commissions taxable under Case VI of Schedule D but which is exempt because it is applied for the purposes of the scheme

10.1 £ ☐

Q11 Did you receive any trading income?

NO ☐   YES ☐   If yes, fill in boxes 11.1 to 11.4

• Turnover and other business receipts etc   **11.1** £ ☐

• Expenses allowable for tax   **11.2** £ ☐

• Net profit   **11.3** £ ☐

• Allowable loss   **11.4** £ ☐

Q12 Did you receive any income under a deed of covenant?

NO ☐   YES ☐   If yes, fill in boxes 12.1 to 12.3

	Amount after tax deducted	Tax deducted	Gross amount before tax
• Income received under a deed of covenant	**12.1** £	**12.2** £	**12.3** £

Q13 Were any payments or charges on the scheme's income paid under deduction of tax?

NO ☐   YES ☐   If yes, fill in boxes 13.1 to 13.4

Enter all charges on the scheme's income paid under deduction of tax (do not include pensions paid under PAYE or payments made under the Construction Industry Scheme).

	Gross amount before tax deduction	Tax deducted
• Amounts paid under deduction of tax	**13.1** £	**13.2** £

	Gross amount before tax deduction	Tax deducted
• Interest, rent etc paid under deduction of tax to anyone who normally lives abroad	**13.3** £	**13.4** £

Q14 Did you receive any other income which you have not already entered elsewhere in this Return? (Make sure you fill in any supplementary Pages before answering Question14)

NO ☐   YES ☐   If yes, fill in boxes 14.1 to 14.4

• Description of income   **14.1** ☐

	Amount after tax deduction	Tax deducted	Amount before tax deduction
	14.2 £	**14.3** £	**14.4** £

BMSD 12/98   Pension Scheme Tax Return: page 4

548

Appendix 37

OTHER INFORMATION

Q15 Do you want to calculate the tax (or repayment) due? NO [ ] YES [ ]   If yes, do it now and fill in boxes 15.1 to 15.4

- Tax due for 1998-99 **before** you made any payments on account (put the amount in brackets if a repayment)   **15.1** £ [ ]

- Your first payment on account for 1999-2000, if appropriate   **15.2** £ [ ]

- tick box 15.3 if you are making a claim to reduce payments on account for 1999-2000 and say why in the 'Additional information' box **15.3** [ ]

- tick box 15.4 if you do not need to make payments on account **15.4** [ ]

Q16 Do you want to claim a repayment? NO [ ] YES [ ]   If yes, fill in boxes 16.1 to 16.12 as appropriate
(If you tick 'No', or the amount you are owed is below £10, I will set any amount you are owed against the next tax bill.)

Should the repayment (or payment) be sent
- to you? *tick box16.1* **16.1** [ ]

or

- the Scheme's bank or building society account or other nominee? *tick box 16.2* **16.2** [ ]

If you ticked either box 16.2 or 16.8, fill in boxes 16.3 to 16.7, 16.9 to 16.12 as appropriate.

Please give details of your bank (or your nominee's) bank or building society account for repayment

The Scheme's (or its nominee's) bank or building society **16.3** [ ]

Branch sort code **16.4** [ ] – –

Account number **16.5** [ ]

Name of Account **16.6** [ ]

Building Society ref. **16.7** [ ]

If your nominee is your agent, tick box 16.8 and complete boxes 16.9 to 16.11 **16.8** [ ]

Agent's ref. for you **16.9** [ ]

Name of nominee/agent

I authorise **16.10** [ ]

Nominee's address **16.11** [ ]

Postcode

to receive on my behalf the amount due

This authority must be signed by you. A photocopy of your signature will not do.

16.12 [ ]

Signature

Appendix 37

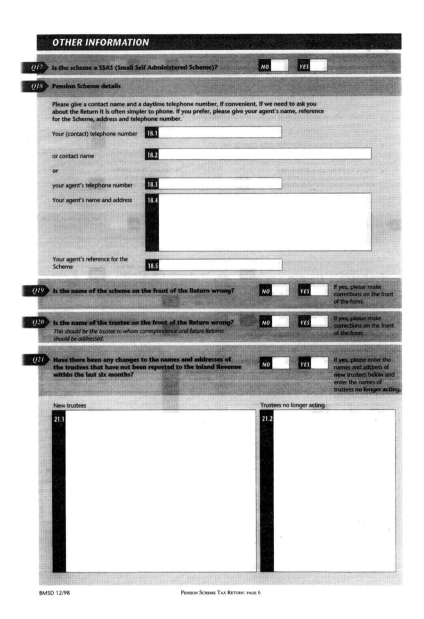

OTHER INFORMATION

Q17   Is the scheme a SSAS (Small Self Administered Scheme)?   NO ☐   YES ☐

Q18   **Pension Scheme details**

Please give a contact name and a daytime telephone number, if convenient. If we need to ask you about the Return it is often simpler to phone. If you prefer, please give your agent's name, reference for the Scheme, address and telephone number.

Your (contact) telephone number   **18.1** ☐

or contact name   **18.2** ☐

or

your agent's telephone number   **18.3** ☐

Your agent's name and address   **18.4** ☐

Your agent's reference for the Scheme   **18.5** ☐

Q19   Is the name of the scheme on the front of the Return wrong?   NO ☐   YES ☐   If yes, please make corrections on the front of the form.

Q20   Is the name of the trustee on the front of the Return wrong?   NO ☐   YES ☐   If yes, please make corrections on the front *This should be the trustee to whom correspondence and future Returns should be addressed.*   of the form.

Q21   Have there been any changes to the names and addresses of the trustees that have not been reported to the Inland Revenue within the last six months?   NO ☐   YES ☐   If yes, please enter the names and address of new trustees below and enter the names of trustees no longer acting.

New trustees   Trustees no longer acting

21.1 ☐   **21.2** ☐

BMSD 12/98   Pension Scheme Tax Return: page 6

OTHER INFORMATION

Q22 Tick box 22.1 if this Tax Return contains any figures that are provisional or estimated because you do not have final figures. Page 9 of the Pension Scheme Tax Return Guide explains the circumstances in which Tax Returns containing provisional figures may be accepted   **22.1** ☐

Give details in the 'Additional information' box below indicating which boxes are affected.

Additional information

Appendix 37

OTHER INFORMATION

Q23 Declaration - you must complete this part

I have filled in where required and am sending back to you the following Pages:

Tick

Pages 2 to 8 of this Tax Return ☐

Non-residence ☐

Income and gains from assets not held for the purposes of the scheme or where a percentage restriction applies ☐

Before sending back the completed Tax Return you must sign the statement below.

If you give false information or conceal any part of the Pension Scheme's income or chargeable gains you may be liable to financial penalties and/or you may be prosecuted.

23.1 I declare the information I have given on this Tax Return is correct and complete to the best of my knowledge and belief.

Signature of trustee   Date

Print name in full here

Printed in the UK by St Ives Direct, St Ives plc. R2H 2084 12/98.

552

Appendix 38

Revenue Inland

Tax Return Guide for Trustees of approved
self-administered Pension Schemes

for the year ended 5 April 1999

How to fill in your Tax Return

This Guide provides details
to help you fill in your
Tax Return.

Most of your questions will be
answered here. If you need
more help, please telephone
your Tax Office - the
telephone number is shown on
the front of your Tax Return.

Contact the Orderline for any
supplementary Pages, leaflets
or Help Sheets mentioned in
this Guide (see page 2).

SA975

Appendix 38

Your Tax Return for Trustees of approved self-administered Pension Schemes asks for details of the Scheme's income and capital gains. It applies to trustees of exempt approved self administered Schemes only. If the Scheme is neither exempt approved nor self administered, **do not** complete this Return. Please send it back to me, explaining why it is not appropriate to your Scheme. With the Tax Return I have sent two guides; this one to help you fill in the Tax Return, and another to help you calculate your tax bill (if you want to).

You are required to complete the Tax Return even if for 1998-99:

- the Scheme does not have to pay Income Tax or Capital Gains Tax on the income received by it
- there is no repayment or further repayment due to the Scheme.

Completion will not mean that you will have to pay any more tax than you would have had to pay without completing the Tax Return.

If accounts have been prepared for a 12 month period ending in the year to 5 April 1999, you may complete the Return using the figures included in the accounts. If accounts have not been prepared for a 12 month period ending in the year to 5 April 1999, complete the Tax Return for income received in the year ended 5 April 1999.

Trustees of every Scheme get the first 8 pages of the Tax Return. There are supplementary Pages for some types of income and gains. For example, there are Pages if some or all of the Scheme's income is not exempt from Income Tax or Capital Gains Tax.

It is your responsibility to make sure that you complete the right supplementary Pages.

You must send the ones you need to complete back to me on time with the rest of your Return. Otherwise you will be liable to an initial automatic penalty of £100, and further penalties for continued delay.

First, fill in page 2 of the Tax Return. This tells you which supplementary Pages you must complete. Pages 4 and 5 of this Guide will help.

Next, if you need any supplementary Pages phone the Orderline. It can provide any of the supplementary Pages, leaflets or Help Sheets mentioned in this Guide.

Decide if you want me to calculate the tax (or repayment) for you. If so, make sure your completed Tax Return reaches me by 30 September 1999. It will save you time and effort if you leave it to me.

If you miss the deadline of 30 September you need to calculate the tax (or repayment) and make sure your completed Tax Return reaches me by 31 January 2000.

Do not delay doing your Tax Return. You do not have to wait for the deadline shown on the front of the Tax Return. Tackling it earlier means you will have more time to get help if you need it. Sending it earlier does not mean you have to pay tax any sooner.

If you are not sure what to do, please ask for help before you start to fill in your Tax Return.

A Bank PLC
Statement

BUILDING SOCIETY
Statement

Gather together information about the Scheme's circumstances for 1998-99. For example, if accounts were prepared for a 12 month period ending within the year ended 5 April 1999, you will need these. Whether or not accounts were prepared you will need any building society statements, dividend vouchers and other financial records. Do not send these with your Tax Return; keep them safe.

You are now ready to fill in your Tax Return. Pages 4 and 5 of this Guide tell you what to do, and the rest of the Guide will help you fill in the boxes. If you need more help ask your Tax Office or tax adviser.

If after sending me your Tax Return, you find that you have made a mistake, let me know at once. Similarly, you should correct any provisional figures as soon as you can. You will only be penalised if your Tax Return is incorrect through fraud or negligence or if there is unreasonable delay in providing corrected figures once they are known to you. The penalties can be up to 100% of the difference between the correct tax due and the amount that would have been due on the basis of the figures you returned. You could also be prosecuted.

Remember, you are responsible for the accuracy of your Tax Return.

In its dealings with you, the Inland Revenue is governed by the Taxpayer's Charter set out on page 10 of this Guide. Page 10 also explains how to complain if you are dissatisfied with the way the Inland Revenue handles your tax affairs.

When I get your completed Tax Return I will process it based on your figures, to work out whether the Scheme owes any tax and if so, how much, or how much the Inland Revenue owes you. If I see any obvious mistakes - for example in the arithmetic - I will put them right and tell you what I have done.

I will send you my calculation of your tax if you have asked the Inland Revenue to do it for you. If you have calculated your tax, I will let you know if it is wrong.

Later, I will send you a statement of your account with the Inland Revenue. This will explain how to pay any tax due - see the notes on page 9 of this Guide.

Once your Tax Return has been processed it will be checked. I have until 31 January 2001 to do this (later if you send your Tax Return late). I may make enquiries about your figures and ask you to send me the records from which you took them. I will also check your figures against any details received from other sources, such as your building society or bank.

Read page 9 of this Guide if your Tax Return was delivered to you after 31 July 1999.

1998

You must, by law, have kept all records.

* Failure to do so could give rise to penalties.

April 1999

You receive your Tax Return:

* find your records
* fill in your Return.

30 September 1999

Send back your completed Tax Return if you want me to:

* calculate your tax in time for the 31 January 2000 payment, if one is due.

31 January 2000

This date is important for three reasons. This is the date by which you must:

* let me have your completed Tax Return
* pay the balance of any tax you owe
* pay your first payment on account for the 1999-2000 tax year, if appropriate.

You must send me your Tax Return and pay what you owe by this date to avoid automatic penalties and interest.

Appendix 38

Filling in your Tax Return

Answer all the questions. If you tick 'No', go to the next question. If you tick 'Yes', fill in the Pages and boxes that apply to you.

- Write clearly using blue or black ink and only in the spaces provided.

- Use numbers only, when you are asked for amounts.

- Please do not include pence - round down your income and gains, to the nearest pound, and round up your tax credits and tax deductions - for example, if your Building Society interest is £3,500.87 after tax deductions, enter £3,500 in box 6.1

- Do not delay sending your Tax Return just because you do not have all the information you need - see the notes for box 22.1 on page 8 of this Guide.

If you need help, look up the question number in the notes.

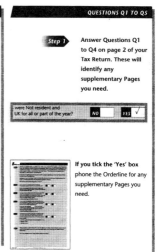

Step 1 Answer Questions Q1 to Q4 on page 2 of your Tax Return. These will identify any supplementary Pages you need.

If you tick the 'Yes' box phone the Orderline for any supplementary Pages you need.

Page 2 of the Tax Return

Step 2 Fill in the supplementary Pages that apply to you.

Please enter your name and tax reference on each copy.

Questions 5 to 14 should be completed only if **all** the income of the Scheme was received from assets held for the purposes of the Scheme or no percentage restriction applies. If it was not, or a percentage restriction applies, then ask the Orderline for the Pages, 'Income and gains from assets not held for the purposes of the Scheme or where a percentage restriction applies'.

Step 3 Fill in pages 3 to 8 of your Tax Return

Example of filling in page 3 of the Tax Return

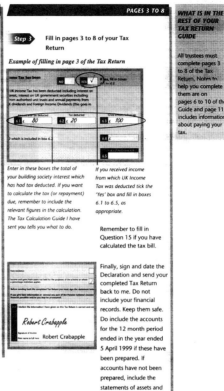

Enter in these boxes the total of your building society interest which has had tax deducted. If you want to calculate the tax (or repayment) due, remember to include the relevant figures in the calculation. The Tax Calculation Guide I have sent you tells you what to do.

If you received income from which UK Income Tax was deducted tick the 'Yes' box and fill in boxes 6.1 to 6.5, as appropriate.

Remember to fill in Question 15 if you have calculated the tax bill.

Finally, sign and date the Declaration and send your completed Tax Return back to me. Do not include your financial records. Keep them safe. Do include the accounts for the 12 month period ended in the year ended 5 April 1999 if these have been prepared. If accounts have not been prepared, include the statements of assets and liabilities at 6 April 1998 and 5 April 1999.

All trustees must complete pages 3 to 8 of the Tax Return. Notes to help you complete them are on pages 6 to 10 of the Guide and page 11 includes information about paying your tax.

Appendix 38

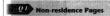 **Non-residence Pages**

Fill in the Non-residence Pages if you are claiming the trustees were not resident and not ordinarily resident in the UK for all or part of the year to 5 April 1999.

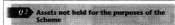 **Assets not held for the purposes of the Scheme**

If the Scheme's assets were not held exclusively for the purpose of the Scheme, ask the Orderline for the Pages 'Income and gains from assets not held for the purposes of the Scheme or where a percentage restriction applies'.

Assets that are held for the purposes of the scheme

This phrase is used in various places throughout the Tax Return and supplementary Pages.

Pension schemes are exempt from Income Tax and Capital Gains Tax on income and gains received from deposits or investments held for the purposes of the scheme. There is a specific exemption for stock lending fees. There is also an exemption for underwriting commissions where the underlying activity does not fall to be treated as a trading activity. Contracts entered into in the course of dealing in financial futures or traded options are regarded as investments. Any other income and gains that are received are **not** exempt from Income Tax and Capital Gains Tax .

Assets held by the Trustees of an exempt approved scheme are regarded as held for the purposes of the scheme so long as, and for as long as, they are held on trust for the purposes stated in the scheme rules of providing retirement and death benefits for employees and their families. If the stated purposes are being met then the exemption is available.

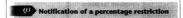 **Notification of a percentage restriction**

If the Pension Schemes Office have notified you that a Sch 22 para 7 restriction applies, ask the Orderline for the Pages 'Income and gains from assets not held for the purposes of the Scheme or where a percentage restriction applies'.

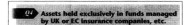 **Assets held exclusively in funds managed by UK or EC insurance companies, etc.**

You only need to answer Questions 1 to 6 and Questions 15 to 23 if the Scheme's assets were held exclusively in funds managed by UK or European Community insurance companies, policies or contracts.

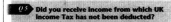 **Did you receive income from which UK Income Tax has not been deducted?**

Your bank or building society or deposit taker's statement will show you the interest you have received without tax deducted (gross). Add up all the amounts you received during 1998-99 for all your accounts and enter the total in box 5.1

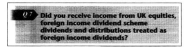 **Did you receive income from which UK Income Tax has been deducted?**

Interest is generally paid after lower rate tax has been deducted. The amount of tax deducted, the amount of interest before tax was deducted and the amount of interest after tax will usually be shown on the scheme's:

- bank or deposit taker's statement or pass book, **or**
- certificate of tax deducted provided by the company which pays interest on any loan made by the scheme.

If you do not have all three figures, they can be worked out as follows.

Either like this:
Tax deducted   = amount **after tax**   x 25%
Statement shows interest of £80 after tax
So tax is £80 x 25% = £20

or like this:
Tax deducted   = amount before tax x 20%
Statement shows interest of £100 before tax
So tax is £100 x 20% = £20

The amount of your gross interest is the same as the amount of your net interest with the tax added back on.

Only the amount of Income Tax deducted that has not been repaid to you during 1998-99 is still repayable. You must not include in any other repayment claim any Income Tax that has been repaid to you (enter such amounts in box 6.4). If none of the tax in box 6.2 has been repaid to you during 1998-99, the figure of tax repayable now, and to be entered in box 6.5, is the same as that entered in box 6.2. If, exceptionally, the figure to be entered in box 6.5 is a *minus* figure then add this figure in box P25 of the Tax Calculation Working Sheet, if you are calculating the tax (or repayment) due.

The deemed distribution element of share buybacks and dividends from authorised unit trusts should be included in Question 7.

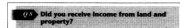 **Did you receive income from UK equities, foreign income dividend scheme dividends and distributions treated as foreign income dividends?**

Tax credits from this income are not repayable and there is no need to enter the total of the tax credits.

Include in this question deemed distributions from **all** share buybacks.

If the scheme took up an offer of shares in place of a cash dividend, this is a 'scrip' or 'stock' dividend. Your dividend statement should have the 'appropriate amount in cash' on it - this is the amount to include in box 7.1.

Foreign income dividends are dividends paid by a company under the foreign income dividend scheme, or qualifying distributions, which are treated as foreign income dividends. Your dividend voucher should show the dividend and notional tax. As with tax credits, this notional tax is not repayable and should not be included in box 7.1.

Q 8 **Did you receive income from land and property?**

Enter in boxes 8.1 and 8.2 the **net** income arising from the receipt of income from land and property in 1998-99. This will be the same figure that appears in the Scheme's accounts or statement of income.

Appendix 38

How to fill in your Pension Scheme Tax Return

Certain forms of income from land and property are regarded as trading income and should be included in Question 11. Such sources of income include the following, although the list is not complete:

- canals and inland navigations and docks
- mines and quarries, including sand pits, gravel pits and brickfields
- rights of markets and fairs, tolls, bridges and ferries.

Overseas tax

If overseas tax was deducted, do not include the income in this Question but include it in box 9.1.

Proceeds from disposals of land or property

Gains from the disposal of land and property should be included only if they arose from assets not held for the purposes of the Scheme. In this case they are appropriate to the 'Income from assets not held for the purposes of the scheme' supplementary Pages, available from the Orderline.

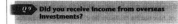 **Q 9 Did you receive income from overseas investments?**

Include income in box 9.1 even if UK Income Tax has not been deducted.

Income should be translated to sterling at the rate of exchange prevailing when the income arose. If you are unsure of the exchange rate to be applied ask your Tax Office or tax adviser.

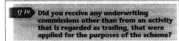 **Q 10 Did you receive any underwriting commissions other than from an activity that is regarded as trading, that were applied for the purposes of the scheme?**

Include commissions, other than own insurance commissions, received from the underwriting of any share issue floated on the Stock Exchange. Where such underwriting commissions are applied to assets held for the purposes of the scheme, see page 6 of this Guide, then the income is exempt from tax and the amount(s) should be included in box 10.1. However, if you know that the activity giving rise to the income, or part of it, amounts to trading, do not include that income in box 10.1, but include it or that part of it in box 11.2 in Question 11.

If underwriting commissions were received but were not applied to assets held for the purposes of the scheme, do not include the income in box 10.1. Instead, ask the Orderline for the 'Income from assets not held for the purposes of the scheme' supplementary Pages.

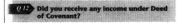 **Q 11 Did you receive any trading income?**

If at any time in the year to 5 April 1999 the Scheme carried on a trade, you should attach any trading accounts prepared for the period and complete boxes 11.1 to 11.4. If you need help to arrive at the Scheme's net profit, ask the Tax Office or your tax adviser.

The Scheme should have records of all its business transactions. These must be kept until at least 31 January 2005 in case the Tax Office asks to see them.

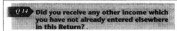 **Q 12 Did you receive any income under Deed of Covenant?**

Enter the total amounts in boxes 12.1 to 12.3. Income Tax deducted from income received from Deeds of Covenant is not repayable.

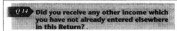 **Q 13 Were any payments or charges on the scheme's income paid under deduction of tax?**

Include in boxes 13.1 and 13.2 the total charges on the Scheme's income that were paid under deduction of tax. Do not include the totals of any interest or rent etc paid under deduction of tax to anyone who lives abroad. These payments should be included in boxes 13.3 and 13.4.

Do **not** include payments of pensions made under PAYE or payments under the construction industry scheme in any of the boxes in this question.

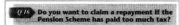 **Q 14 Did you receive any other income which you have not already entered elsewhere in this Return?**

Include income of whatever nature including from futures contracts and options contracts that has not been included elsewhere within the Tax Return. You may wish to refer back to Questions 1 to 4 on page 2 of this Tax Return in case the income is covered in those questions, in which case complete the appropriate supplementary Pages.

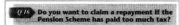 **Q 15 Do you want to calculate the tax (or repayment)?**

Calculating the tax (or repayment) is optional. If you tick 'No' to this question I shall assume that you want me to calculate the tax for you, and you must send the completed Tax Return to me by 30 September 1999. See page 9 of these notes if your Tax Return was issued after 31 July 1999.

If you wish to calculate your tax or repayment, then complete the Working Sheet in the Tax Calculation Guide and copy figures to Question 15.

I need this information so that I can check that you have got it right.

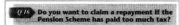 **Q 16 Do you want to claim a repayment if the Pension Scheme has paid too much tax?**

If you wish to claim a repayment, fill in boxes 16.1 to 16.12 as appropriate. If you do not claim a repayment, one will not be sent to you automatically. Any amount you are owed will be set against your next tax bill.

We would normally prefer not to make repayments of small amounts, because of administrative costs. So if the overpaid tax is below £10 we will normally set it against your next tax bill. But if you do not agree with this set-off, please contact your Tax Office.

Tick box 16.1 if you want the repayment sent to you.

Tick box 16.2 if you want the repayment sent direct to your bank or building society account or to someone else. Fill in boxes 16.3 to 16.7 to give details of your account or, if you want the repayment to go to a nominee, or that nominee's account. If you want the repayment to go to your agent fill in boxes 16.8 and 16.9. Fill in boxes 16.10 and 16.11 to give details of your nominee or agent. **You must sign box 16.12.**

Please note that the Inland Revenue reserves the right not to make a repayment to your nominee, and will not normally make a repayment to an overseas nominee.

No vouchers are required with this Return.

Appendix 38

How to fill in your Pension Scheme Tax Return

These questions **must** be completed. The information will help me keep my records up to date.

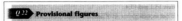

Do not delay sending your Tax Return just because you do not have all the information you need. You must do your best to obtain the information, but if you cannot provide final figures by the time you need to send back your Return, then estimate the amount.

Tick box 22.1 and describe in the Additional Information box:

*   which figures are provisional (refer to the appropriate box numbers on the Return)
*   why you could not give final figures, **and**
*   when you expect to give me your final figures.

I will not normally regard a Tax Return as incomplete simply because it contains provisional figures, provided you have taken all reasonable steps to get the final figures, and you ensure that they are sent as soon as they are available. I would not, however, regard pressure of work either on you, or your tax adviser, or the complexity of the Scheme's affairs, as reasons for accepting a provisional figure.

You must ensure that any provisional figures you do include are reasonable and take account of all the information available to you.

If you negligently submit a provisional figure, which is either inaccurate, or unnecessary, you may be liable to a penalty.

Other estimates (including valuations)

In some situations you may need to provide an estimated figure or valuation which you do not intend to amend at a later date. Broadly, this will be the case when:

*   a valuation is required (for example, of an asset at a certain date for the purposes of calculating Capital Gains Tax liability), **or**
*   there is inadequate information to enable you to arrive at a reliable figure (for example, where the records concerned have been lost or destroyed), **or**
*   while there is inadequate information to arrive at a precise figure, a reliable estimate can be made.

You should identify any valuations you have used by indicating the figure in the 'Additional information' box on page 7 of your Tax Return, and giving details of the valuation.

You should also identify any figures in your Tax Return, which may not be very reliable; where appropriate, explain how the figure has been arrived at. If you are including an estimate which, while not a precise figure is sufficiently reliable to enable you to make an accurate Tax Return, there is no need to make specific reference to it.

Q 23 Declaration

Tick the boxes to show which pages of the Tax Return and supplementary Pages you have filled in. Remember to send back:

*   the Tax Return
*   any supplementary Pages that you have completed
*   the accounts for a twelve month period ending in the year ended 5 April 1999, or
*   statements of assets and liabilities at 6 April 1998 and 5 April 1999.

If you have filled in the Tax Return

Sign and date the Return in box 23.1. This **must** be signed by a trustee of the Scheme, who has been nominated by the trustees of the Scheme.

If you have had the Tax Return filled in for you by someone else

If you have had the Tax Return filled in for you by someone else, acting on your behalf, you must still sign the Return yourself to confirm to us that, to the best of your knowledge, it is correct and complete. This applies whether you have paid for the services of an accountant or other tax practitioner, or have simply had help from a friend or relative.

You should always allow sufficient time for checking and signing the Tax Return if it has been completed by someone on your behalf (particularly if you are likely to be abroad near the deadline for sending the Return back to me). Failure to make appropriate arrangements could mean that you miss the deadline and are charged penalties and interest.

Appendix 38

Paying your tax

■ Your Statement of Account

If you send me your completed Tax Return by 30 September 1999, I will send you a statement showing how much tax you owe us, or we owe you, before any final payment is due on 31 January 2000. It will also explain how to pay.

If you send me your completed Tax Return later than 30 September 1999, I cannot guarantee to process it in time to let you know how much to pay on 31 January 2000, although I will let you have instructions on how to pay your tax.

This might mean that you have to estimate how much to pay. If you pay too little, you will have to pay interest (and perhaps a surcharge). If you pay too much and have claimed a repayment, I will repay it with any interest due. If you do not claim a repayment I will set the amount due, plus any interest, against your next tax bill.

■ If you make payments on account

Some trustees may have to make payments on account, each normally equal to one half of the previous year's tax liability (net of tax deducted at source and tax credits on dividends). The first payment is due on 31 January 1999 and the second is due on 31 July 1999.

If the payments on account add up to less than you owe for 1998-99, you must pay the difference by 31 January 2000. That amount can be calculated by completing boxes P26 to P30 in the Tax Calculation Guide Working Sheet.

If you have paid more than you needed to for your 1998-99 tax bill I will repay the difference if you claimed a repayment in Question 16, or set it against your next tax bill.

When you settle your tax bill for 1998-99 by 31 January 2000 you will also need to make your first payment on account for 1999-2000 if one is due. The second payment on account for 1999-2000 should be made by 31 July 2000.

If you have asked me to calculate your tax, I will tell you how much to pay on account.

If you are calculating your tax, complete boxes P26 to P30 in the Tax Calculation Guide Working Sheet.

Any Capital Gains Tax included in your 1998-99 tax bill will be excluded from the calculation of your 1999-2000 payments on account. If you have asked me to calculate your tax, I will exclude it from the amount I tell you to pay on account. If you are calculating your tax, the calculation excludes Capital Gains Tax when you work through the boxes to calculate your payment on account.

You can make a claim to reduce these payments if you expect your tax bill (net of tax deducted at source and tax credits on dividends) to be lower in 1999-2000 than in 1998-99. The Tax Calculation Guide will tell you what to do if you wish to claim to reduce your payments on account.

■ How to pay

Pay to the Accounts Office by one of the following methods:
- Bank Giro
- Girobank transfer
- BACS or CHAPS - you can use these payment methods to transfer funds electronically. Please ask the Accounts Office if you want further details.
- post.

The address of the Accounts Office and further details of how to pay are given on the back of the Statement of Account I will send you.

■ If you do not pay your tax on time?

Interest will be charged on all late payments from the date the tax becomes due until it is paid. A surcharge will also be made on any tax for the year ending 5 April 1999, which is due by 31 January 2000, but is still unpaid at 28 February 2000. This surcharge will be:
- 5% of tax outstanding at 28 February 2000
- a further 5% of any tax still outstanding at 31 July 2000.

■ If you pay too much tax

If you do not claim a repayment, then the amount you are owed, plus any interest due, will be set against your next tax bill.

If you do claim a repayment by ticking the 'Yes' box in Question 16, I will repay it, plus any interest due on the amount overpaid.

■ If your Tax Return is incorrect

If your Tax Return is incorrect and you have:
- **paid too much tax**, then I will repay it, plus any interest due on the amount overpaid, if you have claimed a repayment (otherwise I will set it against your next tax bill), or
- **not paid enough tax**, then I will ask for further tax. I may require you to pay interest from the original due date, penalties and a surcharge.

■ If the notice requiring you to make your Tax Return was given after 31 July 1999.

If the notice requiring you to make your Tax Return was given on or after 31 July 1999, you must send it back to me:
- within two months of the date the notice was given to you if you want me to calculate your tax, or
- by the later of 31 January 2000 and three months after the date the notice was given if you want to calculate the tax.

If the notice requiring you to make your Tax Return was given after 31 October 1999 and you had notified me by 5 October 1999 of income and gains taxable for the year 1998-99, then the tax is due three months after the date the notice was given. In all other cases, the tax is due on 31 January 2000. You will be charged interest on any tax paid after the due date. A surcharge of 5% will also be made on any tax still unpaid more than 28 days after the due date.

The notice requiring you to make your Tax Return is 'given' on the day it is delivered to you. I will normally assume, for example, for the purpose of charging automatic penalties for the late submission of your Tax Return, that delivery will have taken place not more than seven days after the date of issue shown on the front of it.

561

Appendix 38

If you have a complaint that the Officer in Charge of the Tax Office dealing with your Pension Scheme cannot settle, you should contact the Inland Revenue Regional Director responsible for the area dealing with tax affairs of the Pension Scheme. Leaflet *IR120: You and the Inland Revenue* tells you how to do that. It is available from the Orderline or any Tax Enquiry Centre or Tax Office.

If the Regional Director does not settle your complaint to your satisfaction, you can ask the Adjudicator to look into it and recommend appropriate action.

The Adjudicator, whose services are free and who is an impartial referee whose recommendations are independent, can be contacted at:

Adjudicator's Office
Haymarket House
28 Haymarket
London SW1Y 4SP

Telephone 0171 930 2292

At any time you can ask a Member of Parliament to refer a complaint to the Independent Parliamentary Ombudsman (officially the Parliamentary Commissioner for Administration). Further details can be obtained from the Ombudsman's office at:

Church House
Great Smith Street
London SW1P 3BW

Telephone 0171 276 2130/3000

The Adjudicator will not look at complaints which have been taken up by the Ombudsman, but the Ombudsman can look at complaints that the Adjudicator has investigated.

The Taxpayer's Charter

You are entitled to expect the Inland Revenue

To be fair

- by settling your tax affairs impartially
- by expecting you to pay only what is due under the law
- by treating everyone with equal fairness

To help you

- to get your tax affairs right
- to understand your rights and obligations
- by providing clear leaflets and forms
- by giving you information and assistance at our enquiry offices
- by being courteous at all times

To provide an efficient service

- by settling your tax affairs promptly and accurately
- by keeping your private affairs strictly confidential
- by using the information you give us only as allowed by the law
- by keeping to a minimum your costs of complying with the law
- by keeping our costs down

To be accountable for what we do

- by setting standards for ourselves and publishing how well we live up to them

———— ✦ ————

If you are not satisfied

- we will tell you exactly how to complain
- you can ask for your tax affairs to be looked at again
- you can appeal to an independant tribunal
- your MP can refer your complaint to the Ombudsman

In return, we need you

- to be honest
- to give us accurate information
- to pay your tax on time

The Inland Revenue is a Data Controller under the Data Protection Act. We hold information for the purposes specified in our notification made to the Data Protection Commissioner, and may use this information for any of them.

We may get information about you from others, or we may give information to them. If we do, it will only be as the law permits, to

- check accuracy of information
- prevent or detect crime
- protect public funds.

We may check information we receive about you with what is already in our records. This can include information provided by you as well as by others such as other government departments and agencies and overseas tax authorities. We will not give information about you to anyone outside the Inland Revenue unless the law permits us to do so.

These notes are for guidance only, and reflect the position at the time of writing. They do not affect any rights of appeal.

Appendix 39

 Inland Revenue | **Pension Scheme Tax Calculation Guide**

for the year ended 5 April 1999

How to calculate your Tax

*Also see the Pension Scheme
Tax Return Guide*

 This Guide has step by step instructions and a Working Sheet to help you calculate the Scheme's tax (or repayment).

Keep your Guide in case you want to check any calculations I send you.

You do not have to calculate the tax or repayment if your completed Tax Return reaches me by 30 September.

If I receive your Tax Return after 30 September and you have not done the tax calculation, I will do it for you, but you may not receive it in time to know what to pay by 31 January. If you do not pay enough, you will also have to pay interest and perhaps a surcharge.

As with any other part of the Tax Return, you can ask your Tax Office for help if you have difficulty with particular parts of the calculation. But we can do the calculation for you only when you have sent your Tax Return.

SA976

Appendix 39

Calculating your tax bill

How to use this Guide

The Working Sheet in this Guide will help you calculate the tax bill or the amount of repayment due to the Scheme.

If you have answered 'No' to Questions 11 to 14 and you did not need to complete the 'Income and gains from assets not held for the purposes of the scheme or where a percentage restriction applies' supplementary Pages, and:

* there are entries in boxes 6.5 or 9.4, then the Scheme does not owe any tax and there is a repayment due. **In this case, only complete box P25 in the Working Sheet,**

or

* there are **no** entries in boxes 6.5 or 9.4, then the Scheme does not owe any tax and there is no repayment due. In this case, the Working Sheet does not need to be completed. Enter £0 in box 15.1 in the Tax Return.

However, if you answered 'Yes' to Questions 11 to 14 or completed the 'Income and gains from assets not held for the purposes of the scheme or where a percentage restriction applies' Pages then read the next section below and complete the Working Sheet.

Key steps in calculating your tax

* Work out your total taxable income for 1998-99
* Work out the Income Tax due on this income
* Deduct tax paid or deducted from the taxable income
* Add any Capital Gains Tax due
* Work out the total tax due on income and gains
* Deduct any Income Tax available for repayment
* Work out the total tax owed or overpaid for 1998/99
* Work out if you need to make payments on account for 1999-2000

Working out your total taxable income for 1998-99

Transfer the income details from the Tax Return or supplementary Pages to boxes P1 to P8 inclusive, as indicated.

Box P9 is the total of the figures in boxes P1 to P8.

Complete box P10 only if the Scheme had any trading losses and deduct that figure from box P9 to arrive at the figure in box P11. If there were no trading losses, then copy the figure in box P9 to box P11.

Working out the Income Tax due on this income

The figure of Income Tax due in box P12 is the amount in box P11 at 34%.

If there are any entries in boxes 13.2 or 13.4, copy the totals to box P13 and add this figure to the one in box P11 to arrive at the figure in box P14. Otherwise, copy the figure from box P12 to box P14.

Deduct tax paid or deducted from the taxable income

Transfer the figures of tax deducted to boxes P15 to P20 as indicated in the Working Sheet and total the amounts in box P21.

If there is a figure in box P10

boxes P18, P19 and P20 Overseas tax and notional tax can only be used to reduce liability to UK Income Tax; they cannot be repaid by the Inland Revenue. The amounts of overseas tax and notional tax to be transferred to boxes P18, P19 and P20 in the calculation Working Sheet will depend on whether there are trading losses in box P10 that have been set against income.

If there are **no trading losses in box P10**, transfer the figures of tax deducted to boxes P15 to P20 as indicated in the Working Sheet, and total the amounts in box P21.

If there are **trading losses in box P10**, transfer the figures of tax deducted to boxes P15 to P17, as indicated in the Working Sheet. The figures to be transferred to boxes P18 to P20 may need to be restricted.

If the amount of notional tax/tax credit in box 2.15 is more than the figure in box P12, restrict the amount to be transferred from box 2.15 to box P18 to the figure in box P12. Otherwise, copy box 2.15 to box P18.

If the total of boxes P18 and 2.21 is more than the figure in box P12, restrict the overseas tax from box 2.21 to the amount by which box P12 exceeds box P18, and copy the restricted amount to box P19. Otherwise, copy box 2.21 to box P19.

If the total of boxes P18, P19 and 2.27 is more than the figure in box P12, restrict the overseas tax from box 2.27 to the amount by which box P12 exceeds the total of boxes P18 and P19, and transfer the restricted amount to box P20. Otherwise, transfer box 2.27 to box P20. Otherwise, transfer box 2.27 to box P20. The full amount of UK Income Tax from box 2.26 should be transferred to box P20, irrespective of the box P12 figure.

If there is a figure in box P21, deduct it from the P14 figure to arrive at the entry for box P22. If box P21 is blank, copy the figure from box P14 to P22. If the figure in box P21 is greater than the figure in box P14, put brackets around the *minus* figure which results. This should never be more than the amount of UK tax deducted in boxes P15 to P20.

Add any Capital Gains Tax due

If there is an entry for capital gains in box 2.41, the Capital Gains Tax due in box P23 is the amount of the gain in box 2.41 at 34%.

Work out the total tax due on income and gains

Add the figure in box P23 to the one in box P22 to arrive at box P24, the amount of total tax due. If there was no capital gain, then copy the figure from box P22 to box P24.

Deduct any Income Tax available for repayment

The only amount of Income Tax that can reduce the amount of total tax due in box P24 is the total of UK Income Tax that has still to be repaid to the Scheme for 1998-99. This is the total of the amounts entered in boxes 6.5 and 9.4 on page 3 of the Tax Return and boxes 2.10 and 2.30 in the 'Income and gains from assets not held etc' supplementary Pages. Income Tax deducted from income received from Deeds of Covenant (box P15) is **not** available for repayment.

Working out your payments on account for 1999-2000

box 15.2 in the Tax Return Some pension schemes will have to make two payments on account for 1999-2000, each equal to half of the Income Tax liability for 1998-99. The first payment is due on 31 January 2000, and the second is due on 31 July 2000.

No payments on account for 1999-2000 will be necessary if the tax bill for 1998-99 is below a threshold of £500, or if most (80%) of the tax is collected at source.

Follow the instructions for boxes P31 and P32 on the Working Sheet, and the notes below.

box P31 To work out whether payments on account are needed, where box P22 is equal to or more than £500, multiply box P14 by 20% and enter the result in box P31.

If box P22 is less than box P31, no payments on account are needed. If box P22 is equal to or more than box P31, payments on account are necessary. Fill in box P32.

Copy box P32 *(including pence)* to box 15.2 in the Tax Return, **unless you are claiming to reduce the payments on account.**

Calculating your tax bill - *continued*

Reducing payments on account

box 15.3 in the Tax Return Tick box 15.3 if you want to make reduced payments on account. This might happen if:

- you expect the income in 1999-2000 to be lower than the income in 1998-99, **or**
- you expect that more of the income will be taxed at source.

If you want to reduce the payments on account:

- you must make a reasonable **estimate on the basis of the information you have now** of the difference between the Income Tax you expect to pay for 1999-2000 and the Income Tax for 1998-99 on this Tax Return. You can reduce each of the payments on account by half this difference.
- enter the amount of each reduced payment on account in box 15.2
- tick box 15.3
- write the reason for reducing the payments on account in the 'Additional information' box on page 7 of the Tax Return.

If you decide later that you have reduced the payments on account by too little, you should write to the Tax Office giving the reason why you are claiming to reduce the payments further.

You should ensure that the payments you make by 31 January 2000 and 31 July 2000 add up to your best estimate of the final liability for 1999-2000.

If the payments on account turn out to be different from the tax bill for 1999-2000:

- if you have paid more than you needed to, you will be credited with interest
- if you have paid less than you needed to, you will be charged interest.

The two payments on account only need to add up to the smaller of:

- the actual Income Tax due for 1999-2000, (net of tax deducted at source and tax credits on dividends), **or**
- the actual Income Tax due for 1998-99 (net of tax deducted at source and tax credits on dividends).

If you have been fraudulent or negligent in claiming a reduction in payments on account, you may be charged a penalty.

If you decide later that you have reduced the payments on account by too much, you can make a claim to revise the amounts upwards and/or pay additional amounts in line with your revised estimate. If you do not make a claim, additional amounts paid may be allocated to other outstanding liabilities.

box 15.4 in the Tax Return Tick box 15.4 if you do not need to make payments on account.

These notes are for guidance only, and reflect the position at the time of writing. They do not affect any rights of appeal.

Appendix 39

Tax Calculation Working Sheet

Total income that is not exempt from tax:

- *Other income* (from boxes 14.4 or 2.38) — **P1** £
- *Trading profits* (from box 11.3) — **P2** £
- *Covenant income* (from box 12.3) — **P3** £
- *Income from which no UK Income Tax deducted* (from box 2.2) — **P4** £
- *Income from which UK Income Tax deducted* (from box 2.8) — **P5** £
- *UK equities etc* (from box 2.16) — **P6** £
- *Income from land and property* (from boxes 2.18 and 2.20) — **P7** £
- *Overseas investments* (from box 2.28) — **P8** £

Total **P9** £

Deductions

- *Trading losses* (from box 11.4) — **P10** £

Income minus deductions — box P9 *minus* box P10 — **P11** £

Income Tax due — box P11 x 34% — **P12** £

Plus recoverable tax on charges (from boxes 13.2 and 13.4) — **P13** £

Income Tax due — box P12 + box P13 — **P14** £

Tax paid or deducted at source

- *Covenants* (from box 12.2) — **P15** £
- *Other income* (from box 14.3 or 2.33) — **P16** £
- *UK Income Tax deducted* (from box 2.7) — **P17** £
- *UK equities etc* (from box 2.15, and see note) — **P18** £
- *Foreign land or property* (from box 2.21, and see note) — **P19** £
- *Overseas investments* (from boxes 2.26 and 2.27, and see note) — **P20** £

total boxes P15 to P20 — **P21** £

Income Tax due — box P14 *minus* box P21 — **P22** £

- *Capital Gains Tax due* (from box 2.41 x 34%) — **P23** £

Total Tax due — box P22 + box P23 — **P24** £

- *Income Tax available for repayment* (from boxes 6.5, 9.4, 2.10 and 2.30) — **P25** £

Tax Calculation Working Sheet

▶ Work out the total tax owed or overpaid for 1998-99

box P24 minus box P25

P26 £

Copy the figure in box P26 to
box 15.1 in the Pension
Scheme Tax Return

Minus payments already made (from your Statements of Account)   P27 £

box P26 minus box P27

P28 £

Tax you owe for 1998-99 (where box P28 is a *positive* figure)   P29 £

OR

Tax you have overpaid for 1998-99 (where box P28 is a *negative* figure)   P30 £

▶ Work out if you need to make payments on account for 1999-2000

If box P22 is less than £500, you do not need to make payments on account.
If it is equal to or more than £500, carry on to boxes P31 and P32.

box P14 x 20%

P31 £

If box P22 is less than box P31, you do not need to make payments on account.
If it is equal to or **more** than box P31, you do have to make payments on account.
Fill in box P32.

box P22 x 50%

This is the amount of each payment on account for 1999-2000   P32 £

Copy the figure in box P32 to
box 15.2 in the Pension
Scheme Tax Return

▶ Work out the total amount of tax due by 31 January 2000

Figure from box P29 (a *positive* figure)   £

OR

Figure from box P30 (a *negative* figure)   £

PLUS the figure from box P32   £   P33 £

*If this figure is positive
then this is the amount
owing by 31 January 2000*

Appendix 40

GN9: Retirement Benefit Schemes—Actuarial Reports

Classification

Practice standard

Legislation or Authority

Pensions Act 1995, section 41(1) and (2)(c).

The Occupational Pension Schemes (Minimum Funding Requirement and Actuarial Valuations) Regulations 1996 (SI 1996 No 1536). (Hereinafter called "the Valuation Regulations".)

The Occupational Pension Schemes (Disclosure of Information) Regulations 1996 (SI 1996 No 1655). (Hereinafter called "the Disclosure Regulations".)

Application

Any actuary responsible for preparing a formal actuarial report on funding (or where funding is covered) when a retirement benefits scheme is set up, or at intervals thereafter when an actuarial valuation is to be prepared.

It applies to, but is not limited to, reports on valuations which are required under Section 41(2)(c) of the Pensions Act 1995, and so to the Actuarial Statement required under Regulation 30(7) and Schedule 6 to the Valuation Regulations.

In relation to defined contribution schemes and to small self-administered schemes, this Guidance Note should apply if the advice given is on the funding required to meet a level of benefit (other than lump sum deaths benefits) or on the benefits the funds will support, but not otherwise.

Version 5.1 can be followed for valuations with effective dates before 1 August 1997 and this should be indicated in the report.

Author

Pensions Board.

Status

Approved under Due Process.

Version	Effective from
1.0	01.04.84
2.0	01.04.87
3.0	01.04.88
3.1	01.09.90
4.0	29.09.92
5.0	01.03.93
5.1	01.06.94
6.0	01.08.97

1   Introduction

1.1   This Guidance Note applies to all formal actuarial valuation reports which are required by the scheme governing documentation or by legislation or are specifically requested by the actuary's client.

568

1.2　In the case of schemes to which MFR legislation applies. Regulation 30 of the Valuation Regulations sets forth the time limits attaching to the effective dates of valuations and to the passing of the reports to the actuary's clients. The actuary is encouraged to remind the trustees or managers appropriately when valuations are due, and should comply with the legislation over production of the report.

1.3　In the case of other schemes, and not withstanding any longer intervals permitted by the scheme documentation, the actuary should encourage trustees or managers to have valuations made at appropriate intervals.

1.4　Generally the report should be in the hands of the actuary's client within one year of its effective date.

1.5　Where an event occurs which under the Trust Deed and Rules commences a discontinuance procedure, this Guidance Note continues to apply and the actuary should consider whether it would be appropriate to advise the trustees that an actuarial valuation should be carried out.

2　Purpose of the Guidance

2.1　The purpose of the Guidance Note is to ensure that reports contain sufficient information to enable the current funding level of a scheme to be understood and also, in the case of a defined benefit scheme, to enable the expected future course of a scheme's contribution rates to be understood. It is not intended to restrict the actuary's freedom of judgement in choosing the method of valuation and the underlying assumptions.

2.2　Although any report will be addressed to the actuary's client (normally the trustees but in some circumstances the employer) the actuary needs to bear in mind that the advice may be made available to third parties who can reasonably be expected to rely on it. In connection with actuarial reports required under the Pensions Act, Regulation 7 of the Disclosure Regulations specifies third parties including statutory bodies to whom trustees must make reports available.

3　The Report

3.1　Introduction

3.1.1　The items in 3.2 to 3.11, except where otherwise indicated, are normally regarded as essential components of a report. Other information may often desirable and suitable explanations of some features may be very important, for example the effect on the funding level of an improvement in benefits with retroactive effect.

3.1.2　The report should be in writing. Should a priliminary report be issued not including all the components listed below, in the expectation that a further and full report will be made, it must be made clear in the preliminary report that it does not conform to GN9 but that the further report will do so.

3.1.3　A report on a scheme subject to the Minimum Funding Requirement may incorporate the actuary's statement (prepared in accordance with Guidance Note GN27) on that Rquirement if it is appropriate to do so, i.e. the prescribed calculations have been made by the appointed Scheme Actuary and the report is addressed to the trustees. Care should, however, be taken that the results of calculations with different objectives are clearly identified.

3.2　Basic information

3.2.1　The report should make it clear to whom it is directed, by specifying the client. This will normally be the trustees of a trust-based scheme but in some circumstances will be the employer or both, jointly. An opening statement should state the purpose for which the valuation is made and the dates as at which the current valuation and, if applicable, the immediately preceding valuation were conducted.

3.2.2　It is desirable that the opening statement should also refer to the appropriate sections of the legal documentation of a scheme under which the valuation is being made.

3.2.3　The report should include a statement of the benefits which have valued (for example, by a summary of the terms of a scheme or by reference to appropriate documents). Reference should be made to the extent to which allowance has been made for discretionary increases in benefit (and the recent practice in granting such increases) or discretionary benefits.

3.2.4　The report should include a brief but clear description of the membership and financial data on which the investigation is based, including a desription of the assets. If the actuary has relied on information or opinions provided by others, he should carry out appropriate investigations to assess the accuracy and reasonableness of the data being used. If the actuary has any reservations as to the reliability of the data, such explanation or qualification as appropriate should be given. In particular, if audited accounts as at the date of valuation are not available. this fact should be stated.

Appendix 40

3.2.5 Reference should also be made to any insurance arrangements in place for the benefit of the scheme or any insolvency insurance. This would include, for example, group life assuance held by trustees.

3.2.6 In the case of a scheme in discontinuance, there should be a statement of when benefits ceased to accrue.

3.3 Inter-valuation period

3.3.1 The report should include a statement of the rates of contribution due during the inter-valuation period; and a commentary on any material developments in the scheme during that period, and on any significant variations in experience from the assumptions made at the previous valuation.

3.3.2 In the case of a defined contribution scheme, there need only be a statement of the rates of contributions due.

3.4 Funding objectives

3.4.1 In the case of a defined benefit scheme, the report should explain the funding objectives and the method being employed to acheive those objectives. A statement should be made as to the extent to which there have been changes in the objectives or the method since the last report of a similar nature. Implications in terms of stability of contribution rates and of future funding levels should be explained. If the scheme is subject to the Minimum Funding Requirement comment should be made on the difference from the objectives of that requirement.

3.5 Valuation assumptions and methods

3.5.1 The report shuld contain a statement of both the demographic and economic assumptions made, explicitly or implicitly, in valuing both the liabilities and the assets and, in the case of a defined benefit scheme, the method employed in deriving the contribution rate in 3.6.1. Attention should be directed particularly to those assumptions to which the contribution rate is sensitive. A statement should be made as to the extent to which there have been changes to the assumptions used since the last of a similar nature.

3.5.2 Where appropriate, the report should state whether and in what way future entrants have been taken into account in the valuation.

3.5.3 The report should comment on the compatibility of the basis of valuing the assets with that of valuing the liabilites. The actuary should also comment on any notable or particular risks in the investment stategy of a scheme relative to the form and incidence of the liabilities. The actuary is encouraged to comment on the sensitvity of the funding to future investment market changes. Where relevant, attention should be drawn to such aspects as concentration of assets, levels of self-investment, and currency mismatching. If the assets include derivatives, the actuary should consider the requirements of GN25.

3.6 Contribution rate

3.6.1 In the case of a defined benefit scheme, the report should recommend appropriate contributions consistent with the funding objectives for the period until the next anticipated formal actuarial valuation. If appropriate, the actuary may recommend different contribution rates for different groups of members, or different contribution rates payable for different intervals in the period to such a valuation. Alternatively, if the contribution rate is determined elsewhere, e.g. in governing documentation, so that a recommendation by the actuary is inappropriate, the report should include comment on the adequacy of the rate.

3.6.2 The report should also address the issue of the expected future course of a scheme's contribution rates in the longer term on current methodology and assumptions.

3.7 Minimum Funding Requirement

3.7.1 In the case of a scheme subject to the Minimum Funding Requirement, the Minimum Funding Requirement funding level as given in the most recent statement should be stated with appropriate explanation.

3.8 Current funding level—discontinuance assumption

3.8.1 The purpose of the statement on this subject is to give an indication of the accrued solvency position of a scheme in discontinuance or were the scheme to become a scheme in discontinuance at the valuation date and, in particular, if there were no further contributions due from the scheme sponsor. The actuary should adopt an approach with that principle in mind.

3.8.2   The report should state whether or not, in the actuary's opinion, the assets would have been sufficient at the valuation date to cover liabilities arising (including any dependants' contingent benefits) in respect of pensions in payment, preserved benefits for members whose pensionable service has ceased and accrued benefits for members in pensionable service, the last of which will normally be related to pensionable service to, and pensionable earnings at, the date of valuation including revaluation on the statutory basis (or on such higher basis as has been promised). The accrued benefits of all active service members should be included irrespective of the preservation legislation. If the assets were not sufficient, the report should indicate the level of coverage.

3.8.3   If the scheme is not already in discontinuance, the actuary must make a judgement as to whether, in the event of contributions from a scheme sponsor terminating, a wind-up would be likely in the short term. If a wind-up were likely, the statement should be based on assets valued at market value and liabilities in respect of active service members and deferred members either as cash equivalents or as an estimate of the cost of deferred annuities or as a combination of both. For pensioners (and contingent pensioners) an estimate of the cost of immediate annuities will normally be appropriate. A reminder should be given that market conditions change. If a wind-up were not likely, closed fund approach should be adopted. The report should state whether a closed fund approach or a wind-up approach has been adopted. If a wind-up approach has been adopted, the report should also state whether liabilities in respect of active service members and deferred members have been valued as a cash equivalent or as an estimate of the cost of deferred annuities, or as a specified combination of both.

3.8.4   Provision for future expenses should be made. The provison should be appropriate to the approach adopted under 3.8.3. The report should give the basis of the provision and point out that it is a provision, not an estimate or quotation.

3.8.5   Where appropriate, having regard to the approach adopted under 3.8.3, it should be pointed out that the value of the liabilities may not represent the cost required to secure the liabilities of a scheme were a scheme to wind-up as at the date of the valuation.

3.8.6   The report should include a description of the consequences (without necessarily quantifying) of the priority clause in the Trust Deed and Rules as overriden by the Pensions Act 1995 and regulations.

3.9   Current funding level—on going assumption

3.9.1   If the scheme is not already in discontinuance, the report should include a statement as to the funding position on the assumption that both scheme and the scheme sponsor(s) are on-going. The statement should include, where relevant, a comparison between assets and accrued liabilities, the latter with pensionable salaries projected where appropriate to assumed end of pensionable service, if this is not otherwise conveyed by the comments on the funding objectives and the contribution rate.

3.10   Reconciliation

3.10.1   A reconciliation of the valuation should be made with the position disclosed by the previous valuation, and a statement included in the report quantifying the financially material items of actuarial gain or loss, including changes in the valuation method and of the valuation assumptions.

3.11   General

3.11.1   A statement should be made in the report whether the valuation has been prepared in accordance with GN9 current at the effective date of the valuation report.

3.11.2   There should be a statement indicating any departures GN9. The actuary is expected to comply with GN9, unless the actuary is convinced that full compliance would be inappropriate, in which case a complete explanation and justification of all departures should be given.

4   The Actuarial Statement

4.1   This section relates only to the Actuarial Statement required under Regulations 30(7) and Schedule 6 to the Valuation Regulations.

Appendix 40

4.2 A Statement will normally follow a formal valuation to which the earlier parts of this Guidance Note apply. A revised statement can, however, be issued at any time.

4.3 Section 1 of the Statement requires an opinion from the actuary on the adequacy of the resources of a scheme 'in the normal course of events'. In interpreting this expression at the date of each Statement, the actuary should take a prudent view of the future without taking into account every conceivable unfavourable development. The actuary should regard this as excluding the possibilities of events—including those external to a scheme—which cannot reasonably be expected to have been allowed for in a conservative approach to the matter. The actuary will not generally need to give a negative or qualified opinion provided that the contribution rate specified reflects that referred to in 3.6.1 and provided that any Statement under 3.9.1 and provided that any Statement under 3.9.1 does not indicate cause for concern. If a negative or qualified opinion is given, attention should be drawn to the relevant sections of the last valuation report.

4.4 For the purpose of Section 2 of the Statement, use may be made of the names of commonly used valuation methods in GN26: *Pension Fund Terminology*. It is sufficient to describe the *key* funding assumptions; these are not necessarily limited to the financial assumptions. Readers should be referred to the latest valuation report for fuller details.

4.5 Care should be taken to avoid confusion between MFR liabilities, liabilities on an ongoing valuation basis and discontinuance liabilities.

4.6 If the Statement has been based on data (either in respect of assets or liabilities) which the actuary considers to be unreliable, mention should be made of the actuary's reservations. Particular reference should be made if the statement is not based on audited accounts.

4.7 Regulation 30 refers to the issue of a revised Statement during the inter-valuation period. This is not designed to require the actuary to monitor the situation continuously; however, if he or she is made aware or becomes aware of developments which materially affect the continuing validity of the latest Statement, then a revised Statement should be prepared and issued under Regulation 30.

Maximum Permissible Funding Rates For Small Self-Administered Schemes (Ssass) (SSAS 1996 Method)
Practice Notes Appendix IX

1   **Introduction**

These notes set out the method (the SSAS 1996 Method) fixed by *IR SPSS* calculate maximum contributions to SSASs from 1 June 1996 for approvable retirement benefits. The method makes allowance for the earnings cap (the '*permitted maximum*') where applicable and applies to money purchase and defined benefit SSASs.

The method for calculating maximum *special contributions* to SSASs is described in Section 8.

2   **Transitional arrangements**

SSASs established prior to 1 June 1996 are not required to comply fully with the SSAS 1996 Method until later of:

(*a*)   1st June 2001, and

(*b*)   The effective date of the second triennial actuarial valuation report after 31 May 1996.

By this time, the maximum joint contributions by employer and employee should then be no higher than the maximum allowed under the SSAS 1996 Method. The following events during the transitional period will trigger the SSAS 1996 Method:

Where *special contributions* are paid after 31 May 1996 and which were recommended by an actuary after 1 December 1995.

Where it is proposed to increase contributions during the transitional period for an existing member above the maximum ordinary contribtuion recommended by an actuary in the last valuation or because a new member joins the scheme: (the SSAS 1996 Method need not apply at that time to other continuing members whose contributions are not being increased).

Where undisclosed *retained benefits* come to light which, when expressed in terms of pension, exceed £260 in aggregate, or (for Class C members only) lump sums of £2,500 in aggregate.

If the contribution made on one of the above trigger events is more than the maximum under the *IR SPSS* 1996 Method then the increase may not be made but the existing contribution does not have to be reduced at that time. If the contribution is less than the maximum under the PSO 1996 Method but the increase would take it over then a partial increase up to the maximum may be made.

A replacement scheme will enjoy these transitional arrangements if, and only if, one of the reasons for continuation set out in Practice Notes IR12 (1991), Appendix III, applies. This is irrespective of which maximum limits basis applies to the member.

A member who belongs to an insured scheme before 1 September 1994 and who becomes a member of a SSAS may be able to benefit from the transitional arrangements until 1 September 1999 (provided none of the trigger events described above occurred). See PSO Update No 16.

3   **De minimis limit**

No check against the maximum funding rate is required for a member where:

(*a*)   the annual aggregate contributions to all schemes, excluding contributions for death in service benefits, for the same employment do not exceed 17.5% of *remuneration* (within the permitted maximum); and

(*b*)   contributions (including special contributions) have not been at a higher amount than the figure determined from this limit in any earlier year.

There is no corresponding de minimis limit for *special contributions*

Appendix 41

4   **Current valuation of existing assets (V)**

The value of assets (V) is to be taken as the market value, as shown in the scheme accounts in respect of the member concerned.

If the maximum funding rate is being assessed on a date other than the scheme's accounting date, then the value of the assets should be taken at market value. If this is not readily available the assets may be taken as the value at the most recent accounting date increased (or decreased, as appropriate) by the monies received by the scheme between that date and the date of assessment, all accumulated at the rate of 8.5% per annum compound.

Assets under any other 'Money Purchase' schemes relating to the same employment are to be brought into account. In addition, for Class A members, the value of benefits from all connected schemes and *associated employments* must be brought into account as explained in PN 7.19. Assets under *free-standing AVC schemes* (but not in-house AVCs) may be ignored. Concurrent benefits in respect of the same employment from defined benefit schemes are dealt with in 7C below.

Where PN 7.9 applies in determining maximum benefits, the value of retirement annuities or personal pension benefits is to be taken as the transfer value at the date of assessment (or if exceptionally a transfer value is not available, the present value of the projected benefits at retirement calculated on a basis consistent with the financial assumptions specified in paragraph 2 of the Appendix to these notes.

5   **Special contributions (s)**

The amount of any *special contributions(s)* which is to be paid at the time of calculation is also to be taken into account as indicated in 7D below. The method of calculating the maximum *special contribution* is described in Section 8.

6   **Expenses**

Where a scheme meets its own expenses, these should be justified and clearly identified in the actuary's report. A reserve for such expenses excluding investment-related expenses may be incorporated in the calculations equal to the capitalised value of all expected future administration costs to be borne by the scheme.

7   **Method of calculation**

Factors [1] to [14] are described in the Appendix to these notes.

A   **Value of *Retained Benefits (R)***
The figures represented R1 and R2 in section B below are arrived at as follows:

R1 = transfer value of the *retained benefit* at the assessment date ÷ Factor [1]

R2 = transfer value of the *retained benefit* at the assessment date ÷ Factor [3].
Retained benefits may be ignored (i.e. R1 and R2 taken as zero) in the circumstances described in PN 7.5 etc. If the *retained benefit* is already in payment, then it should be taken at its current value (and including the amount of any lump sums already paid – PN 16.35).

B   **Calculation of the Maximum Permissible Pension at the Normal Retirement Date**
The calculation varies depending on which basis of Revenue limits applies i.e. post 1989 (Class A), pre 1 June 1989 (Class B), or pre 17 March 1987 (Class C) members. For Class A members it is necessary to calculate separately the maximum permissible pension on the basis of current *remuneration* (P1) and the current *permitted maximum* (P2).

'Either "*final remuneration*" (as defined in PN Appendix1) or "*current remuneration*" can be used for the calculations. There is no requirement to use just one approach for all members of a particular SSAS.

"*Final remuneration*" should be used in every case for the three year period immediately prior to NRA.

Where contributions are to be fixed as level amounts for the period (to be longer than three years) until the next valuation, that can be reflected in the calculation of *Factor [2]* and *Factor [4]* (which are defined in the Appendix to this note). Otherwise, those contributions factors should allow for *remuneration* to increase every year in line with the assumptions specified in that appendix.

The maximum total benefits at *normal retirement date* derived from this calculation applies to the aggregate benefits from all schemes relating to the current employment and for Class A members *associated employment/connected schemes*.

574

(I) Class A Members

P1 = The greater of

(*a*) NS (maximum 40)/60 × *remuneration* and

(*b*) the lesser of

    (i)   NS (maximum 20)/30 × *remuneration* and

    (ii) 2/3 × *remuneration* – R1

P2 = The greater of

(*a*) NS (maximum 40)/60 × *remuenration* and

(*b*) the lesser of

    (i)   NS (maximum 20)/30 × *permitted maximum* and

    (ii) 2/3 × *permitted maximum* – R2

(II) Class B Members

The calculation of P1 is the same as for Class A members.

The calculation of P2 is not required.

(III) Class C Members

P1 = The greater of

(*a*) NS (maximum 40)/60 × *remuneration* and

(*b*) the lesser of

    (i)   The uplifted scale (PN7.39) × *remuneration* and

    (ii) 2/3 × *remuneration* – R1

The calculation of P2 is not required.

C **Allowance for Concurrent Benefits under a Defined Benefit Scheme**

If the employee is a concurrent member of a defined benefit scheme in respect of the same employment scheme then V must be increased either by

the value of the prospective pension under that scheme at the *normal retirement date* based on current pensionable earnings in that scheme or,

by the value of the prospective pension under that scheme at the *normal retirement date* based on the current *permitted maximum*.

The value must be assessed on a basis consistent with that used for calculating the maximum contribution C below.

D **Calculation of the Maximum Regular Contribution (C)**

For Class A members, the maximum regular contribution (C) is the lesser of the amounts calculated on the basis of remuneration (C1) and the current *permitted maximum* (C2).

For Class B and C members, C1 always applies and C2 is not calculated.

$$C1 = \frac{P1 \times Factor\ [1] - V - S}{Factor\ [2]} \times 1.05$$

$$C2 = \frac{P2 \times Factor\ [3] - V - S}{Factor\ [4]} \times 1.05$$

The value V used in these calculations must be adjusted to allow for concurrent defined benefit scheme membership (see 8C).

The amount calculated above in C is the maximum annual figure to all schemes relating to the current employment.

It should be noted that the value of S cannot be negative.

8 **Method of calculation of maximum special contributions**

Special contributions should not be made to fund benefits in advance of the maximum justifiable by reference to service to date.

For a post 1989 (Class A) member the maximum is the lesser of S_1 and S_2 where

$$S_1 = (\tfrac{N}{NS} \times P1 \times \text{Factor [1]}) - V \quad S_2 = (\tfrac{N}{NS} \times \text{Factor [3]}) - V$$

For Class B and C members S_1 always applies

P1 and P2 are calculated as described in Section 7.

9   *Reassessment of maximum contribution level*

     A   *3 Year reassessment*

         The contribution limit must be reassessed within 3 years of the date that the maximum contribution C has been established unless it has been previously amended in accordance with 9B below (in which case the 3 year period runs from the date of the most recent change in 9B).

         The revised value of C must apply from the effective date of the assessment. A new 3 year period will then commence.

     B   Special Contributions

         A reassessment of the maximum contributions must be made whenever a *special contribution* outside that shown in an actuarial report is paid. The revised value of C must apply immediately (increase or decrease) and, if necessary, future regular contributions reduced. A new 3 year period will commence for the purpose of 9A above.

10   Death in service benefits

       Contributions towards insurance of approvable death-in-service benefits may be paid in addition to the contributions being paid for post retirement benefits.

11   **Review of assumptions**

       The financial and demographic assumptions underlying the factors in the Appendices to these notes will be reviewed from time to time by the Pension Schemes Office in consultation with the Government Actuary's Department and the Association of Pensioneer Trustees.

Annex to Appendix IX

1   **Definitions**

       T means the period between the *normal retirement date* of the member and the date of calculation.

       NRA means the age of the member at the *normal retirement date*.

2   **Financial assumptions**

rate of investment return	8.5%p.a.
Rate of future salary growth	6.9% p.a.
Rate of post retirement pension increases	5.3% p.a.
Rate of price inflation	5.3% p.a.

3   **Factors**

       Factors [1] is the present value at the date of calculation of a pension of £1 pa payable at NRA allowing for future salary increases up to NRA.

       Factor [2] is the present value at the date of calculation of a future contribution of £1 p.a. until NRA increasing in line with earnings. The frequency of the increases is to be in accordance with paragraph 7B.

       Factor [3] is the present value at the date of calculation of a pension of £1 payable at NRA allowing for future price inflation to NRA.

       Factor [4] is the present value at the date of calculation of a future contribution of £ p.a. until NRA increasing in line with prices. The frequency of the increases is to be in accordance with paragraph 7B.

The annuity factors may be calculated as a life annuity guaranteed five years and payable in accordance with the likely payment frequency using mortality PA(90) ultimate minus two years age. A contingent post-retirement spouse's pension may be included if the member is married at the date of calculation, or if there is a nominated financial dependent. The actual age of the spouse may be used where known: otherwise it may normally be assumed that in the case of a male employee he is married to a wife 3 years younger than himself, and in the case of a female employee, that she is married to a husband 3 years older than herself.

Appendix 42

Pension Schemes: Loss of Tax Approval

Inland Revenue
Press Office

North West Wing
Bush House
Aldwych
London WC2B 4PP

Media enquiries:
071 438 6692/6706/7327/7356
Fax: 071 438 7541
Non-media enquiries:
Your own tax office or
071 438 6420/6425

2 November 1994

PENSION SCHEMES:
LOSS OF TAX APPROVAL

The Financial Secretary to the Treasury, Sir George Young Bt MP, today announced that the Government intends to introduce legislation in the next Finance Bill to discourage the exploitation of the pensions tax reliefs by certain approved occupational pension schemes.

In reply to a written Parliamentary Question today, the Financial Secretary said:

"The tax approval system gives pension schemes very favourable tax treatment if certain conditions are met concerning the amount, timing and form of the benefits to be paid. The purpose of the tax reliefs is to encourage the provision of pensions to employees during their retirement.

Arrangements are now being encountered under which the trustees of some small self-administered occupational pension schemes have exploited the tax approval system. These arrangements involve initially taking advantage of the tax reliefs but then engineering loss of tax approval when access to the accumulated funds, in circumstances not allowed by the tax approval conditions, is desired by the scheme members or the sponsoring employer. An example is where the scheme wishes to lend all or a large part of its funds to the sponsoring employer.

The tax approval system is not intended to be used in this way. Arrangements of this kind undermine the pensions purpose for which the tax reliefs are given. Where a pension scheme wishes to take advantage of those reliefs it must accept all the conditions on which approval is granted.

In order to discourage the misuse of the tax approval system in this way a special 40 per cent tax charge will be levied on the value of funds held by these schemes at the time tax approval is withdrawn. This new tax charge will apply where tax approval ceases on or after today. Further details are given in an Inland Revenue Press Release published today."

/The text of

1.

578

The text of the proposed Finance Bill Clause is set out in the Annex to this Press Release.

DETAILS

1.   Tax approved occupational pension schemes benefit from a number of tax reliefs. In particular:

- contributions by employees and employers are tax deductible (and the employer's contributions are not treated as part of the employees' taxable income);

- the investment income and capital gains of the schemes build-up tax-free; and

- pension benefits are taxable (but part can be taken as tax-free lump sums).

2.   The aim of the tax reliefs is to encourage employers and employees to set aside part of current earnings in order to provide an income in retirement. This is normally done through an employer setting up a pension scheme which is subject to a trust (so that the scheme assets are kept separate from those of the employer and the beneficiaries).

3.   Where an approved scheme fails to comply with the tax approval conditions, or the terms of a scheme are altered in an unacceptable way, tax approval can be withdrawn. Withdrawal is normally effective from the date when the failure to observe the approval conditions occurred. The tax treatment of a scheme and any payments it makes following loss of approval will be subject to the normal provisions applying to non-approved schemes. In particular this will mean that any benefits paid will be treated as the taxable income of the recipient.

4.   The trustees of some small occupational pension schemes (those with less than 12 members) manage the schemes' investments themselves. These are known as small self-administered pension schemes. Typically, these schemes are set up to provide benefits for directors with controlling interests in the sponsor company. Usually the directors are also the pension scheme trustees.

5.   Some small self-administered schemes which have benefited from the tax reliefs given to approved schemes have deliberately broken the tax approval conditions in order to secure loss of approval. This, for example, has enabled the whole of the accumulated funds to be paid to the directors or to be invested in the employer's business. In certain circumstances the funds may escape tax altogether. The tax approval rules were never intended to be used in this way.

/ In order to

2.

579

6.   In order to prevent this exploitation of the system of tax approval a new tax charge is to be introduced. Its aim is to discourage pension schemes from breaking the tax approval rules. The tax charge will:

- apply where approval of a scheme ceases on or after today;

- affect those schemes that have either -

    (i) less than 12 members, or

    (ii) 12 or more members which include, or have included, a controlling director of a company that participates in the scheme;

- be set at 40 per cent and will, except for debt due from the employer (or any connected person) which will be taken at face value, be levied on the market value of the scheme assets at the effective date from which approval ceases.

Press enquiries to: Diane Gee
                     Lynn Simpson

          on: 071-438-6692/6706/7327
                  (out of hours 0860 359544)

3.

580

Appendix 43

Exemption from Actuary's Statement

Under *regulation 6(1)(a)* of *SI 1996/1655* a copy of the latest actuarial statement (whether or not a revised statement) shall be made available no later than seven months after the end of the scheme year if required by regulations made under *section 41(1)* and *41(2)(c)* of the *Pensions Act 1995*.

Money purchase schemes do not have to produce such a statement, by virtue of section 56 of the Act which exempts them from the minimum funding requirement as shown in the extract below.

Part I - Occupational Pensions:
Minimum Funding Requirement:

56.–(1)   Every occupational pension scheme to which this section applies is subject to a requirement (referred to in this Part as "the minimum funding requirement") that the value of the assets of the scheme is not less than the amount of the liabilities of the scheme.

(2)   This section applies to an occupational pension scheme other than-

(a)   a money purchase scheme, or

(b)   a scheme falling within a prescribed class or description.

(3)   For the purposes of this section and sections 57 to 61, the liabilities and assets to be taken into account, and their amount or value, shall be determined, calculated and verified by a prescribed person and in the prescribed manner.

(4)   In calculating the value of any liabilities for those purposes, a provision of the scheme which limits the amount of its liabilities by reference to the amount of its assets is to be disregarded.

(5)   In sections 57 to 61, in relation to any occupational pension scheme to which this section applies-

(a)   the amount of the liabilities referred to in subsection (1) is referred to as "the amount of the scheme liabilities",

(b)   the value of the assets referred to in that subsection is referred to as "the value of the scheme assets",

(c)   an "actuarial valuation" means a written valuation prepared and signed by the actuary of the scheme of the assets and liabilities referred to in subsection (1), and

(d)   the "effective date" of an actuarial valuation is the date by reference to which the assets and liabilities are valued.

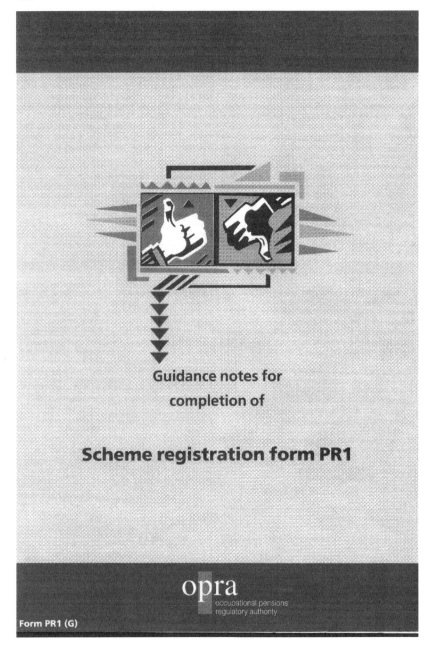

Guidance notes for
completion of

Scheme registration form PR1

opra
occupational pensions
regulatory authority

Form PR1 (G)

What is a "Registrable scheme"?
A registrable scheme is an occupational or personal pension scheme which either;

a. is established in the United Kingdom, or

b. has a place at which its management is conducted in the United Kingdom and has a representative appointed to carry out the functions of a trustee in the United Kingdom, and which either;

c. is a scheme in respect of which a person has applied for, or received, the approval of the Board of Inland Revenue for the purposes of sections 590 or section 591 (other than subsection (2)(g)) of the Income and Corporation Taxes Act 1988 (conditions for approval of retirement benefits scheme and discretionary approval), or for the purposes of Chapter IV of Part XIV of that Act (personal pension schemes), or

d. is a scheme which is a public service scheme, and which;

e. has more than one member, and

f. provides benefits which are not solely payable on the death of a member;
and for the purposes of these Regulations, an occupational pension scheme which is a retirement benefits scheme approved under section 591(2)(h) (discretionary approval) of the Income and Corporation Taxes Act 1988 shall be treated as a personal pension scheme.

When should a scheme register?
A scheme should provide the Pension Schemes Registry with the information required for registration within 3 months.

Scheme Membership Upon Registration
Total membership means the number of members on the day on which the scheme becomes a registrable scheme .

A member means any person who:-

1. is in pensionable service under the scheme, or

2. has rights under the scheme by virtue of pensionable service under the scheme, or

3. has rights under the scheme by virtue of having been allowed transfer credits under the scheme.

other than a member in respect of whom entitlement under the scheme is only for benefits payable on his death.

Levy Payments
In general every registrable occupational pension scheme with two or more members is liable for the payment of both a general and compensation levy towards meeting the cost of the Occupational Pensions Advisory Service, the Pensions Ombudsman, the Occupational Pensions Regulatory Authority, the Occupational Pensions Compensation Board and the Registrar of Occupational and Personal Pension schemes. The levies are calculated by reference to the total membership of the scheme. A levy calculation sheet is enclosed.

What is meant by "Registrable date"?
Levy payments are due from the beginning of the registration year in which the scheme became registrable. These instructions apply to schemes with a registrable date of the 1st April 1997 or later.

If a scheme has a registrable date earlier than the 1st April 1997 different rules and levy rates will apply. If applicable then please contact the Pension Schemes Registry on 0191-2256393/4/6/8 for advice.

Exemption from payment of the Compensation Levy.
Although there is a general requirement to pay the compensation levy, a registrable scheme will be exempt from the requirement in the specific circumstances listed below:

a. which has fewer than 12 members, all of whom are trustees and under the rules of which all trustees decisions must be made by unanimous agreement, save that the non-participation of a pensioneer trustee in any such decision shall be disregarded;

b. which is a public service scheme;

c. which is a relevant lump sum retirement benefits scheme;

d. in respect of which any Minister of the Crown has given a guarantee or made any other arrangements for the purpose of securing that the assets of the scheme are sufficient to meet the liabilities;

e. which is a section 615(6) scheme meaning:-

a scheme with such a superannuation fund as is mentioned in section 615 (6) of the Income and Corporation Taxes Act 1988

f. any occupational pension scheme in respect of which the employer cannot become insolvent within the meaning given by section 123 PSA 1993 (interpretation of Chapter II of Part VII PSA 1993).

Appendix 44

An exemption will remain in force indefinitely whilst the above criteria apply.

Circumstances in which the requirement to pay the compensation and general levies will be waived
Payment from both levies may be waived where:-

a. there is no employer in relation to the scheme, or

b. the employer in relation to the scheme is insolvent,

and one of the following applies:

1. for money purchase schemes, there are insufficient unallocated assets to meet the levy liabilities; or

2. for final salary schemes, a "minimum funding requirement actuarial valuation" shows the value of scheme assets is less than 100% of liabilities; or

3. for final salary schemes where there has not yet been a "minimum funding requirement valuation" prepared,

the last "actuarial disclosure valuation" shows the amount by which scheme assets exceed liabilities is less than the levy liabilities.

A new application for waiver must be made annually.

Multi Employer Schemes
When occupational pension schemes with more than 1 employer are divided into 2 or more sections for administration purposes the Occupational and Personal Pension Schemes (Levy) Regulations 1997, regulation 9 may apply for the purposes of calculation and waiver of the levies. The legislation should be read in full for specific details and schemes may wish to seek independent advice. If you wish to register a scheme as a multi employer scheme, advise the Registrar who will provide the format in which scheme information should be presented.

This information is provided for general guidance and should not be taken as an authoritative statement of the law.

Please read the following notes to help you complete the form

BOX 1(a) - Full Name of Scheme

Enter the full name of the scheme as given in the Trust Deed or any subsequent amending deed.

BOX 1(b) - Previous Name(s)

Enter any other names under which the scheme has been known and the names of the schemes which in whole or in part have merged with, or been replaced by it, since 6 April 1975.

BOX 2 - Address of Scheme

Enter the place or, if more than one, the principal place in the United Kingdom at which the management of the scheme is conducted.

BOX 3 - Scheme Status

Open Scheme
An open scheme means a registrable scheme which has members who are in pensionable service under the scheme and to which new members may be admitted.

Frozen Scheme
A Frozen Scheme is one under which benefits continue to be payable to existing

members, and to which no new members may be admitted and no further contributions are payable by or in respect of existing members, and no further benefits accrue to existing members although benefits which have already accrued to them may be increased.

Closed Scheme
A Closed Scheme is one to which no new members may be admitted, but to which contributions are or may be payable by or in respect of, and benefits accrue to, existing members.

BOX 4 Type of Scheme

Money Purchase

Benefits other than money purchase - e.g. salary related and average salary benefits.

Combination of benefits specified above - this is intended to cover mixed benefit schemes, hybrid schemes and schemes where there is an underpin.

Benefits derived from transfer credits, from member's voluntary contributions or death in service only should be disregarded

584

Appendix 44

BOX 5 - **Date Scheme became Registrable**

Enter the date the scheme became a registrable scheme, see General Information.

BOX 6 - **Total Membership**

In relation to an occupational pension scheme a member means any person who:-

(a) is in pensionable service under the scheme, or
(b) has rights under the scheme by virtue of pensionable service under the scheme, or
(c) has rights under the scheme by virtue of having been allowed transfer credits under the scheme;

other than a member in respect of whom entitlement under the scheme is only for benefits payable on his death.

The total membership of a scheme, is the number of members on the date at which the scheme became a registrable scheme.

BOX 7 - **Amount of General Levy**

Enter the appropriate amount.

Amount of Compensation Levy

Enter the appropriate amount.

TOTAL

Enter the amount of total levy due.

BOX 8 - **Cheque Number**

Enter the cheque number.

BOX 9 - **Bank Sort Code**

Enter the bank sort code.

BOX 10 - **Inland Revenue Pension Schemes Office (PSO) Reference Number**

If you are unsure of the PSO reference number, please leave this section blank and confirm the number later.

BOX 11- **Insured Details**

If the scheme benefits, or any of them, are secured by a contract of insurance or an annuity contract tick the appropriate box and complete boxes 12 & 13. If not go to box 14.

BOX 12 - **Name of Insurer**

Enter the name of Insurer.

BOX 13 **Address of Insurer**

Enter the address of the insurer and insert the policy number, if known.

BOX 14 **Name of all Scheme Trustees**

Enter the name of the trustees as shown on the Trust Deed(s) and complete the official trustee address if different from the scheme address.

BOX 15 **Name of Scheme Administrator**

Enter the name of the scheme administrator.

BOX 16 **Current Principal Employer's Name**

Enter the name of the principal employer.

BOX 17 **Principal Employer's Address**

Enter the current address of the principal employer. Beneath boxes 16 and 17 enter any previous principal employers or any previous names by which the principal employer has been known and any previous addresses.

BOX 18 **Employers Currently Associated with the**
and 19 **Scheme**

Enter the names and addresses of all employers currently associated with the scheme.

BOX 20 **Employers Previously Associated with**
and 21 **the Scheme**

Enter the names and addresses of all employers who have been associated with the scheme.

Box 22 **Continuation Sheets**

Enter the number of continuation sheets you have used, if appropriate.

A registrable scheme should report changes to the information provided either by letter or on form PR10.

585

Occupational Pensions Regulatory Authority
Pension Schemes Registry
PO Box 1NN
Newcastle upon Tyne
NE99 1NN

Telephone: 0191 2256393/4/6/8

Registration of Occupational Pension Scheme

You should use this form if you are providing information about an occupational pension scheme for the first time. Refer to the enclosed guidance notes for help before completion of this form. Please PRINT replies in CAPITAL LETTERS.

Details of Pension Scheme to be Registered

1	Full name of scheme	(a)	
	Previous name(s)	(b)	
2	Address of scheme		
		postcode	
3	Scheme status - *tick appropriate box*		☐ Open ☐ Frozen ☐ Closed
4	Benefit type - *tick appropriate box*		☐ Money Purchase ☐ Benefits other than money purchase ☐ Combination of benefits specified above
5	Date scheme became registerable		
6	Total membership		
7	Amount of general levy	£	
	Amount of compensation levy (see levy calculation sheet PR5 (97))	£	
	Total	£	
8	Cheque number		
9	Bank sort code		
10	Inland Revenue Pension Schemes Office (PSO) reference number		

For the purpose of providing information under section 6 of the Pension Schemes Act 1993 and corresponding Northern Ireland legislation.

Form PR1 (97)

Page ONE

11 Insured details:
Are the scheme benefits, or any of them, secured by a contract of insurance or an annuity contract?

-tick appropriate box

If yes complete boxes 12 and 13
If no go to box 14

☐ yes

☐ no

12 Name of Insurer

13 Address of Insurer (where the pensions department is located)

postcode

Life Office Reference/Policy number, if known

About the scheme trustees

14 Name of all scheme trustees

From the 6th April 1997, all of the following persons are disqualified from being a trustee of an occupational pension scheme:

Anyone who has a **conviction** (except a spent conviction) for an offence involving dishonesty or deception.

Any undischarged **Bankrupt.**

Anyone whose property in Scotland is subject to a **sequestration order.**

Anyone **disqualified by an order of the** Occupational Pensions Regulatory Authority (OPRA)

Anyone **disqualified** from being a company director by an order under the Company Directors Disqualification's Act 1986.

Anyone subject to an order under **section 429 of the Insolvency Act** 1986.

Anyone who has entered into a **composition contract** or an arrangement with, or **granted a trust deed** for the benefit of, his creditors and has not been discharged in respect of it.

A **Scottish Partnership** with a partner who is disqualified from being a trustee.

A **company** with a director who is disqualified from being a trustee.

You may be prosecuted if you act as a trustee or continue to act as a trustee while disqualified. On conviction you may be fined or sent to prison or both.

Page TWO

587

Appendix 44

Trustee contact address if different
from scheme address

postcode

About the scheme administrator

15   Name of scheme administrator

About the principal employer *(where relevant)*

16   Principal employer's (current) name

17   Principal employer's address

postcode

**Previous principal employer or previous
name(s) by which the principal employer has
been known and any previous addresses**

(Details required are those of all the
employers to which the scheme has
been related since 6th April 1975).

Employer's name

Employer's address

postcode

Employer's name

Employer's address

postcode

If necessary please continue on the
continuation sheet on page 6.

About current employers associated with the scheme

18 Employer's name

19 Employer's address

postcode

Employer's name

Employer's address

postcode

Employer's name

Employer's address

postcode

Employer's name

Employer's address

postcode

If necessary please continue on the continuation sheet on page 6.

Appendix 44

(Details required are those of all the employers to which the scheme has been related since 6th April 1975).

20 Employer's name

21 Employer's address

postcode

Employer's name

Employer's address

postcode

Employer's name

Employer's address

postcode

If necessary please continue on the continuation sheet on page 6.

22 Number of continuation sheets

590

Continuation sheet
(please indicate relevant box numbers)

Employer's name

Employer's address

postcode

Employer's name

Employer's address

postcode

Employer's name

Employer's address

postcode

Employer's name

Employer's address

postcode

If there is not enough room on this page for the entries you have, please photocopy the page as required. Any photocopied pages should be enclosed with this form.

Page SIX

591

Appendix 44

The Register of Occupational and Personal Pension Schemes Regulations 1997, SI 1997/371, make it a criminal offence for a trustee to fail without reasonable cause to supply information in accordance with those regulations.

1   Please make sure the form is completed correctly.

2   Please give the name, address and telephone number of the person(s) to whom any enquiries about this form should be sent:

Name:

Address:

Tel No:

Signature:

3   Please send the form and the cheque for the total amount of the levy to the address shown at the bottom of this page. The crossed cheque should be endorsed either "A/C Payee" or "not negotiable" and made payable to "OPRA LEVY ACCOUNT".

(This should be a scheme trustee or a person authorised to act on behalf of the trustee(s))

Name:

(Please PRINT in CAPITAL LETTERS)

Status:

Date:

Please send this form to:

If you require confirmation that your scheme details have been recorded on the Register, please enclose a stamped addressed envelope.

Occupational Pensions Regulatory Authority
Pension Schemes Registry
PO Box 1NN
Newcastle upon Tyne
NE99 1NN

Telephone: 0191 2256393/4/6/8

Note:

If any of the information required on the form is not available at the time of registration you should inform the Registrar of the reason why it cannot be provided. But you should supply as much information as is practicable within the time limit laid down, and pay the levy.

Page SEVEN

592

FOR OFFICIAL USE ONLY

SCHEME NUMBER _____

ONLINE _____ VERIFIED _____

Page EIGHT

593

Appendix 45

Social Security Press Release:
New Measures to Protect Occupational Pensions

Social Security Press Release:
New Measures to Protect Occupational Pensions

89/477   7 November 1989

NEW MEASURES TO PROTECT OCCUPATIONAL PENSIONS

Tony Newton,Secretary of State for Social Security,today
announced that there would be greater protection for members of
pension schemes whose companies are involved in takeovers
or mergers.He also announced that he would be setting up a
Pensions Ombudsman.

Mr Newton also announced:

* a tracing service based on a register of pension schemes to
help people track down pensions held with their previous
employers;and

* increased help and advice for members of occupational
and personal pension schemes by a strengthening of the
voluntary Occupational Pension Advisory Service.

These measures will improve both the value and security of
pension benefits.

Speaking to the Society of Pension Consultants tonight Mr Newton
said that the Ombudsman for the pensions industry would have
power to settle individuals' grievances. There would be a
statutory requirement that the pensions industry abide by the
Ombudsman's decisions.

Turning to the Occupational Pensions Advisory Service, Mr Newton
said,"We must put its finances on a sound basis so that its
future is guaranteed.

                         - MORE -

Issued by: DSS, Richmond House, 79 Whitehall, London SW1A 2NS Telephone 01-210 5968

"What is more,at present it is only able effectively to help
pensioners of occupational schemes. It would surely be a great
advance if it could help all members of all types of schemes,
including personal pensions.OPAS has certainly indicated that
it would like to do so."

To improve benefit security for present and future pensioners Mr
Newton proposed four measures.

"First,we will strengthen the protection for early leavers from
occupational pension schemes which we introduced in 1985 by
requiring schemes to revalue all future early leavers' preserved
pension rights. Pension rights which go beyond the Guaranteed
Minimum Pension will have to be revalued in line with prices,up
to a maximum of 5 per cent a year.

"Second, where a pension scheme winds up, the same revaluation
requirement will also apply to future pensions and to pensions
in payment.

"Third,again on wind-up,any deficiency in a scheme's assets to
meet scheme liabilities,including these new liabilities,will
become a debt on the employer.

"Fourth,we shall introduce a new ceiling on self-investment for
pension schemes which will allow them to hold no more than 5 per
cent of their assets in the employer's business."

NOTE TO EDITORS

The Occupational Pensions Board report,"Protecting
Pensions : Safeguarding Benefits in a Changing Environment",was
published on 1 February 1989.The then Secretary of State, John
Moore, launched a consultation exercise on that day.Today's
announcement takes into account the views expressed by
respondents.

- ENDS -

Appendix 46

SI 1992 No. 246

The Occupational Pension Schemes (Investment of Scheme's Resources) Regulations 1992

Made:12th February 1992
Laid before Parliament: 171h February 1992
Coming into force: 9th March 1992

The Secretary of State for Social Security, in exercise of his powers under sections 166(1) to (3) and 168(1) of, and Schedule 20 to, the Social Security Act 1975(a), sections 56A(l), 57A(1), and 66(2) and (4) of the Social Security Pensions Act 1975(b) and of all other powers enabling him in that behalf, after considering the report of the Occupational Pensions Board on the proposals referred to them(c), hereby makes the following Regulations:

1 Citation, commencement and interpretation

(1) These Regulations may be cited as the Occupational Pension Schemes (Investment of Scheme's Resources) Regulations 1992.

(2) These Regulations shall come into force on 9th March 1992.

(3) In regulations 2 to 5–

"member" means a person who is in pensionable service for the purposes of the scheme in question or, as the case may be, a person who qualifies for benefits under the scheme in question by reason of his pensionable service;

"pensionable service" has the same meaning as in paragraph 3(1) of Schedule 16 to the Social Security Act 1973(d) (preservation requirements: interpretation);

"scheme" means an occupational pension scheme;

and any reference to a numbered regulation or paragraph is a reference to the regulation or paragraph which bears that number in these Regulations.

2 Schemes to which Regulation 3 applies

(1) Subject to paragraph (2), regulation 3 applies to schemes–

(a) which either—

(i) are approved for the purposes of Chapter I of Part XIV of the Income and Corporation Taxes Act 1988(e) (retirement benefit schemes) or are the subject of an application for such approval which has not been determined; or

---

(a) 1975 c.14. *See* definitions of "prescribe" and "regulations" in Schedule 20. Sections 166(1) to (3) and 168(1) apply, by virtue of section 66(2) of the Social Security Pensions Act 1975 (c.60), to the exercise of certain powers conferred by that Act.
(b) 1975 c.60. Section 56A(l) was inserted by Schedule 2 to the Social Security Act 1985 (c.53). Section 57A was inserted by paragraph 3 of Schedule 4 to the Social Security Act 1990 (c.27).
(c) *See* section 61(2) of the Social Security Pensions Act 1975.
(d) 1973 c.38.
(e) 1988 c.1.

        (ii)   are exempt from income tax under section 608 of that Act (exemption for superannuation funds approved before 6th April 1980); and

    (b)   which have at least one member in the United Kingdom and either–

        (i)   are established in the United Kingdom; or

        (ii)   have one or more trustees resident in the United Kingdom.

(2)   Regulation 3 shall not apply to schemes–

    (a)   which have less than 12 members;

    (b)   each of whom is a trustee of the scheme; and

    (c)   the rules of which provide.that before any investment of the resources of the scheme is made in an employer-related investment, each member shall agree in writing to the making of that investment.

3 Restriction on self-investment

(1)   Subject to paragraph (2) and regulation 5, not more than 5 per cent. of the current market value of the resources of a scheme may at any time be invested in employer-related investments.

(2)   The restriction prescribed in paragraph (1) shall not apply to any employer-related investment of resources to which regulation 4 applies.

4 Investments to which the restriction does not apply

(1)   This regulation applies to–

    (a)   any employer-related investment of resources in an account (including a current, deposit or share account) with a building society as defined in the Building Societies Act 1986(a) or an institution authorised under Part 1 of the Banking Act 1987(b); or

    (b)   any employer-related investment of resources which have been derived from voluntary contributions within the meaning of section 12 of the Social Security Act 1986(c) (voluntary contributions) and are invested in employer-related investments with the written agreement of the member who paid those contributions.

(2)   This regulation applies to any employer-related investment of resources in the purchase of a policy of insurance or an annuity contract so as to provide benefits in respect of the pensionable service of a member (whether or not that policy or contract also relates to any other member) where—

    (a)   the policy or contract is specifically allocated to the provision of those benefits for that member or any other person mentioned or described in–

        (i)   that policy or contract; or

        (ii)   the scheme rules or a nomination thereunder; and

    (b)   that member–

        (i)   has the right under the rules of the scheme to choose the policy or contract in question; and

        (ii)   has agreed in writing that the resources in question may be invested in employer-related investments.

5 Existing cases

(1)   Where on 9th March 1992 the resources of a scheme which are invested in employer-related investments exceed the limit prescribed by regulation 3, those investments may be retained in accordance with paragraph (2).

(2)   To the extent that the employer-related investments mentioned in paragraph (1) consist of–

    (a)   employer-related loans which are in being on 17th February 1992, they may be

---

(a) 1986 c.53.   (b) 1987 c.22.   (c) 1986 c.50.

retained until 8th March 1994 or, where repayment cannot be required on or before that date, they may be retained until the earliest date on which repayment can be enforced.

(b)   securities which are listed on a recognised stock exchange on 9th March 1992, they may be retained until 8th March 1994;

(c)   employer-related securities that are traded in a second tier market of a recognised stock exchange on 9th March 1992, they may be retained until 8th March 1997;

(d)   employer-related investments to which sub-paragraphs (a) to (c) above do not apply, they may be retained without limit of time.

(3)   There shall be no new investment in employer-related investments where the resources of a scheme which have been retained in employer-related investments by virtue of paragraph (2) exceed the restriction prescribed by regulation 3.

(4)   In this regulation—

"loans" does not include any sums regarded as loans under section 57A(3) of the Social Security Pensions Act 1975 (restrictions on investments of scheme's resources in employer-related assets);

"recognised stock exchange" has the same meaning as in section 841 of the Income and Corporation Taxes Act 1988 (recognised stock exchange and recognised investment exchanges);

"retained", in relation to a loan, means left undischarged;

"resources" does not include any resources to which regulation 4 applies.

6 Amendment of the Disclosure Regulations

(1)   The Occupational Pension Schemes (Disclosure of Information) Regulations 1988(a) shall be amended in accordance with the following paragraphs of this regulation.

(2)   In regulation 9(1)(c) (availability of audited accounts, actuarial statements and other information) for the number "15" there shall be inserted the number "17".

(3)   The following paragraphs shall be added after paragraph 15 of Schedule 5 (information to accompany audited accounts and actuarial statement)–

"16. Where the scheme has employer-related investments within the meaning of section 57A of the Act(b) (restrictions on investment of scheme's resources in employer-related assets)–

(a)   a copy of a list of those investments;

(b)   a copy of a statement on the proportion of the scheme's resources that are invested in employer-related investments;

(c)   if that proportion exceeds 5 per cent, information on whether and, if so, how it is intended to reduce that percentage.

17   Where the Occupational Pensions Schemes (Investment of Scheme's Resources) Regulations 1992(c) apply, a copy of a statement on whether the investments of the scheme are invested in accordance with those Regulations.".

Signed by authority of the Secretary of State for Social Security.

Henley
Paliamentary Under-Secretary of State,
Department of Social Security

12th February 1992

(a) S.I. 1986/1046, amended by S.I. 1987/1105.
(b) Section 57A was inserted by paragraph 3 of Schedule 4 to the Social Security Act 1990 (c.27).
(c) S.I. 1992/246.

Appendix 47

Members' Agreement Form

Name of Scheme ....

....

We, the undersigned, being all the members of the above scheme hereby AGREE to the making of the following investment by the Trustees of the Scheme:-

....

....

....

(brief description of investment)

Signed ....

Name in Capitals ....

Signed ....

Name in Capitals ....

Signed ....

Name in Capitals ....

Signed ....

Name in Capitals ....

Signed ....

Name in Capitals ....

dated this   day of   200

Appendix 48

Model letter of appointment for scheme trustees to send to the scheme auditor where a statutory audit is required

XYZ Pension Scheme

Notice of Appointment of Scheme Auditor

In accordance with Section 47 of the Pensions Act 1995 and Regulations 5 of the Occupational Pension Schemes (Scheme Administration) Regulations 1996, we hereby give you written notice of your appointment as auditor of the Pension Scheme with effect from [date].

In connection with your appointment as Scheme auditor, you should take instructions in relation to the audit Scheme from [name and position] and you should report to [name and position].

We confirm that, under Section 27 of the Pensions Act 1995, no trustee of the scheme is connected with or an associate of [name of audit firm], which would render [name of audit firm] ineligible to act as auditor to the scheme.

We should be grateful if you would write to acknowledge receipt of this notice of appointment and your acceptance of this appointment as scheme auditor within one month of the date of this letter.

Yours faithfully

For and on behalf of the Trustees of the XYZ Pension Scheme

Note
This letter should be typed on the scheme trustees' headed notepaper

Appendix 49

Model letter of appointment for scheme trustees to send to the auditor of the scheme acting as professional adviser (where a non-statutory audit is to be undertaken)

XYZ Pension Scheme

Notice of Appointment as Professional Adviser to act as Auditor in accordance with the Trust Deed and Rules

In accordance with Section 47 of the Pensions Act 1995 and Regulation 5 of the Occupational Pension Schemes (Scheme Administration) Regulations 1996, we hereby give you written notice of your appointment adviser to act as auditor of the XYZ Pension Scheme with effect from [date].

In connection with your appointment as professional adviser in the above capacity, you should take instructions in relation to the audit of the Scheme from [name and position] and you should report to [name and position].

We confirm that, under Section 27 of the Pensions Act 1995, no trustee of the scheme is connected with or an associate of [name of audit firm], which would render [name of audit firm] ineligible to act as auditor to the scheme.

We should be grateful if you would write to acknowledge receipt of this notice of appointment and your acceptance of this appointment in the above capacity within one month of the date of this letter.

Yours faithfully

For and on behalf of the Trustees of the XYZ Pension Scheme

Note
This letter should be typed on the scheme trustees' headed notepaper.

601

Appendix 50

(Unqualified audit report for a money purchase SSAS which has prepared statutory accounts and a payment schedule)

Auditors' report to the trustees of the XYZ Pension Scheme

We have audited the accounts on pages 00 to 00.

Respective responsibilities of trustees and auditors

As described on page 00, the scheme's trustees are responsible for obtaining audited accounts which comply with applicable United Kingdom law and Accounting Standards. They are also responsible for making available, commonly in the form of a trustees' report, certain other information about the scheme which complies with applicable United Kingdom law. Further, as described on page 00, they are responsible for ensuring that a payment schedule of contributions payable to the scheme is prepared and maintained and for procuring that contributions are made to the scheme in accordance with that schedule. Our responsibilities as independent auditors are established in the United Kingdom by statute, the Auditing Practices Board and by our profession's ethical guidance.

Bases of opinions

We conducted our audit in accordance with Auditing Standards issued by the Auditing Practices Board. An audit includes examination, on a test basis, of evidence relevant to the amounts and disclosures in the accounts. It also includes an assessment of the significant estimates and judgements made by or on behalf of the trustees in the preparation of the accounts, and of whether the accounting policies are appropriate to the scheme's circumstances, consistently applied and adequately disclosed. The work that we carried out also included examination, on a test basis, of evidence relevant to the amounts of contributions payable to the scheme and the timing of those payments.

We planned and performed our audit so as to obtain all the information and explanations which we considered necessary in order to provide us with sufficient evidence to give reasonable assurance that the accounts are free from material misstatement, whether caused by fraud or other irregularity or error, and that contributions have been paid in accordance with the payment schedule dated [. . .], prepared in accordance with the *Pensions Act 1995*. In forming our opinions we also evaluated the overall adequacy of the presentation of the information in the accounts.

Opinions

In our opinion, the accounts show a true and fair view of the financial transactions of the scheme during the scheme year ended [. . .], and the amount and disposition at that date of the assets and liabilities (other than liabilities to pay pensions and benefits after the end of the scheme year) and contain the information specified in the Schedule to the *Occupational Pension Schemes (Requirement to Obtain Audited Accounts and a Statement from the Auditor) Regulations 1996* made under the *Pensions Act 1995*.

In our opinion, contributions have been paid in accordance with the payment schedule dated [. . .].

Chartered Accountants
Registered Auditors

[Date]
[Address]

Appendix 51

(Unqualified non-statutory audit report)

Auditors' report to the trustees of the XYZ Pension Scheme

We have audited the non-statutory accounts on pages 00 to 00, which have been prepared for the reasons set out in note 1.[1]

Respective responsibilities of trustees and auditors

As described on page 00, the scheme's trustees are responsible for the preparation of the non-statutory accounts which comply with applicable United Kingdom Accounting Standards and Statements of Recommended Practice.[2] Under the terms of our engagement, our responsibilities as independent auditors are established in the United Kingdom by the Auditing Practices Board and by our profession's ethical guidance.

We report to you our opinion as to whether the accounts give a true and fair view and if we have not received all the information and explanations we require for our audit.

[We read the other information accompanying the accounts and consider whether it is consistent with those accounts. We consider the implications for our report if we become aware of any apparent misstatements or material inconsistencies wiht the accounts.][3]

Basis of opinion

We conducted our audit in accordance with Auditing Standards issued by the Auditing Practices Board. An audit includes examination, on a test basis, of evidence relevant to the amounts and disclosures in the accounts. It also includes as assessment of the significant estimates and judgements made by the trustees in the preparation of the accounts, and of whether the accounting policies are appropriate to the scheme's circumstances, consistently applied and adequately disclosed.

We planned and performed our audit so as to obtain all the information and explanations which we considered necessary in order to provide us with sufficient evidence to give reasonable assurance that the accounts are free from material misstatement, whether caused by fraud or other irregularity or error. In forming our opinion, we also evaluated the overall adequacy of the presentation of the information in the accounts.

Opinion

In our opinion, the non-statutory accounts show a true and fair view of the financial transactions of the scheme during the year ended [. . .] and of the amount and disposition at that date of the assets and liabilities (other than liabilities to pay pensions and other benefits after the end of the scheme year) [and contain the information specified in the Schedule to the *Occupational Pension Schemes (Requirement to Obtain Audied Accounts and a Statement from the Auditor) Regulations 1996*, as if those regulations applied].[4]

Chartered Accountants

[Date]
[Address]

---

[1] Note 1 should set out the reasons why accounts have been prepared, which will in most cases be because the trust deed of the scheme specifies that audited accounts should be prepared.

[2] The statement of trustees' responsibilities should refer to that fact the trust deed requires the trustees to prepare audited accounts.

[3] This paragraph should be included if the non-statutory accounts are included in a scheme annual report.

[4] If the non-statutory accounts do not contain the information specified in te schedule, this sentence should be deleted. Where the notes to the accounts do not contain a statement that the acccounts have been prepared in accordance with the SORP, the following sentence should be added after '. . . after the end of the scheme year)': 'and contain the information specified in the Statement of Recommended Practice, Financial Reports of Pension Schemes.'

Appendix 52

Statement of trustees' responsibilities

The audited accounts are the responsibility of the trustees. Pension scheme regulations require the trustees to make available to scheme members, beneficiaries and certain other parties, audited accounts for each scheme year which:

(*a*)   show a true and fair view of the financial transactions of the scheme during the scheme year and of the amount and disposition at the end of the scheme year of the assets and liabilities, other than liabilities to pay pensions and benefits after the end of the scheme year; and

(*b*)   contain the information specified in the Schedule to the *Occupational Pension Schemes (Requirement to Obtain Audited Accounts and a Statement from the Auditor) Regulations 1996*, including a statement whether the accounts have been prepared in accordance with the Statement of Recommended Practice, 'Financial Reports of Pension Schemes'.[1]

The trustees have supervised the preparation of the accounts and have agreed suitable accounting policies, to be applied consistently, making estimates and judgements on a reasonable and prudent basis. They are also responsible for making available each year, commonly in the form of a trustees' annual report, information about the scheme prescribed by pensions legislation, which they should ensure is consistent with the audited accounts it accompanies.

The trustees are responsible under pensions legislation for ensuring that there is prepared, maintained and from time to time revised a payment schedule showing the rates of contributions payable towards the scheme by or on behalf of the employer and the active members of the scheme and the dates on or before which such contributions are to be paid. The trustees are also responsible for keeping records of contributions received in respect of any active member of the scheme and for procuring that contributions are made to the scheme in accordance with the payment schedule.

The trustees also have a general responsibility for ensuring that adequate accounting records are kept and for taking such steps as are reasonably open to them to safeguard the assets of the scheme and to prevent and detect fraud and other irregularities.

---

[1] In addition to the statutory requirements, the trust deed and rules of some schemes require auditors to report whether contributions have been paid to the scheme in accordance with the rules of the scheme and with the recommendations of the actuary, where on is appointed. In such cases, to make it clear that compliance with the rules and recommendations is in the first instance a matter for the trustees' references to the 'payment schedule' in the paragraphs set out above will need to be extended to include 'the scheme rules [and recommendation of the actuary, if appointed]'.

Appendix 53

Statement of trustees' responsibilities where non-statutory accounts are audited

Where a SSAS's trustees have decided to have an audit and the accounts are not statutory, the trustees' responsibilities statement needs to refer to this fact.

The non-statutory accounts are the responsibility of the trustees. The trust deed and rules of the scheme require the trustees to prepare audited accounts for each scheme year which:

(*a*) show a true and fair view of the financial transactions of the scheme during the scheme year and of the amount and disposition at the end of the scheme year of the assets and liabilities, other than liabilities to pay pensions and benefits after the end of the scheme year; and

(*b*) contain the information specified in the Statement of Recommended Practice, 'Financial Reports of Pension Schemes'.

The trustees have supervised the preparation of the accounts and have agreed suitable accounting policies, to be applied consistently, making estimates and judgements on a reasonable and prudent basis.

The trustees are responsible for keeping records of contributions received in respect of any active member of the scheme and for procuring that contributions are made to the scheme in accordance with the payment schedule.

The trustees also have a general responsibility for ensuring that adequate accounting records are kept and for taking such steps as are responsibly open to them to safeguard the assets of the scheme and to prevent and detect fraud and other irregularities.

Appendix 54

1997 No 570

Company Accounts (Disclosure of Directors' Emoluments) Regulations 1997

Made: 4th March 1997

The Secretary of State in exercise of the powers conferred on him by section 257 of the Companies Act 1985 and of all other powers enabling him in that behalf hereby makes the following Regulations of which a draft has been laid before Parliament in accordance with section 257(2) of that Act and approved by a resolution of each House of Parliament:—

1   Citation, commencement and interpretation

(1)   These Regulations may be cited as the Company Accounts (Disclosure of Directors' Emoluments) Regulations 1997.

(2)   These Regulations shall come into force on 31st March 1997 and shall have effect as respects companies' financial years ending on or after that date.

(3)   In these Regulations—

"the Act" means the Companies Act 1985;

"Schedule 6" means Schedule 6 to the Act (disclosure of information: emoluments and other benefits of directors and others).

2   Aggregate amount of directors' emoluments etc

For paragraph 1 of Schedule 6 there shall be substituted the following paragraph—

"Aggregate amount of directors' emoluments etc

1—(1)   Subject to sub-paragraph (2), the following shall be shown, namely—

(a)   the aggregate amount of emoluments paid to or receivable by directors in respect of qualifying services;

(b)   the aggregate of the amount of gains made by directors on the exercise of share options;

(c)   the aggregate of the following, namely—
(i)   the amount of money paid to or receivable by directors under long term incentive schemes in respect of qualifying services; and
(ii)   the net value of assets (other than money and share options) received or receivable by directors under such schemes in respect of such services;

(d)   the aggregate value of any company contributions paid, or treated as paid, to a pension scheme in respect of directors' qualifying services, being contributions by reference to which the rate or amount of any money purchase benefits that may become payable will be calculated; and

(e)   in the case of each of the following, namely—
(i)   money purchase schemes; and
(ii)   defined benefit schemes,
the number of directors (if any) to whom retirement benefits are accruing under such schemes in respect of qualifying services.

(2)   In the case of a company which is not a listed company—

(a)   sub-paragraph (1) shall have effect as if paragraph (b) were omitted and, in paragraph (c)(ii), "assets" did not include shares; and

(b)   the number of each of the following (if any) shall be shown, namely—
(i)   the directors who exercised share options; and
(ii)   the directors in respect of whose qualifying services shares were received or receivable under long term incentive schemes.

(3)   In this paragraph "emoluments" of a director—

608

(a)   includes salary, fees and bonuses, sums paid by way of expenses allowance (so far as they are chargeable to United Kingdom income tax) and, subject to paragraph (b), the estimated money value of any other benefits received by him otherwise than in cash; but

(b)   does not include any of the following, namely—

  (i)   the value of any share options granted to him or the amount of any gains made on the exercise of any such options;

  (ii)   any company contributions paid, or treated as paid, in respect of him under any pension scheme or any benefits to which he is entitled under any such scheme; or

  (iii)   any money or other assets paid to or received or receivable by him under any long term incentive scheme.

(4)   In this paragraph "long term incentive scheme" means any agreement or arrangement under which money or other assets may become receivable by a director and which includes one or more qualifying conditions with respect to service or performance which cannot be fulfilled within a single financial year; and for this purpose the following shall be disregarded, namely—

(a)   bonuses the amount of which falls to be determined by reference to service or performance within a single financial year;

(b)   compensation for loss of office, payments for breach of contract and other termination payments; and

(c)   retirement benefits.

(5)   In this paragraph—

"amount", in relation to a gain made on the exercise of a share option, means the difference between—

(a)   the market price of the shares on the day on which the option was exercised; and

(b)   the price actually paid for the shares;

"company contributions", in relation to a pension scheme and a director, means any payments (including insurance premiums) made, or treated as made, to the scheme in respect of the director by a person other than the director;

"defined benefits" means retirement benefits payable under a pension scheme which are not money purchase benefits;

"defined benefit scheme", in relation to a director, means a pension scheme which is not a money purchase scheme;

"listed company" means a company—

(a)   whose securities have been admitted to the Official List of the Stock Exchange in accordance with the provisions of Part IV of the Financial Services Act 1986; or

(b)   dealings in whose securities are permitted on any exchange which is an approved exchange for the purposes of that Part;

"money purchase benefits", in relation to a director, means retirement benefits payable under a pension scheme the rate or amount of which is calculated by reference to payments made, or treated as made, by the director or by any other person in respect of the director and which are not average salary benefits;

"money purchase scheme", in relation to a director, means a pension scheme under which all of the benefits that may become payable to or in respect of the director are money purchase benefits;

"net value", in relation to any assets received or receivable by a director, means value after deducting any money paid or other value given by the director in respect of those assets;

"qualifying services", in relation to any person, means his services as a director of the company, and his services while director of the company—

(a)   as director of any of its subsidiary undertakings; or

(b)   otherwise in connection with the management of the affairs of the company or any of its subsidiary undertakings;

"shares" means shares (whether allotted or not) in the company, or any undertaking which is a group undertaking in relation to the company, and includes a share warrant as defined by section 188(1);

"share option" means a right to acquire shares;

"value", in relation to shares received or receivable by a director on any day, means the market price of the shares on that day.

(6)   For the purposes of this paragraph—

(a)   any information, other than the aggregate amount of gains made by directors on the exercise of share options, shall be treated as shown if it is capable of being readily ascertained from other information which is shown; and

(b)   emoluments paid or receivable or share options granted in respect of a person's accepting office as a director shall be treated as emoluments paid or receivable or share options granted in respect of his services as a director.

(7)   Where a pension scheme provides for any benefits that may become payable to or in respect of any director to be whichever are the greater of—

(a)   money purchase benefits as determined by or under the scheme; and

(b)   defined benefits as so determined,

the company may assume for the purposes of this paragraph that those benefits will be money purchase benefits, or defined benefits, according to whichever appears more likely at the end of the financial year.

(8)   For the purpose of determining whether a pension scheme is a money purchase or defined benefit scheme, any death in service benefits provided for by the scheme shall be disregarded."

3   Aggregate amount of directors' emoluments etc

(1)   For paragraphs 2 to 6 of Schedule 6 there shall be substituted the following paragraph—

"Details of highest paid director's emoluments etc

2—(1)   Where the aggregates shown under paragraph 1(1)(a), (b) and (c) total £200,000 or more, the following shall be shown, namely—

(a)   so much of the total of those aggregates as is attributable to the highest paid director; and

(b)   so much of the aggregate mentioned in paragraph 1(1)(d) as is so attributable.

(2)   Where sub-paragraph (1) applies and the highest paid director has performed qualifying services during the financial year by reference to which the rate or amount of any defined benefits that may become payable will be calculated, there shall also be shown—

(a)   the amount at the end of the year of his accrued pension; and

(b)   where applicable, the amount at the end of the year of his accrued lump sum.

(3)   Subject to sub-paragraph (4), where sub-paragraph (1) applies in the case of a company which is not a listed company, there shall also be shown—

(a)   whether the highest paid director exercised any share options; and

(b)   whether any shares were received or receivable by that director in respect of qualifying services under a long term incentive scheme.

(4)   Where the highest paid director has not been involved in any of the transactions specified in sub-paragraph (3), that fact need not be stated.

(5)   In this paragraph—

"accrued pension" and "accrued lump sum", in relation to any pension scheme and any director, mean respectively the amount of the annual pension, and the amount of the lump sum, which would be payable under the scheme on his attaining normal pension age if—

(a)   he had left the company's service at the end of the financial year;

(b)   there were no increase in the general level of prices in Great Britain during the period beginning with the end of that year and ending with his attaining that age;

(c)   no question arose of any commutation of the pension or inverse commutation of the lump sum; and

(d)   any amounts attributable to voluntary contributions paid by the director to the scheme, and any money purchase benefits which would be payable under the scheme, were disregarded;

"the highest paid director" means the director to whom is attributable the greatest part of the total of the aggregates shown under paragraph 1(1)(a), (b) and (c);

"normal pension age", in relation to any pension scheme and any director, means the age at which the director will first become entitled to receive a full pension on retirement of an amount determined without reduction to take account of its payment before a later age (but disregarding any entitlement to pension upon retirement in the event of illness, incapacity or redundancy).

(6)　Sub-paragraphs (4) to (8) of paragraph 1 apply for the purposes of this paragraph as they apply for the purposes of that paragraph."

(2)　Nothing in paragraph 58(2) of Schedule 4 to the Act (corresponding amounts to be shown for previous financial year) shall apply to any amount which, in relation to a financial year of a company ending before 31st March 1998, is shown by virtue of paragraph 2(2) of Schedule 6 as substituted by paragraph (1) above.

4　Excess retirement benefits of directors and past directors

For paragraph 7 of Schedule 6 there shall be substituted the following paragraph—

"Excess retirement benefits of directors and past directors

7—(1)　Subject to sub-paragraph (2), there shall be shown the aggregate amount of—

(a)　so much of retirement benefits paid to or receivable by directors under pension schemes; and

(b)　so much of retirement benefits paid to or receivable by past directors under such schemes,

as (in each case) is in excess of the retirement benefits to which they were respectively entitled on the date on which the benefits first became payable or 31st March 1997, whichever is the later.

(2)　Amounts paid or receivable under a pension scheme need not be included in the aggregate amount if—

(a)　the funding of the scheme was such that the amounts were or, as the case may be, could have been paid without recourse to additional contributions; and

(b)　amounts were paid to or receivable by all pensioner members of the scheme on the same basis;

and in this sub-paragraph "pensioner member", in relation to a pension scheme, means any person who is entitled to the present payment of retirement benefits under the scheme.

(3)　In this paragraph—

(a)　references to retirement benefits include benefits otherwise than in cash; and

(b)　in relation to so much of retirement benefits as consists of a benefit otherwise than in cash, references to their amount are to the estimated money value of the benefit;

and the nature of any such benefit shall also be disclosed."

5　Compensation to directors for loss of office

(1)　In sub-paragraph (2)(b) of paragraph 8 of Schedule 6 (compensation to directors for loss of office), the words from "and shall distinguish" to the end shall be omitted.

(2)　For sub-paragraph (4) of that paragraph there shall be substituted the following sub-paragraphs—

"(4)　In this paragraph, references to compensation for loss of office include the following, namely—

(a)　compensation in consideration for, or in connection with, a person's retirement from office; and

(b)　where such a retirement is occasioned by a breach of the person's contract with the company or with a subsidiary undertaking of the company—
(i)　payments made by way of damages for the breach; or
(ii)　payments made by way of settlement or compromise of any claim in respect of the breach.

Appendix 54

(5)   Sub-paragraph (6)(a) of paragraph 1 applies for the purposes of this paragraph as it applies for the purposes of that paragraph."

6   Minor and consequential amendments

(1)   For subsection (3) of section 246 of the 1985 Act (special provisions for small companies) there shall be substituted the following subsection—

"(3)   The company's individual accounts for the year—

    (a)   may give the total of the aggregates required by paragraphs (a), (c) and (d) of paragraph 1(1) of Schedule 6 (emoluments and other benefits etc. of directors) instead of giving those aggregates individually; and

    (b)   need not give the information required by—
        (i)   paragraph 4 of Schedule 5 (financial years of subsidiary undertakings);
        (ii)   paragraph 1(2)(b) of Schedule 6 (numbers of directors exercising share options and receiving shares under long term incentive schemes);
        (iii)   paragraph 2 of Schedule 6 (details of highest paid director's emoluments etc); or
        (iv)   paragraph 7 of Schedule 6 (excess retirement benefits of directors and past directors)."

(2)   In paragraph 10 of Schedule 6 (supplementary)—

    (a)   in sub-paragraph (1), for the words "paragraphs 1, 7, 8 and 9" there shall be substituted the words "this Part of this Schedule", and

    (b)   sub-paragraph (3) shall be omitted.

(3)   In paragraph 11(1) of that Schedule, for the words "paragraphs 1, 7, 8 and 9" there shall be substituted the words "this Part of this Schedule".

(4)   In sub-paragraph (2) of paragraph 13 of that Schedule (interpretation), the words "(including any provision of this Part of this Schedule referring to paragraph 1)" shall be omitted.

(5)   For sub-paragraph (3) of that paragraph there shall be substituted the following sub-paragraph—

"(3)   The following definitions apply—

    (a)   "pension scheme" has the meaning assigned to "retirement benefits scheme" by section 611 of the Income and Corporation Taxes Act 1988;

    (b)   "retirement benefits" has the meaning assigned to relevant benefits by section 612(1) of that Act."

Appendix 55

1994 No 3013
Value Added Tax (Buildings and Land) Order 1994

Made: 29th November 1994

The Treasury, in exercise of the powers conferred on them by section 51 of the Value Added Tax Act 1994 and of all other powers enabling them in that behalf, hereby make the following Order:

1   This Order may be cited as the Value Added Tax (Buildings and Land) Order 1994 and shall come into force on 30th November 1994.

2 . . .

NOTES
Amendment
        This article amends the Value Added Tax Act 1994, Sch 10, para 2(1) and inserts paras 2(3A), 3(8A).

Appendix 56

Customs give new Concessions on Property Transactions

11/96   28 February 1996

CUSTOMS GIVE NEW CONCESSION ON PROPERTY TRANSACTIONS

Customs & Excise have today published an extra statutory concession to mitigate further the effect of an anti-avoidance measure on property transactions.

The VAT (Buildings and Land) Order 1994 S.I. 3013 was introduced on 30 November 1994 to counter tax avoidance schemes involving the acquisition or development of property for use by businesses in exempt sectors. It provides that an option to tax does not apply in relation to a grant made between connected persons if either is not fully taxable.

It is common practice for a small self-administered pension scheme to own the trading premises of the associated trading company, which occupies the premises under a lease granted by the pension scheme. Many small self-administered pension schemes are not fully taxable, because of activities in the exempt finance and property sectors.

If the scheme and the company are connected, then the Order prevents recovery of the tax incurred on the acquisition of trading premises for the use of the trading business even where that business is fully taxable. Were the premises acquired directly by its occupant, the tax on the acquisition would be recoverable. That is not the avoidance the Order sought to prevent, where another party is involved in the acquisition of the property because the eventual occupant of the property could *not* recover the tax on its acquisition.

By concession, **"for the purposes of paragraph 3(8A) of Schedule 10 to the VAT Act 1994, a small self-administered pension scheme may be treated as a fully taxable person."**

614

The effect of the concession is that where a grant is made between a small self-administered pension scheme and a connected person, the taxable status of the scheme is essentially ignored, and the Order will disapply an election only if the other party is not fully taxable. The other party may take advantage of the earlier '80 per cent' concession in determining whether he is fully taxable.

The concession will have retrospective effect, and is available with effect from 30 November 1994.

Customs will consider individual cases where businesses are not able to take advantage of the concession, but which are not motivated by tax avoidance, and for which there is a clearly demonstrable ordinary commercial motivation and justification. Applications should be made via local VAT enquiry offices.

Notes for Editors

An extra - statutory concession allows taxpayers something to which they would not be entitled under the strict letter of the law. Such concessions may be granted where there are minor or transitory anomalies under legislation, to meet hardships at the margins where a statutory remedy would be difficult to devise, or to alleviate the unintended effect of a piece of legislation, or the unintended effects of the interaction between two pieces of legislation.

The concession is being introduced because the VAT (Buildings and Land Order) 1994 was intended to counter tax avoidance, but it has had the unintended effect of disturbing ordinary commercial activities where no tax avoidance is attempted. The background to the Order, and the granting of a concession from it, were described in News Release 62/95.

Customs' extra-statutory concessions are intended to have general application, but all the circumstances of any particular case must be taken into account in considering the application of a concession. A concession will not be given in any case where an attempt is made to use it for tax avoidance.

For further information traders and their advisers should contact their local VAT enquiry office listed under Customs and Excise in the telephone book.

MEDIA ENQUIRIES ONLY TO THE CUSTOMS AND EXCISE PRESS OFFICE, NEW KING'S BEAM HOUSE, 22 UPPER GROUND, LONDON SE1 9PJ. TELEPHONE 0171 865 5468/5470/5471.

Appendix 57

Memorandum No 101

MEMORANDUM NO 101

Joint Office of
Inland Revenue Superannuation Funds Office and
Occupational Pensions Board

October 1989

Lynwood Road
Thames Ditton
Surrey KT7 0DP

01-398 4242

PERSONAL PENSION SCHEMES
PART I — INVESTMENT OF MEMBERS' CONTRIBUTIONS
PART II — USE OF SCHEME FUNDS

Issued by the Inland Revenue Superannuation Funds Office

PART I — INVESTMENT OF MEMBERS' CONTRIBUTIONS

1   In his Budget statement the Chancellor proposed that personal pension scheme (PPS) members should have the opportunity to become more involved in decisions about how their contributions are invested. This Memorandum contains the further guidance promised in paragraph 59 of Memorandum No 99.

2   This guidance applies to all personal pension schemes, regardless of the type of provider (bank, building society, friendly society etc), which wish to give members a degree of investment choice.

3   Decisions on the extent of choice which scheme members can have are matters for each scheme to decide. There will be no Revenue requirements on this point. Some schemes may choose to limit individual involvement to selecting the parameters of the investment portfolio, leaving the selection of particular investments to a fund manager. On the other hand, others may give the members a direct say as to the specific investments to be held and when they should be bought or sold.

Range of acceptable investments

4   The SFO will, therefore, now consider for approval schemes whose rules allow members to choose, if they wish, how their contributions should be invested. Investments available can be any of the following.

> Stocks and shares (eg equities, gilts, debentures etc.) quoted on the UK Stock Exchange including securities traded on the Unlisted Securities Market.
>
> Stocks and shares traded on a recognised overseas stock exchange.
>
> Unit trusts and investment trusts.
>
> Insurance company managed funds and unit-linked funds.
>
> Deposit accounts.
>
> Commercial property.

PART II — USE OF SCHEME FUNDS

5   There will need to be some controls on investment activities and the way in which the scheme is administered. This is because the sole purpose of an approved PPS must be the provision of annuities or lump sums as required by Section 633 of the Taxes Act. So, from the date of this Memorandum it will be a condition of approval for all personal pension schemes,

irrespective of the type of provider, that the documents must contain provisions expressly prohibiting investments of the types described in paragraphs 6 to 8 below.

Loans

6   Scheme funds must not be used to provide loans to members or any persons connected with a member. Further, no loan from any source made to an individual who is a member of the scheme should in any way affect the return on the investments representing that members' interest in the scheme.

Other Investments

7   Schemes must not, except in the circumstances described in paragraph 8, enter into any investment transactions with a member or any person connected with a member. The acquisitions by the scheme of a member's commercial property or portfolio of stocks and shares are such transactions, as is the subsequent acquisition by the member of any of the scheme's assets. All transactions in quoted UK or overseas securities should take place through a recognised stock exchange.

8   Schemes must not hold directly as an investment residential property or land connected with such a property, or personal chattels capable in any way of private use. This does not apply to commercial land and property (subject to paragraph 7 above). Where commercial property is leased to a business or partnership connected with the member, the scheme rules should ensure that the lease, including the rent payable, is on commercial terms determined by a professional valuation.

Connected Transactions

9   For the purposes of paragraphs 6 to 8 above a person is connected with a member if that person falls within the definition of "connected persons" in Section 839 of the Taxes Act. The duty of ensuring that a transaction is not one with a connected person must be placed on the scheme administrator.

Transactions completed before the issue of this Memorandum

10   Investment transactions which conflict with the requirements in paragraphs 6 to 8 above, but which were completed by an approved (or provisionally approved) scheme before the issue of this Memorandum will not normally be treated as giving rise to unapprovable benefits.

Existing Schemes

11   Schemes which have already received full approval will be required to amend their rules accordingly, and should submit appropriate amendments to this Office. In the meantime no transactions as described in paragraphs 6 to 8 above should be entered into.

12   Schemes which have received provisional approval will be required to include the new restrictions in the rules before substantive approach is given. In the meantime the administrator's undertaking that the scheme does not make provision for any benefit other than those mentioned in the Taxes Act should be regarded as preventing any of the transactions described in paragraph 6 to 8 above.

13   Schemes which have already submitted rules, and which are capable of, but have not yet received, provisional approach in all respects except for paragraphs 6 to 8 above will be granted provisional approach on the understanding that the administrator will interpret his undertaking as in paragraph 12 above.

New Schemes

14   The rules should contain the restrictions in paragraphs 6 to 8 above before provisional approval can be given. The form of application for approval (SF PP1) will be amended in due course to require an indication of where in the scheme documents the new restrictions are to be found. In the meantime applications should include in part 3 of the SF PP1 a note

Appendix 57

showing which rules contain these provisions. If rules have already been executed without these provisions this Office may be prepared to grant provisional approval upon receipt of an assurance from the administrator that he will interpret his undertaking as in paragraph 12 above.

Model Rules

15   The model rules coded IMR/APP/88 and IR/PP/88 will be amended in due course to incorporate provisions permitting members' investment choice and the restrictions described above.

Appendix 58

**Application for tax approval of a
Personal Pension scheme under
Chapter IV Part XIV of Income and
Corporation Taxes Act 1988
(ICTA 1988)**

Please write in CAPITALS, using blue or black ink

1 Existing scheme details

Are you converting an existing Chapter I scheme to a Chapter IV scheme?

☐ No ▶ *go to section 2*

☐ Yes Current scheme name

> [blank box]

Name of Principal Employer

> [blank box]

Tax approval reference number

> S F [blank]

Are you contracted out?

☐ No
☐ Yes

Please give details of contracting out numbers

Scheme
Contracted-out Number S [blank]

Employer
Contracted-out Number E [blank]

Proposed
date of conversion   / /

What are you converting?

☐ The whole scheme ▶ *go to section 2*
☐ Part of the scheme

Please give details of the employments, sections, or parts of the scheme converting to Chapter IV
Please use a separate sheet if necessary

> [blank box]

▶ *go to section 2*

2 Personal Pension scheme details

Name of scheme

> [blank box]

Date the scheme was established
As shown in the establishing deed declaring when the scheme is established.
For converting schemes, this will be the date shown on the original establishing deed.

> / /

Under which part of Section 632 of ICTA 1988 does the person establishing the scheme qualify as a Provider?

> [blank box]

Name and address of the Provider
This is the person who is establishing the scheme.
For trust-based schemes, this is the person who sets up the trust.
For non trust-based schemes, this is the person who declares the establishment of the scheme by deed poll.

Full name

Address

Postcode

Appendix 58

2 Personal Pension scheme details *continued*

Company Registration Number (CRN) of the Provider *if applicable*

Unique Taxpayer Reference (UTR) Number of the Provider

Registered Charity Number of the Provider *if applicable*

Corporation Tax/Schedule D Inland Revenue office to which the Provider's accounts are submitted

Name of the office

Inland Revenue office Number

How is the scheme established?
All schemes must be established under irrevocable trust, except those provided by an insurer with contributions wholly invested in insurance or annuity contracts, or where, irrespective of the type of Provider, the contributions are invested wholly in Individual Pension Accounts (IPAs).

☐ Deed poll/Board resolution
☐ Irrevocable trust

What is the relevant clause number in the establishing deed where the trust is declared?

Does the scheme consist of individual irrevocable trusts?
► *see Note 1 below*

☐ No
☐ Yes

What is the relevant clause or rule number where the trust is declared?

Note 1: A scheme may itself be under irrevocable trust, or may consist of individual irrevocable trusts for each member. Unless the arrangements to be made under the scheme are in the form of insurance contracts, it will be necessary for each member to enter into a formal agreement, by deed. This deed must state that the member will not require the withdrawal of trust funds, or income from those trust funds to be paid to them, except for the payment of benefits under the scheme at the time provided by the rules. Approval will only be available for the scheme as a whole, and if it uses individual trusts it must contain a rule requiring the benefits for each member to be subject to a trust in a form agreed by the Pension Schemes Office (PSO).

If the scheme is set up under an irrevocable trust, does it have a corporate trustee?

☐ No Please complete the separate *Personal Pension Scheme Trustees' information, form* PSPP103

☐ Yes Please give the corporate trustee's details here

Full name

Address

Postcode

If there are additional trustees, complete form PSPP103

Type of investment mode *tick as many options as apply*
☐ Individual Pension Account (IPA)
☐ Insurance policies
☐ Annuity contracts
☐ Unit trusts
☐ Investment of contributions on deposit
☐ Other, please specify

Is the scheme operated as a Self-Invested Personal Pension (SIPP)? *as defined in the Personal Pension Schemes (Restriction on Discretion to Approve) (Permitted Investments) Regulations 2000*
☐ No
☐ Yes

The Scheme Administrator
This is the person resident in the UK who will be responsible for the management of the scheme.

Full name

Address

Postcode

3 Scheme rules

To assist Providers, model rules coded IMR2000 have been published. These are available on request from PSO on 0115 974 1670, or at the Inland Revenue website www.inlandrevenue.gov.uk/pso

Have model rules been adopted without amendment?
☐ Yes *This application should be accompanied by a copy of the executed document establishing the scheme and Schedule A to IMR2000.*
☐ No *This application should be submitted with a full copy of the rules in addition to a copy of the executed establishing document.*

4 Details for tax repayments

Scheme Administrators must complete the details below.
Administrators of existing approved Personal Pension schemes should
enter details of the account they currently use.

Name and address of bank/building society

| Full Name |
| Address |
| |
| |
| Postcode |

Account details

| Branch sort code | | | |

| Account number | | | | |

| Account name |

| Type of account | ☐ Current | ☐ Investment |

Building society reference number *if applicable*
18 characters max

| | | | | | | | | | | | | | | | | | |

Account name used by BACS *18 characters max*

| | | | | | | | | | | | | | | | | | |

Details of up to five authorised signatories to sign tax repayment claims
Authorised signatories should be appointed by resolution of your Board, or of an equivalent managing body,
which we will need to see, along with original specimen signatures for each individual.
Administrators of existing approved Personal Pension schemes, please enter details of the current authorised signatories.
You do not need to send in the resolution of your Board, or of an equivalent managing body, or original specimen signatures.

Full name	Status

Details of two people appointed to provide day-to-day contact about tax repayments
with the Financial Intermediaries and Claims Office (FICO)
These people may also, if desired, be authorised signatories.

Contact full name	Status	Full phone number

5 Correspondence details

Enter details of the person to whom correspondence should be directed about tax approval of this scheme. This may be an authorised
agent, or a corporate trustee, or a nominated trustee if there is more than one. If this section is left blank, correspondence for trust-based
schemes will be with the corporate trustee or first-named trustee on form PSPP103, and for non trust-based schemes, with the Provider.

| Full Name |
| Address |
| |
| |
| Postcode |

Your reference number *if applicable*

| |

Full phone number

| |

PSPP101: Page 3

Appendix 58

6   Declaration

Where applicable, references to Great Britain legislation shall be taken to include references to corresponding Northern Ireland legislation.

I apply for:

- tax approval under Section 631 Income and Corporation Taxes Act 1988 of the Personal Pension scheme described in this form.

I declare that:

- to the best of my knowledge and belief, the information given in this application is correct and complete.

I confirm that:

- the scheme to which this application relates is a Money Purchase scheme

- the application form used to evidence the contract between the member and the scheme complies with the details shown at Appendix 19 of IR76 (2000), which satisfies the Personal Pension Schemes (Relief at Source) (Amendment) Regulations 2000

- the application form used to evidence the transfer of funds into the scheme complies with the details shown at Appendix 20 of IR76 (2000), which complies with the Personal Pension Schemes (Transfer payments) Regulations 2000

- any subsequent changes to the information relating to this scheme will be declared, in writing, to the Pension Schemes Office.

I certify that, in the case of a scheme which is being wholly or partly converted to a Chapter IV scheme:

- the scheme fund does not exceed the amount required to pay benefits

- the transfer value of the fund for each controlling director or prescribed member does not exceed the prescribed amount. Regulation 7 of the Personal Pension Schemes (Conversion of Retirement Benefits Schemes) Regulations 2000.

- the scheme assets have been identified in respect of each member who is to become a member of the Personal Pension scheme and those assets will become assests of the Personal Pension scheme

- I am able to identify at all times which part of the scheme each member and their benefits belong in.

I enclose, in the case of a scheme which is being wholly or partly converted to a Chapter IV scheme:

- a statement showing how the assets are to be earmarked for each member

- documents evidencing compliance with Regulations 6 and 7 of the Personal Pension Schemes (Conversion of Retirement Benefits Schemes) Regulations 2000.

As trustee/Provider of the scheme, I authorise the person detailed at section 5:

- to act on our behalf in connection with matters in relation to the scheme.

This declaration must be signed by the person establishing the scheme, and ALL the trustees.

Please attach photocopies of this page if further space is required.

Signature of the person who is establishing the scheme

Signature	Date
Name	

☐ Director ☐ Company secretary ☐ Authorised signatory

Signatures of the trustees

Signature	Date / /
Name	

Signature	Date / /
Name	

Signature	Date / /
Name	

Signature	Date / /
Name	

Signature	Date / /
Name	

Signature	Date / /
Name	

Signature	Date / /
Name	

PSPP101: Page 4

622

Appendix 58

7 What to do now

First, tick below to show which of the
following documents you are enclosing:

*Office
use only*

☐ Resolution of the Board, or equivalent
managing body, authorising
signatories for tax repayment claims   ☐

☐ Specimen signatures of authorised
signatories   ☐

☐ Document establishing scheme   ☐

☐ Copy of Schedule A to IMR2000
*where model rules have been
adopted without amendment*   ☐

☐ Copy of rules
*where model rules have not been
adopted*   ☐

☐ Completed *Personal Pension
scheme trustees' information*,
form PSPP103, detailing trustees'
names and correspondence addresses
*this is required if the scheme is
established under trust and there is no
corporate trustee*   ☐

☐ Statement showing how the assets
on converting to a Personal
Pension scheme are to be earmarked
for each member *this is required if the
scheme is converting from Chapter I*   ☐

☐ Documents evidencing compliance
with Regulations 6 and 7 of the
Personal Pension Schemes
(Conversion of Retirement Benefits
Schemes) Regulations 2000
*this is required if the scheme is
converting from Chapter I*   ☐

☐ Relevant application to contract-out
if applicable   ☐

☐ Individual irrevocable trust document
if applicable   ☐

Next, fill in all other relevant forms.

Then send this form, with the
documents listed above to:

Pension Schemes Office
Yorke House
PO Box 62
Castle Meadow Road
Nottingham
NG2 1BG

*If any of the required documents are missing, we may not be
able to process your application.*

PSPP101: Page 5

623

Appendix 58A

**Personal Pension scheme
trustees' information**

1 Personal Pension scheme details

Name of scheme

Tax approval reference number *if applicable*

S F

2 Trustees' information

Please use a separate sheet if necessary

Full Name	Full Name
Address	Address
Postcode	Postcode
Nature of change	Nature of change
Date of change / /	Date of change / /

Full Name	Full Name
Address	Address
Postcode	Postcode
Nature of change	Nature of change
Date of change / /	Date of change / /

Office use only ☐ REJ ☐ ACC ☐ APP

Ref No S F

Trustees' information continues on the next page

PSPP103: Page 1

10/00

624

Appendix 58A

2 Trustees' information *continued*

Full Name	Full Name
Address	Address
Postcode	Postcode
Nature of change	Nature of change
Date of change	Date of change
/ /	/ /

3 Declaration

I declare that to the best of my knowledge and belief, the information given in this form is correct and complete.

Signature

Signature	Date / /
Name	

☐ Administrator ☐ Provider ☐ Trustee

4 What to do now

Your next steps will depend on what you are using this application for.

If you are	Send
making an initial scheme application	this form and PSPP101 to PSO
adding trustee details	this form and a deed of appointment to PSO
removing trustee details	this form and a deed of retirement to PSO
amending trustee details	this form and a deed of amendment to PSO

All documents for PSO should be sent to:
Pension Schemes Office
Yorke House
PO Box 62
Castle Meadow Road
Nottingham
NG2 1BG

PSPP103: Page 2

625

Appendix 59

CONTENTS

INTRODUCTION

These notes are for guidance only and reflect the tax position at the time of writing. It should be borne in mind that they are not binding in law and in a particular case there may be special circumstances which need to be taken into account.

INTRODUCTION

Before the 1989 Finance Act, retirement provision by employers had to comply with Inland Revenue tax rules for approved pension schemes. This meant that tax law effectively constrained the total pensions employers could pay to their employees.

The 1989 Act has ensured that employers can now provide whatever retirement benefits they see fit. Tax relief is of course restricted by the maximum benefit limits and the earnings cap, but benefits outside the confines of the tax privileged scheme are unlimited. Non-approved pension schemes give new opportunities and choices to employers which allow them to arrange the retirement package needed to recruit and retain staff.

Employers can now set up non-approved schemes which give flexibility to, for example

- offer a pension greater than the normal two thirds of final salary

- provide a full two-thirds pension even if the normal rules do not allow it – for example, if the employee cannot complete 20 years service with the final employer

- provide lump sum benefits in addition to those allowed under the terms of approved schemes

- give employees who are affected by the earnings cap on tax privileged benefits, pensions and lump sums on earnings above the cap.

But non-approved schemes will not, of course, attract any special tax privileges. And so the purpose of this booklet is to explain in general terms the tax treatment of non-approved pension schemes – which are referred to throughout as "top-up" schemes.

The guidance in this booklet deals only with those social security rules which interact with tax matters – this concerns transfers of pension rights. Any question on how top-up schemes are affected by other Social Security requirements should be sent to the Department of Social Security.

PART 1

DEFINITION OF A TOP-UP PENSION SCHEME

1.1 What is a Top-up Pension Scheme?

1.1.1 Top-up pension schemes do not have to adopt any particular form. there are no tax rules which govern the structure of schemes, the type of benefits or their amount. These are all matters for employers, employees and their advisers to decide, within the context of general law.

1.1.2   The guidance in this booklet relates only to the tax treatment of schemes which are "retirement benefits schemes" as defined in the Income and Corporation Taxes Act 1988 ("the Taxes Act"). Such schemes will also be subject to other legislation relating to equal treatment, preservation of benefits and so on. These matters are the responsibility of the Department of Social Security to whom any enquiries should be sent.

1.1.3   A retirement benefits scheme is defined in section 611 of the Taxes Act. It means, broadly, a scheme providing benefits for employees or their families which include "relevant benefits" as described in paragraph 1.2.1. The scheme does not have to be set up in any particular way: indeed, a decision to give a relevant benefit on a voluntary basis will be enough to constitute a scheme. More formal arrangements for setting up a scheme may involve a deed, agreement, or other arrangement and it may cover a group of employees or be for just one. For example, a provision in a contract of employment would be enough to establish a retirement benefits scheme.

1.2   Meaning of "relevant benefits"

1.2.1   No matter what form the scheme takes, it is a retirement benefits scheme only if it includes "relevant benefits" among the benefits it gives. Relevant benefits are defined in section 612 of the Taxes Act. They include a pension, lump sum, gratuity or other similar benefit which is, or will be, given

● when a person retires or dies

● in anticipation of retirement

● after a person has retired or died (if the reason for payment is in recognition of past service)

or

● as compensation for any change in the conditions of a continuing employment.

1.2.2   Disability benefits (whether regular payments or lump sums) are not relevant benefits if they are payable solely because of an employee's death or disablement by accident while employed.

1.2.3   Some schemes which are not intended to be retirement benefits schemes could come within the legislation on top-up schemes. An example is a sick pay scheme which includes a lump sum death in service benefit. On the other hand, redundancy schemes which provide lump sum payments on severance of employment will not normally be affected. This is because redundancy lump sums are payable because of severance of service and not because of retirement or a change in the conditions of a continuing employment.

1.3 Relationship with approved schemes

1.3.1   A tax approved scheme cannot offer non-approvable benefits: they must be kept entirely outside its trust deed and rules. A scheme can only be split into approved and unapproved parts where there are separate classes of employee. For example, where a multi-national employer has a single scheme for its worldwide workforce, it may be possible to approve that part of it covering employees of the UK branch or subsidiary. But only if the types and amounts of benefits payable under the scheme to the UK employers are approvable.

1.3.2   The guidance in this booklet is also relevant to the tax treatment of a scheme, and of payments made to or by it, where its approval is not backdated to commencement, resulting in a period of non-approved status. In such a case the tax privileges that go with approval are available only from the effective date of approval. Prior to that date, the scheme will be treated as a non-approved scheme.

PART 2   TAX TREATMENT OF TOP-UP PENSION SCHEMES

2.1   General

2.1.1   Top-up pension schemes are often referred to as being either

- funded (where money is set aside in advance to meet the benefits promised)
- unfunded (where the promised benefits are met on a pay-as-you-go basis when the employee retires or dies).

In fact, the Taxes Act contains no such distinctions. So although terms like "funded" and "unfunded" are useful labels, they are no more than that. A scheme may combine both approaches (for example, unfunded retirement benefits and funded (insured) death in service benefits).

2.1.2   There are tax consequences when top-up schemes make or receive payments. This Part covers

- the tax treatment of payments to schemes
- the tax treatment of payments by schemes
- the tax treatment of the schemes themselves.

2.2   Tax treatment of payments to schemes

2.2.1   Payments to top-up schemes normally come from contributions by the employer and/or by the employee.

Contributions by the employee

2.2.2   Employee contributions to a top-up scheme are not deductible as an expense in assessing income tax under Schedule E. So where an employee makes direct payment to the scheme no tax relief can be claimed (except on the first £100 each year of premiums paid to secure annuities for a widow and provision for children – section 273 Taxes Act). Where the employer deducts the contributions from pay and passes the money to the top-up scheme, the contributions should come out of taxed income (like, for example, trade union subscriptions and other similar deductions).

2.2.3   As no tax relief is normally due for the contributions, there are no upper or lower limits on the amounts the employee may pay into the scheme. an employee would therefore be better advised to pay additional voluntary contributions, within the normal limits, to a tax approved scheme where that option is available.

Contributions by the employer

2.2.4   Where an employer contributes to a top-up scheme to provide relevant benefits, the contribution counts as the employee's taxable income (section 595(1) Taxes Act). If the scheme is for one employee it is easy to identity the amount chargeable. Where the scheme benefits have been insured, the whole premiums are chargeable to tax. But where the scheme is self-administered, only the contributions used towards providing relevant benefits are chargeable: a tax charge does not arise on separately identifiable contributions which meet the scheme's establishment and administration expenses.

2.2.5   Where an employer pays a contribution for more than one employee, section 595(4) requires the sum to be shared between all of the employees who can benefit from it. The employer, or scheme administrator, should tell the Tax Office how each contribution should be split between the employees. The tax charge will usually be based on these figures.

2.2.6   An employer should notify employees about payments which are chargeable under section 595. *This notice is important and should be retained by the employee.* It may be needed, when benefits become payable, to show that income tax is not payable under section 596A Taxes Act 1988 on all or part of the benefits (see paragraph 2.3.1).

2.2.7   If an employer wants to meet the employee's tax liability on the contributions they may agree on a grossing arrangement: the consent of the local Tax Office is not needed. But, under section 311 Companies Act 1985, it is not lawful for a company to pay a director remuneration free of income tax or varying with the amount of his or her income tax.

2.2.8   Where a grossing arrangement operates, the grossed-up equivalent of the actual chargeable contribution, and the tax figure, should then be included on the employer's pay record (form P11) for the pay period in which the contributions are paid.

Example

A monthly-paid employee is liable to higher rate tax. The employer pays a contribution of £6,000 to a top-up scheme on 6 March. the grossed-up equivalent of the contribution should be included in emoluments, and tax included in tax deducted, for the pay period to 31 March. the employee's top rate of tax is 40%. So the gross contribution, and tax, are

$$£6,000 \times \frac{100}{60} = £10,000$$

Tax on £10,000 at 40% = £4,000.

2.2.9   Contributions paid by an employer without a grossing arrangement should be notified by the employer at the end of the year to the Tax Office on a form P9D or P11D. The amount of the contribution will then be included in a Schedule E assessment made on the employee who will be asked to pay any resulting tax underpaid.

2.2.10   Benefits in kind can also be chargeable to income tax under section 154 Taxes Act where they are payable to an employee or to members of his or her family or household. But in the case of pensions, lump sums and similar retirement benefits, section 155(4) and Extra Statutory Concession A72 provides exemption from this tax charge. This avoids the possibility of a double charge to tax: once under section 595 and again under section 154.

2.2.11   The borderline between there being a tax charge under section 595 or not can be a fine one. The position will depend upon whether sums have been paid by an employer under a scheme with a view to the provision of benefits for employees. So, for example, payments by an employer to meet the costs of establishing or administering a scheme are not chargeable under section 595. But in other situations the Tax Office will need to consider all the relevant factors before reaching a view.

2.2.12   One example of a borderline case is the creation of a fixed or floating charge on some of the employer's assets. The purpose of such a charge would be to provide security for an unfunded benefit promise. Normally the charge will be called in only if the employer became insolvent or failed to pay the benefits when due. In these cases, the value of the charge would not count as the employee's taxable income when it is created.

2.2.13   On the other hand, if the charge should at any time be called in, that will involve a payment by the employer that could lead to a section 595 charge (even if the employee is then retired or no longer in service). In practice, the tax treatment may depend upon when happens to the funds realised. If they are all paid immediately to the employee, it will often be simpler to charge tax on the benefit paid under section 596A Taxes Act (see paragraph 2.3.1). But where the funds are to be held by trustees on trust until, say, the employee reaches a specified age, then the section 595 tax charge would be applied.

2.2.14   Key man insurance is another difficult area. This insurance is normally used to protect the employer's profits against the loss of a director or other key employee. If used in its conventional form (to protect the employer's profits from the loss of services of a key employee), premiums are not within section 595. But if the insurance contract is part of the arrangements for providing the promised benefits, or to provide security for that promise, then the premiums will be chargeable under section 595(1). The tax treatment in a particular case can be decided by the relevant Tax Office only after seeing the policy and other agreements involved.

2.3   Tax treatment of payments by schemes

2.3.1   The tax treatment of benefits depends on what happened while they accrued. In particular all benefits from a top-up scheme are chargeable to income tax under section 596A Taxes Act unless

- the benefit is chargeable under section 19(1)1 Taxes act (and section 596a does not produce a greater tax liability)

  or

- it can be shown that the benefit is attributable to sums taxed under section 595(1).

Benefits where sums are charged under Section 595

2.3.2   If benefits are paid as lump sums, no tax is chargeable. This is because of the exemptions in section 189(b) Taxes Act (where benefits are paid to the scheme member) or in section 5596A(8) (in other cases). These exemptions apply to benefits payable on retirement or on death.

2.3.3   But pensions and other periodical payments will be chargeable to tax even though they come from sums taxed under section 595(1). In the case of pensions tax will be chargeable under section 19(1) 2 or 3 Taxes Act and where annuities or other annual payments are paid the charge will arise under Case III of Schedule D. In both cases it will be the payer's responsibility to deduct the tax due when making the payment.

2.3.4   If the employee prefers a pension to a lump sum benefit, it will generally be best to give him or her the cash value of the benefits. the money could then be used to buy a life annuity. By arranging matters in this way the annuity will qualify for special tax treatment under which tax is only charged on the income element of each annuity instalment.

If the top-up scheme bought the annuity, the whole of each instalment would be taxable.

Benefits where there is no section 595 charge

2.3.5   Pension payments are taxable under section 596A.

2.3.6   Other types of benefit – whether payable on retirement or death, or as lump sums or benefits in kind – are chargeable under section 596A. That section treats the payments made to an individual as Schedule E income. In the case of cash benefits the payer has to deduct and account for tax under PAYE when the payment is made. Where the benefit is not in cash, details should be given by the scheme administrator to the Tax Office within 3 months of its payment.

2.3.7   In some cases an employer might choose to capitalise an unfunded pension promise at retirement and purchase an annuity. But the cost of the annuity would count as the retired employee's taxable income. Also, the annuity would not qualify for the tax relief given for purchased life annuities: the whole of each instalment would be taxable.

2.3.8   Securing benefits in this way could lead to hardship if the employee did not have the cash to meet the tax liability. An alternative would be for the employer to pay the capital value (less income tax under PAYE) to the employee. The balance of the money could then be used to buy the annuity if he or she wished. In this way, the annuity instalments would be taxable only on the income element, not on the whole amount.

2.3.9   Top-up pension schemes are not regulated by tax rules. So payments do not have to be made to the employee or his or her family. For example, the employee could nominate payment to a club or association. These payments would not fit well within a Schedule E charge. Section 596A therefore makes the pension scheme administrator liable to a Case VI, Schedule D tax charge on payments other than to an individual.

2.3.10   There is no statutory provision requiring this tax charge to be deducted from the payments. Authority for doing so should, if needed, be included in the rules or terms of the top-up scheme.

2.3.11   Where the scheme administrator incurs a Case VI Schedule D liability on a payment, the details should be reported to the Tax Office dealing with its affairs. The report, covering all payments of this kind which were made in the accounting period, should be made within 3 months after the end of that period.

2.3.12   Section 596A also taxes benefits in kind which continue after retirement. The measure of the tax charge is on the cash equivalent of the benefit. The cash equivalent is calculated under section 596B according to the type of benefit.

2.3.13 Details of the benefit should be included by the person receiving it on his or her tax return. He or she should be told that if they do not receive a tax return they are legally obliged to tell the Tax Office about the benefit so that it can be assessed.

2.4 Benefits from schemes which formerly were approved

2.4.1 When a retirement benefits scheme ceases to be tax approved, it immediately comes within the tax regime for top-up schemes. Employer contributions payable after tax approval ceases will be chargeable on the members under section 595(1). Lump sum benefits which relate to sums assessed under section 595(1) will be exempt from tax. But any lump sum which relates to the period when the scheme was approved will be chargeable in full under section 596A (even though if the scheme had still been approved, such payments would have been tax exempt).

2.5 Inheritance tax position

2.5.1 It is not possible to give firm guidance on the inheritance tax position since this can only be determined when all the relevant facts about a particular scheme are known. But some general points can be made.

2.5.2 Most top-up schemes (whether funded or unfunded) are likely to be "sponsored superannuation schemes" as defined in section 624 Taxes Act because, even where the employee is charged to income tax under section 595(1), that tax charge does not cover separately identifiable costs of setting up and running the scheme. Where several employers are contributing to a scheme it does not matter whether, or how, participating employers allocate the setting up or administrative costs between themselves as it is the scheme that must bear this cost if it is to qualify as a sponsored superannuation scheme.

2.5.3 For inheritance tax, this means that top-up schemes set up under trust which are also sponsored superannuation schemes will fall within section 151 Inheritance Tax Act 1984. As a result, the normal inheritance tax charges on settled property will not apply. So, for example, benefits paid out under such schemes will be free of any inheritance tax trust charges. there are no special provisions in the Inheritance Tax Act for benefits payable under non-trust arrangements.

2.5.4 Broadly, it is only death benefits that may be liable to inheritance tax. Tax is chargeable if the benefit is expressed to be payable only to the deceased's estate. But commonly, death benefits may be paid at the employer's or scheme administrator's discretion to one or more of a specified group of possible beneficiaries. In these cases inheritance tax will not generally be payable if the employee's estate is excluded from this group.

2.5.5   However, if the employee's estate is included as a possible beneficiary under the discretionary power there may be an inheritance tax gifts with reservation (GWR) charge under section 102 Finance Act 1986. (The provisions outlined in the Inland Revenue press release of 9 July 1986 – which excluded a GWR charge on death benefits under tax approved schemes held on discretionary trusts – do not apply where the scheme is unapproved. "Tax approved schemes" in this context include approved personal pension schemes.)

2.6   Tax treatment of transfer payments

2.6.1   The rules of approved pension schemes do not allow them to make transfer payments to, or accept transfer payments from, an unapproved pension scheme. Benefit rights which have accrued under a top-up scheme may therefore, in practice, be transferred only to another top-up scheme.

2.6.2   There are no tax problems where a cash equivalent is paid between funded schemes. The funds held in the transferring scheme will have accrued from contributions, investment income and gains which have been taxed. For this reason there will not be any tax liability on the transfer payment. and the benefits, when payable, will be subject to the normal tax treatment that applies to funded schemes.

2.6.3   Transfers from a funded scheme of one employer to an otherwise unfunded one of another are also straightforward in tax terms. Once again, the transfer will not itself be a taxable payment. and the benefits derived from the transfer payment will be tax-free if paid as a lump sum, but taxable if paid as pensions. but the unfunded benefits for service with the later employer will all be taxable.

2.6.4   The situation most likely to give rise to complications is transfers from an unfunded scheme. As an unfunded scheme holds no assets, the employer would have to provide the money to pay the cash equivalent, but this would result in a tax liability for the employee under section 595(1) – even if the employee had by then already left service. This may not be an attractive result if the employee did not have the resources to meet the tax liability.

2.7   Income and gains of top-up pension schemes

2.7.1   The tax position of the income and gains of top-up schemes, and the persons chargeable, will depend on the particular structure the scheme takes. A firm ruling on the tax treatment in a particular case can be given by a Tax Office only after considering all the relevant facts. It is therefore possible here to give guidance in only general terms.

2.7.2   Unfunded schemes will not normally have tax complications. the benefit promise will exist on paper, but the scheme will hold no assets. When benefits are due, the employer will at that time provide the funds to pay them and tax liabilities will arise then on the benefits as described in paragraphs 2.3.5 to 2.3.13.

2.7.3   Funded schemes are another matter. In many cases they will be set up under trust (although that is not a tax requirement), and the trustees will be responsible for holding the scheme assets. Some schemes may be wholly insured with premiums paid on insurance contracts. In these cases the trustees will not normally have tax liabilities for those contracts (but see paragraph 3.2.1 to 3.2.4 about the employer's tax position). Any tax due on investment income and gains on the funds which underwrite the contracts will normally be the insurance company's responsibility.

2.7.4   In other cases the scheme may be self-administered. The tax treatment of the income and gains will depend on the particular structure that the scheme takes. Generally, if the scheme is a trust where the trustees have discretion as to the payments to be made or can accumulate surplus income, there will be potential liability to both basic rate and additional rate tax. But, if the only benefits provided by the scheme are "relevant benefits" (see paragraph 1.2.1), it will be exempt from the additional rate tax charge (section 686(2)(c)(i) Taxes Act). The rate of capital gains tax will also normally be restricted to basic rate income tax (section 100 Finance Act 1988). The normal rules for capital gains tax will apply but the trustees will generally be entitled to half the personal annual exemption rather than the full personal exemption (£5,500 for 1991–92).

2.7.5   The "benefit to settlor" rules in Part XV Taxes Act and Schedule 10 Finance act 1988 can apply to top-up pension schemes. But this is not likely to be the case where the structure and operation of a scheme are broadly similar to an approved pension scheme.

2.7.6   Funded self-administered schemes will have to prepare annual accounts and these should be submitted by the scheme's administrator to the scheme's Tax Office so that the appropriate assessments to income tax and capital gains tax may be made.

PART 3   EMPLOYER'S TAX POSITION

3.1   Deductibility of payments

3.1.1   The 1989 Finance Act introduced new rules affecting an employer's right to a deduction for payments to provide non-approved benefits. A right to a deduction now depends on whether those payments are chargeable to tax.

3.1.2   Section 76 Finance Act 1989 disallows the costs incurred by an employer in providing non-approved benefits except where

- the benefits payable under the scheme are taxable
  or

- payments made to provide benefits in future are treated as the scheme member's income under section 595(1).

3.1.3   The section also ties the timing of the deduction to the actual payment of the taxable sums. This prevents an employer claiming a deduction in advance of the payments being chargeable to tax. So, in the case of unfunded schemes, it will not be possible to obtain a deduction for an accounts provision which reflects the liability to pay the future benefits. The deduction will be due only when taxable payments are actually made under the scheme.

3.1.4   Section 76 does not apply to payments made specifically to meet the establishment or running costs of a top-up scheme. Decisions as to whether a deduction is due for these payments are matters for the employer's Tax Office to consider under normal principles.

3.2   Gains on life insurance policies and annuities

3.2.1   The Finance Act 1989 extended the charge on company owned life policies and annuity contracts and on those held on trusts set up by companies.

3.2.2   The company is taxable on any gain made (unless paragraph 3.2.4 – second part – applies). This is, broadly, the difference between the premiums paid and the proceeds. All amounts received from a policy, for example on a partial withdrawal, come into the calculation.

3.2.3   However, in the case of a life policy, the gain on a death is computed by reference to the surrender value of the policy immediately before death. This is particularly important for single policies insuring more than one life ("group policies"). With these, on each death a gain is computed on the surrender value immediately before the death plus all sums paid on earlier deaths. So, instead of using group policies, it will generally be best for each scheme member to have a separate policy. this will ensure that the insurance is individually rated so that liability under section 595 (see paragraph 2.2.4) relates exactly to the premiums paid for the member; the policy benefits can also be tailored more closely to the member's wishes.

3.2.4   Liability arises even on the proceeds received by non-approved pension trusts, but the gain is not charged to tax under these provisions if policy benefits are otherwise chargeable to tax (for example, in the case of Key Man Insurance – see paragraph 2.2.14).

PART 4   REPORTING REQUIREMENTS

4.1.1   Section 605(3)(a) Taxes Act requires an employer to report the existence of a top-up scheme to the Revenue. the report should be made to the Tax Office dealing with the employer's accounts.

4.1.2   This notification should be made within 3 months of the date when the scheme first comes into operation for any employee. This means the date a taxable event first arises; for example, the payment of a contribution or a benefit.

4.1.3   So, in the case of a funded scheme with one or more members, the report should be made within 3 months of the scheme being set up. If separate funded schemes are set up for each employee – such as where the benefits are secured by individual insurance policies – the Tax Office should be told about each new scheme.

4.1.4   But with unfunded schemes, no taxation consequences normally arise until benefits become payable. So, no reports will be required until then.

4.1.5   Section 605 also gives the Board of Inland Revenue the power to call for information. In particular

- Section 605(3)(b) requires the employer to comply with a notice requiring details about

    — top-up schemes
    and

    — the employees who benefit under those schemes.

- Section 605(4) places similar duties on the administrator of a top-up scheme.

Appendix 60

Inland **Revenue** | **Trust and Estate Tax Return** | **for the year ended 5 April 1999**

Tax reference

Date

Issue address

⌐   ⌐

Tax Office address

⌐   ⌐
Officer in Charge

L   ⌐

L   ⌐

Telephone

For
Reference

▌ Please read this page first

*The green arrows and instructions will guide
you through the Trust and Estate Tax Return*

*T*his Notice requires you by law to send me
a Tax Return for the year from 6 April 1998
to 5 April 1999. Give details of all the income
and capital gains on which the trust or estate
may be charged to tax using:

- this form and any supplementary Pages
  you need, OR

- other Inland Revenue approved forms, OR

- the Electronic Lodgement Service (ELS).

**Make sure the Tax Return, and any documents
asked for, reaches me by:**

- *the later of 30 September 1999 and
  2 months after the date this notice was
  given if you want me to calculate the trust or
  estate's tax, OR*

- *the later of 31 January 2000 and 3 months
  after the date this notice was given, at the
  latest, or you will be liable to an automatic
  penalty of £100.*

Make sure your payment of any tax the trust or
estate owes reaches me by 31 January, or you will
have to pay interest and perhaps a surcharge.

All Tax Returns will be checked. Please remember
that there are penalties for supplying false
information.

The Trust and Estate Tax Return

I have sent you pages 1 to 12 of the Tax Return.

- *Page 2 tells you about supplementary Pages
  for some types of income and gains. For
  example; there are Pages for income from
  land and property.*

- *Pages 3 and 4 are for details of other income.*

- *Pages 5 to 12 are for other information.*

*You are responsible for making sure you have
the right supplementary Pages. Use page 2 to
find out which ones you need.*

I have also sent you:

- *a Trust and Estate Tax Return Guide to help
  you fill in the Trust and Estate Tax Return
  (read pages 2 to 7 of the Guide before you
  start) and*

- *a Trust and Estate Tax Calculation Guide to
  help you if you are calculating the trust or
  estate's tax.*

If you need help:

- *refer to the Trust and Estate Tax Return
  Guide, OR*

- *ring the number above - most questions can
  be answered by telephone, OR*

- *when the office is closed, phone our
  Helpline on 0645 000 444 for general advice.
  It is open each evening and at weekends, OR*

- *if you do not want to explain your question
  on the phone, call in at a Tax Enquiry
  Centre - look under 'Inland Revenue' in the
  phone book.*

SA900

Inland Revenue

INCOME AND CAPITAL GAINS *for the year ended 5 April 1999*

Step 1

- see notes on page 6 of the Trust and Estate Tax Return Guide

You can go straight to Question 18 on page 10 if:

Tick if this applies ▼

1) you are the trustee of a bare trust (read the notes on page 4 of the Trust and Estate Tax Return Guide), that is one in which the beneficiary(ies) has/have an immediate and absolute title to both capital and income, **or** ☐

2) you are the personal representative of a deceased person **and all** the points below apply:
- all the income arose in the UK
- you do not wish to claim reliefs
- no annual payments have been made out of capital
- all income has had tax deducted before you received it
- you have made no chargeable disposals

- there are no accrued income charges or reliefs,
- no income from relevant discounted securities, offshore income gains, or gains on life insurance policies, life annuities or capital redemption policies that are not treated as having been taxed at the basic rate. ☐

3) you are the trustee of an interest in possession trust **and all** the points below apply:
- you do not wish to claim reliefs
- no annual payments have been made out of capital
- no capital payments have been made to or for the benefit of the minor unmarried children of the settlor during his/her lifetime
- the trust has never been non-resident and has never received any capital from another trust which is or at any time has been non-resident

- you have made no chargeable disposals
- no further capital has been added to the settlement
- there are no accrued income charges or reliefs, no income from relevant discounted securities, gilt strips, company buy-backs, offshore income gains or gains on life insurance policies, life annuities or capital redemption policies

and provided that
a) no income arose to the trust, **or** ☐
b) you have mandated all the trust income to the beneficiary(ies), **or** ☐
c) all the income arose in the UK and has had tax deducted before you received it, **or** ☐
d) you have mandated part of the income to the beneficiary(ies) where the part you have not mandated comprises only income arising in the UK which has had tax deducted before you received it. ☐

If you would have ticked one of the boxes in 2) or 3) except for the fact that you have chargeable disposals you need only answer Questions 5 and 6 at Step 2, Question 7 and Questions 16 to 21. **In any other case,** including if you are the trustee of a unit trust scheme that is not an authorised unit trust, you should go to Step 2.

Step 2

Answer Questions 1 to 6 below to find out if you need any supplementary Pages. Read pages 8 and 9 of the Trust and Estate Tax Return Guide if you need help. The questions are colour coded to help you identify the supplementary Pages and the guidance notes. If you answer 'No' go to the next question. If you answer 'Yes', you must complete the relevant supplementary Pages. **Ring the Orderline on 0645 000 404 between 8am and 10pm for any you need; make sure you ask for the supplementary Pages for the Trust and Estate Tax Return.**

Make sure you have the right supplementary Pages and then tick the box below when you have filled them in.

Q1 Did the trust or estate make any profit or loss from a sole trade? (Read page 8 of the Trust and Estate Tax Return Guide if you were the personal representative of a deceased Name at Lloyd's) | NO ☐ | YES ☐ | TRADE YES ☐

Q2 Did the trust or estate make any profit or loss or have any other income from a partnership? | NO ☐ | YES ☐ | PARTNERSHIP YES ☐

Q3 Did the trust or estate receive any rent or other income from land and property in the UK? | NO ☐ | YES ☐ | LAND & PROPERTY YES ☐

Q4 Did the trust or estate receive any income from foreign companies or savings institutions, offshore funds or trusts abroad, or income from land and property abroad, or gains on foreign life insurance policies? | NO ☐ | YES ☐

Is the trust or estate claiming relief for foreign tax paid on foreign income or gains, or relief from UK tax under a Double Taxation Agreement? | NO ☐ | YES ☐ | FOREIGN YES ☐

Q5 Capital gains
- did the trust or estate dispose of assets worth more than £13,600 in total? | NO ☐ | YES ☐
- were the trust's or estate's chargeable gains more than their annual exemption? | NO ☐ | YES ☐

Does this Return include the disposal of assets for either a Trust/Settlement with separate funds, or for just one of those 'separate funds'? Read page 9 of the Trust and Estate Tax Return Guide. | NO ☐ | YES ☐ | CAPITAL GAINS YES ☐

Q6 Is the trust claiming to be not resident in the UK, or dual resident in the UK and another country for all or part of the year for:
- Income Tax | NO ☐ | YES ☐
- Capital Gains Tax? | NO ☐ | YES ☐ | NON-RESIDENCE ETC YES ☐

Step 3

Please use blue or black ink to fill in the Trust and Estate Tax Return and please do not include pence. Round down, to the nearest pound, income and gains and round up tax credits and tax deductions. Now fill in any supplementary Pages BEFORE going to Step 4.

Step 4

You must answer Question 7 and then Questions 8-20 as directed.

BMSD 12/98 ■ TRUST AND ESTATE TAX RETURN: PAGE 2

INCOME AND CAPITAL GAINS *for the year ended 5 April 1999* continued

Q7 Are you completing this Tax Return in the capacity of personal representative? NO ☐ YES ☐

Are you completing this Tax Return as the trustee of an unauthorised unit trust? NO ☐ YES ☐

If you are the trustee of a Funded Unapproved Retirement Benefit Scheme (FURBS) have you provided any non-relevant benefits to any of the scheme's beneficiaries? NO ☐ YES ☐

If you are a trustee, is the trust liable to tax at the special 'rate applicable to trusts' (34%)? NO ☐ YES ☐   See page 10 of the Trust and Estate Tax Return Guide.

INCOME *for the year ended 5 April 1999*

Q8 Did the trust or estate receive any other income not already included on the supplementary Pages? NO ☐ YES ☐   If yes, fill in boxes 8.1 to 8.44 as appropriate.

- If you are the trustee of a (non-interest in possession) trust where the income is treated as the settlor's for tax purposes because the settlor has retained an interest (if in doubt ask the Orderline for *Help Sheet IR270: Trusts and settlements - income treated as the settlor's*) only include income which has had tax deducted before you received it if there is accrued income scheme relief to set against the interest or, if you are claiming reliefs (Question 9) which exceed the untaxed income, or if you are claiming losses against general income, or if its exclusion would make you liable to make payments on account which would not be due if you included it – see page 7 of the Tax Calculation Guide for Trusts and Estates, concerning payments on account **before** following this guidance.

- If you are the trustee of an interest in possession trust, only include income which has had tax deducted before you received it if:
  (i) that income has not been mandated to the beneficiary and there is accrued income scheme relief to set against the interest or you are claiming losses against general income, or
  (ii) its exclusion would make you liable to make a payment on account which would not be due if you included it - see page 7 of the Tax Calculation Guide for Trusts and Estates concerning payments on account following this guidance.

- If you are the personal representative of a deceased person only include income which has had tax deducted before you received it if there is accrued income scheme relief to set against the interest. If the reliefs claimed at Question 9 on page 5 exceed untaxed income you will need to include estate income that has had tax deducted to ensure a repayment can be calculated.

Tick this box if you received any taxed income which is not included in this Trust and Estate Tax Return. **A** ☐

■ *Interest*

- Interest from UK banks, building societies and deposit takers

	Taxable amount
- where **no tax** has been deducted	**8.1** £

	Amount after tax deducted	Tax deducted	Gross amount before tax
- where **tax has been** deducted	**8.2** £	**8.3** £	**8.4** £

- Interest distributions from UK authorised unit trusts and open-ended investment companies (dividend distributions go below)

Amount after tax deducted	Tax deducted	Gross amount before tax
8.5 £	**8.6** £	**8.7** £

- National Savings (other than FIRST Option Bonds)

Taxable amount
8.8 £

- National Savings FIRST Option Bonds

Amount after tax deducted	Tax deducted	Gross amount before tax
8.9 £	**8.10** £	**8.11** £

- Other income from UK savings and investments (except dividends)

Amount after tax deducted	Tax deducted	Gross amount before tax
8.12 £	**8.13** £	**8.14** £

BMSD 12/98 ■ TRUST AND ESTATE TAX RETURN: PAGE 3 **Please turn over** ➡

Appendix 60

■ *Dividends*

	Dividend/distribution	Tax credit	Dividend/distribution plus credit
● Dividends and other qualifying distributions from UK companies	8.15 £	8.16 £	8.17 £

	Dividend/distribution	Tax credit	Dividend/distribution plus credit
● Dividend distributions from UK authorised unit trusts and open-ended investment companies	8.18 £	8.19 £	8.20 £

	Dividend	Notional tax	Dividend plus notional tax
● Scrip dividends from UK companies	8.21 £	8.22 £	8.23 £

	Dividend	Notional tax	Dividend plus notional tax
● Foreign income dividends from UK companies	8.24 £	8.25 £	8.26 £

	Dividend	Notional tax	Dividend plus notional tax
● Foreign income dividend distributions from UK authorised unit trusts and open-ended investment companies	8.27 £	8.28 £	8.29 £

		Notional tax	Taxable amount
● Non-qualifying distributions and loans written off	8.30 £	8.31 £	8.32 £

■ *Gains on UK life insurance policies, life annuities and capital redemption policies*

	Amount of gain
● without notional tax	8.33 £

	Notional tax	Amount of gain
● with notional tax	8.34 £	8.35 £

■ *Other income*

	Amount after tax deducted	Tax deducted	Gross amount before tax
● Other income	8.36 £	8.37 £	8.38 £

	Losses brought forward	Loss used in 1998-99
	8.39 £	8.40 £

	Losses sustained in 1998-99
	8.41 £

	Taxable amount
● Deemed income etc. (see page 17 of the Trust and Estate Tax Return Guide)	8.42 £

	Notional tax	Taxable amount
● Company purchase of its own shares	8.43 £	8.44 £

642

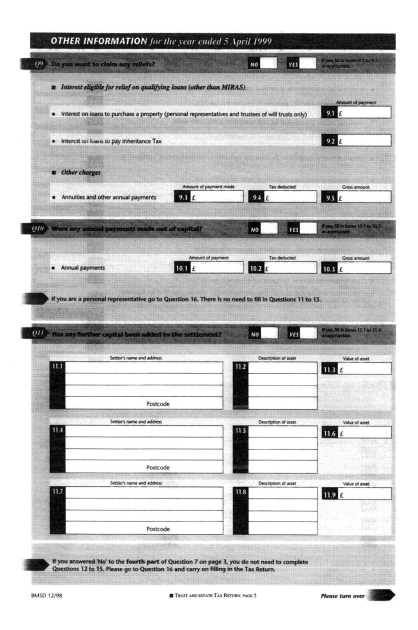

OTHER INFORMATION *for the year ended 5 April 1999*

Q9 **Do you want to claim any reliefs?**   NO ☐   YES ☐   *If yes, fill in boxes 9.1 to 9.5 as appropriate.*

■ *Interest eligible for relief on qualifying loans (other than MIRAS)*

	Amount of payment
● Interest on loans to purchase a property (personal representatives and trustees of will trusts only)	9.1 £
● Interest on loans to pay Inheritance Tax	9.2 £

■ *Other charges*

	Amount of payment made	Tax deducted	Gross amount
● Annuities and other annual payments	9.3 £	9.4 £	9.5 £

Q10 **Were any annual payments made out of capital?**   NO ☐   YES ☐   *If yes, fill in boxes 10.1 to 10.3 as appropriate.*

	Amount of payment	Tax deducted	Gross amount
● Annual payments	10.1 £	10.2 £	10.3 £

▶ If you are a personal representative go to Question 16. There is no need to fill in Questions 11 to 15.

Q11 **Has any further capital been added to the settlement?**   NO ☐   YES ☐   *If yes, fill in boxes 11.1 to 11.9 as appropriate.*

Settlor's name and address	Description of asset	Value of asset
11.1 _____ Postcode	11.2	11.3 £
11.4 _____ Postcode	11.5	11.6 £
11.7 _____ Postcode	11.8	11.9 £

▶ If you answered 'No' to the **fourth part** of Question 7 on page 3, you do not need to complete Questions 12 to 15. Please go to Question 16 and carry on filling in the Tax Return.

BMSD 12/98   ■ TRUST AND ESTATE TAX RETURN: PAGE 5   *Please turn over* ▶

Appendix 60

Q12 Is any part of the trust income not liable to tax at the rate applicable to trusts? NO ☐ YES ☐ If yes, fill in boxes 12.1 to 12.16 below. If no, fill in boxes 12.9 to 12.16.

- Amount of income chargeable at the lower rate treated as that of the settlor — **12.1** £

- Trust management expenses applicable to the income in box 12.1 — **12.2** £

- Amount of income chargeable at the basic rate treated as that of the settlor — **12.3** £

- Trust management expenses applicable to the income in box 12.3 — **12.4** £

- Amount of income chargeable at the lower rate applicable to beneficiaries whose entitlement is not subject to the trustees' (or any other person's) discretion — **12.5** £

- Trust management expenses applicable to the income in box 12.5 — **12.6** £

- Amount of income chargeable at the basic rate applicable to beneficiaries whose entitlement is not subject to the trustees' (or any other person's) discretion — **12.7** £

- Trust management expenses applicable to the income in box 12.7 — **12.8** £

- Amount of income chargeable at the lower rate allocated to specific purposes — **12.9** £

- Trust management expenses applicable to the income in box 12.9 — **12.10** £

- Amount of income chargeable at the basic rate allocated to specific purposes — **12.11** £

- Trust management expenses applicable to the income in box 12.11 — **12.12** £

- Total amount of deductible trust management expenses (see notes on page 18 of the Trust and Estate Tax Return Guide) — **12.13** £

- Expenses set against income not liable at the rate applicable to trusts — **12.14** £ boxes 12.2 + 12.4 + 12.6 + 12.8 + 12.10 + 12.12

- Total income not liable to UK Income Tax and not included elsewhere on this Trust and Estate Tax Return (non-resident trusts only) — **12.15** £

- Exceptional deductions — **12.16** £

Q13 Have discretionary payments of income been made to beneficiaries? (See notes on page 19 of the Trust and Estate Tax Return Guide before filling in these boxes) NO ☐ YES ☐ If yes, fill in boxes 13.1 to 13.15 as appropriate. If no, fill in box 13.15 only.

Name of beneficiary	Amount of payment	Tick the box if the beneficiary was a minor and unmarried child of the settlor and the settlor was alive when payment was made.
13.1	**13.2** £	☐
13.3	**13.4** £	☐
13.5	**13.6** £	☐
13.7	**13.8** £	☐
13.9	**13.10** £	☐
13.11	**13.12** £	☐
13.13	**13.14** £	☐

- Amount, if any, of unused tax pool brought forward from last year (enter '0' if appropriate) — **13.15** £

Appendix 60

OTHER INFORMATION for the year ended 5 April 1999

Q14 Have the trustees made any capital payments to, or for the benefit of, minor, unmarried children of the settlor during the settlor's lifetime?   NO ☐   YES ☐   If yes, fill in box 14.1.

If there were capital transactions between the trustees and settlors, fill in boxes 14.2 to 14.13 as appropriate

● Total capital payments   Amount paid
                                            14.1 £

■ *Capital transactions between the trustees and settlors* (Read page 19 of the Trust and Estate Tax Return Guide)

Date	Amount	Name of company (if appropriate)
14.2 / /	**14.3** £	**14.4**

Registered office
14.5

Postcode

Date	Amount	Name of company (if appropriate)
14.6 / /	**14.7** £	**14.8**

Registered office
14.9

Postcode

Date	Amount	Name of company (if appropriate)
14.10 / /	**14.11** £	**14.12**

Registered office
14.13

Postcode

Q15 Has the trust at any time been non-resident or received any capital from another trust which is or at any time has been non-resident?   NO ☐   YES ☐

If YES, have the trustees made any capital payments to or provided any benefits for beneficiaries?   NO ☐   YES ☐   If yes, read pages 19 and 20 of the Trust and Estate Tax Return Guide and if appropriate fill in box 15.1.

● Total capital payments or value of benefits provided   **15.1** £

Please give details of the payments in box 15.1 in the boxes below. If there are insufficient boxes please provide the additional details on a separate sheet.

Name of beneficiary	Name of beneficiary
15.2	**15.3**

Address of beneficiary	Address of beneficiary
15.4	**15.5**
Postcode	Postcode

Amount/value of payment/benefit	Amount/value of payment/benefit
15.6 £	**15.7** £

BMSD 12/98   ■ TRUST AND ESTATE TAX RETURN: PAGE 7   *Please turn over* ➡

645

Appendix 60

Name of beneficiary
15.8

Name of beneficiary
15.9

Address of beneficiary
15.10

Postcode

Address of beneficiary
15.11

Postcode

Amount/value of payment/benefit
15.12 £

Amount/value of payment/benefit
15.13 £

Name of beneficiary
15.14

Name of beneficiary
15.15

Address of beneficiary
15.16

Postcode

Address of beneficiary
15.17

Postcode

Amount/value of payment/benefit
15.18 £

Amount/value of payment/benefit
15.19 £

Name of beneficiary
15.20

Name of beneficiary
15.21

Address of beneficiary
15.22

Postcode

Address of beneficiary
15.23

Postcode

Amount/value of payment/benefit
15.24 £

Amount/value of payment/benefit
15.25 £

If you have received capital from any other trust which is or at any time has been non-resident please provide the following details:

Name of trust
15.26

Date of trust
15.27 / /

Address of trustee
15.28

Postcode

Amount of value received
15.29 £

646

OTHER INFORMATION *for the year ended 5 April 1999*

Q16 Do you want to calculate the tax? NO ☐ YES ☐

If yes, do it now and then fill in boxes 16.1 to 16.7 below. The Trust and Estate Tax Calculation Guide will help you.

- Total tax due for 1998-99 (put the amount in brackets if an overpayment)   **16.1** £ ☐

- Tax due for earlier years   **16.2** £ ☐

- Tick box 16.3 if you have calculated tax overpaid for earlier years (and enter the amount in the 'Additional information' box on pages 11 and 12)   **16.3** ☐

- Your first payment on account for 1999-2000 (include the pence)   **16.4** £ ☐

- Tick box 16.5 if you are making a claim to reduce your payments on account and say why in the 'Additional information' box   **16.5** ☐   Tick box 16.6 if you do not need to make payments on account   **16.6** ☐

- 1999-2000 tax you are reclaiming now   **16.7** £ ☐

Q17 Do you want to claim a repayment if the trust or estate has paid too much tax? NO ☐ YES ☐   *If yes, fill in boxes 17.1 to 17.12 as appropriate.*

(If you tick 'No', or the tax overpaid is below £10 I will use the amount you are owed to reduce the next tax bill.)

Should the repayment (or payment) be sent
- to you? *(tick box and go to Question 18)*   **17.1** ☐

or
- a bank or building society account or other nominee? *(tick box 17.2)*   **17.2** ☐

If your nominee is your agent, tick box 17.8   **17.8** ☐

If you ticked either box 17.2 or 17.8, fill in boxes 17.3 to 17.7, 17.9 to 17.12 as appropriate

Agent's ref. for you   **17.9** ☐

Please give details of the bank or building society account for repayment

I authorise   **17.10** ☐   Name

Name of your (or your nominee's) bank or building society   **17.3** ☐

Nominee's address   **17.11** ☐

Branch sort code   **17.4** ☐ – ☐ – ☐

Postcode

Account number   **17.5** ☐

to receive on my behalf the amount due

Name of account   **17.6** ☐

This authority must be signed by you. A photocopy of your signature will not do.   **17.12** ☐

Building society ref.   **17.7** ☐

Signature

Appendix 60

Q18 Trustee or personal representative details

- Please give a daytime telephone number if convenient. If we need to ask you about the Return it is often simpler to phone.

Your telephone number **18.1** [   ]   or, if you prefer, your agent's telephone number **18.2** [   ] (and give your agent's name and reference in the 'Additional information' box on page 11 or 12).

Q19 Have there been any changes to the names and addresses of the trustees or personal representatives? **NO** [ ] **YES** [ ] If yes, fill in boxes 19.1 to 19.12, as appropriate.

- Retiring trustees' or personal representatives' names and addresses

19.1 [ ]
Postcode

19.2 [ ]
Postcode

19.3 [ ]
Postcode

19.4 [ ]
Postcode

- New trustees' or personal representatives' names and addresses

19.5 [ ]
Postcode

19.6 [ ]
Postcode

19.7 [ ]
Postcode

19.8 [ ]
Postcode

- Existing trustees' or personal representatives' with new addresses

19.9 [ ]
Postcode

19.10 [ ]
Postcode

19.11 [ ]
Postcode

19.12 [ ]
Postcode

648

OTHER INFORMATION *for the year ended 5 April 1999*

Q20 **Other information**

- If the trust was terminated or the administration period ceased during the year, please enter the date of cessation.

Date 20.1 / /

- If this Trust and Estate Tax Return contains any figures which are provisional because you do not yet have final figures, please tick the box and enter details in the 'Additional information' box below. Page 20 of the Trust and Estate Tax Return Guide explains the circumstances in which Tax Returns containing provisional figures may be accepted.

20.2

- If any 1998-99 tax was refunded directly by the Tax Office, or (personal representatives only) by the DSS Benefits Agency, please enter the amount in the box.

Amount 20.3 £

Additional information

649

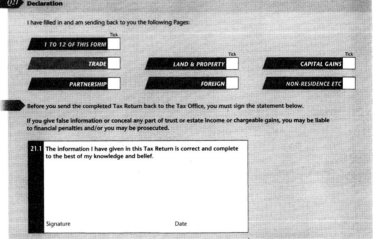

Appendix 61

Main Applicable Tax Rates for 2001/2002

Surplus AVCs

The repayment is net of basic rate tax (22%). The *section 599A* rate is 32%. A higher rate taxpayer (40%) will have to pay additional tax on the grossed up amount and return it on his or her return of income.

Personal Taxation

First £1,880 of taxable income (i.e. over £4,535 for a single person): 10%

£1,881–£29,400: 22%

Over £29,400: 40%. 20% below basic rate limit and 40% above that limit.

Capital Gains

Taxed at £7,500. (Taxed at 10% below the starting rate limit, 20% between the starting rate and basic rate, and 40% above the basic rate.)

Inheritance Tax

40% (tapers on gifts made within 7 years of death)

£242,000 exempt sum

(Domicile spouse's exemption)

VAT

17.5%

(registration level is £54,000)

Insurance Premium Tax

5% of gross premium

Full Corporation Tax Rate

30%

Appendix 61

Small companies' rate of Corporation Tax

20% (Profits up to £300,000, increase to 30% on a sliding scale up to profits of £1.5m. A small companies rate of 10% from April 2000 for profits up to £10,000 tapered to £50,000.)

Withdrawal of approval – small schemes/Controlling Director membership – Personal Pension Schemes from 1998

40% on the fund value

Serious ill-health/triviality commutation (Exempt Approved Schemes)

20% on the excess over the amount shown in *ICTA 1988, s 599.*

Ex-Gratia Payments

Taxed at Schedule E rates

(£30,000 exemption)

Earnings Cap

£95,400

Capital Gains rate applicable to trusts

34% (this also applied to 'interest in possession' trusts from 6 April 1998, previously taxed at 23 per cent)

Appendix 62

Permitted SIPP Investments

List agreed between IR SPSS and SPG, as at 10 March 1998

Note: Schemes must not enter into any investment transactions with a member or any person connected with a member, except in the circumstances described in item 7A. Connected persons are defined in *section 839 Income and Corporation Taxes Act 1998.*

1. Stocks and shares of companies (including investment trust companies and Open-Ended Investment Companies (OEICs)) listed on any stock exchange recognised by the Board of the Inland Revenue (including the Alternative Investment Market (AIM) but not OFEX):

    –   equities;

    –   fixed interest securities issued by Government or other bodies;

    –   debenture stock and other loan stock;

    –   warrants (equity);

    –   permanent interest-bearing shares;

    –   convertible securities.

2. Futures and options traded through a relevant exchange.

    –   currency, equity and bond futures – either long or short positions;

    –   currency, equity and bond options – either put or call options.

3. Unit Trusts:

    –   resident in the UK and authorised for that purpose under the *Financial Services Act*;

    –   resident outside the UK which are subject to regulation for that purpose under the *Financial Services Act*;

    –   'tax exempt' unauthorised unit trusts within the UK;

    –   U.S. Mutual Funds recognised by the Financial Services Authority in the UK under *sections 86, 87* or *88* of the *Financial Services Act.*

4. Stocks and shares in investment trusts purchased and held through investment trust savings schemes or investment plans operated by persons:

–   resident in the UK and authorised for that purpose under the *Financial Services Act*;

–   resident outside the UK but subject to regulation for that purpose in terms of the *Financial Services Act*.

5.   Insurance company managed funds and unit-linked funds:

–   investment policies or unit linked funds of a UK insurance company or an insurance company within the European Union authorised under *Article 6* of the *First Life Insurance Directive 79/267 EEC*.

–   traded endowment policies provided that such investments are transacted on a commercial basis through a recognised market maker.

6.   Deposit accounts with any authorised financial institution. However, speculation in foreign currency fluctuation is not permitted.

7.   Commercial property:

–   commercial property in or outside the UK (whether freehold or leasehold) purchased from an unconnected party;

–   land in or outside the UK including development land, farm land and forestry purchased from an unconnected party;

–   borrowing may be permitted provided it is authorised and monitored by the scheme administrators. No borrowing may be undertaken in respect of any scheme member's arrangements where pension date has been reached.

7A.   As an exception to the rule described in the Note above, it is permissible for a scheme to lease a commercial property to a business or partnership connected with the member including the member's own business. But the scheme should ensure that the lease, including the rent payable, is on commercial terms and is determined by a professional valuation.

7B.   Schemes must not hold directly as an investment residential property or land connected with such a property. It is permissible for commercial property to include a residential element but only to the extent that the element:

–   is occupied by an employee as a requirement of their job and that employee is not a connected person (e.g. a caretaker's house); or

–   is an integral part of business premises (e.g. a flat above a shop) and is occupied by an unconnected person.
It is important therefore that schemes should continually monitor the nature of commercial property to ensure that it does not become capable of residential use other than as permitted (e.g.

land for development as residential property would not be permitted).

7C. No commercial property may be purchased in respect of a scheme member asfter the late of age 65 or pension age.

Appendix 63

2000 No 2316

Personal Pension Schemes (Information Powers) Regulations 2000

Made: 29th August 2000
Laid before the House of Commons: 31st August 2000
Coming into force: 1st October 2000

The Commissioners of Inland Revenue, in exercise of the powers conferred on them by section 651A of the Income and Corporation Taxes Act 1988, hereby make the following Regulations:

PART I
INTRODUCTORY

1 Citation and commencement

These Regulations may be cited as the Personal Pension Schemes (Information Powers) Regulations 2000 and shall come into force on 1st October 2000.

2 Interpretation

(1) In these Regulations unless the context otherwise requires—

"approved", "member", "personal pension scheme" and "scheme administrator" have the meanings given by section 630(1);

"the Board" means the Commissioners of Inland Revenue;

"excluded person" means any person who, on ceasing to act in relation to the scheme or, as the case may be, provide administrative services to the scheme, transferred all documents in his possession or under his control relating to the scheme to another person who succeeded him in acting in relation to the scheme or in providing administrative services to the scheme;

"friendly society" has the meaning given by section 116 of the Friendly Societies Act 1992;

"insurance company" has the meaning given by section 659B;

"notice" means notice in writing;

"personal pension arrangements" has the meaning given by section 630(1); and references in these Regulations to "arrangements" in connection with personal pension schemes shall be construed accordingly;

"pooled fund" in relation to a personal pension scheme means a fund—

(a) which is open to the public and is described in the documents establishing the fund as being a standard fund open to all members,

(b) in relation to the management of which the scheme administrator is not required to consult with any member of the scheme except to the extent that an investment offers choices that are available to any person (whether or not a member of the scheme), and

(c) the value of which is applied to all members and not segregated among certain members or linked to certain members by reason of particular assets comprised in the fund;

"the relevant date" means the date which is 6 years from the end of the scheme year in which an event specified in regulation 9(4) occurs;

"scheme provider" in relation to a personal pension scheme for which there is for the time being no scheme administrator or for which the scheme administrator cannot be traced means—

(a)   the person who established the scheme, or

(b)   any person by whom that person has been directly or indirectly succeeded in relation to the provision of benefits under the scheme;

"scheme year" means—

(a)   a year specified for the purposes of a personal pension scheme in any document comprising the scheme or, if no year is specified, a period of 12 months commencing on 1st April or on such other date as the scheme administrator selects; or

(b)   such other period (if any) exceeding 6 months but not exceeding 18 months as is selected by the scheme administrator—
(i) respect of the scheme year in which the scheme commences or terminates, or
(ii) connection with a variation of the date on which the scheme year is to commence;

"self-invested personal pension scheme" has the meaning given by regulation 3;

"the Taxes Act" means the Income and Corporation Taxes Act 1988.

(2)   For the purposes of these Regulations and subject to paragraph (3), any question whether a person is connected with another person shall be determined in accordance with section 839.

(3)   A person shall not be regarded as connected with another person for the purposes of these Regulations where the connection arises as a result of a transaction entered into in the course of normal investment management by a scheme in relation to a fund that is a pooled fund.

(4)   In these Regulations references to a particular provision, without more, are references to that provision of the Taxes Act.

3   Definition of self-invested personal pension scheme

(1)   In these Regulations "self-invested personal pension scheme" means a personal pension scheme the arrangements made in accordance with which by a member—

(a)   are arrangements under which the member is able to direct the manner in which some or all of the contributions paid to the scheme are to be invested by or on behalf of the scheme administrator, and

(b)   are not arrangements falling within paragraph (2).

(2)   Arrangements fall within this paragraph if they are either—

(a)   arrangements under which—

   (i)   all the investments held for the purposes of the scheme comprise contracts of insurance or units in unit trust schemes, and

   (ii)   in managing those investments, the scheme administrator or the person acting on his behalf does not consult with any member of the scheme except to the extent necessary by virtue of the scheme offering choices that are available to any person (whether or not a member of the scheme); or

(b)   arrangements under which—

   (i)   all contributions paid are, after deduction of expenses, invested in deposits with deposit-takers, and

   (ii)   the payment of interest on those deposits comprises the only income of the scheme from its investments.

PART II
INFORMATION REQUIRED WITHOUT NOTICE

4 Investment and borrowing transactions of self-invested personal pension schemes

    (1)   The scheme administrator of an approved personal pension scheme that is a self-invested personal pension scheme is a person who is prescribed for the purposes of this regulation.

    (2)   The scheme administrator of an approved personal pension scheme that is a self-invested personal pension scheme shall furnish to the Board, at the time prescribed by paragraph (3), such information (including copies of any relevant books, documents or other records) as—

        (a)   is specified on the relevant form supplied by the Board, and

        (b)   relates to any transaction entered into by the scheme or under arrangements made in accordance with the scheme that—

            (i)   is of a kind specified in paragraph (4), and

            (ii)   is entered into by or on behalf of the scheme administrator on or after the date of coming into force of these Regulations.

    (3)   The time prescribed is any time not later than 90 days after the date of the transaction in question.

    (4)   The transactions specified in this paragraph are—

        (a)   the acquisition or disposal of land;

        (b)   the borrowing of money;

        (c)   the purchase, sale or lease of any asset other than land.

5 Reporting of chargeable event

    (1)   The scheme administrator of an approved personal pension scheme is a person who is prescribed for the purposes of this regulation.

    (2)   The scheme administrator of an approved personal pension scheme shall furnish to the Board, at the time prescribed by paragraph (3), such information (including copies of any relevant books, documents or other records) relating to the event specified in paragraph (4) as is specified on the relevant form supplied by the Board.

    (3)   The time prescribed is any time not later than 30 days after the end of the year of assessment in which the event occurs.

    (4)   The event specified is any payment under arrangements made in accordance with the scheme to which section 648B(1) applies (return of contributions after pension date).

PART III
NOTICES REQUIRING PARTICULARS AND DOCUMENTS

6 Approved personal pension schemes

    (1)   The Board may by notice require any of the persons prescribed by paragraph (2), within the time prescribed by paragraph (3), to furnish to the Board such particulars, and to produce to the Board such documents, as they may reasonably require relating to—

        (a)   any monies received or receivable by an approved personal pension scheme or under approved personal pension arrangements made in accordance with that scheme, or

        (b)   any investments or other assets held by that scheme or under those arrangements, or

        (c)   any monies paid or payable out of funds held under that scheme or those arrangements, including any monies paid by way of repayment of contributions to a member of that scheme or his employer.

    (2)   The persons prescribed are—

(a)   the person who is for the time being the scheme administrator in relation to the scheme concerned;

(b)   any person who was at any time prior to the relevant date the scheme administrator in relation to that scheme, other than an excluded person;

(c)   any person who is, or has been at any time prior to the relevant date, a scheme provider in relation to that scheme, other than an excluded person;

(d)   any person who provides, or has at any time prior to the relevant date provided, administrative services to that scheme, other than an excluded person.

(3)   The time prescribed is such time (not being less than 28 days) as is provided by the notice.

(4)   A notice under paragraph (1) may require particulars to be furnished, and documents to be produced, relating to more than one scheme.

7 Annuity contracts

(1)   The Board may by notice require any of the persons prescribed by paragraph (2), within the time prescribed by paragraph (3), to furnish to the Board such particulars, and to produce to the Board such documents, as they may reasonably require relating to any annuity contract issued by that person by means of which benefits provided under an approved personal pension scheme or under approved personal pension arrangements made in accordance with that scheme have been secured.

(2)   The persons prescribed are—

(a)   the insurance company which issued the annuity contract, where that company is a body corporate;

(b)   the chief executive and the manager, within the meaning of section 96D of the Insurance Companies Act 1982, of the insurance company which issued the annuity contract;

(c)   the person referred to in section 659B(6) or (8);

(d)   the friendly society which issued the annuity contract, where that friendly society is a society incorporated under the Friendly Societies Act 1992;

(e)   the chief executive and the secretary, any assistant chief executive and deputy chief executive, and any assistant secretary and deputy secretary, of the friendly society which issued the annuity contract.

(3)   The time prescribed is such time (not being less than 28 days) as is provided by the notice.

(4)   A notice under paragraph (1) may require particulars and documents relating to more than one annuity contract.

PART IV
INSPECTION AND RETENTION OF RECORDS

8 Inspection of records

(1)   The Board may by notice require any of the persons prescribed by paragraph (2) to make available for inspection by an officer of the Board authorised for that purpose, within the time prescribed by paragraph (3), all books, documents and other records in his possession or under his control relating to—

(a)   any monies received or receivable by an approved personal pension scheme,

(b)   any investments or other assets held by that scheme,

(c)   any monies paid or payable out of funds held under that scheme, or

(d)   any annuity contract by means of which benefits provided under that scheme have been secured.

(2)   The persons prescribed are—

    (a)   the person who is for the time being the scheme administrator in relation to the scheme concerned;

    (b)   any person who was at any time prior to the relevant date the scheme administrator in relation to that scheme, other than an excluded person;

    (c)   any person who is, or has been at any time prior to the relevant date, a scheme provider in relation to that scheme, other than an excluded person;

    (d)   any person who provides, or has at any time prior to the relevant date provided, administrative services to that scheme, other than an excluded person.

(3)   The time prescribed is such time (not being less than 28 days) as is provided by the notice.

(4)   A notice under paragraph (1) may require books, documents and other records relating to more than one scheme to be made available for inspection.

(5)   Where records are maintained by computer the person required to make them available for inspection shall provide the officer making the inspection with all the facilities necessary for obtaining information from them.

(6)   The authorised officer may take copies of, or make extracts from, any books, documents or other records made available for inspection in accordance with paragraph (1).

9   Retention of records

(1)   Each of the persons prescribed by paragraph (2) shall preserve, for the time prescribed by paragraph (3), all books, documents and other records in his possession or under his control relating to—

    (a)   any monies received or receivable by an approved personal pension scheme or under approved personal pension arrangements made in accordance with that scheme;

    (b)   any investments or other assets held by that scheme or under those arrangements;

    (c)   any monies paid or payable out of funds held under that scheme or those arrangements; or

    (d)   any annuity contract by means of which benefits provided under that scheme or those arrangements have been secured.

(2)   The persons prescribed are—

    (a)   the person who is for the time being the scheme administrator in relation to the scheme concerned;

    (b)   any person who was at any time prior to the relevant date the scheme administrator in relation to that scheme, other than an excluded person;

    (c)   any person who is, or has been at any time prior to the relevant date, a scheme provider in relation to that scheme, other than an excluded person;

    (d)   any person who provides, or has at any time prior to the relevant date provided, administrative services to that scheme, other than an excluded person.

(3)   The time prescribed—

    (a)   in the case of accounts relating to the scheme, including books, documents and other records on which such accounts are based, is 6 years from the end of the scheme year in which falls the date on which the accounts were signed;

    (b)   in the case of books, documents or other records containing information which is required to be furnished pursuant to regulation 4, is 6 years from the end of the scheme year in which the transaction in question occurred;

    (c)   in the case of books, documents or other records containing information which is required to be furnished pursuant to regulation 5, is 6 years from the end of the scheme year in which the event specified in paragraph (4) of that regulation occurred;

    (d)   in the case of books, documents or other records relating to an event specified in paragraph (4), is 6 years from the end of the scheme year in which the event occurred.

(4)   The events specified are—

(a)   the provision by the scheme or under the arrangements of any benefit to a member of the scheme or other person;

(b)   the payment of contributions to the scheme by a member or his employer;

(c)   the repayment to a member or his employer in accordance with section 638(3) of an excess amount of contributions paid to the scheme;

(d)   the payment of transfer values or the purchase of annuities under the scheme or the arrangements;

(e)   the acquisition or disposal of any asset by the scheme or under the arrangements;

(f)   the undertaking of any transaction for the purposes of the scheme or the arrangements;

(g)   the receipt by the scheme of any income resulting from—

(i)   the investment of assets held by the scheme or under the arrangements, or

(ii)   any trading activity carried on by the scheme or under the arrangements.

(5)   The duty under paragraph (1) to preserve books, documents and other records may be discharged by the preservation of information contained in them.

EXPLANATORY NOTE

(This note is not part of the Regulations)

These Regulations make provision for the furnishing of information and documents to the Board of Inland Revenue in connection with personal pension schemes approved by the Board, and for the inspection and retention of records relating to such schemes. The Regulations specify the information and documents to be furnished, the persons responsible for furnishing them, and the time within which they are to be furnished.

The Regulations are in a number of Parts of which Part I, comprising regulations 1 to 3, is introductory. Regulation 1 provides for citation and commencement, and regulation 2 for interpretation. Regulation 3 defines "self-invested personal pension scheme" for the purposes of the Regulations.

Part II, comprising regulations 4 and 5, deals with information which is to be furnished by approved personal pension schemes without the need for the Board to serve a notice requiring that information. Regulation 4 provides for the furnishing of information in relation to investment and borrowing transactions entered into by self-invested personal pension schemes or under arrangements made in accordance with such schemes. Regulation 5 provides for the furnishing of information in relation to the return of a member's contributions after the member's pension date.

Part III, comprising regulations 6 and 7, deals with particulars and documents relating to approved personal pension schemes, arrangements made under such schemes, and annuity contracts which the Board may by notice require any person prescribed by those regulations to furnish or produce within the time specified. Regulation 6 deals with approved personal pension schemes and arrangements, and regulation 7 with annuity contracts.

Part IV, comprising regulations 8 and 9, deals with inspection of records of approved personal pension schemes and annuity contracts by an officer of the Board (regulation 8), and the retention by prescribed persons of records relating to such schemes and contracts, and to arrangements made under such schemes (regulation 9).

Appendix 64

2000 No 2317

Personal Pension Schemes (Establishment of Schemes) Order 2000

Made: 31st August 2000
Laid before the House of Commons: 31st August 2000
Coming into force: 1st October 2000

The Treasury, in exercise of the powers conferred on them by section 632(4) of the Income and Corporation Taxes Act 1988, hereby make the following Order:

Citation and commencement

This Order may be cited as the Personal Pension Schemes (Establishment of Schemes) Order 2000 and shall come into force on 1st October 2000.

(1)   Section 632 of the Income and Corporation Taxes Act 1988 shall be amended as follows.

(2)   In subsection (1) for the word "The" there shall be substituted the words "Subject to subsection (1A), the".

(3)   After subsection (1) there shall be inserted the following subsection—

'(1A) The Board may approve a personal pension scheme established by any person other than a person mentioned in subsection (1)(a) to (e) if the scheme is established under a trust or trusts.'

EXPLANATORY NOTE

(This note is not part of the Order)

Section 632(1) of the Income and Corporation Taxes Act 1988 provides that the Commissioners of Inland Revenue shall not approve a personal pension scheme established by any person other than those mentioned in that sub-section. Section 632(4) provides that the Treasury may by Order amend that section.

This Order, which comes into force on 1st October 2000, provides that a personal pension scheme set up in the form of a trust may be established not only by the existing categories of persons in section 632(1), but also by any other person.

Appendix 65

2000 No 2692

Personal Pension Schemes (Payments by Employers) Regulations 2000

Made: 30th September 2000
Laid before Parliament: 6th October 2000
Coming into force: 6th April 2001

The Secretary of State for Social Security, in exercise of the powers conferred upon him by section 111A(4)(b), (5), (6), (7) and (15)(b), 181(1), 182(2) and (3) and 183(1) of the Pension Schemes Act 1993 and of all other powers enabling him in that behalf, after consulting such persons as he considered appropriate, hereby makes the following Regulations:

1 Citation, commencement and interpretation

(1)   These Regulations may be cited as the Personal Pension Schemes (Payments by Employers) Regulations 2000 and shall come into force on 6th April 2001.

(2)   In these Regulations—

"the 1993 Act" means the Pension Schemes Act 1993;

"scheme" means a personal pension scheme;

"stakeholder pension scheme" has the meaning given by section 1 of the Welfare Reform and Pensions Act 1999 (meaning of "stakeholder pension scheme");

"statement year" has the meaning given by regulation 18(3) of the Stakeholder Pension Schemes Regulations 2000 (disclosure of information to members);

"trustees or managers", in relation to a scheme, means—

(a)   in the case of a scheme established under a trust, the trustees of the scheme; and

(b)   in any other case, the managers of the scheme.

2 Record of direct payment arrangements

For the purposes of section 111A(4)(b) of the 1993 Act (record of direct payment arrangements must satisfy prescribed requirements) the prescribed requirements are that the record contains separate entries for the rates of contributions payable under the direct payment arrangements—

(a)   on the employer's own account in respect of the employee; and

(b)   on behalf of the employee out of deductions from the employee's earnings.

3   Prescribed time in which an employer is to make a record of direct payment arrangements available to trustees or managers

For the purposes of section 111A(5) of the 1993 Act (employer must within the prescribed period send a copy of the record to the trustees or managers) the prescribed period after the preparation or any revision of the record within which the employer must send a copy of the record or, as the case may be, of the revised record to the trustees or managers of the scheme is such period which is likely to result in the copy of that record being available to the trustees or managers of the scheme no later than the date upon which the first contribution payable by reference to that record falls due for payment.

4 Time limits for giving notice to the Regulatory Authority and to the employee that any contribution which is payable has not been paid and the circumstances in which such notice need not be given

(1)   Subject to paragraph (2), for the purposes of section 111A(6) of the 1993 Act (except in prescribed circumstances notice to be given by the trustees or managers to the Regulatory Authority and to the employee within a prescribed period that any contribution which is payable has not been paid on or before its due date) the prescribed period within which the trustees or managers of the scheme must, where any contribution shown by the record to be payable under the direct payment arrangements has not been paid on or before its due date, give notice of that fact—

(a)   to the Regulatory Authority, is the period of 30 days beginning with the day following that due date; and

(b)   to the employee, is the period of 90 days beginning with the day following that due date, unless payment has been made before the end of the period of 60 days beginning with the day following that due date.

(2)   The prescribed circumstances in which the trustees or managers of the scheme need not give notice to the Regulatory Authority or the employee or both the Regulatory Authority and the employee that any contribution referred to in paragraph (1) has not been paid on or before its due date are when the Regulatory Authority have informed the trustees or managers—

(a)   that it or the employee or both it and the employee need not be notified that any future contribution shown by the record to be payable under the direct payment arrangments has not been paid on or before its due date; and

(b)   when, if at all, they must resume giving notice in accordance with section 111A(6) of the 1993 Act to the Regulatory Authority or the employee or both the Regulatory Authority and the employee that any future contribution shown by the record to be payable under the direct payment arrangements has not been paid on or before its due date.

5 Prescribed period for the purpose of calculating the due date for the payment of any contribution on behalf of an employee

For the purposes of section 111A(15)(b) of the 1993 Act (meaning of "due date" where a contribution payable under the direct payment arrangements falls to be paid on behalf of the employee) the prescribed period is the period of 19 days commencing on the day following the last day of the month in which the deduction was made from the employee's earnings.

6 The issue of payment statements to an employee

(1)   For the purposes of section 111A(7) of the 1993 Act (trustees or managers to send the employee a statement of payments made during a prescribed period before the end of prescribed intervals) the prescribed period for which the statement must set out the amounts and dates of the payments made under the direct payment arrangements is the period specified in paragraph (2) or (3), as the case may be.

(2)   Where the scheme is not a stakeholder pension scheme the prescribed period is—

(a)   in the case of the first statement referred to in paragraph (1), the period beginning with—

(i)   6th April 2001, or the date the employee joins the scheme, whichever is the later, in the case of an employee who is or becomes a member of a scheme during the period from 6th April 2001 to 5th April 2002; or

(ii)   the date the employee joins the scheme, in the case of an employee who becomes a member of a scheme on or after 6th April 2002,

and ending with the date of the last payment which appears on that statement; and

(b)   in the case of the second or any subsequent statement (the relevant statement), a period of not more than 12 months beginning with the day following the date of the last payment which appeared on the statement immediately preceding the relevant statement.

(3)   Where the scheme is a stakeholder pension scheme the prescribed period is the period which is, in accordance with regulation 18(3) of the Stakeholder Pension Schemes Regulations 2000, the statement year in relation to that scheme.

(4) For the purposes of paragraph (2)(a) the date of the last payment referred to in that paragraph must be no later than—

    (a) 5th April 2003, where paragraph (2)(a)(i) applies; or

    (b) 12 months after the date the employee joined the scheme, where paragraph (2)(a)(ii) applies.

(5) The prescribed intervals before the end of which the trustees or managers must send the employee the statement referred to in paragraph (1) are those specified in paragraph (6) or (7), as the case may be.

(6) Where the scheme is not a stakeholder pension scheme the prescribed intervals are—

    (a) in the case of the first statement referred to in paragraph (1)—

        (i) the period beginning with 6th April 2001 and ending with 5th April 2003, where paragraph (2)(a)(i) applies; or

        (ii) the period of 12 months beginning with the date the employee joined the scheme, where paragraph (2)(a)(ii) applies; and

    (b) in the case of—

        (i) the second statement, the period of 12 months beginning with the next anniversary of the date the employee joined the scheme following the date the trustees or managers sent the employee the first statement; and

        (ii) the third or any subsequent statement, the period of 12 months beginning with the anniversary of the date the employee joined the scheme.

(7) Where the scheme is a stakeholder pension scheme the prescribed interval is 3 months after the end of the statement year to which that statement relates.

7 Revocation

Regulation 5A of the Personal Pension Schemes (Disclosure of Information) Regulations 1987 (member to be informed when contributions not received) is revoked.

EXPLANATORY NOTE

(This note is not part of the Regulations)

These Regulations make provision concerning the monitoring of employers' payments to personal pension schemes under section 111A of the Pension Schemes Act 1993 (c 48).

Regulation 1 provides for citation, commencement and interpretation.

Regulation 2 sets out the prescribed requirements for the contents of the record of direct payment arrangements.

Regulation 3 specifies the period within which the employer must send a copy of the record of direct payment arrangements to the trustees or managers of the personal pension scheme.

Regulation 4 specifies the time limits within which the trustees or managers of the personal pension scheme must give notice to the Occupational Pensions Regulatory Authority and to the employee that any contribution which is payable by the employer under the direct payment arrangements has not been paid and the circumstances in which such notice need not be given.

Regulation 5 specifies the period to be used for the purpose of calculating the due date for the payment by the employer of any contribution paid on behalf of an employee.

Regulation 6 provides for the period which a payment statement sent to an employee by the trustees or managers of a personal pension scheme or a stakeholder pension scheme must cover, and the frequency with which such statements must be sent to the employee.

Appendix 65

Regulation 7 revokes regulation 5A of the Personal Pension Schemes (Disclosure of Information) Regulations 1987.

The impact on business of these Regulations was included in the Regulatory Impact Assessment for the Welfare Reform and Pensions Act 1999 (c 30), by virtue of which, these Regulations are made. A copy of that Assessment has been placed in the libraries of both Houses of Parliament and can be obtained from the Department of Social Security, Regulatory Impact Unit, 3rd Floor, The Adelphi, 1–11 John Adam Street, London WC2N 6HT.

Appendix 66

2001 No 117

Personal Pension Schemes (Restriction on Discretion to Approve) (Permitted Investments) Regulations 2001

Made: 23rd January 2001
Laid before the House of Commons: 24th January 2001
Coming into force: 6th April 2001

The Commissioners of Inland Revenue, in exercise of the powers conferred on them by section 638A of the Income and Corporation Taxes Act 1988, hereby make the following Regulations:

1 Citation and commencement

These Regulations may be cited as the Personal Pension Schemes (Restriction on Discretion to Approve) (Permitted Investments) Regulations 2001 and shall come into force on 6th April 2001.

2 Interpretation

(1) In these Regulations unless the context otherwise requires—

"approved pension arrangement" means a pension scheme—

   (a) which is an "approved pension arrangement" as defined in section 660A(11), and

   (b) under which all the benefits that may be provided are money purchase benefits;

"authorised unit trust scheme" means a unit trust scheme in the case of which an order under section 78 of the Financial Services Act 1986 is in force;

"the Board" means the Commissioners of Inland Revenue;

"commercial property" includes land;

"company" means any body corporate or unincorporated association, but does not include a partnership;

"depositary interest" means the rights of the person mentioned in paragraph (b) of this definition under a certificate or other record (whether or not in the form of a document) which acknowledges—

   (a) that a person holds relevant investments or evidence of the right to them, and

   (b) that another person is entitled to rights in or in relation to those or identical relevant investments, including the right to receive such investments, or evidence of the right to them or the proceeds from such investments, from the person mentioned in paragraph (a);

667

"deposit-taker" has the meaning given by section 481(2);

"EEA Agreement" means the Agreement on the European Economic Area signed at Oporto on 2nd May 1992, as adjusted by the Protocol signed at Brussels on 17th March 1993;

"EEA State" means a State, other than the United Kingdom, which is a Contracting Party to the EEA Agreement;

"employee" includes the holder of an office;

"employer" in relation to a scheme—

(a) means an employer who, by virtue of the governing instrument, is entitled to pay contributions to the scheme, and

(b) includes a person under whom an office is held;

"feeder fund" means a feeder fund within the meaning (and complying with the requirements) of paragraph 2 of Part I of Schedule 1 to the Personal Pension Schemes (Appropriate Schemes) Regulations 1997 (including a constituent part of an umbrella personal pension unit trust which is regarded as a feeder fund for the purposes of those Regulations);

"governing instrument" in relation to a scheme means a trust deed, or other document by which the scheme is established, and any other document which contains provisions by which the administration of the scheme is governed;

"insurance company" has the meaning given by section 431(2);

"investment company with variable capital" has the meaning given by regulation 3(2) of the Open-Ended Investment Companies (Investment Companies with Variable Capital) Regulations 1996;

"member" in relation to—

(a) a personal pension scheme has the meaning given by section 630(1),

(b) an approved pension arrangement falling within Chapter I of Part XIV of the Taxes Act, has the same meaning as "scheme member" in section 611(6)(a) and (b), and

(c) an approved pension arrangement approved under Chapter III of Part XIV of the Taxes Act, means an individual referred to in section 618(2);

"open-ended investment company" except in relation to the phrase "qualifying EEA open-ended investment company"—

(a) has the meaning given by section 468(10), and

(b) also includes a UCITS situated in a member state other than the United Kingdom which has been authorised by the competent authorities of that member state and is a recognised scheme;

"personal pension scheme" has the meaning given by section 630(1), and "scheme" shall be construed accordingly;

"personal pension unit trust" means a personal pension scheme which is an authorised unit trust scheme of a kind mentioned in Part I of Schedule 1 to the Personal Pension Schemes (Appropriate Schemes) Regulations 1997;

"pooled fund" in relation to a personal pension scheme means a fund—

(a) which is open to the public and is described in the documents relating to the scheme as being a fund open to all members,

(b) in relation to the management of which the scheme administrator is not required to consult with any member of the scheme except to the extent that an investment offers choices that are available to any person (whether or not a member of the scheme), and

(c) the value of which is applied to all members and not segregated among certain members or linked to certain members by reason of particular assets comprised in the fund;

"qualifying EEA investment company" means a company—

    (a)   which is formed under the law of an EEA State and complies with the requirements specified in section 266(2) of the Companies Act 1985,

    (b)   which may lawfully offer its shares to the public in an EEA State, and

    (c)   in relation to which, on the basis of its last published annual accounts, the ratio between the company's loan capital and the value of its ordinary shares is 50 per cent or less;

"qualifying EEA open-ended investment company" means an open-ended investment company within the meaning given by section 75(8) of the Financial Services Act 1986 which—

    (a)   is formed under the law of an EEA State,

    (b)   is not a UCITS, and

    (c)   may lawfully offer its shares to the public in an EEA State;

"qualifying UK investment company" means an investment company within the meaning of section 266 of the Companies Act 1985—

    (a)   which is incorporated in the United Kingdom, and

    (b)   in relation to which, on the basis of its last published accounts, the ratio between the company's loan capital and the value of its ordinary shares is 50 per cent or less;

"recognised futures exchange" has the meaning given by section 288(6) of the Taxation of Chargeable Gains Act 1992;

"recognised scheme" has the meaning given by section 86 of the Financial Services Act 1986;

"recognised stock exchange" has the meaning given by section 841;

"relevant investments" in relation to the definition of "depositary interest" means investments listed in the Schedule to these Regulations as investments which are permitted to be held by a self-invested personal pension scheme;

"residential property" means property normally used, or adapted for use, as one or more dwellings;

"scheme administrator" means the person referred to in section 638(1);

"self-invested personal pension scheme" has the meaning given by regulation 3;

"the Taxes Act" means the Income and Corporation Taxes Act 1988;

"UCITS" means an undertaking for collective investment in transferable securities within the meaning of Article 1 of Council Directive 85/611;

"umbrella personal pension unit trust" means a personal pension unit trust which is constituted as an umbrella fund within the meaning of the Financial Services (Regulated Scheme) Regulations 1991;

"unauthorised unit trust" has the meaning given by paragraph 2(4) of Schedule 10 to the Finance Act 1996;

"unit trust scheme" has the meaning given by section 75(8) of the Financial Services Act 1986;

"51 per cent subsidiary" has the meaning given by section 838.

(2)   For the purposes of these Regulations and subject to paragraph (3), any question whether a person is connected with another person shall be determined in accordance with section 839.

(3)   A person shall not be regarded as connected with another person for the purposes of these Regulations where the connection arises as a result of a transaction entered into in the course of normal investment management by a scheme in relation to a fund that is a pooled fund.

(4)   References in these Regulations to a freehold or leasehold interest in commercial or residential property include, as respects Scotland, the estate or interest of the proprietor of the dominium utile or, in the case of property other than feudal property, of the owner of such property, and the interest of a tenant in such property subject to a lease.

Appendix 66

(5) In these Regulations references to a particular provision, without more, are references to that provision of the Taxes Act.

3 Definition of self-invested personal pension scheme

(1) In these Regulations "self-invested personal pension scheme" means a personal pension scheme the arrangement made in accordance with which by a member—

    (a) are arrangements under which the member is able to direct the manner in which some or all of the contributions paid to the scheme are to be invested by the scheme administrator, and

    (b) are not arrangements falling within paragraph (2).

(2) Arrangements fall within this paragraph if they are either—

    (a) arrangements under which—

        (i) all the investments held for the purposes of the scheme comprise contracts or policies of insurance, units in unit trust schemes or shares in open-ended investment companies, and

        (ii) in managing those investments, the scheme administrator does not consult with any member of the scheme except to the extent necessary by virtue of the investment offering choices that are available to any person (whether or not a member of the scheme); or

    (b) arrangements under which—

        (i) all contributions paid are, after deduction of expenses, invested in deposits with deposit-takers, and

        (ii) the payment of interest on those deposits comprises the only income of the scheme from its investments.

4 Definition of individual pension account

(1) For the purposes of regulations 6(2) and 7(4) "individual pension account" means an account within which investments may be held and which satisfies the following conditions.

(2) The first condition is that the funds of the account consist only of—

    (a) monies received from the trustees, managers or administrators of approved pension arrangements, or monies held for the purposes of approved pension arrangements that are designated to be held within the account, and

    (b) income and gains arising from those monies when held as funds of the account.

(3) The second condition is that any monies so received consist of one or more of the following—

    (a) contributions to an approved pension arrangement by a member, or the employer of a member, of that approved pension arrangement,

    (b) amounts transferred to an approved pension arrangement from another approved pension arrangement,

    (c) minimum contributions referred to in section 638(6)(c),

    (d) minimum payments within the meaning given by section 8(2) of the Pension Schemes Act 1993.

(4) The third condition is that the funds and other assets of the account—

    (a) are held—

        (i) by the trustees, managers or administrators of the approved pension arrangements whose members subscribe to the account as account holders, and

        (ii) on behalf of the individual account holders as beneficial owners subject to the account rules, or

    (b) in the case of assets consisting of units in a personal pension unit trust or, where the personal pension unit trust is an umbrella personal pension unit trust, in the respective parts of the umbrella personal pension unit trust—

670

(i)   are registered in the names of the individual account holders, and

(ii)   are issued subject to the terms of the trust deed and the rules constituting the personal pension unit trust.

(5)   The fourth condition is that the funds and other assets of the account are used only to provide benefits for individual account holders under approved pension arrangements and subject to the limits and rules of those approved pension arrangements.

(6)   The fifth condition is that the assets of the account, other than cash awaiting investment, consist of one or more of the following investments—

   (a)   units in an authorised unit trust scheme or in a unit trust scheme that is a recognised scheme,

   (b)   shares in a qualifying EEA open-ended investment company,

   (c)   units in a UCITS formed under the laws of a member state other than the United Kingdom which has been authorised by the competent authorities of that member state and is a recognised scheme,

   (d)   shares in a body corporate which is a qualifying UK investment company,

   (e)   shares in a body corporate which is a qualifying EEA investment company,

   (f)   shares in an investment company with variable capital, and

   (g)   investments falling within paragraph 3 of Part I of Schedule I to the Financial Services Act 1986 (Government and public securities).

(7)   The sixth condition is that, where monies are received by the account that comprise an individual's investment in more than one approved pension arrangement, the amount relating to each approved pension arrangement is separately identified by the administrator of the account.

(8)   The seventh condition is that, whenever required to do so by an officer of the Board, the administrator of the account has provided to that officer the following information—

   (a)   the names of individuals who are the account holders,

   (b)   details of the approved pension arrangements of which those individuals are members,

   (c)   the amount of the funds, and the description and value of the assets, held on behalf of each account holder,

   (d)   the amount of income and gains accruing to each account holder from funds and assets held on that individual's behalf,

   (e)   transfers of funds to another individual pension account on behalf of an account holder.

(9)   The eighth condition is that, whenever required to do so by an officer of the Board, the administrator of the account has enabled that officer to audit and inspect all aspects of the management and administration of the account, including records and systems relating to the management or administration of the account.

(10)   The reference in paragraph (6)(a) to units in an authorised unit trust scheme, where the authorised unit trust scheme is an umbrella personal pension unit trust that is constituted as a feeder fund or comprises feeder funds, comprises both the units in the feeder fund or feeder funds that are issued to the individual account holder and the underlying units held by the feeder fund or feeder funds.

5   Restrictions on discretion to approve—general

Regulations 6 to 10 impose, subject to regulation 11, restrictions on the Board's discretion to approve personal pension schemes under Chapter IV of Part XIV of the Taxes Act.

6   Restriction on investments—self-invested personal pension schemes

(1)   No investments may be held directly or indirectly for the purposes of a self-invested personal pension scheme other than the investments listed in the Schedule to these Regulations.

(2)   Investments listed in the Schedule that are also specified in regulation 4(6) may be held within an individual pension account.

671

(3) Subject to paragraphs (4) to (8), no amount may be borrowed by a self-invested personal pension scheme for any purpose.

(4) A self-invested personal pension scheme may borrow an amount towards the purchase of a freehold or leasehold interest in commercial property to be held directly or indirectly as an investment for the purposes of the scheme, or towards the development of commercial property held directly or indirectly as an investment for the purposes of the scheme, but the amount borrowed—

    (a) must not exceed 75 per cent of the purchase price of the property concerned, or 75 per cent of the costs of any development,

    (b) must be secured only on that property or on any other asset of the scheme, and

    (c) where the property is subsequently sold, must be repaid on completion of the sale of the property.

(5) A self-invested personal pension scheme may borrow an amount to defray any liability to VAT arising on the purchase or development of commercial property in accordance with paragraph (4), but the period over which the amount is borrowed must not exceed—

    (a) the period commencing on the date on which the purchase or development of the property is completed and ending on the day that is 12 weeks after that date, or

    (b) the period commencing on the date on which the purchase or development of the property is completed and ending on the day on which the amount of the liability to VAT is refunded to the purchaser,
    whichever is the shorter.

(6) A self-invested personal pension scheme may borrow an amount ("a replacement loan") to replace a loan falling within paragraph (4).

(7) The amount of a replacement loan must not exceed the amount outstanding, as at the date on which the replacement loan is made, of the loan that is replaced.

(8) In this regulation—

    (a) references to the purchase price of commercial property include references to legal and other costs incidental to the purchase of the property;

    (b) references to the development of commercial property include references to—

        (i) the erection of, or extensions to, buildings, or

        (ii) the refurbishment or renovation of, or any other improvements to, buildings.

7 Restriction on investments—personal pension schemes other than self-invested personal pension schemes

(1) This regulation applies to personal pension schemes other that self-invested personal pension schemes.

(2) None of the assets specified in paragraph (3) may be held directly or indirectly as an investment by a personal pension scheme.

(3) The assets specified in this paragraph are—

    (a) any personal chattels other than choses in action (or, in Scotland, any movable property other than incorporeal movable property);

    (b) any residential property other than that specified in paragraph (5).

(4) Assets which a personal pension scheme is not restricted under paragraph (2) or (3) from holding as an investment and which are also specified in regulation 4(6) may be held within an individual pension account.

(5) The residential property specified in this paragraph is—

    (a) property which is, or is to be, occupied by an employee, whether or not a member of the personal pension scheme or connected with a member of the scheme, who is not connected with his employer and is required as a condition of his employment to occupy the property, and

(b) property which is, or is to be, occupied by a person who is neither a member of the personal pension scheme nor connected with a member of the scheme in connection with the occupation by that person of business premises held as an investment by the scheme.

(6) For the purposes of paragraphs (2) and (3), a personal pension scheme shall not be regarded as indirectly holding as an investment residential property where the scheme holds as an investment units in a unit trust scheme that holds residential property and—

(a) is an authorised unit trust scheme or a recognised scheme, or

(b) is an unauthorised unit trust whose gains are not chargeable gains by virtue of section 100(2) of the Taxation of Chargeable Gains Act 1992.

(7) For the purposes of paragraphs (2) and (3), a personal pension scheme shall not be regarded as indirectly holding as an investment residential property where—

(a) the scheme holds as an investment a right which confers entitlement to receive payment of any ground rent, rentcharge, ground annual, feu duty or other annual payment reserved in respect of, or charged on or issuing out of, that property, and

(b) the property is not occupied by a member of the scheme or a person connected with him.

8 Restrictions on lending

(1) A self-invested personal pension scheme may not lend money to any person (whether or not that person is an individual who is a member of the scheme).

(2) A personal pension scheme that is not a self-invested personal pension scheme may not lend money to a member of the scheme or a person connected with him.

(3) A personal pension scheme shall be regarded, for the purposes of paragraphs (1) and (2), as lending money to a member of the scheme or a person connected with him in circumstances where—

(a) the scheme holds as an investment, whether directly or indirectly, assets of a person,

(b) that person lends money to the member concerned or a person connected with him, and

(c) the loan has the effect of limiting or reducing in any way the return on the investment.

9 Restrictions on transactions with scheme member and others

(1) Subject to paragraphs (2) and (3), no interest in an asset may be acquired by a personal pension scheme in circumstances where a member of that scheme, or a person connected with him, has an interest in that asset or, at any time in the period of three years prior to the date of the acquisition, had an interest in that asset.

(2) Paragraph (1) does not apply in relation to the transfer of eligible shares in a company in accordance with section 638(9) and (12).

(3) Paragraph (1) does not apply in relation to the acquisition at market value by a self-invested personal pension scheme ("scheme A") of an interest in commercial property in which another self-invested personal pension scheme ("scheme B") also has an interest in circumstances where—

(a) the commercial property is leased by scheme A to—

(i) the member of scheme A for the purposes of a trade or profession carried on by him, whether or not in partnership with another person or persons, or

(ii) a company which is connected with the member of scheme A, for the purposes of a business carried on by the company,

(b) the lease is granted on normal commercial terms,

(c) the amount of the rent payable under the lease accords with a commercial rate and is supported by an independent professional valuation, and

(d) either—

(i) the member of scheme A is, or becomes within a reasonable time after the acquisition by scheme A of the interest in the commercial property, a partner in a partnership carrying on the trade or profession in question, and the member of scheme B is also a partner in that partnership, or

    (ii)   the member of scheme A is, or becomes within a reasonable time after that acquisition, a director of the company to whom the commercial property is leased, and the member of scheme B is also a director of that company.

(4)   Except in the circumstances specified in paragraphs (3) and (5), no interest in an asset may directly or indirectly be sold or leased by a personal pension scheme to a member or a person connected with him.

(5)   Commercial property an interest in which is acquired at market value by a self-invested personal pension scheme otherwise than in a case to which paragraph (1) applies may, subject to the conditions specified in paragraph (6), be leased by the scheme to—

    (a)   the member for the purposes of a trade or profession carried on by him, whether or not in partnership with another person or persons, or

    (b)   a company which is connected with the member, for the purposes of a business carried on by the company.

(6)   The conditions specified in this paragraph are that—

    (a)   the lease is granted on normal commercial terms, and

    (b)   the amount of the rent payable under the lease accords with a commercial rate and is supported by an independent professional valuation.

(7)   For the purposes of paragraph (4) a sale by the scheme shall not be regarded as a sale indirectly to a member, or a person connected with him, if the purchase by the member or the person connected with him took place three years or more after the sale by the scheme.

(8)   In paragraphs (3) and (5) "business" means a trade, profession or any other activity carried on by the company except the activity of making or managing investments unless—

    (a)   those investments consist wholly of shares in 51 per cent subsidiaries of the company, and

    (b)   those subsidiaries do not themselves carry on the activity of making or managing investments.

(9)   In this regulation "market value" means the price which the interest in the commercial property might reasonably be expected to fetch on a sale in the open market.

10   Restrictions on investments relating to members of self-invested personal pension schemes

(1)   A self-invested personal pension scheme may not set up after the pension date of a member of the scheme either—

    (a)   a borrowing arrangement for that member, or

    (b)   in the case of a serialised borrowing arrangement in existence at the time of the pension date, a further instalment of the loan for that member.

(2)   Paragraph (1) applies notwithstanding that the purpose of the borrowing arrangement or, as the case may be, the further instalment of the loan would be to acquire particular investments in accordance with the member's direction.

(3)   No commercial property may be acquired by a self-invested personal pension scheme in respect of a member of the scheme after the member's pension date or his attaining the age of 65, whichever is the later.

(4)   In paragraphs (1) and (3) "pension date" has the meaning given by section 630(1).

11   Schemes awaiting approval

(1)   Where at the date of coming into force of these Regulations a personal pension scheme is in existence and either—

    (a)   has not yet been submitted to the Board for approval, or

    (b)   is before the Board for approval,
        the Board shall not be prevented from approving it under Chapter IV of Part XIV of the

Taxes Act by reason only that it contains a provision or provisions of a description specified in any of sub-paragraphs (a) to (c) of paragraph (2).

(2)   The description of provisions specified in this paragraph is—

(a)   a provision which authorises the scheme to retain as an investment an asset—

(i)   which is held by the scheme immediately before the date on which these Regulations were made, and

(ii)   the holding of which directly or indirectly as an investment would, by virtue of regulation 6 or 7, prevent the Board from approving the scheme;

(b)   a provision which authorises the scheme to continue to lend money to a person in circumstances which, by virtue of regulation 8, would prevent the Board from approving the scheme;

(c)   a provision which authorises the scheme to acquire, sell or lease any interest in an asset in circumstances which, by virtue of regulation 9, would prevent the Board from approving the scheme.

SCHEDULE
List of Investments that may be Held Directly or Indirectly for the Purposes of a Self-Invested Personal Pension Scheme

Regulation 6

1   Stocks and shares listed or dealt in on a recognised stock exchange.

2   Futures and options, relating to stocks and shares, traded on a recognised futures exchange.

3   Depositary interests.

4   Units in an authorised unit trust scheme.

5   Units in a unit trust scheme which—

(a)   is an unauthorised unit trust whose gains are not chargeable gains by virtue of section 100(2) of the Taxation of Chargeable Gains Act 1992, and

(b)   does not hold any freehold or leasehold interest in residential property other than that specified in paragraph 13 or 14 of this Schedule.

6   Eligible shares within the meaning of section 638(11) received by the self-invested personal pension scheme as contributions to the scheme.

7   Shares in an open-ended investment company.

8   Interests (however described) in a collective investment scheme that is either a recognised scheme or a designated scheme within the meaning of section 86 or 87 of the Financial Services Act 1986.

9   Contracts or policies of insurance linked to insurance company managed funds, unit-linked funds or investment funds of an insurance company resident in the United Kingdom or authorised in accordance with Article 6 of Council Directive 79/267 (First Council Directive on Direct Life Assurance).

10   Traded endowment policies transacted with a person regulated by the Financial Services Authority.

11   Deposits in any currency held in deposit accounts with any deposit-taker.

12   A freehold or leasehold interest in commercial property where the interest is acquired from any person other than a member of the scheme or a person connected with him, or the interest is acquired from a member of the scheme or a person connected with him in circumstances in which regulation 9(3) applies.

13   A freehold or leasehold interest in any residential property which is—

    (a)   property which is, or is to be, occupied by an employee, whether or not a member of the self-invested personal pension scheme or connected with a member of the scheme, who is not connected with his employer and is required as a condition of his employment to occupy the property, and

    (b)   property which is, or is to be, occupied by a person who is neither a member of the self-invested personal pension scheme nor connected with a member of the scheme in connection with the occupation by that person of business premises held as an investment by the scheme.

14   Ground rents, rent charges, ground annuals, feu duties or other annual payments reserved in respect of, or charged on or issuing out of, property, except where the property concerned is occupied by a member of the scheme or a person connected with him.

EXPLANATORY NOTE

(This note is not part of the Regulations)

These Regulations impose restrictions on the Board of Inland Revenue's discretion to approve a personal pension scheme by restricting the investments in which the scheme may invest.

Regulation 1 provides for citation and commencement, and regulation 2 for interpretation.

Regulation 3 defines a "self-invested personal pension scheme" for the purposes of these Regulations.

Regulation 4 defines "individual pension account" for the purposes of regulations 6 and 7 of these Regulations.

Regulation 5 introduces regulations 6 to 10 which impose restrictions on the investments in which a personal pension scheme may invest.

Regulation 6 provides that a self-invested personal pension scheme may only invest in those investments listed in the Schedule to these Regulations, and stipulates restrictions on a self-invested personal pension scheme's borrowing powers.

Regulation 7 prohibits personal pension schemes other than self-invested personal pension schemes from investing in personal chattels or, subject to specified exceptions, residential property.

Regulation 8 prohibits self-invested personal pension schemes from lending to any person, and personal pension schemes that are not self-invested personal pension schemes from lending to members of the scheme or persons connected with members.

Regulation 9 prohibits personal pension schemes from purchasing, selling or leasing assets from or to members of the scheme or persons connected with members (subject to exceptions relating to commercial property).

Regulation 10 prohibits self-invested personal pension schemes from setting up borrowing arrangements for a member, or issuing further instalments of an existing serialised loan, after an annuity first becomes payable to the member under the scheme or the member elects to defer the purchase of an annuity ("the member's pension date"). The regulation also prohibits such schemes from acquiring commercial property for a member after the member's pension date or he attains 65, whichever is the later.

Regulation 11 contains transitional provisions with regard to personal pension schemes which had not yet been submitted for approval, or were awaiting the Board's approval, when these Regulations came into force.

Appendix 67

2001 No 118

Personal Pension Schemes (Conversion of Retirement Benefits Schemes) Regulations 2001

Made: 23rd January 2001
Laid before the House of Commons: 24th January 2001
Coming into force: 6th April 2001

The Commissioners of Inland Revenue, in exercise of the powers conferred upon them by paragraphs 2 and 4 of Schedule 23ZA to the Income and Corporation Taxes Act 1988, hereby make the following Regulations:

1 Citation and commencement

These Regulations may be cited as the Personal Pension Schemes (Conversion of Retirement Benefits Schemes) Regulations 2001 and shall come into force on 6th April 2001.

2 Interpretation

(1) In these Regulations—

"administrator"—

    (a) in relation to a retirement benefits scheme, has the meaning given by section 611AA and, in relation to a scheme which secures relevant benefits falling within section 591(2A) by means of an annuity contract, includes the insurance company with which the contract is made; and

    (b) in relation to a personal pension scheme, means the person referred to in section 638(1);

"the Board" means the Commissioners of Inland Revenue;

"continuing member" means a person who—

    (a) is a member of the eligible scheme which is the subject of the application under paragraph 3 of Schedule 23ZA; and

    (b) is to remain a member of the scheme if it becomes a personal pension scheme;

"controlling director" means a person who is, or was within the 10 years immediately preceding the date of the application under paragraph 3 of Schedule 23ZA, in relation to a relevant employer—

    (a) a director (as defined in section 612(1)); and

    (b) within paragraph (b) of section 417(5);

"conversion assets value" means the sum which has been calculated, within the period of three months ending with the date of the application under paragraph 3 of Schedule 23ZA, as representing a member's benefits under the retirement benefits scheme which is the subject of that application;

"conversion payment" means the amount to be held subject to a personal pension scheme representing an individual member's benefits at the date of change;

677

Appendix 67

"date of change" has the meaning given in paragraph 3(2) of Schedule 23ZA;

"eligible scheme" means a retirement benefits scheme to which Schedule 23ZA applies;

"Part XIV" means Part XIV of the Taxes Act (pension schemes etc);

"permitted amount" has the meaning given by regulation 7(4);

"personal pension scheme" has the meaning given in section 630;

"prescribed member" means a person who falls within one or more of the classes prescribed by regulation 6;

"qualifying scheme" means a retirement benefits scheme which, if the conditions prescribed under paragraph 2(3)(d) of Schedule 23ZA were met, would be an eligible scheme;

"relevant employer" means an employer by reference to employment with whom a continuing member is entitled to benefits under the eligible scheme;

"relevant year" means the year of assessment in which the application for approval as a personal pension scheme is made;

"retirement benefits scheme" has the meaning given in section 611; and

"the Taxes Act" means the Income and Corporation Taxes Act 1988.

(2) In these Regulations, except where the context otherwise requires—

    (a) a reference to a numbered regulation is a reference to the regulation bearing that number in these Regulations;

    (b) a reference in a regulation to a numbered paragraph is a reference to the paragraph bearing that number in that regulation;

    (c) a reference in a paragraph to a lettered sub-paragraph is a reference to the sub-paragraph bearing that letter in that paragraph; and

    (d) a reference to a numbered section or Schedule is a reference to the section of, or Schedule to, the Taxes Act bearing that number.

3 Application to convert eligible scheme to personal pension scheme

(1) The trustees of a qualifying scheme may apply to the Board for approval of the scheme as a personal pension scheme if the conditions prescribed in paragraphs (2) and (3) are satisfied.

(2) The first condition is that regulation 7 (valuation of prescribed member's benefits) has been complied with in respect of each prescribed member of the scheme.

(3) The second condition is that the value of the fund of a prescribed member, who is to be a continuing member of the scheme, does not exceed the permitted amount.

4 Documents to accompany application

(1) An application for approval under paragraph 3 of Schedule 23ZA must—

    (a) state the date from which the trustees propose the approval should have effect; and

    (b) be accompanied by the statements specified in paragraph (2) and the documents specified in paragraph (3).

(2) The statements, which must be signed by or on behalf of the trustees, are—

    (a) a statement that assets have been identified in respect of each continuing member's entitlement under the proposed personal pension scheme;

    (b) a statement showing how the assets referred to in sub-paragraph (a) were identified; and

    (c) a statement showing for each individual whom the trustees propose should be a continuing member, if approval is given, whether the whole of each asset so identified has been appropriated to that individual's personal pension fund and, if not, what part of the asset has been so appropriated.

(3)   The documents are—

(a)   a copy of the rules and other scheme instruments which the trustees propose should apply to the personal pension scheme if approval is given;

(b)   the written consent, to the making of the application, of each relevant employer; and

(c)   documents showing how the requirements of regulations 7 and 8 were satisfied.

5   Board's discretion to refuse approval: prescribed descriptions of retirement benefits scheme

(1)   The descriptions of eligible scheme which are prescribed in respect of the Board's discretion to refuse approval under Schedule 23ZA are all descriptions of eligible scheme other than a simplified defined contribution scheme.

(2)   In this regulation "simplified defined contribution scheme" has the meaning given by regulation 2 of the Retirement Benefits Schemes (Restriction on Discretion to Approve) (Additional Voluntary Contributions) Regulations 1993.

6   Board's discretion to refuse approval: prescribed classes of individual member

(1)   The classes of individual member of an eligible scheme which are prescribed for the purposes of paragraph 4(1) of Schedule 23ZA are—

(a)   in the case of a scheme of which a controlling director is to be a continuing member, the classes mentioned in paragraph (2); and

(b)   in any other case, the class mentioned in paragraph (3).

(2)   The classes referred to in paragraph (1)(a) are those comprising—

(a)   controlling directors;

(b)   persons who are connected with a person falling within sub-paragraph (a); and

(c)   members of the scheme—

(i)   whose age at the proposed date of change will be not less than 45 years; and

(ii)   whose remuneration derived from their employment with the relevant employer is, or was, for any year of assessment falling (wholly or partly) during the period of six years prior to the date on which the application is made, more than the permitted maximum for the year of assessment in which the application is made.

(3)   The class referred to in paragraph (1)(b) is that comprising members of the scheme—

(a)   whose age at the proposed date of change will be not less than 45 years; and

(b)   whose remuneration derived from employment with the relevant employer is, or was, for any year of assessment falling (wholly or partly) during the period of six years prior to the date on which the application is made, more than the permitted maximum for the year of assessment in which the application is made.

(4)   For the purposes of paragraph (2) a person is connected with another if he is—

(a)   that person's husband or wife;

(b)   that person's brother, sister, parent or remoter forebear, child or remoter lineal descendant;

(c)   the husband or wife of a brother, sister, parent or remoter forebear, child or remoter lineal descendant of that person; or

(d)   a brother, sister, parent or remoter forebear, child or remoter lineal descendant of that person's husband or wife.

(5)   In this regulation—

"permitted maximum" has the meaning given in section 590C(2); and

"remuneration" has the meaning given in section 612(1).

7   Valuation of prescribed member's benefits

(1)   Before making an application for approval as a personal pension scheme, the trustees of a qualifying scheme shall ascertain whether the conversion assets value, in respect of any prescribed member to whom they intend the proposed personal pension scheme to apply, exceeds the permitted amount.

(2)   The conversion assets value must be calculated in accordance with normal actuarial practice.

(3)   If the conversion assets value in respect of a prescribed member exceeds the permitted amount, regulation 8 applies to that member.

(4)   In these Regulations "the permitted amount" means the maximum amount as described in regulation 8(3) of the Personal Pension Schemes (Transfer Payments) Regulations 2001.

8   Prescribed members whose conversion assets value exceeds permitted amount

(1)   If—

(a)   this regulation applies to a prescribed member; and

(b)   the Board have exercised their discretion under section 611(3) to treat the eligible scheme as two (or more) separate schemes;
      the restriction in paragraph (2) applies to the prescribed member.

(2)   The restriction is that the prescribed member may not become a member of the resultant personal pension scheme at the date of change, unless, before that date, the value of the prescribed member's fund, calculated in accordance with normal actuarial practice, is shown to be less than or equal to the permitted amount.

9   Restriction on discretion to approve: conversion of qualifying scheme

(1)   The Board shall not approve a qualifying scheme as a personal pension scheme unless the proposed personal pension scheme complies with the restrictions imposed by regulations 10 and 11 in the case of an individual to whom paragraph (2) applies.

(2)   This paragraph applies to an individual who is a controlling director and whom the trustees of the scheme which is the subject of the application under Schedule 23ZA intend should be a continuing member.

10   Restriction on discretion to approve: controlling directors' death benefits

(1)   The restriction imposed by this regulation is that the accumulated value must be applied, after the death of a controlling director, in accordance with paragraph (3) or (4).

(2)   In this regulation "the accumulated value" means the total of—

(a)   the conversion payment; and

(b)   any sum attributable to growth through investment of the conversion payment.

(3)   If the controlling director has died before any benefits have been paid to him under the arrangements represented by the accumulated value, the accumulated value must be applied—

(a)   wholly to secure the payment of an annuity which satisfies the conditions in section 636 (annuity after death of member);

(b)   to secure the payment of income withdrawals with respect to which the conditions in section 636A (income withdrawals after death of member) are satisfied and, as to any amount not used for that purpose, to secure the payment of such an annuity as is referred to in sub-paragraph (a); or

(c)   as to not more than 25 per cent, to secure the payment of a lump sum and, as to the balance, to secure the payment of such an annuity as is referred to in sub-paragraph (a) or of such income withdrawals and annuity as are referred to in sub-paragraph (b).

This paragraph is subject to the qualification in paragraph (4).

(4) If the administrator of a personal pension scheme is satisfied, having taking all reasonable steps—

    (a) that there is no surviving spouse to whom an annuity referred to in paragraph (3)(a), or income withdrawals referred to in paragraph (3)(b), can be paid; and

    (b) if the arrangement so requires, that there is no dependant to whom such an annuity or income withdrawals can be paid;

    the whole of the accumulated value may be applied to secure the payment of a lump sum.

11 Restrictions on discretion to approve: lump sum benefits to controlling directors under proposed personal pension scheme

(1) The restrictions imposed by this regulation are those specified in paragraphs (2) and (3).

(2) The restriction specified in this paragraph is that no amount may be paid to a controlling director by way of a lump sum on his pension date (as defined in section 630(1)) out of the conversion payment unless, within six months beginning with the date of change, the administrator of the retirement benefits scheme which is the subject of the application under Schedule 23ZA has given such a lump sum certificate as would be required under the rules of the retirement benefits scheme if it were making a transfer payment to a personal pension scheme.

(3) The restriction specified in this paragraph is that the amount that may be paid by way of lump sum as mentioned in paragraph (2) shall not exceed the sum found by the formula in paragraph (4).

(4) The formula referred to in paragraph (3) is—

$B \times EF$

Here—

B is the amount shown in the certificate mentioned in paragraph (2); and

EF is the greater of 1 and the fraction in paragraph (5).

(5) The fraction referred to in paragraph (4) is—

$R1/R2$

Here—

R1 is the value of the retail prices index for the last month for which that index had been published at the date when the lump sum referred to in paragraph (2) was calculated; and

R2 is the value of that index for the last month for which that index had been published at the time of the approval by the Board of the application under Schedule 23ZA.

(6) The references in paragraph (5) to the retail prices index shall be construed in accordance with section 833(2) as if that paragraph were contained in the Income Tax Acts.

EXPLANATORY NOTE

(This note is not part of the Regulations)

These Regulations prescribe the way in which retirement benefits schemes which are money-purchase schemes ("occupational money purchase schemes") may apply to the Inland Revenue for approval as personal pension schemes. Schedule 23ZA to the Income and Corporation Taxes Act 1988 (c 1), inserted by paragraph 27 of Schedule 13 to the Finance Act 2000 (c 17), introduces the possibility of conversion of occupational money purchase schemes into personal pension schemes.

Regulation 1 provides for the citation and commencement of the Regulations and regulation 2 provides definitions for terms used in them.

Regulation 3 prescribes the conditions to be satisfied before an application can be made for conversion from an occupational pension scheme to a personal pension scheme, whilst regulation 4 prescribes the documents which are to accompany an application.

Appendix 67

Regulation 5 prescribes descriptions of scheme in respect of which the Board may refuse applications for conversion under Schedule 23ZA unless prescribed conditions are satisfied. These are all schemes other than simplified defined contribution schemes.

Regulation 6 prescribes classes of member of a scheme in respect of whom specific requirements are imposed ("prescribed members"). There are two classes of schemes for the purposes of this regulation. In the case of a scheme of which a controlling director is a member, the classes of prescribed members are controlling directors, those who are persons connected with them and those who are aged not less than 45 years at the proposed date of change and who have, or in the preceding six years have had, earnings exceeding the cap on earnings for the calculation of pension benefits prescribed by section 590C(2) of the Income and Corporation Taxes Act 1988 for the year in which the application under Schedule 23ZA is made. In the case of a scheme of which no controlling director is to be a continuing member, the prescribed members are those aged not less than 45 years at the date of change and who have, or in the preceding six years have had, earnings exceeding the cap.

Regulation 7 prescribes a requirement as to the valuation of the assets held to provide benefits in respect of a prescribed member.

Regulation 8 prescribes action to be taken before a prescribed member, in respect of whom the conversion assets value exceeds the permitted amount at the time of the valuation, may become a member of the resulting personal pension scheme.

Regulations 9, 10 and 11 impose restrictions on the Board's discretion to approve an application under regulation 3 in respect of the lump sum benefits payable to controlling directors and the death benefits payable to their dependants.

Appendix 68

2001 No 119

Personal Pension Schemes (Transfer Payments) Regulations 2001

Made: 23rd January 2001
Laid before the House of Commons: 24th January 2001
Coming into force: In accordance with regulation 1

The Commissioners of Inland Revenue, in exercise of the powers conferred on them by section 638(2) and (7A) of the Income and Corporation Taxes Act 1988, hereby make the following Regulations:

Part I
Introductory

1 Citation, commencement and effect

(1) These Regulations may be cited as the Personal Pension Schemes (Transfer Payments) Regulations 2001 and shall come into force for the purposes of—

(a) regulations 13 and 14, and

(b) regulation 3 so far as it relates to regulation 13,
on 14th February 2001, and for all other purposes on 6th April 2001.

(2) Regulation 10 shall have effect in accordance with regulation 15(1).

2 Interpretation

In these Regulations, unless the context otherwise requires—

"administrator"—

(a) in relation to a retirement benefits scheme has the meaning given by section 611AA of the Taxes Act and, in relation to a scheme which secures relevant benefits falling within section 591(2A) of the Taxes Act by means of an annuity contract, includes the insurance company with which the contract is made, and

(b) in relation to a personal pension scheme means the person referred to in section 638(1) of the Taxes Act;

"approved retirement benefits scheme" means a retirement benefits scheme approved by the Board for the purposes of Chapter I of Part XIV and includes an annuity contract which secures relevant benefits as mentioned in paragraph (a) of the definition of "administrator";

"the Board" means the Commissioners of Inland Revenue;

"the certifying requirements" means any requirement to give a lump sum certificate—

(a) under regulation 5, 6 or 13,

(b) under the Personal Pension Schemes (Transfer Payments) Regulations 1988, or

(c) under the rules of a scheme or fund making a transfer payment to a personal pension scheme;

"Chapter I" means Chapter I of Part XIV;

"controlling director" means a director within the meaning of section 612(1) of the Taxes Act who falls within the provisions of subsection (5)(b) of section 417 of that Act (read with subsections (3), (4) and (6) of that section);

"dependant" and "surviving spouse" have the respective meanings, and shall be determined at the time, given by section 636(2) of the Taxes Act;

"electronic signature" has the meaning given by section 7(2) of the Electronic Communications Act 2000;

"the 1999 Act" means the Welfare Reform and Pensions Act 1999;

"the 1999 Order" means the Welfare Reform and Pensions (Northern Ireland) Order 1999;

"Part XIV" means Part XIV of the Taxes Act;

"pension credit" means a credit under section 29(1)(b) of the 1999 Act or Article 26(1)(b) of the 1999 Order, "transferee" means the person who becomes entitled to the pension credit under either of those provisions, and "pension debit" means a debit under section 29(1)(a) of that Act or Article 26(1)(a) of that Order;

"pension date" has the meaning given by section 630(1) of the Taxes Act;

"pension sharing order or provision" means any such order or provision as is mentioned in section 28(1) of the 1999 Act or Article 25(1) of the 1999 Order;

"personal pension scheme", except in regulation 3, means a personal pension scheme approved by the Board for the purposes of Chapter IV of Part XIV;

"personal pension protected rights premium" means a premium payable under section 55(1) of the Pension Schemes Act 1993 or section 51(6)(d) of the Pension Schemes (Northern Ireland) Act 1993;

"protected rights" shall be construed in accordance with section 10 of the Pension Schemes Act 1993 and section 6 of the Pension Schemes (Northern Ireland) Act 1993;

"relevant statutory scheme" has the meaning given by section 611A(1) of the Taxes Act;

"remuneration" shall be construed in accordance with section 612(1) of the Taxes Act;

"retirement annuity contract" means a retirement annuity contract approved by the Board under Chapter III of Part XIV, and "trust scheme" means a trust scheme approved by the Board under that Chapter;

"scheme member" in relation to an approved retirement benefits scheme or relevant statutory scheme means—

    (a)   a member of the scheme to whom benefit is currently accruing as a result of service as an employee, or

    (b)   a person who is an ex-spouse of a member of the scheme and whose rights under the scheme derive from a pension sharing order or provision;

"the Taxes Act" means the Income and Corporation Taxes Act 1988;

"transfer payment" in regulations 5 to 7 and 12 includes a payment under paragraph 1(3) of Schedule 5 to the 1999 Act or under paragraph 1(3) of Schedule 5 to the 1999 Order;

"transfer request" means a request in writing in accordance with regulation 4(1), save that a request shall be regarded as in writing if it is furnished by telephonic facsimile transmission, or by electronic communication containing an electronic signature of the individual in question.

3   Requirements under section 638(2) of the Taxes Act

The provision for the making, acceptance and application of transfer payments, which is required to be made by a personal pension scheme, in order that the scheme may be approved by the Board for the purposes of Chapter IV of Part XIV, is the provision set out in regulations 4 to 13 (to be construed using the relevant definitions in regulation 2).

Part II
Provision for the Making of Transfer Payments

4 Basic obligations

(1)   Subject to paragraph (2) and regulation 8, where the administrator of a personal pension scheme is requested so to do in writing by an individual who is a member of the scheme, he shall make a transfer payment from the scheme to—

    (a)   another personal pension scheme; or

    (b)   an approved retirement benefits scheme of which the individual is an existing scheme member (otherwise than in relation to the transfer payment); or

    (c)   a relevant statutory scheme of which the individual is an existing scheme member (otherwise than in relation to the transfer payment);
but not to any other approved retirement benefits scheme or relevant statutory scheme.

(2)   The transfer payment shall, in respect of arrangements made by the individual in accordance with the scheme which are (wholly or partly) the subject of the transfer request, comprise the whole of the accumulated funds held in connection with those arrangements except that, where the fund—

    (a)   includes protected rights, or

    (b)   has been, or will be, used to pay a personal pension protected rights premium,

        the amount of the funds which represents those rights or has been, or will be, so used may be excluded from the transfer payment.

(3)   Before making a transfer payment the administrator shall take all reasonable steps to ensure that the payment is being made to a scheme referred to in paragraph (1)(a) to (c).

(4)   The reference in the words of paragraph (1) preceding sub-paragraph (a) to an individual who is a member of a scheme shall be treated as including a reference to a surviving spouse or dependant mentioned in regulation 14(3)(c).

5   Transfer payments from one personal pension scheme to another—additional obligation to hand over a lump sum certificate where any of the payments originated from certain schemes mentioned in Chapter I

(1)   Subject to paragraph (2), the administrator of a personal pension scheme ("the paying scheme") from which a transfer payment is made in the circumstances described in paragraph (3) shall, on the making of the payment, give the certificate referred to in paragraph (3)(b) to the administrator of the personal pension scheme to which the payment is made ("the receiving scheme").

(2)   Where only one (or some) of the arrangements made by the individual in accordance with the scheme is being transferred, the administrator of the paying scheme shall apportion any amount shown on the certificate on a proportionate basis, and shall prepare and sign replacement certificates in respect of each part of the funds (including in a case where the amount is nil), and shall give the replacement certificate relating to the funds transferred to the administrator of the receiving scheme.

(3)   The circumstances described in this paragraph are where the transfer payment is made from the paying scheme to another personal pension scheme and—

    (a)   the payment or part of the payment had its origin in a transfer payment ("the original payment") from an approved retirement benefits scheme or a relevant statutory scheme, and

    (b)   the administrator of the paying scheme holds a certificate which was given in relation to the original payment or any other event showing either—

        (i)   that an amount is payable out of that payment by way of lump sum to the individual in respect of whom the transfer payment will be made, on his pension date, or

(ii)   that no amount is payable out of that payment by way of lump sum to that individual on his pension date.

6 Transfer payments from a personal pension scheme to certain schemes mentioned in Chapter I— additional obligation to hand over a "nil" lump sum certificate where any of the payments originated from such schemes

(1)   Subject to paragraph (2), the administrator of a personal pension scheme ("the paying scheme") from which a transfer payment is made in the circumstances described in paragraph (3) shall, on the making of the payment, give the certificate referred to in paragraph (3)(b) to the administrator of the approved retirement benefits scheme or relevant statutory scheme to which the payment is made ("the receiving scheme").

(2)   Where only one (or some) of the arrangements made by the individual in accordance with the scheme is being transferred, the administrator of the paying scheme shall prepare and sign replacement certificates, each in the amount of nil, in respect of each part of the funds, and shall give the replacement certificate relating to the funds transferred to the administrator of the receiving scheme.

(3)   The circumstances described in this paragraph are where the transfer payment is made from the paying scheme to an approved retirement benefits scheme or a relevant statutory scheme and—

(a)   the payment or part of the payment had its origin in a transfer payment ("the original payment") from an approved retirement benefits scheme or relevant statutory scheme, and

(b)   the administrator of the paying scheme holds a certificate which was given in relation to the original payment or any other event showing that no amount may be paid out of that payment by way of lump sum to the individual in respect of whom the transfer payment will be made.

Part III
Provision for the Acceptance of Transfer Payments

7 Basic obligation

Subject to regulations 4 and 8, a personal pension scheme may accept a transfer payment from—

(a)   another personal pension scheme;

(b)   an approved retirement benefits scheme;

(c)   a relevant statutory scheme;

(d)   a retirement annuity contract or trust scheme; or

(e)   a fund to which section 608 of the Taxes Act applies; but shall not accept a transfer payment from any other source without the prior written approval of the Board.

8 Prohibition of acceptance of certain transfer payments from certain schemes mentioned in Chapter I unless the administrator has obtained a certificate as to the value of the proposed transfer payment

(1)   A personal pension scheme shall not accept a transfer payment from—

(a)   an approved retirement benefits scheme (other than an annuity contract securing relevant benefits as described in section 591(2)(g) of the Taxes Act where that contract is made before 6th April 2001), or

(b)   a relevant statutory scheme, ("the paying scheme") in the circumstances described in paragraph (2) unless the administrator of the personal pension scheme has obtained the certificate referred to in paragraph (3) from the administrator of the paying scheme.

(2)   The circumstances described in this paragraph are circumstances where, in relation to any employment to which the proposed transfer payment, or any part of it, relates—

(a) the individual is, or has been at any time during the period of ten years prior to the date of the proposed transfer payment ("the proposed transfer date"), a controlling director, or

(b)

    (i) the individual's annual remuneration is, or was, for any year of assessment falling (wholly or partly) during the period of six years prior to the proposed transfer date, more than the allowable maximum (within the meaning of section 640A(2) of the Taxes Act) for the year of assessment in which the proposed transfer date falls, and

    (ii) the individual's age at the proposed transfer date will be not less than 45 years.

(3) The certificate referred to in this paragraph is a certificate, signed by the administrator of the paying scheme, which shows that the proposed transfer payment does not exceed the maximum amount which may be transferred from an approved retirement benefits scheme or relevant statutory scheme to a personal pension scheme calculated in accordance with Appendix XI of "Occupational Pension Schemes Practice Notes (IR 12)" published by the Board on 22nd January 2001.

Part IV
Provision for the Application of Transfer Payments

9   Basic obligations

Subject to regulations 10 to 14, any transfer payment accepted by a personal pension scheme in accordance with these Regulations shall only be used for providing benefits listed in section 633(1) of the Taxes Act or for making a further transfer payment subject to the provisions of these Regulations.

10   Application of transfer payments to a personal pension scheme from or originating from certain schemes mentioned in Chapter I for the provision of "death benefits"

(1) Where a personal pension scheme has in the circumstances described in regulation 8(2) (omitting the word "proposed" wherever it occurs) accepted a transfer payment from—

(a) an approved retirement benefits scheme, or

(b) a relevant statutory scheme, or

(c) another personal pension scheme in circumstances where the transfer payment, or part of it, had its origin in a transfer payment from an approved retirement benefits scheme or a relevant statutory scheme,
the accumulated value arising from that transfer payment or, as the case may be, that part shall be applied after the death of the individual referred to in regulation 8(2) in accordance with paragraph (2) or (3), in the events described in paragraph (2).

(2) Where the individual dies before any benefits have been paid to him under an arrangement under which the transfer payment falls to be held, the accumulated value arising from that transfer payment or, as the case may be, that part shall be applied—

(a) wholly to secure the payment to a surviving spouse or (if the arrangement so provides) a dependant of an annuity which satisfies the conditions in section 636 of the Taxes Act, or

(b) to secure the payment of income withdrawals by the surviving spouse or (if the arrangement so provides) the dependant with respect to which the conditions in section 636A of the Taxes Act are satisfied and, as to any amount not used for that purpose, to secure the payment to the surviving spouse or (if the arrangement so provides) the dependant of such an annuity as is referred to in sub-paragraph (a), or

(c) as to not more than 25 per cent to secure the payment of a lump sum and as to the balance to secure the payment to the surviving spouse or (if the arrangement so provides) the dependant of such an annuity as is referred to in sub-paragraph (a), or of such income withdrawals and annuity as are referred to in sub-paragraph (b).

(3)   In the events described in the words of paragraph (2) preceding sub-paragraph (a), subject to sub-paragraphs (a) to (c) of that paragraph, the whole of the accumulated value may be applied to secure the payment of a lump sum.

11   Application of transfer payments to a personal pension scheme from or originating from certain schemes mentioned in Chapter I for the provision of lump sums to the member

(1)   Where in the circumstances described in regulation 8(2) (omitting the word "proposed" wherever it occurs) a personal pension scheme ("the receiving scheme") accepts a transfer payment from—

(a)   an approved retirement benefits scheme, or

(b)   a relevant statutory scheme, or

(c)   another personal pension scheme in circumstances where the transfer payment or part of it had its origin in a transfer payment ("the original payment") from an approved retirement benefits scheme or a relevant statutory scheme, ("the paying scheme") the provisions of paragraph (2) shall apply.

(2)   Where the provisions of this paragraph apply—

(a)   no amount may be paid to the individual in respect of whom the transfer payment is made by way of lump sum on his pension date out of the transfer payment or, as the case may be, the part of that payment unless the administrator of the receiving scheme has obtained from the administrator of the paying scheme the lump sum certificate required by the certificating requirements; and

(b)   the amount which may be so paid by way of lump sum may not exceed the aggregate of the amount shown in any such certificate ("the basic amount") and any amount by which the basic amount may be enhanced at the date of payment.

(3)   For the purposes of paragraph (2) the amount by which the basic amount may be enhanced is the result of applying to the basic amount the percentage increase in the retail prices index between—

(a)

(i)   in a case falling within paragraph (1)(a) or (b), the month in which the transfer payment referred to in the words preceding paragraph (1)(a) was received, or

(ii)   in a case falling within paragraph (1)(c), the month in which the original payment was made, and

(b)   the last month for which that index had been published at the date of the payment by way of lump sum.

(4)   The reference in paragraph (3) to the retail prices index shall be construed in accordance with section 833(2) of the Taxes Act as if it were a reference in the Income Tax Acts.

12   Application of transfer payments to a personal pension scheme where a "nil" lump sum certificate is held

Where—

(a)   a personal pension scheme has accepted a transfer payment in accordance with regulation 7, and

(b)   the administrator of the scheme holds a certificate given under any of the certificating requirements with regard to the transfer payment or any other event, showing that no amount is payable out of that payment by way of lump sum to the individual in respect of whom the transfer payment was made on his pension date, no such lump sum may be paid out of the accumulated value arising from that transfer payment.

13 Obligations where there is a pension sharing order or provision

(1) Where—

(a) a transfer payment has been accepted by a personal pension scheme in the circumstances described in regulation 5(3) (omitting sub-paragraph (b)(ii) and the word "either" preceding sub-paragraph (b)(i)), and

(b) a pension sharing order or provision is subsequently made against the individual in respect of whom the payment was made,
the administrator of the receiving scheme shall recalculate the amount shown on the certificate referred to in regulation 5(2) or (3)(b), according to any debit to which the individual's rights under the scheme become subject by virtue of that order or provision, and shall prepare and sign a replacement certificate in respect of the individual's rights remaining after the reduction referred to in section 29 of the 1999 Act or Article 26 of the 1999 Order has taken place.

(2) Where—

(a) a transfer payment has been accepted by a personal pension scheme in the circumstances described in regulation 5(3) (omitting sub-paragraph (b)(i) and the word "either" which precedes it), and

(b) a pension sharing order or provision is subsequently made against the individual in respect of whom the payment was made,
the administrator of the receiving scheme shall prepare and sign a certificate in respect of the pension credit to which the transferee becomes entitled, showing that no amount may be paid out of the original payment by way of lump sum to the transferee.

(3) Where, after the date which is a member's pension date in relation to the arrangements in question, a pension sharing order or provision is made against that member, the administrator of the scheme shall prepare and sign a certificate in respect of the pension credit to which the transferee becomes entitled, showing that no amount may be paid out of the pension credit by way of lump sum to the transferee.

(4) The reference in paragraph (1) to a certificate referred to in regulation 5(2) or (3)(b) includes a reference to a certificate given under regulation 4 of the Personal Pension Schemes (Transfer Payments) Regulations 1988.

Part V
Exceptions to Section 638(7A) of the Taxes Act and Supplemental

14 Exceptions to section 638(7A) of the Taxes Act

(1) Paragraphs (2) and (3) prescribe situations which fall within the exception in section 638(7A) of the Taxes Act with regard to the making of transfer payments.

(2) The first situation is where—

(a) the transfer payment is from the personal pension scheme ("the paying scheme") to another personal pension scheme ("the receiving scheme");

(b) income withdrawals are being made by the member from the paying scheme with respect to which the conditions in section 634A of the Taxes Act are satisfied, and the period of deferral of the purchase of an annuity has not ended;

(c) the transfer payment comprises the whole of the funds held under any arrangement which is the subject of the transfer payment;

(d) where any of the funds referred to in sub-paragraph (c) was the subject of, or represents the proceeds of, an earlier transfer payment made in accordance with this paragraph ("the earlier transfer payment"), the period between the earlier transfer payment and the transfer payment referred to in sub-paragraph (a) is not less than one year;

(e) the arrangements made in accordance with the receiving scheme ("the new arrangements") were set up by the member for the purpose of accepting the transfer payment, or a previous or contemporaneous transfer payment which fell or falls within this first situation, and prohibit the acceptance of—

689

(i)   contributions, or

(ii)   further transfer payments which do not fall within this first situation;

(f)   under the new arrangements the member elects to defer the purchase of such an annuity as is mentioned in section 634 of the Taxes Act, and to make income withdrawals as mentioned in sub-paragraph (b), and that election takes effect simultaneously with the transfer payment; and

(g)   no benefit referred to in section 633(1)(b) or (d) of the Taxes Act is payable under the new arrangements.

(3)   The second situation is where—

(a)   the transfer payment is from the paying scheme to another personal pension scheme ("the receiving scheme");

(b)   the member referred to in section 634 of the Taxes Act ("the original member") has died;

(c)   a surviving spouse or dependant referred to in section 636 of the Taxes Act is making income withdrawals from the paying scheme with respect to which the conditions in section 636A of the Taxes Act are satisfied, and the period of deferral of the purchase of an annuity has not ended;

(d)   the arrangements made in accordance with the receiving scheme by the surviving spouse or dependant ("the substitute member") were set up for the purpose of accepting the transfer payment, or a previous or contemporaneous transfer payment which fell or falls within this second situation, and prohibit the acceptance of—

(i)   contributions, or

(ii)   further transfer payments which do not fall within this second situation;

(e)   under the arrangements referred to in sub-paragraph (d) ("the new arrangements") the substitute member elects to defer the purchase of an annuity and to make income withdrawals with respect to which the conditions in section 634A of the Taxes Act are satisfied;

(f)   the income withdrawals referred to in sub-paragraph (e) cannot be made after the original member would have attained the age of 75 or, if earlier, after the substitute member attains that age;

(g)   the election referred to in sub-paragraph (e) takes effect simultaneously with the transfer payment;

(h)   any benefit under the new arrangements corresponds to a benefit which would have been payable to the same person under the paying scheme (and "the same person" means the same individual, without having regard to the way in which that or any other individual is defined in the new arrangements); and

(i)   the conditions in paragraph (2)(c), (d) and (g) are satisfied (construing the references in paragraph (2)(d) to "this paragraph" and "sub-paragraph (a)" as if they were references to the present paragraph and sub-paragraph (a) of this paragraph).

15   Revocations and transitional provision

(1)   Regulations 8 and 9 of the Personal Pension Schemes (Transfer Payments) Regulations 1988 shall cease to have effect where the death of the individual referred to in the former regulation occurs on or after 6th April 2001, and regulation 10 of these Regulations shall have effect where the death of the individual referred to in that regulation occurs on or after 6th April 2001.

(2)   The Personal Pension Schemes (Transfer Payments) Regulations 1988, the Personal Pension Schemes (Transfer Payments) (Amendment) Regulations 1989 and the Personal Pension Schemes (Transfer Payments) (Amendment) Regulations 1997 shall otherwise cease to have effect.

(3)   Any transfer payment made under, and any certificate supplied or obtained under a provision of, the Personal Pension Schemes (Transfer Payments) Regulations 1988 shall be treated for the purposes of these Regulations as if made, supplied or obtained, as the case may be, under the corresponding provision (if any) of these Regulations.

EXPLANATORY NOTE

(This note is not part of the Regulations)

Section 638(2) of the Income and Corporation Taxes Act 1988 ("section 638(2)" and "the Taxes Act" respectively) provides that the Commissioners of Inland Revenue ("the Board") shall not approve a personal pension scheme unless it makes such provision for the making, acceptance and application of transfer payments as satisfies any requirements imposed by or under regulations made by the Board. These Regulations amend and consolidate those requirements.

Regulation 1 provides for citation and commencement and regulation 2 contains definitions.

Regulation 3 provides that the requirements referred to in section 638(2) are to make the provision set out in regulations 4 to 13.

Regulations 4, 5 and 6 set out the provision for the making of transfer payments to other personal pension schemes, certain retirement benefits schemes and statutory schemes.

Regulations 7 and 8 set out the provision for the acceptance by personal pension schemes of transfer payments from other personal pension schemes, retirement benefits schemes, relevant statutory schemes and retirement annuity contract or trust schemes.

The publication "Occupational Pension Schemes Practice Notes (IR 12)" referred to in regulation 8(3) may be obtained from the PSO Stationery Order Line, Pension Schemes Office, Yorke House, PO Box 62, Castle Meadow Road, Nottingham NG2 1BG (tel: 0115 974 1670), or from web site: *www.inlandrevenue.gov.uk* (Revenue leaflets).

Regulations 9 to 12 set out provision for the application of transfer payments made to personal pension schemes. Regulation 13 imposes obligations relating to the preparation of lump sum certificates where a pension sharing order or provision has been made.

Regulation 14 prescribes exceptions to section 638(7A) of the Taxes Act, allowing the transfer of funds which are subject to income drawdown in the circumstances specified.

Regulation 15 contains revocations and provides for the continuity of transfer payments made, and certificates given, under the revoked Regulations.

The Regulatory Impact Assessment for these Regulations can be obtained from Inland Revenue (Capital and Savings), Room 134, New Wing, Somerset House, Strand, London WC2R 1LB or from web site: *www.inlandrevenue.gov.uk*

Appendix 69

Income Tax

Inland **Revenue**

Tax Office reference

Tax Office Date stamp

Personal Pension Contributions and Free Standing Additional Voluntary Contributions other than contributions made to or for your employer's occupational pension scheme

Claim for year 6 April _____ to 5 April _____

Client's name _____
where form issued to an agent

If you are either an employee or a self employed person, you may be able to claim tax relief in respect of contributions you make to a personal pension scheme or to a pension scheme separate from your employer's pension scheme.

• **Employees**

> If you are an employee and pay tax under PAYE tax relief at basic rate will be given at source by the pension scheme administrator to whom to you make your pension scheme contributions. Unless you are liable to tax at a higher rate no further relief will be given by your Tax Office.

> If you are liable to tax at a higher rate the additional relief due i.e. the difference between the higher rate and basic rate will be given as an allowance in your code number. You can claim your relief either by including it in your tax return or by using this form. If you use this form to make your claim please complete it overleaf and send it to your Tax office as soon as possible to claim the additional relief. You should show the gross contributions (that is before tax has been deducted) you paid to your pension scheme administrator.

• **Self employed**

> If you are self employed and make contributions to a personal pension scheme you may be able to claim tax relief on the contributions you make. The relief will not be given at source by the scheme administrator but you will instead receive relief from your own Tax Office by set off against outstanding liabilities or by way of repayment. You can claim your relief either by including it in your tax return or by using this form. If you use this form to make your claim please complete it overleaf and send it to your Tax Office as soon as possible to claim the relief. You should show the gross contributions you actually paid to your personal pension scheme administrator.

If you make contributions to more than one personal pension scheme or for more than one employment please give details for each scheme or employment. If you need more space please use a separate piece of paper and attach it to this form.

You should indicate in respect of each pension scheme

> • the employment or self employment to which it refers

> • the contributions paid in the previous year to 5 April and the contributions to be paid in the current year to 5 April.

There is no need to send in the Personal Pensions Contributions Certificate (PPCC), Voluntary Contributions Certificate (VCC) or contribution receipts with your claim but these should be retained as the Revenue may call for these in selected cases under Self Assessment.

If you would like more information ask your Tax Office for Help Sheet IR 330.

PP120

35825 3.99 Niceday Stationery & Print Limited   BMSD11/98   R0K4118

	1st scheme	2nd scheme	3rd scheme
Nature of employment/self employment			
Name and address of employer (and PAYE reference if known) **or** place of business (and reference if known).			
Name of approved pension scheme and scheme reference number.			
Name and address of Scheme Administrator			
Contributions paid in the previous year to 5 April _____			
Contributions to be paid in the current year to 5 April _____			
Date of birth			
	4th scheme	5th scheme	6th scheme
Nature of employment/self employment			
Name and address of employer (and PAYE reference if known) **or** place of business (and reference if known).			
Name of approved pension scheme and scheme reference number.			
Name and address of Scheme Administrator			
Contributions paid in the previous year to 5 April _____			
Contributions to be paid in the current year to 5 April _____			
Date of birth			

It is a serious offence to make a false declaration.

To the best of my knowledge and belief the information given on this form is correct and complete.

Name (in CAPITAL letters) _____

Signature [   ]   Date [/   /   ]

Private address _____

_____ Postcode _____

National Insurance Number [| | | | |]

Appendix 70

PERMITTED INVESTMENTS FOR SIPPS

- Stocks and shares traded on any recognised stock exchange (including the AIM), including:

  - equities

  - fixed interest securities issued by governments or other bodies

  - debenture stock and other loan stock

  - warrants (for equities)

  - permanent interest bearing shares

  - convertible securities

- Futures and options traded on any recognised stock exchange whether currency, equity or bonds and either long or short positions or options

- Unit trusts:

  - resident in the UK and authorised under Financial Services Act (FSA);

  - resident outside the UK but subject to regulation for that purpose in terms of the FSA, including US mutual funds recognised under s86-88 FSA;

  - tax exempt unauthorised unit trusts

- Investment trusts:

  Stocks and shares in investment trusts purchased and held through investment trust savings schemes or investment plans operated by persons:

  - resident in the UK and authorised for that purpose under FSA

  - resident outside the UK but subject to regulation for that purpose in terms of the FSA

- Open ended investment companies (OEICs)

- Insurance company managed funds and unit-linked funds, investment policies or unit linked funds of a UK insurance company or an insurance company within the EEC authorised under Article 6 of the First Life Insurance Directive 79/267/EEC

- Endowment policies traded by a FSA regulated person (TEPs)

- Deposit accounts with any authorised institution in any currency

- Commercial property (including land whether development land, farmland or forestry) in or outside the UK

- Borrowing to finance the purchase or development of a commercial property. Or to pay for VAT liability arising from the purchase of any such property

- Undertaking for Collective Investment Schemes in Transferable Securities (UCITS)

- Ground rents

- Foreign currency deposit accounts

- Public houses

- Depository Interests (including CREST Depository Interests)

- Individual Pension Accounts (IPAs)

- Hotels, motels and guest houses

- Nursing homes

Appendix 71

PROHIBITED INVESTMENTS FOR SIPPS

- Premium bonds

- Loans to any party

- Milk quotas

- Fishing quotas

- Residential property

- Gold bullion

- Shares traded on OFEX

- Unlisted shares (except in a site maintenance company, for the necessary extent needed to purchase a commercial property)

- Leisure property (e.g. golf courses) or property with an affiliated leisure interest such as sporting rights

- Any land or property directly adjacent to any land or property owned by the member or any party connected with the member

- Personal chattels (e.g. paintings, antiques, fine wine and jewellery)

- Borrowing other than that specified in 11.24,11.26 or 11.27 of Part 11

Glossary

The descriptions of the terms which appear in this glossary are not intended to be comprehensive definitions. They are intended as guides for ease of reference to the particular paragraphs in the book where the term or concept is defined and/or discussed in more detail.

1987 Member—As described in 4.12(*c*)

1989 Member—As described in 4.12(*d*)

Actuary—A Fellow of the Institute of Actuaries in England or of the Faculty of Actuaries in Scotland. The term is defined in *section 47* of the *Pensions Act 1995* in relation to an occupational pension scheme.

Additional voluntary contributions (AVC)—Additional payments to an occupational pension scheme made by a member of up to 15 per cent of his remuneration per tax year.

Administrator—The person or persons having the management of the scheme and who is or are responsible to the Inland Revenue for fulfilling certain statutory duties under *section 611AA*.

Appropriate Personal Pension Scheme—A personal pension scheme for the purpose of contracting-out of SERPS, as described in *Chapter I* of *Part III* of the *Pension Schemes Act 1993*.

Approval, and approved— Approval of a scheme under *ICTA 1988, Ch I* of *Pt XIV*.

Auditor—*An individual or firm who or which satisfies the requirements of the Pensions Act 1995* in relation to auditors of occupational pension schemes.

Authorised insurance company—An insurance company as described in *ICTA 1988, s 659B*, and acceptable under the *Pension Schemes Act 1993, s 19*. Such companies include certain European Community insurers (Update No 3 and No 19).

Authorised provider—A person authorised under *section 632* who may establish a personal pension scheme. Such a person includes anyone authorised under the *FSA 1986* to carry on investment business, e.g. a LO or authorised unit trust, or a bank or a building society or Friendly Society.

Basis year—a tax year chosen by a member of a personal pension scheme, the net relevant earnings for which are used to validate contributions in that year and the following five tax years–as defined in *s 646B(1)*.

Break year—a tax year in which a member of a personal pension scheme has no relevant earnings–as defined in *s 646D(1)(a)*.

Glossary

Buy-out policy or section 32 buy-out policy—A single life deferred annuity on the life of the member taken out with an insurance company to satisfy the rights of an early leaver who selects this option on the termination of his pensionable service.

Cash equivalent—The amount which a member of a pension scheme may require to be applied as a transfer payment to another approved pension scheme or to a buy-out policy.

Cessation year—a tax year preceding a *break year* in which the member of a personal pension scheme had relevant earnings–as defined in *s 646D(1)(b)*.

Chapter I scheme—a retirement benefits scheme.

Chapter IV scheme—a personal pension scheme.

Common trust fund—Investments made under trust where the interests of the beneficiaries (members in a pension scheme) lie against all the assets of the trust and not against any specific asset.

Commutation—The right to convert part of an income pension entitlement into a cash lump sum. Permissible within certain limits for all forms of Inland Revenue approved pension provision.

Continued rights—The status conferred on an individual by virtue of *SI 1988 No 1436* or *SI 1990 No 2101* in order that such person may benefit from the pre-*F(No 2)A 1987* or the pre- *FA 1989* tax regime (see 4.5, 4.10 to 4.15).

Contracting-out—The *Occupational Pension Schemes (Contracting-out) Regulations 1996*, and any other regulations in respect of contracting-out which permit contracting-out of the State Earnings-Related Pension Scheme.

Contribution credit—Such an amount as calculated by the actuary as represents the member's interest in the scheme.

Contributions Agency—An executive of the DSS. The COEG branch dealt with contracting-out since 6 April 1997. Responsibility for NICs and contracting-out transferred to the Inland Revenue (NICO) on 6 April.

Controlling Director—a director who, as described in the Glossary to Practice Notes IR12 issued by the Inland Revenue, together with associated persons owns or controls 20% or more of the ordinary shares of the employer company—as described in APPENDIX 10.

Deferred SSAS—A SSAS established by a Life Office where all investments are held in insurance policies from the outset, but with provision in its rules to invest elsewhere later and to become a fully fledged SSAS.

Defined benefit scheme—A type of pension scheme under which the amount of pension and related benefits of the member are defined by reference to final remuneration. Also known as a 'Final salary scheme'.

Defined contribution scheme—A type of pension scheme under which the pension and related benefits of the members depend entirely on the amount of contributions paid into the scheme by the company and by the employee/ members themselves, albeit subject to final salary limitations in the case of a *Chapter I* scheme. Also known as a money-purchase scheme.

Definitive deed—Comprehensive deed setting out the powers and duties of the trustees to which will commonly be attached the full rules of the scheme (see 3.16 to 3.41). To be distinguished from the interim deed.

Disclosure Regulations—The *Occupational Pension Schemes (Disclosure of Information) Regulations 1996*.

Dynamisation—A means of increasing final remuneration for particular basis periods in line with the increase in RPI.

Earnings Cap—The limit imposed on pensionable earnings as described in *section 590C (2)* and, for personal pension schemes, *section 640A* and on pensionable service with companies within a trading group (see APPENDIX 25).

Earnings Threshold—upper limit of contributions payable to a personal pension scheme in any one tax year, without reference to an individual's net relevant earnings—as defined in *s 630(1)*. It is currently £3,600 but can be changed by Treasury Order.

Employer-Related Investments—Investments by the trustees in loans to the company, in property and land leased to the company and in shares of the company.

Equal access—The requirement imposed under *PSA 1993, s 118* and subsequent legislation that membership of a pension scheme must be open to both men and women on equal terms

Final remuneration—The term commonly used to describe what pay of an employee/member, and over what period, is to count in the calculation of pensionable pay. Subject to numerous restrictions (see 4.16 to 4.27).

Fluctuating emoluments—Remuneration received by an employee on an irregular basis or not as part of basic remuneration which may be included in final remuneration (see 4.21, 4.25).

Free-standing AVC (FSAVC)—A contract between an individual who is a member of an occupational pension scheme and an independent pension provider to which the member can make additional voluntary contributions up to the general limit of 15 per cent of his remuneration per tax year.

Full 1989 Member—as described in 4.12(*a*).

Fund—The monies, investments and property held by a scheme for the purpose of providing benefits for members and other beneficiaries. For a group personal pension scheme or an earmarked scheme, the fund in respect of an individual member shall mean the invested value of the contributions paid in by and on behalf of such person, net of any outgoings.

Fund manager—A person who manages the investments of an occupational pension scheme as described in *section 124(1)* of the *Pensions Act 1995*—see also *Investment manager.*

Hybrid scheme—A partly insured, as opposed to fully self-administered, occupational pension scheme under which up to, usually, 50 per cent of the fund is invested in an insurance policy and the remainder is self-invested.

Index—The Index of Retail Prices published by the Department of Employment or such other authority of Her Majesty's Government as shall apply from time to time (see RPI).

Inland Revenue Savings, Pensions, Share Schemes (IR SPSS)—a new 'business stream' of the Inland Revenue of which the former Pensions Schemes Office (PSO) is now a part.

Interim deed—Deed between the company and the trustees under which the scheme is established. To be distinguished from the definitive deed.

Investment business—Business mainly or wholly concerned with the making of investments, or a company whose income is mainly investment income.

Investment company—As defined in *ICTA 1988, s 130.*

Investment manager—A person or body appointed to manage scheme investments (see also fund manager).

Member-nominated director—As defined in *section 18(2)* of the *Pensions Act 1995.*

Member-nominated trustee—As defined in the *section 16(2)* of the *Pensions Act 1995.*

Minimum funding requirement—As defined in *section 56* of the *Pensions Act 1995.*

Model deed—A definitive deed agreed by a practitioner with the standards section of the IR SPSS for use on that practitioner's SSAS or SIPPS.

Net relevant earnings—Applies to the income of employed or self-employed persons, as defined in *ICTA 1988, s 646*:

- For an employed person whose income is assessable to tax under Schedule E it is described in *section 646* and *section 646A* as his or her Schedule E chargeable income exclusive, by virtue of section 644, of pensions and some non-pensionable elements (similar to the exclusions which apply to schemes approved under *ICTA 1998, Ch I of Pt XIV*).

- For a self-employed sole trader or partner whose income is assessable to tax under Schedule D Case I or Case II it is his or her income net of deductible expenses received from a trade, profession or vocation in which he or she is engaged, but before deduction of personal allowances (see *ICTA 1988, ss 644, 646* and *646A*).

Normal retirement age—The age at which a member of a scheme is normally expected to retire from service with the employer. Under *ICTA 1988, s 590(3)(a)*, this should be within the ages 60 to 75. However, IR SPSS may agree an age outside this band for a specific profession or job.

Occupational pension scheme—As described in *section 1* of the *Pensions Schemes Act 1993*.

Occupational Pensions Board—This body closed on 6 April 1997. It was mainly replaced by the Contributions Agency. Most of its powers concerned contracting-out of SERPS.

Occupational Pensions Regulatory Authority—The regulatory body for occupational pension schemes with effect from 6 April 1997.

Ordinary annual contributions—The regular contributions made by the company in line with the actuary's recommendations to the trustees of its pension scheme and is to be distinguished from a special contribution.

Pension date—As defined in *ICTA 1988, s 630* (as amended by *s 638ZA*) for personal pension schemes.

Pension Schemes Office (PSO)—Now part of *Inland Revenue Savings, Pensions, Share Schemes (IR SPSS)*.

Pension Schemes Registry—The Registrar of Occupational and Personal Pension Schemes, which is Opra. This body provides a tracing service and collects the pension schemes levies.

Pensioneer trustee—An individual or body corporate widely involved with occupational pension schemes and approved to have dealings with the IR SPSS.

Pensions Advisory Service—Known as OPAS. This is an independent and voluntary organisation which gives free advice to the public who have problems with pensions matters.

Pensions Compensation Board—A compensation scheme for occupational pensions which provides compensation on employer insolvency and any dishonest removal of scheme assets with effect from 6 April 1997.

Pensions Ombudsman—Deals with disputes about pension entitlement and maladministration.

Personal pension scheme—A scheme approved under *ICTA 1988, Ch IV* of *Pt XIV* and defined in *section 1* of the *Pension Schemes Act 1993*, and (where the

Glossary

context requires) such a scheme as is categorised as an appropriate personal pension scheme.

Post cessation year—any of the five tax years following a *cessation year*–as defined in *s 646D(4)*.

Pre 1987 Member—As described in 4.12(*b*).

Preservation—Broadly the requirements imposed under the *Preservation Regulations* that certain early leavers are to be no less favourably treated in the way in which their pension and related benefits are calculated than those who retire at normal pension age. The term also refers to the statutory revaluation of deferred pensions.

Preservation Regulations—*The Occupational Pension Schemes (Preservation of Benefit) Regulations 1991*, as amended by the *Pension Schemes Act 1993* and the *Pensions Act 1995*.

Protected rights—Contracted-out rights as described in *Chapter I* of *Part III* of the *Pension Schemes Act 1993*.

Qualifying post cessation year—any *post cessation year* where a member of a personal pension scheme has no relevant earnings and is not a member of a retirement benefits scheme–as defined in *s 646D(5)*.

Reference years—the six tax years preceding a *break year*–as defined in *s 646D(1)(c)*.

Regulated individual—in relation to transfers to and from personal pension schemes, an individual who is, or was during the ten years prior to the transfer, a controlling director or whose earnings for any year of assessment falling (wholly or partly) in the six years prior to the transfer, exceed the earnings cap for the tax year in which the transfer falls, and is aged 45 or over at the date of transfer.

Regulations—The Inland Revenue statutory provisions contained in *SI 1991 No 1614* restricting or banning certain features and investments of SSASs and laying down reporting requirements effective from 5 August 1991 (see APPENDIX 4).

Relevant benefits—Broadly these are the permitted classes of benefit which an occupational pension scheme may provide (see *section 612 (1)* and CHAPTER 4).

Relevant earnings—As defined in *ICTA 1988, s 644*.

Relevant superannuation scheme—As described in *ICTA 1988, s 645*.

Relevant statutory scheme—A statutory scheme as defined in *ICTA 1988, s 611A*.

Resident— Means resident for tax purposes.

Retirement annuity contract—A pension policy providing certain pension and related benefits, principally for the self-employed (see *ICTA 1988, Ch III of Pt XIV*).

Retained benefits/Retained death benefits— The benefits and death benefits payable under separate pension arrangements which members of an occupational scheme, or their dependants as the case may be, must take into account when determining whether the total level of benefits from the occupational pension scheme exceeds Inland Revenue maxima (see 4.40).

Retirement benefits scheme—A scheme which provides relevant benefits as described in *ICTA 1988, s 611*.

Section 608 scheme—A superannuation fund approved prior to 6 April 1980.

Section 615 scheme—A scheme approved for persons not resident in the UK, as described in *ICTA 1988, s 615*.

Self-investment—See Employer-Related Investments.

SERPS—The state earnings-related pension scheme applicable to those in employment who are not members of contracted-out occupational pension schemes or (after June 1988) of personal pension schemes contracted-out of SERPS.

Special contribution—A contribution made by a company to the trustees of its pension scheme which is not part of the regular pattern of contributions. It may be made in order to fund for a particular liability, e.g. an increase in pension entitlement, or to meet a deficiency in the assets of the fund.

Sponsored superannuation scheme—A scheme defined in *ICTA 1988, s 624* meaning a scheme which makes provision for the future retirement, leaving service, death etc. of an employee or employees and to which the employer makes some contribution (which may only involve payment of administration or establishment expenses).

SSAS 1996 Method—The method of funding a SSAS from 1 June 1996 including the actuarial assumptions and calculations set out in the Exposure Draft published in December 1995 (see APPENDIX 39).

Stakeholder scheme—a personal pension scheme which meets the conditions set out in the *Welfare Reform and Pensions Act 1999, s 1*, and *The Stakeholder Pension Schemes Regulations 2000 (SI 2000 No 1403)* (as amended).

Statutory scheme—A scheme defined in *ICTA 1988, s 612(1)*.

Taxation of Pensions Benefits—A Tolley publication by Alec Ure, a Senior Adviser in the Employee Benefits Department at Gissings, being a guide to the provisions and taxation of retirement and death benefit schemes.

Transfer payment—The amount paid by the trustees of one scheme to the trustees of another scheme or personal pension scheme when members change employer from one company to another and at the same time join the new company pension scheme or a personal pension scheme (see 4.58, 14.74 and 14.75). A transfer payment could also take place where a member leaves one scheme and joins another scheme of the same employer.

Trust-busting—The winding-up of a tax-approved pension scheme contrary to its rules usually with the intention of members acquiring the investments or the cash realised from their sale.

Unit trust scheme—An authorised unit trust within the meaning of *section 468(6)* or where all the unit holders are wholly exempt from CGT or corporation tax (otherwise than by reason of residence) if they dispose of their units.

Whistle blowing—The statutory obligation placed on the auditors and actuaries of occupational pension schemes to notify Opra if they believe any statutory obligation of the trustees has not been complied with and the breach is likely to be of material significance.

Some Useful Addresses

Association of Pensioneer Trustees
c/o Hymans Robertson
221 West George Street
Glasgow G2 2ND
Tel: 0141 300 7717
Fax: 0141 300 7803

Inland Revenue Central Unit (PP)
St John's House
Merton Road
Bootle
Merseyside L69 9BB
Tel: 0151 472 6000
Fax: 0151 472 6003

IR Savings, Pensions, Share Schemes
Yorke House
PO Box 62
Castle Meadow Road
Nottingham NG2 1BG
Tel: 0115 974 1600
Fax: 0115 974 1480
www.inlandrevenue.gov.uk/spss/

National Association of Pension
Funds
NIOC House
4 Victoria Street
London SW1H 0NX
Tel: 020 7808 1300
Fax: 020 7222 7585
E-mail: membership@napf.co.uk
www.napf.co.uk

National Insurance Contributions
Office
Longbenton
Newcastle upon Tyne NE98 1ZZ
Tel: 0191 225 7655

Occupational Pensions Advisory
Service
11 Belgrave Road
London SW1V 1RB
Tel: 020 7233 8080
Fax: 020 7233 8016
E-mail: enquiries@opas.org.uk
www.opas.org.uk

Pensions Ombudsman
11 Belgrave Road
London SW1V 1RB
Tel: 020 7834 9144
Fax: 020 7821 0065
E-mail: enquiries@
pensions-ombudsman.org.uk
www.pensions-ombudsman.org.uk

The Pension Schemes Registry
PO Box 1NN
Newcastle upon Tyne NE99 1NN
Tel: 0191 225 6316
Fax: 0191 225 6390

Revenue Adjudicator's Office
Haymarket House
28 Haymarket
London SW1Y 4ST
Tel: 020 7930 2292
Fax: 020 7217 2298
E-mail: adjudicators@gtnet.gov.uk

SIPP Provider Group
Pointon York Ltd
10 St Mary at Hill
London EC3R 8EE
Tel: 020 7283 6240
Fax: 020 7623 5400

Index

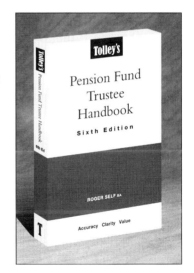

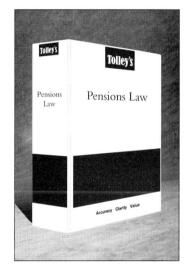

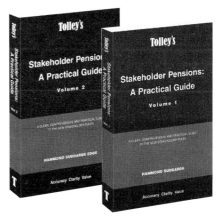

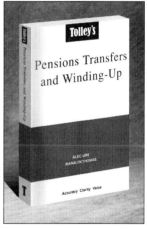